# BU ME BƐ: Proverbs of the Akans

# BU ME BƐ: Proverbs of the Akans

By
Peggy Appiah
Kwame Anthony Appiah
Ivor Agyeman-Duah

ayebia

An Adinkra symbol meaning
*Ntesie matemasie*
A symbol of knowledge and wisdom

Copyright © 2007 Ayebia Clarke Publishing Limited
Copyright © 2007 Introduction Peggy Appiah, Kwame Anthony Appiah and Ivor Agyeman-Duah

This edition first published in the UK by Ayebia Clarke Publishing Limited, 2007.
7 Syringa Walk
Banbury
OX16 1FR
Oxfordshire
UK

First edition published by the Centre for Intellectual Renewal in Ghana in 2001

British Library Cataloguing-in-Publication Data
A catalogue record of this book is available from the British Library.

Bu Me Bɛ: Proverbs of the Akans /Appiah, Peggy/Appiah, Kwame Anthony/Agyeman-Duah, Ivor

Cover design by Amanda Carroll at Millipedia
Cover artwork © gold weights Peggy Appiah
Picture research by Ivor Agyeman-Duah, Amanda Carroll and Nana Ayebia Clarke
Typeset by Tech-Set Ltd, Gateshead, Tyne & Wear.
Printed and bound in Great Britain by CPI Group (UK) Ltd, Croydon, CR0 4YY

ISBN 978-0-9555079-2-2

Available from www.ayebia.co.uk or email info@ayebia.co.uk
Distributed in Africa, Europe & the UK by TURNAROUND at www.turnaround-uk.com

# Dedication

Otumfuo, Osei Tutu II
(Asantehene or King of Asante)
And in memory of Peggy Appiah
(1921–2006)

# Acknowledgements

We cannot claim to have invented these proverbs. They are an essential part of our cultural heritage and what we have strived for years to understand and put them together and to interpret them to the best of our ability. During the compilation, many people helped to shape this project and we gratefully acknowledge them through the Preface and the Research Associates page.

We would like to express our appreciation to Ayebia Clarke Publishing Limited in Oxfordshire for publishing this collection as a first under the Ayebia Heritage Series. In particular, we also thank Nana Ayebia, herself a Queen Mother or Adantahemaa from Akuapem Larteh in Ghana and also her husband David. Thanks go also to the staff of the Centre for Intellectual Renewal in Ghana and supporters, Joseph Boateng, Joe Amoako Adusei and Abena Appiah who worked on the Asante goldweights photo collection. We would also like to thank our earlier editorial advisor, language and cultural consultant, Yaw Adusi-Poku of Kumasi.

In addition, Nana Ayebia would like to thank Dr Kwadwo Osei-Nyame who teaches Twi at the School of Oriental and African Studies (SOAS), University of London, for his dedication in going through the whole text with a fine tooth-comb; and to Amanda Carroll, for the design of the cover.

# Contents Page

# Biographies of Contributors

**Peggy Appiah,** who was awarded the MBE by Queen Elizabeth II for the distinguished promotion of Anglo–Ghanaian cultural and creative industries, died at the age of 84 (1921–2006) in Kumasi. Daughter of Sir Stafford Cripps, Chancellor of the Exchequer in the first post-war British Labour Government, she had lived in the Asante capital for over 50 years before and after the death of her statesman husband, Joe Appiah. Though she travelled as a painter but more as a writer to Namibia, Nigeria and the United States, her writings (over 30 books mainly for children) reflected the cultural dynamics of the Asante and Akan people of Ghana. They include popular ones such as: *A Smell of Unions; Ananse the Spider: Tales from an Ashanti Village; Tales of an Ashanti Father; The Children of Ananse; The Pineapple Child and Other Tales from Ashanti; The Lost Earring: Yao and the Python and The Gift of Mmotia.*

**Kwame Anthony Appiah,** currently the Laurance S. Rockfeller University Professor of Philosophy at the University Centre for Human Values, Princeton University, is one of the world's leading philosophers in Ethics of Philosophy. He has taught Philosophy and African–American Studies in Ghana, where his parents Peggy and Joe Appiah lived for years and at Clare College, Cambridge University, where he completed his Doctorate in Philosophy. He has also previously taught at Harvard, Duke, Cornell and Yale Universities. His published works include the Herskovits Award-winning *In My Father's House* (1992): *Colour Conscious: The Political Morality of Race* (1996); *Thinking it Through: An Introduction to Contemporary Philosophy* (2003); *The Ethics of Identity (2005); Cosmopolitanism: Ethics in a World of Strangers (2006)* and *Experiments in Ethics (forthcoming).*

**Ivor Agyeman-Duah,** founder of The Centre for Intellectual Renewal in Ghana, has been a Visiting Scholar-in Residence at The College of Arts and Letters, California State University in Pomona and a League of Women's Voters Visiting Writer at the University of Nebraska. His published books include two editions of *Between Faith & History: A Biography of J.A. Kufuor* (2003, 2006) and the co-authored *Pan-Africanism: Caribbean Connections* (2007). He has also been advisor to the Andrew Mellon Foundation of New York on its Itaka–Aluka cultural and economic data preservation project and has also worked as the culture and communication advisor at the Ghana Embassy in Washington, DC and the Ghana High Commission in London.

# Introduction to the 2nd Edition

Peggy Appiah, the leading author of this collection, died in Kumasi in February 2006 aged 84. For over half a century, Kumasi, capital city of the historically powerful 19th century Asante Kingdom, was truly a new home away from her original home in Filkins, Gloucestershire, where her parents, Isobel Cripps and Sir Stafford Cripps, Chancellor of the Exchequer in the post-war British Labour Government, had nurtured Peggy, who was their fourth and youngest child.

Peggy, who had migrated in 1954 from this English landed gentry with a long lineage of prestige and fame was the grandchild on her paternal side of Lord Parmoor, himself a descendant of Potter, who in turn was the sister of the famous Beatrix Webb, a relative of the great merchants who built up the cotton trade in Manchester and the Canadian Pacific Railway. Peggy's mother held China's oldest and prestigious decoration – *The Order of the Most Brilliant Star of China* and she was the granddaughter, as the records say, of the great inventor Eno, of *Eno's Fruit Salts* fame. Peggy herself had a fulsome life of love and marriage with the famous Ghanaian statesman Joe Appiah.

Her burial next to the tomb of her beloved husband at the Tafo Cemetery in Kumasi and her funeral as a whole was a traditional durbar of national respect. The President of the Republic of Ghana, John Agyekum Kufuor and his wife and First Lady, Theresa, attended the ceremony. President Kufuor had a tribute read, which recounted Peggy's contribution through her writing to the preservation of Ghanaian culture. As a mark of traditional respect, the King of Asante Otumfuo Osei Tutu II made a similar gesture of appreciation. This achievement had also been recognized in a different sense by Queen Elizabeth II of England with the conferment upon Peggy of an MBE.

Peggy's work was an important part of the post-colonial cultural movement in Ghana and Africa. She wrote extensively on Asante folklore and made an interesting contribution to Ghanaian cultural studies with publications such as *Ananse the Spider: Tales from an Ashanti Village* (1966): *The Pineapple Child and Other Tales from Ashanti* (1969); *A Smell of Onions* (1971); *Gift of the Mmotia* (1972); *A Dirge Too Soon* (1976); *Tales of an Ashanti Father* (1989); *Afua and the Mouse* (1991); and *Kofi and the Crow* (1991) among others.

In addition to this remarkable collection of books on indigenous Asante cultural wisdom and folklore, Peggy also collected gold weights in many villages throughout the land of Asante and endeavoured to decipher their proverbial meanings. She would spend days and weeks speaking with several individuals and groups of people, among who were the ordinary villagers of the land, the courtiers at the palace of chiefs, the care-takers of shrines and the elite within society. Some of the latter group in particular included the cultural avant-gardists of her generation such as the celebrated Ghanaian inventor and musicologist Ephraim Amu, Alex Atta Yaw Kyerematen and the Asantehenes or Kings of Asante, Otumfuo Sir Osei Agyeman Prempeh II and Otumfuo Opoku Ware II. The last two mentioned in particular offered Peggy a very sophisticated and wonderful window of appreciation into the cosmology of the Asante, including their traditional beliefs, philosophy and culture in general.

Peggy's husband and greatest supporter Joe Appiah related to her many of the stories and proverbs which now make up her impressive corpus of anthropological and philosophical literature. By the 1960s, she felt so much at home in Ghanaian society that according to a quote published in her obituary in *The Times* of London, she told Ghana's first President, Osagyefo Kwame Nkrumah that: "Over the years, I have come to regard this country as my own and I genuinely feel Ghanaian." That feeling derived more from a sense of cultural emplacement and familiarity than anything else. Yet this was a woman who, having studied the History of Art in Italy and learnt about painting in London, had travelled with her father to Iran, Mexico, China and other non-African nations, and thus had very little knowledge of Africa apart from the numerous anti-colonial agitations by African students in London that she was witness to. Her parents had supported these anti-colonial movements and had particularly followed the activities of the West Africa Students Union (WASU) of which Joe Appiah, Peggy's husband-to-be, was President.

Significantly, Peggy Appiah's migration to Ghana would coincide with the intellectual renaissance in African cultural self-awareness and self-understanding that would flourish especially in West and East Africa as part of the anti-colonial movement as a whole. Many researchers including the highly respected Ghanaian Africanist J.H. Kwabena Nketia, the scholar Joseph Agyeman-Duah, the politician and Prime Minister of Ghana from 1969-72, Dr Kofi Abrefa Busia, and the English historians Ivor Wilks and Basil Davidson were collecting stool histories, lyrics of music and oral traditions of African history for the first time. In Ghana, it helped as other consciousness raising activities in Africa did to contest and overturn the ignorant and misinformed view of the 20th English Regius Professor of Modern History at Oxford University, Hugh Trevor-Roper that Africa was "a continent of darkness" and that "darkness" was "not a subject of history." Trevor-Roper's presumptions that Africans had no history and that history in Africa started with the arrival of the Europeans would be rendered untenable by the huge work-in-progress then and even now, which delved into the African past in a process of historical retrieval and cultural self-recuperation.

Though the immediate post-independent years after British colonialism in Africa provided the occasion for several African writers to rewrite the glorious histories of African empires, civilizations and societies, it was also an era of great urban expansion and migration from the villages to the towns and cities. This was thus also a period of disproportionate Westernisation. As a result, the process of cultural and ideological decolonization suffered a setback. This affected some aspects of Ghanaian culture for example. It is for this reason that many Ghanaians were and still are unconsciously impressed with Western and European knowledge systems with undue reverence for the works, quotations and thoughts of such English writers as William Shakespeare, William Wordsworth, Charles Dickens, Jane Austen and other writers of empire. While there is absolutely nothing wrong with admiring the work of others from a different culture, a significant repercussion has been that some Africans have ended up downgrading the rich cultural heritage of African, Asian and Caribbean societies. An obvious and striking example is the Trinidadian writer V.S. Naipaul, who has written a lot about so-called underdeveloped Caribbean cultures.

In Ghana too, the syllabus for primary and secondary education especially that relating to language development, has not shown the necessary reverence for Ghanaian languages and other important aspects of our indigenous cultures such as proverbs. It is in this respect that one finds particularly useful the many works and co-initiatives of Peggy Appiah. Of her several works, the one that stands out most in repudiation of Trevor-Roper's racially prejudiced assertions despite remaining unpublished for many years is *Bu Me Bɛ: Proverbs of the Akans*. First published locally in 2001 by *The Centre for Intellectual Renewal* in Ghana, it belongs to an important school of Ghanaian philosophical thought. This work was produced late on in Peggy's life as she neared the end of her productive days and years. Interestingly, as she began to lose her memory, she wanted very much to see the publication of this collection, which she started alone, but which was later joined by her son Kwame Anthony Appiah, whose many interests include the theory of Art and Philosophy.

Anthony Appiah grew up in Kumasi before he attended English boarding school and then went on to the University of Cambridge to study Philosophy after abandoning Medicine, which he did not find interesting. He spoke and still speaks Twi and remembers when his mother started this collection:

> I learned about art growing up in my hometown in Kumasi, the capital of Asante, an old Akan Kingdom at the heart of the new republic of Ghana. There were paintings and drawings on our walls; there were sculptures and pots, in wood and ivory and earthenware and brass; and there were art books in the bookcases. But above all, my mother collected Asante gold weights: small figures or geometrical shapes, cast in brass, usually from wax originals, that had been weighing gold dust when it was our currency (and continued well into this century). These figurative gold weights were wonderfully expressive: they depict people and animals, plants and tools, weapons and domestic utensils, often in arrangements that will remind the Asante who looks at them of a familiar proverb....'

In this second edition of *Bu Me Bε* by Ayebia, an emergent and important press on African studies in the UK and internationally, in which we have aimed for an international readership, the text has apart from this introduction hardly changed shape from its original. Peggy, who in a sense is still living through her *Preface* to the work, gives the history of this publication from the moment over thirty years ago when it started. She writes of the people she started with as well as the many intellectual debts she incurred along the way. Important among these is the precedent set by the German missionary, philologist, and linguist Johann Gottlieb Christaller (1827–1895), who has been described as the "founder of scientific linguistic research in West Africa." Christaller did missionary work in many villages of the then Gold Coast and translated the Bible into Twi. He was the same man who had earlier in the mid-nineteenth century started a similar project to Peggy's, which ended up as the compilation *Three Thousand Six Hundred Ghanaian Proverbs: From the Asante and Fante Languages*. This work was first published by the Basel Mission in 1879. *Bu Me Bε: Proverbs of the Akans* can be said to be without question the most extensive and up-to-date book since Christaller's important publication on Twi proverbs. This is a major achievement given that in Africa to date, Christaller's *Three Thousand Six Hundred Ghanaian Proverbs: From the Asante and Fante Languages* is still one of the most important sources of Asante and Akan proverbial lore and wisdom.

Anthony Appiah's "Introduction," which follows the *Preface* is a manifestation of how these proverbs can compare to philosophical musings anywhere from Greece to England and beyond. Himself a deep thinker in the theory and philosophy of language, Appiah demonstrates how these Akan proverbs could be interpreted within the tested and contested theories of meaning and literary production. To understand these proverbs, however, one also needs to understand the culture from which they come. It is worth stating here therefore that the matrilineal Akan culture traces familial lineage from the mother's side. Hence we say that a child may resemble his father, but he has a family – the family being a reference to one's mother and to others within the mother's bloodline. This helps to partially define Akan familial construction, and is a pointer to Akan religion and to the many figurative beliefs and political systems, which include access to capital, labour and land within the entire economic system.

"Akan Cultures: A Brief Introduction", the discussion which precedes this second "Introduction", is also meant to help the reader understand some of the contexts within which some of the proverbs were derived although not in an extensive manner. The bibliography is also a major help to a fuller and more meaningful understanding. The complexity of language may also potentially unfaze the reader. Although these proverbs and their interpretation are by no means a conventional alphabetical dictionary of words and meanings, we have provided a note about their ordering and arrangement which somewhat parallels the form of a dictionary. We hope and say so also on behalf of the deceased lead author Peggy Appiah that you will enjoy this latest edition. Our fervent hope is that a fair amount of cultural understanding will be generated among all peoples of the world wherever this collection is read.

*Ivor Agyeman-Duah*
*London*
June 2007.

# Preface

*The genius, wit and spirit of a Nation are discovered by their proverbs.*

So wrote Francis Bacon in 1594. But, whereas Westerners no longer seem to consider proverbs as words of wisdom, but rather as commonplaces, to be used in everyday conversation, in many countries of Africa, and, in particular, amongst the Akan, a truly educated and cultured person is one who can make use of proverbs and whose speech is full of the imagery and the innuendo that they make possible. Proverbs contain the philosophy, humour, symbolism and religion of the peoples who use them. They are imbued with a deep knowledge of the surrounding world, physical and spiritual, and of social realities.

No one can appreciate the philosophy and beliefs of the Akan without studying their proverbs. Even today the use of an appropriate proverb in public oratory is deeply appreciated and is often the final word in an argument. One short proverb can provide the equivalent of pages of philosophical discussion.

## The proverb

*Though we carry gunpowder, we smoke tobacco*

(**No. 5699**) is a good example of this. Even in a dangerous situation, you must enjoy the good things of life, or, as a friend once explained to me:

"Even if things are very, very bad, we must enjoy fufuo".

Thus, if people need money to pay debts, it is better, an elder will tell you, to pay the debt for them than to give them the money: for the money they might be tempted to use it for every day enjoyment. Risks must be taken to enjoy life, whatever the theoretical priorities may be.

The famous symbol of the crocodiles, with a single central stomach but two heads and tails, which illustrates the proverb

*Stomachs mixed up, crocodiles' stomachs mixed up, they both have one stomach but when they eat they fight because of the sweetness of the swallowing*

(**No. 2402**) reflects the dilemmas and the complexities of the family system. All individual actions affect the family in general (that is, all food goes in one stomach); but, as the crocodiles reply, the taste is in the throat—enjoyment is an individual and not a group experience.

Education in traditional society involved oral and not written communication; and proverbs were a way of reinforcing moral and social precepts. They teach the philosophy and way of life of the community, its customs and its prejudices. Before a person can become well versed in customary behaviour, they must have a broad knowledge of proverbs to illustrate and emphasize their statements. This knowledge is, and was, learnt by listening to the elders. It is in the village context, where the elders gather together to discuss village and state affairs, to reminisce and to pass on their wisdom to the young, that the richness of the proverb is most manifest. In Chieftaincy or Stool affairs, above all, knowledge of proverbs are essential. It is one of the main qualifications of the Stool linguist. An aspiring Akan orator is expected to know many proverbs and to be able to cite to provide points of comparison, illustrating general truths about human behaviour, during legal proceedings and on deliberative occasions. Proverbs can be used to summarize what would otherwise be a long and tedious disquisition. They can, also, like the folk tales, be used as a polite—and oblique—form of criticism, when direct speech would cause offence, and they are thus a way of avoiding quarrels or conflict.

The Akan do not always favour clear and direct statement, and proverbs are used when people do not want to be immediately and directly understood, or where a double meaning or a prevarication is required. Proverbs can also be used to emphasize a statement or argument, especially where it is desired to show that there is precedent for a certain action. Present actions are interpreted in terms of the past, and given the aura of the conventional by their association with familiar forms of words.

This collection of proverbs has been made over many years and has been obtained in many different ways. The greatest debt is owed to Christaller, whose collection of 3,600 proverbs in Fante and Akuapem-Twi, made in the mid–nineteenth century, has formed the basis of every collection since published in Europe. His dictionary, from Twi into English, is still the only good one available, and he cross-referenced it with the proverbs, making their translation substantially easier. This collection of over 7,000 is, however, in the Asante-Twi dialect, which is slightly different from Akuapem-Twi. Most of the proverbs are common to the two dialects, but we have always used the Asante-Twi version in this collection.

Mr. C. E. Osei, one of the elders of the last generation, generously gave his written collection of proverbs, some of which confirmed those already collected, some of which were new. Almost all the translation and some of the collection have been done in collaboration with Yaw Adusi-Poku, whose book, in part, this is. He has spent patient hours chewing over the translations of the written Asante-Twi versions. Mr. K. Nsiah, who is a gifted recorder of the old oral tradition and whose own proverbs are indistinguishable from the main tradition, has given us his own collection, and, by consulting the elders in his family, has helped to explain some of the difficulties and, in particular, the historical allusions. Mr. A. C. Denteh, the Twi scholar, provided us with invaluable advice and criticism. A list of other sources, including some of the individuals who have helped, appears at the end of the book. (Appendix B).

My own individual contribution has been the proverbs collected while doing research on the Asante goldweights, in Asante, Brong-Ahafo and other Twi-speaking areas. Sitting in village compounds and in the houses of their chiefs, I was able to record many proverbs not actually needed for their association with the weights. Wandering conversations on objects and artefacts used in the village, the farm and the forest, produced many stories which later allowed me to understand some of the more difficult proverbs. Amongst the aged there is nostalgia for the past, for a time in which, as imaginative memory has it, the boundaries between fiction and reality were blurred. As one old man told me sadly:

> "In the old days if I had told you this stone was a tortoise, you would have seen it get up and walk!"

Village life changes slowly and the proverbs and spider stories—the Anansensɛm—often seem, as one sits in the village, more real than modern life. Since so few books have been published in Asante-Twi, some of the words, such as the names of plants, birds, insects and animals, have been hard to verify, and we have probably made some mistakes in translation. In addition, just as in the English language, words have changed through the years, and one image has sometimes taken the place of another, making the meaning difficult to recover. There are many very local varieties of the same proverbs (and words) and the ones I have recorded may not be the favourite versions in all Akan areas. After listening to hour-long conversations as to exactly what certain proverbs mean or as to whether the wording is one way or another, in the end I have had to make a personal choice. One difficulty in translating or explaining a proverb is the number of different contexts within which a single proverb may be used. It is impossible to explain all the uses, even if one is aware of them; it is the occasion that brings a proverb to mind and a skilled user will exploit the subtleties of a proverb to the maximum.

Finally, the proverbs provide a richness of poetic imagery and vision which makes them a distillation of the best of Akan languages and oral literature. They give inspiration to drum and horn language, give depth to the funeral dirges and the appellations of the chiefs, and are used symbolically in many items of stool paraphernalia, where visual designs have associated proverbial meanings. To those who use them and to us who collect them alike, the proverbs are a treasure beyond price. For me, the gathering of them has been a great joy; and I have spent many hours immersed in their study and arrangement. They should be preserved and cherished in all their richness profound or punning, profane or philosophical, obvious (occasionally) and, (more often) illuminatingly obscure. They are, in sum, the verbal shrine for the soul of a nation.

Those mistakes in recording and vocabulary that remain I must regret. Such a collection should be a challenge to Akan scholars—to correct, add to and adapt according to their own knowledge and vision. This is only a first effort to publish a portion of this rich tradition with accompanying translations and glosses, so that it shall not be lost to the world in general and to the future generations of the Akan in particular.

Peggy Appiah
Ghana
2000.

# Introduction

*Asɛm a ehia Akanfoɔ no na Ntafoɔ de goro brɛkɛtɛ.*
A matter which troubles the Akan people, the people of Gonja take to play the
*brɛkɛtɛ* drum. (Proverb 5480)

*Kaka ne ɛka ne ayafunka fanyinam ɛka.*
Toothache and indebtedness and stomachache, debt is preferable. (Proverb 3010)

*Kampesɛkwakye se: sɛ onim sɛ abɛ rebɛbere a, anka wankɔware adɔbɛ nkonto.*
The drongo says: if he had known that the palm nuts were going to ripen, then he
would not have married the raffia palm with a twisted leg.
(Proverb 3019)

These proverbs are but three of the 7000-odd proverbs that my mother has collected over roughly the period of my lifetime, and she and some colleagues have been trying to understand them for the last two decades; latterly I have joined them in setting out to prepare this book, which records many of these sayings for the first time in writing, that glosses them in English, and that offers also, in each case what I have just offered you: what we call a literal translation.

Coincidentally, I have spent much of the same decade working in what philosophers call the theory of meaning: in the activity of trying to say what an adequate theoretical account of the meanings of words and phrases and sentences should look like.

It would seem natural enough, *prima facie*, to bring these two activities – of translating and theorizing about meaning – together, because of the simplest of beginning thoughts about translation: namely that it is an attempt to find ways of saying in one language something that means the same as what has been said in another. What I would like to do in this introductory essay is to explore some of the reasons why it is that this *prima facie* thought should be resisted: most of what interests us in the translations that interest us most is not meaning, in the sense that philosophy of language uses the term; in many cases, as the proverbs surely show, and for reasons they exemplify, getting the meaning, in this sense, right is hardly even a first step towards understanding.

\*\*\*

Let me start again with a simple thought: what we translate are utterances, things said and written by men and women, with voice or pen or keyboard; and those utterances are the products of actions, which like all actions, are undertaken for reasons. Since reasons can be complex and extensive, grasping an agent's reason can be a difficult business; and we can easily feel that we have not dug deeply enough, when we have told the best story we can. Utterances – ordinary everyday remarks – are, in this respect somewhat unusual: for while it may not be easy to give a *full* account of why someone has, for example, uttered the words "It's a lovely sunny day," in the ordinary course of things English speakers will be inclined to suppose that anyone who says this to them has, as one reason for uttering, the intention to express the thought that it is a lovely sunny day.

I say "in the ordinary course of things" because, in odd enough circumstances, we might suppose no such thing; and that is because in odd enough circumstances it might not be true. Perhaps – to impose on you one of those bizarre fantasies that mark the style of the philosopher – this is a speaker who has been told this is an English sentence without being told what it means; perhaps, she is uttering it not to express that thought – which she does not know it expresses – but to mislead us into thinking she is Anglophone. Perhaps we know all this. Perhaps. Still esoteric utterances do ordinarily propose themselves as motivated, at least in part, by a desire to express a certain specific thought.

This is easy enough, of course, to explain: part of what is distinctive about utterance as a kind of action, with distinctive sorts of reasons, is that it is *conventional*; and the thought we normally take someone to be intending to express in uttering a sentence is the thought that the conventions of language associates with it.

The philosopher H.P. Grice once suggested that we could say what an utterance meant by identifying the belief that it was conventionally intended to produce; and he identified, correctly in my view, the heart of the mechanism by which these beliefs are supposed to be produced. Roughly, he suggested that when a speaker communicates a belief by way of the utterance of a sentence, she does so by getting her hearers to recognize *both* that this is the belief she intends them to have *and* that she intends them to have that belief in part *because* they recognize that primary intention. This is the heart of utterance-meaning; the conventions of language associate words with roles in determining *which* belief is to be communicated by an utterance, but it is by way of the Gricean mechanism that this communication occurs, when it does.

The general theoretical point here is that it is possible to have the reasons we ordinarily have for uttering only because there exists within any community of speakers of a single language a specific structure of mutual expectations about reasons for uttering. Learning the grammar and the lexicon of a language is learning a complex set of instructions for generating acts that are standard and intended to achieve their effects in others who know the same instructions and precisely by way of a recognition of those intentions.

When somebody speaks, therefore, in the ordinary course of things and in the absence of contrary evidence, she will be taken and will expect to be taken, by participants in the conventions of her language to have the intentions that those conventions associate, by way of grammar and lexicon, with her utterance.[1] To be able to identify *those* intentions is to know the literal meaning of what she has said; and the literal meanings of words and phrases are determined by the way in which they contribute to fixing the intentions associated with the speech-acts in which they can occur. Let me call these the *literal* intentions. While each utterance of a sentence will be surrounded and motivated by more than its literal intentions, will have (in other words) more reasons than these; and while *some* utterances will not even have these intentions – because, for example, they are clearly ironically intended; it remains true that explanations of what a speaker is doing in uttering a sentence will almost always involve reference to the standard intentions, even in the cases where they are absent.

\*\*\*

If, as I originally suggested, translation is an attempt to find ways of saying in one language something that means the same as what has been said in another; and if, as I have recently suggested, the literal meaning of an utterance is a matter of what intentions a speaker would ordinarily be taken to have in uttering it; then a literal translation ought to be a sentence of, for example, English, that would ordinarily be taken to be uttered with the intention that the original, for example, Twi, sentence, was conventionally associated with.

This thought has been rejected more often than it has been affirmed in recent philosophy because, for a variety of reasons, it has been thought that what language you speak affects what thoughts you can have. If what language you speak determines what thoughts or intentions you can have, translation, thus conceived, will always be impossible.

Perhaps because I was brought up between several languages, not all of them varieties of English, I have never quite believed that this could be right. Of course there are some thoughts that it is hard to imagine someone having without *some* language – the thought that a particle is an atomic nucleus, for example – and others that require linguistic knowledge constitutively – the thought that Ronald Reagan's cat is smarter than my dog surely requires that I know Mr. Reagan's name. But surely there are thoughts – "It's a cat," say – that you can have without speaking English; have, uncontroversially, no questions begged. And if that is so, can we not see how you could have the thought that this is an atomic nucleus, not because you know the words "atomic nucleus" but because you know some other words that refer, in some other language, to the same thing. So, at least, I think, though I shall not argue it here; because what I want to notice, now, is that even if this is right, we need only consider

---

[1]Of course the conventions may make the intentions depend on features of the context – what is perceptually salient, what has just been said, what time it is, and a whole host more such features.

the case of proper names to see that it will often be a matter of luck whether the relevant intentions are possible for both of the two communities, between which we are translating. To make the point at its least complicated, it is no surprise that you cannot exactly say in Twi that the colour of the wall is "burnt Sienna."

This impossibility, though of the first importance in translation, is not theoretically puzzling; explanations of why Twi does not have the concept of burnt Sienna or of an atomic nucleus are too obvious to be worth giving. What I am inclined to deny is the more exciting claim – which follows from any view that involves holism about meanings – that we cannot translate any talk at all, because, for example, every sentence in which it can occur subtly shades the meaning of every word, so that "table" and "Tisch" do not mean the same, because nothing adequately gets the sense of "Der Tisch ist gemütlich." In standard circumstances the literal intentions with which I utter "It's a table" and Hans says "Es ist ein Tisch" are, for all the arguments I know, the same.

On this topic I am only saying where I stand, not making arguments: if I am right there are barriers to translation to be noted here, but, as I say, while they are important to an understanding of why translation is so difficult, they do not seem theoretically puzzling. If you cannot conventionally communicate a certain literal intention in language A and you can in language B, then the translator cannot produce a literal translation; that is all it amounts to.

***

Let us look back at the proverbs with which I began, and explore them for a moment with some of these distinctions in mind. What you need now, along with all this apparatus, is a little richer contextualization. These sayings belong to a *genre* – what I have called the proverb, which in Twi is called εbε (pl. mmε) – that is well known to speakers of that language. In the case of the last proverb – the drongo says: if he had known that the palm nuts were going to ripen, then he would not have married the raffia palm with a twisted leg – it is recognizable by its *form* as a proverb; speaker and hearers of such a proverb, know that drongos don't speak and that one kind of bε begins "The such–and–such says: ..." and thus have mutual knowledge, in the ordinary course of things, that this is, indeed, mmεbuo, proverb-making.[2]

The first immediate consequence of this mutual recognition is that the literal intentions are, so to speak, cancelled. Just as, when I begin a narration with the words "Once upon a time, ..." I withdraw the usual license to suppose that I believe what I am saying to be, as we say, literally true, so recognition that I am uttering an εbε cancels the implication that what I am saying is literally true. (It does not carry the implication that what I say is literally *false*, however). What makes this case different from the fairy-tale "Once upon a time ... " is that a different intention is now conventionally implied: an implication to the effect that, starting with the literal meaning – starting from the very literal intentions I have "cancelled" – and building on mutually known fact (some of it, perhaps, extremely context-bound) you can work out a truth that I *do* intend to express.

Thus, in a typical use of the first proverb, for example – A matter which troubles the Akan people, the people of Gonja take to play the brεkεtε drum – I might utter it in the midst of an argument with my father about whether it matters that I do not want to go to church with him one Sunday; our contrasting attitudes, he will infer, are being likened to the contrasting attitudes of Dagomba and Akan peoples – for the brεkεtε drum is one they play for entertainment at dances, and represents fun. Different peoples have different attitudes, is the generalization that seems to cover both cases, the one we may suppose he will grasp, by the Gricean mechanism, as my target thought. In this inference the literal intentions of the proverb-sentence have to be identified to go through the reasoning – the literal meaning is there and is what the sentence means; but it is not, so to speak, what I mean by it.

Proverbs have utterance meanings, and those utterance meanings are the ones that convention associates with those words in that order. But in the broader sense of meaning, in

---

[2]This proverb would naturally be used in a context where someone has expressed vain regrets. The thought is something like this: that if you (the drongo) had known that one person (the palm–nuts) would prosper, you would not have relied on a person who was less successful (the crippled raffia–palm).

the sense of meaning which has to do with understanding adequately why someone has spoken as she has–where that means, minimally, *understanding* what she *intends* us to understand by way of the Gricean mechanism–it is plain that proverbs do not mean only what they say.

\*\*\*

I have been essentially accepting the thought that meaning in the broadest sense is what is communicated by the Gricean mechanism. Literal intentions work in the Gricean way; I have suggested that the proverbs do, too, though I have not said much about how. It is clear, I think, that metaphor works like this, however the details go. On one sort of contemporary view, "Juliet is the sun" is a literal falsehood which invites us to think of Juliet as standing to the speaker as the sun stands to the world; on another, resurrected by Bob Fogelin, it is elliptical for a simile whose rough meaning is that "Juliet has a significant number of the (contextually) salient features of the sun."[3] So she is central, a source of warmth and nourishment, enlivening, important and–one must add prosaically– ... and so on. But on either view the metaphor is supposed to work by getting you to see how it is supposed to work and getting you to recognize that that is how I want you to understand it. And here both convention (*metaphor*, however it works in detail, is known to all of us) and specific features of the mutual knowledge of speaker and hearer that derives from context interact to produce meaning.

What philosophers of language have largely attended to in thinking about meaning are these Gricean aspects of meaning–they include both what are normally thought of as semantical and as pragmatic phenomena, and they broadly, as I say, exhaust the range of philosophical interest in language. Having identified this interest and its scope, my argument from now is directed towards examining the ways in which the point of much translation transcends what I am calling the Gricean aspects of meaning.

\*\*\*

And to begin to see why, let us observe that the sorts of things I have been saying about meaning are not much favoured by those who spend their time in literary studies, in part, I think, because faced with a real live text, it seems bizarrely inappropriate to spend one's time speculating about the author's intentions: the author may be long dead, unknown to us, uninteresting, and surely, it will seem, her intentions have nothing to do with what we are interested in. Nor do I disagree with any of this: whether a work is fictional or not, our literary interest in it has usually very little to do with psychological facts about its historical author. But it remains true that in order to begin to have a literary understanding of many texts, we must usually first know its language well enough to be able to identify what the intentions conventionally associated with each of its sentences are: that we must begin with the literal meanings of words, phrases, sentences. More than this, in understanding many of the texts that we address as literary, we must grasp not merely the literal intentions but the whole message that would be communicated by the utterance of the sentence in more ordinary settings: metaphor and implicature, as they occur in fiction, occur also outside it. These more complex elements of the Gricean message of the utterance in its context also occur with the usual intentions suspended: we do not have to believe that Jane Austen tells us that it is a truth universally acknowledged that a single man in possession of a fortune must be in need of a wife in order to express her own ironic attitude to the relations of marriage, gender and property, but we are plainly meant to rely on our understanding of the fact that an utterance of this sentence would convey that ironic attitude outside the fiction.

Many, perhaps most texts, in other words, require us to grasp the Gricean burden that the words would bear in ordinary uses. But only "most"; for with some texts–symbolist poems, the late James Joyce, the productions of the dada "poets"–it seems that, while we often need to understand the roles that the words in those texts play in their more normal habitats, there is no intention at all that our language associates with the strings of words that fall between periods. And sometimes, as in Joyce (and Jabberwocky), we do not even have

---

[3]Robert J. Fogelin *Figuratively Speaking* (New Haven: Yale University Press, 1988).

word-meanings to rely on: the words themselves often have no established meaning - no rules for how they should contribute to determining literal intentions; and what we then do is either to see them as made from existing words, invoking those meanings, or to rely on associations of sound and thought that are based on other things than meanings, or, perhaps, to give up altogether!

But even in the case of narrative fiction, where the sentences do not raise these problems of identifying the literal intentions, I agree, as I say, that the literal intentions can hardly be the point of the matter, since to be packaged as fiction is to be offered with the literal intentions cancelled.

It is a serious question, I think, why on earth we should have the practice of producing language whose understanding requires us both to grasp what would have been its literal intentions and to accept that these are not the writer's intentions in the present case. It is a question about whether we can *justify* the practice of fiction externally. It is plain, that we *can*, though the story is complicated and has many elements, but that is not an issue to pursue now. What *is* important now is that literary practice, like linguistic practice, is conventional - which is to say it is governed by a specific structure of mutual expectations - but that these literary conventions - unlike linguistic conventions - do not usually invoke the Gricean mechanism.

Akan uses of proverbs are, in this respect, quite atypical. To use a proverb *as such* is, to imply that, starting with the literal meaning - starting from the very literal intentions I have "cancelled" - and building on mutually known fact (some of it, perhaps, extremely context-bound) you can work out a truth that I *do* intend to express, even though it is not the truth associated with the literal intentions. This is a feature that proverbs share with two genres of fiction - the parable and the fable - but not with most others. While the form of the novel is constrained by historically developing conventions, those conventions do not carry a message: are not, that is, supposed to operate in such a way as to allow us to read off the governing intentions of the author, to answer the question why did she write this. And it is for this reason, I think, that attention to intentions - in the novel and in many other genres - is likely to strike us as a mistake.

Literary conventions, simply put, make possible acts that can be defined by reference not only to the meanings - both literal and non-literal, direct and indirect - of utterances; but also to features that are broadly formal - alliteration, meter, rhyme, plot-structure. What they do not usually do - and here, proverbs are an exception - is determine how we should construct a meaning - in the sense of a set of intentions operating through the Gricean mechanism, for the work.

Because the novel and the sonnet are not conventionally constituted by a process of meaning-generation, there is no set of conventions to which we can refer, analogous to the conventions of literal meaning, for deciding what the work means; there are no literary intentions, conventional and Gricean, to correspond to literal intentions. Because there are literal intentions we can say what a literal esoteric utterance is for - it is to communicate such-and-such information; it may be possible, then, in literal translation, to find a sentence in a target language that has more or less the same literal intentions as the utterance in the object-language. If it is not possible, it may be clear enough why: there is no way of expressing that thought in the target language, perhaps because the referent of some term is unknown there, or because a social practice in which the utterance is embedded - the curse, say - is absent. Success and failure at this level are well enough defined.

But for literary translation our object is not to produce a text that reproduces the literal intentions of the author - not even the ones she is cancelling - but to produce something that shares the central literary properties of the object-text; and, as is obvious, these are very much under-determined by its literal meaning, even in the cases where it has one. A literary translation, aims at producing a text whose relation both to the literary and to the linguistic conventions of the culture of the translation is relevantly like the relations of the object-text to its culture's conventions. A precise set of parallels is likely to be impossible, just because the chances that metrical and other formal features of a work can be reproduced while preserving the identity of literal and non-literal, direct and indirect, meaning, are vanishingly small.

And, in fact, we may choose, rightly, to translate a term in a way that is unfaithful to the literal intentions, because we are trying to preserve formal features that seem more crucial. But even if we did not have to make such choices, even if we could, *per impossibile*, meet all the constraints of the Gricean meaning and all the literary conventions, we would not have produced the perfect translation: we could do better, we could aim to reproduce literary qualities of the object–text that are not a matter of the conventions.

So that the reason why we cannot speak of the perfect translation here is not that there is a definite set of desiderata and we know they cannot all be met; it is rather that there is no definite set of desiderata. A translation aims to produce a new text that matters to one community the way another text matters to another: but it is part of our understanding of why texts matter that this is not a question that convention settles; indeed, it is part of our understanding of literary judgement, that there can always be new readings, new things that matter about a text, new reasons for caring about new properties.

***

There is then no perfect translation of a proverb, in this sense of a literary translation, because proverbs are used over and over again in different contexts for different reasons. We have sought in our more literal translations to capture Twi word order and sentence structure, so that someone who knows very little of the language can still see how it works. Some of the proverbs have obvious uses that flow from their literal meanings and these few we have not given explanatory glosses. In the glosses that occur in parentheses after most translations, on the other hand, we have tried to give you some indication of at least one way that the proverb might be used: but a really skillful orator would find new ways to new proverbs, new and surprising contexts in which he can persuade us that they are relevant. Being able to do this requires a rich understanding of the way proverbs live in Akan life; the sort of understanding that will leave you able both to understand the truth in the words with which I began:

> Asεm a εhia Akanfɔ no na Ntafɔ de goro brεkεtε.
> A matter which troubles the Akan people, the people of Gonja take to play the brεkεtε drum.

Kwame Anthony Appiah
Boston, 2001.

# Akan Cultures:
# A Brief Introduction

As social anthropologists often discover, some of those things that we take most for granted within one culture, cannot be assumed in another. And so it is when we come to consider the organisation of the family in Akan societies. For, unlike many other African societies and most of those in contemporary Europe and North America, Akan societies are matrilineal: children belong to the families of their mothers. If we call a group of living people who share common descent through the female line a matriclan, we can say that the Asante family is a sub-group of the matriclan, usually consisting of a group with a common ancestress in their grandmother or great-grandmother. This group is what is usually referred to as the *abusua*.

The head of the family is typically a child's maternal uncle – his or her mother's brother or *wɔfa* – but it may be a great-uncle, a nephew or a brother. For the senior male member of this group need not be the eldest member. This head of the family holds property in trust for the whole group and is responsible for the maintenance and the behaviour of its members. Property descends in the matriclan, again typically from uncle (*wɔfa*) to sister's son (*wɔfaase*) though there are a number of exceptions to this rule. (Thus, for example, jewellery passes from elder to younger females in the matriclan and a hunter's gun may pass to his son).

Wider than the matrilineal family is the maternal clan, which is also called the *abusua* or *ntɔn*. There are 7 or 8 clans into which all of Asante is divided: but the functioning group for most people consists of fellow clansfolk who live in the same village or town. Associated with the *ntɔn* are a number of taboos: restrictions on food, for example, or on the utterance of certain words.

Membership of this maternal group is held to flow from the fact that a person's body *(nnipadua)* is made from the blood of the mother (the *mogya*) hence the *abusua* is sometimes called the *bogya*. The other two components of a person are the *sunsum* and the ɔkra. The former – the *sunsum* – derives from the father at conception; the ɔkra is a sort of life force, which departs the body only at the person's last breath (and is sometimes, as with the Greeks and the Hebrews, identified with breath) and is sent to a person at birth, from God. (The child also acquires at birth a "day-name," the name for a male or female child born on that day of the week). Despite the primary descent group being matrilineal, Asante people also belong to a paternal clan, called the *ntorɔ*, which also has its associated taboos. These taboos are seen as arising out of the fact that the members of the *ntorɔ* have souls that share a common source and similarities of personality between father and son are held to derive from this inherited *sunsum*.

Both *abusua* and *ntorɔ* were traditionally exogamous: that is it was incestuous to marry a member of the same matriclan or patriclan. Since, therefore, my father's sister or brother is bound to marry someone who belongs to a different *ntorɔ* (for I and my father's siblings are in the same exogamous patriclan) and may quite possibly marry someone who is not in my mother's (and therefore his) matriclan, there is no barrier to his marrying his paternal cousin. To marry your mother's sister's child, however, would be incestuous: you belong to the same *abusua*.

To someone who is used to seeing the children of the siblings of either parent as cousins, distinguishing between one group, as being totally prohibited in marriage and another as not only not prohibited but sometimes encouraged is no doubt confusing. But it must be remembered that as a child's mother's brother is very often the head of his or her family, he or she may actually live in the maternal uncle's household and be brought up with the children of other maternal aunts. To marry within this group would, in effect, be like marrying a brother or sister. Indeed, my mother's sisters I call "mother," and their children I call by the same term I use to call my siblings.

The *sunsum,* unlike the ɔkra, may leave the body during life and does so, for example, in sleep, dreams being thought to be the perceptions of a person's *sunsum* on its nightly peregrinations. Since the *sunsum* is a real entity, dreaming that you have committed an offence is evidence that you have committed it, and, for example, a person who dreams that he has had sexual intercourse with another man's wife, is liable for the adultery fees which are paid for daytime offences.

Asante, the largest of the Akan societies, from which most of the proverbs in this book derive, is a monarchy, headed by a King, the Asantehene, on the male side, and the Asantehemaa, or Queen Mother on the female side. Though the Asantehene takes precedence over the Queen Mother, he is the only person that does and he is supposed to treat her with great respect. The positions of King and Queen Mother are both inherited within the matriclan so that Kings may be succeeded by their sister's children, or their brother's, but never by their sons. And likewise Queen Mothers are succeeded often by nieces or great-nieces.

Below the King, are the great Paramount chiefs, each with his queen mother. And beneath the Paramount Chiefs are lesser chiefs, in a hierarchy that descends to the level of the village chief and his queen mother.

Both the Asantehene and the Asantehemma and every other chief and queen mother have their palaces, their courtiers and their stools. The stool is the symbol of rule in Asante and the King has a Golden Stool and the Queen a silver one, which symbolize their rule. This Golden Stool is not sat upon, save at the King's enthronement, when he is lifted over to it for a moment. And it has its own palace and servants. Asante people say that the Golden Stool contains the sunsum of the Asante Nation and that it was brought down from heaven by Ɔkomfo Anɔkye the priest who with the great King Osei Tutu founded the modern Asante nation.

Amongst the courtiers at every chief's court will be found a group of *mpaninfoɔ* (elders), who advise the king and *akyeame* (or linguists), who speak for him on special occasions, as well as heralds (*asene*) who announce his coming. There are many spiritual agencies in the Akan world, beginning at the head of the pantheon with the sky-God, Nyame, or Onyankopɔn. Nyame is not particularly close to the everyday world, and has no special priests or temples or cult. There are myths about why Nyame removed himself from close proximity to humankind. Nevertheless, almost every traditional compound or group of dwellings has outside the main entrance to the main courtyard a cleft-stick with a bowl in the cleft, which is called a *Nyame Dua*, a tree of God. This usually contains, apart from offerings of food and drink that may be placed in it, a small stone, called a *Nyame Akuma* (an axe of God). These are believed to be sent down in lightning bolts (hence "axe"-they cut down trees) and it is believed that wherever lightning strikes one of these enters the earth. Archeologists would recognize them as Neolithic celts.

To say that Nyame has no special cult is emphatically not to say that he is not regularly mentioned in prayer. Almost every prayer to a lesser divinity will begin with a mention of Nyame, and the Nyame Dua receives regular offerings. But Nyame is different in having no special shrine or priests. Many Asante proverbs evidence a belief in Nyame's ubiquity and power.

Nyame had sons, of whom he sent four to earth. These four are associated with great waters. The senior Tano is associated with the Tano River, Bosomtwe is a lake in Asante, Bea is a river, and Ɔpo is the Atlantic Ocean. Each of these has its associated taboos: foods, words and so on which the priests and those seeking help from the god may not use. Tano had, in the 1920's when Rattray was writing the classical ethnography of Asante, temples at Tano Ɔboase. There lived the priests of Tano, to whom people could go to make requests in important matters: Kings would go there before great military campaigns, for example.

Apart from Nyame and the main gods, who are his sons, there is Asaase Yaa, the Earth Goddess. (Asaase means earth. Yaa is a day-name for Thursday, which is her special day). She, like Nyame, has no special priests or cult and like him is mentioned in the prayers at most shrines. She is treated with respect and, in the past, it was a capital offence to have sexual intercourse on the bare earth, as this was thought to be an offence to her. Below Nyame, his sons, and Asaase Yaa, there is a large number of lesser gods or spirits, the *abosom*. These may be found associated, for example, with trees or rocks. They would have offerings and prayers made to them. Following Ghanaian English, we have usually translated "*abosom*" as "fetishes." Just as the priests of Tano are called akɔmfoɔ, so too are the priests who serve the *abosom*. Indeed the main obvious differences between the four great gods who are children of the sky–God and other lesser gods or *abosom*, are

a) that an appeal to an *abosom* would usually be made by people who live relatively near its shrine, while Tano, for example, used to be visited by people from all over Asante; and
b) that a single priest might serve an *abosom*, while Tano had a large organized priesthood.

Some *abosom* speak through their priests while in trance but not all do so. Where an *abosom* resides in a tree, the tree itself is not the object of the priest's rites. But there are rites in which the spirits of certain trees (and animals), those in particular which have the power to do harm, are propitiated. Thus, of the main trees that are used in carving, people would say: "Ɛnyɛ koraa." And when a woodcarver is cutting such a tree he will address it, offer it, say, an egg, and ask it not to let the knife cut him. (The spirit of the tree may be asked in a later ritual to come and inhabit the stool that the carver makes).

I have mentioned the high gods and the lower gods, and I have mentioned that animals, plants and people have spirits: and when people die they become *samanfoɔ,* the spirits of ancestors. These sometimes roam the earth as ghosts, but the more respected of them have shrines set up to them in the households of their *abusua.* Here senior members of the family may seek advice – with a member of the family perhaps being "taken over" by the spirit of an ancestor – or ask for help in important projects.

Apart from the sky–God and his sons, the Earth Goddess, the *abosom* and the ancestor spirits, there are four other sorts of spiritually significant creatures: *mmotia* (the little creatures), *Sasabonsam,* (a forest monster) and *obayifoɔ* and *bonsam* (male and female witches). *Mmotia* are thought to be about a foot high, come in three colours, red, white and black and converse by whistling. They live in the forest, but run through the rafters of houses at night. The black ones are harmless, but the white and the red ones are thought to be the cause of great mischief. (They are not to be confused with dwarfs). The *mmotia* often are found serving *abosom* as their messengers and agents and many priests claim to have learned their knowledge of healing and the making of *suman,* or charms, from them.

*Sasabonsam* is a larger creature, and is believed to be found in remoter parts of dense forest. Covered with long hair, it has large blood–shot eyes (in Twi "my eyes are red" means I am angry), and long legs with a full turn at the knee, so that their feet, too, face backwards. It is disposed to sit on the branches of trees hanging its legs down to hook the hunter who does not take care where he is going. *Sasabonsam* is in league with witches – sasa means charged with magical power (usually for evil) and *bonsam* means witch – and with the bad red and white *mmotia*.

Finally, witches. As in many cultures, the majority of witches are thought to be female (a*bayifo*) and they are thought to be unable to do harm to people outside their clan. Odd–looking women (for example those with much facial hair) are often accused of witchcraft. Witches were sought out by witchfinders and executed, if found, by the King's executioners. Since their blood must not be shed, they were strangled.

Witches – and again the ideas are familiar – are believed to be in league with each other, can turn themselves into birds, (owls, crows, vultures and parrots) animals, (elephants, bush–cow and other *sasa* animals) and also into such things as houseflies. They are thought sometimes to glow at night.

The association of witches with darkness or nightly agenda shows the extent of its assumed evil countenance. Anthropologists would tell you that the belief also existed for centuries in pre–modern European societies as shown in the literary works of William Shakespeare. It could be argued as being part of the evolutionary belief system of pre–modern societies including the Akans.

# Appendix A
# A Note on the Ordering

In Asante-Twi nouns often have an initial vowel when they occur as the first word in a sentence, and this vowel is dropped in some other positions. All forms of the verb elide with a personal pronoun which precedes them, but not with a proper noun, and all pronouns begin with M, W, _ or Y. Furthermore, plurals for nouns are often formed by prefixing an initial M or N; and where an M precedes a B or an N precedes a D, they are elided to produce MM and NN respectively. The same elision occurs in the negative form of the verb, which is formed with an M before B M or P, and an N otherwise. A listing of proverbs that proceeded in alphabetical order by initial letter would thus have considerable disadvantages. A proverb which begins "Worekɔ..." (You (singular) are going), for example, would be listed under W and next to Woreko (You singular) are fighting), but far distant from "Yerekɔ" (We are going) which would be under Y; and a proverb beginning "Ɔbaa..." (Woman), would be under Ɔ, while proverbs beginning "Mmaa..." (Women) would be under M.

In view of these facts it is now usual, when listing Asante words, as, for example in the word-list mentioned in the bibliography, to do so according to principles close to those set out below. These principles are likely to seem complex to those familiar with alphabetic ordering of the sort found in a modern English dictionary; but we have found by experience that they provide satisfactory solutions to the sorts of problems mentioned above. We have felt that a system based on orthography was preferable to one based on a classification by subject matter for three major reasons.

First, the ordering we have used, though arbitrary from a semantic point of view, is objective. It allows anyone who wishes to find a proverb he or she knows to do so. Second, a classification by subject matter, apart from being less objective, misses the essentially fluid, situational character of the uses to which proverbs are put. Proverbs have uses not meanings – and a subject-based classification belies this fact. Third, most proverbs, even in their standard uses, are not really about just one subject matter.

Here then are the principles:
1. The basic rule is that words are put in alphabetical order by their first consonant, and proverbs are put in order by their first words. The Asante alphabet is given below.
2. Once the first consonant has been identified, words with the same first consonant go in alphabetical order by the succeeding letters. Thus "Ɔba" (Child) comes before "Abɛ" (Palmnut).
3. If two words have the same letters after the first consonant, but different vowels before it, they are put in alphabetical order by these vowels. Thus "Aba" (Seed) comes before "Ɔba" (Child). (An initial pronominal adjective, however, though written as a separate word, will be treated as part of the noun that it modifies, with the first consonant being that of the noun).
4. Plural forms, however, beginning with M or N (and sometimes with another letter) are placed immediately after their singular forms. So "Ɔbaa" (Woman) comes before "Mmaa" (Women); and "Da" (Day) is followed immediately by "Nna" (Days).
5. With verbs a slightly different principle operates. First the initial consonant of the root verb is identified; this gives the letter under which the word will be listed. Thus "Meremma" (I won't come) is listed under B, because the root verb is "Ba" (Come). The word is then placed in the list according to the alphabetical order of the succeeding letters in the root verb. Thus all forms of "Ba" come before "Baako" (One), including "Mebaeɛ" (I came). To put the various forms of the verb in order, we place all positive forms before all negative ones; and then put the words in alphabetical order in the standard (English) way.

6. We put the proverbs in order by their first word, order first words by these principles. If the first words are the same we put them in order by the second word, using the same principles. If the first two words are identical, we use the third, and so on.
7. It follows from the above rules that all proverbs must be listed under consonants. But the order of the whole alphabet, vowels included, is given below, since vowels play a part in the ordering.

   ABDEƐFGHIK(L)MNOƆPRSTUWY.
   abdeɛfghik(l)mnoɔprstuwy.

(The letter L is used only in adopted foreign words. In traditional spoken Twi English L and R are allophones: they are equivalent sounds. The only initial L in the list is in Lɔre (Lorry)).

8. It will be clear that these principles are not based purely on spelling; for they depend upon a prior distinction between verbs and other words. It is thus not possible to find a proverb without knowing the grammatical category of the initial words.
9. Where alternative versions of a proverb exist, in which one word or phrase may be substituted for another, the variants have been indicated as follows:

   "Spare the (rod)/(birch), spoil the (child)/(bairn)".

Since the alternatives are sometimes roughly synonymous, alternatives are not given in the translation where they make no substantial difference.

# Appendix B
# Informants

Abetifi
Ɔpanin Kofi Kuma
Ɔpanin Kofi Sono
Ɔbaa-panin Yaa Atonsu
Kwasi Sɛn
Kwasi Ntiamoah
Kwaku Ɔpɔn

Agona
Nkonnwa-Soafohene
Abonkro - Mampong
Ɔpanin Kofi Kyei
Osei Asibe (Custodian of the Town's Shrine)
Akomadan
Nana Kofi Nti
Mpanimfoɔ
Akrokerri
Nana Kwadwo Wusu (Benkumhene)
Nana Okyekohene, Kwadwo Ankam
Ɔpanin Anyan
Owura Mensa
Charles Amano-Kwarteng

Ampabame
Teachers from the school

Amakom, Kumasi
Ɔhemmaa Abenaa Akyeaa
Ɔkyeame Ahenkan
Ɔkyeame Atuku
Ɔkyeame Boakye
Gyasehene Kwame Boakye
Ɔpanin Kwaku Kuma
Ɔpanin Saakɔdeɛ

Antoa
Nana Antoahene
Papa Agyei
Asamankroma - Offin
J.B. Amponsah
Asarekurom
Nana Kofi Akɔkoma
Ayeduase
Kwaku Twumasi
Kwame Nsiah
Banko
Nana Spain
M.A.E. Amankwah
Abenaa Afrokoma
Afua Donkor
Baman-Bonwire
Ɔpanin Yaw Boakye
Bechem
Paul Asante

## - B -

**1. Ɛba a, ɛka oni.**
*If it comes it affects your relatives.*
(Trouble which affects one person affects their whole family group).

**2. "Ɛreba a, mɛbɔ ano ban" ne "Ɛtoto a, mɛsane", wɔn mu hwan na wowɔ n'afa? Mewɔ "Ɛreba a, mɛbɔ ano ban" afa.**
*"If it is coming, I will prevent it", and "When it is entangled, I will disentangle it", which of them will you follow? I will follow "If it is coming, I will prevent it".*
(Prevention is better than cure).

**3. "Ɛreba ɛreba na ɛyɛ hu" na ɛnya ba a, ɛnyɛ hu biom.**
*"It is coming, it is coming" is frightening; but when it actually comes it is not frightening any longer.*
(This refers to awaiting something with great expectation or fear. Once the event or phenomena occurs all the previous excitement or trepidation dissolves into normality).

**4. "Mereba, ma ɛnyɛ ansa" na ɛmaa kwakuo dua kaa hɔ.**
*"I'm coming, let this be finished first" made the monkey's tail remain.*
(This refers to a folk-tale in which delay saved the monkey from losing its tail. Hence: Sometimes delay is to your advantage. Contrast with Proverb 10).

**5. Yɛbaa mmɛbuo a, anka yɛso nkuma.**
*If we had come to "fell" proverbs, then we would carry axes.*
(Because "Ɛbɛ" (Proverb) and "Abɛ" (Palm) have the same final syllable, and "bu" is used both for "felling" (of trees) and for "making" (of proverbs) the pun here is on "felling a palm" (Bu abɛ) and "making a proverb" (Bu ɛbɛ). Since nouns beginning with B form their plurals in MM, and verbal nouns from "Bu" end in "Buo", we get "Mmɛbuo" meaning both "Palm-felling" and "Proverb-making". Proverbs are often used to prevent violence, rather than to provoke it, even though they are often thrown out in a kind of challenge. Hence: you defeat your enemy with clever words (making proverbs) rather than with violence (the axe). This proverb, like others involving puns,is also used to make the point that similarity of sound (in words) does not entail similarity of meaning; or, more generally, that objects that appear the same may not be so).

**6. Aba wo bo a, na ɛsi w'adaka mu.**
*If it has come to you, then it is in your box.*
(And if it is in your box, then you can take it out and show it. Hence: Don't boast unless you are sure you can perform what you boast about).

**7. "Bra bɛhwɛ bi" nkyerɛ sɛ "Bɛhunu sene me".**
*"Come and look too" doesn't mean "See it better than I".*
(If someone offers you something, you shouldn't take more than your fair share).

**8. "Bra bɛhwɛ nahoɔfɛ", na ɛyɛ fɛ, na ɛnyɛ "Bra besie no bi ma me".**
*"Come and see its beauty", is fine, but not "Come and help me bury".*
(You should share your advantages and not your problems, with friends).

**9. "Bra bɛhwɛ" ne deɛ woahunu.**
*"Come and see" is what you have already seen.*
(You can only talk about what you have experienced).

**10. Woamma ntɛm a, woma odwan.**
*If you don't come quickly, you give a sheep.*
(Sheep are used to pay fines. Hence: Delays may cost you dear. Contrast with Proverb 4).

**11. Aba a ɛtɔ nyinaa na efifiri a, anka obi rennya dua ase kwan.**
*If all seeds that fall were to grow, then no one could take the path under the trees.*
(If everyone were prosperous, no one would work).

**12. Ɔba a ɔbɛkyɛ no, yɛmmɔ no suman.**
*A child who will live long, we do not make it a protective charm.*
(We only try to protect what we think is in danger).

**13. Ɔba a ɔbɛyɛ yie, [yɛnnya]/[yɛnyɛn] no kɛtɛpa so nko.**
*A child which is going to turn out to be any good, we do not rear only on a special mat.*
(Kɛtɛpa is a specially luxurious sleeping mat woven out of silk yarn and raffia and used for chiefs' children. Hence: Spare the rod, spoil the child).

**14. Ɔba firi ɔse yam na ɔkɔtɔ oni yam.**
*The child comes from its father's sexual organs and it goes to its mother's womb.*
(The father provides the sunsum which creates the child, but the mother contributes mogya - blood - and nurtures it. Both are necessary. Hence: used to point out that each of the two things are essential).

**15. Ɔba gyegyefoɔ na ɔma ɔbayifoɔ adidie da adie.**
*A provocative child betrays the witch's meal.*
(People insult the mother of a naughty child by calling her a witch. Thus: One person's bad behavior brings trouble to another).

**16. Wo ba kɔ sumena so na ɔwɔ ka no a, wontwa hɔ ntwene na woyɛ no aduro.**
*If your child goes to the rubbish heap and a snake bites it, you don't cut off the place (where it was bitten), but you give it medicine.*
(If someone close to you is in real trouble, you do all you can to remedy the situation).

**17. Wo ba korɔ wu a, na wo kosua korɔ abɔ.**
*If your only child dies, your single egg is broken.*
(Said when someone has missed their last opportunity).

**18. Wo ba ne gu wo serɛ so a, wode baha na wontwa ntwene.**
*If your child defecates on your lap, you take a sponge to wipe it off, you don't take a knife and cut off the place.*
(See 16).

**19. "Ɔba no yɛ ba bɛn?" yɛse: "ɔno na ɔda hɔ no".**
*"What sex is the child?" We say: "There it lies".*
(Said when a question to which the answer is easily available is asked. Also: Seeing is believing).

**20. Ɔba nyini ɔse fie, nanso ɔnka hɔ, ɔwɔ abusua.**
*A child grows in its father's house, but it does not stay there, it has a matriclan.*
(When you grow up you belong to your mother's family not your father's, even if you were reared by the latter).

**21. Ɔba san borɔ a, yɛmmo no.**
*If a child passes the age of (lit. is finished with) being beaten, we don't beat it.*
(We treat a person according to their station).

**22. Ɔba sɛ ɔse, nanso ɔwɔ abusua.**
*A child resembles its father, but belongs to its matriclan.*
(Appearances can be deceptive).

**23. Ɔba nsɛ oni a, ɔsɛ ɔse.**
*If a child doesn't resemble its mother, then it resembles its father.*
(There are only two possibilities).

**24. Ɔba nsu a, yɛma no num.**
*If a baby does not cry, we still give it a drink.*
(Used where, for example, someone owes money but the creditor has not asked for it back, and the speaker wishes to say that the debt should be paid anyway. You don't wait to be asked for something you know you should give someone).

**25. Wo ba sa asabɔne a, se no sɛ: "Wasa nyɛ fɛ," na nse no sɛ: "Ɔkra, tete gu mu".**
*If your child is dancing badly, tell it: "Your dancing is not beautiful," but don't tell it: "Little one (lit. spirit), dance as you like".*
(Don't pamper your children)

**26. Wo ba sisi wo kora ba a, ɛnyɛ; nanso wo kora ba sisi wo ba a, ɛnyɛ.**
*When your child cheats your co-wife's child, it is no good; but when your co-wife's child cheats your child it is also not good.*
(Two wrongs don't make a right. Do as you would be done by).

**27. Abaa a yɛde bɔ nkwaseafoɔ no, onyansafoɔ dane kwasea a, yɛde bɔ no bi.**
*The stick which we take to beat foolish people, if a wise person turns foolish, we use to beat them also.*
(We punish people for their offenses, not for their character).

**28. Abaa a yɛde bɔ efie aboa no, yɛmfa mmɔ wiram aboa.**
*The stick which we take to beat the tame animal, we do not take to beat the forest animal.*
(You treat a stranger differently from a relative or a friend).

**29. Abaa a yedɛbɔ Takyi no, ɛno ara na yɛde bɔ Baa.**
*The stick we use to beat Takyi is the same one we use to beat Baa.*
(Your turn will come!)

**30. Abaa da fie a, yɛnma ɔkraman nkeka nnipa.**
*If there is a stick in the house, we don't allow the dog to bite people.*
(If we have a way of preventing trouble, we use it. See Proverb 48).

**31. Ɔbaa a ɔbɛbɔ adwaman, nnim sɛ wakɔ aware pa.**
*If a woman is going to commit adultery, it doesn't matter that she has a good marriage.*
(If you are going to commit an offence, you will do so however good your circumstances).

**32. Ɔbaa a ɔda nkunkyire na ɔpene kɔtekɔm.**
*A woman who sleeps with her husband is the one who asks for sex.*
(The person who has a right to something will ask for it).

**33. Ɔbaa a ne kunu nni hɔ na yɛdi no.**
*It is the woman whose husband is absent that we have sex with.*
(When the cat's away, the mice will play).

**34. Ɔbaa a n'ani ateɛ no, yɛdi no dantuo mu.**
*A devious woman we have sex with in an unfinished room.*
(If you have a bad character, you will be treated without respect).

**35. Ɔbaa a ɔnyem na ɔnim ne kunu.**
*A pregnant woman knows her husband.*
(Only those most intimately concerned know the real facts of a case).

**36. Ɔbaa a ɔpɛ ne ho animguase na ne kunu gye ne ho ayefere wɔ ahemfie.**
*A woman who likes disgrace, her husband collects pacification fees from the palace (i.e. in public).*
(Don't wash your dirty linen in public).

**37. Ɔbaa a ɔpɛ ne kunu, ɔse: "Mehwɛ wo ara".**
*A woman who loves her husband says: "I look up to you".*
(A loving woman respects her husband. More generally: if you trust someone, you look up to them).

**38. Ɔbaa a ɔso, na ne twɛ so no; woware no a, wontɔ mpa.**
*If a woman is fat, her vagina is also fat; if you marry her, you don't buy a bed.*
(If you have something good (i.e. in this case, to lie on), you don't use a substitute).

**39. Ɔbaa biara te sɛ deɛben ara, na ɔgyae awareɛ, gyae awareɛ a, n'anim mma nyam.**
*No matter how beautiful a woman is, if she is always divorcing (lit. stops marriage, stops marriage) she has no respect.*

**40. Ɔbaa bɔne na yɛfiri no ntoma kɔkɔɔ.**
*A bad woman, we give her a red cloth on credit.*
(A red cloth is used for funerals. Hence: We want trouble to come to those we dislike).

**41. Ɔbaa bɔne na ɔyɛ nkontomire nkwan a, ɔsa ani ngo.**
*A bad woman that is making coco-yam leaf soup collects the palm oil out of it.*
(Bad people cheat in whatever way they can).

**42. Ɔbaa bonoaa na ɔde kotokuro yi ne twɛ soɔ.**
*A tough woman uses a cutlass to shave her pubic hair.*
(You act according to your character).

**43. Ɔbaa bonoaa na ɔyi ne kɛtɛsosɛm adie.**
*A vulgar woman is one who publicizes her night-time activities (lit. sleeping mat business).*
(Discretion is a virtue).

**44. Ɔbaa brɛfoɔ kɔ awareɛ a, ɔde ade pa ba fie.**
*If a hard-working woman gets married, she brings good things into the house.*

45. Ɔbaa da ɔbarima akyi.
*A woman lies behind a man.*
(A man always takes first place, but it is the woman who backs him up).

46. Ɔbaa da ayeya a, na ɔgye ne twɛ adeɛ.
*If a woman lies on her back, then she takes her vagina's thing.*
(When you act appropriately, you get the expected results).

47. Ɔbaa de "fɛɛfɛ" nko ara kɔ awareɛ a, ɔnnya.
*If a woman uses "beauty" only to get married, she will not be successful.*
(You need more than good looks to succeed in life).

48. Ɔbaa de ka a, ɔde ne twɛ na ɛko.
*If a woman is in debt, she uses her vagina to get rid of it.*
(If we have a way of preventing trouble, we use it. See Proverb 30).

49. Ɔbaa di ɔbaa adeɛ, na ɔbarima di ɔbarima adeɛ.
*A woman inherits a woman's things, a man inherits a man's things.*
(There must be order in society; conventions must be followed).

50. Ɔbaa dɔ ne twɛ ho bebrebe a, ɔkɔ awareɛ a, ɔnnya.
*A woman who constantly withdraws from sex (lit. withdraws her vagina), if she marries, she has no success.*
(What you put into life determines what you get out of it).

51. Ɔbaa dwamanfoɔ na ɔto mmarima mmɔnaa.
*A lecherous woman (lit. a prostitute) rapes men.*
(People with strong desires will use force to get what they want).

52. Ɔbaa dwamanfoɔ se: "Nyɛ atopa a anka ɔnte mpoma mu".
*A lecherous woman (lit. a prostitute) says: "If it were not for the way I shake my hips, I would not stay at the window".*
(If you are provocative, you will get a reaction).

53. Ɔbaa ho bɔn a, na ɛfiri ne twɛ.
*If a woman stinks, it is because of her vagina.*
(Internal cleanliness is as important as external cleanliness).

54. Ɔbaa ho yɛ fɛ a, na ɛfiri ɔbarima.
*If a woman is beautiful it is because of a man.*
(Male chauvinism!)

55. Ɔbaa ahoɔden wɔ n'atofo mu.
*A woman's strength is in her bustle.*
(Women sometimes wear their cloth in a kind of roll at the back - "atofo", a bustle - where they may keep their money and other valuables, and on which it is easy to carry a child. This bustle stands both for her wealth and for her femininity. Hence: However weak someone may be, they also have their strengths).

56. Ɔbaa kɛseɛ na ne pim so.
*A bulky woman has a large clitoris.*
(Everything is in proportion).

57. Ɔbaa kɔ adwareɛ na ɔmma ntɛm a, na ɔresiesie ne ho.
*If a woman goes to the bathroom and she doesn't come back quickly, she is tidying herself up.*
(Every action has a reason).

58. Ɔbaa kɔkɔɔ, yɛware no ti pa.
*A light-skinned woman, we marry her if we are lucky.*
(Light-skinned women are supposed to bring good luck. Hence: Lucky people get the best things in life).

59. Ɔbaa kɔn dɔ kɔteɛ a, ɔse: "Me kunu mmɔ me akɔnhoma".
*If a woman is eager to have sex (lit. loves a penis), she says: "My husband does not give me a daily allowance".*
(You sometimes have to find a roundabout way to get what you want).

60. Ɔbaa korafoɔ awareɛ yɛ ya.
*A jealous woman's marriage is grievous (lit. hurts).*
(Jealousy brings misery).

61. Ɔbaa kuta a, ɔtwa no abenkum mu.
*If a woman holds it, she cuts it from the left.*
(The left hand is unlucky. Hence: If anything important goes to a woman, she misuses it!)

62. Ɔbaa kwadwofoɔ kɔ awareɛ a, wɔde praeɛ na ɛpam no.
*If a lazy woman goes to get married, they take a broom to drive her away.*
(If you don't work, you don't prosper).

63. Ɔbaa kwadwofoɔ na ɔtena afikyire pene kɔtekɔm.
*A lazy woman who sits in the backyard asks for sex.*
(If you are not busy you leave yourself time to reflect on unsatisfied desires).

64. Ɔbaa kwasea na ɔkɔ awareɛ a, ɔnya adeɛ ne mma.
*If a stupid woman marries, she gets property and children.*
(If you achieve something, you achieve its advantages).

65. Ɔbaa kyerɛ wia a, yɛnnyina so nnye no.
*If a woman admits to adultery, we don't use it in a divorce against her.*
(If a woman confesses to adultery, it is believed that her ancestors forced her to confess. It would, therefore, be ungrateful to them to divorce her provided she promises not to do it again. Hence: If someone confesses their faults, we do not hold it against them).

66. Ɔbaa na onim ne kunu yam kɔm.
*A woman knows when her husband is hungry (lit. her husband's stomach's hunger).*
(It is a wife who best knows her husband's needs).

67. Ɔbaa na ɔwo ɔbarima.
*It is a woman that gives birth to a man.*
(A weak person may enable a strong one to succeed).

68. Ɔbaa ne ɔbarima hyia a, ɔbaa yɛ ɔbaa na ɔbarima nso yɛ ɔbarima.
*When a woman and a man meet, the woman remains (lit. is) a woman and the man remains (lit. is) a man.*
(You do not change your nature when you change the company you keep).

69. Ɔbaa ne ne kunu asɛm, obi nnim mu.
*The affairs of a woman and her husband, nobody knows them.*
(Used normatively also: Don't interfere in the marital (or, more generally, private) affairs of others).

70. Ɔbaa animuonyam ne awareɛ.
*A woman's glory (lit. what causes her to be respected) is marriage.*

71. Ɔbaa nitefoɔ kɔ awareɛ a, ɔnnya.
*If a too clever woman gets married she does not succeed.*
(Men do not like their womenfolk to be cleverer than they. Hence: Cleverness is no guarantee of success).

72. Ɔbaa nya adepa a, obi nte; ɔnya amaneɛ a, na ɔbarima anya amaneɛ.
*If a woman gets a fortune, no one hears of it; if she has trouble then a man has trouble.*
(Women share their disadvantages, but not their advantages, with their men).

73. Ɔbaa nya adwareɛ pa dware a, ɔkyɛre ne hɔ.
*If a woman has a good bathroom to bathe in, she stays there a long time.*
(If you get what you want, you hold onto it as long as you can).

74. Ɔbaa nya ne ho a, ɔdane ɔbarima.
*If a woman becomes wealthy, she changes into a man.*
(You cannot order about a woman who has money. Hence: Wealth brings authority).

75. Ɔbaa nyansafoɔ na ɔse: "Mehwɛ deɛ abusua bɛka".
*A wise woman says: "I look forward to what my matriclan will say".*
(Well-behaved people do not fear the judgement of their superiors).

76. Ɔbaa nyinsɛn na wanwo ɔbaa a, ɔwo ɔbarima.
*If a pregnant woman doesn't give birth to a girl, she gives birth to a boy.*
(There are only two possibilities).

77. [Ɔbaa mmɔdemmɔfoɔ]/[Ɔbaa sima] na ne ba hyɛ n'akyiri a, ɔsoa nnooma.
*If the [hard-working]/[ideal] woman puts her child on her back, she carries a load at the same time.*
(An industrious worker is prepared to take on an extra burden).

78. Ɔbaa pa de apaterɛ bɛtem yɛ nkwan ma ɛyɛ dɛ; nanso ɔbaa bɔne de dwannam bɛyɛ nkwan a, ɛrenyɛ dɛ.
*A good woman takes tilapia fish to put in the soup to make it good, but if a bad woman takes mutton to make soup, it is not tasty.*
(Mutton is considered preferable to fish in Asante. Hence: It is the quality of the work that matters, not necessarily the quality of the materials used).

79. Ɔbaa pa na ntɛtia kɔkɔɔ nam n'apakyie aseɛ.
*A good woman, small red ants crawl over the back of her gourd.*
(The ants appreciate tasty food. Hence: A good woman is valued by all).

80. Ɔbaa pa ne deɛ ɔtie ne kunu asɛm.
*A good woman is she who listens to her husband's advice.*

81. Ɔbaa pɛ wo, na abaa da wo kɔn ho a, ɔse "Dɔbroba".
*If a woman loves you and a stick lies on your shoulder, she says "(It is a) double-barrelled gun".*
(Love is blind).

82. Ɔbaa pɛ wo na ɔhunu wo kɔkɔbo a, ɔse: "Kyemetam".
*If a woman loves you and she sees the inside of your rectum, she says "(It is a) silk loin cloth".*
(Beauty is in the eye of the beholder. See also 81).

83. Ɔbaa mpɛ wo a, ɛnnim sɛ woatete sika.
*If a woman doesn't love you, it doesn't help if you splash money out on her.*

84. Ɔbaa mpɛ wo a, ɔmpɛ wo ka.
*If a woman doesn't love you, she doesn't love your debt. (i.e. doesn't want you to be in debt).*
(If you are free of women, you are free of expenses).

85. Ɔbaa mpɛ wo a, ɔse: "Me ba nyiniɛ".
*If a woman doesn't desire you, she says:"My child has not yet grown."*
(Rearing young children and sexual dalliance are incompatible. Hence: Dislike breeds excuses).

86. Ɔbaa se ɔbehyɛ torɔsa a, momma ɔnhyɛ, na ɛbɛto ne dwonso.
*If a woman says she is going to put on trousers, let her put them on, and she'll have problems urinating.*
(Leave people to learn from their own mistakes).

87. Ɔbaa [sene bɔama]/[yɛ kyɛm] a, ɛtwere ɔbarima dan mu.
*(Even) if a woman [carves a drum]/[makes a shield], she keeps it in a man's room.*
(Whatever a woman may do she needs a man).

88. Ɔbaa sini nim sɛ ɔbɛwo ba ama ɔba ahwɛ no a, anka wansɛe ne twɛ.
*If a prostitute knew that she was going to give birth to a child, to let it look after her, she would not have spoiled her vagina.*
(If you know profit can be made out of something, you care for it).

89. Ɔbaa asobrakyeɛ so amaneɛ.
*A stubborn woman causes trouble.*

90. Ɔbaa ansua adeɛ yɔ, na ɔkɔ awareɛ a, wɔde ne nkwan gu ahina mu kyɛrɛ ɔman.
*If a woman has not learned how to do things, and gets married, they pour her soup into a water-pot and show it to the public.*
(Because she doesn't know how to make soup. Hence: Lack of adequate preparation leads to disgrace).

91. Ɔbaa te sɛ borɔdeɛ, n'ase mpa mma.
*A woman is like a plantain tree, which sprouts all the time.*
(We depend on the fruitfulness of women).

92. Ɔbaa te sɛ akokɔ; yɛde Aburowna ɛsɔne no.
*A woman is like a chicken; we use maize to lure her.*

(You need to coax people with something good, to get what you want from them).

**93. Ɔbaa te sɛ ohuriiɛ; ɔnom mogya na ɔmma mogya.**
*A woman is like the tsetse fly; she drinks blood but she doesn't give blood.*
(Women are parasites).

**94. Ɔbaa tentene so abɛ a, ɔnwam di bi.**
*If a tall woman carries palm-nuts, the hornbill eats some.*
(The hornbill normally swoops to take palm-nuts from the tree, but does not fly very low. The carrier of a head load, if tall, would be about the right height for it. Hence: If you put temptation in people's way, you can't blame them if they succumb to it).

**95. Ɔbaa tɔ odwan a, ɔbarima na ɔyɛn no.**
*If a woman buys a sheep, it is a man who rears it.*
(Certain jobs are appropriate for women, others for men).

**96. Ɔbaa tɔn nnuadewa na, ɔntɔn atuduro.**
*A woman sells garden-eggs, but she doesn't sell gunpowder.*
(Women should do what is appropriate to them and not interfere in men's affairs).

**97. Ɔbaa, yɛware no (wɔ) n'anom, na yɛnware no (wɔ) n'ase.**
*A woman, we marry her for her words (lit. mouth), but we do not marry her for her vagina.*
(Your essential nature is revealed through your speech, not through your body).

**98. Ɔbaa wo awobɔne a, ɔte ne twɛ nka.**
*If a woman gives birth to a stubborn child, she hears talk of her vagina.*
(A very grave insult in Asante refers to your mother's vagina. Hence: If you have troublesome relations, people will curse you).

**99. Ɔbaa wɔ mpempem a, ɔbarima na ɔhwɛ ne soɔ.**
*However rich a woman may be (lit. If a woman has thousands and thousands), it is a man that looks after her.*
(Whatever a woman may do she needs a man).

**100. Ɔbaa Yaa Ataa se n'ani yɛ den, nso yɛde ne twɛ so nwi na ɛto hyeɛ.**
*The woman Yaa Ataa says she is wild (lit. her eyes are hard), but we use the hair of her vagina to mark the boundary.*
(There are ways of subjugating even a forceful person. Ataa is the name of a female twin).

**101. Ɔbaa yare a, ne twɛ nyare bi.**
*If a woman is sick, her vagina is not sick also.*
(Sickness does not affect all members of a family in the same way).

**102. Ɔbaa bɛyɛ yie a, na efii ɔbarima.**
*If a woman does well (i.e. becomes rich), it is because of a man.*

**103. Ɔbaa nyɛ a, ne kunu na ɔka.**
*If a woman is no good, it is her husband who tells.*
(We are best known to those with whom we are most intimate).

**104. Mmaa dodoɔ kunu ntoma yɛ fi a, ɔnɔ ara na ɔsie.**
*If the husband of many women has a dirty cloth, he himself washes it.*
(A man uses his own cloth to cover the woman he is sleeping with. If he is constantly changing women, then none of them will want to wash the cloth which has covered the others; and if he asks one of them, the others will all be jealous. Therefore he is forced to do the work himself. Hence: Too many cooks spoil the broth).

**105. Mmaa dodoɔ kunu wu a, na ɛkɔm na aku no.**
*If the husband of many women dies, it is because hunger has killed him.*
(It is the custom for the wife who is sleeping with a man to cook for him. If, however, he has too many wives, each will expect another to cook for him and so he will get no food. Hence: Too many cooks spoil the broth. See 104).

**106. Mmaa dodoɔ awareɛ mu nni biribi sɛ ohia.**
*To marry many women is nothing but poverty.*
(Too many obligations keep you poor).

**107. Mmaa nnyae ankaa adwareɛ; na nhohoɔ ho bɔn.**
*Let women stop using lime to bathe with; for the red ant stinks.*
(The red ant lives in the lime tree. Hence: Don't substitute scent for washing; and, more generally, appearance for reality).

**108. Mmaa rekamfo wo duaforo no na wɔrekamfo w'akyakya.**
*At the same time as women praise your tree-climbing, they praise your hunchback.*
(You may be praised for one your strengths and censured for your weakness at the same time).

**109. Mmaa rekamfo w'ahoɔfɛ no na wɔrekamfo w'akabɔ.**
*At the same time as women praise your good looks they praise your ability to spend money.*
(Flatterers are expensive).

**110. Mmaa kɔ afuom, na sɛ wo yere ba a, na mmaa no nyinaa aba.**
*The women go to the farm, but if your wife comes back, all the women come.*
(Birds of a feather flock together).

**111. Mmaa pɛ ɛdɛ, kyiri ɛka.**
*Women like pleasure (but) abhor debt.*
(Women like a profitable relationship).

**112. Mmaa pɛ deɛ [adeɛ]/[sika] wɔ.**
*Women love (to be) where [possessions are]/[money is].*

**113. Mmaa se: "Wo ho yɛ fɛ!" a, ɛne ka.**
*If women say: "You are handsome!", it leads to debt.*
(Flattery often has an ulterior motive. See also 109).

**114. Mmaa te sɛ mmɛrekyie, adidie mma wɔnte asɛnnyea.**
*Women are like goats, feeding makes them immune to abuse.*
(If you concentrate on one thing, you disregard all others).

**115. Mmaa atopagyengyen na ɛkum mmarima.**
*Women's energetic shakings of the hips kill (i.e. give them power over) men.*
(Women use sexual guile to keep men in tow).

**116. Baabaadɔm ma kurɔ bɔ.**
*Communal ownership destroys the town.*
(Everyone's work is no one's work).

**117. Baabi a aboa no awu ada, ɛhɔ na yɛfiri kan n'asinisini.**
*Where the animal has died and lies, it is there that we start counting its pieces.*
(We settle a case from its origins).

**118. Baabi a aburopata wɔ no, ɛhɔ na akokɔ bɔ mprɛ korɔ.**
*Wherever the cornshed stands, there the chicken moves around.*
(A person will be found in the situation that benefits them most).

**119. Baabi a ɔdɔ wɔ na asomdwoeɛ wɔ.**
*Where there is love there is peace.*

**120. Baabi a yɛfa kɔ na yɛfa ba.**
*The place we pass through in going, we pass through in returning.*
(If you obtain what you want through someone's help, you must also work through them if you want to do other things. Or: You come back to where you start from).

**121. Baabi a yɛnam foro no, ehɔ na yɛnam siane.**
*The place through which you pass in climbing, is the place you pass through in descending.*
(See 120).

**122. Baabi a onipa animuonyam duru no, n'animguase a, ɛtra hɔ.**
*Wherever a person's good reputation reaches, if he or she is disgraced, it goes beyond that place.*
(Bad news travels swifter than good).

**123. Baabi a yɛnom no, yɛnnware hɔ.**
*Where we drink, we do not wash (there).*
(You don't spoil a place from which you benefit).

**124. Baabi a piredwan ahwie aguo no, asia mpa hɔ da.**
*There where a piredwan (of gold-dust) has been scattered, an asia (of gold dust) always remains.*
(A piredwan is a large weight; an asia is a small weight. Hence: If you are rich, you always have something to spare).

**125. Baabi a nsa asuhina abɔ aguo no, nsahua mpa hɔ da.**
*Where the palm-wine pot has broken and poured out (its contents), the scent of palm wine remains for ever.*
(A thing or person worth remembering is not forgotten).

**126. Baabi a esia abu aguo no, mmabaa mpa hɔ da.**
*Where the Petersia Africana tree has fallen, pieces of stick are always present.*
(This tree makes good firewood. Hence: If a rich person dies, he or she leaves much behind).

**127. Baabi a esiaboɔ aguo no, moaba mpa hɔ da.**
*Where an esiaboɔ (of gold-dust) has poured out, a moaba (of gold dust) is always present.*
(Esiaboɔ is a weight; moaba is the smallest notional weight, about one rice grain. Hence: An important person is never entirely forgotten. See 125).

**128. Baabi a ɛsono awu ada no, nnompe mpa hɔ da.**
*Where the elephant has died and lies, bones will always be present.*
(A great person is never forgotten).

**129. Baabi dehyeɛ kɔsom a, na wɔfrɛ no afanaa.**
*Where a freeman's child goes into service, she is called a female slave.*
(Someone well thought of in their own community may be regarded as of little worth in another place).

**130. Baabi yɛ sum na woto sika pɛ hɔ a, ɛhɔ te.**
*Where it is dark, if you put money there, the place is bright.*
(With money nothing is impossible).

**131. Baabiara nni hɔ a wotena we atadwe a, ɛnyɛ dɛ.**
*There is no place where, if you chew a tigernut, it is not sweet (tasty).*
(If something is good, it is good wherever it is).

**132. Baabiara yɛ nwa tareberɛ.**
*Anywhere is the snail's dwelling-place.*
(A vagabond does not care where he stays).

**133. Abaabo ya nti na wokum ɔwɔ a, ɔdane ne yam.**
*It is because of the bitterness of being beaten with a stick, that if you kill a snake it turns up its stomach.*
(You reveal your weakness in times of adversity).

**134. Baafoɔ, wowɔ adeɛ a, wonkɔ afoɔ.**
*Forager, if you had possessions you would not be looting.*
(Used when a person boasts of wealth but behaves as if they have nothing; i.e. in Asante terms, behaves ungenerously).

**135. Ɔbaako so nyɛ katana.**
*One thing is not hard to cover.*
(You can hide small troubles, but not big ones).

**136. Ɔbaako yɛ ya.**
*A person alone hurts.*
(To be alone is sad).

**137. Ɔbaakofoɔ di ɛwoɔ a, ɛnyane ne yam.**
*If one person (alone) eats the honey, it awakens his stomach (he gets diarrhea).*
(Greed brings suffering).

**138. Ɔbaakofoɔ di due-ne-amane-hunu.**
*A solitary person deserves condolences.*
("Due ne amane" is a greeting to someone who has been bereaved. Hence: Solitude is suffering).

**139. Ɔbaakofoɔ di awu a, ɔsoa ne funu.**
*If a single person kills another, he carries the corpse.*
(If you commit an offence on your own, you alone suffer for it).

**140. Ɔbaakofoɔ akɔhunu, ɔdansefoɔ ne hwan? Woka kyerɛ nyansafoɔ a, ɔregye wo akyinnye.**
*If a single person goes to see, who is their witness?*

*If you tell the wise man, he argues with you.*
(A person who has no companions has no friends, nor are their stories believed).

### 141. Ɔbaakofoɔ nkyekyere kuro.
*One person does not build a town.*
(One person cannot on their own achieve great things).

### 142. Ɔbaakofoɔ nkyere bɔdamfoɔ.
*One person alone does not arrest a lunatic.*
(There is safety in numbers).

### 143. Ɔbaakofoɔ na ɔto tuo na ɛdɔm guo.
*A single man fires a gun and defeats the enemy.*
(Used where one person's decision determines the outcome).

### 144. Ɔbaakofoɔ nnante anadwo.
*One person alone does not walk at night.*
(Take care!)

### 145. Ɔbaakofoɔ na ɔkum ɛsono ma amansan twe nkuma kɔdwa die.
*A single person kills an elephant to enable his fellow-citizens to collect axes to chop it up to eat.*
(The well-being of the state may depend on a single individual).

### 146. Ɔbaakofoɔ ani nkyɛre bere.
*One person alone easily becomes anxious.*
(If you have no one to share your troubles, you suffer).

### 147. Ɔbaakofoɔ nsa nso Nyame ani kata.
*A single person cannot cover God's eyes (the sky).*
(You cannot achieve anything worth while on your own).

### 148. Ɔbaakofoɔ nua ne sika.
*The brother of a single person is money.*
(If you are rich, money can make up for lack of family and friends).

### 149. Ɔbaakofoɔ tirim nni adwen.
*The head of a single person has no thoughts.*
(It is difficult to come to wise decisions on your own).

### 150. Ɔbaakofoɔ werɛ aduro a, ɛgu.
*If one person goes to collect medicine, it falls (to the ground).*
(The bark of trees is often used as medicine. To scrape it from the tree you need a helper to hold the tools. Hence: People need others to help them in their lives).

### 151. Ɔbaakofoɔ yɛ akoa.
*One person alone is a slave.*
(If you have no support, you are at everyone's beck and call).

### 152. Ɔbaakofoɔ nni nsɛm.
*An individual does not judge a (court-)case.*
(It takes more than one person to judge a case).

### 153. Ɔbaakofoɔ nyɛ ɔbarima.
*A single person is not a warrior (lit. adult male).*
(You need to have someone to fight to be shown to be brave).

### 154. Baakoyɛ nyɛ fɛ a, hwɛ nkrane a ato santene.
*If unity is not a good thing, look at the black ants as they form a straight line.*
(Cooperation results in advancement).

### 155. Baanu ka a, ɛkyene dodoɔ.
*If two people get on with each other, it is better than many (friends).*

### 156. Baanu ko a, deɛ ɔtia baasa yɛ ɔpatafoɔ.
*If two people are fighting, then he who is a third must be the peacemaker.*

### 157. Baanu so (dua) a, ɛnmia.
*If two people carry (wood), it does not weigh them down.*
(Help lightens work).

### 158. Baanu wea kɔ kukuo mu.
*The tree hyrax belonging to two people goes into the cooking pot.*
(The thought is that two people are more likely to be more successful in hunting than one. Hence: Some problems can only be solved by sharing).

### 159. Ɔbaapɛfoɔ nyɛ anem.
*A person who loves his woman does not bear grudges against her.*
(People excuse those they love).

### 160. Ɛmmaapɛ mu wɔ adeɛ a, anka ɔpapo da apakan mu.
*If there were something to be gained from desiring women, then the he-goat would ride in a palanquin.*
(As in some other cultures, the he-goat typifies lust. The palanquin (in which a chief rides) represents chieftaincy. Hence, this proverb suggests that lust is not to one's advantage).

### 161. Ɔbaasadefoɔ twe ade pa ba fie.
*A lucky woman draws good things to the home.*
(A lucky person enables others to share their luck).

### 162. Ɔbaatan kasa agyinam na ɔnkasa badwam.
*A motherly woman speaks at a private meeting but not in public.*
(If you are considerate you don't disgrace people in public).

### 163. Ɔbaatan kɔ ne mpampuro mu a, ɔde ne to bini ba fie.
*If a motherly woman goes to her bamboo plantation, she comes home with unclean buttocks (lit. she brings the feces of her buttocks home).*
(Bamboo leaves are used to clean the bottom after excretion. Hence: A good woman gives everything to her family (especially her children) and is left with nothing herself).

### 164. Ɔbaatan kɔdi asika a, ɔnnya ne ba hɔ.
*If a good woman goes to collect gold, she does not leave her child behind.*
(However great the reward, a good woman will never desert her child).

### 165. Ɔbaatan na ɔnim deɛ ne ba bɛdie.
*A motherly woman knows what her child will eat.*
(A good person will make provision for their dependents).

**166. Ɔbaatan nnim ba bɔne.**
*A motherly woman does not know a bad child.*
(If a woman knows how to care for children properly, they will not misbehave. Hence, more generally: If you show real concern for people, they will respond by helping you).

**167. Ɔbaatan asɛnhia hwehwe abonimma aso.**
*A motherly woman's serious matter is thought trivial by a barren woman.*
(You can't understand or sympathize with what you haven't experienced).

**168. Ɔbaatan wɔ fie a, yɛmmisa deɛ ne ba ane.**
*If a motherly woman is in the house, we don't ask whose child it is that has defecated.*
(You don't ask after the ownership of something, when it's obvious).

**169. Ababaawa a ɔnnim nkwan yɛ awareɛ ansɔ a, na ɛfiri ne nkwammɔne.**
*If a young-woman-who-cannot-make-soup's marriage has not been successful, then it is due to the badness of her soup.*
(It is our weaknesses that let us down).

**170. Ababaawa animuonyam ne ne to.**
*A young woman's reputation lies in her buttocks.*
(You take an interest in women because of their female attributes).

**171. Babadua dɔnkɔ: onipa te n'ase a, ɔmpɛ.**
*Babadua (Thalia near geniculata) the slave: if a person stands on their own feet, then they are dissatisfied.*
(The babadua is a strong cane, with swollen joints, used in building. Thickets of it are extremely difficult to penetrate. This is a form of proverb in which a view is ascribed to something other than a person. There is usually some connection between the nature of the thing here, perhaps, the sturdy independence of the plant and the "message". The thought here is that human beings when they are independent seek someone or something on which they can become dependant).

**172. Babadua se: "Ɔfamfoɔ yɛnwae no".**
*Babadua (Thalia near geniculata) says: "He who has stuck firmly, we cannot loosen".*
(See 171. The relevant feature of the babadua here is presumably its capacity to entrap one in a thicket. This proverb is used when a person stays too long in one place and is unwilling to lose contact with it).

**173. Babadua se nyɛ ne mu apɔapɔ a anka ɔne ne [mfɛfoɔ pɛ]/[sibire sɛ].**
*Babadua (Thalia near geniculata) says that if it weren't for the bumps on its stems, it and [its contemporaries would be equal]/[the reed would be the same].*
(See 171. The relevant feature of the babadua here is the fact that it has swollen joints on its stem. This proverb is used where someone is held back by some hindrance or infirmity).

**174. Ɔbabɔne yɛku no abosom mu.**
*A bad child we kill through the fetish.*
(You use clever means to get rid of a difficult person).

**175. Ɔbabɔne nnim [kasakyerɛ]/[afotuo].**
*A bad child does not know (how to take) advice.*

(Used of a person who seems incapable of acting reasonably).

**176. Ɔbabɔne te sɛ ɛtoɔ, ɛfam onipa ho; wotwa twene a, ɛnyɛ yie.**
*A bad child is like the buttocks that are part of a person; if you (try to) cut them off, it doesn't work (i.e. you cannot).*
(Your children are yours, good or bad).

**177. Ababunu nti na yɛdi aberewa a, yɛma no adeɛ.**
*It is because of the virgin that, if we have intercourse with the old woman, we give her things (gifts).*
(If you desire to please someone, you may have to begin by pleasing those around them first).

**178. Ababunu wu na yɛde aberewa di n'adeɛ a, ayie no na yɛatu ahyɛ ɛda.**
*If a virgin dies and we take an old woman to inherit her property, it is the funeral that we are putting off to another day.*
(If you lose or spoil a good thing and replace it with a bad one, you will have to replace it again soon).

**179. Ɔbadeyɔfoɔ de ahobrɛaseɛ nya baabi tena.**
*An industrious child uses politeness to get somewhere to stay.*
(Virtue has its rewards).

**180. Badwa na mma okouroko anni amim.**
*A public gathering makes it impossible for a bully to dominate (through violence).*
(Violence can be controlled by public opinion. A man can act quite differently in public and in private).

**181. Ɔbadueduefoɔ nto oni funu.**
*The wandering child does not meet with his mother's corpse.*
(A warning to those who stay too long from home. They will miss their mother's funeral).

**182. Abadwadeɛ yɛ wo dɛ a, w'afuo yɛ ketewa.**
*If you enjoy getting your court fees (for attending an arbitration), your farm will be small.*
(A warning to those who hang around the ahemfie (palace), rather than going out to work. Also, more generally: You can't be in two places at once. Or: If you want to prosper tend to your own affairs).

**183. Badwafoɔ nyɛ a, ɔbaakofoɔ mfa nkyeyere n'akyi.**
*Even if the arbitrators are not good, a single person cannot influence them all (lit. carry everyone of them on his back).*
(Safety in numbers. For instance: one corrupt person on a panel of arbitrators cannot carry the day).

**184. Ɔbadwemma hwɛ ade-dada so yɛ foforɔ na ɔnto ade-dada ntwene nyɛ foforɔ.**
*A wise person looks at an old thing in order to make a new one, and he does not throw away the old before making the new.*
(Tradition must be maintained).

**185. Ɔbaeɛ ankɔ a, yɛfrɛ no [aboa bi]/[akoa bi].**
*If he who has come does not go, we call him a [beast]/[slave].*
(Both "akoa" and "aboa" are relatively grave insults in Asante. Hence: If you overstay your welcome, you invite insult).

186. **Bafan da ayeya a, ɔhwɛ ne twɛdeɛ.**
*If a cripple lies on his back, he thinks only of how he can give a blow.*
(If a physically helpless person keeps quiet, they may be planning how to achieve what they want).

187. **Bafan nnim biribi a, ɔnim abɔnsamu.**
*If a cripple does not know anything else, he knows how to clap hands.*
(Everyone has something they can do, however slight).

188. **Bafan se ɔbebɔ wo boɔ a, na ewɔ deɛ waforo atena soɔ.**
*If a cripple says he will stone you, then it means he has climbed something and is sitting on it.*
(A weak person prepares before they act).

189. **Bafan se ɔreyɛ oni abrɔ, ɔnnim sɛ ɔresɛe ne to.**
*The cripple says he is deceiving his mother; he does not realize he is spoiling his own buttocks.*
(Deception works to the disadvantage of the deceiver).

190. **Mmagum na ɛkum dɔm.**
*Reinforcements lead to the defeat of the enemy.*
(There is strength in numbers).

191. **Ɔbagyegyefoɔ na ɔma ɔbayifoɔ adidie da adie.**
*The mischievous child brings to light the witch's feasting.*
(Witches are supposed to feed on the blood of their victims and to have to sacrifice members of their own abusua (matriclan) for this purpose. A witch's feast is thus an affair of mischief. Hence: It takes a thief to catch a thief).

192. **Ɔbagyimifoɔ yɛn yɛ yɛnna.**
*Raising a stupid child is hard. (lit. A stupid child's raising is a hard raising).*

193. **Abahyɛbɔne nti na kɔkɔsakyi di sɛbeɛ.**
*Because of bad upbringing the vulture eats dung.*
(People live by example; those brought up with bad examples have bad habits).

194. **Bakoma, yɛdi no wɔ yɛn ni gya ho, na yɛnni no obi ni deɛ ho.**
*Spoilt man, we show our pride at our mother's fireside, not at somebody else's mother's.*
(Don't be arrogant in someone else's home).

195. **Ɔbakwasea rehonhono a, ɔse ɔreyɛ kɛse.**
*If a stupid person is developing a swollen body, he says he is going to be fat.*
(A fool cannot recognize the truth).

196. **Ɔbakwasea na yɛbu no bɛ a, yɛkyerɛ no asɛe.**
*If we tell a fool a proverb, we explain its meaning to him.*
(You need to explain everything to a foolish person).

197. **Ɔbakwasea na ɔhwe ase mprenu.**
*A foolish person falls down twice.*
(A fool disregards a warning).

198. **Ɔbakwasea na ɔse: "Wɔde me yɔnko na wɔnne me".**
*A foolish person says: "They refer to my companion and not to me".*
(A fool does not learn from the experience of others).

199. **Ɔbakwasea, ne kuro tutu no na ɛgyae no tutuo a, ɔse awu.**
*A fool, if he feels pains in his sore and then the pain lessens, thinks it is healed.*
(Just because something is not worrying us, it does not mean it is not there).

200. **Ɔbakwasea nnim biribiara, ɔnim ayɛase-sa.**
*If a fool knows nothing (else), he knows how to dance at a funeral.*
(There are some things everyone, however humble or foolish, can do).

201. **Ɔbakwasea ano resɔ nsuo a, ɔse ɔretwa tii.**
*If saliva drops from the mouth of a fool, he says he is making tea.*
(Foolish people joke about their own faults).

202. **Ɔbakwasea, yɛntia ne dua so mprɛnu.**
*A foolish person, we do not step on his penis (lit. tree) twice.*
(Once bitten, twice shy. Even a fool has some sense).

203. **Ɔbamumuu se: sɛ wanya ɔba ansoma no a, na nyɛ krawa na ɔyɛ, na mmom na ɔbaa na wannya bi anware no, na wawo ɔba.**
*An ugly man says: if he did not have a child in order to send it, it does not mean that he was impotent, but it was because he could not get a woman to marry so that he could have a child.*
(If someone did not achieve something it does not necessarily mean they were incapable of doing so. Or: People will find excuses for their incompetence).

204. **Aban bɛgu a, ɛfiri yam.**
*If the state is going to be destroyed, it is from the inside (lit. the stomach).*
(It is your own weaknesses that bring about your downfall).

205. **Ɛban kata asɛm so.**
*The fence round the house conceals its secrets.*
(People are entitled to a certain amount of privacy).

206. **Bankye nte sɛ bayere na yɛasi no pam.**
*The cassava is not like the yam that we have to support it.*
(Someone who is tough can stand on their own feet without support. The cassava plant does not need staking).

207. **Bankye nyɛ a, egya na ɛka.**
*If the cassava is no good, the fire can judge it.*
(i.e. the fire on which it is cooked. Hence: The expert is the best judge of his craft).

208. **Abanoma nsene ɔba-pa.**
*A step-child is not better than one's own child.*
(Blood is thicker than water).

209. **[Ɔbanyansafoɔ]/[ɔnyansafoɔ], yɛbu no bɛ, na yɛnka no asɛm.**
*We speak to a wise person in proverbs and not in stories.*
(A word to the wise is sufficient).

210. Ɔbanyansafoɔ na ɔdi kosua a, ɔbɔ kasɛɛ mu.
*If a wise person eats an egg, he breaks a bone in it.*
(The wise person detects the chicken that would have come from the egg. Hence: A wise person uses the little capital he has to provide for the future. There is a tale of two people who were given eggs. One ate his. The other hatched his out and in time had many chickens so that he could eat both eggs and chickens whenever he wanted).

211. Ɔbanyansafoɔ na ɔkɔto asantrofie a, ɔnya ne ho teteɛ.
*If a wise person meets a nightjar he is able to free himself from all eventualities.*
(The nightjar is considered to be a bird of ill omen. Hence: A wise person knows his way out of a problem).

212. Ɔbanyansafoɔ na yɛkyerɛ no adeɛ soro a, ɔhwɛ fam.
*A wise person, if we show them something above, looks on the ground.*
(A wise person considers all sides to a question).

213. Ɔbarima a ɔdi mmaafodie na ɔsoa bokiti.
*A man who follows women too much carries a bucket.*
(If you are subservient to women, they will make use of you to do their work).

214. Ɔbarima fa tifa ko sa a, wɔfa no dɔmmum.
*If a worthy man goes half-heartedly (lit. half-headedly) to war, they take him captive.*
("Ɔbarima," unqualified, often means not just a male but a man who has manly virtues. You do not succeed unless you put your whole self into what you are doing).

215. Ɔbarima mfa kyiniiɛ nsi ne so mma ɔbaa nso mfa kyiniiɛ nsi ne so.
*A man does not use an umbrella so that a woman may also use an umbrella to put over her.*
(Women should not usurp the privileges of the male. Women do not use umbrellas traditionally. The Queen Mother has large fans which replace the chief's state umbrella).

216. Ɔbarima bɛfrɛ ne ho katakyie no, na ɔnhunuu asɛm a ɛyɛ hu.
*When a man is going to call himself by a brave title he has not seen any terrible things.*
(Actions speak louder than words. You are not brave merely because you say you are).

217. Ɔbarima gyae adwooguo a, ne nan po.
*If a man withdraws from an uncompleted venture, his legs become shaky.*
(If you don't carry through what you should, you become timid).

218. Ɔbarima ho reba a, ɔnka sɛ: "Koteɛ fefe".
*If a man discharges he does not say: "(My) penis vomits".*
(There is a suitable language for every occasion).

219. Ɔbarima hufoɔ na ne to so.
*A cowardly man has big buttocks.*
(It is believed that in men large buttocks are the sign of a coward. Hence: Sometimes we know a man's character from his appearance).

220. Ɔbarima nkata ne koko so na ɔmfa ne nsa nsi ne yɔnko barima bo.
*A man does not cover his own chest in order to take his hand to beat his male companion's chest.*
(You don't sacrifice your praise for another).

221. Ɔbarima hyɛ ɔbarima na ɔbaa hyɛ ɔbaa.
*A man trains a man and a woman a woman.*
(There is a correct way of doing things).

222. Ɔbarima bɛko a, ɛwɔ ne tirim.
*If a man is going to fight, it is in his head.*
(If you are serious about something, you don't need to chatter about it).

223. Ɔbarima kɔtekɛseɛ na ɔte sika ma ɔbaa a, ɔnnwene ho.
*If a man with a big penis gives money to women, he doesn't think about it.*
(Satisfaction makes some people careless).

224. Ɔbarima na ɔbɔ ntoa.
*It is a (brave) man who wears a cartridge belt.*
(Only the brave prepare for war).

225. Ɔbarima na ɔnom aduro a, ɛyɛ nwono.
*It is a (real) man who takes bitter medicine. (lit. If a man takes medicine, it is bitter).*
(A courageous man faces up to any situation).

226. Ɔbarima nim ninkunu twe a, ɔnkɔtwe ninkunu wɔ dua a abu atɔ ne yere afuom kwan soɔ so.
*If a man suspects that his wife commits adultery, he should go and suspect the fallen tree across the path to his wife's farm.*
(However jealous you are there must be limits to your jealousy).

227. Ɔbarima pagya ne nsa a, ɔdi si ɔnoara ne bo.
*If a man raises his hand, he puts it on his own chest.*
(Men like to emphasize their manly qualities).

228. Ɔbarima se ɔbɛpere ɛtwe ho a, ma ɔmpere; na ne ho ba a, na ɔbɛhunu sɛ ɛtwe nyɛ aduane.
*If a man says he will struggle over a vagina too much, let him; but when he has "come," he will see that the vagina is not food.*
(We sometimes mistake desire for necessity).

229. Ɔbarima se ɔyɛ dwamanfoɔ a, ɔnsene keteke.
*If a man says he is lecherous, he is not as much so as a railway engine.*
(Nothing can excel the expert. The old steam engines had a piston which worked continuously and which people sometimes considered in this context).

230. Ɔbarima nse ne yɔnko barima sɛ: "Mɛhwe wo".
*No man says to his male companion: "I shall beat you".*
(Don't boast of your prowess or presume on your strength and wealth).

231. Ɔbarima nsi asuo mu na waham.
*A brave man does not step in the water and draw in his breath.*
(A brave man does not show his feelings).

232. Ɔbarima nsuro wuo.
*A brave man does not fear death.*

233. Ɔbarima bɛyɛɛ bi, na wammɛyɛ ne nyinaa.
*A man came to perform some (task), but not to finish it entirely.*
(When you have done what you set out to do, you can retire gracefully).

234. Ɔbarima nyɛ sumiɛ na ɔbaa de ne ti ato no so.
*A man is not a pillow for a woman to lay her head on.*
(A woman should not overdo her demands on her husband).

235. Mmarima mu nni ɔketewa.
*Among men there is no inferior.*
(All men are equal. Or: Despise no man).

236. Mmarima nni fie a, mmaabasiaa yi wɔn ho kyerɛ.
*If men are not present, then women expose themselves.*
(When the cat's away, the mice will play).

237. Mmarima nni kurom a, na akyakya tu mmirika kyerɛ mmaa.
*If there are no (real) men in town, the hunchback runs to show off before women.*
(A weak man swaggers when he knows there is no one to challenge him).

238. Ɔbarintwerɛboɔ na ne ho bɔn atuduro.
*A warrior smells of gunpowder.*
(If an expert spends all his time using something, he shows it).

239. Abasa se ɔware a, ɔnsene tiri tenten.
*If the arm says it is long, it is not longer than the head.*
(Thoughts go further than physical deeds).

240. Abasini twe adeɛ bɔn mu na amma a, na ɛmfiri ne nsa, na mmom biribi ntira.
*If a person with one arm amputated pulls something from a hole and it does not come, it is not because of his arm but because of something else.*
(It is not always because of your shortcomings that you do not succeed).

241. Bata bɔne yɛ animguaseɛ.
*A fruitless venture (lit. a bad "bata") is shameful.*
("Bata" is the word used for long distance trade or travelling in search of a fortune. If such a venture is not successful you are shamed. Or: A poor bargain puts you to shame).

242. Bata ɛnyɛ wo yie a, yɛfrɛ wo "Ayebiaguo".
*If travelling in search of a fortune does not succeed, we call you a ne'er-do-well.*
(A person who goes abroad to make his fortune and returns as poor as he left is not respected).

243. Abatadie wɔ hɔ yi, yɛkɔ no anibue.
*Trading abroad being what it is, we go into it with open eyes.*
(If you are to be successful at something you have to know all the "tricks of the trade").

244. Abatafoɔ gya, "agoo" wɔ akyire.
*The itinerant trader's light, a knock on the door follows it (lit. "agoo" is behind it).*
(When someone arrives at the door of a house they say "Agoo" to ask for entry. In the old days a travelling trader was entitled to ask for lodging at any house along the way. Thus the appearance of his light would indicate he would soon be knocking on someone's door. Hence: The appearance of one thing, gives warning of what will follow).

245. Batafoɔ se: anyɛ n'ano, ɛnyɛ n'ano, na (ɛyɛ) n'ano ara ne no.
*The wild pig says: it is not its mouth, it is not its mouth, but it is its mouth all the same.*
(Said when someone is evading responsibility which they should by rights accept).

246. Ɔbatafoɔ ntoatoa nti na ɛmaa kurotwiamansa nyaa awia wuo.
*Because the wild pig is garrulous the leopard met his death in the afternoon.*
(If you are too keen on obtaining something, you may not take adequate precautions about the risks).

247. Batam nkasa agyina mu.
*A fool does not talk in a council.*
(We accept only the advice of the wise).

248. Batire nna baabi na woatwa wo ba bɔne ti akɔtɔ ho.
*There is not another shoulder (torso) somewhere on which you can put the head of your bad child if you cut it off.*
(A warning to deal leniently – if firmly – with your offspring).

249. Ɔbawerɛmfoɔ nte aduro.
*A recalcitrant child should not collect medicine.*
(Don't give a job which needs care to an untrustworthy person).

250. Abawuo na ɛde sodeɛ ba.
*Infant mortality results in a sodeɛ ceremony.*
(Sodeɛ is normally the ceremony at the first death of a baby or young child in the family, although it is also carried out when the first adult of a generation dies. Hence: Certain things can only happen as a consequence of earlier events).

251. Abayɛn te sɛ obi a ɔkuta ngo ne koraa; [ɔsom]/ [ɔsɔ mu] dɛnn na anhwie agu.
*Caring for a child is like someone who holds a calabash full of palm oil; s/he holds it carefully so that it does not pour out.*
(If you have responsibility, you must take care).

252. Bayerɛpa nti na yɛtɔ afaseɛ a yɛtua ka.
*It is because of the good yam that we have to pay for the water yam.*
(You make do with substitutes hoping thereby to get the best in the future).

253. Bayerɛpa nyɛ noa-na.
*A good yam is not hard to cook.*
(With good material you can do a good job).

254. Bayerɛ a ɛrenyɛ yie na ɛyɛ dufudufu.
*The yam which is not good for eating is of weak and poor quality.*
(You can tell the value of a person by his ability to be useful. "Dufudufu" means something which is weak and feeble).
(You can tell the value of a person by his ability to be useful. "Dufudufu" means something which does not become sticky like fufuo).

**255. Bayerɛ kɔkɔrɔ nti na Asafoman bɔeɛ.**
*Because of the inner part of the roasted yam the town of Asafo was ruined.*
(A quarrel between two small boys over a piece of yam once caused all the town of Asafo to take sides and the resulting civil strife nearly destroyed it; this is also said of Abotakyi town. Hence, either: Don't join in a fight without good reason. Or: Don't quarrel over small things).

**256. Wo bayerɛ ammɔ a, na ɛfiri w'asaase.**
*If your yams don't flourish, it is from the nature of your soil.*
(A person needs the right environment to flourish).

**257. Bayerɛ ammɔ a, ne ti nyera.**
*If the yam tuber does not grow big, it will not lose its head.*
(The head of the yam is used for planting if it is of good quality. Hence: If you are not ostentatious or wayward you do not catch the eye of those who may harm you).

**258. Bayerɛ ammɔ kɛseɛ a, wɔmpam no kɛse.**
*If the yam does not grow big, you don't dig deep for it.*
(Only big things are worth a big effort).

**259. Bayerɛ se ne ho adɔ no, ɔkyɛne akyekyedeɛ a ɔda abena mu.**
*The yam says it is very hot, it excels (i.e. is hotter than) the tortoise lying in its shell.*
(Said when you are hot, thirsty and dying for a drink).

**260. Bayerɛ se da ne nkaseɛ so a, woda.**
*If the yam says sleep on its thorns, you sleep.*
(You depend on it so you have to accept what is asked of you. Hence: Good things are worth suffering for).

**261. Bayerɛ ti nyɛ a, na ne forɔ nyɛ.**
*If the top of a yam is not good, its bottom is not good either.*
(What is bad, is bad throughout).

**262. Bayie fata aberewa, nanso ebia na akɔdaa na ɔnyɛ.**
*Witchcraft befits an old lady, but it may happen that a young person is also bad.*
(Sin is not found only among the old).

**263. Ɔbayifoɔ ba wu a, ɛyɛ no ya.**
*If a witch's child dies, it grieves her.*
(Female witches are believed to cause the deaths of the children of co-wives. Hence: If you inflict suffering on others, you should expect to feel it yourself in similar circumstances).

**264. "Ɔbayifoɔ rekɔ o! ɔbayifoɔ rekɔ o!" na wonyɛ ɔbayifoɔ a, wontwa w'ani.**
*"A witch is passing! a witch is passing!" but if you are not a witch you do not turn to respond.*
(If abuse does not apply to you, don't take any notice of it).

**265. Ɔbayifoɔ kum wadi-wanma-me na ɔnkum wama-me-na-ɛsua.**
*The witch kills he-ate-and-gave-me-nothing, but does not kill he-gave-me-a-little.*
(People dislike those who refuse to share, but are grateful for small mercies. If you arouse the dislike of a witch, he or she may harm you. Hence: It is better to share what you have, even if you can afford to give only a little).

**266. Ɔbayifoɔ nkum wo a, na wodi mfensa.**
*If a witch does not kill you, then you live for three years.*
("Three years" is a conventional way of saying a very long time. Hence: If no one harms you, you may live a long life).

**267. Ɔbayifoɔ anom yɛ nnam a, ɔdidi asuogya na ɔntumi mfa ntwa asuo.**
*However sharp a witch's mouth may be, she eats on her own side of the stream but cannot cross the water.*
(A witch is believed to be able to harm only members of her own family. Hence: However powerful you are you cannot act outside your own territory).

**268. Ɔbayifoɔ nsuo, ɔbaako nnware.**
*The witch's pool, one man does not swim in it.*
(Some misfortunes are shared by many. Used to comfort those who think they alone suffer).

**269. Bayi-kwasea na aduro kye no.**
*It is a foolish witch who is caught by fetish.*
(People who are like each other know how to avoid being troubled by each other. Anti-witchcraft shrines and protective charms were used against witches and it was the job of the fetish priest to protect his clients from them).

**270. Abɛ baako na ɛseɛ mmɛ-duasa nsa.**
*One palm tree's wine can spoil the palm wine from thirty.*
(Because the wine from many sources may be mixed in a single container. Hence: One bad man can ruin a community).

**271. Abɛ bere a, woso fa, meso fa.**
*If the palm nuts ripen, you carry half and I carry half.*
(Used to warn someone who is not living up to expectations. Hence: Responsibility lies on both of us).

**272. Abɛ de ne mpapa na ɛyɛ mmarinsɛm.**
*It is the branches of the palm tree which make it formidable.*
(A man's supporters make him strong).

**273. Abe ntini sua, nso [aboa biara ntumi ntu no gye ɛsono]/[mframa ntumi ntu no].**
*The palm tree's roots are small, but [no animal can uproot them except for the elephant]/[the wind cannot uproot it].*
(Some apparently weak people can only be overcome by the most powerful).

**274. Abɛ ho mmire, yɛnkyiri bi nni bi.**
*The mushrooms on the palm tree, we don't taboo some and eat some.*
(You should be consistent in your actions. You cannot deal with some members of a family and refuse to have anything to do with others).

**275. Abɛ ho nni nam a, yɛtwerɛ no saa ara.**
*If the palm nut does not have much flesh, it is chewed all the same.*
(You use what you have even if it is not perfect).

276. Abɛ ho nnɔɔma aduasa nkron, ayɛ kyribi dibi.
*Thirty-nine things may be obtained from the palm tree, some you dislike, others you enjoy.*
(You cannot like everything about a person or situation. Tastes and standards differ).

277. Abɛ nkon mu adeɛ yɛ fɛ.
*The thing round the neck of the palm tree (its new flowers and fruit) is beautiful.*
(People admire what is productive)

278. Abɛ mpapa nnim ɔmanni.
*The branches of the palm tree do not know who is a citizen of the state.*
(If you are to be victimized it does not make much difference if it is by friend or foe).

279. Abɛ pii a ɔbɛtwani atoto yi, ɔbenya aketekyiwa wɔ he de ne agu aseɛ.
*All the many palm trees the tapper is uprooting, from where will he get pots for the wine from them?*
(Said of someone who does not plan ahead).

280. Abɛ se wannya opuro dwonsɔ a, anka ɔremmere da.
*The palm tree says if it had not got the urine of the squirrel, it would never have ripened.*
(Some important people achieve success because they are helped by insignificant ones. Hence: One should never despise the help of anyone, however humble).

281. Abɛ tɔ baabiara a ɛyɛ mpɔeɛ mu.
*Whatever its position is, the palm tree can be tapped.*
(People retain their essential nature wherever they are. In some places, palm trees are tapped while still standing; in Asante, they are usually felled first).

282. Abɛ tɔ fam a, na ɛyi nsa.
*You must fell the palm tree before you tap it (lit. remove the wine).*
(First things first).

283. Abɛ rebɛwu a, na ɛso.
*If the palm tree is going to die, it gives more palm wine.*
(Some people are at their most productive late in life).

284. Ɛbɛ bi ne bɛ bi nsɛ a, yɛmfa nto ho mmu.
*If one proverb is not like another, we don't quote one to illustrate the other.*

285. Bea a ɔtomfoɔ gyene n'ani bɔ no, na mfomsoɔ wɔ hɔ.
*Where the blacksmith concentrates to work, that is where the fault is.*
(Repairs are done where they are needed).

286. Abebe na ɔkaa n'asɛm sɛ: "Yɛrekyɛ no pɛ pɛ pɛ".
*It is the grasshopper that has a saying that: "We are dividing it equally."*
(Said when someone tries to cheat comrades out of their fair share of the proceeds of work. There is a story about the butterfly and the grasshopper in which the latter was cheated out of his share of a reward. The proverb is what he is supposed to say when he is chirruping).

287. Abebeɛ ho nyɛ fɛ, nso ɔtua mpanimfoɔ ano.
*The water snail is not beautiful, but it is found in the mouths of the elders.*

(Beauty is not usefulness or wisdom. The water snail is eaten by being sucked out of its shell).

288. Abebeɛ se: "Gyesɛ wotwa me ti ne me to, ansa na woafe me!"
*The water snail says: "Unless you cut my head and bottom you cannot suck me."*
(Some small things can only be dealt with considerable effort).

289. Abebeɛ se: woreku no a wode sekan, nanso wode mframa na ɛdwa no.
*The water snail says: if you are killing it, you use a knife, but when you are preparing it to eat you use air.*
(You make use of different tools for different operations).

290. Bɛbɔdam firi fie.
*Insanity is from the home.*
(You behave strangely at home before you do so outside).

291. Bebrebe yɛ mmusuo.
*Too much causes trouble.*
(Enough is as good as a feast).

292. Ɔbedɛ mma Kumase a, nyɛ Asomase bɛdɛ.
*If a palm leaf carrying basket is not allowed to come into Kumasi, it is not Asomase's basket.*
(In former times carrying baskets made out of palm leaves were not allowed to be brought into Kumasi. However, after the downfall of Asumegya a certain subject of Asansu is said to have found some of the state heirlooms and to have taken a share to the Asantehene tied up in palm leaves. Hence: There are exceptions to every rule).

293. Ɔbedɛ mu nni akyamfoɔ.
*There is no distinction among baskets.*
(All ordinary people are of equal importance).

294. Bɛdɛ ayɛyie ne sumina so.
*A palm basket's reward is (to be thrown on) the rubbish heap.*
(Used when ingratitude is shown to an old and faithful servant or helper).

295. Abedeɛ bɔ bum a, ɔde ne sumieɛ ne ne kɛte na ekɔ.
*If a red duiker runs suddenly away, it takes its pillow and its mat and goes.*
(If you clear out of a place you take everything with you).

296. Abɛdua a ogya aka no nsa na ano yɛ hyeɛ.
*A palm tree that has been scorched, its palm wine is powerful.*
(Fire is used to get the last wine out of a palm tree which has been felled. Hence: We grow through suffering).

297. Abɛdua, gyae ahohoahoa, na bɛtene hyɛ aseɛ na ɔne wo pɛ.
*Short palm tree, stop showing off, for when the tall palm tree began life it was like you.*
(Don't boast. Or: Don't imagine there is anything special about what you are doing).

298. Abɛdua pɛ nkwa a, na ɛbata odum.
*If a young palm tree wants life, it grows beside the odum tree.*
(The helpless seek help from the powerful).

299. Mmɛdua ase mpa mmɛfua.
*Palm nuts are not scarce under the palm tree.*
(Where there is plenty you can expect to profit a little).

300. Bɛfua korɔ yɛntwɛre no mprenu.
*One palm nut cannot be ground twice.*
(You cannot cheat a man twice running).

301. Bɛfua kyim, yɛdi no afonom.
*One single cooked palm nut, we eat it only once.*
(Some things are too small to share. Only one person can enjoy them).

302. Bɛkoe din fata no a, yɛhu no akono na ɛnyɛ nnyedua ase.
*If "the one who was born to fight" deserves the name, he must earn it on the battle field and not sitting under a tree.*
(Your real qualities are only shown in action. A great name is earned and not inherited).

303. Ɔbɛmmɔne didi bɛmpa kɔte ano.
*A bad man eats from the mouth of a good man's penis.*
(A man who has no wife depends on his friends who have).

304. Wobɛn nsuo ho a, na wote sɛ ɔkɔtɔ rebɔ wa.
*If you get close to a river, you hear the crab coughing.*
(It is when you go to a man's home that you see his real character).

305. Abɛn korɔ wɔnhyen no "puu" na wɔahyɛn no "paa!"
*A single horn, they can't blow it "puu" and "paa" at the same time.*
(Paa-puu is the signal note before playing. An orchestra is made up of several horns and each has its own note. You can only play one at a time. Hence: You can only be master of one art at a time).

306. Abɛn nyɛ dɛ mpo a, ɛtua onipa ano.
*Even if the horn is not sweet, it is played by a person.*
(Some things must be taken seriously, whether you like them or not).

307. Wobene bene a, wohye.
*If you fortify yourself too much (lit. fortify, fortify), you burn-up.*
(Fortifying means protecting yourself by means of magic and herbs against disaster. If you use too much juju to protect yourself it destroys you. Hence: You can have too much of a good thing).

308. Benkum dware nifa na nifa dware benkum.
*The left (hand) washes the right and the right washes the left.*
(You scratch my back, I'll scratch yours).

309. Ɔbɛnnoburobo tafere ne nsa a, ɔde kamfo ne yere nkwan.
*If an unmannerly man licks his hand, he does it in praise of his wife's delicious soup.*
(There is a reason for every action, however unattractive).

310. Abɛntia fata abɔgyeɛ a, yɛde ma no.
*If the short horn deserves a jawbone it gets one.*
(In the old days jawbones of defeated enemies were used to decorate the war horns. Hence: If a man fights bravely he wins success).

311. Ɔbɛnya-adeɛ kra nkyiri biribi.
*The soul of a man born wealthy has no taboos.*
(Wealth buys freedom to act as you like. If you are pre-destined to be rich you will be rich whatever you do).

312. Bepɔ yɛforo no nkyɛn-nkyɛn.
*We climb a hill diagonally.*
(A hard problem must be tackled in the best way possible).

313. Bepɔ-dwuma, obi nhwɛ obi anim.
*Working on a hillside, no one watches the face of another.*
(A difficult job requires concentration).

314. Bepɔso dua, yɛsɔ mu home, na yɛnsɔ mu ntu aseɛ.
*The tree on a slope, we hold on to it to rest, but we don't hold on to it to uproot it.*
(If someone is helping you, you don't do them harm).

315. Aberanteɛ ano nyinaa wɔ hɔ mpo, yɛse n'ano nnuru dwam, na yɛatwa soɔ.
*When a young man's mouth was all there, we said his mouth (voice) did not reach the public, how much less now his lips are cut.*
(In the old days people's lips might be cut off for vicious gossip or slander. If something does not function when it is in good condition, nor will it if it is damaged).

316. Aberanteɛ tɔn atomdeɛ a, ɔbɔ ka wɔ mmabaawa nsa ano.
*If a young man sells meat, he will be in debt to a young woman.*
(Money that comes to a man, goes out to a woman).

317. Mmeranteɛ [baanu]/[mmienu] te nsuo ho a, ɛgu.
*If two youths sit by the water, it spills over.*
(Only one person can do a job at a time. Too many cooks spoil the broth).

318. Mmeranteɛ bo yɛ sika a, anka nnipa nyinaa anya bi pɛn.
*If youthful pride were wealth, every man has had some before now.*
(A warning against arrogance).

319. Aberantewaa firi mantamu bɛhyem a, anyɛ sotorɔ na obi abo no a, na ɛyɛ nkwanne na wasa.
*If a teenager comes from the gap between two houses to clear his nose, (and) if he has not been slapped by someone, it is sweet soup that he has eaten.*
(An experience must be either bad or good. Spicy soup makes your nose and eyes water).

320. Berɛ a bese kɔɔ Sraha na kube kɔɔ Asante.
*At the time cola went to Salaga, coconut went to Asante.*
(The give and take of trade).

321. Berɛ a Ɔfosu nkɔdɔɔ nkatefuo wɔ Aprade no, na ɛhɔ amoakua didi.
*At the time Ɔfosu went to make a ground nut farm at Aprade, the place's ground squirrels (already) ate there.*
(Used to challenge originality, as in: Before the birth of Mohammed there were many prophets).

322. Berɛ a Agyaba repɛ baabi ada ahome no, na Enaba rekɔ n'anim, na waduru ntɛm.
*At the time Father's child was looking for somewhere to lie and rest, Mother's child was going ahead so that they could arrive early.*
(Everyone reacts to life in their own way. Two people do not necessarily come to the same conclusion).

323. Berɛ a [Agyinamoa]/[Ɔkra] de ne ho bɔɔ Kurotwiamansa, sɛ asɛm ba a wako agye no; nanso Kurotwiamansa dii nkoguo wɔ Ɔsono nsa ano, na ɔde ne ho bɔɔ Ɔsono; na Ɔsono nso dii nkoguo wɔ Ɔbɔfoɔ cɔfcɔ, na ɔde ne ho bɔɔ Ɔbɔfoɔ no, na ɔgye di sɛ ɔbarima akyi nii ɔkokoɔdurufoɔ bio. Nanso, berɛ a [ɔbaabaseaa]/[Ɔbɔfoɔ yere] tumi de wɔmafunu pamoo ne kunu firi fie, ɛhɔna Agyinamoa hunu sɛ sɛɛ wokwati ɔbaa a, na woahwere wo ho adeɛ.
*Time was that Cat went to serve Leopard so that, if trouble came, he would defend him, then Leopard was defeated by Elephant, and he went to serve Elephant, and then Elephant too was defeated by Hunter, which made him go to serve Hunter, for he thought that after man there was no braver creature. But, when an ordinary woman (Hunter's wife) was able to drive her husband from the house with a pounding stick, that made Cat see that if you bypass the woman, you have lost the greatest of all.*
(Woman is the greatest).

324. Berɛ a nkɔnkɔnsa afiti kurotia no, na nnabraba te kurom retwen no.
*At the time intrigue enters the outskirts, falsehood is (already) in the town to meet it.*
(Society is never without hypocrites).

325. Berɛ a ɔkɔropɔn rekata ne ntakara soɔ no, na aserewa nso rekata ne deɛ so.
*At the time the eagle covers his feathers, the sunbird is busy covering his.*
(Big or small, we have to deal with similar problems).

326. Berɛ a akwatia beyɛ sɛ ɔtenten no, na ɔtenten deɛ ɔnsene wiase bio.
*At the time the dwarf becomes a tall person, the tall person will not fit into the world at all.*
(It is not possible for all men to be equal).

327. Berɛ a mmoa rekɔhyɛ mmara no na ɔsebɔ nsa si apɛse so.
*At the time all the animals came to an agreement, the leopard had its paws on the brush-tailed porcupine.*
(Violence was from the beginning of time).

328. Berɛ a mmusuo renyini no, na mpatadwan nso renyini.
*At the same time as a bad omen is growing up, the sheep for pacification is growing up.*
(Just as there are problems, so do solutions develop).

329. Berɛ a onyansafoɔ adwene kɔ aporɔ no, na kwasea deɛ te n'anan mu.
*At the same time as the wise man's mind is going on a journey, the fool's remains in one place (lit. is on his feet).*
(While the thoughtful man tries to do something about a situation, the thoughtless man makes no contribution).

330. Berɛ a mpanin ada no, na mmɔfra reyi amaneɛ.
*When the elders sleep, the young initiate trouble.*
(However careful you may be, your children may still lead you into trouble. Also: When the cat's away, the mice will play).

331. Berɛ a aprawa wuiɛ no, mmoadoma kɔgyam no. Ɔda bamma soɔ no, na anibereɛ mmaeɛ. Ɛduru ne koraberɛ no na wɔhunuu sɛ aka wɔn nko.
*At the time when the pangolin died, all the animals went to condole for him. When he was lying in the alcove they did not feel it much. It came to the time of burial, then they realized that he had left them alone.*
(It is when a person is really buried that you feel the loss most).

332. Berɛ a osua rekɔdi adeɛ no na abera barima ani afiri.
*At the time the white-nosed monkey was going to be enstooled, the red monkey's grandchild was already mature.*
(Said to quieten a boasting upstart - he is not the first to be successful).

333. Berɛ a supurupu redom sɔprɔpɔ no na sɔprɔpɔ redom supurupu.
*At the time the turtle is helping the sopropo, the sopropo is also helping the turtle.*
(There is a plant like an African cucumber called sɔprɔpɔ and the proverb probably refers to this. The turtle eats the fruit of the plant and presumably distributes its seeds. Hence: Mutual help).

334. Berɛ a Ata ne Ata ne Atakorata ne wɔn Ntantaban twaree asuo kɔ Nta sɛ wɔrekɔpɛ Ntakwan adi a, wɔkaeɛ na ɔtwo atwe ne ho, na kɔkɔte ate ne ho ahwe mu, na ɔdabɔ ada ne hɔ soɔ, na ɛbeɛ se "Mabe me ho," na sisire akɔsie, na ɔforɔteɛ aforo atɛ, na ɔtrɔmo atrom ne ho abɔ ne ho adwaa no, ɛhɔ na Ata ne Ata ne Atakorata ne wɔn Ntantaban hunuu sɛ, sɛɛ ɛbɛtɔ da na brɛdee adane brɛguo.
*When Ata and Ata (the twins) and Atakorata and all their entourage crossed the Volta to go see the North to collect savannah meat, as they went along, the Maxwell duiker sneaked out of their way, and the bush pig turned tail, and the bay duiker also got ready (to flee), and the forest hog said "I can't face up to the situation," and the badger hid himself, and the kob climbed an anthill, and the bongo slipped away and hid, so that Ata and Ata and Atakorata and their entourage realized that sometimes determination is fruitless.*
(Success in life can be thwarted by circumstances. This proverb contains a good deal of wordplay: Ata and Ata go to Nta (the North) crossing Ntantaban (the Volta); and the actions of the animals are described in language that audibly echoes their names).

335. Berɛ a tɔkua denden afiti kurotia no, na mpata denden rehyia no.
*When a tough quarrel makes its appearance at the outskirts of town, a serious peace effort meets it.*
(Every cloud has a silver lining).

**336. Berɛ a woretwa sa akɔtu ahu no, na woreyɛ obi amumuyɔ.**
*At the same time as you are making a path to find a treasure, you are causing harm to someone else.*
(Something may help you but harm another).

**337. Berɛ a ɔtwe nhunuu adukuro no na ɔda.**
*At the time that the duiker saw the hollow tree, it already knew how to sleep (lit. it slept).*
(The duiker is supposed to seek protection in such hollow trees. Hence: People existed before all the conveniences of life. Or: One can live even without a protector).

**338. Berɛ a owura de n'ano reya akoa no, na akoa de n'adwene regu owura.**
*When a master is insulting his slave verbally, the slave is insulting his master in his mind.*
(Even if you cannot answer back openly, your thoughts can kill. Or: Don't think a dependent does not mind how you treat him, just because he refrains from answering back).

**339. Berɛ a meyɛn akokɔ na meyɛn obirekuo yi deɛ adekyeeɛ renkɔfa me mpa ase da.**
*At the time I rear chickens and Senegal coucals the morning will never find me in bed.*
(Both these birds cry in the morning and wake people up. Hence: Said by someone who diversifies and so provides against the failure of one project).

**340. Ɛberɛ, yɛnni nka so.**
*Time, we don't remain with it.*
(There is an end to all things).

**341. Ɛberɛ nsoeɛ a, yɛnkra nkɔ.**
*If the time has not arrived, you don't say farewell to your host.*
(There is a correct time for everything).

**342. Ɛberɛ te sɛ anomaa, ɔtu a worenhu no bio.**
*Time is like a bird, it flies and you see it no more.*

**343. Mmerɛ dane a, yɛdane yɛn ho bi.**
*If times change, we change ourselves too.*
(You must adapt yourself to circumstances as they are).

**344. Mmerɛ di adanneɛ.**
*Times change.*

**345. Mmerɛkɛnsono a adi kan wɔ abɛ ho na ɛdane mpapa.**
*The young palm shoot that has emerged first from the tree turns into a palm frond.*
(The person who takes the lead becomes prosperous).

**346. Mmerɛkɛnsono si ne tiri ase a, na ɛwɔ deɛ asaase reka kyerɛ no.**
*If the young palm shoot bends its head to the earth, it means that there is something the earth wishes to tell it.*
(When someone does something unusual there must be a good reason for it).

**347. Ɔberɛmpɔn nyina si hɔ kunkonn ayɛ ara ɛbɛso dua ba bi ama amanfoɔ ate bi adi, sɛɛ na atentirehuo na ɛrebɛso ama atɔ mmɔfra ani.**
*The great silk-cotton tree (Ceiba pentandra) stands enormous there as if it is going to bear edible fruit for*

the citizens to pluck and eat. It has not realized that it will grow cotton to fly into the eyes of children.
(Mere size is no indication of value).

**348. Ɔberɛmpɔn wuo mfono ɔsafoɔ.**
*A great man's death does not disturb the warrior.*
(A brave man is brave, whatever happens).

**349. Aberewa a ɔnni se no, n'atadwe gu ne kotokuo mu.**
*The old lady who has no teeth, leaves her tiger nuts in her pocket.*
(Don't be a dog in the manger).

**350. Aberewa bɛdi twɛdeɛ a, ɛfiri n'ano.**
*If the old lady received a blow, it is because of her mouth.*
(If you provoke violence with your talk you should accept the result).

**351. Aberewa hwe ase a, ɔde hyɛ ne poma.**
*If an old woman falls down, she blames her walking stick.*
(We always try and blame others for our own weaknesses).

**352. Aberewa kɔ asuo a ɔbɛba, na ne ntɛm.**
*If an old lady goes for water she will come back, but how soon?*
(Don't expect speed from the aged. People can only work within their capacity).

**353. Aberewa nim adeɛ a, ɔnyɛ ne ban.**
*If the old woman knows (how to do) something, let her build her fence.*
(If you know how to do something, do it! Self help).

**354. Aberewa nsampana yie.**
*An old lady never dresses well.*
(Age becomes careless).

**355. Aberewa nsuro kaka.**
*An old lady does not fear toothache.*
(Old people often have no teeth. Hence: You don't fear what can't harm you).

**356. Aberewa atomdeɛ ne ɛfan.**
*An old woman's meat is ɛfan (Justicia galeopsis).*
(This is a small herb used for making soups and stews. The proverb is used of a humble person who accepts their position).

**357. Bese te kwaeɛ mu, na kube te mpoano.**
*Kola grows in the forest, but coconut grows by the sea.*
(Each person to his own place).

**358. Bese-pa ne konini ahahan, yɛtaase no ɔbanyansafoɔ.**
*The leaves of bese-pa and konini (two kinds of cola trees) are separated with wisdom.*
(Both fruits need careful handling to make the best use of their products. A red dye is obtained from the surface of konin-bixa orellana-seeds and is known commercially as bixine. Intelligence is necessary in even apparently simple jobs).

**359. Besebese na ɛma yɛtɔn akoa.**
*Grumbling makes us sell the slave.*
(A person who grumbles all the time is always unpopular).

360. Wobɛte mako na wobu so a, na ɛwuo.
*If you are picking peppers and you break the stem, it dies.*
(If you use the profits on an investment it continues to produce but if you spend capital it comes to an end).

361. Abeteɛ anim gu ase a, ebi ka nkuruma.
*If cassava dough becomes disgraced then the okro is also disgraced.*
(If those you work with or your relatives are in trouble, so are you).

362. Abɛtia gyae apinisie na wo ba ne kwaabɛtene.
*Short palm tree, stop complaining, for the young palm tree is your child.*
(Whatever your difficulties, if you have offspring your care is assured. Your children may achieve what you could not).

363. Abɛtia na ɛnyini yɛ bɛtene.
*The short palm tree grows into a tall palm tree.*
(It is a child that grows into a man).

364. Abɛtia pɛ nkwa a, ɛbata odum.
*If the short palm tree wants long life, it grows beside the odum tree.*
(If you have a protector you prosper).

365. Abɛtia yi wira a, ɛgu ne kɔn mu.
*If the short palm tree picks leaves, it spreads them round its neck.*
(You bear the consequences of your own actions).

366. Ɔbɛtwani a, ɔkɔwensani bɔɔ ne kɔraa, ɔse: "Monnyae no, na ɔkyena ɔbɛgye deɛ ɔde bɛnom nsa".
*The palm-wine tapper whose gourd was broken by the drunkard says:*
"Leave him alone, because tomorrow he will take what he will use to drink wine".
(If you know you can benefit from something in the future, you should take care of it).

367. Ɔbɛtwani tɔn nsa korɔ mprenu a, yɛbɔ no nimo.
*If the tapper sells the same wine twice, we spoil his name.*
(If someone cheats us we warn others and ruin their reputation).

368. Bɛyɛɛfieyie na owuo ni no.
*A person who is benevolent in the home is well known to death.*
(Death does not discriminate).

369. Ɛbi da bi so.
*Everyone depends on someone else.*

370. Ebi da w'anom a, na woto bi a ɛbene.
*If a morsel is in your mouth, then you can wait a little until it (the food) is well roasted.*
(Even a small installment can satisfy a creditor. Or: You are more likely to be successful if you already have something to live on).

371. Ebi akyiri woɔ bi.
*There is something better somewhere.*
(Don't brag. There is always someone better or better off than you).

372. Ebi anyɛ wo dɛ a, womma bi nyɛ wo nwono.
*If one thing was not sweet to you, you don't expect another to be bitter.*
(If you cannot appreciate one thing you can't say another is distasteful to you. You must try two things before you make a choice between them).

373. Obi a, Ɔbɔadeɛ de biribi pa bi bɔɔ no mpo, yayere no agye ne nsam; na wo a wofaa wo deɛ wɔ asaase so, na wobɛnya dɛn ayɛ wo ho?
*Even someone the Creator endowed with something good, they have taken it from his hands; how much more so, you who have taken something from the land (by your own effort).*
(When the top people are at a disadvantage, then those below really suffer).

374. Obi a ɔda fam nsuro ahweaseɛ.
*He who is down needs fear no fall.*

375. Ɔbi a ɔde n'ahwedeɛ na owe n'ase.
*The person who has the sugarcane, chews the lower part.*
(This part is the sweetest. The owner has first choice).

376. Obi a ɔde ne "Tanɔ" na ɔnim ne kasa-kyerɛ.
*The one who owns his own Tano fetish, knows how to address it.*
(Apart from the main fetish shrines, such as Tano, people had smaller individual shrines in their own houses. Hence: The owner of something knows best how to use it).

377. Obi a ɔdi mmire nkwan no, yɛnsrɛ no bonam.
*If someone eats mushroom soup, we don't ask them for game (soup).*
(If you know someone has not got something, don't ask them for it).

378. Ɔbi a ɔdi wo yere ama woadi no bi, nyɛ ya sɛ deɛ ɔredi no agye no aware.
*Someone who is sleeping with your wife and also allowing you to do so as well, does not cause as much pain as the one who sleeps with her and takes her to marry.*
(Temporary suffering is not as bad as permanent loss).

379. Obi a ne din da wo soɔ na wo ne no dware asukorɔ mu.
*It is the person whose name you bear that you bathe in the same water with.*
(You do things in common with your relatives and intimates).

380. Obi a wakɔhunu ɔsaman yarefoɔ abɛka no, ɔmamfoɔ rekɔpɛ no ahwɛ a, wɔnkɔ nnya no akyire.
*A person who has discovered a sick ghost and reported it, if the citizens are going to see it, they don't go and leave that person behind.*
(The person who starts something should be allowed to participate in it. Or: A person who tells a tall story should be prepared to prove it).

381. Obi a akyakya si n'akyi na yɛhu no mmɔbɔ, na nyɛ deɛ si n'anim.
*If someone has a hump on his back, we are sympathetic, but not if it is on his chest.*
(You will be pitied for a trouble which could not be foreseen, but not for something you did not try and prevent).

**382. Obi a n'akyi apaeɛ no, ɛnyɛ ɔno ara na ɔpam.**
*Someone whose back is broken, it is not he himself that mends it.*
(Even a good doctor cannot always heal himself. There are some jobs that must have help).

**383. Obi a n'akyiri nni bie no, ɔpɛ bosea a, ɔnnya.**
*One who has no backing, when he is after a loan, cannot get it.*
(Unless people are prepared to vouch for you, you cannot get credit).

**384. Obi a ne nsa gu n'akyi nni ahotɔ.**
*A person who has their hands behind their back is not free.*
(If you are in someone's grip, you are in for real trouble).

**385. Obi a yɛni no awia no, yɛnsɔ kanea nhwɛ n'anim anadwo.**
*The person that we know in the daytime, we don't light a lamp to see his face in the night.*
(A familiar person is always familiar).

**386. Obi a onim atoɔ na yɛmma ɔgyina twenenoo soɔ.**
*It's the person that knows how to shoot whom we put on the track of an animal.*
(The skilled man is the first to be put on a job).

**387. Obi a ne pɛtea hyɛ wo nsa no, na woyɛ [n'akoa]/[n'afenawa].**
*It's the person whose ring is on your finger whose [slave]/[maid] you are.*
(In Akan society rings were given to sons or daughters; children had to obey parents. Hence: If you accept someone's gifts you are under permanent obligation to them).

**388. Obi a ɔresum ne fidie wɔ [abotan]/[ɛsie] soɔ no, ɔno ara na ɔnim faako a ɔde ne kuntunu bɛbɔ.**
*Someone who sets his trap on a [vast stone]/[ant-hill], he himself knows the place that he is going to put his stick.*
(The stick is part of the trap. Hence: Don't judge someone's actions without knowing the full story).

**389. Obi a ɔti abɔntenso nim ne fie awerɛhoɔ.**
*Someone who stays outside (still) knows the afflictions of his home.*
(Absence does not always mean ignorance).

**390. Obi a wato adwan mmienu de baako ato "Hwɛ-wo-ho-yie" na ɔde baako ato "Tena-w'ase" no, na ɛfiri deɛ wahunu ntira.**
*Someone who names two sheep and names one "Look-after-yourself-well" and the other "Stay-where-you-are", it is out of his own experience (lit. what he has seen).*
(If an experienced person warns you indirectly to be careful, he may nevertheless mean it seriously).

**391. Obi a wawuo na yɛsu no.**
*It is a person who has died that we weep for.*
(We sympathize with those in real trouble).

**392. Obi a ɔyɛ obubuafoɔ yɛ n'adeɛ.**
*Even a lame person does his own thing.*

**393. Obi abawuo keka obi asom.**
*The death of one person's child disturbs another person.*

(The death of another person's child reminds us of the mortality of our own families. Hence (paradoxically): Our deepest feelings have to do with our own concerns).

**394. Obi aberewa yɛ no dɛ.**
*Someone's old woman is precious to them.*
(You care for those who are close to you).

**395. Obi mmisa ɔkɔrɔmfoɔ sɛ: "Wɔkyeree woɔ no wɔboroo wo?"**
*No one asks a thief: "When you were caught, were you beaten up?"*
(Don't ask the obvious).

**396. Obi mmisa ɔkwatani se: "Ɛbini wɔ wo to?"**
*One does not ask a leper if his anus is dirty.*
(A leper has no fingers to use for personal hygiene and so cannot keep himself clean. Hence: Don't embarrass someone by pointing out their shortcomings).

**397. Obi mmisa Mowire aberewa sɛ ɔpɛ mmɔmɔne.**
*No one asks the old lady from Mowire if she likes fermented fish.*
(Mowire is by the sea and they dry fish there. Hence: You don't ask someone if they like something they use all the time).

**398. Obi bɔ wo dua sɛ: "Ma ɔnwu!" a, ɛnyɛ ya sɛ ɔse: "Ma ohia nka no!"**
*If someone invokes a fetish against you saying: "Let him die!" it is not as painful as if he were to say: "Let poverty lay hold on him!"*
("Bɔ dua" is to knock a piece of wood into the ground and at the same time to invoke a curse and call on the fetish to harm someone. Hence: Poverty is worse than death).

**399. Obi bɔ wo awerɛkyekyerɛ suman na ɔde nkɔmmɔ due ano a, na wannya papa bi anyɛ wo.**
*If someone makes you a comforting charm and then rests on their condolences, they have not done you any good.*
(This is difficult to translate word for word. It means unfulfilled promises do people no good. Don't make promises unless you can keep them).

**400. Obi mmɔ nkɔkora nto mu atuo.**
*No one goes into hiding and fires a gun there.*
(If you want to be anonymous, you don't call attention to yourself).

**401. Obi mmɔ w'asom da a, ɛnyɛ deɛ ɔreyi woɔ.**
*If someone has not boxed your ears before, it is not the person who shaves you.*
(Some experiences are common to all, whatever their position).

**402. Obi mmɔ ntoa wiram, nnya no wiram.**
*No one prepares building earth in the bush and leaves it in the bush.*
(You don't work to no purpose).

**403. Obi mmoro obi, na ɔmmra no su.**
*No one beats someone up and forbids them to weep.*
(You don't harm someone and expect them not to react).

**404. Obi mmoro ɔyarefoɔ na ɔnka sɛ: "Mako".**
*No one beats a sick man and says: "I have fought a war".*

(If you do something despicable, don't boast and pretend that it is good.

**405. Obi mmu dua nnya so aba.**
*No one cuts down a tree and expects fruit to remain on it.*
(You can't expect profit from something you have destroyed).

**406. Obi mmua n'ano nni fɔ.**
*One should not remain silent to be pronounced guilty.*
(Every man has a right to defend himself).

**407. Obi abusudeɛ yɛ obi akradeɛ.**
*One man's curse is another man's blessing.*

**408. Obi busuyefoɔ ne obi nnipa pa.**
*One man's enemy is another man's friend.*

**409. Obi de kusie yɛ wo nkwan a fa mmire yɛ ne nkwan, ɛfiri sɛ ne nyinaa firi esie mu.**
*If someone makes you soup from the rat, make them soup from mushrooms because both (lit. all) are from the anthill.*
(Rats make their holes in the white-ant mounds and mushrooms grow on them. Do as you would be done by).

**410. Obi deɛ aba no, na obi deɛ nam kwan so.**
*One person's troubles have come and another's are also on the way.*
(Trouble comes to us all sooner or later).

**411. Obi adeɛ dada kɔ obi nsam a, ɛyɛ no foforɔ.**
*If someone's old thing gets into someone else's hands, it is as new to him.*

**412. Obi ade-fo yɛ no ade-pa.**
*Someone's bad thing pleases them all the same (lit. is their good thing).*
(If something is yours, it is what you think of it that matters).

**413. Obi nni kosua mmɔ dompe mu.**
*One does not eat an egg and crush a bone in it.*
(You don't expect to find anything hard in an egg. This is said for instance of a safe job where you can't get into trouble).

**414. Obi nni n'akra-duane na n'anom nhyehye no.**
*Someone does not eat his favorite food to burn his mouth.*
(No one admits to being harmed by what he likes).

**415. Obi nni nkwankwaasɛm nsuro nimmomu.**
*One does not behave ostentatiously and fear slander.*
(If you want to be known in public you must be prepared for criticism).

**416. Obi nni Amantena asɛ nnya Kwankyewaa Bɛdɛ.**
*One does not trace the history of Amantena and leave out the Queen Mother Kwankyewaa Bɛdɛ.*
(This Queen Mother of Amantena in Bompata (Asante Akim) lived to a very old age. When she was captured by the Asantes they treated her with great respect as she was found to be able to trace all the history of the area. When her son Apenten wanted her to fight the Asantes, she advised him not to. He did and was captured and killed. Hence: Don't leave out an essential person).

**417. Obi nnii nnɛte-dwini maa ɛmmɔɔ no da.**
*One does not do the potter's work (i.e. make pots) to get into debt.*
(When materials are free it does not cost you anything but energy to do a job, therefore don't claim such work has led to great expenses).

**418. Obi nni aponkyerɛne akyi mmɔ akokompe.**
*No one imitates a frog in hopping.*
(It is no good trying to rival the expert).

**419. Obi nni ɛsono akyiri mmoro hasuo.**
*One does not follow an elephant and get wet with the dew from the undergrowth.*
(If you follow a powerful man, you are protected).

**420. Obi nnidi mma ne werɛ mfiri wuo.**
*One does not eat and forget death.*

**421. Obi nnidi nnu ne ho.**
*One does not eat to repent.*
(You don't regret something from which you have benefitted).

**422. Obi dɔ wo a, na ɔka ba wo ho.**
*If someone loves you, then they come closer to you.*

**423. Obi dɔ wo a, ɔfrɛ wo asanom.**
*If someone loves you, then they call you to drink with them.*

**424. Obi dɔ wo a, ɛnkyerɛ sɛ watɔ wo.**
*If someone loves you, it does not mean they have bought you.*
(Love is not absolute possession).

**425. Obi dɔ wo a, na ɔfa wo dɔmum.**
*When someone loves you, they make you a prisoner of war (instead of killing you).*
(You don't destroy what you like).

**426. Obi dɔ wo a, na ɔto wo badin.**
*If someone loves you, they name their child after you.*
(You want your child to take on the character of those you love. Among the Akan it is believed that a child takes on the character of the person he or she is named after. Naming is, therefore, very important).

**427. Obi dɔ wo a, na ɔsrɛ wo hɔ adeɛ.**
*If someone loves you, they will beg something from you.*
(Amongst the Akan, if you like someone you ask them to do things for you as a kind of compliment. For instance, if you ask someone to cook for you it means that you enjoy their cooking and feel they are intimate enough to do it for you with love. People like to be remembered in little gifts as well).

**428. Obi dɔ wo a, na ɔyi wo bɔne adi kyerɛ woɔ.**
*If someone loves you, then they point out your faults to you.*

**429. Obi nnɔ ne nnan ho nnɔ n'akoa nnan ho.**
*Someone does not love his feet and love his slave's feet as well.*
(If a job has to be done and you spare yourself from doing it, then someone else must do it. Hence: You can't have things both ways).

**430. Obi ne aduane ne sika nyɛ aka.**
*No one's food and money quarrel together (lit. cut off relationships).*
(To be "aka" with someone is to stop all contact with them as the result of a disagreement. You cannot separate your food and your money. Hence: There are certain basics in life that you cannot do without).

**431. Obi nnɔ ne yɔnko na ɔntane ne ho.**
*Someone does not love their companion and hate themselves.*
(Everyone should have self-respect before respecting others).

**432. Obi dwan wu a, na obi anya nkwan.**
*If someone's sheep dies, then someone else has soup.*
(One man's curse is another man's blessing).

**433. Obi dwane toa wo a, na ɔde asɛm akyɛ wo.**
*If someone pleads with you to act on their behalf, then they have committed you (lit. they have given the matter to you).*

**434. Obi nnwane mfiri adepa ho.**
*One does not run away from a good thing.*

**435. Obi nnwen wuo nnwen porɔ.**
*One does not think of death (and) think of decay.*
(Something which is inevitable should not be thought about too much).

**436. Obi mfa badwafoɔ nyɛ nkoa.**
*One does not treat councilors as slaves.*
(You must respect the people who help you).

**437. Obi mfa bayerɛ pa mfua nhanoa.**
*One does not take a good yam to plant at the edges of the farm.*
(You care for what is good and don't put it where it may be neglected, stolen or lost).

**438. Obi mfa obi adeɛ nhoahoa ne ho.**
*One does not take someone else's thing and boast about it.*

**439. Obi mfa aboa anim mmɔ homa.**
*One does not go in front of an animal to tie a knot in a rope.*
(You don't make it obvious you want to catch someone out).

**440. Obi mfa bɔdwesɛ hunu nkɔ Basel asɔre.**
*One does not take only a beard to go to the Presbyterian church.*
(The early Presbyterian or Basel Mission church was very strict about dress. Those who went and who could not afford to dress in European style could take little part in the worship. Hence: If something requires expenditure and you have no money, you can't take part in it).

**441. Obi mfa abofuo nto anomaa boɔ.**
*One does not use anger to throw a stone at a bird.*
(You have to use patience to deal with a difficult person).

**442. Obi mfa ɔbɔmu nho gya so.**
*One does not smoke the whole carcass over the fire.*
(You must consider in depth before coming to a decision).

**443. Obi mfa n'abusua mu asɛm nkɔto serewa.**
*One does not take his matriclan's affairs (outside) and joke about them.*
(Family affairs should be kept within the family and treated with respect. Traditionally you did not reveal family secrets to those outside, nor the secrets of one stool to the followers of another. From his first days a child was taught to be discrete about family matters).

**444. Obi mfa deɛ wawuo suman nka sɛ: "Mɛma wo akwanhosan".**
*One does not take a dead person's good luck charm and say: "Protect me from an accident".*
(You do not use something which has already failed).

**445. Obi mfa adeɛ nkɔyi mmusuo wɔ kurotia, na ɔnsan nkɔfa bio.**
*One does not take something to make a ritual sacrifice at the outskirts and (then) bring it back again.*
(If you decide to give something valuable away, you don't expect to take it back again).

**446. Obi mfa ne dɛɛfoɔ nyɛ foɔ mmɔ ne ho asu.**
*No one uses his benefactor as a colobus monkey in order to purify himself.*
(In the old days, this monkey was sacrifices in certain purification ceremonies. Don't show ingratitude to your benefactors).

**447. Obi mfa ade-kɔkɔɔ nsisi bayifoɔ.**
*One does not use a red thing to deceive a witch.*
(A witch deals with blood and fire, both of which are red. Hence: You cannot cheat an expert. Or: You can't fool someone who knows what you are doing).

**448. Obi mfa adidie mfa adepɛ.**
*One does not combine gluttony with acquiring wealth.*
(You cannot eat your cake and have it too).

**449. Obi mfa adidie ne kasa.**
*One does not combine eating and talking.*
(Amongst the Akan it is not done to talk while you are eating a meal; it is bad manners. Hence: Concentrate on one thing at a time).

**450. Obi mfa dɔkonsini nkwankyɛn na ɔmmisa deɛ ɔbuu soɔ.**
*One does not pick up a bit of kenkey by the roadside and ask for the person who broke it off.*
(Don't look a gift horse in the mouth).

**451. Obi mfa fɛreɛ nkɔdwa [Ampɔfo]/[ɔkwatani].**
*One does not out of respect (lit. someone does not take respect to) shake hands with [Ampɔfo]/[a leper].*
(Ampɔfo was a famous man who was a leper. Shaking hands is customary but in this case dangerous. Hence: You don't go out of your way to endanger yourself).

**452. Obi mfa fɛreɛ nware obi nuaba a ne paam pɔ.**
*One does not out of respect marry someone's sister who has a lump on her clitoris.*
(In this case "bashfulness" might be a better translation of "fɛreɛ." You don't do something foolish just because you are afraid to say "No!").

**453. Obi mfa n'afuru mmutu aburopata so mma ne mfɛfoɔ ntwetwe mfa n'ase.**
*One does not lie on a pile of corn cobs to let his neighbor pull some from under him.*

(A man should enjoy the fruit of his own labors. A man's reputation should not be spoilt by the dishonesty of others).

### 454. Obi mfa ohia nsisi apempem.
*One does not use poverty to extort money.*
(A warning against extortion in any circumstances).

### 455. Obi mfa ohia nto dɔtebɛ.
*One does not out of poverty fell a palm tree in a swamp.*
(If you are in want you don't create extra difficulties for yourself).

### 456. Obi mfa n'ahoɔden nsie mma ɔkɔm nne no.
*Someone does not preserve his strength and allow hunger to overcome him.*
(If you don't make use of what you have you cannot improve your situation. It is no good saving and starving).

### 457. Obi mfa hyire nti deɛ watɔ wiram.
*One does not take white clay and pursue someone who has escaped into the forest.*
(White clay is used to smear on people who have something good to celebrate – a victory in court, release from prison, victory in elections and so on. Someone who has run away because they are guilty is not congratulated. Hence: Don't pervert justice).

### 458. Obi mfa kokuroko nni amim.
*Someone should not use his size or strength to oppress.*

### 459. Obi mfa ɔkyena nhoahoa ne ho.
*Some one does not take tomorrow to show off.*
(Don't boast of what you may do in the future for death may come at any time).

### 460. Obi mfa koma-bɔne nkɔ Anum.
*One does not go to Anum with arrogance.*
(Anum people have a reputation for pride. Hence: Don't show off in front of a proud man).

### 461. Obi mfa nkonyaayie nkɔ mmoatia kurom.
*One does not take magic to the town of the little people.*
(The mmoatia or little people are the fairies of the Akan people. They are possessed of magic and can travel great distances in a short time. I have even been told of one who went overseas to remove evidence from a police file so that the nephew of my informant could not be taken to court. Hence: Don't carry coals to Newcastle).

### 462. Obi mfa ne [kɔre]/[ɔsansa] takra nkɔsesa pɛtɛ takra.
*One does not exchange an [eagle's]/[hawk's] feathers for those of a vulture.*
(You don't change good for bad).

### 463. Obi mfa nkwadaasɛm nsisi kontromfi.
*One does not take childish ploys to trick a baboon.*
(You can't trick a clever man with simple tricks).

### 464. Obi mfa nwoma nto nsuo mu na ɔnnya kɔ ahemfie.
*One does not put a hide to soak in water and leave it and go to the chief's palace.*
(You never know how long you will be kept on an important person's business so you don't leave work half-done when you go to them).

### 465. Obi mfa amaneɛ a wahunu ntutu ka.
*Someone does not use his misfortunes to seek to excuse a debt.*
(You must honor an obligation whatever you are suffering).

### 466. Obi mfa namɔn tenten nkɔ Ɔseɛ Tutu fie nkɔhunu agyapadeɛ na ɔnni ahurisie.
*Someone does not use his long legs to hurry to Osei Tutu's (the Asantehene's) palace to see his heirlooms and become happy.*
(Don't concern yourself about what is not your business. Or: Don't worry about what you cannot emulate).

### 467. Obi mfa ne nnan mmienu nsusu asuo.
*One does not use two feet to test the depth of the water.*
(Be cautious and don't jump into things without knowing what you are letting yourself in for. Or: Don't put everything into one venture).

### 468. Obi mfa ne nsa benkum nkyerɛ n'akuraase kwan.
*Someone does not use his left hand to show the way to his village.*
(It is rude and unlucky to point the way with your left hand in Akan society. Hence: Do not belittle your own origins but treat them with respect).

### 469. Obi mfa ne nsa hunu ne gyata nni ako.
*One does not challenge a lion with bare hands.*
(You do not challenge a powerful man unless you are sure you have the means with which to fight him).

### 470. Obi mfa ne nsa nhyɛ ne dammirifa mu na ɔnsu hyia.
*Someone does not keep his hands between his thighs and complain of poverty.*
(Unless you work, you don't prosper).

### 471. Obi mfa "pan" nhwe "pen" so.
*One does not take a "punch (fist)" to beat a "thwack (stick)."*
(You must meet strength with equal strength).

### 472. Obi mfa asamanfoɔ ntwa mpasua.
*One does not take the spirits of the dead to encamp against enemy lines.*
(You meet material things with material things. Do not rely on those who may not give practical help).

### 473. Obi mfa asɛmpa nyɛ nsɛmma-nsɛmma.
*One does not treat an important matter as if it were a mere trifle.*

### 474. Obi mfa ne se mmobɔ adwe mma ne yɔnko mmɛfa nwe.
*Someone does not use his teeth to crack a palm kernel to give to his companion to chew.*
(You don't take unnecessary risks for someone outside the family).

### 475. Obi mfa toa-num nkɔsrɛ ngo.
*One does not take an unopened gourd to beg for palm oil.*
(Its no use asking for help if you do not have the means to use it).

**476. Obi mfa atofo kɛseɛ mpam okusie nkye no.**
*No one wears a big bustle to chase a rat and catch it.*
(You don't dress up to do a strenuous job. Dress for the occasion).

**477. Obi mfa ntwa-wo-ho nsisi kɔmfoɔ.**
*One does not use turning-around to cheat the fetish priest.*
(The fetish priest whirls around when he is under possession and is dancing. Hence: You don't try and cheat someone in a way which is well-known to him).

**478. Obi mfiri ɔbaa akyi ntu ne tam.**
*One does not pull the loin cloth off a woman behind her back.*
(Some things can only be done with the agreement of the person involved).

**479. Obi mfiri Nsabaa a yɛtɔ onipa taku ne damma mma Kwenyako mmesu sɛ: "Menko menam".**
*One does not come from Nsabaa where we buy a slave for a taku and a damma and come to Kwenyako and weep that: "I walk alone."*
(A taku and a damma is a small amount of gold dust. Make the best of your opportunities when they occur or don't complain afterwards. Both towns were in the Fante area of Ghana).

**480. Obi mfiri ɛsono akyi nkɔbɔ aserewa boɔ.**
*One does not leave an elephant to throw stones at a sunbird.*
(Don't permit a small thing to lose you a large one).

**481. Obi mfiri sudwaresɛn ho nhohoro ne ho.**
*One does not by-pass the washing pot to wash himself.*
(Use the correct thing for the job and don't go elsewhere).

**482. Obi mfiri tan akyi nsie ɔba.**
*One does not by-pass a mother to bury her child.*
(No one does a service for someone most concerned without consulting them).

**483. Obi mfiri Takyiase nkɔdi Anowuo asɛm.**
*One does not come from Takyiase to go to try a case from Anowuo.*
(Don't poke your nose into other people's concerns).

**484. Obi mfiri awoeɛ mmɛgye feam.**
*One does not come from the place of birth to fetch a charm for easy birth.*
(One does not make provision for something which has already happened).

**485. Obi fom kum a, womfom nnwa.**
*If someone errs and kills an animal, you don't flay it in error.*
(If someone offends you without consideration you don't need to retaliate and put yourself on the level with them).

**486. Obi foro abɛ te hwe a, na ɛnkyerɛ sɛ obi ntwa abɛ bio.**
*If someone climbs a palm-nut tree and falls, it does not mean that no one should cut palm-nuts again.*
(Just because one person fails at a job it does not mean that others will not do it again).

**487. Obi mforo gyamma nsiane mma fam mmɛpɛ kɔtɔkoro.**
*One does not climb the Christmas bush (alchornea cordifolia) and come down to look for a hooked stick.*
(This small tree is used for making hooked sticks for work on the farm and its fruits are also used for trapping birds. Hence: You don't return from the place where you can get something and ask for it elsewhere).

**488. Obi afuo so a, yɛmfa mpampa na ɛfom.**
*However great a person's farm may be, we don't plunder the crops with large headpans.*
(Don't be over greedy or presume on a friend's generosity).

**489. Obi nnyae abawuo nkɔdi akorasɛm.**
*Someone does not leave the death of a child to go and involve themselves in quarrels of fellow wives.*
(You don't leave something deeply serious and where you are needed, to involve yourself in trivial squabbles).

**490. Obi nnyae ngo so tare nkɔtare adwe so.**
*One doesn't stop covering the palm oil pot in order to go and cover palm kernels.*
(You deal with the most immediate problems first).

**491. Obi nnyae ɔsono akyiri die nkɔdi aserewa akyi.**
*Someone does not stop following an elephant in order to chase a sunbird.*
(You don't give up something big for a trifle).

**492. Obi agyimi a ne ɛnkyerɛ sɛ n'ani afura.**
*If someone is foolish it does not mean he is blind.*
(Not all shortcomings are alike).

**493. Obi ahiasɛm hwehwe obi aso.**
*One person's important affair is seldom understood by another.*

**494. Obi ho atwa na yɛde sa yɛn ho yareɛ.**
*Someone's scars are what we use to cure our diseases.*
(We learn by experience).

**495. Obi nhuhu mma obi nkeka.**
*Someone does not blow (on food) for another person to eat it.*
(You blow on food to cool it for yourself. Hence: You don't work for another to benefit).

**496. Obi nhunta mmɔ wa.**
*One does not cough when in hiding (lit. Someone does not hide to cough).*
(If you wish to keep something private, don't draw attention to it).

**497. Obi nhunta mpunu ahina**
*Someone does not smoke out the water pot when in hiding. (lit. Someone does not hide to smoke out the water pot).*
(See Proverb 496).

**498. Obi nhunta nsɔ gya.**
*One does not light a fire when in hiding (lit. Someone does not hide to light a fire).*
(See Proverb 496).

**499. Obi nhunu obi da koro na ɔnse no sɛ: "Woafɔn".**
*One does not see someone else for only one day and
say: "You have grown lean".*
(Don't make on the spot judgements).

**500. Obi nhunu obi kwabrane nni ahurisie.**
*One does not see someone else's strong slave and
dance for joy.*
(You do not rejoice over someone else's good
fortune).

**501. Obi nhunu ne nsono ho mfe.**
*Someone does not see his (own) intestines and vomit.*
(However nasty something which belongs to you is,
you don't reject it).

**502. Obi nhunu "anka," nkata "anka," nnyae "anka," na
ɔnka sɛ: "Mehunuiɛ a, anka".**
*One does not see "Had I known," hold "Had I known,"
release "Had I known," and then say: "If only I had seen
Had I known".*
(It is no good having vain regrets after opportunities
pass).

**503. Obi nhunu Frempɔn mma nson nnakaberɛɛ ho na
ɔnyɛ ne ho brakasimane.**
*Someone does not see Frempɔn's seven childrens'
gold coffin and then hide himself.*
(Frempong had seven sons who all travelled away from
home. When they returned they bought a golden coffin
for their father and hid it. When their father died, they
brought out the magnificent coffin for the funeral.
Hence: If something is interesting you can't take your
eyes off it).

**504. Obi nhunu nimdeɛ nkɔ ayie ase na ɔsɔre a,
wasere.**
*A person with sense does not go to a funeral and
laugh when he gets up to leave. (lit. Someone does
not see wisdom and go to a funeral and if he gets up,
he laughs).*
(You must have a sense of propriety. If you do
something, then do it properly).

**505. Obi nhunuu wo two da a, nyɛ dware-sen.**
*If no one has seen (lit. If someone has not seen) your
hydrocele, it is not the bucket from which you bath.*
(A hydrocele is a swelling in the scrotum. Hence:
Nothing can be completely secret from those intimate
with you).

**506. Obi hwɛ obi anim na ɔnom abɛsini nsa.**
*It is because a person respects another that he drinks
the dregs of the palm wine.*
(The dregs of the palm wine do not taste good.
Hence: Some things are done out of respect rather
than for pleasure. Or: Don't look a gift horse in the
mouth).

**507. Obi nhwɛ obi ba nka ɔnsoma no.**
*One person does not bring up another's child and not
send it on errands.*
(If we take responsibility for someone else's child, we
should treat them as we do our own).

**508. Obi nhwɛ kɔm so nni awu.**
*One does not out of hunger assassinate someone.*
(Hunger is more easily overcome than death).

**509. Obi nhwɛ kuro anim mfa dua nwɔ mu.**
*One does not look at an open sore and prick it with
a stick.*
(Don't add insult to injury).

**510. Obi [nhwɛ]/[nhunu] tumm ntiam.**
*One does not [look at]/[see] a dark spot and tread on
it.*
(It may be a hole. You don't run into danger open-
eyed).

**511. Obi nhwɛ ɛtwe tia hɔ mmu ne kwasea.**
*One does not look at the short vagina to despise it (lit.
to regard it as foolish).*
(You can't judge what you don't know).

**512. Obi nhyira ne busuyɛfoɔ.**
*One does not bless one's ill-wisher.*

**513. Obi nhyira ne ho na ɔmmɔ ne yɔnko dua.**
*Someone does not bless himself and curse his
companion.*
(Do as you would be done by).

**514. Obi nhyira yɛ obi duabɔ.**
*One person's blessing is another's curse.*

**515. Obi ka kyerɛ wo sɛ: "Ɔkraman ani yɛ nan" a, ɔboa;
mmienu yɛ nwi.**
*If someone tells you: "The dog has four eyes," he is
lying; two are tufts of hair.*
(Don't take every exaggeration literally).

**516. Obi nka obi.**
*One person does not bite another.*
(This is often used as an emblem of peace and desire
for reconciliation and is the name of an abstract adinkra
design which is also used on stool paraphernalia).

**517. Obi nka nkyerɛ obi sɛ: "Tɔ nkyene di na w'anom
akum."**
*No one tells someone else: "Buy salt to eat because you
have lost your appetite".*
(Don't interfere in other people's personal affairs
unless they ask you to).

**518. Obi nka nkyerɛ ɔsafoɔ sɛ ɔmfa ahina nsi ho.**
*No one tells the palm wine seller to put a drinking pot
by the palm wine.*
(You don't instruct an expert).

**519. Obi nka sɛ: "Kum wo dwan ma menni na mentu
ne srɛ mma wo".**
*No one says: "Kill your sheep for me to eat so that I
give you the haunch."*
(You don't repay generosity with stinginess).

**520. Obi nka sɛ: "Putuo nhye ma yɛnni dwo". Nanso
putuo ɛhye a, yɛbɛhua bayerɛ no bi adi.**
*No one says: "Let the yam shed burn to let us eat
baked yam." But if the shed does burn we shall all help
ourselves to yam to eat.*
(No one wishes for adversity, but if it comes, all will
share in any benefits which may come out of it).

**521. Obi kae wo yafunu mu kɔm a, ɔkae wo hia.**
*If anyone reminds your stomach of its hunger, he
reminds you of poverty.*
(One thing automatically reminds you of another).

**522. Obi nkae ne wuda mfɔn.**
*No one remembers his day of death to grow lean.*
(We all know that we shall die one day, but we don't let it get us down).

**523. Obi nkari piredwan mma obi mfa.**
*No one weighs out a piredwan (of gold dust) for someone else to take it.*
(You don't work for someone else to profit).

**524. Obi nkasa nwie na wagu nsa.**
*No one ends their speech before pouring a libation.*
(You call on the ancestors, the earth and so on as you pour out a libation before commencing discussions. Hence: Everything has its appropriate time).

**525. Obi nkɔ obi akura nkɔkyerɛ n'ase.**
*One does not go to someone else's village in order to reveal his origins.*
(In Akan society it is not done to reveal another man's origins at any rate. Your own family affairs are private to your family. Hence: You do not go to Rome to revile the Pope!)

**526. Obi nkɔ obi kurom na ɔnkɔfrɛ ne ho Agyeman.**
*No one goes to another man's town to boast that he is the Savior.*
(You don't throw your weight about in another man's home).

**527. Obi nkɔ, obi mma; ɛbɛyɛ dɛn na yɛahunu sɛ ɔkwan mu yɛ hu?**
*No one goes, no one comes; how is it then that we know that the path is frightening?*
(You have to involve yourself in something before you know its true nature).

**528. Obi nkɔ ahua na ɔnkɔka nkwan nhwɛ.**
*One should not go begging and ask to taste the soup.*
(Beggars can't be choosers).

**529. Obi nkɔ ahua na ɔnto aduane ho pe.**
*No one goes begging and criticizes the food he gets.*
(Don't look a gift horse in the mouth).

**530. Obi nkɔ ahweɛ ngu ɛpo mu.**
*No one goes to fish and throws the water into the sea.*
(People dam a stream or river and then splash the water out below the dam to catch the fish. Hence: Don't add insult to injury).

**531. Obi nkɔɔ Kɔdiabɛ da nanso ɔte ne din a, ɔhunu sɛ abe nkanka.**
*No one has been to Kɔdiabɛ (Go-and-eat-palm-nuts), but when they hear its name they can realize it is not properly laid out.*
(Some names indicate the nature of the person or place. The bunch of palm nuts is a shape not suitable for the lay-out of a well-planned town. Therefore, when you hear it you have a bad picture of the town).

**532. Obi nkɔ Korɔbo nkwati boɔ.**
*No one going to Korɔbo avoids stones.*
(A play on words. Korɔbo is the name of a place; Kuro-boɔ means town of stones. Hence: Some things are the automatic consequences of certain actions and cannot, therefore, be avoided).

**533. Obi nkɔ Ananse amu so nkɔtu asaasedeɛ.**
*No one goes to Ananse's grave to collect a windfall.*

(Ananse the Spider is a cunning character who would never leave anything precious for a stranger to take and go free. Hence: A clever man never leaves anything to chance).

**534. Obi nkɔ aponkyerene fie nka sɛ: "Ma me akonnwa ntena so."**
*No one goes to the house of a frog and asks him to give him a seat.*
(You don't ask someone to give you what they obviously don't use).

**535. Obi nkɔ asamando na ɔnsan mmɛka abibisɛm.**
*No one goes to the underworld and returns to tell African tales.*
(No amount of imagination will enable you to return from death).

**536. Obi nkɔ asuo so ntware kwarifa.**
*No one goes to the stream to intercept the rat.*
(If you want to find someone, look in the right place).

**537. Obi akoa de Ahima a, ɔnhima no kwa.**
*Even if someone's slave is called "Punishment", he does not punish him without reason.*
(Ahima was a name given to slaves. Hence: A person may have got a bad name, but that doesn't mean he is always guilty).

**538. Obi akoa di piredwan na woma asuasa tɔ no a, ɔyi ka sua ma wo tua.**
*If a slave is worth a piredwan and you buy him for asuasa he will incur a debt of a sua which you will have to pay.*
(A piredwan is a large quantity of gold-dust and asuasa is much less. A sua is a quarter of a piredwan. Hence: You can't get things cheap in life. If you try to save you will lose in the long run).

**539. Obi nkɔfa obi dɔkono sini na ɔmpae deɛ ɔtwaa soɔ.**
*No one goes to take someone's remaining piece of kenkey and asks for the person who cut it off.*
(You don't show concern for the person from whom you steal).

**540. Obi nkɔgye ɔbɔfoɔ adeɛ nni na ɔnyɛ no hammusuo.**
*No one goes to collect a hunter's meat to eat and hinders him.*
(You don't harm the person who is helping you).

**541. Obi nkɔhwɛ sika-kɛseɛ anim mmuanna.**
*No one in the presence of a large sum of money goes hungry to bed.*
(You will not starve in the house of a rich man. Also a warning to the miser).

**542. Obi akɔnnɔdeɛ ne dompo nsono.**
*Someone's favorite food is the marsh mongoose's intestines.*
(One man's meat is another man's poison).

**543. Obi nkɔte bese kyɛm mfa mfra besetorɔ nkɔtɔn mma ne manni.**
*No one mixes dry and fresh cola and sells it to their own townsmen.*
(You don't try and cheat people with whom you are dealing all the time).

544. Obi nkɔtena wiram nkɔyɛ amumuyɔ mma fie.
*No one goes to stay in the bush to commit a crime and returns home.*
(i.e. you never get back home, or you don't get home safe. Hence: You never escape the results of your offenses, wherever you commit them).

545. Obi ankɔtɔ obi biribi a, anka obi nne obi ka.
*If someone does not go and buy something from someone, then no one owes anyone a debt.*
(You have to do something to incur a debt. If you avoid getting into debt you don't have to involve yourself in trouble).

546. Obi nkɔtoa ɔhahani wɔ ne bɔn ano na ɔnse sɛ: "Wo ho bɔn".
*No one follows the stinking ant to the mouth of its hole and says: "You stink!"*
(You don't pontificate in someone else's home. What they do and are there is entirely their own business).

547. Obi nkɔtoto mmane ngu hɔ na ɔnkɔsrɛ koobi mmɛbɔ borɔdedwo so.
*No one puts herrings on to roast and goes to beg stinking fish to eat with roasted plantains.*
(No one, having something good, goes after something inferior).

548. Obi rekra ne nyame na obi nnyina hɔ.
*When someone was promising his "god", no one was standing by.*
(Before coming to Earth the Akan believe that a soul is given a choice by God of what his station in life will be. No one else shares this choice, it is for him alone. Hence: Everyone has his own individual destiny).

549. Obi anku wo a wo ara wowu.
*If no one kills you, you yourself die.*

550. Obi nkukuru ɔpanten mmɔ kahyire mfa nsoa ne [nana]/[mma].
*No one makes a carrying pad out of an adder and asks his [grandchild]/[children] to carry it.*
(Kahyire, a carrying pad, is the piece of material that people place on their heads when carrying a load. Hence: You do not wittingly put members of your family in danger).

551. Obi akum sono amma amansan adi a, na ɛkyerɛ sɛ watua pɔn ɔha.
*If someone has killed an elephant for the nation to enjoy, it is as if he had paid a hundred pounds.*
(Giving service is as good as giving money).

552. Obi nkum Ananse; wokum Ananse a, ɔman bɛbɔ; wogyae Ananse a, ɔbɛdane kyɛmfoɔ abɛka wo.
*No one kills the spider; if you kill the spider, the state will be ruined; if you let the spider go, it will change into a bird spider and bite you.*
(It is regarded as unlucky to kill a spider amongst the Akan. If you kill it, you waste wisdom. This proverb is used when you have two equally unattractive options; a "Hobson's choice").

553. Obi kwan nkyɛre na asi obi deɛ mu.
*One man's path does not take long to join another's.*
(Our paths in life are always crossing).

554. Obi kwan nsi obi kwan.
*No man's path crosses another's.*
(Each person takes his or her own path).

555. Obi nkwati Afram nkɔ Nta.
*No one by-passes the Afram river to go to Gonja.*
(In order to get from the South to Gonja you have to cross the Afram river. Hence: Some obstacles can never be avoided).

556. Obi nkwati kokurobotie mmɔ pɔ.
*No one avoids the thumb and makes a knot.*
(You can't dispense with the indispensable).

557. Obi nkwati Tanɔ nkɔ ko.
*No one omits (to call on the fetish) Tano in going to war.*
(Chiefs used to consult fetishes before going to war. The Tano fetish was a very powerful one and was consulted by the Asantes before they went to war. Hence: No one takes an important action without doing everything they can to see that it will be successful).

558. Obi kyɛ wo adeɛ a, (na) woda no ase.
*If someone gives you a gift, you thank them.*

559. Obi nkyekyere nyansa kotokuo mfa nkɔto adaka mu mmɛgyina adihɔ nse sɛ: "Kyerɛ me asɛm".
*No one collects wisdom in a bag, to put it in a box and come out and say: "Teach me wisdom".*
(Make use of what you have before asking for more).

560. Obi nkyɛn mu yɛ tenana.
*It is difficult to live with someone who is not your relative.*
(Make special efforts in your relationships with those outside the family. Living with others is a generally difficult human task. One therefore has to be careful in relating to others).

561. Obi kyerɛ wo awia-kwan na woammfa so a, ɔkyerɛ wo anadwo-kwan.
*If someone shows you the path in the daytime and you don't take it, he shows you a path in the night.*
(If you don't accept the truth then people will persuade you with lies).

562. Obi nkyerɛ obi nwe a, obi nso mfa obi anum nyi kwan.
*If no one catches anyone to eat, then also no one should make their mouth a road to pass through.*
(If there were no persecuted there would be no persecutors).

563. Obi nkyerɛ abɔfra Nyame.
*No one needs to show a child God.*
(A child has pre-natal inherent knowledge of God and does not need to be persuaded of His existence. You do not need to point out the obvious).

564. Obi nkyerɛ [gyahene]/[ɔsebɔ] ba atoɔ.
*No one teaches the leopard's cub to spring.*
(Some talents and knowledge are inherited, or acquired in the ordinary course of things. Hence: Don't teach someone what they already know).

565. Obi nkyerɛ agyinamoa [korɔno-bɔ]/[apakyi mu hwɛ].
*No one needs to teach the cat how to [steal]/[look into the gourd].*
(See Proverb 564).

**566. Obi nkyerɛ katakyie nto dɔm ano mmisa no efiesɛm.**
*No one tells a valiant man to go to the war front and then asks him how it is at home.*
(If you send a man away to do something for you, you don't expect him to know conditions at home as well).

**567. Obi nkyerɛ akokɔbaatan abu ko.**
*No one teaches the good hen how to hatch eggs.*
(See Proverb 564).

**568. Obi nkyere akokɔnini na ɔnkɔbisa birekuo sɛ "Adeɛ bɛkye dabɛn?"**
*No one detains the cock and goes and asks the Senegal coucal when the day will break.*
(Both birds cry in the early morning and wake people up. Hence: If you have the means of knowing something at hand you don't go round asking for a substitute).

**569. Obi nkyerɛ kɔmfoɔ ba akɔm.**
*No one teaches a fetish priest's child (how to call on the) fetish.*
(Said when someone has been brought up in surroundings where he cannot fail to have picked up certain knowledge).

**570. Obi nkyerɛ [kontromfi]/[kwafea] mma ɔnni [ɔsɔn]/[sorɔno] aba.**
*No one forces the [baboon]/[red monkey] to eat the fruit (or seed) of the [tamarind tree – Tamarindus Indica]/[locust bean – Parkia Clappertonia].*
(You don't need to tell someone to do what they enjoy doing).

**571. Obi nkyerɛ kramoni ba kɔtefekyere.**
*No one shows a Moslem's child how to pull back the foreskin from his penis.*
(Moslems are usually circumcised but in the Akan areas this was not the custom. Hence: You don't show someone how to do something they don't need to do).

**572. Obi nkyerɛ ɔkwakuo abɛ wɔ.**
*No one teaches the monkey how to pound palm nuts.*
(You don't teach someone an unnecessary skill).

**573. Obi nkyerɛ apantweaa ba akɔmfo hyɛ.**
*No one teaches the bat's child how to hang.*
(See Proverb 564).

**574. Obi nkyerɛ ɔsansa ba adwareɛ na ɔnkyerɛ no nkuraase kwan nka ho.**
*No one teaches the kite's child how to swoop (on its prey) and also teaches it the way to the village.*
(The kite goes after chickens and other small birds. Hence: You don't help someone who may one day work against you).

**575. Obi nkyerɛ ɔtomfoɔ ba atono.**
*No one teaches a blacksmith's child how to forge.*
(A son learns from his father if he is an expert, or he does not learn at all).

**576. Obi nkyiri kooko na ɔnni ne mma.**
*No one taboos cocoyam and eats its offspring.*
(i.e the leaves of the cocoyam, which are also eaten. Hence: If you have nothing to do with one member of a family you avoid the rest of it).

**577. Obi nkyiri ɔpɛtɛ nni ne nkosua.**
*No one taboos the vulture and eats its eggs.*
(See Proverb 576).

**578. Obi bɛma wo a, nte sɛ woama wo ho.**
*If someone says that they will give you something, it is not like providing for yourself.*
(Self–sufficiency is best).

**579. Obi bema wo fufuo adi a na ɔde apɛsie di wo adanseɛ.**
*If someone is going to give you fufuo to eat then he gives you boiled plantain first to testify to that fact.*
(If people are going to favor you in a big way, they show it by little acts of kindness first).

**580. Obi mma bafan ni due da.**
*One never commiserates with a cripple's mother.*
(It should be taken for granted that you are sorry for someone unfortunate. By calling attention to it you make it worse. Hence: Don't rub it in).

**581. Obi mma ne ho amo.**
*No one congratulates himself.*
(Don't advertise your own achievements).

**582. Obi amaneɛ sane obi.**
*One person's problems affects another person.*
(We are all interdependent).

**583. Obi mee Memeneda a, na ɔmee Kwasiada.**
*If one feeds well (lit. is full) on Saturday one feeds well on Sunday.*
(One good thing follows another).

**584. Obi mmia ne ho kuro na ɔnsu.**
*No one dresses his own sore and cries.*
(You do not complain about your own actions).

**585. Obi remiamia wo mfe a, na ɔrepɛ wo nsono ani ahwɛ.**
*If someone is putting a dressing on your ribs, they also want to see your intestines.*
(If you are too free with someone, they may learn too much about you for your own comfort).

**586. Obi mmuna ntena sum mu.**
*No one who is gloomy should stay in the dark.*
(If you don't voice out your worries you continue to be depressed).

**587. Obi ne kurotwiamansa mmo mperɛ wɔ adukuro mu.**
*No one shares the roots of a tree with a leopard.*
(Don't try to become intimate with a dangerous person).

**588. Obi ne amim nsɛɛ kɛte nnaeɛ nsenneeɛ da.**
*No one willingly spreads out the (sleeping) mat to let a bully sleep.*
(You don't willingly help a disagreeable person. A bully is not a good bed–fellow).

**589. Obi ne wo ka a, na ɛfiri dabi asɛm.**
*If someone likes you, it is because they remember the past.*
(An intimate relationship has a source).

**590. Obi ne yafunu [ntwe manso]/[nyɛ aka].**
*No one [bears their stomach a grudge]/[quarrels with their stomach].*
(See Proverb 430. You don't bear a grudge against someone on whom you depend).

**591. Obi ni yɛ frɛna.**
*It is difficult to appeal to someone else's mother.*
(It is to your own mother you appeal in time of trouble, so value her!)

**592. Obi ni ayie ase na obi su ne ni.**
*At someone else's mother's funeral you weep for your own mother.*
(Someone else's sorrow reminds you of your own).

**593. Obi nni wo a, ɔfrɛ wo aboa bi.**
*If someone does not know you, he may call you a beast.*
(If you don't make yourself known to someone you are dealing with he may treat you with lack of respect).

**594. Obi anika dwom tuatua obi aso.**
*One person's sweet song disturbs another's ear.*
(One man's meat is another man's poison).

**595. Obi nim deɛ owuo wɔ a, anka ɔrensi hɔ ara da.**
*If someone knows where Death lives, then he doesn't ever stop there.*
(You don't knowingly court disaster).

**596. Obi nim nsanom a, ɔnsene asɔmorɔdwe.**
*Even if someone knows how to drink he cannot surpass the palm beetle.*
(Said of a well-known drunkard or a man able to drink a great deal. No one can surpass the expert).

**597. Obi nim sɛ ohia bɛhia no a, anka ɔkɔɔ Aburokyire mma wɔwoo no.**
*If someone had known he would become poor, then he would have been born outside Africa.*
(Aburokyire is now used to mean Europe or North America, though it probably originally meant simply "abroad." Hence: It is no good having vain regrets about one's situation in life).

**598. "Obi nnim a," ɛyɛ nyansakyerɛ.**
*"No one knows," is to profess wisdom.*

**599. Obi nnim (adeɛ) a, obi kyerɛ (no).**
*If one man does not know (something) then another teaches (him).*

**600. Obi nnim obi a, ɔnsɔ ne ka mu.**
*If one person does not know another he does not stand surety for him.*

**601. Obi nnim obi ase a, ɔnkyerɛ n'ase.**
*If someone does not know the origins of another person, he should not try and reveal them.*
(Don't say what you don't know).

**602. Obi nnim obi tirim a, ɔmfa n'adepa nnya no.**
*If someone does not know what kind of a person someone else is (lit. does not know what is in another's head), they do not trust them with their property.*
(You only give responsibility to those you know are capable of holding it).

**603. Obi nnim obi tirim a, ɔnsoma no adwadie.**
*If someone does not know what kind of a person someone else is (lit. does not know what is in another's head), he does not send him to trade.*
(See Proverb 602).

**604. Obi nnim obi tirim a, nyɛ nwanwento.**
*If someone does not know what is in another person's head, it is not a snail shell.*
(Said of someone who is regarded as completely empty-headed or an idiot).

**605. Obi nnim obi awieɛ.**
*No one can foresee destiny.*

**606. Obi nnim bɔdɔm bi a, ɔnsɔ ne nkawa mu.**
*If you don't know the dog, you don't handle its rings (i.e its chain).*
(Beware of trusting strangers).

**607. Obi nnim deɛ ɔbɛhwɛ bie.**
*No one knows who will look after whom.*
(We don't know on whom we shall depend in the future).

**608. Obi nnim deɛ ɛsono diiɛ a ɔyɛɛ kɛseɛ.**
*No one knows what the elephant ate to grow so large.*
(It is not known what conditions a man's position in life).

**609. Obi nnim adekyeɛ mu asɛm.**
*No one knows what the morning will provide.*
(We cannot foresee the future).

**610. Obi nnim dwonkuo a adeɛ bɛkyɛ soɔ.**
*No one knows which hip-bone will see the light of day.*
(We cannot foresee our fate).

**611. Obi nnim n'akyi a, ɔntɔ adeɛ.**
*If someone does not know what is in stock (at home) they do not buy something.*

**612. Obi nnim ɔpemfoɔ a, ɛnyɛ deɛ n'afura ahunu.**
*If someone doesn't know a pregnant woman, it's not the person who has experienced pregnancy.*
(You can't hide the obvious from those in the know).

**613. Obi nnim "Ɔtorɔmo-Saakwa" abɔsuo.**
*No one knows how the Bongo came about.*
(The origins of some people are mysterious. The Bongo is supposed to have a strong spirit and if you kill it you have to perform certain rituals or its spirit may damage you).

**614. Obi nnim tuo tirim.**
*No one knows what is in the gun's mind.*
(You cannot calculate the thoughts of a dangerous man).

**615. Obi nnim Twumwaa ne Sampa hyeɛso.**
*No one knows the vagina and the anus's boundary.*
(No one knows what goes on in private between two intimate people. The words Twumwaa and Sampa are nick-names for the vagina and the anus).

**616. Obi nnoa aduane-fini nkɔte nkwanta nhwehwɛ ɔmanni.**
*No one cooks stale food to go and place it at the cross-roads to search for fellow citizens.*
(No one expects praise for what is not praise-worthy).

**617. Obi nnom aduro mma ɔyarefoɔ.**
*No one takes medicine for a sick man.*
(Some things in life you can only do yourself).

**618. Obi nnom nsa nkɔkyere ɔwɔ.**
*No one gets drunk to catch a snake.*
(You need to be sober to do a dangerous job).

**619. Obi nnom nsa mmɔ koraa.**
*No one takes strong drink and breaks the calabash.*
(If you want to do something again, don't destroy your prospects of doing so).

**620. Obi nnom nsuo nsie Opɛ.**
*No one can drink and store water against the harmattan.*
(Don't attempt the impossible. The harmattan is the season of the year when there is no rain and the hot dry winds blow in from the Northern deserts - about December to February).

**621. Obi nnome deɛ obɛwu na wawu.**
*No one curses someone who is going to die before he dies.*
(You don't persecute a man when he is down).

**622. Obi bɛnya wo a, na ɛfiri yareɛ.**
*If someone will get you, it is because of sickness.*
(People become vulnerable when weak).

**623. Obi nnya sɛ Ɔberɛmpɔn Ntiamoa awo no.**
*A person would not be pained if he had been born of Paramount Chief Ntiamoa.*
(Ntiamoa was a well-known, brave and rich chief in the nineteenth century in Asante. No one fears to be born into the best families).

**624. Obi nnya sɛ ɔda ayeya na mfenemfenemadeɛ asɔ agu n'anom.**
*No one would be unhappy to lie on their back for sweet things to fall into their mouth.*
(No one avoids good fortune).

**625. Obi rennya sɛ yɛde ne mpena abɛsi ne ni awowa.**
*No one would be unhappy to see that his girl friend has been given to his own mother as a pawn.*
(In the old days families used to "pawn" members to those to whom they were in debt. When the debt was repaid then the person could return home. Hence: No one objects to luck coming their way).

**626. Obi rennya sɛ dwumfoɔ awo bafan.**
*No one minds that the metal worker has given birth to a child without proper use of its legs.*
(A smith needs someone to work his bellows. A disabled child (bafan) will be tied down and be more willing to work. Hence: Even something which is generally disliked may be acceptable to somebody).

**627. Obi nnya sɛ ananse ne padeɛ anya.**
*No one is as intimate as the spider and the ceiling.*
(You are closest to what you know best).

**628. Obi nnya sɛ wato boɔ ama akɔbɔ n'akonta akoa tirim.**
*No one minds that you have thrown a stone and hit the head of your brother-in-law's servant.*
(If something bad happens it is better that it should happen inside the family).

**629. Obi nnya ne ti mma edwie.**
*No one grows his hair for the benefit of lice.*
(You don't work for someone else to benefit).

**630. Obi nnyina akono nnwene kyɛm.**
*No one stops at the battle front to weave a shield.*
(You must take adequate precautions before facing adversity. It is no use preparing when you are already overtaken by events).

**631. Obi pae w'apampam a, na ɔrehyɛ wo akɔnmuden.**
*If someone strikes the top of your head, he imparts strength to your neck.*
(Adversity hardens).

**632. Obi pamo wo firi sadwaase a, na woahwere wo to ankonnwa.**
*If someone drives you away from the palm-wine tapper's bar, then you have lost your seat (drinking place).*
(If you are at someone's mercy they can punish you as they like).

**633. Obi pamo wo firi sadwaase a, wo sika ho dwo no.**
*If someone drives you from the drinking bar, your money becomes peaceful.*
(If you are not tempted to spend, you save).

**634. Obi mpata adaban mmienu nhyɛ gyam.**
*No one joins two iron bars without putting them in the fire.*
(You can't do a job without using certain necessary processes).

**635. Obi patu pɔ ne se apɔmono a, [ɛtu]/[mogya ba].**
*If anyone cleans his teeth too thoroughly, [he loses them]/[blood comes].*
(All things in moderation).

**636. Obi mpatu nya adeɛ a, ɛnsɛ sɛ ɔnya.**
*No one suddenly acquires something which he does not deserve.*
(What you acquire without effort you lose without effort).

**637. Obi pɛ kɔkɔɔ, ena obi na ɔpɛ tuntum, nti na ɛmma akunafoɔ nyɛ kyɛ na.**
*Someone likes fair-colored women and another likes dark-skinned ones, that is why it is easy to share out widows.*
(In Akan society, when a man dies, the man who inherits him may marry his widows if he wishes. Hence: Every man has his taste).

**638. Obi pɛ sɛ ɔsisi wo a, na ɔka abakɔsɛm a, ɔse wo sɛ: "... na wɔnwoo wo".**
*If someone wants to deceive you and he tells you a history, he says: "... then you were not yet born".*
(A liar does not want a witness to his story).

**639. Obi repɛ wo asisi wo a, na ɔne wo bɔ abusua wɛ ntɛsie ase.**
*If someone wants to cheat you, they first make friends by playing at marbles.*
(A clever person finds a way to gain your confidence before cheating you).

**640. Obi repɛ wo atoto wo awe a, wonhuri ntra ne gya.**

*If someone wants to make it hot for you, you do not hurry to get near the fire.*
(You keep away from people who wish you ill).

**641. Obi mpɛ obi yie.**
*No one wishes well for another.*

**642. Obi mpɛ da bi nyɛ papa na ɔmpɛ da bi nyɛ bɔne.**
*No one chooses a day to be kind and chooses another day to be cruel.*
(People should act consistently).

**643. Obi mpɛ dabere mmaa adeɛ nkyee no da.**
*No one ever searched for a sleeping place until dawn broke.*
(However difficult circumstances are, one can find some relief).

**644. Obi mpɛ adeɛ ngu Asante na ɔnnyina Akuapem nkamfo.**
*No one collects things and puts them in Asante and stands in Akuapem to admire them.*
(Akuapem is the state to the south of Asante. Use what you have, where you are).

**645. Obi mpɛ adeɛ mma ne wura mma n'ani mmere ne ho.**
*No one searches for something for his master and becomes annoyed.*
(If something is your job, you do it without complaint).

**646. Obi mpɛ ntɛm mfa akyekyedeɛ.**
*You don't need to go fast to catch a tortoise.*
(Said when something is easy to achieve).

**647. Obi apɛse-buroo anyɛ yie a, yɛmfa yɛn nan ase akum suman nkɔfa mu (aseɛ).**
*If someone's maize planted in August does not grow well you don't walk on it with your ankle killing charm.*
(If someone is not doing well, don't give them a chance to blame you for failure).

**648. Obi mpopa ne to wɔ kɔtɔkɔ akyi.**
*No one brushes his bottom with a porcupine's back.*
(The porcupine is the symbol of the Asante nation. You do not challenge an Asante, or you will have the whole nation against you. Hence: Keep away from dangerous people).

**649. Obi mpra na obi ansa.**
*No one sweeps for another to collect the rubbish.*
(If you start a job, finish it).

**650. Obi ara yere nkwan yɛ no dɛ.**
*Every man finds his own wife's soup sweet.*
(You enjoy what you are familiar with and what has been made to your taste).

**651. Obi nsa n'akyɛnkyɛnkyɛ ngu dwa so.**
*No one spreads his palm kernels in a public place.*
(No one reveals his secrets to a stranger).

**652. Obi se: "Bɔ wo bra yie" a, na ɔnni wo atɛn.**
*If someone says: "Be careful!" he has not scolded you.*
(Appreciate advice given in good faith).

**653. Obi se boro ne ba a, na ɔnse boro no ku no.**
*Someone may say that you can beat their child, but*

they don't say you can beat and kill it.
(You have permission but not unlimited license).

**654. Obi se ɔdɔ wo a, ebia na ɔreka wo.**
*If someone says they love you, they may still be back-biting.*
(People may pretend they like you but go on telling stories behind your back).

**655. Obi se fa wo yam-kɔm kɔdo a, woma w'adɔ yɛ tia.**
*If someone tells you to go hungry to weed, you make the work short.*
(If you are not treated well, you don't work well).

**656. Obi se ɔbɛforo dunsini a, ma ɔmforo na ɔrekɔso ho asan aba.**
*If someone says he will climb a tree stump, let him climb for he will go and come in vain.*
(Let people learn from their own mistakes).

**657. Obi se gye aduane hyɛ w'ano pipiripie mu a, na ɔnnii wo atɛm.**
*If someone tells you to get food to put through your heavy lips, he has not abused you.*
(If someone is helping you, you don't take it as an offence when he teases you).

**658. Obi se gye n'akokɔ yɛne no a, yɛmfa.**
*If someone asks us to rear their chicken, we don't take it.*
(You don't take on work which brings no profit in the future).

**659. Obi se gye ntoma kɔma ne yere, wogyina kurotia retrɛ mu; ɛware a, wo bɛtwa no anaasɛ, ɛyɛ tia a wobɛtoa so?**
*If someone asks you to take a cloth to his wife, you stop at the village outskirts to spread it out. If it is too long will you cut off a bit, or if it is too short will you add a bit?*
(Just because you are doing someone a favor don't think you have license to interfere in his affairs).

**660. Obi se ɔbɛhuri atena ahomoankaa mu a, ma ɔnhuri, na ɔhuri a, na ɔbɛhunu.**
*If someone says he will jump onto the hammock, let him jump, and if he jumps he will see the outcome of it.*
(See Proverb 656).

**661. Obi se: "Hyɛ wo sapɔ mu nsuo," a, na ɔnni wo atɛm.**
*If someone says: "Put water on your sponge", he is not scolding you.*
(In this context, "put water on your sponge" means "work hard". Hence: Don't spurn encouragement).

**662. Obi se n'akoa ne wo na ɛyɛ nokorɛ a, na ɔnnii wo atɛm**
*If someone says that you are his slave and it is true, then he does not insult you.*
(The truth is not insulting).

**663. Obi se ɔkyɛne wo ammirika a, huri hwe nkwankyɛn, na fa akyire ne anim to ne hɔ.**
*If someone says he can run faster than you, jump to the roadside and leave the way open to him, behind and before.*
(If someone boasts that he can outdo you, let him try and you will then see the truth of the matter).

664. Obi seɔbɛmawo[adefenemfenem]/[adɔkɔdɔkɔdeɛ] adi na ɔma wo sika a, na wawie wo ma.
*If someone says he will give you something sweet to eat and he gives you money, he has already fulfilled his promise.*
(Money is sweet).

665. Obi se obɛma wo ane a, ɛnte sɛ wo ara woane wo ho.
*If someone says he will let you defecate, it is not as if (as good as) you do it yourself.*
(It is better to do things for yourself without waiting for others to tell you to).

666. Obi se ɔsen wo a, ma ɔnsen wo; na ɔno nso wɔ obi a ɔsen no.
*If someone claims he excels you, let him do so; for someone else also excels him.*
(Everyone has a superior. Boasting will get you nowhere).

667. Obi se wosɛ wo se a, mpɛ ntɛm mma w'ani nnye, ɛfiri sɛ ebia na wo se yɛ mmɔnaatoni.
*If someone tells you you resemble your father, don't be in a hurry to be happy, for perhaps your father is a rapist.*
(Don't take all compliments at their face value).

668. Obi se ɔbɛsoa wo a, wonsɛ: «Mɛnante.»
*If someone says he will carry you, you don't say: «I will walk".*
(Don't reject help willingly offered).

669. Obi se wo yam kɔm a, ma wo nkrantɛ ano nyɛ nam.
*When someone tells you your belly hungers, you must sharpen your cutlass.*
(If you are in need, you yourself must do something about it).

670. Obi se ɔwɔ apem na ɔsrɛ wo takunam, fa wo damma yɛ awerɛkyekyerɛ
*If someone says he has a thousand and asks you for takunam, take your damma to console yourself with.*
(Takunam and damma are both small weights of gold dust. Hence: If someone pretends to be rich but acts poor, then the poor man must be happy with less).

671. Obi se wu a, nya nkwa ma ɔnhwɛ.
*If someone says die, live for him to see!*

672. Obi nse n'aberewa sɛ: "Sɔre na menhwe wo!"
*No one tells his old lady: "Get up and let me beat you".*
(Respect your elders).

673. Obi nse obi sɛ: "Fa wo nnipa-pa sɔre firi me so," mmom ɔka sɛ: "Fa wo nnipa-bɔne sɔre me so."
*No person says to another: "Take your good person away from me", but rather says: "Take your bad person away from me".*
(You don't rebuff kindness, but rather unkindness).

674. Obi nse birekuo sɛ: "Su!" na wasu.
*No one says to the Senegal coucal: "Cry!" before it cries.*
(The expert does not need prompting. This bird is sometimes called the Clock Bird and is supposed to call on the hour).

675. Obi nse aburobua a ɛwɔ anom sɛ: "Bɛdi nkɔmmɔdɔm".
*No one says to the small clay pipe (made in Europe) that is being smoked: "Come and mock my suffering".*
(You do not expect a sympathetic person to mock at suffering).

676. Obi nse sɛ putuo nhye ma yɛnni dwo, nanso ɛhye a, yɛdi.
*No one asks for the yam heap to catch fire, but if it does, we eat.*
(Every cloud has a silver lining).

677. Obi nse twurodo mma toa.
*No one makes a gurgling noise for a bottle.*
(A person must speak for himself).

678. Obi asɛm ba, na woamfa ho biribi a, wofa ntɔdie.
*If someone's case comes and you don't get anything at all from it, (at least) you get expenses (for food).*
(If you don't make a profit from what you do, at least you get enough to eat from it).

679. Obi asɛm nware ka.
*No one becomes talkative for no reason.*

680. Obi asɛm yɛ obi asɛm.
*One man's trouble is another man's trouble.*

681. Obi nsene deɛ wawuo nna.
*No one can sleep as much as the dead.*
(You can't beat the expert).

682. Obi nsene fasuo akotoku-se.
*No one excels a wall at carrying a bag.*
(A bag or sack is usually hung on a wall. Hence: You can't beat the expert. Compare Proverb 681).

683. Obi nsene mɛwe-mɛwe akɔtɔ-bɔ.
*No one excels the chewer (lit. I will chew-I will chew) in hunting crabs.*
("We" (chew) is the verb used for eating crabs. Hence: If you are vitally interested in the outcome of your work, you work well).

684. Obi nsene ne ni nua dehye-yɛ.
*No one excels their mother's sister at being royals.*
(The heir to an Akan woman is either her sister or daughter, but the former has precedence. Hence: You cannot avoid tradition).

685. Obi nsene nwowa mpammɔrɔ di.
*No one exceeds the bees in attacking someone.*
(If you trouble one member of a powerful family the rest descend upon you).

686. Obi sere kyerɛ wo a, wohunu n'anom na wonhunu ne tirim.
*If someone smiles at you, you see his mouth but you don't see his mind.*
(Beware of being taken in by a pleasant expression).

687. Obi nsere hia.
*No one laughs at want.*

688. Obi nsi kwaeɛfuo nnɔ no da koro.
*No one starts a new farm in the forest and digs it on the same day.*
(Rome was not built in a day).

**689. Obi nsi apini kwa.**
*No one sighs heavily without cause.*
(There is no smoke without fire).

**690. Obi nsiane ne kɛtɛ no nna fam.**
*No one by-passes their sleeping mat and sleeps on the ground.*
(If you have something useful, use it).

**691. Obi nsie obi funu.**
*One does not bury someone else's corpse.*
(That is, a corpse that belongs to a matriclan other than one's own. Funerals are the responsibility of the matriclan. Hence: There is a correct procedure for every situation).

**692. Obi nso daeɛ nkɔ baabi a yɛbɛku no.**
*No one dreams of going where he will be killed.*
(You do not willingly walk into danger).

**693. Obi nso gya ngu ne kotokuo mu.**
*No one collects embers from the fire to put in his bag.*
(You don't deliberately do something stupid).

**694. Obi resoa wo a, wonnane mmɔ ne so.**
*If someone helps you to carry a load, you do not leave it all to him.*
(If someone offers to help, don't presume that they will do all the work).

**695. Obi soma wo anomaato na woannya egya a, ne nan nhye.**
*If someone sends you to roast a bird and you don't have any fire, its leg does not get burnt.*
(If a job is not done you should not lose anything through it).

**696. Obi soma wo ayeretɔkwa a, ɔsoma wo ayerepata.**
*If someone sends you to quarrel with his wife, he also sends you to patch it up.*
(If you start a job, you will be asked to finish it).

**697. Obi nsoma obi soro na ɔnhwan n'ase atwedeɛ.**
*No one sends another aloft and removes the ladder from beneath him.*
(You do not ask someone to do something for you and then remove his means of support).

**698. Obi nsoma abɔfra nhwe n'anim.**
*No one sends a child and looks at his face.*
(That is, looks to see what the child's response is. Hence: If you want someone to do something, you disregard their reaction to doing it).

**699. Obi nsoma abɔfra na ɔmfa ne so abofu.**
*No one sends a child on an errand and gets angry with him if he does not do it well.*
(Do not expect from people what they cannot perform. If you ask a child to do something, remember that he is only a child).

**700. Obi nsoma ɔsansani paadie na ɔnkyerɛ no deɛ ɔmfa deɛ ɔbenya nkɔ.**
*No one sends a useless person to work for pay and then directs him where to take his wages to.*
(If you earn money, it is up to you to decide what to do with it).

**701. Obi resu na obi nso resere.**
*While one man is weeping another too is laughing.*
(All men are not alike in their reactions. Life is made up of sorrow and joy).

**702. Obi susu asɛm ho kyerɛ wo na ɔmpɛ wo nyansa ahunu a, na ɔrepɛ wo kwasea na ahunu.**
*If someone brings a problem to you and he does not want to see your wisdom, then he wants to see your foolishness.*
(A person must have some motive for doing something).

**703. Obi nsusu ɛsono yam mmu ahahan.**
*No one, in order to measure an elephant's stomach, breaks off a leaf.*
(A big job needs a big effort).

**704. Obi tan wo a, na ɔbɔ w'ayɛmmoa.**
*If someone hates you, he beats your household pet.*
(If someone can't get at your personally, they attack what is dear to you).

**705. Obi tan wo a, na ɔfa wo yere.**
*If someone hates you, then he takes your wife.*
(If people hate you they harm you in any way they can).

**706. Obi tan wo a, ɔnsrɛ wo adeɛ.**
*If someone hates you, he will not beg from you.*
(Among the Akan, it is the custom to ask people you like to do things for you - this being a kind of compliment. Hence: If someone does not like you, they won't come to you for things).

**707. Obi tan wo a, ɔnte w'asɛm ase.**
*If someone dislikes you, they don't understand you.*
(You tend to misunderstand deliberately the people you don't like).

**708. Obi nte, obi nte, na apem ate.**
*No one should hear, no one should hear, then a thousand have heard.*
(Things told often in secret are soon public knowledge).

**709. Obi nte mmerɛkɛnsono aduasa mfa nkɔbɔ werefoɔ.**
*No one collects thirty palm leaves and ties them round his own kinsmen.*
(Palm leaves are used to express condolence to a bereaved person. If wrongly used, they would bring back luck. Hence: You don't present someone you care for with a bad omen).

**710. Obi ntee obi asɛm a, ɔnnye no anyaado.**
*If one has not heard another person's version of a case, one should not congratulate him.*
(Consider all sides of a question before coming to a conclusion).

**711. Obi ntena obi srɛ so nnye asisiduro.**
*No one sits on someone's lap and collects medicine for waist pains.*
(We don't complain if someone is supporting us).

**712. Obi ntena obi serɛ so nsum no.**
*No one sits on another person's lap and pushes him over.*
(You don't destroy your own means of support).

**713. Obi ntena mfofo ho mma ɛnnane no kwaeɛ.**
*No one stands among the fofo plants to watch them turn into forest.*
(Fofo (pl. mfofo) is a small yellow weed; a farmer would cut them back. Hence: You don't wait for a small case to become a big one before taking action. A stitch in time saves nine).

**714. Obi ntena akwannya nni akwannya asɛm.**
*No one stops on the side of the road and settles things on the spot (lit. deals with the side of the road business).*
(We take care in dealing with important matters).

**715. Obi ntena asɛm ho nni mu abadwadeɛ na ɔmfrɛ no sɛ saadwuma.**
*No one sits on a case and receives his share of the fine and later on says the whole business of having a trial was a waste of time.*
(You don't denigrate what you profit from).

**716. Obi ntena sie so mmɔ [ɔkwarifa]/[kusie] akutia.**
*No one sits on an ant-hill in order to slander a rat.*
(Rats make their holes in anthills. Hence: If you slander a person, be careful he is not within hearing range).

**717. Obi ntie obi ano asɛm na ɔnnyae ne nkwankwaasɛm di.**
*No one listens to another person and stops showing off.*
(It's no good giving advice to an incorrigible person).

**718. Obi tiri boɔ nni wo fotoɔ mu a, wommu no dɔnkɔ.**
*If someone's head price is not in your weight bag, you can't call him a slave.*
(The "head price" is the cost of buying the slave. Hence: What you can't afford, you can't have).

**719. Obi to wo kɔtie, na woanto no bi a, ɔse wo serɛ yɛ tia.**
*If someone kicks your penis and you don't retaliate, he says your thigh is short.*
(It is a weak man who does not respond to a challenge).

**720. Obi nto anansesɛm nkyerɛ Ntikuma.**
*No one tells spider stories to Ntikuma.*
(Ntikuma is the son of Kwaku Ananse the Spider, to whom all stories ("Ananse-(a)sɛm") belong. Hence: Don't give someone what they already have. Or - since Ananse is a master trickster: Don't try to cheat someone who already knows all the tricks).

**721. Obi nto apakye nkɔwia Kukurantumi dwan.**
*No one who is lame goes to steal a sheep at Kukurantumi.*
(Kukurantumi is a town on steep hills which are difficult to negotiate even if you have two good legs. Hence: You don't put obstacles in your own way).

**722. Obi nto susu mmua nna.**
*No one pays a subscription to go hungry to bed.*
(If you have money anywhere you don't starve).

**723. Obi nto tuo mma obi ntafere twerɛboɔ ano.**
*One person should not fire a gun for another to lick the flint.*
(You should clear up your own mess and look after your own tools).

**724. Obi nto yareɛ asaworam na wagyae asa.**
*No one leaves a sickness uncared for and then leaves to dance.*
(Be consistent in what you do. Treat serious things seriously).

**725. Obi ntɔ ade-fɛɛfɛ mfa nhunta.**
*No one buys a beautiful thing to hide it.*
(Don't hide your light under a bushel).

**726. Obi ntɔ akoa ma ɔmmɛhyɛ ne so.**
*No one buys a slave to control his own actions.*
(No one obtains something to be used to his own detriment).

**727. Obi ntɔ akokɔnini mma ɔnkɔbɔn wɔ obi akuraa.**
*No one buys a cock for it to crow in someone else's village.*
(You don't invest in something which brings profit to others but not to you).

**728. Obi nto kosua mmɔ akorɔma a wakyere akokɔ.**
*No one throws an egg at the hawk that has already caught (their) chicken.*
(Don't throw good money after bad).

**729. Obi ntɔ mansotwe amena mu mfa ne ho tɔtorɔtɔ.**
*No one steps in the hole of litigation and escapes scot-free.*
(Any kind of legal case costs money, whether you are guilty or innocent).

**730. Obi ntɔ nantwinamɔn.**
*No one buys a cow's footprint.*
(No one buys a pig in a poke).

**731. Obi ntɔ sɛn foforɔ mfa nsi pata so.**
*No one buys a new cooking pot and puts it in the rafters.*
(You don't acquire something useful and hide it away).

**732. Obi toa wo asamando a, woyi w'ano nsamampɔ mu.**
*If someone summons you in the land of the spirits, you have to answer the charge in the spirit grove.*
(The spirits of the departed are supposed to return periodically to their place of burial and it is there that you are expected to propitiate them. Hence: There is a right place for everything).

**733. Obi ntɔn obi busuani.**
*No one pawns someone from another family.*
(Formerly an uncle could pawn his sister's children if he was unable to pay a debt and they would have to work for the creditor until the debt was paid. Hence: You do not usurp the rights of others).

**734. Obi ntɔn n'akokɔbereɛ kwa.**
*No one sells his laying hen for no reason.*
(No one parts with something profitable unless they have to).

**735. Obi ntoto namporɔeɛ mfa nhyɛ ne yɔnko anom nse no sɛ: "W'anom bɔn."**
*No one bakes rotten meat and puts it in his companion's mouth and says to him: "Your mouth stinks."*
(You do not blame someone for something for which you are yourself responsible).

**736. Obi ntra ne kafoɔ aboboɔ-ano nkɔsom obi.**
*No one crosses his creditor's threshold to go and serve another.*
(You serve where you owe).

**737. Obi ntu abɛ na obi mpene.**
*No one fells a palm tree for another to groan for it.*
(You should not suffer for the actions or misdeeds of another).

**738. Obi tu gya hye w'ano a, wo nso wotu bi hye ne to.**
*If someone takes fire and burns your mouth, you take fire and burn his buttocks.*
(You take your revenge on those who harm you).

**739. Obi ntu mmire nsie sie so.**
*No one uproots mushrooms and hides them on an anthill.*
(Mushrooms often grow around anthills. Hence: You don't take trouble to collect something and then put it back in the place you took it from).

**740. Obi ntu mmirika nkɔtena kurotia nkɔserɛ amanneɛ mfa nto ne ho so.**
*No one runs to stay at the outskirts to go and ask for trouble to bring upon himself.*
(You don't go looking for trouble).

**741. Obi ntu mmirika nkɔpɛ Owuo akyiri kwan.**
*No one runs to search around for Death.*
(Death comes without invitation).

**742. Obi ntua n'akɔnnɔdeɛ nwu.**
*No one stops taking his favorite things and then dies.*
(If you don't indulge yourself you might as well be dead).

**743. Obi turu wo kɔhwɛ nkwa a, woturu no kɔhwɛ Owuo.**
*If someone carries you on the back to see life, you also carry him to see Death.*
(If someone cares for you when young, you too care for him and show your gratitude in old age).

**744. Obi nturu yarefoɔ nkɔ sa.**
*No one carries a sick person on his back when going to war.*
(When on a serious mission, you don't encumber yourself with extra burdens).

**745. Obi ntwa obi ho nhyɛne ne dan mu.**
*No one overtakes someone else and enters his room.*
(An owner takes precedence).

**746. Obi ntwa odwan nna afa.**
*No one slaughters a sheep and sleeps by its side.*
(A sheep was often the fine charged at traditional courts. Hence: When you are found guilty don't expect to benefit from your own punishment).

**747. Obi ntwa akokɔ ano mma akye.**
*No one says "good morning" before the cock.*
(No one can beat the expert).

**748. Obi ntwa ne mene nhyɛ Adinkra.**
*No one cuts his own throat to attribute it to Adinkra.*
(Adinkra, Chief of Gyaman was renowned for beheading people and was finally captured and decapitated by the Asantes. Hence: You don't harm yourself in order to cast blame on someone else).

**749. Obi ntwa poma mma ɛnsene no tenten.**
*No one cuts a walking stick so that it is taller than he is.*
(You don't bring up a child to lord it over you).

**750. Obi ntware kwan nwie na ɔnsan nkɔpɛ n'akwano.**
*No one completes a journey and then goes back to look for the beginning.*
(If you have finished something, you don't need to involve yourself in it again).

**751. Obi ntware asuo Kwasiada na adeɛ nkɔkye no nsuo no ano Dwoada.**
*No one crosses a stream on Sunday and waits for the dawn to meet him on Monday.*
(If you have escaped from danger you don't rest on your laurels).

**752. Obi ntwɛn Firaw ansa na wasi ne ntoma.**
*No one waits to reach the Volta before washing his cloth.*
(Certain jobs are done automatically and not delayed for a special occasion or until they become easy).

**753. Obi nware ne kunu saman kwa.**
*No woman marries her husband's ghost for nothing.*
(When a man dies, his heirs take responsibility for the wives unless they prefer to "divorce," in Akan Society. If a wife is young or wants to marry again she may prefer to be free. Hence: Before a widow marries her husband's heir she must have something to gain from it).

**754. Obi nware ne kuru-mani nnu ne ho.**
*No one marries someone from the same town and regrets it.*
(It is best to marry within your own community. Hence: Better the devil you know).

**755. Obi nware ne yere foo kwa.**
*No one marries his bad wife in vain.*
(If you choose to be with someone, however bad, you have a good reason for it).

**756. Obi wo mma du a, ɔyarefoɔ ba mu.**
*If anyone has ten children, then there will be one sick child amongst them.*
(Not everything in the world can be perfect. If you are involved in a lot of things, some of them are bound to go wrong).

**757. Obi nwo ba nto "Ayɛbiaguo" na ɔnnyae nni abarinsɛm.**
*No one gives birth to a child and names it "Defeated One" and at the same time expects it to be bold.*
(Naming among the Akan is very important. If you name your child after someone who has not good a good reputation, you have only yourself to blame if he does not succeed. Hence: You should not expect someone to act out of character).

**758. Obi nwo obi saman.**
*No one gives birth to someone else's ghost.*
(What should remain inside the family cannot go outside. A departed spirit is reincarnated in its own clan in its next existence).

**759. Obi anwo wo a, ɔnni wo.**
*If someone has not given birth to you, they do not know you.*
(You are really only known properly to members of your own family).

760. Obi wu a, na n'agyapadeɛ da edwa.
*If someone dies, his heirlooms become public.*
(When someone dies you can find out what he was
worth).

761. Obi awuo, obi nna.
*Someone dies, someone else does not sleep.*
(One man's fate affects another).

762. Obi yaa wo na woyaa no bi a, na ne ho yɛ no den.
*If someone scolds you and you scold them back, then
they become more determined.*
(Retaliation is no end to a quarrel).

763. Obi nyare ntoto na obi nyare anom–deɛ.
*No one gets ill with baking for someone else to get ill
with eating it.*
(An owner benefits from his own work).

764. Obi nyare ayamka nkye nkyewee mfa nsa ne ho
yareɛ.
*No one who has a stomach ache roasts parched corn
to cure the sickness.*
(Apply the right remedy).

765. Obi yɛ wo papa a, na waha wo.
*If someone is generous to you, then he has troubled
you.*
(You are under an obligation to those who help you).

766. Obi nnye obi hyɛberɛ.
*No one collects someone else's destiny.*
(Our destinies are unchangeable).

767. Obi nnye obi asia mma ɔnka dwam.
*No one demands an asia from someone, leaving him
stranded in court.*
(An asia is a small quantity of gold dust. If you ask a
penniless man for money in public you disgrace him.
Used when someone is in a defenseless state and you
go on pressing him for answers. He can't leave but he
can't do anything about it either).

768. Obi nnye ɔboafoɔ kyɛm ntwitwa mu na ɔnse no
sɛ: "Boa me!"
*No one cuts to pieces the shield of a helper and then
says to him: "Help me".*
(Don't bite the hand that feeds you).

769. Obi nnye bɔmmɔfoɔ adeɛ nni nyɛ no hammusuo.
*No one collects a hunter's game to eat and tries to
bring him bad luck in his hunting.*
(You don't harm those who are helping you).

770. Obi nyɛ akokɔhwedee adwuma na ɔnkɔnom
asabia nsuo.
*No one works for the bush fowl and goes to drink the
red-flanked duiker's water.*
(You take your reward from where you work).

771. Obi nyɛ yie nnya bɔne.
*No one gets on well and avoids bad.*
(However good you are you will by all means do some
bad things. To err is human).

772. Obi nyi obi a asuo refa no mfiri asuo mu na ɔmfa
no nto gya mu.
*No one takes someone who the river is drowning out
of the river and puts him into the fire.*
(Don't make things worse).

773. Obi nyi akokɔ nan ase adeɛ nkɔto akokɔhwedeɛ
nan ase mma ɔmfa ntu nkɔ wiram.
*No one takes something from a chicken's leg and puts
it on the francolin's leg for it to run off with into the
bush.*
(You don't take something from the family and give it
to a stranger to be misused).

774. Obi nyi mmusuo mfa mmusuo.
*No one removes misfortune in order to take it again.*

775. Obi ayie ase na yesu yɛn ni ne yɛn se.
*It is at someone's funeral that we mourn for our
mother and our father.*
(Thinking of other's sorrows reminds us of our own).

776. Obi nyini nni akura.
*No one grows to eat a mouse.*
(You grow up to acquire wisdom not foolishness).

777. Obi nyiyi mmire mu mmoaa.
*No one removes the maggots from a mushroom.*
(Some jobs are too time-wasting to be worth doing).

778. Abia, ne hyɛ fata ɔsebɔ abakɔm, nanso adowa na
oni awuo.
*Seed bracelets, putting them on would beautify the
leopard's wrists, but it is the antelope's mother who
has died.*
(And the antelope who has therefore inherited them.
Hence: It is not always the most suitable person who is
entitled to something).

779. Abia nyɛ ahweneɛ bi, nanso yɛannya no a, yɛnsina
kyekyerekona.
*The creeper seeds are not beads but if you don't get
them you can't thread a chief's necklace.*
(Seeds of various plants were used with beads to
make up some necklaces. Some insignificant things
are nonetheless indispensable to doing a job
properly).

780. Ebia wobɛdi ɛsono mu, ɛrenhia wo, nanso wodi
apataa a, na kasɛɛ ahia wo.
*You may eat a whole elephant and not choke, but when
you eat a fish, the bone may stick in your throat.*
(Little things may be responsible for your downfall).

781. Biakoyɛ yɛ.
*Unity is good.*

782. Obiara de ankaa-twadeɛ dware a ne ho yɛ huam,
nhohoɔ nko ara de dware a, na ne ho agye nka.
*If anyone uses lime to bathe they smell good; the tree-
ant is the only one who, if he goes to bath, his body
stinks.*
(Some people do not benefit from what helps the
majority and are correspondingly unlucky).

783. Obiara adeɛ yɛ n'adeɛ.
*Every person's belongings are theirs alone.*
(We have a right to our possessions).

784. Obiara kurom bosom yɛ nam.
*Every town's fetish is powerful.*
(People support and believe in what they are familiar
with).

785. Obiara ani gye ɔbakwasea ho nanso ɔmpɛ sɛ oni
wo bi.

*Everyone is interested in a foolish child, but they don't want their mothers to produce one.*
(You take interest in other people's troubles but don't want to have to face them also).

### 786. Obiara pe deɛ ɛyɛ dɛ na waka.
*Everyone likes the tasty part of something to bite.*
(We all wish to enjoy what is good).

### 787. Obiara wɔ n'ahoɔfɛ a Onyame de bɔɔ no.
*Everyone has his God-given beauty.*

### 788. Obiara nni hɔ a ne werɛ firi n'adidiyowa.
*No one forgets his eating dish.*
(You don't forget essentials).

### 789. Obiara nni hɔ a wɔwoo no owudifoɔ, ɔbra mu nsɛm na ɛkyerɛ onipa suban.
*There is no one who was born a criminal, circumstances influence people's character.*
(Social conditions shape people's actions).

### 790. Obibini dane buroni a, yɛkyi.
*If an African turns into a European, it is a taboo.*
(Every man should stick to his own customs).

### 791. Ebini bɔn na wosi ho a, na ɛbɔn wura wo hwene mu.
*If excrement stinks and you step into it, then the smell enters into your nose.*
(If you involve yourself in a dirty business, you get soiled).

### 792. Ebini ntoatoasoɔ na ekum nwansenampobire.
*The piling up of feces kills the dung fly.*
(You can have too much of a good thing).

### 793. Ebini yɛ wo tane a, womfa wo nsa nto mu.
*If you dislike excrement, they you don't put your hand into it.*
(If you don't like something bad, then keep away from it altogether).

### 794. Birebire amma a, Amaneɛ nso amma.
*Birebire didn't come, so Amaneɛ too did not come.*
(After a war, Dankyira and Adanse made peace and each sent a slave to work for the other. After a time Adanse sent people to demand their slave Amaneɛ but did not return Dankyira's Birebire. Ntim Gyakari, then Dankyirahene, asked why this was so and the messengers could give no answer. So he did not return Amaneɛ to Adanse. The proverb means therefore "Do as you would be done by").

### 795. Obirekunam yɛdi no hyhyeehye.
*The Senegal coucal's meat, we eat it very hot.*
(The meat of this bird is supposed to be very tough. Hence: A tough case should be settled quickly).

### 796. Obirekuo se anka ɔne akokɔ na ɛte fie, nanso abosonsom nti na watu akɔtena wiram ama ne to aporɔ.
*The Senegal coucal says that it and the chicken used to be living in the house, but because of fetish worship (on the part of the chicken) it went to stay in the bush, which resulted in its buttocks becoming rotten.*
(Avoiding one problem may lead to a different problem. No place is perfect).

### 797. Obirekuo su anadwo a, yɛkyi.
*If the Senegal coucal cries in the night, we taboo it.*
(It's believed to be unlucky for the coucal to cry at night. Hence: Don't act out of turn or contrary to custom).

### 798. Wobirekyi a, wode w'akyi akyɛ.
*If you turn your back on someone, you give your back as a gift.*
(The moment you depart from home, you no longer have authority there).

### 799. Abirekyie ba: woma no so kɔ soro a, wogyaa no brɛo!
*The kid: if you lift it high above you, you lower it gently.*
(You treat vulnerable things carefully).

### 800. Abirekyie fra nnwanten mu a, wɔyi no.
*If the goat is mixed up with sheep, they remove it (easily).*
(It is easy to separate the goat from the sheep. It is easy to identify the odd man out).

### 801. Abirekyie na ɔde dwantene kɔ adidie.
*A goat can lead a sheep to graze.*
(The cleverest man leads, even if he is not a citizen of the area).

### 802. Abirekyie nya wura pa a, na ɔfu abɔdwesɛ.
*It is when the goat has a good master, that it grows a beard.*
(The fate of a servant or slave is in the hands of his master).

### 803. Abirekyie mpo ɔnim ta, na ɛnte sɛ ofui.
*Even the goat knows how to fart, how much more the hyena.*
(No one can beat the experts).

### 804. Abirekyie se: "Wobrɛ na wodi a, obi mmu wo asebuo".
*The goat says: "When you're tired (from work) and you eat (what you produce), people don't make insinuations about you."*
(If you enjoy the fruits of your own labor, people don't talk against you).

### 805. Abirekyie se: "Abusua-tɔkwa yɛsoa no kyirenn na yɛagyaa no brɛɛ."
*The goat says: "A family quarrel begins hotly but ends calmly".*
(Quarrels inside the family may be violent but they should end in an amicable settlement).

### 806. Abirekyie se, ɔbɛdane odwan a, tuntum mpa mu da.
*If the goat says it will turn into a sheep, there is bound to be a black spot.*
(If someone pretends to be what they are not, some action or characteristic will show them up).

### 807. Abirekyie se: "Obi nnante nkɔwu".
*The goat says: "No one walks deliberately to his death".*
(Said when someone is not in a position to avoid disaster).

### 808. Abirekyie se: "Deɛ ɛbɛba, aba dada".
*The goat says: "What will happen has already happened".*
(There is nothing new under the sun).

809. Abirekyie se: "Deɛ adedie wɔ na abogyabum wɔ".
*The goat says: "Where there is food there is much blood".*
(Death threatens when profits are greatest).

810. Abirekyie se: adeɛ rebɛkye ama wawu a ɔbedi hene.
*The goat says: the day before his death he will be a chief.*
(When the goat is going to be killed, it is carried like a chief in his palanquin. Hence: If you know you will die you do what you like most beforehand).

811. Abirekyie se: "Adwaman kotokuo, ɔbaako nse".
*The goat says: "The prostitute's bag, no single person wears it".*
(Prostitution is common).

812. Abirekyie se: mfumdie nti na ɔnam a [ɔmmo amoaseɛ no]/[ɔrenware da].
*The goat says: because of impromptu intercourse that [it does not wear a loin cloth]/[it will not get married].*
(If you enjoy something, you have to make sacrifices for it).

813. Abirekyie se: sɛ yɛbɛfrɛ no kwasea deɛ, yɛmfrɛ no aniɛden.
*The goat says: if we call him a fool, he would rather we called him stubborn.*
(People will admit to being obstinate but not foolish).

814. Abirekyie se: "Akoa mfu abɔdwesɛ".
*The goat says: "A slave does not grow a beard".*
(If you are not free, you cannot prosper).

815. Abirekyie se: "Kotromua twedeɛ ntumi ɔbrane".
*The goat says: "A blow from the fist does not defeat a tough person".*
(A stubborn person is not easily put off).

816. Abirekyie se: ɔsuro ayeferɛ nti ɔrekɔfa ne na, sɛɛ n'agya yere ne no.
*The goat says: because he fears paying adultery fees he is going to take his mother, but the mother is his father's wife.*
(Fear of paying small debts may lead you into greater ones. More generally: Fear of a small danger may lead to a greater one).

817. Abirekyie se: "Wɔtɔɔ me ni na wɔantɔ me".
*The goat says: "They bought my mother but they did not buy me."*
(Said when someone disowns friend or family when they get into trouble).

818. Abirekyie se: ɔyɛɛ sɛ nantwie a, anka gye ne nwoma na ɛbɛfiri serɛm aba Asante.
*The goat says: if it had grown (as big) as a cow, only its skin would have come from the long grasses to Asante.*
(The savannah, the country of the long grasses, is to the north of the Akan peoples; thus serɛm could be translated as "the North." Cattle are driven down from the North to Asante for slaughter. But you can't drive goats because they resist. Hence: A good fighter cannot be defeated easily).

819. Abirekyie nni afuo, nanso ɔdidi daa.
*A goat has no farm, but it always eats.*
(Some people always live off others. In conditions of plenty, no one goes hungry).

820. "Obiri, hwɛ deɛ yɛde reyɛ Oben".
*"Obiri, look what is happening to Oben".*
(Take warning from the sufferings of your friends).

821. Obiri nti na yɛnom basini nsa.
*It is because of Obiri that we drink the drink of the one-armed man.*
(It is said that Obiri was a chief who had a palm wine tapper with one arm and a stump. The stump was infected and the people were afraid to drink the wine, yet they did so out of respect for the chief. Hence: Said of someone who does something unpleasant out of respect for the person who asks him to).

822. Biribi anka ayowa mu a, yɛntafere mu.
*If there is nothing in the pot, you don't lick it.*
(There's no profit from an empty purse).

823. Biribi nkyɛn ogya kɔkɔɔ.
*Nothing is redder than fire.*
(The ultimate punishment cannot be exceeded).

824. Wo biribi ne akyenkyena a, anka ɛka rempa wo so da, ɛfirisɛ obi repae n'adeɛ a, ɔgye ma ne ho sɛ: "Mea! Mea!"
*If your relation is an allied hornbill, then you will not stop paying debts, because whenever someone is shouting for a lost thing, it takes responsibility crying: "It is I, it is I!"*
(A person who invites trouble causes constant anxiety to his relatives. This bird, by its call, accepts responsibility for what goes wrong in the village).

825. Biribi ankɔka papa a, papa nyɛ grada.
*If something is not done to the palm frond, the palm frond does not rustle.*
(There is no smoke without fire).

826. Biribiara a ɛfiri ɔdɔfoɔ nsam som bo.
*Everything that comes from a well-loved person is worthwhile.*
(The actions of a benevolent person are appreciated by those they serve and are liable to bring good results).

827. Wo biribi ne kankabi a, ɔwu a, ɔgya wo nkawa.
*If your relation is a millipede and he dies, he leaves you rings.*
(When the millipede dies it dries up and breaks into sections which children use as rings. Hence: No matter how useless a person seems to be, he leaves something behind).

828. Wo biribi ne Kobuobi a, anka worenka sɛ twene kɛsɛɛ fata no.
*If your relative were to be Kobuobi, then you would not say that the big drum suits him.*
(Kobuobi is a slave's name. No one expects their relative to do a slave's job and be praised for it).

829. Wo biribi ne aponkyerɛne a, wonnyae no dammirifua ma da.
*If your relative is a frog, people never stop sympathizing with you.*
(If you have a troublesome or handicapped member of the family, you will be exhausted).

830. Wo biribi ne prako a, wo nsa mpa boɔ so da.
*If you have a pig as a relation, your hand will never be free of a stone.*

(A troublesome member of the family brings constant worry).

**831. Wo biribi ne asɔkwaa a, anka wobɛkye no aka no yomo.**
*If your relation were the white-crested hornbill, then you would catch him and dye his hair for him.*
(You only take trouble over those who are members of your family).

**832. Wo biribi ne ɔtwea a, anka woremma no aduane fam.**
*If you had a bitch as a relative, you would not give her food on the ground.*
(You dare not treat relatives as badly as strangers).

**833. Biribi ansɛe a, biribi nyɛ yie.**
*If something does not spoil, something does not keep well.*
(Nothing ventured, nothing gained).

**834. Biribi wɔ soro a, ɛtwa sɛ ɛba fam.**
*Whatever is above must come to earth.*
(Everything must end some day).

**835. Biribi nni baabi a, anka yɛda a yɛnto pono mu.**
*If there is nothing anywhere, we would not close the door when we sleep.*
(i.e. If we had nothing, we would not need protection. Hence: People have reason to protect themselves).

**836. Biribi nni bɔtɔ a, ne sane [yɛ sanena]/[nyɛ anigye].**
*If nothing is in the bag, [you are reluctant to untie it]/[untying it is not a happy occasion].*
(You don't bother to explore unprofitable situations).

**837. Biribi nni fie a, yɛnka sɛ: "Pɛ biribi di ma yɛnkɔ abayerɛ."**
*If there is nothing in the house we don't say: "Find something to eat and let us go and look for wild yam."*
(When you know someone does not have anything, don't rub it in by asking for it).

**838. Biribi nni wo nsam a, wommua so mma yɛntiti akyire.**
*If you have nothing in your palm, you don't close your fist to make us scratch the back of your hand.*
(Don't hide poverty for others to drag it out of you).

**839. Biribi yɛ wo a, nnu wo ho, na ebia anka deɛ ɛreba so.**
*If something bad happens to you, don't regret it, for perhaps what was to have happened to you might have been worse.*
(Be grateful things are not worse than they are).

**840. Biribi anyɛ wo a, worenhunu ho nyansa.**
*If something does not happen to you, you don't gain wisdom from it.*
(We learn from our experiences in life).

**841. Biribiara a ɛyɛ hu, onipa na ɔyɛ.**
*Everything which is dangerous is caused by a human being.*
(Man is the root of all evil).

**842. Biribiara wɔ ne berɛ.**
*Everything has its time.*
(Every dog has its day).

**843. Biribiara nni hɔ a ɛkwati Nyame.**
*There is no single thing that can by-pass God.*

**844. Abirida ne Sadandan hyia da a, wɔnna no, na ɛfiri deɛ ɛfiri.**
*If Abirida and Sadandan meet to have sex together and they do not have sex successfully, it is for some reason (lit. it is the result of what it is the result of).*
(Abirida and Sadandan stand for husband and wife. Hence: If something unusual happens there must be a good reason for it).

**845. Biribiara nyɛ ya sɛ aniwuo.**
*Nothing is as hurtful as shame.*

**846. Yɛbisa kose ansa na yɛakɔyi ɔwea.**
*We ask for nightfall before we go after the tree-bear.*
(The tree-bear or hyrax is active in the night when you can hear its child-like cries from the trees. Hence: You look for someone when you know they are around).

**847. Woabisa akyeremadefoɔ ama wɔse wɔne wo bɛgoro ama adeɛ akyi?**
*Have you asked the drummers whether they are prepared to play for you until daybreak?*
(Don't take favors for granted).

**848. Wobisa wo to ansa na womene adɔbɛ.**
*You ask your anus before swallowing the fan-palm nut.*
(You consult those who will be affected before you take a drastic action).

**849. Obisabisafoɔ nto [mfom]/[kwan].**
*One who asks the way does not lose the road.*
(When you need to, ask and don't wait for things to go wrong).

**850. "Mabo no na ɔreba" nyɛ amanenya.**
*"I have beaten him and he is coming" is not an offense.*
(Things said as a joke should not offend).

**851. "Bɔ me na memmɔ wo" nyɛ agodie.**
*"Hit me and let me hit you" is no game.*
(An eye for an eye and a tooth for a tooth is not a good philosophy).

**852. Wobɔ obi akoa safohene a, ɔse: "Mehwɛ wo ara", nanso wotɔn no di deɛ a, ɔkɔbɔ ne wura amanneɛ.**
*If you make someone's slave paramount chief, he says, "I look up to you," but if you let him down, he goes to inform his master.*
(If you do good to someone they admire you, but if you criticize them they will turn on you).

**853. Wobɔ [abirekyie]/[ɔkraman] a, ɔkyerɛ wo ne wura fie kwan.**
*If you beat a [goat]/[dog], it shows you the way to its master's house.*
(A subordinate looks for his superior's support in time of trouble).

**854. Yɛbɔ bono-pakyie asom ansa na abue.**
*We beat a gourd on the ears before it opens.*
(Some people only act when forced to do so).

855. **Wobɔ bosea de tua wo ka a, ɛte sɛ woatu amena asi amena.**
*If you take a loan to pay your debt it is as if you were to dig a hole to fill a hole.*
(You don't create a difficulty to solve a difficulty).

856. **Wobɔ bra-pa a, wote mu dɛ.**
*If you live a good life you find it sweet.*
(Virtue brings its own reward).

857. **Yɛbɔ nnawuta mu a, na ato abeseweɛ.**
*If we play the double gong-gong, then it is time to chew cola.*
(Some things are kept for serious occasions. Cola is chewed in place of food at funerals, during court-cases, or if plans are being made for war).

858. **Yɛbɔ wo din hyɛ mmara a ɛnyɛ, ɛna yɛbɔ wo din nso tu mmara gu mu a, ɛnyɛ.**
*If through your action we make a law that is bad, that is as bad as if through your action we discard a (good) law. (lit. If we call your name to make a law that is bad, and if we call your name to discard a law, it is not good).*
(You should behave in a way that avoids doing harm in society).

859. **Yɛbɔ wo din noa na woanni bi a, ɛyɛ ya.**
*If we mention your name in cooking something and you do not eat any of it, it is sad.*
(If someone does something for you and you can't benefit from it, you regret it).

860. **Wobɔ dokum kyɛnee yane ɔtwea a, ɔtwetwe no ase.**
*If you tie plenty of raffia around the neck of a bitch, it drags on the ground.*
(If you give an ignorant person something good, it is misused).

861. **Wobɔ afɛkuo a, wonwu w'akrawuo.**
*If you get into bad company you don't die a natural death.*
(Bad company leads to a bad end).

862. **Wobɔ ahina ho a, na wohunu deɛ ekam da.**
*If you tap the pot, you see where the crack is.*
(If you test a man you find his faults).

863. **Wobɔ kabɔne ma wo yɔnko a, wotua bi.**
*If you make a bad debt for your companion, you pay part of it.*
(If you cheat a friend, you also cheat yourself).

864. **Wobɔ koro firi wo kurom a, ohia amfa wo amma fie a, ɛka de wo ba fie.**
*If you desert your town, if poverty does not bring you back, debt brings you back.*
(In times of difficulty, you return to your own people).

865. **Wobɔ nkuro bɔne ma wo wɔfa a, wo wɔfa akoa bɔ bi ma wo.**
*If you lodge a bad complaint against your uncle, your uncle's slave will lodge one against you.*
(In Akan society, you would have inherited the slave who might act against you too. Hence: Do as you would be done by).

866. **Bɔ mu tafere a, wonyɛ no dɔbɔre doo.**
*If you share the taste of the food, you don't face problems alone.*
(Don't be greedy).

867. **Wobɔ onifrani asom a, na ɔhunu sɛ w'ani abere.**
*If you box a blind person's ears, then they see that you are angry (lit. your eyes are red).*
(A blind person would not see that your eyes were red, i.e. that you were angry, so they have to find out in other ways. Hence: If people are stubborn there are positive ways of making them realize you are serious).

868. **Yɛbɔ wo nnimmo na antumi wo a, ɛtete wo ntoma.**
*If we slander you too much, and you don't suffer for it, your cloth becomes tattered.*
(If slander does not affect you personally it may lead to poverty).

869. **Yɛbɔ wo nsabrane na ɛnni wo so a, wopusu w'awan.**
*If we give you an honorary title but if it does not fit you, you shrug your shoulders.*
(Don't take any notice of idle flattery).

870. **Wobɔ nsamamfɛ a, wokyere na adeɛ na wonnya.**
*If you adopt someone, you get your praises but you don't get possessions.*
(If you adopt someone outside the family you get kudos from it but you incur expenses).

871. **Wobɔ nsɛkuro a, amanneɛ mpa wo so da.**
*If you gossip, you are never free of cases.*
(A gossiper is in constant trouble).

872. **Wobɔ asantrofie dua a, ɔno ara na ɔsu "Kɔkɔtwea, kɔkɔtwea".**
*If you curse the nightjar, it itself sings: "It may not happen, God forbid".*
(In singing these words, the nightjar lifts the curse; this is the force of "it itself." Normally a curse must be lifted by the curser; it is believed, however, that certain people have protection from evil. Hence: An exceptional person is immune from outside attacks).

873. **Wobɔ twafoɔ asom a, wonsuro n'ahweaseɛ.**
*If you slap a person who suffers from fits, you don't fear his falling down.*
(If you know what the consequences may be before you act, you are not taken by surprise at the results of your action).

874. **Wobɔ wa a, wonte korɔmfoɔ.**
*If you cough, you don't hear the thief.*
(If conditions are not suitable for something to happen, you don't expect it).

875. **"Wo bo yɛ duru a bra", yɛ akekasɛm na nyɛ akudie.**
*"If you are brave, come (and face me)" is mere saying, it is not coming to blows.*
(Easier said than done).

876. **Wobɔ ayamuɔnwono kan na wonya sika, na woyɛ ayɛ a, wodi nna.**
*If you are stingy from the onset and later you become more prosperous and give big donations, you are well-regarded.*
(If you are a reformed sinner, people respect you).

877. Woammɔ wo bra yie a, na mmaa siɛ wo asekanseɛ.
*If you don't succeed in life, women ask you to sharpen knives for them.*
(A failure must do as he is asked).

878. Yɛmmɔ adagya (wɔ) abɔntenso na yɛnkuru ngu so (wɔ) dampɔn mu.
*We don't become naked in public and dress up in our own room.*
(It is no good behaving well at home if you can't behave in public).

879. Woammɔ wo kunu kɔte so dwie a, ɛsae wo.
*If you don't squash the louse on your husband's penis, it will come to you too.*
(If you don't help others out of trouble, you will get into trouble yourself).

880. Yɛmmɔ ɔkwaberane bɛdɛ.
*We don't carry a strong man in a palm basket.*
(You can't use weak tools to do a tough job).

881. Yɛmmɔ asisirapɛ mfra nkyeweɛ.
*We don't hunt for the flying ants amongst the fried corn.*
(Some people eat the flying ants after removing their wings and frying them. We don't mix ordinary people with aristocrats).

882. Yɛboa hata nkyene kwa, yɛde begu nsuo mu.
*We dry the salt in vain, (after all) we shall put it in the water.*
(Used for an unprofitable action which appears to waste time).

883. Woboa akobɔfoɔ ano a, woma wo danta ano yɛ duru.
*If you gather vagabonds around you, you make the end of your loincloth heavy (with money tied into it).*
(It costs a lot to entertain dependents. Don't take them on unless you are prepared to pay for it).

884. Yɛboa yɛn ase afuyɛ mu na yɛmmoa yɛn ni ba.
*We help our in-laws in farming, but we don't help our mother's child.*
(We work on our in-law's farm not on our brother's, for our children may stand to inherit the former. Hence: You invest in what you know will benefit your children in the future. This proverb runs against the standard notion that Akan people take primary responsibility for their matriclans).

885. Aboa a ɔbɛba nnim wa.
*The animal that will come does not care if you cough.*
(What will be, will be).

886. Aboa a ɔbɔfoɔ ato afom no biara nyɛ aboa ketewa.
*The animal which the hunter shot at but which escaped is never a small animal.*
(We always think that what we lose is greater than what we have).

887. Aboa a ɔnnaeɛ na ɔtutu mmirika kɔnyane deɛ wada.
*An animal which has not gone to sleep runs to waken the one who sleeps.*
(It is the wary who warn the carefree).

888. Aboa a fidie ayi no na ɔda adwaa mu.
*An animal which has been trapped is in bondage.*
(A person who is under restraint suffers without redress).

889. Aboa a ɔrehyia bɔfoɔ nnim deɛ ɛwɔ n'anim.
*An animal which is approaching the hunter does not know what is coming to him.*
(You are unaware of your destiny until it comes to pass).

890. Aboa a yɛkum no kane na yɛanhunu ne din a, deɛ ɔdi hɔ no yɛ kane deɛ no bi ara.
*If we could not tell the name of the animal that was first killed, the one that follows is the same as the one which was killed.*
(A first offence may not be recognized but if it is repeated you take notice of the first offense as well).

891. Aboa a ne tiri nni soɔ die yɛ din.
*The animal whose head is not on its body is difficult to eat.*
(You need to know the nature of a thing before you consider using it).

892. Aboa a ɔno nko ara nam, nnim n'anim asɛm.
*An animal which wanders alone does not know what is lying in wait for it.*
(A solitary person has no one to warn him of trouble on the way).

893. Aboa a ɔsebɔ antumi ankye no anwe no, ɔkra mfa no fo.
*If the leopard cannot kill and eat an animal, neither can the cat make light work of it.*
(If a strong man cannot achieve something, neither can a weaker).

894. Aboa a ɔsɔ na ɔmene ne yɔnko.
*It is the big animal that swallows its companion.*
(Privileges are for the more powerful. When a man obtains power he may destroy erstwhile comrades).

895. Aboa na ɔsɔ na ne nwoma so.
*If an animal grows so does its skin.*
(The greater your position the greater your responsibilities).

896. Aboa a ɔwɔ dua-puo na yɛsɔ mu.
*If an animal has a tail, that is what we hold.*
(You can make use of someone who is equipped to help).

897. Aboa a ɔnni wura na obi tɔn no di.
*It is the animal that has no master that someone sells to eat.*
(Everyone needs a strong protector).

898. Aboa a ɔnni dua, Nyame na ɔpra ne ho.
*It is the animal that has no tail that God brushes flies off.*
(God defends the defenseless).

899. Aboa baako, yenyi ne ho ayan mprenu.
*One animal, we do not get two chests from it.*
(You should not suffer two punishments for one crime).

**900. Aboa abɛbɛ su sɛ: Pɛpɛ, pɛpɛ ,**
*The grasshopper cries: «Evenly, evenly".*
(The grasshopper and the butterfly once shared in a job and the butterfly cheated the grasshopper by using Ananse's trick of saying of three pence: "I take one, you take one, and I take one." The grasshopper only realized he had been cheated when he got home and ever since has been crying about it. Hence: All profits should be shared equally among those who do similar work).

**901. Aboa bi reka wo a, ɔfiri wo ntoma mu.**
*If an animal is biting you, it is from inside your cloth.*
(A person close to you is the most likely to harm you).

**902. Aboa bi nkaa wo da a, wode wo nan ne wo nsa na ɛprɛ no.**
*If an animal has never bitten you, you use your leg and your hand to push it away.*
(If you never had cause to fear someone, you treat them casually).

**903. Aboa biara bɛdi m'aduane a, ɛrenyɛ me ya sɛ kontromfi a, ne nsa hya nkrantɛ, nanso ɔse ɔrennɔ.**
*If all animals are going to eat my food, it does not hurt me as much as the baboon as its hand can hold a cutlass but it says it won't cultivate.*
(If someone is able but unwilling to do a job, he is disliked more than someone who can't do it anyway).

**904. Aboa biara didi kɔ deɛ n'asom bɛdwo no.**
*Every animal eats where he is free from disturbance.*
(We cannot thrive if we are constantly disturbed).

**905. Aboa biara rebɛdɔre sradeɛ a osua prako.**
*Every animal which grows fat is copying the pig.*
(Said of a boaster whose achievement is not original).

**906. Aboa biara nni soro a ɔdi kube.**
*There is no animal above that eats the coconut.*
(Some problems are too tough for anyone to tackle).

**907. Aboa abirekyie na ɔbu ne bɛ sɛ: "Ade pa na yɛkata soɔ".**
*The goat has a proverb which says: "A good thing is sure to be covered over."*
(People hide their valuables and what is precious to them).

**908. Aboa abubumabaa ɔse: "Merehwɛ adeɛ".**
*The bag insect in its case says: "I am looking to see something."*
(Said of the passive watcher).

**909. Aboa adanko na obu ne bɛ sɛ: "Yɛanya awo wo barima yi na aka wo ne ɔyɛguo."**
*The hare has a proverb which runs: "When we are born male we are destined to face the misfortunes of life".*
(Misfortune is the lot of man).

**910. Aboa deɛ ɔwe wira wɔ wiram.**
*It is the animal which eats grass that lives amongst it.*
(Wira is grass; wiram, the bush (i.e. the grasses). You live where you can thrive).

**911. Aboa dompo nnim asudwareɛ nti na ɔnam asuo ho bɔ akɔtɔ.**
*Because the marsh-mongoose has made no preparation for the washing of its soul, that is why it walks by the water digging for crabs (to offer the soul).*

(See introduction for soul-washing. People always have reasons for what they do or fail to do, even if they are not obvious).

**912. "Aboa ahweaa, w'ano sɛ hwerɛma nso nyɛ wo na wo bɔ, bontontwufo na ɔbɔ".**
*"Cusimanse, your mouth may looking suitable for whistling but it is not you who should do it but the bontontwufo bird."*
(It is not appearance that counts but inherited rights and character).

**913. Aboa ako nni nsa nanso ɔforo dua.**
*The parrot has no hands but it is able to climb a tree.*
(There is not only one way of doing something).

**914. Aboa kɔkɔsakyi pɛ abɔfono nso ɔsuro ɔsommɔfono.**
*The vulture likes an animal's carcass but it fears the dead elephant.*
(Some people are so powerful that they are feared even in death).

**915. Aboa kɔkɔsakyi se atennidie nti na waka sumina soɔ.**
*The vulture says he stays on the rubbish heap to avoid scolding.*
(Said of someone who keeps out of trouble by being humble).

**916. Aboa kɔkɔsakyi nni tuo nso ɔtɔn asommɛn.**
*The vulture has no gun but it sells elephant tusks.*
(Said of someone who lives off other people's achievements).

**917. Aboa koterɛ se, sɛ ɔdasani didi mee a, ɔbɔ dam.**
*The lizard says, if a human being eats until completely satisfied, he will go mad.*
(Life without desire would be deadly).

**918. Aboa kɔtɔ ɔnka na ne nkyea na ɛyɛ ya.**
*The crab does not bite but its handshake is hard!*
(Everyone is strong in some point).

**919. Aboa ɔkra (ɔkraman) nim sɛ ntwe-mu yɛ dɛ a, anka ɔbɛtwe ne mu aduru aburokyire.**
*If the [cat]/[dog] knows that stretching is pleasant, then it will stretch till it reaches overseas.*
(If what you enjoy doing (or lazing around) were profitable, you would be rich).

**920. Aboa [ɔkra]/[ɔkraman] se ntwe-mu nti na wantɔ akoa.**
*The [cat]/[dog] says it was because of stretching that it did not buy a slave.*
(If you are over self-indulgent, you achieve little in life).

**921. Aboa ɔkra nni biribi a, ɔwɔ mmɔwerɛ.**
*Even if the cat has nothing else, it has claws.*
(Everyone has something useful and some means of defense).

**922. Aboa ɔkraman na ɔkae sɛ: "Da fam, ma menna fam, na ɛmaa ayɔnkogorɔ sɔeɛ".**
*It is the dog that says: "Lie down, let me lie down, makes a friendly game interesting".*
(The advantages of sharing equally. Dogs when playing, whether big or small, lie down alternatively, pretending to be the 'under-dog.')

**923. Aboa-kuntun-kantan da hɔ na n'akyi ka Nyame a, yɛmmisa deɛ ɔsɔre a ɔbɛduru.**
*If an enormous animal lies on the ground and he can reach the sky- God, we don't ask him when he gets up where he can reach to.*
(If a man is all-powerful, you don't question his ability to get to wherever he wants to).

**924. Aboa kuntunu, yɛnsum no nsɛmma.**
*The hyena, we do not set a trap for him.*
(You don't waste time over someone who is useless to you).

**925. Aboa kusie nya fufuo a, ɔbɛdi, na wɔmma na ɛrenkɔ ne bɔn mu.**
*If the rat gets fufu, it will eat it, but the pestle will not go into its hole.*
(If wishes were horses, beggars would ride. With all the will in the world there are some things you cannot achieve).

**926. Aboa kwakuo nim sɛ ɛkɔm bɛba nti na ɔkwatri korɔ ho.**
*The monkey knows there will be famine, therefore it reserves part of the seed of the tree (Albizia).*
(Said of people who provide for the future).

**927. Aboa kwakuo se: "Aduane dwetire yɛ bɔ na".**
*The monkey says: "To stock-up food is a difficult task".*
(It is hard to start saving).

**928. Aboa kwakuo se: "Mmarinsɛm, yɛdi no dua so na yɛnni no nsuo ase."**
*The monkey says: "Male bravery we practice it in the tree but not down in the water".*
(A man is king of his own castle, not of another man's).

**929. Aboa kye wo a, ɔhwɛ wo nam.**
*If an animal catches you, he examines your flesh.*
(Animals usually only kill when they need to eat. Hence: No one acts without a motive).

**930. Aboa akyekyedeɛ nni ntoma, nso awɔ nne no da.**
*The tortoise has no cloth, but it does not feel the cold.*
(God gave us all the equipment we need in life).

**931. Aboa Amemenenhoma memene nhoma na ɔmmemene nnompe.**
*The animal (called) Ropeswallower swallows ropes, not bones.*
(Because you have one talent, that does not mean you have another).

**932. Aboa nanka nim adekyeeɛ a, anka ɔnna awia-nna.**
*If the adder knew when it was dawn, it would not sleep in the daytime.*
(Said of someone who acts out of time).

**933. Aboa no da a, ɔde n'ani to deɛ obɛbuma no.**
*When the animals sleeps, he thinks of who will capture him.*
(Be vigilant).

**934. Aboa no de "Agyaakwaa" a, yɛnnyae no kwa.**
*If a beast is called "Don't go free", we don't simply let it go free.*

(If you are expected to behave in one way, that is how we make you behave).

**935. Aboa no de ne ho hu na ɛwɛre n'afuo.**
*The animal uses its fearful personality to watch its farm.*
(A person's reputation protects his property).

**936. Aboa no din de "Da bi yɛ bio".**
*The name of an animal is "Another day will come".*
(If you cheat someone they may get back at you in the future).

**937. Aboa no anha wo brɛ a, wonsɛe n'abɔn.**
*If an animal does not trouble you, you don't destroy its hole.*
(Let sleeping dogs lie).

**938. Aboa no nhunta nnya ne dua.**
*The animal does not hide to leave its tail behind.*
(If you wish something to be secret, don't leave evidence around).

**939. Aboa no ka deɛ n'ano kɔso.**
*An animal bites wherever its mouth reaches.*
(A person wishing to harm you will do so in whatever way they can).

**940. Aboa no ka anibereɛ.**
*An animal bites out of anger.*
(This refers to snakes. People only act when provoked).

**941. Aboa no ani ammere a, ɔnkyere ɔbɔfoɔ.**
*If an animal does not become angry, it does not catch the hunter.*
(Only if you annoy someone, will they take the trouble to find the resources to harm you).

**942. Aboa no repɛ efie aba a, na ɔsisi sumina so.**
*When an animal wishes to come into a house, it stands on the rubbish heap.*
(If someone wishes to join your group or family, they will try to associate with one of its members in order to work their way in).

**943. Aboa no repɛ kɔkɔɔ ayɛ nti na ɔde ne ho kɔtwere esie.**
*An animal that wants to become red, rubs itself against an anthill.*
(If you want to achieve something, you take the actions necessary to do so).

**944. Aboa no nya wo na ɔrenka wo a, ɔmfee ne se nkyerɛ wo.**
*If an animal is not going to bite you, it does not bare its teeth at you.*
(Take warning from threats).

**945. Aboa no se ɔreyɛ dua na ɛhia no a, ɔde apra ne ho.**
*The animal says it is growing a tail so that when it is in need it can brush itself.*
(Its good to plan ahead).

**946. Aboa nwoma bɛyɛ yie a, gye sɛ akorabɔɔ abɔ apare no.**
*An animal's skin will be good, unless a bullet spoils it.*
(You don't damage what you intend to make use of).

**947. Aboa patuo reka "Nhuu, nhuu", no nyinaa, na asɛm ara nko.**
*The owl cries "Hoo, hoo," when there is a real problem.*
(Elders say "hmm, hmm", when they do not want to discuss a serious matter. Used in a very serious situation which you should keep quiet about).

**948. Aboa patuo muna wo a, wonhunu.**
*If the owl gets angry with you, you don't see it.*
(The owl always looks imperturbable. An enemy does not necessarily show himself up).

**949. Aboa apatuprɛ se: "Ɔhɔhoɔ nnim a, ɔmanni nim".**
*The bulbul says: "If a stranger does not know, a citizen knows".*
(A local person knows local affairs better than a stranger).

**950. Aboa ɔpɛtɛ di obi bini nso obi nni ne deɛ.**
*The vulture eats others' excrement but no one eats its own.*
(Said of people who exploit others but do not want to be exploited themselves).

**951. Aboa pɛtɛ nni biribi a, ɔwɔ dunsin a ɔsi anim.**
*If the vulture has nothing else, it has the stump of a tree to perch on.*
(God provides everyone with some comfort).

**952. Aboa apetebie su sɛ: "Adeɛ yɛyɛ no n'ano, n'ano".**
*The striped squirrel cries out: "Everything is done from the beginning, from the beginning".*
(You must begin at the beginning).

**953. Aboa aponkyerɛne se: sɛ yɛdi ne ni konkontimaa nam a, anka ɔwɔ animuonyam wɔ nnipa anim.**
*The frog says: if we were to eat the meat of the tadpole its mother, it would be more respected by people.*
(If you come from a family which is not respected, neither will you be respected).

**954. Aboa prako nim sɛdeɛ ɔteɛ, nti na ɔnante mfikyire.**
*The pig knows what it is like, so it walks (i.e. lives) in the back yard.*
(People live in the place and have the status that suits them).

**955. Aboa aprawa se: sɛ ntɛtiadie na ɛyɛ honam yie a, anka ne ho nyɛ werɛkyerɛ werɛkyerɛ.**
*The pangolin says: if eating tree ants made one's skin smooth, then his skin wouldn't be so rough.*
(It is no good indulging in wishful thinking. You can't change your inherited characteristics).

**956. Aboa ɔsebɔ nnim akokɔ kasɛɛ mu asɛm nti na ɔne akokɔ nni aweretɔ.**
*Because the leopard does not know what is inside the chicken's bone, that is why it does not attack it.*
(You are not interested in something good unless you know the use of it).

**957. Aboa sika domfo-kumfo, womuna a, yɛde ma wo, wosere a, yɛde ma wo, na akyire asɛm!**
*The animal money, comforter and killer, if you frown, we give it to you, if you smile, we give it to you, but what matters is the result.*
(You need tact in obtaining money so that you can retain your reputation).

**958. Aboa tɛtia bɛtware asuo no, na ɛfiri babaa.**
*If the ant is going to cross the stream, it is because of a stick.*
(There are some things we cannot achieve without help).

**959. Aboa atwaboa se: "Ɔsoro adeɛ yɛ duru. (Adeɛ a ɛyɛ hare mpo hwe ne so a, na wawu).**
*The grass-cutter says: "Things above are weighty".*
*(Even if a light object falls on him from above, he dies).*
(When a person more powerful than you wishes to destroy you, he can do so easily).

**960. Mmoa no bɔ mu "Yaa" na wɔase "Yaa".**
*Creatures come together to act together (lit. Creatures join (in saying) "Yaa" and then they say "Yaa").*
(This is supposed to refer to solider ants. Unity is strength).

**961. Mmoa nyinaa di abɛ na opuro nko ara kɔdi bi a, yɛse: "N'ano kɔɔ".**
*All animals eat palm nuts, yet when the squirrel alone eats a few, we say: "Its mouth is red".*
(Everyone may cheat but only one person is made a scapegoat).

**962. Mmoa nyinaa tu mmirika dwane; nantwie nkoara tu mmirika dwane a yɛse wabɔ dam.**
*All animals run and flee; only the cow runs and flees and they say that it is mad.*
(Said of someone who is criticized for doing what everyone else does).

**963. Wommoaa wo ho a, wonkɔ asupɔnhweɛ.**
*If you are not well-prepared you don't go to fish in the big river.*
(This kind of fishing involves damming a river. Hence: You need to prepare carefully for difficult tasks).

**964. Mmoadoma a, wɔannya baabi antena yie, nni baabi pa ma wɔn dua.**
*The animals which don't get anywhere to sit comfortably, their tails have nowhere proper to lodge.*
(If an important person does not succeed nor does the less important).

**965. Mmoadoma nyinaa bɛnya dabere a, ɛnyɛ ɔnwam.**
*If all creatures have a sleeping place, that does not apply to the hornbill.*
(Don't show sympathy for someone whose position is his own fault).

**966. Mmoadoma pɛ Amiri kurom.**
*Animals like Amiri's town.*
(Amiri was a famous hunter. A good hunter is never without meat or a good worker without the rewards of his labor).

**967. Mmoadoma mpo wɔ wɔn hene.**
*Every type of animal has its chief.*
(Every community has its leader).

**968. Aboadeɛ nti na yɛbɔ nkuro.**
*Because of a court fee we take a case to court.*
(Used in justification for the taking of legal action against someone).

**969. Boafo-apatuprɛ kuruwa, ɔte mako a, ɔnte no kwa, ɔde yɛ ne ho aduro.**

*When Boafo the bulbul picks pepper, it does not do so for no reason, but to make medicine to cure itself.*
(Bulbuls are very fond of pepper. Hence: People do not act without reason. Or: One doesn't take medicine without hope of a cure).

**970. Oboafoɔ yɛ na.**
*Helpers are rare.*

**971. Woboapa yare a, ɔyarepa de ne ho gye mu.**
*If you pretend that you are sick, a real illness comes upon you.*
(Don't tempt fate; you may get more than your bargained for).

**972. Boapea se ne kasa yɛ nnipa ahi, nti na sɛ ɔrene a, ɔbɔ apee no.**
*The diana monkey says people don't like its language and that is why when it is defecating it makes a contemptuous sound (i.e a fart).*
(If people do not respect you, then you, too, do not respect them).

**973. Aboateaa se nkete nkete nso ɔka wo a ɛnni aduro.**
*The snake's teeth are small yet when it bites there is no medicine.*
(Small things can be fatal).

**974. Aboatia tɔ amena mu a, yɛde kwadu dada no.**
*If one of the little people falls into a hole, you use ripe bananas to entice him out.*
(The little people are supposed to be very fond of sweet things like tiger nuts, bananas and sweet drinks. Hence: If you want to attract someone who is shy, you use what you know they like best to do so).

**975. Wobobɔ w'adɔtɔ mu homa a, owia hye wo.**
*If you clear away all the lianas in your thicket, you allow sunshine to burn you.*
(If you get rid of all your protection, you suffer).

**976. Worebobɔ odupɔn mu na ɛregyegye ɔtwe aso mu.**
*When you are cutting down the big tree it reverberates in the duiker's ear.*
(The duiker sleeps between the buttresses of a big tree. Hence: The fate of a big man reacts on his dependents).

**977. Bɔbɔmfradaa dɛ nti na amamfoɔ hunu a na wɔrepere no.**
*The Bɔbɔmfradaa (fruit): it is because of its good flavor that fellow citizens flock to it when they see it.*
(Good food advertises itself. Or: A popular person is always the center of attraction).

**978. Abobɔnnua se ɔde ne ti bɔ dua mu a na ɔnya biribi die, na ɛnyɛ sɛ ɔde ne ti bobɔ mu kwa.**
*The woodpecker says it is only when it hits its head against the tree that it gets its daily bread, but it does not use its head to hit for no reason.*
(If you see someone doing something hard or unpleasant, it must be because he has to earn a living that way).

**979. Abobɔnnua korɔsen, obi nhunu deɛ ɔrepɛ ayɛ a, da biara ɔde "po, po, po", ɔbobɔ nnua mu nso ɔno a ɔnsene kodoɔ, na ɔnsene ta nso.**
*The woodpecker, no one can see what it is driving at; every time you hear it "knock, knock, knock", it is making a hole in the tree, but it is neither making a vessel nor a ladle.*
(Said when you cannot see what someone is achieving through hard work).

**980. Ɔbɔdamfoɔ a yɛato no dawɛmfoɔ na ɔkaa n'asɛm sɛ: "Dawɛmfoɔ adaworoma na ama ɔmamfoɔ ahyɛ me nso".**
*A madman who is kept in shackles told his tale thus: "Thanks to the shackles I am recognized by all the people in the state".*
(Some people court publicity at any cost. Used sarcastically).

**981. Ɔbɔdamfoɔ kɛtɛgo yɛ n'adepa.**
*A mad man's tattered mat is valuable to him.*
(We all have special things to which we are attached).

**982. Ɔbɔdamfoɔ na ɔdidi sumina soɔ.**
*It is a madman who eats on the rubbish heap.*
(If you are not normal you act abnormally).

**983. Ɔbɔdamfoɔ na ɔmfɛre adeɛ a, ne mma fɛre.**
*If a madman is not ashamed, his children are ashamed.*
(The bad actions of one member of a family affect all its members).

**984. Ɔbɔdamfoɔ nan, yɛtwe no nyaa.**
*The leg of a madman, we pull it cautiously.*
(Be careful how you approach an unpredictable person).

**985. Ɔbɔdamfoɔ pa ne ntoma gu a, wompa wo deɛ ngu bi.**
*If a mad man throws away his cloth and lets it fall, you don't take off drop yours.*
(You don't copy something abnormal).

**986. Ɔbɔdamfoɔ se ne dam kɔ a, na nyɛ ɔde hunahuna mmɔfra.**
*If a madman says his madness has gone, a little remains for frightening children*
(Once you have evolved some habit it may be difficult to get rid of it altogether).

**987. Ɔbɔdamfoɔ wo ba a, ɔwo no ma amansan.**
*If a mad person gives birth to a child, she gives it to the state.*
(Every citizen, however insignificant, belongs to the state).

**988. Abodin-akeka nti na ɛkoɔ nyaa yamtuo.**
*Because of negative gossip the bush-cow had diarrhea.*
("Abodin-akeka" literally means the mentioning of your name in a derogatory manner. Hence: If you hear too much criticism of yourself you become nervous).

**989. Abodin-akeka nti na owuo nam akwan hodoɔ so fa nnipa.**
*Because of negative gossip, Death uses different ways of taking people.*
(A clever person disguises his intentions. See Proverb 988).

**990. Abodin-akeka nyɛ dɛ.**
*Negative gossip is not good.*
(See Proverb 988).

**991. Bɔdwese bɔ onyini ho dawuro.**
*A beard spreads the news of old age (lit. plays the gong-gong for old age).*
(Some characteristics are symbolic of prevailing circumstances).

**992. Bɔdwesɛ bɛtoo anintɔnnwi.**
*The beard came to meet the eyebrows.*
(It is not size but seniority which counts).

**993. Ɔbofoɔ mmɔfra ho nyɛ fɛ da.**
*A mean person's children are never attractive.*
(The word "ɔbofoɔ" means someone who is a destroyer (mean person) and who does not want others to prosper. Hence: Like father, like son, the destroyer's son never has a good reputation or image).

**994. Ɔbofoɔ na ɔbɔ akosɛm.**
*A mean person spreads rumors of war.*
(A trouble maker has no regard for suffering, but makes trouble for its own sake. See Proverb 993).

**995. Ɔbofoɔ nim deɛ ɔbɛdi adowa-tire a, anka ɔhoo no yie.**
*If a mean person knew the one who would eat the head of the royal antelope then he would have singed it well.*
(If you don't do a job properly, you may be the one who stands to lose by it. See Proverb 993).

**996. Ɔbofoɔ ntɔ akoa.**
*A mean person does not buy a slave.*
(A person who begrudges everyone else's successes, won't look after-and thus gain the loyalty of-others. See Proverb 993).

**997. Ɔbofoɔ a mmoa ayi no akwa na ɔkum ɔpɛtɛ.**
*The hunter who has been outwitted by other animals kills the vulture.*
(In time of need we take anything we can get).

**998. Ɔbofoɔ a worekɔdi no ayaw na etuo apae aka ne nsa yi; na wo deɛ woso nkonkonte-bɛdɛ rekɔyɛ deɛn?**
*The hunter you are going to assist has injured his hand when the gun exploded, and you, why do you still carry a basket of dried cassava?*
(If the person on whom you depend is out of action it is no use your doing your part of the work which depends on him finishing his).

**999. Ɔbofoɔ a wakum ɔpɛtɛ wasɛe n'atuduro.**
*The hunter who has killed a vulture has expended his powder in vain.*
(Said when effort and expense are spent on obtaining something useless).

**1000. Ɔbofoɔ a ɔkum sono no, sɛ ɔto dɔtɔ mu tuo na aberɛbeɛ firi mu tɔ a, ɔne ne mma de toto borɔdedwo (we).**
*The hunter who kills an elephant, if he fires into the thicket and a palm civet drops down, he and his children use it with toasted plantain (to eat).*
(If you expect great things, you may treat small ones with disdain but you nonetheless use them).

**1001. Ɔbofoɔ a ɔkum sono mpo wannya ne ho, na wo a worekɔwɔ abɛ atɔn na wobɛnya wo ho?**
*The hunter who killed the elephant has not become wealthy, how much less you who pound palm nuts.*
(If the powerful man does not get what he wants, how can the poor man succeed?)

**1002. Ɔbofoɔ a wakum tɛnkwa, meremma w'annan so na woabɔ dam ato tuo abɔ me.**
*O hunter who has killed the bongo, I will not come to your camp so that if you should go mad you would shoot me.*
(The Bongo is a sasaboa-an animal with a very strong spirit-which can destroy the hunter who shoots at it, unless he performs certain rituals. Hence: You avoid someone who you believe may get into trouble and drag you down with them).

**1003. Ɔbofoɔ ba, wɔnkyerɛ no abeɛ.**
*The hunter's child, we do not teach it songs.*
(There are many hunting songs, used by the hunters when they are returning to the village and also by the villagers who welcome them. A hunter's child would learn them automatically. Hence: You don't need to be taught something which you have learned through your upbringing).

**1004. Ɔbofoɔ din bata sonnam ho.**
*The hunter's name is attached to the meat of the elephant.*
(A man's reputation depends on his deeds).

**1005. Ɔbofoɔ firi wiram ba na ɔkuta mmire a, yɛmmisa no ahayɔ mu asɛm.**
*If a hunter comes out of the forest carrying mushrooms, you don't ask him about his hunting.*
(If a man obviously has not been successful you don't rub it in by asking him to recount his achievements).

**1006. Ɔbofoɔ ho suro nti na ɔtwe da a, ɔso daebɔne.**
*It is from fear of the hunter that when the duiker sleeps, it has evil dreams.*
(When you fear someone you are constantly troubled by them in your mind).

**1007. Ɔbofoɔ anhyehyɛ toa yie a, ɛbɔ.**
*If a hunter does not pack his gourd well (with gunpowder) it breaks.*
(If you prepare carelessly, you fail).

**1008. Ɔbofoɔ nka ahamusɛm nyinaa.**
*A hunter does not tell all the story of the chase.*
(People tend to tell only the part of a story which resounds to their credit and to forget the mistakes or disasters).

**1009. Ɔbofoɔ kɔ wiram na wamma a, yɛpɛ no nnanso.**
*If the hunter goes to the forest and does not return, we look for him at his hunting cottage.*
(You start looking for a person in the place that he most frequents).

**1010. Ɔbofoɔ kɔ wiram ma osuo tɔ hwe no, ma ntummoa keka ne ho, ma awɔ de no, ma hwerɛmo wɔ no a, ne nyinaa ɛyɛ due na yɛde ma no.**
*If the hunter goes to the bush and the rain beats him, the sandflies bite him, he feels cold and is scratched by thorns; for all these things we give him sympathy.*
(No matter how great the suffering or misfortune it is the same sympathy that you give to someone for it).

**1011. Ɔbofoɔ kɔte dua na aboa amma a, ɔsan ba fie.**
*If the hunter goes to lie in wait for the game and if the animals don't come, he returns home.*
(One can only do one's best, even if it does not succeed).

1012. Ɔbɔfoɔ: Womaa anomaa-tewa biribi diiɛ a anka woate n'ano kasa pa.
*Hunter: If you had given the small bird something to eat, then you would have heard something good from its beak.*
(Don't disregard apparently insignificant people for they may be the ones to lead you to achievement).

1013. Ɔbɔfoɔ ne deɛ ne nam gu apasoɔ.
*The hunter is the one who has his meat roasted.*
(The person who has evidence of achievement is accepted for what he is).

1014. Ɔbɔfoɔ nnim aboa yarefoɔ.
*A hunter does not distinguish a sick animal.*
(Your enemies are your enemies whatever the circumstances).

1015. Ɔbɔfoɔ annya biribi a, na ɛfiri kataeɛ.
*If the hunter does not get anything, it is because of his gun-lock cover.*
(Even an apparently insignificant helper may cause you to fail).

1016. Ɔbɔfoɔ annya aduane pa a, deɛ ɔdie ne opuro ti.
*If the hunter does not catch good food, he eats the head of a squirrel.*
(If you don't succeed in life you have to be content with what you can get).

1017. Ɔbɔfoɔ annya agyapadeɛ na ɛfiri nkwanne.
*If the hunter has not been able to accumulate heirlooms it is because of delicious soup.*
(Too much love of good things stops one from achieving wealth in life).

1018. Ɔbɔfoɔ repɛ wo abɔ wo atirimuɔden a, na ɔse kɔkɔte nni nnwa nam.
*If the hunter wishes to be stingy, then he tells you that the bush pig has no meat for the flayer.*
(Said of a close-fisted man who refuses to give someone their legitimate reward).

1019. Ɔbɔfoɔ werɛ firi ne tuo a, gyata pamo no.
*If the hunter forgets his gun, the lion chases him.*
(A man in a dangerous position cannot afford to be caught off-guard).

1020. Abɔfono, yɛfa no wo adukuro mu, na yɛmfa no nkwanta so.
*The carcass, we collect it from the buttress of the tree, and we do not collect it at the crossroads.*
(There is a right place for everything. See Proverb 732).

1021. Abɔfra a ɔnni hwɛfoɔ na asɛm bɔne kotokuo sɛn n'aboboɔ-ano.
*A child who has no guardian, has a container of evil hanging on its threshold.*
(Without supervision, the young are in constant danger).

1022. Abɔfra bɔ nwa na ɔmmɔ akyekyedeɛ.
*A child can break a snail but not a tortoise (shell).*
(You should only attempt what you are able to do. People's strengths differ).

1023. Abɔfra bɔ mmusuo nkoron a, ɔfa mu nsia de sane n'abusuafoɔ.
*If a child commits nine taboos he takes six of them to his matriclan.*

(A family suffers for the misdoings of its members however irresponsible they are).

1024. Abɔfra didi panin atɛm a, [ɔnnyini nkyɛre]/[ne hwene bu gu mu.]
*If a child insults an elder, [he does not grow to an old age]/[his nose breaks off].*
(Lack of respect of the elders will cause you trouble).

1025. Abɔfra nsam adeɛ nyɛ hyɛna.
*A child's present is not hard to find.*
(A child or a simple person is easily pleased with little things).

1026. Abɔfra se ɔbɛyɛ mpaninneɛ a, ma ɔnyɛ; ebia na ɔrebɛyɛ ɔpanin a, obi nnim.
*If a child says he will act as an elder, let him do so; perhaps he will really become an elder, no one knows.*
(Let children live their dreams).

1027. Abɔfra se ɔbɛsɔ gya mu a, ma ɔnsɔ mu, na ɔhye no a, ɔbedane atwene.
*If a child says he will catch hold of fire, let him catch hold of it, for if it burns him, he will throw it away.*
(We learn through experience, even though it may be painful).

1028. Abɔfra sika [yɛ]/[tesɛ] nyankomaa-gya; wotwa so a, na adum.
*A child's gold [is]/[is like] the branch of a custard-apple tree, when it is broken up it is soon burnt.*
(A small amount disappears in no time).

1029. Abɔfra su a, yɛmmɔ no duam.
*When a child cries, we don't tie him to a log.*
(You don't punish a child cruelly because he weeps, but rather find the cause).

1030. Abɔfra su mpanin su a, yɛma no besehene.
*If a child weeps like an adult, we give him the best cola (to chew).*
(If children behave like adults, they will be treated as such).

1031. Abɔfra resua adwini di a, ɛnyɛ ɔsebɔ-nwoma na ɔde sua.
*If a child is learning his craft, it is not on a leopard's skin that he learns.*
(You do not give the best materials to a learner; let him start on something which it does not matter spoiling).

1032. Abɔfra nto biribi nni mmɔ ka mma yɛnnye no kɔkɔsakyi mpensa ahaasa.
*A child does not toast something to eat and fall into a debt of three thousand three hundred vultures.*
(Some fetishes accept vultures as offerings. Someone who commits small offenses should not be given a harsh punishment).

1033. Abɔfra yɛ deɛ yenyɛ a, ɔhunu deɛ yɛnhunu.
*If a child does what is not done, then he sees what is not meant to be seen.*
(If you go against custom you suffer for it).

1034. Abɔfra yɛ deɛ ɔpanin yɛ a, ɔhunu deɛ ɔpanin hunu.
*If a child does what the elder does, then he sees what the elder sees.*
(If you act like someone else, you get the results they would get).

**1035. Abɔfra yε somakorɔ a, ɔnya n'akɔnnɔdeε di.**
*If a child is obedient in running errands, it gets its reward.*
(Virtue is rewarded).

**1036. Mmɔfra nkɔtu mmire a, wɔanhunu tu; mpanin nkɔtu a, woatiatia so.**
*If children go to gather mushrooms, they don't know how to do it; if elders go to gather, they trample on them.*
(A wrong action of an experienced person is worse than that of an inexperienced).

**1037. Abofuo de asεntenten na εnam.**
*Anger brings with it a long tale.*
(Anger makes people talk too much).

**1038. Abofuo nua ne akayɔ.**
*Anger's brother is quarrelling.*

**1039. Abofuo pamo adepa firi fie.**
*Anger drives something good from the house.*

**1040. Abofuo te sε ɔhɔhoɔ, ɔntena baakofoɔ fie.**
*Anger is like a stranger, it does not stay in only one person's house.*

**1041. Abofuo nti na Ɔhemmaa fua papa.**
*Because of anger the Queen Mother holds the fan.*
(The Queen Mother holds a fan and waves it to show she is annoyed. We use the symbol to illustrate the reality).

**1042. Abofuo yε ɔbrammiri.**
*Anger turns a man into a strong man.*
(Anger makes a weak man violent).

**1043. Bogya bɔne yε adesoa.**
*A bad blood-relation is a burden.*

**1044. Bogya ne asεm.**
*Blood-relationship is what counts.*

**1045. Bogya mpε hia.**
*A blood-relation does not like poverty.*
(If you are poor you are of no use to your family).

**1046. Bogya yεmpepa ngu.**
*Blood-relationship, we don't wash it off.*
(Blood relationships are permanent and cannot be denied).

**1047. Mogya sɔne gu wo ho a, wommisa deε aba.**
*If blood is splashing on you, you don't ask what has happened.*
(You don't question the obvious).

**1048. Bogya afεre, kotoro-bankye afεre.**
*The firefly is shamed, the cassava is shamed.*
(This cassava gives off a phosphorescent light when rotten, the firefly also gives off a small light. If the sun comes out, both are put to shame. Said of people or things which did not help at the proper time, when real help comes and they are put to shame).

**1049. Aboko ba: "Ɔkyena na mekɔ".**
*The stone partridge's chick (says): "Tomorrow I am off".*
(Said by someone who will soon be leaving and is unable to improve the situation before he does so. If you don't live permanently somewhere you are not too concerned about the situation there).

**1050. Bɔgyaeε sene yarewuo.**
*A long illness is worse than a mortal illness.*
(Suffering is worse than death).

**1051. Abɔgyeε anna a, εyare kaka.**
*The jaw, if it does not sleep, gets toothache.*
(If you don't rest, you get ill).

**1052. Ɛbɔhyε sene akadan.**
*Promise is stronger than demand.*
(Used once you've promised to carry out an obligation, to ask someone to stop making demands and rely on your word).

**1053. "Bɔ-me-ma-menni" na ede asε ba na nyε "anka-me".**
*"Hit me but I will render the blow harmless" brings trouble but not "avoidance".*
(You can keep out of trouble by refusing to retaliate).

**1054. "Bɔ-me-ma-menni" ne "anka me," deε εwɔ hene na εyε?**
*"Strike me but I will render the blow harmless" and "avoidance", which of them is better?*
(Prevention is better than cure. Compare Proverb 1053).

**1055. Ɛbɔmfoɔ repε wo ahwe wo a, na wɔse: "Ma yεnkɔ Nwabe ahweε".**
*If the people of Ɛbɔm want to beat you up, they say: "Lets go to the river Nwabe to fish".*
(Ɛbɔm is near Mampɔnten, Asante. The people of Asante villages dam the streams to collect fish in baskets through which the water flows. Hence: If someone wants to cheat you, he first lures you away to where he has you at his mercy).

**1056. Obomokyikyie firi nsuo ase bεka kyerε wo sε ɔdεnkyεm [awu a]/[yare a], yεnnye no akyinne.**
*If the river fish (Mochokidae synodontis) comes out of the water to tell you that the crocodile [is dead]/[is sick], don't disbelieve it.*
(Apart from both being in the river the fish is reputed to kill the crocodile if swallowed by sticking its fins in the liver. Hence: Don't doubt someone who is in a position to know).

**1057. Obomokyikyie agorɔ nyε ago-pa.**
*The river fish's game is no safe game.*
(There can be no good outcome from playing with a dangerous man. See Proverb 1056).

**1058. Bɔmmɔte de asuo na εbua ɔne ɔdasani asεm.**
*The skink uses the water to judge a case between it and a human being.*
(These lizard-like reptiles are reputed to have a poisonous bite. If you get to water before the one that bites you, it dies. If it reaches water first, you die! The bite is not in fact poisonous but the head of the reptile looks very like a snake, which may account for its reputation. Hence: If you are honest you accept the judgement of a higher authority).

**1059. Bɔne akatua ne owuo.**
*The wages of sin are death.*

**1060. Bɔne mu na papa firi ba.**
*It is from bad things that good things come.*
(We learn from our mistakes).

1061. Bɔne ne papa te sɛ nsuo ne ngo, ɛntumi nni afra.
*Evil and good are like water and oil, they cannot mix.*

1062. Bɔne te sɛ mframa: ɛmfa ɔbaakofoɔ ho.
*Evil is like the wind: it does not blow on one person alone.*
(Evil is everywhere, you cannot avoid it).

1063. Bɔne te sɛ ahwanhwanniɛɛ: ɛka wo ho a, ɛdi w'akyi.
*Evil is like a strong perfume: if you apply it, it follows you around.*
(You can never rid yourself of the effects of your evil deeds).

1064. Bɔne te sɛ emee: wode sie a, ɛyi wo adi.
*Evil is like a pleasant-smelling herb: if you hide it, it calls attention to itself.*
(However hard you try and hide evil deeds, they come to light in the end).

1065. Bɔne te sɛ nwira, ɛmpa deɛ ɛfifiri.
*Evil is like weeds, it is never completely uprooted.*
(Human nature being what it is, you can never rid the world of evil).

1066. Bɔnkɔ a ɔda nsuo mu: sɛ woanhwɛ a, worennya no.
*The shrimp in the river: if you don't clear away the water, you can't catch it.*
(If you don't separate someone from their protector, you can't do anything to them).

1067. Bɔne nyɛ, nso obiara di bi.
*Evil is not good, but everyone indulges in it a bit.*

1068. Bonniayɛ, di deɛ woadie na worenni adi bio.
*Ungrateful person, eat what you have already eaten as you won't get any more!*
(Lack of gratitude discourages the donor).

1069. Bonniayɛ, ne nyaatwom, ne dinsɛe yɛ ahanasa.
*Ingratitude, hypocrisy and calumny are triplets.*
(Vices that create a false impression are equally bad).

1070. Bonniayɛ nua ne Kaeda-bi.
*An ungrateful person's brother is Think-of-the-future.*
(See Proverb 1069).

1071. Bonniayɛ te sɛ Kumawu Koterefeni.
*Ungratefulness is like the Kumawu Koterefeni.*
(This chief was rescued from captivity in the war against Domena but killed his rescuer, fearing he would boast of his doings. The proverb is used when someone rewards a benefactor with treachery).

1072. Bonniayɛfoɔ didi ntɛntɛm na wapepe n'ano.
*An ungrateful person eats fast and wipes his lips.*
(An ungrateful person tries to hide his obligation to his benefactor).

1073. Ɔbonsam a ɔyɛ wo manifoɔ yɛ ma wo sene Ɔsoro Boafoɔ a wonni no nse no.
*The devil who is your fellow citizen does things for you better than the Angel you don't know.*
(Better the devil you know).

1074. Ɔbonsam ka ne twene na ɛsɛ sɛ wosa a, wosa.
*If the devil plays his drum and you have to dance, then you dance.*
(You do what you are predestined to do).

1075. Mmɔbɔnsɛ Agyewaa, ɔne opitire ntumi mpere mwansɛn mu.
*The young shrimp Agyewaa does not compete with the mudfish in the soup pot.*
(Said for instance of an orphan who cannot compete with the children of the house).

1076. Bonsua kyɛre ahina mu a, ɛbɔ.
*If the cup keeps long in the water pot, it breaks.*
(Familiarity breeds contempt).

1077. Abɔntenso bayie bɛdi wo nam a, na ɛfiri fie.
*If witchcraft from without is going to eat your meat, it is because of your family (lit. home).*
(Witchcraft can be most effective against blood relations. A witch is required to "eat" one of his or her own family. Hence: If anyone wishes you harm it is because of something your own family has done).

1078. Obonto mfa ne ho mmɔ nkawa.
*A tadpole should not mix itself up with small fish.*
(Don't pretend to be what you are not).

1079. Obonto se ɔrepɛ hwefoɔ, nanso hwefoɔ mpɛ no.
*The tadpole says he wants (to be caught by) the fishermen, but the fishermen do not want him.*
(Said of a person who tries to get attention by all means but is wanted by no one).

1080. Obontu se: ɔreyɛ yie na ɔwu a, ɔde agyae ne mma.
*The long-haired goat says: he is putting things in order so that when he dies his children can inherit.*
(Example is better than precept).

1081. Bontuku Kramo se ɔbɛforo tagyammoɔ a, ɔne ne pɔnkɔ nansini.
*If the Moslem from Bondougou says he will climb the great stone there, he and his three-legged horse will do it.*
(There was a great stone at Bondougou on top of which Moslems worshipped. They were only allowed to climb it on horse-back. Thus if a man had only a crippled horse he was in difficulty. The proverb means: "If you say you can do something apparently impossible, let us see you do it!")

1082. Bonwoma bata brɛboɔ ho a, ɛyɛ twana.
*If the bile is attached to the liver, it is difficult to separate them.*
(If a small man attaches himself to an important one it is not easy to harm the former).

1083. Ɛboɔ a ɛtim fam mpo mframa de no rekɔ, na kampesɛ ahahan?
*If even a stone that is lying on the ground is taken by the wind, how much more the leaf.*
(If a difficult task is accomplished there is no trouble over an easier one).

1084. Ɛboɔ da ɔboɔ so a, na yɛfrɛ no bopɔ.
*If there is one stone on top of another, we call it a hill.*
(There is strength in numbers).

**1085. Ɛboɔ mu nni adɔmma.**
*A stone has no tenderness.*
(You can't get blood out of a stone).

**1086. Ɔboɔ dwo a, otanfoɔ asom dwo no.**
*If anger abates, an enemy becomes peaceful.*
(Even enemies can become friends when they cool off).

**1087. Ɛboɔ twerɛboɔ da nsuo ase a, ogya mpa mu da.**
*If a flintstone lies in the water, it is still not without fire.*
(You can recognize a man's natural gifts wherever he is).

**1088. Bopɔ-foro kwokwa a, nka Kusa mmerewa de wɔn akyi na ɛforo mmopɔ.**
*If climbing a hill can be got used to, then the old ladies of Kusa (in Adanse) would climb the steep hill in reverse.*
(If we could all acquire equal skills we should be able to overcome every obstacle easily).

**1089. Ɔbɔpɔn ko tɔ a, kɔkɔsakyi bɔ hyire.**
*If any great animal dies, then the vulture rejoices (lit. puts on white).*
(One man's sorrow is another man's joy).

**1090. Ɔbɔrakɔmfo se ɔsuro kum, nti na wayɛ ne kɔn tia.**
*The Bɔra fetish priest says that because he is afraid of execution he has made his neck short.*
(Prevention is better than cure).

**1091. Woboro aberewa nana a, wote adomankomasɛm.**
*If you beat an old lady's grandchild you hear expressions that are hidden from every day use.*
(Be careful how you treat the relatives of an important person as your action may bring unanticipated consequences).

**1092. Woboro gyata a, wo tiri na ɛpae wo.**
*If you beat a lion, it is your own head which aches.*
(Don't bite off more than you can chew).

**1093. Woboro ahenkwaa a, na woaboro ɔhene.**
*If you beat a stool servant, you beat the chief.*
(If you trouble a powerful man's followers it is as if you had troubled him).

**1094. Yɛboro akɔdaa a ɔbɛsu na yɛmmoro deɛ ɔbɛseree.**
*We beat a child who will cry and not one who after beating will laugh.*
(We advise the obedient and not the stubborn).

**1095. Woboro nsa wɔ nsamanpɔ mu a, na woawie ayie yɛ.**
*If you get drunk in the cemetery, you have finished celebrating the funeral.*
(Some taboos end all taboos).

**1096. Yɛboro wo a, wanka sɛ: "Mekyiri atɛnnie".**
*If we beat you up, you don't say: "I taboo abuse".*
(If something serious happens to you, you don't complain of minor things).

**1097. Yemmoro aberewa nkɔ sa.**
*We don't beat up an old lady and then go to war.*
(Bad luck follows maltreatment of those we should respect. You don't do something dangerous after provoking a curse on yourself).

**1098. Aborɔ nti na kotokurodu yɛ ɛwoɔ a, nsuo nni mu.**
*Because of mischief, when the black wasp makes honey, it has no liquid in it.*
(Some people are determined that others shall not benefit from their work).

**1099. Aborɔbɛ dɛ nko na ankaa nso dɛ nko.**
*The pineapple's sweetness is one thing and the orange's another.*
(Tastes and people differ).

**1100. Aborɔbɛ amfa ne kɔkɔɔ a, ɛnyɛ dɛ.**
*Unless a pineapple emulates its own ripe color, it is not sweet.*
(The color of ripe fruit is "kɔkɔɔ". A truly superior person must emulate his own achievements to be supreme).

**1101. Aborɔbɛ ase ntu.**
*The pineapple hardly gets extinct.*
(Some things are endowed with prolific blessings).

**1102. Borɔdeɛ bɛboa ɔdeɛ.**
*The plantain came to help the yam.*
(The new came to help the old).

**1103. Borɔdeɛ se: "Ɔdeɛ agye din kwa, me na meyɛn mma".**
*The plantain says: "Yam's name has spread in vain, it is I who raise the children".*
(Small children are especially fond of ripe plantain. Hence: A person who is sure of their own merit does not accept the counterclaims of another).

**1104. Borɔdeɛ se: "Mankanu, gyae w'ahantan no, na wo ho mfasoɔ ne yareɛ".**
*The plantain says: "Cocoyam, stop your pomposity, for your end result (lit. profit) is sickness".*
(A boaster merits a sharp reprimand).

**1105. Borɔdeɛ se: "Mankanu, sɛ woamma a, anka me yɛn me mma ara".**
*The plantain says: "Cocoyam, it you had not come, I would still have reared my children".*
(Some people are capable of caring for themselves and their families unaided, even if others say they help. If you boast too much about helping someone, they may reject you).

**1106. Borɔdeɛ se ne ho yɛ fɛ nanso ɔda egya mu a na wɔredanedane no.**
*The plantain says it is beautiful but when it is in the fire people turn it over and over.*
(It is not beauty but usefulness that matters to most people).

**1107. Borɔdedwo ne nkateɛ nnyae dɛ yɛ da.**
*Roasted plantain and groundnuts never stop being sweet.*
(Used of something classic which never loses its charm).

**1108. Borɔdekɔkɔɔ ne nkateɛ, wodi na anyɛ wo dɛ a, na ɛfiri wo se.**
*If you eat ripe plantain and groundnuts and don't find them good , then it must be because of your teeth.*
(If you don't like something universally popular then there must be something wrong with you).

1109. Borɔdeɛ hane a, na ne wuo aduro so.
*If the plantain is about to bear fruit, then it is nearing its time of death.*
(As we prosper and produce so death approaches).

1110. Borɔdeɛ hane a, na ato ne twa.
*When the plantain is about to bear fruit, you anticipate its cutting.*
(See Proverb 1109).

1111. Aborɔdwomma se: "M'aforo boɔ afɛre".
*The sweet potato says: "I have climbed the rock to my shame".*
(Said by someone who has toiled in vain or refused to accept good advice and has been proved wrong).

1112. Borɔferɛ a ɛyɛ dɛ, na dua da aseɛ.
*The pawpaw that is sweet, a stick lies under its tree.*
(If something is good there is always some evidence of its popularity).

1113. Borɔferɛ a eyɛ dɛ, na ɛnsee kɔso ayie.
*It is the sweet pawpaw of which the woodpeckers attend the funeral.*
(People gather together where their needs will be satisfied).

1114. Borɔferɛ ammere dua soɔ, ɛdɛ biara nni mu.
*The pawpaw which does not ripen on the tree never becomes really sweet.*
(Things which deviate from their natural course cannot be expected to give the best results).

1115. Borɔferɛ se: "Ɛnyɛ me na ɔkom ba a, mehwɛ nkurɔfoɔ mma".
*The pawpaw says: "It is not I who, if famine comes, should take care of people's children"."*
(Said of someone who is unwilling to help others in need even if able to do so).

1116. Aborɔfo adaworoma na yɛn nyinaa furafura ntoma.
*Because of the mercy of Europeans that is why we all wear cloth.*
(Some people prosper as the result of the work of others).

1117. Aborɔfo de nyansa na ɛforo po.
*Whitemen use wisdom to launch into the sea.*
(Use your head!)

1118. Aborɔfo nyansa gyina koroyɛso.
*The wisdom of the whiteman depends on togetherness.*
(Europeans coming to Ghana in the old days worked either for a company or for the colonial government, from which they derived their power. Hence: Power needs backing. Or: Unity is strength).

1119. Ɔborɔfotefoɔ na ɔma oburoni yɛ ayɛ.
*It is the person who knows English who makes the whiteman give presents.*
(An interpreter is in a strong position. If someone is intimate with another he has influence on his policy).

1120. Aborɔkɔborɔkɔ yoyo: "Meyɛ adwene na me tiri na ɛnyɛ".
*The wriggly eel says: "I am a fish but I am unlucky".*
(Said by someone who has an obvious physical disability and resents it).

1121. Boron mpakyie na yɛbɔ n'asom ansa na abue.
*The Brong gourd, unless you slap it, it won't open.*
(A stubborn person needs forcing).

1122. Aborɔnoma se: "Ɔkwantia yɛ mmusuo".
*The dove says: "Shortcuts are dangerous".*
(This bird flies a long way round to reach its destination. Hence: More haste, less speed).

1123. Aborɔnoma se: ɔrepɛ fie nsɛm ahunu, nti na ɔbɔ kuro mpɛmpɛ.
*The pigeon says: it wants to know all that goes on in the home, that is why it patrols the town.*
(It is necessary to have know a place well, before you get what you want from its people).

1124. Aborɔnoma da soro, odwansaeɛ da fam.
*The pigeon sleeps above, the ram below.*
(Each man to his own place).

1125. Aborɔnoma te fie nso ɔnte kasa, wama aboa ako firi wiram abɛte kasa agya no.
*The pigeon stays in the house and cannot understand the language but the parrot comes from the bush and can understand.*
(Said when a person who should know something, does not, but a stranger does).

1126. Aborɔsan bɛbu a, ɛfiri pam.
*If a story building collapses it is from within.*
(It is a man's own weaknesses which often cause his downfall).

1127. Mmɔborowa, sɛ ɛbi wɔ nsuo bi mu a, na ɛkyerɛ sɛ ɛnam wɔ saa nsuo no mu.
*The Mmɔborowa fishes, if you find them in some water, it means that there is plenty of fish (lit. flesh) in that water.*
(Said of something the presence of which indicates that a place is suitable for some specific use).

1128. Aboseaa na ɛkum nnomaa.
*Small stones kill birds.*
(Small things can bring success as well as large ones).

1129. Abɔsobaa na ɛma ogya paeɛ.
*The mallet helps to split the firewood.*
(You need help in life).

1130. Ɔbosom a ɔnnii dwan da, na ɔhunu odwan ani ase nkyene a, ɔse: "Ɛyɛ sradeɛ".
*The fetish that has never eaten a sheep, if it sees the matter from a sheep's eye, it says: "It is fat".*
(If you have never had the best things, then even if you are offered the least part of them, you appreciate it).

1131. Ɔbosom a ɔnkasa na yɛto no aboɔ.
*It is the fetish that does not talk that we throw stones at.*
(We despise someone who does not do their work properly).

1132. Ɔbosom a ɔma mma, na ɔfa mma.
*The fetish which brings children also takes children.*
(There is good and bad in everything).

1133. Ɔbosom a ɔnya wo a, ɔrenku wo no na ɔkyerɛ wo n'akyiwadeɛ.
*The fetish which gets you and is not going to kill you is the one which tells you what it needs to pacify it.*
(If you offend someone it is only they who can tell you how to purge your offence. Only those who like you care if you apologize).

1134. Ɔbosom a ɔnni kɔmfoɔ no, yɛto no abuo.
*If a fetish has no priest, we put it on one side.*
( Sometimes the spirits taking possession of a fetish desert it and it becomes like an empty house. It is only when it is re-possessed that people take notice of it. Hence: You only serve someone when it is profitable to do so).

1135. Ɔbosom a ɔyɛ nam na ɔdi aboadeɛ.
*An effective fetish receives its offerings.*
(Success is self-evident. See Proverb 1134).

1136. Ɔbosom gye aboadeɛ di boa.
*A fetish gets a promising gift to eat and helps.*
(If someone is helping you, you give them something).

1137. Ɔbosom ankɔda a, na ɛfiri nnyegyesoɔ.
*If a fetish spirit does not rest, it is due to adulation.*
(An important man is spoiled and exhausted by sycophants).

1138. Ɔbosom kɔm a, na ɛmfiri nnyegyesoɔ.
*If the spirit possesses, it is not because of adulation.*
(A man sometimes acts from a sense of duty or purpose and not just to get praise).

1139. Ɔbosom kyerɛ nantwie a, yɛmfa mfa abɔnten, yɛmfa mfa afikyire, nso ɛwo deɛ yɛde fa.
*If the fetish indicates a cow, we do not lead it in public (lit. outside), we do not lead it behind the houses, but nevertheless there is a way that we will take it.*
(The fetish indicates the cow it wants as a sacrifice. Hence: If something is important to be done, you do it somehow. Or: A thing that is predestined will happen).

1140. Ɔbosom na ɛkyerɛ ɔkomfoɔ ntwaho.
*It is the fetish that teaches the priest to whirl around.*
(It is the spirit which directs men to act).

1141. Ɔbosom anim, yɛkɔ no mprɛnsa.
*One goes to consult an obosom three times. (lit. The face of the obosom, we go to it thrice).*
(Three is a lucky number. Hence: Try, try and try again).

1142. Ɔbosom bɛnya wo a, na ɛfiri nnipa.
*If the fetish is going to get you, it is because of people.*
(Most of our trouble is caused through other people).

1143. Abosom nyinaa yɛ Onyame mma.
*All fetishes are the children of God.*
(People go to the shrines of the abosom with requests. Hence: You should not discriminate between those who help you).

1144. Ɔbosom pa na yɛkɔ akɔm to no.
*A good fetish we go to serve en masse.*
(A good thing is appreciated by all).

1145. Ɔbosom pa na yɛsosɔ ne soɔ, na nye ɔbosommɔne.
*A good fetish we praise but not a bad one.*
(We only acclaim what we believe to be good).

1146. Abosom bebrebe bɔ kuro.
*Too many fetishes destroy the town.*
(Too many cooks spoil the broth).

1147. Ɔbosomakoterɛ ho ntoma fata obiara.
*The cloth worn by the chameleon suits everyone.*
(A turn-coat agrees with everyone).

1148. Ɔbosomakoterɛ hunu asafoakwa a ɔtwe nwonom.
*When the chameleon sees palm branches prepared for a bed, it hides itself.*
(Everything hides from obvious danger).

1149. Ɔbosomakoterɛ hyɛ ɔhye a, ɔhye.
*If the chameleon is predestined to burn, it burns.*
(Predestination).

1150. Ɔbosomakoterɛ se: ɔde brebre bekɔ deɛ ɔfiri.
*The chameleon says: slowly, slowly, he reaches his destination.*
(Slow but sure).

1151. Ɔbosomakoterɛ se: "Onyankopɔn bɔɔ wiase na ɔnka ho, nti ɔtia asaase so a, ɔtia no brɛ brɛ".
*The chameleon says: "God made the world without his aid, and that is why, when he steps on the earth, he steps slowly".*
(If you don't own something, be careful how you use it).

1152. Ɔbosomakoterɛ se: "Ntɛm yɛ, ntoboaseɛ yɛ. Wotutu mmirika a wonya, wodwo w'ani nso a, wonya."
*The chameleon says: "Quick is good, slow is good. If you hurry you succeed, and if you are patient, too, you succeed".*
(More haste, less speed).

1153. Ɔbosomakoterɛ se: ɔye ahobrɛaseɛ ma Onyankopɔn nti na obiara nkyɛn no ahodeɛ.
*The chameleon says: he is humble before God, therefore no one is wealthier than he is.*
(Humility brings its rewards).

1154. Ɔbosomakoterɛ tumi dane deɛ ɛfura woɔ, na ɔntumi nnane deɛ ɛwo adaka mu.
*The chameleon can change color according to what you wear, but it cannot change according to the contents of the box.*
(The contents of the box are hidden. Hence: A witness can only give evidence of what he has actually seen).

1155. Ɔbosomakoterɛ wɔ awoɔ aduro a, anka ɔrebɛwo a, ne yam rempae.
*If the chameleon had medicine for delivery, it would not have its stomach split when giving birth.*
(If you can avoid trouble, you naturally do so).

1156. Bosome mmfiri faako.
*The moon does not appear in one place alone.*
(You cannot monopolize grace and favor).

1157. Ɔbosomfoɔ ka ne nkonim na ɔnka ne nkoguo.
*A priest tells of his triumphs but not of his failures.*

(People boast of success and keep quiet about their failures).

**1158. Ɔbosomfoɔ anom asɛm nsa da.**
*A priest's advice is never exhausted.*
(A good professional is never at a loss in his own profession).

**1159. Bosommɔne ntam ne: "Ka me fituom".**
*A bad fetish's oath is: "Swear on my loneliness".*
(An inefficient person shows up his own weakness).

**1160. Bosompo a ɔnni akoa, ɔno ara na ɔbɔ asorɔkye de pra ne fie anim.**
*The sea which does not have a slave, he alone makes the waves beat to sweep the entrance of his home.*
(Bosompo is the name of the Atlantic Ocean, which is an obosom because it is one of the children of Nyame, the sky-God. Hence: If you have no help you must do the work yourself).

**1161. Bosompo bɛtoo abotan.**
*The sea came to meet the stone.*
(The stone was there before the sea came. Hence: Size does not replace seniority. See Proverb 1160).

**1162. Bosomtwe ho nnua ara ne nketewa no.**
*The trees around (Lake) Bosomtwe are the small ones you see.*
(Sometimes an important man's supporters are all insignificant. See Proverb 1164).

**1163. Bosomtwe mu apaterɛ na yɛyi ma Nana Asantehene die.**
*The (Lake) Bosomtwe apaterɛ fish is what we give the Asantehene to eat.*
(A food fit for kings! A Chief is the first to profit from the produce of his own state. See Proverb 1164).

**1164. Bosomtwe na ɔnim n'akwan.**
*Lake Bosomtwe knows its own way.*
(Lake Bosomtwe in Asante is a lake formed by a meteorite and has no outlet. It loses water by evaporation, however. People there believe that it has its own secret way of escaping. Hence: Everyone knows their own business best. Or: Where there is a will there is a way).

**1165. Wobotabota wo ho a, wohwere dabrɛ.**
*If you scarify yourself, you lose a place to stay.*
(Scarification is produced by cutting the skin. "Bota" basically means "cut". Hence: If you have no mercy on yourself, others will not help you).

**1166. Abotan kɔtɔ: mewɔ adayɛ, m'akyiri twere boɔ, me yam fam aban.**
*The rock crab: I have a good situation, my back leans against a stone, my stomach clings to a stone house.*
(A man who has powerful protectors does not fear anything).

**1167. Aboterɛ ma nkonim.**
*Patience leads to success.*

**1168. Aboterɛ ma asɛm twa.**
*Patience leads to solving a problem.*

**1169. Aboterɛ ma awareɛ sɔ.**
*Patience makes a marriage succeed.*

**1170. Aboterɛ tutu mmopɔ.**
*Patience removes mountains.*

**1171. Abotesɛm nti na amaniannɔ mpue awia.**
*Because of abhorrence the rat does not come out of its hole in the daytime.*
(Said when someone stays at home rather than risk rudeness outside).

**1172. Botire nhommɔ mma berɛboɔ nka.**
*The head of the animal should not be over-cooked for the liver to remain.*
(The most difficult work is finished, then the easier work should be completed too).

**1173. Botire nyera nkwan mu.**
*The animal's head is not lost in the soup.*
(You don't lose sight of an important man. This proverb is often portrayed on stool paraphernalia such as linguist's sticks).

**1174. Abotokura bɔ fɛ a, ɛbi ka n'ani.**
*If the striped mouse injures someone, he also suffers from the action.*
(If you get your neighbor into trouble, you will, by all means, suffer too).

**1175. Abotokura ano wɔ borɔ, nanso no ho nyɛ hu nti yɛnsuro no.**
*The striped mouse's mouth is poisonous, but because it does not instill fear we don't fear it.*
(We judge by appearances. Or: We don't fear those who do not threaten us).

**1176. Botom-nam, woatwa na woantwa no yie a, sekan twa wo nsa.**
*Meat-in-a-sack, if you want to cut it and you don't cut it carefully (lit. well), the knife cuts your hand.*
(If you try to do things in a hidden way, you may come to no good).

**1177. Bɔwerɛ taa tu a, nsateaa na ɔhunu amaneɛ.**
*If the nail is constantly removed, it is the finger that suffers.*
(One man's downfall affects those nearest to him).

**1178. Bowerɛ tuatua nsateaa ano.**
*Nails are attached to the ends of the fingers.*
(One thing leads to another).

**1179. Bra ne brakyerɛ, nkwanta da mu.**
*Manner of life and how life ought to be lived are different things.*
(The fact and the ideal are different).

**1180. Ɔbra ammɔ yie a, na yɛdan abusuafoɔ.**
*If life is not going well, then we depend on the matriclan.*
(We fall back on those nearest to us in times of trouble).

**1181. Ɔbra bɔne sɛe ɔbra pa.**
*Bad behavior (lit. A bad life) spoils good.*

**1182. Ɔbra ne deɛ wo ara woabɔ.**
*Character (lit. life) is what you alone have formed.*

**1183. Ɔbra te se ahwehwɛ.**
*Life is like a mirror.*
(You get from life what you put into it).

# 64

# Proverbs of the Akans

**1184. Ɔbra te sɛ ntenten, yɛtete no nyansafoɔ.**
*Life is like a cobweb, we unwind it with wisdom.*
(Patience! It takes time to solve difficult problems).

**1185. Ɔbra yɛ bɔ-na.**
*Life is hard.*

**1186. Abrabɔ a, ɛwiee nnora no, n'ahyeaseɛ ne nnɛ.**
*If a way of life ended yesterday, the beginning is today.*
(If one way of life ends, another starts).

**1187. Abrabɔ ho nhoma-nhoma, yɛde anantenanteɛ na ɛtete mu.**
*A way of life's strings, we use walking about to tear them.*
(The strings of a way of life bind you. So: If you want to get on in life you have to make an effort).

**1188. Abrabɔ nyɛ bɔna a, anka akokɔ mo tɔma.**
*If a way of life were not difficult, then the hen would wear beads round her loins.*
(If we all had the same opportunities we would all have the same advantages).

**1189. Ɔbrane nkyere brane.**
*A strong man does not catch a strong man.*
(People of equal standing do not easily defeat each other).

**1190. Ɔbrane nni biribi a, ɔwɔ nhyɛsoɔ.**
*If the strong man has nothing else, he has the ability to oppress.*
(No strong person is powerless).

**1191. Yɛbrɛ di, na yɛmmerɛ mma yɛn yɔnko.**
*We get tired in order to eat, we don't get tired in order to give to our companion.*
(We work for our living and not to support others).

**1192. Wobrɛ odwanini ase a, womfa apɔnkye nyɛ aga.**
*If you overpower a ram, the male goat is of no consequence to you.*
(If you beat a strong man, you don't respect a weaker one).

**1193. Wobrɛ wo ho a na wonya wo ho.**
*If you are industrious you profit.*

**1194. Ɔbrɛ twa owuo.**
*Tiredness ends in death.*
(Don't overdo it!)

**1195. Brɛbrɛ ammaa, amaneɛ nso mma.**
*If tiredness has not come, trouble also does not come.*
(This proverb is ascribed to Asantehene Osei Tutu. Said when, if one thing hadn't happened, another wouldn't have happened).

**1196. Brebre yɛnnwa! Nyɛ nsɛm nyinaa na yɛka.**
*Abena Biri (Brebre) we don't grasp her hand. It is not all things that we mention.*
(It is said that Abena Biri (the dark), known as Brebre, was a favorite wife of a Dankyirahene. She was captured, but the Amakom and Tafo chiefs recommended she should be returned. However the Asantehene decided to keep her and he ruled that no one should touch her. The others were critical but could say nothing; so the proverb was coined to

use when you wanted to criticize high authority but were afraid to do so. Hence: If you want to criticize someone in authority you must do it in a circumspect way).

**1197. Brɛmanfoɔ hye bidie, na Konkorifoɔ nso we abebeɛ.**
*The Breman people make charcoal whilst the Konkori people eat water snails.*
(Everywhere has its own customs).

**1198. Ɔbrempɔn pagya akonnwa a, ɔnim deɛ ɛsie.**
*If a Paramount chief lifts the stool up, he knows its proper place.*
(An experienced person knows the correct thing to do).

**1199. Ɔbrempɔn rebɛwu a, na odwan tiri keka.**
*If the paramount chief is going to die, then the sheep's head moves.*
(When an important man dies many of his followers suffer).

**1200. Ɔbrempɔn yera a, yese watu kwan.**
*If a noble person is missing, we say he has travelled.*
(An important man is not disgraced).

**1201. Abrɛnsa nnom nsuo.**
*The person who brings alcohol does not drink water.*
(A donor shares his gift).

**1202. "Abridiabrada" na ɛma ɔkɔmfoɔ bu abugyen.**
*"Caning" led the priestess to a premature death.*
(A fetish priestess once started her possession by singing a song in which she included the words "beat me." The crowd took it literally and beat her to death. Hence: Careless words may lead to disaster).

**1203. Yɛrebu Ahafo nkuro a, yɛmmu Adorobaa no, na ɛfiri sɛ ɛhofoɔ firi Kumase.**
*When we are considering the Ahafo towns, we don't include Adorobaa, because the people there come from Kumasi.*
(You don't count your own people among strangers).

**1204. Wobu bɛ kyerɛ onyansafoɔ a, ɔnkyɛre aseɛ te.**
*If you speak in proverbs to a wise man, he does not take long to understand.*

**1205. Wobu ohiani kwasea a, ɔde ma Nyame.**
*If you treat a poor man as a fool, he will complain to God.*
(God protects the poor).

**1206. Wobu wo ho kokuroko a, na yɛde akuma twa woɔ.**
*If you think yourself great, we will take an axe to fell you.*
(Pride comes before a fall).

**1207. Wobu wo ho kokuroko a, wotɔ mpenteneso.**
*If you think yourself great, you die an accidental death.*
(Pride comes before a fall).

**1208. Wobu wo ho kokuroko a, wotua piredwan.**
*If you think yourself great, you will pay a piredwan (fine).*
(A piredwan is a large amount. Hence: If you act big you have to pay a lot for it).

**1209. Wobu ɔkaa dua a, wowie we.**
*If you break the tail of the fish, you finish eating it.*
(Once started, a job must be finished).

**1210. Wobu kɔtɔ kwasea a, Onyame hwɛ wo to.**
*If you cheat a crab, God sees your bottom.*
(You have to bend over to get at a crab's hole. Hence: If you deceive the helpless you will surely get your punishment).

**1211. Wobu ɔkwasea bɛ a, ɔbisa wo asɛ.**
*If you speak to a fool in proverbs, he asks for an explanation.*
(Wisdom is for the wise).

**1212. Wobu na woammobɔ na wohye a, wobrɛ.**
*If you fell (trees) and you don't cut them into pieces and you burn them, you exhaust yourself.*
(A burnt tree is very hard to cut up. Hence: If you don't do a job properly at first, the job will be more difficult later. Or: Laziness prolongs a task).

**1213. Yɛbu nam a, wose kɔtɔ!**
*We are talking of meat and yet you mention crab.*
(We are talking of important things; don't bring in irrelevant trifles).

**1214. Wobu wo sekantia animtia a, ɛbota wo.**
*If you regard your short cutlass as unimportant, it cuts you.*
(If you despise a servant he serves you ill).

**1215. Ebu so a, ebu ma deɛ ɛyɛ ne dea.**
*If things are abundant, they are so for the owner.*
(Warning against taking what is not yours, even if there is plenty).

**1216. Wobu wo suman asumamma a, ɛkyɛ wo.**
*If you imply that your amulet is a poor amulet, then it will take vengeance on you.*
(Don't underestimate and therefore antagonize a friend).

**1217. Wobu wo yɔnko aboa a, ɔbu wo sɛbeɛ.**
*If you regard your companion as a beast, he will regard you as mere dirt.*
(You get what you give in life).

**1218. Yɛmmu ahahan nhyɛ ɛsono anom na yɛnyi.**
*We do not break leaves and put them in the mouth of an elephant and then withdraw them.*
(You don't placate a powerful man and then insult him).

**1219. "Memmu ɔpanin" yɛse: "Asɛm bɛba da bi!"**
*(To) "I do not respect an elder" we say: "Trouble will come one day".*
(If you don't respect the elders, then when you're in trouble, they will not give you advice).

**1220. Worebua ada a, wonse sɛ: "Mekyiri nkoa aduane".**
*If you are going to bed hungry, you don't say: "I taboo the food of slaves".*
(In adversity, all men are equal).

**1221. Abua se: "Nnipa nyinaa nom me nanso wɔmpɛ me nyɛ aga".**
*The pipe says: "All people smoke me but they don't regard me".*
(This is said by someone whom everyone makes use of without gratitude).

**1222. Abuada tenten nte ayika so.**
*Long fasting does not reduce the debt of funeral rites.*
(Fasting is one thing and debt-paying another).

**1223. Bubɛ ne Tebɛ te kurom a, tɔkwa mpa.**
*If Proverb-maker and Proverb-hearer stay in the same town, there is bound to be trouble.*
(Bubɛ makes proverbs and Tebɛ understands (lit. hears) proverbs. Hence: Experts seldom agree).

**1224. Abubummabaa adaka, sɛ ɔnweneeɛ na ɔkɔɔ mu o, sɛ ɔkɔɔ mu na ɔnweneeɛ o, obi nnim.**
*The bag-worm's case, if it wove it and went inside, or if it went inside and then wove it, no one knows.*
(These insects belong to a family of moths known as the Psychidae which is very well represented in Africa. The female is fat and maggot-like and never leaves the bag in which she develops, which looks like a little bundle of sticks. The male is winged but has a very short life and dies after fertilizing the eggs the female has laid, and which replace her in the bag before her death. Hence: Which came first, the chicken or the egg?)

**1225. Obuo nyɛ suro.**
*Respect is not fear.*

**1226. Aburobia ahahan kɔ kwaem a, na anwonomo ahahan reba ofie.**
*When the canna leaves go to the forest, the anwonomo leaves come back to the house.*
(This refers to the custom of exchanging gifts between town and village. The canna is a decorative town plant and the anwonomo is used for wrapping kenkey and other things in the village. Hence: We give presents and we receive them too).

**1227. Burodua dodonku se: "Woto me twene a, mɛsan maba".**
*The empty corn-cob says: "If you throw me away, I return".*
(A new crop will grow. Individuals die but the family will flourish).

**1228. Aburokyire a merekɔ, ɛnhia me; mpoano na ɛhia me.**
*(The thought of) Europe, where I am going, does not distress me; it is the sea shore that distresses me.*
(See Proverb 597. Used when it is the means and not the ends for which you are working that worries you).

**1229. Aburokyire adeɛ, ɔha damma, nanso ne mmaeɛ mu na ɛhia.**
*European goods, a hundred for damma, but the way of importing them is hard.*
(See Proverb 597. Damma is a small sum. Hence: What your eye can see, your hand cannot easily touch).

**1230. Aburokyire nyɛ kɔna, na po.**
*To go to Europe is not a hard thing, except for the ocean.*
(See Proverb 597. If you do not have the means of doing something, you find a good excuse).

**1231. Oburomsonsɔn nni yɔnkoɔ a, ɔfa ɔforoteɛ yɔnkoɔ.**
*If the Western Hartebeeste has no companions, he joins the company of the kob antelope.*
(If your associates are absent, you are forced to mix with similar strangers).

**1232. Oburoni a ɔte aborɔsan soɔ, se ɔwu a, na ɔbɛda fam.**
*The white man who lives in a story building, when he dies, lies in the ground.*
(Death the Leveller).

**1233. Oburoni a ɔtɔn yiwan tiri tumi fu gu ne kɔn mu.**
*The white man sells razors yet his hair grows down his neck.*
(Just because you sell something, it does not mean that you make use of it).

**1234. Oburoni adeɛ sɛe a, ɛgu po mu.**
*If a white man's things spoil they are poured into the sea.*
(Whatever goes on is within the orbit of the person most concerned).

**1235. Oburoni rekɔ aborokyire a, yɛmmane no.**
*If a European goes overseas, we don't send him for something.*
(You don't ask a stranger for a favor).

**1236. Oburoni nyansa a gyina kroyɛ so.**
*The wisdom of a white man depends on his ability to bring people together (lit. to make a settlement).*
(Power needs strong backing. See Proverb 1118).

**1237. Aburowne aburow, nanso ɔpeburoo nko ara na ɛpesɛ ɔpɛ berɛ.**
*Maize is maize, but only the maize grown during the harmattan blossoms during the harmattan.*
(People flourish best in the best environment for them).

**1238. Aburow de ne mpɛsɛ rekum nnuadewa.**
*Corn is killing the garden eggs with its tassels.*
(When corn is first planted other smaller vegetables are sometimes grown between. Said when a big man buys up or destroys a humble one).

**1239. Aburowdwane, yɛnti ani.**
*We don't test dry corn with our nails.*
(It is too hard. Hence: If a problem is hard, you must take it seriously).

**1240. Aburowdua ne ho a, ɛtoto.**
*If corn plants itself, it fails to thrive.*
(If someone needs looking after and insists on being on their own, they don't thrive. Or: An orphan does not thrive).

**1241. Aburowahahan, yɛmmɔ no pɔ.**
*The corn leaf, we don't tie it in a knot.*
(Don't expect something from a person which they cannot give).

**1242. Aburowwɔ hɔ yi, yɛyam a, yɛmfrɛ no Aburowbio.**
*Corn as it is, if we grind it, we don't call it corn any more.*
(As people develop they change their status).

**1243. Aburowfua na yɛbu no aburopata.**
*It is through one grain of corn that you fill the corn store.*
(However big the family it originates from one ancestor).

**1244. Aburowfua na ɛyɛ [ɔsan]/[aburowpata].**
*A grain of corn will fill a [storehouse]/[cornshed].*
(Great things grow from small beginnings. Many a mickle makes a muckle).

**1245. Aburowfua tɔ akoa.**
*One grain of corn buys a slave.*
(Everything starts from small beginnings).

**1246. Aburopata hye a, ɛka mmurofua ɔha.**
*Though the cornhouse is burnt, a hundred grains remain.*
(You cannot destroy a whole race).

**1247. Aburuburo kosua: "Adeɛ a ɛbɛyɛ yie nsɛe da".**
*The dove's eggs: "What is destined to prosper cannot be destroyed".*
(Predestination).

**1248. Aburuburo Kwaakye, ɔse: "Adeɛ a ɛwɔ woɔ nyera da".**
*The dove Kwaakye says: "What belongs to you will never be lost".*
(What you are destined to achieve, you will achieve).

**1249. Abusua dɔ funu.**
*A matriclan loves a corpse.*
(As soon as you are dead, people praise you, alive they may let you starve).

**1250. Abusua dɔ wo a, na wɔkyɛ ka a, wɔma wotua bi.**
*If the matriclan likes you and they have a debt, they let you pay part of it.*
(If you are to gain respect, you have to accept responsibility. Or: Friendship brings responsibility).

**1251. Abusua-dua yɛntwa.**
*The tree of the matriclan, we do not cut it.*
(Your family remains your family whatever individual members do. We do not disparage our origins).

**1252. Abusua hwedeɛ gu nkurawa na me nko me deɛ na ogya da mu.**
*The grass of the matriclan grows in groups, mine alone is burning.*
(The family should be united, but my part of it is in conflict).

**1253. Abusua kyɛ di wie a, na ato agorɔ.**
*If the matriclan finishes taking all they can, then they play.*
(When people have got all they can out of you, they cease to bother about you. Or: When problems are dealt with, we can take pleasure).

**1254. Abusua kyɛ ka na wɔnkye adedie.**
*The matriclan shares a debt but they don't share an inheritance.*
(Members of a family share a funeral debt, but it is the individual members who inherit. Hence: A family solves problems as a group, but the benefits go to individuals).

**1255. Abusua kyiri ka.**
*The matriclan taboos debt.*

**1256. Abusua nkyiri: "Fa w'abususɛm kɔ".**
*A matriclan does not taboo: "Take your calamity and go".*
(There is nothing wrong in getting rid of a bad thing).

1257. Abusua nkyiri "Fa w'adeɛ kɔ", nanso wɔsane de ne nyinaa bɛbɔ mu.
*The matriclan does not taboo "Take your things and go," but all belong together.*
(Your family is your family, whatever happens).

1258. Abusua nyinaa yɛ abusua, nanso yɛhwɛ mmɛtema so deɛ.
*Every member of a matriclan is matriclan, but we discriminate in favor of those who are nearest.*
(There is rank and precedence in every organization).

1259. Abusua te sɛ kwaeɛ: wowɔ akyiri a, ɛyɛ kusuu; wopini ho a, na wohunu sɛ dua koro biara wɔ ne siberɛ.
*The matriclan is like the forest: if you are outside, it is dense; if you are inside you see that each tree has its own position.*
(When you know people intimately you know their individual characters but to a stranger they may all seem alike).

1260. Abusua ti ne deɛ ɔbɔ ntampɔ.
*The head of the matriclan is he who strives hard.*
(A hard worker has the respect of all).

1261. Abusua twene, yɛde afafa na ayere; nanso yɛde dadeɛ nkonta ka a, ɛnsuane.
*The matriclan drum is covered in spider's webs; and yet when it is beaten with iron sticks, it does not break.*
(No matter how high feelings are in a family's quarrels, the family does not split up).

1262. Abusua yɛ dɔm, na wo na ba ne wo nua.
*The matriclan is widespread, but your own mother's child is your sibling.*
(In times of need you have to rely on the more intimate family group rather than on more remote relations).

1263. Abusua ayɛ nkɔnsɔnkɔnsɔn: nkwa mu a, ɛtoa mu; owuo mu a, ɛtoa mu.
*The matriclan is like a chain: in life they are joined; in death they are joined.*
(An expression of the strength of the Akan family links, which join those who have gone, those who are here, and those who are to come).

1264. W'abusua nyɛ a, wonto ntwene.
*If your matriclan is no good, you don't throw it away.*
(Your family is your family, good or bad).

1265. Abusuafoɔ kyɛ wo ka tua a, na woasopa.
*If the matriclan shares in paying your debt, you are disgraced.*
(If you are careless about paying debts, people won't respect you).

1266. Abusuafoɔ kyɛ wo ka tua a, wɔn ani nso wo mma.
*If the matriclan shares in paying your debt, they disrespect your children.*
(Like father, like son).

1267. Wo busuani ne abebeɛ a, anka worenka sɛ ɔmfa ne to ntena akonnwa so.
*If your relative were to be a water snail, then you would not ask him to sit on a stool.*
(You don't deliberately embarrass your relatives).

1268. Abusuapanin mpene kɔm.
*The head of the matriclan does not groan from thirst.*
(The man at the top can by all means get enough to satisfy himself).

1269. Obusuyɛfoɔ bɛtena wo fie a, yɛde kosua ne ɛtɔ na ɛpamo no.
*If an evil person comes to stay in your home, we get rid of him with eggs and mashed yam.*
(These offerings are given to the fetish. Hence: Sacrifice is necessary to get rid of evil).

1270. Busuonini tɔn adeɛ a, busuonini na ɔtɔ.
*If a scoundrel sells things, a scoundrel also buys them.*
(Birds of a feather flock together).

1271. Abususɛm nti na yɛmfa asantrofie mma fie.
*It is because of the taboo (against it) that the nightjar is not brought into the house.*
(A warning against bringing trouble into the home. The nightjar is a bird of ill omen).

1272. Yɛmmutu baabi nnwa na yɛadane baabi adwa.
*We don't flay in one place and then turn to another to do the same thing.*
(Every job has its appropriate place).

## - D -

**1273. Woda adagya a, wotɔ ntoma mono.**
*If you are naked, you buy plain cloth.*
(Necessity bars choice).

**1274. Woda fam a, wonse sɛ mesɔre a, mɛbo wo.**
*If you are lying on the ground, you don't say when I rise up, I will beat you.*
(You don't boast in a position of disadvantage or defeat).

**1275. Woda nkudaa mu a, woma noko due.**
*If you have an old sore, you never giving condolences to the soft rotted plantain stem.*
(The plantain stem was formerly used to cover wounds. Hence: One person's problem involves another).

**1276. Woda na w'ani nkum a, na wote mmoadoma su.**
*If you lie down and you are not sleepy, then you hear the birds sing.*
(You only pay attention to something outside if you are not interested in what you are doing).

**1277. Woda na asaaseboa ka wo na wotu no to gyam a, na woda a, w'ani kum.**
*If you sleep and a ground insect bites you, if you pick it and put it in the fire, then you are able to lie down and sleep.*
(It's only when you have dealt with a problem that you can really rest).

**1278. Woda na woso daeɛ pa a, ka kyerɛ nnipa pa; na woso daeɛ bɔne a, aka wo tirim.**
*If you sleep and dream a good dream, tell it to good people; but if you dream a bad dream, keep it to yourself.*
(Good news is always worth spreading, bad news is best kept private).

**1279. "Yɛbɛda anaa sɛ yɛbɛkɔ?" hunu sɛ deɛ ɔkaa kane no, na ɛye n'asɛmpa.**
*"Are we going to sleep or we are going to go?" knows that what he says first is what he really means.*
(Your immediate reaction is likely to be the most honest).

**1280. Woda pata ase na nkyene pore gu w'anom a, wompore ngu.**
*If you are lying beneath the shed and bits of salt fall into your mouth, you don't spit them out.*
(Be grateful for a good thing, however you obtain it).

**1281. Woda ɔsa ano a, ɛsoso w'adaeɛ.**
*If you are a war-leader (lit. if you sleep at the battle front), you have a special sleeping place.*
(A leader is given special treatment).

**1282. "Meda ase, Afi": yɛnse no kwa.**
*"Thank you, Friday born": we do not say without reason.*
(You don't thank someone unless they have done something for you).

**1283. Ɛda wo yɔnko kɔn ho a, wose ɛda bankye akorɛ mu!**
*If the burden lies on your companion's shoulders, you think it lies between the forks of a cassava stick!*
(Said to someone who lacks feeling for another's trouble).

**1284. Yɛnnaeɛ a, yɛnso daeɛ.**
*If we do not sleep, we do not dream.*
(If an occasion does not arise, we don't take the action rising out of it).

**1285. Yɛnna afa mpere afa.**
*We don't sleep at one side and fight for the other side.*
(Once you have chosen your place, keep to it).

**1286. Ɛda a wobɛfura ntoma pa no, wonhyia w'ase.**
*The day you put on a beautiful cloth, you don't meet your mother-in-law.*
(We seldom hit the right time to do the right thing).

**1287. Ɛda a onipa bɛgyae adidie no, na n'asɛm asa.**
*The day that man stops eating, all problems cease.*
(Death solves every problem).

**1288. Ɛda onipa tenten benya, tiatia renya.**
*The day a tall man gets something, a short man does without.*
(One man's meat is another man's poison).

**1289. Ɛda a yɛsi ɔhene no, ɛda no ara na yɛfa adwen a yɛde bɛtu no.**
*The day on which we enstool a chief is the same day that we start planning to destool him.*
(As soon as a man gets power people make note of every fault he commits, until they get enough to use to get him out again).

**1290. Ɛda a woresisi akyakya no na akyakya nso gyina hɔ rehwɛ wo.**
*The day that you cheat a hunchback, another hunchback stands there watching you.*
(Don't think you can get away with bullying the weak, they are, after all, members of a family whose other members may act against you).

**1291. Ɛda a ntoa teɛ no, ɛda no ara na danka bɔ.**
*The day the belt breaks the gunpowder flask breaks.*
(If a powerful man falls, those dependent on him also suffer).

**1292. Ɛda a woretu afu adaka mu no, na afu te hɔ rehwɛ wo.**
*The day you ransack the hunch-back's box, another one sits and watches you.*
(See Proverb 1290).

**1293. "Da bi mɛnya wo," nyɛ nnɛ asɛm.**
*"One day I will catch you," is not today's problem.*
(Sufficient unto the day is the evil thereof).

**1294. Da koro adwuma nyɛ adwuma.**
*One day's work is not work.*
(Only constant labor brings success).

**1295. Da koro na yɛhunu ɔmanni.**
*In one day we get to know a fellow citizen.*
(Friendship comes quickly when you have something in common).

**1296. Da koro yɛ ɔkafoɔ fo.**
*One day is cheap for a debtor.*
(In time of difficulty even a small relief gives great pleasure).

**1297. Da sɛ nnɛ nti na yɛhwɛ obi anim nom nsasin.**
*Because of next week we look at someone's face and drink a half bottle.*
(Because we hope for more in the future we accept less in the present).

**1298. Ɔda mfinimfini nna fam.**
*The one who sleeps in the middle does not sleep on the floor.*
(If you are secure you don't fear anything).

**1299. Daakye bi nti na yɛyɛ papa.**
*Because of some time in the future we behave generously.*
(You help others hoping they will help you in the future if you need it).

**1300. Daakye asɛm nti na yɛpɛ ɔyɔnko pa.**
*Because of what may happen in the future, we value a good companion.*
(Friendship is a provision for the future).

**1301. Ɔdaamani biara nyɛ abɔfra.**
*No middle-aged person is a child.*
(Be your age!)

**1302. Ɔda-ayeya mfa ka.**
*The one who lies on her back incurs no debt.*
(Used of someone who does not commit any fault or do anything which leads them into debt).

**1303. Daban da aburokyire a, ɔtomfoɔ dea.**
*If an iron bar lies abroad, it belongs to the smith.*
(The smith is the only one who can use the iron. Thus if there is a serious case to be settled only the chief has the power to arbitrate).

**1304. Daban da hɔ a, ɛda asɛm so.**
*If the iron bar lies there, it lies there for a reason.*
(You don't leave something valuable lying about for no reason).

**1305. Dabi asɛm nti na yɛdi kwadu a, yɛgya ne hono.**
*Because of the future, when we eat a banana, we leave its skin.*
(There is a story of a man who was left alone in a woman's house and was given bananas to eat. He kept the skins and when later he was accused of eating her ripe plantain he produced them to prove he could not have consumed both. Hence: Said when you need to keep evidence for future reference).

**1306. Dabi asɛm nti na yɛto kwadu a, yɛgyam ho.**
*It is because of the future that when we come across a banana tree we prune it.*
(You care for things which may help you in the future).

**1307. Ɔdabɔ se: "Ɔbɔmmɔfoɔ, wo nam a, bobɔ bɛdɛ saa ara". Ɔbɔmmɔfoɔ nso se: "Ɔdabɔ wo nso, ɛyɛ a, deda adukurom saa ara".**
*The bay duiker says: "Hunter, as you go along, continue making baskets (for meat) like that." The hunter then says: "Bay duiker, you too, if that is good, you also keep on sleeping in the buttress of a tree like that".*
(When one man provokes another, he will retaliate).

**1308. Dabodabo na ɔkaa n'asɛm: sɛ yɛwo tɔ yɛn ti.**
*It is the duck that says: if we give birth, we do so for our own sake.*
(The duck is supposed to be a bad mother who sends her young ahead of her. Hence: Children are an insurance against the future and old age).

**1309. Dabodabo se: ɔrenna na owuo awia no.**
*The duck says: it does not sleep lest death steals it.*
(Said of an unnecessarily fearful person who worries about the inevitable).

**1310. Dabodabo se ɔrenhwete na wadidi.**
*The duck says it is not scratching before it eats.*
(Said of someone who will not stoop to work for others in order to eat).

**1311. Adadowa kyiri deɛ ɔhunuu no.**
*A slow-grower hates the one who has recognized him.*
(A person with disadvantages dislikes the one who recognizes them).

**1312. Ɔdaadaafoɔ na ɔgyegye adeɛ ma ɔpempɛnsifoɔ.**
*It is a swindler who collects things to give to the usurer.*
(Birds of evil feather flock together).

**1313. Ɔdaadaafoɔ na ɔma onipa horan.**
*A flatterer (lit. swindler) makes a man arrogant.*
(Flattery corrupts).

**1314. Ɔdaadaafoɔ na ɔsɛe adamfoɔ.**
*A swindler spoils a friend.*
(Dishonesty corrupts others).

**1315. Dadeɛ, yɛse no boɔ so, na yɛnse no nku so.**
*Iron, we sharpen on a stone but not on shea-butter.*
(Use appropriate tools for the job).

**1316. Dadewa wɔ hɔ yi, anka ɔyɛ panin, na asaa na amma no ahunu ne panin.**
*The nail is the elder, but it is the hammer that has made him lose his position.*
(If it were not for one person's oppression, another would not prospered).

**1317. Dadewa mu dɔnkɔ ne deɛ adeɛ ahia no.**
*The slave among nails is the single one which is needed.*
(Amongst the whole family the unlucky one becomes the victim of circumstances).

**1318. Dagyaweɛ nse kwaterekwa sɛ: "Bɔ me bosea".**
*A naked person does not say to a nearly-naked person: "Make me a loan".*
(The poor are not in a position to help each other).

**1319. Adaka hini deɛ ɔdeɛ.**
*The box opens to its owner.*
(A man reveals himself only to those who have a right to know).

**1320. W'adaka si aburokyire a, deɛ ɛwɔ mu nyinaa wonim.**
*If your box is overseas you still know everything that is in it.*
(You know what is yours, wherever it may be).

**1321. Adam bere afanu a, anka yɛbɛto no piredwan.**
*If the cockle shell were to become red on both sides, then we would have to pay a piredwan for it.*
(Red cockle shells were a popular form of decoration on belts and other stool paraphernalia. A piredwan is a large sum. Hence: If something appreciated for its beauty were doubly beautiful, you would have to pay much more for it).

**1322. Adam mmere afanu.**
*The cockle shell does not become red on both sides.*
(You cannot expect people to be one hundred percent good).

**1323. Damma ankɔ a, piredwan mma.**
*Unless a damma goes a piredwan won't come.*
(A damma is a small amount, a piredwan a large one. Hence: You don't get anything unless you give something. A little generosity or output brings a great return).

**1324. Damaram te ase dada a ɔse ɛrebere, na ɛnteɛ ne sɛ woahwie ngo agu soɔ.**
*If Ashanti Blood (Mussaenda erythrophylla) has been there for a long time and has ripened, how much more so when you have poured palm oil on it.*
(Red stands for anger. In Twi, I am angry is: "My eyes are red." Hence: If you are naturally quarrelsome, how much more so when you have a real cause).

**1325. Damenam da n'amena mu.**
*The dweller in a hole sleeps in it.*
(A self-contained person need never worry).

**1326. "Adamfoɔ, adamfoɔ" ɛne me nnɛ.**
*"Friend, friend" has brought me to my present condition (lit. it is my today).*
(If you are over-friendly, you may lose out in the long run).

**1327. Damfoɔ anyɛ yie, na baafoɔ.**
*Even a comrade is not respected, how much less an acquaintance.*
(If you don't consider those intimate to you, you won't consider a stranger).

**1328. Nnamfoɔ baanu goro ɔbaa baako ho a, ɛde ntoto ba.**
*If two friends flirt with one woman, then quarrels come.*
(Sexual jealousy spoils friendship).

**1329. W'adamfowaa repɛ wo atu wo ne fie a, na ɔse: "Yi wo kyemfrɛ awia mu".**
*If a hostess wishes to eject you from her house, then she says: "Take away your broken pot from the sunshine".*
(If you want to take action against someone you often give trivial pretext for doing so, rather than the real reason, so that they seem to have provoked the trouble).

**1330. Dammirifua firi tete, ɛmfiri nnɛ.**
*Condolences are from ancient times, they are not from today.*
(The causes of events come from the remote past).

**1331. Ɛdan wɔ aso.**
*Walls have ears.*

**1332. Ɛdan nyɛ a, ɛnte sɛ dɔtɔ.**
*Even if the building is not good, it is not like the thicket.*
(Any shelter is better than none).

**1333. Wodan wo na ka a, wokɔto w'agya die.**
*If you request your mother to pay what she owes you, the request goes to your father.*
(It is the boss who has to pay in the long run!)

**1334. Wodane okusie amoakua a, ɔrennane da.**
*If you try and turn a rat into a ground squirrel, you will never succeed.*
(You can't change a man's real nature).

**1335. Yɛnnane ka, ntua ka.**
*We do not demand a repayment, to pay a debt.*
(Don't rely on unreliable means of paying debts).

**1336. Ɔdanka worawora worawora a, na biribi wo mu.**
*If the powderhorn rattles, there is something inside.*
(There is no smoke without fire).

**1337. Adanko na ɔwɔ aso, momfrɛ no na ɔmmɛkyerɛ asɛm ase.**
*It is the hare that has ears, let us call him so that he can explain things to us.*
(If you are doubtful about something, call on the elders to explain it, for after all they have spent much time listening to wisdom).

**1338. Adanko se: obi gye obi nkwa.**
*The hare says: someone saves someone else's life.*
(We are all interdependent).

**1339. Adanko se: "Mmoa wɔ hɔ nti na nnipa wɔ hɔ".**
*The hare says: "Because animals are there, human beings are there".*
(We all depend on something else for our existence and yet we all think we are more important than anyone else).

**1340. Dankwansere da nkwan mu nwene ne se a, ɔnka sɛ nkwan mu da na ɛyɛ no dɛ, na mmom ɔse: "Owuo! obi nnim!**
*If the fruit bat lies in the soup and shows its teeth, it does not say that it likes lying in the soup but rather it says: "Death! Nobody knows!"*
(The teeth of this bat are long and pointed and when it is cooked it seems to smile; hence its name lying-in-the-soup-smiling. This is a warning against complacency-your turn may come any time).

**1341. Dankyira bɔmmɔfoɔ anya biribi a, na ɛfiri obirekuo.**
*If the Dankyira hunter does not get game it is because of the Senegal coucal.*
(The bird warns the animals of the hunter's approach. Hence: Said of someone who interferes and so prevents the successful outcome of a venture, though he reaps no benefit from his actions).

**1342. Dankyira anomaa-werɛmfoɔ, ɔnni yɛnfoɔ, nso aprɛmo resiane no.**
*The miraculous bird from Dankyira, it has no guardian, but the cannons protect it.*
(This refers to the time of the European occupation of the castles on the Ghanaian coast, where those within range of the cannons were protected by them.)

"Anomaa-werɛmfo" is the name given to one of the Akan goldweights of a bird carrying cannons on its back and (sometimes) a gunpowder keg in its beak. (The symbol is also used by some chiefs in stool paraphernalia). Hence: An exceptional person receives protection from unexpected quarters).

### 1343. Dankyiraman abɔ na taasɛn!
*Even the Dankyira State is shattered, how much more the pipes.*
(Don't complain of small troubles when there are plenty of big ones to deal with).

### 1344. Adanse nkɔtɔwa-nkɔtɔwa: obiara butu ne bɔn ano.
*The small crabs of Adanse, each one clings to its own hole.*
(In the early days, the Adanse chiefs were small but independent and only came together under one leader in time of war. Hence: Said of people who value their own individual independence).

### 1345. Adanseɛ nti na mmoadɔma ne ɔkɔtɔ si nkonnwa.
*Because of witnessing that is why animals and the crab sit in council.*
(The crab is reputed to have a good memory. Hence: You need to invite a neutral person to give an impartial view of a case).

### 1346. Adansehyɛ nti na sɛ kurotwiamansa kɔdidi hahan mu wie a, ɔbene kwankyɛn no.
*It is because of producing a witness that the leopard, when it finishes eating in the bush, defecates by the wayside.*
(You have to do something to let people know of your achievements).

### 1347. Adansekurum nua ne amanehunu.
*Perjury's brother is trouble.*
(Once you start lying, you can't avoid trouble).

### 1348. Ɔdansini [nam n'afuru so na ɔwuo]/[ɔwu n'afu].
*A witness dies because of his belly.*
(In the old days a man had to take an oath that he was speaking the truth. If he was proved wrong, he could lose his life. Hunger might tempt him to lie or to take bribes. Hence: A man in need must take risks to live).

### 1349. Ɔdansini mu wɔ adeɛ a, anka ɔkoterɛ nkɔdi ohia.
*If there were something profitable in an unfinished house, then the lizard would not suffer from poverty.*
(If something can't bring wealth, then there is no point in sticking to it).

### 1350. Ɔdanta nya akyiginafoɔ a, ɔkum abɔprɔn.
*Once the danegun gets someone to fire it, it kills the great animal.*
(You need a backer to achieve great things).

### 1351. Darewa a, ɛnam nhyɛ ano ntumi mmɔ ɔkaa.
*A hook which has no meat cannot catch a fish.*
(You have to bait a trap before it can be successful. Hence: You cannot achieve an objective without preparation).

### 1352. Adasamma ani kyiri sɛbeɛ, nso obiara wɔ bi gu ne yam.
*Human beings hate the sight of excreta, but everyone has it in their stomach.*
(Certain things are part and parcel of life, whether we like it or not).

### 1353. Adasamma nim nsɛm ka; wonya wo ho a, ɔse woyɛ obusufoɔ, ɛhia wo nso a, wɔse wayɛ ɔkrabirifoɔ.
*Mankind knows how to make remarks; if you are rich, they say you are an evil person, if you are poor, they say you are a blackguard.*
(Wealth is not virtue, and poverty is not dishonesty. Hence: Put not your trust in appearances!)

### 1354. Dasɛnnɛ nsuo nti na yɛpunu ahina mu.
*Because of this day week's water, we smoke out the water pot.*
(If you smoke the water pot and keep water in it, it gradually becomes good tasting. Hence: We embark on a tedious job because we know we shall profit from it eventually).

### 1355. Dasusuo wo ba a, amansan gye no tu.
*If a wise person gives birth to a baby, the citizens make use of it.*
(The advice of a wise man is appreciated by all).

### 1356. Dawuro se: "Deɛ ɔne me ka-o, deɛ ɔne me nka-o, obiara te me nka a, ɔwɛn n'aso tie me".
*The gong-gong says: "The person who agrees with me, or the person who does not agree with me, when they hear me being beaten, they both have to pay attention and listen to what I have to say".*
(You have to listen to news, good or bad, for you cannot know its nature unless you do).

### 1357. Ɔdawuro ton-ton-san-san, yɛhwehwɛ mu deɛ dɛ na yɛabo.
*The gong-gongs, we search through them to pick and beat the one which sounds best.*
(You choose people for their qualities to work for you).

### 1358. Wode w'adeɛ yɛ wo ho adeɛ a, yɛnkyi.
*If you use what is yours, we do not object.*

### 1359. Wode wo ba ma aponkyerɛne a, ɔwo akorosee.
*If you give your child to a frog in marriage, she gives birth to a long legged frog.*
(In the old days all marriages were arranged and this was a warning against careless arrangements).

### 1360. Yɛde abasakɔnmu na ɛsrɛ akɔdaa adeɛ.
*We put an arm around its shoulders (lit. We use putting-arms-round-the-shoulders) when asking a child for something.*
(Affection is the quickest way to success).

### 1361. Yɛde abeseweɛ na ɛbɔ nnawuta.
*We use cola-chewing when we beat the twin gong-gong.*
(Some things are only used on serious occasions).

### 1362. Wode obi ka na wosom no som pa a, ɔde woka kyɛ wo.
*If you owe someone and you serve him well, he forgives you your debt.*
(Good service will bring its reward).

### 1363. Yɛde biribi na ɛyɛ biribi.
*We use something for doing something.*
(Some actions cannot be performed without help).

1364. **Wode dadu wɔ borɔdeɛ a, ɛrennane bayere da.**
*If you take ten days to beat plantain, it will not turn into yam.*
(You can't make a silk purse out of a sow's ear).

1365. **Wode ɛdɛ yɔ dɔkono-kankyeɛ a, yɛbu no dɛ so.**
*If you use sweetness to make kankyeɛ-kenkey (a kid of sweet kenkey) we eat it with enjoyment.*
(If you try and make people happy they respond).

1366. **Wode w'adeɛ gya ɔkorɔmfoɔ a, ɔnna mfa.**
*If you leave your things with a thief, he does not take them any more.*
(If a man feels trusted, he does his best to live up to the trust).

1367. **Yɛde aderɛ na ɛpere asaase.**
*We use the cutlass in struggling for land.*
(If something gives you your livelihood you should look after it properly).

1368. **Wode adɔyɛ kɔ awareɛ a, wonya aware pa.**
*If you take loving-kindness to get married, you will have a happy marriage.*
(What you give you get).

1369. **Yɛde aduane na ɛgye ahɔhoɔ.**
*We use food to get a stranger (to visit).*
(If you have nothing to offer people they won't come to you).

1370. **Wode odwantire ma deɛ ɔdie a, akɔma tɔ.**
*If you give the sheep's head to the right person, peace reigns.*
(When a sheep is slaughtered and the parts distributed, there is a correct part to give each person. Hence: If you do what is expected of you, you'll have no trouble).

1371. **Yɛde dwannwoma na ɛsrɛ dabrɛ.**
*We take a sheepskin to beg for a sleeping place.*
(If you go somewhere and you are prepared, you are more likely to get what you want).

1372. **Yɛde ɛdwono na ɛyɛ panin a, anka obi nsene asɔkwa panin.**
*If white hair denotes old age, then there is no one older than the white crested hornbill.*
(Appearance is not the only thing that counts).

1373. **Yɛde Ɔfe ho nsuo na ɛnoa n'adwene.**
*It is the water from the Ofin River that is used to cook its fish.*
(It is quite in order to promote a project with its own proceeds).

1374. **Yɛde ngo na ɛdɔn mpɔmpɔ.**
*We take oil to anoint the boil.*
(If you want someone to help you, you take something to them first).

1375. **Wode w'agorɔ hyɛ ɔtwea a, ɔtafere w'ano.**
*If you play too much with a bitch, it licks your mouth.*
(If you are too familiar with a servant, he or she takes advantage of it).

1376. **Yɛde ogya na ɛyi ɛwoɔ.**
*We use fire to collect honey.*
(Bees have to be smoked out before you can collect their honey. Hence: If you want profit you must invest capital).

1377. **Wode ogya to akyekyedeɛ akyi a, na wohunu ne nam.**
*If you put fire on the shell of a tortoise, then you see its meat (body).*
(If you want to find someone, you must take the appropriate measures).

1378. **Wode Agyaakwaa a, yɛnnyae wo kwa.**
*If you are called Dragon-fly, we don't let you go scot-free.*
(There's a pun here. The word for dragonfly sounds like: Leave him free. Just having a good name doesn't guarantee that you'll get the best treatment).

1379. **Wode ahahan bɔ kahyire soa bɛmu a, w'apampam tu kuro.**
*If you use a leaf as a carrying pad to carry the bunch of palm nuts, the top of your head becomes sore.*
(See Proverb 550. If you don't provide proper means of doing something, you suffer).

1380. **Yɛde hia na ɛbua Asante atɛn.**
*Poverty makes us (lit. we take poverty to) give a verdict against the Asante.*
(The Asantes were much feared. Hence: It needs courage to give verdict against a dangerous man, and you only do so when you can't avoid it).

1381. **Yɛde hia na ɛdi ɔkrampa aduane.**
*Poverty makes us (lit. we take poverty to) eat a vulture's food.*
(Beggars can't be choosers).

1382. **Yɛde hia na ɛmo ntampehoma.**
*Poverty makes us (lit. we take poverty to) wear a rope tied round the loins.*
(Want may make us do unattractive things. See also Proverb 1381).

1383. **Yɛde hia na ɛware akyakya.**
*Poverty makes us (lit. we take poverty to) marry a hunchback.*
(See Proverb 1381).

1384. **Yɛde hia na ɛwe dɛnkyɛmmoɔ.**
*Poverty makes us (lit. we take poverty to) chew crocodile's stones.*
(The crocodile is supposed to swallow a stone each year and stones are found in the stomachs of crocodiles. Hence: When you are destitute you take whatever you can get. See also Proverb 1381).

1385. **Wode hia twetwe seperewa a, n'ahoma te.**
*If out of poverty (lit. you take poverty to) you pluck the lute strings, they tear.*
(If your need makes you over-zealous, you destroy your opportunities).

1386. **Wode wo ho bɔ ɔwɔbiefoɔ na ɛhia wo a, ɛnnere wo.**
*If you befriend rich people and you are in need, you need will not be great.*
(The rich man's friend does not go hungry).

1387. **Yɛde ahoɔden na ɛpɛ sika a, anka Akurufoɔ nyinaa anya wɔn ho.**
*If we were to use only strength in making money, then all the Kru people would be rich.*
(The Kru people of Sierra Leone are known along the West Coast of Africa for hard work at fishing and manual

labor. Yet they remain poor. Hence: If brawn counted more than brain, the strong would be wealthy).

**1388. Wode ahopopoɔ pɛ adeɛ a, wosiane ho.**
*If you use haste to get things, you miss them.*
(Haste does not achieve anything).

**1389. Wode hwimhwim adeɛ a, basabasa bisa wo.**
*If you act in a hurried way confusion will seek for you.*
(Gently does it).

**1390. Wode ka dwoa na wonya mu taku a, na aka dwoa-hwan.**
*If you owe dwoa and you are able to repay taku out of it, there remains less than dwoa.*
(Dwoa is a large amount, taku a small one. Hence: Every little bit counts).

**1391. Wode ka na wohunu tutu a, obi nte wo nka.**
*If you owe a debt and you are able to put off paying, no one hears about it.*
(If you are discrete you can get away with a lot).

**1392. Wode ka na wo se te, na wo yere te a, na woawie fɛre.**
*If you owe someone and your father hears of it, and your wife hears of it, then your shame has ended.*
(If you bring something into the open it no longer seems so fearful).

**1393. Wode ka na wotua a, na woho adwo wo.**
*If you have a debt and you pay, you have peace of mind.*
(You cannot really relax when you owe someone something).

**1394. Yɛde nkate-dodoɔ na ɛdi amim.**
*If we have plenty of ground-nuts, we cheat.*
(If people think you are rich, they do things for you in anticipation of a reward; but you may not give it to them).

**1395. Yɛde akokoɔduru na ɛbɔ korɔno.**
*We need bravery to be a burglar.*
(Don't involve yourself in a risky enterprise unless you have plenty of courage).

**1396. Wode kokurobotie kɔ ayie a, yɛde sotorɔ gya wo kwan.**
*If you attend a funeral with your thumb, you are received with a slap in the face.*
(Don't deliberately insult people. They will respond in like manner. Pointing your thumb at someone is an insult).

**1397. Yɛde kokuroko na ɛdi amim a, anka yɛde ɔdade si dan.**
*If we use mere bulk to cheat we should use the baobab tree for building a house.*
(This tree, many parts of which are used for food, medicine, water storage, canoes, rope, cattle food, etc. is not suitable for house building. At times wisdom is more important than mere bulk).

**1398. Yɛde kokuroko na ɛdi anim a, anka ɛsono bɛba fie.**
*If mere bulk were paramount then the elephant would have come into the haunts of man.*
(If bulk were the most important thing then the largest would be supreme).

**1399. Wode nkontompo kyekyere a, gye sɛ wode nokorɛ na ɛsane.**
*If you take falsehood to bind something up, then you take truth to untie it.*
(If you do harm and you wish to restore your reputation, you must first try and put things right).

**1400. Wode nkontompo pata nokorɛ a, ɛntwa.**
*If you use lies to drive away truth, you don't succeed.*
(Truth is more powerful than lies).

**1401. Wode nkontompo pɛ adeɛ mfe apem a, ɔnokwafoɔ gye wo nsam da koro.**
*If you seek a thing for a thousand years through falsehood, the honest man takes it from your hand in a day.*
(Honesty is the best policy).

**1402. Wode nkontompo tu kwan a, woyera.**
*If you start a journey in dishonesty, you get lost.*
(See Proverb 1401).

**1403. Yɛde akorɔkorɔ na ɛgye akɔdaa nsam adeɛ.**
*We use tact to take something from a child's hand.*
(If you need something belonging to a difficult person, you have to use a tact to get it).

**1404. Yɛde nkotodwe refrɛ Nyankopɔn mpo, ɔmma, na ɛnte se kyekye batakari.**
*Even when we use kneeling to invoke God, he does not come, how much less so if we use a bark smock.*
(The bark smock is worn by a fetish priest. Hence: Even those who know those in power find it difficult to get what they want. Those without support find it impossible).

**1405. Wode wo kraa ka, na woantua a, ɔfa wo abofu.**
*If you owe your female slave a debt and you don't pay it, she becomes angry with you.*
(Even a slave has rights).

**1406. Yɛde ɔkraman ho fɛ na ɛtɔ no.**
*We consider a dog's beauty before we buy it.*
(We judge the look of a thing before we obtain it).

**1407. Wode kunkumaboɔ bɔ adwe a, wohwere adwe, fa nsamfi.**
*If you use a ball of clay to crack a palm kernel, you lose the kernel and get a dirty hand.*
(Use the right tools for the job).

**1408. Wode nkwan pa pia hwennorɔ a, wonna nhua asra.**
*If you use good soup to bring up mucus, then you don't need to trouble to take snuff.*
(A strong well-peppered soup, like snuff, will clear the nasal passages. Hence: If you use a good method first, you don't need to use any other).

**1409. Yɛde akyire gya wo a, ɛnka wo nko.**
*If we leave you as a caretaker you are not regarded as being alone.*
(If you represent someone then you add their standing to yours).

**1410. "Wode me a, na wode asɛm", yɛmfa nka asɛm.**
*"If you rely on me then you will have confidence", we don't regard it as serious.*
(Boasting is different from reality).

**1411. Wode wo mena a, wode hwe wo ho mpɛn aduasa.**
*It is your own whisk, you may choose to strike yourself thirty times with it.*
(It is your own funeral if you want to hurt yourself with your own possessions).

**1412. Wode me nam resɛe me yɛ koowaasɛm.**
*You go about spoiling me (my name) is gossiping.*
(Don't gossip in any form).

**1413. Wode amoakua yɛ nkatekwan a, na ɔkɔ n'abusua mu.**
*If you use the ground squirrel for peanut soup, it goes into its own matriclan.*
(Said of someone who is in his own element).

**1414. Yɛde mmɔtɔ reyɛ biribi a, wose dufa.**
*Where we are using juju, you talk of medicine.*
(We are dealing with serious matters and you talk of insignificant ones. See Proverb 1213).

**1415. Yɛde nna dane na ɛka akɔdaa nwoma soɔ.**
*We use tricks to have sexual relations with a young girl.*
(It's easy to fool the naive).

**1416. Yɛde nnɛ adeɛ ma ɔkyena.**
*We take today's things to give to tomorrow.*
(If you don't succeed today, try tomorrow).

**1417. Yɛde ani ketewa na ɛhunu adeɛ.**
*We use the pupil of the eye to see things.*
(It is a small part of what we use that is essential).

**1418. Wode w'ani mmienu hwɛ toa mu a, ɛkoro bɔ.**
*If you use two eyes to look into the bottle gourd, one becomes blind.*
(If you don't concentrate on one thing at a time, you lose by it).

**1419. Wode w'ani mmienu hwɛ toa mu a, wonhunu mu asɛm.**
*If you look into the bottle gourd with your two eyes, you don't see what is inside it.*
(You can only look through the hole with one eye at a time. Hence: If you are over eager you may lose all).

**1420. Wode w'ani to obi kwansɛn so a, wobuada.**
*If you rely on someone else's soup pot, you go hungry to bed.*
(Don't depend on others; they will disappoint you).

**1421. Wode w'ani to wo twɛ so a, wobuada.**
*If you rely on your vagina, you go hungry to bed.*
(See Proverb 1420).

**1422. Wode w'ano dɔ nwerɛ a, ɛbi nwɔ wo.**
*If you weed thorns with your mouth, none of them pricks you.*
("Weeding thorns with your mouth" means just talking about weeding. Hence: Saying is different from doing).

**1423. Wode anobrɛbrɛ tutu ka a, wofa di.**
*If you use tact to pay a debt, you are relieved of it.*
(A soft tongue helps to get you out of trouble).

**1424. Wode nokorɛ di asɛm a, ɛtwa.**
*If you use truth in settling a matter, it settles easily.*

**1425. Wode nokorɛ tutu ka a, wɔbra wo, nanso w'asɛmpa ara na woaka no.**
*If you use truth to settle a debt, they disgrace you, but it is the truth that you have spoken.*
(The way you are treated does not alter the truth of your case).

**1426. Wode nsa frɛ wo bosom na wamma a, na ba ara na ɔremma.**
*If you use drink to invoke a fetish and it does not come, then it has decided not to come.*
(If you use the normal way of doing something and it does not work then it means you are not going to succeed).

**1427. Wode wo nsa ma bɛmu so na woanhwɛ yie a, bɛtema wɔ wo.**
*If you lift up a bunch of palm nuts in your hands and you are not careful, you are pricked by them.*
(Dangerous matters should be handled carefully).

**1428. Wode wonsa bɛte apem ne-adu na yɛtwa kɔtɔkora ma wo a, wonse sɛ: "Ɛyɛ tia".**
*If you are going to remove the hornet's nest with your hand and we cut a hooked stick to give you, you don't say: "It is short."*
(Don't look a gift horse in the mouth).

**1429. Wode wo nsa to wo to a, na woawie atantanneɛ.**
*If you touch your anus with your hand, then you have touched all filthy things.*
(Your own disgrace is as shameful as a stranger's. Or said of a situation which is the worst you can ever expect to handle).

**1430. Wode wo nsa to yarefoɔ aduane mu a, wodi no prɛko.**
*If you put your hand into a sick person's food, you eat it all.*
(One does not withdraw from risk once one has committed oneself).

**1431. Mede me nuaba ama wo aware no a, na mense sɛ: "Di me turumu ka ho".**
*If I give you my sister to marry, I don't say "Use my anus as well".*
(If you do someone a favor, it does not mean that you are willing to do even more).

**1432. Yɛde ntoma dibere na ɛhunu ne boɔ.**
*We consider the quality of a cloth before determining its price.*
(Value is based on real quality not first appearances).

**1433. Yɛde nyansa na ɛkyere nantwie.**
*We use wisdom to catch a cow.*
(You need tact in dealing with a difficult person).

**1434. Yɛde nyansa na yɛsɔ nnyansii mmienu ano wɔ suminaso.**
*We use wisdom to make a fire out of two pieces of wood on the rubbish heap.*
(You need skill to solve a problem).

**1435. Wode safoa to bamma ho na wodi asɛm a, wohunu ano.**
*If you place a key besides the stoop during arbitration, you succeed in solving the case.*
(Wisdom is the key to the solution of a problem).

**1436. Wode sebɔ nwoma sua adwini di a, na wode awie.**
*If you start leather work with leopard skin, you must keep it up.*
(What you start well you must finish well. If you use the best materials you are expected to do fine work).

**1437. Wode sekan twa na antwa a, wofa akuma.**
*If you take the cutlass to cut and it does not cut, then you take the axe.*
(If you can't do a thing one way, do it another).

**1438. Wode asɛm kyɛ a, na womfaa hwee nkyɛɛ.**
*If you forgive a wrong action, you have not done anything to your disadvantage.*
(It is always good to forgive and it does you no harm).

**1439. Wode w'asɛm ma Onyame a, ɔdi ma wo na ntɛm na ɛnyɛ.**
*If you take your problem to God, he solves it for you, but not quickly.*
(God works at his own pace to answer your requests).

**1440. Yɛde asɛm pa na ɛpɛ otwitwagyefoɔ.**
*We use good manners to find a redeemer.*
(If you behave decently people will support you in time of need).

**1441. Wode si anim kyekyere na anyɛ yie a, wode to ho kyekyere.**
*If you cannot join two pieces by the ends you do it by the sides.*
(Where there is a will there is a way).

**1442. Wode sie, de sie a, ɛfa porɔ.**
*If you are always hiding things (lit. hide things, hide things), a part rots.*
(If you are stingy, you lose by it).

**1443. Wode sika tɔ ɔdɔ a, ohia na eseɛ no.**
*If you buy love for money, poverty spoils it.*
(A fair-weather friend is no friend).

**1444. Yɛde sika-mono na ɛsisi [mpoatwafoɔɛ]/[mpɛɛwadifoɔ].**
*We use ready cash to cheat a [greedy man]/[petty trader].*
(If a greedy person sees "physical cash", he will take it even if it is not enough).

**1445. Wode sono nwoma rebu kotokuo, na wode deɛn ahyɛ mu?**
*You are using an elephant's skin to make a bag, then what will you put inside?*
(Don't have ideas above your station in life).

**1446. Yɛde nsuonwunu na ɛfra nsuohyeɛ mu.**
*We mix cold water with hot water.*
(If someone is angry you try and cool them down, not make it worse).

**1447. Wode suro di adɔna a, yɛde wo sekan dwa apetebie.**
*If you fear to show displeasure they use your knife to skin a striped squirrel.*
(If you are not tough, people will take advantage of you in small things).

**1448. Yɛde ntamkeseɛ reka asɛm a, wose: "Meka agya nnan".**
When we use the great oath to enforce our point, you say: "I swear on my father's legs".
(Swearing the Great Oath of Asante was a most serious affair and could lead to your death if what was said was proved untrue when the case was taken before the Paramount Chief. Don't confuse important with trivial matters. See Proverb 1213).

**1449. Wode tenten sesa tiatia a, wonya.**
*If you exchange tall for short, you succeed.*
(If you give more than you get, there is no problem).

**1450. Wode wo tɛkrɛma ma ɔman na woregye a, wɔmfa mma wo.**
*If you give your tongue to the State and you want to get it back, they don't give it to you.*
(If you serve well, people do not want you to retire).

**1451. Yɛde tɛkrɛma pa na ɛwɛn tiri.**
*We take a good tongue to protect the head.*
(With tact we can keep out of trouble).

**1452. Wode tɛkrɛma si asowa a, wontumi mpɔn no.**
*If you pledge your tongue, you cannot redeem it.*
(If you give away your capital, you have nothing to redeem it with).

**1453. Wode tire ma tire wura a, akoma tɔ.**
*If you give the head to the person who is entitled to it, peace reigns.*
(If you follow protocol, there is no trouble).

**1454. Wode atirimuɔden pɛ sika, na wonya bi a, wode adɔyɛ na ɛpa w'aniso aniwuo.**
*If you use hardheartedness to acquire wealth and you get it, you use benevolence to save your face.*
(Not all giving comes from the heart).

**1455. Wode wo tuo bɔ mmɔkwaa gye aboa basa a, ɛpae.**
*If you lend your gun in order to get an animal's foreleg, it bursts.*
(If out of need you part with your capital, you may lose it).

**1456. Yɛde wanterema na ɛyi asaaseboaa.**
*We use long grass to trap the ground insect.*
(Children poke a grass into the hole of this insect, which makes it come out. Hence: There is a right implement for every job).

**1457. Yɛde ayaaseduro na ɛhyɛn abɛn.**
*We blow the horn on a full stomach.*
(A man must eat to work properly).

**1458. Ɛde nka anom.**
*Sweetness does not remain in the mouth.*
(You can't have it good all the time).

**1459. "Ɔdɛ wɔ do," "Ɔdɛ wɔ do", na ɛmaa aboa no wee wisa tema.**
*"Sweetness is further on", "sweetness is further on", made the animal eat the whole bundle of guinea pepper.*
(Constant anticipation of something better makes it possible to endure present suffering).

**1460. Ade-bɔne yɛtɔn no abosiri.**
*A bad thing we sell cheaply.*
(Used in advising people to produce only the best).

1461. Ɔdebɔnyɛni dwane wɔ berɛ a obi mpam no.
*An offender runs away when he's not being pursued by anyone.*

1462. Wɔdeda onipa wie ansa na wɔadi n'adeɛ.
*You see to a person's burial before you inherit from him.*

1463. Ɔdedeɛ nnane akoa.
*The owner does not turn into a slave.*
(If you have authority, you are respected).

1464. Adedie ba a, na abusua hunu "Ɛmfankɔ".
*When (the question of) inheritance arises, the matriclan gets to see "Don't take it away".*
(Different circumstances bring different reactions).

1465. Adedie ba a, na yɛhunu Tawia ne Abamoba.
*When (the question of) inheritance arises, we distinguish between Tawia and Abamoba.*
(Tawia is a child born after twins; Abamoba is literally the child of the twin fetish, so a twin. Hence: Individual competition occurs within the family when inheritance is in question).

1466. Adedie kata ɔhene mmɔfra so.
*Enstoolment (lit. inheritance) covers-up the youthfulness of a chief.*
(Authority makes people forget the one in authority's past misdemeanors).

1467. Adedie mu wɔ adanseɛ.
*Inheritance has a witness.*
(If a person is given a post in the public eye, he is likely to be open to public inquiry).

1468. Adedodoɔ nyɛ mfone.
*Plenty is not nauseating.*
(Things in themselves are neither good nor bad, it is your attitude that makes them so).

1469. Ademadeɛ nhwere ɔdansefoɔ.
*A witness is not denied his legal reward.*
(A laborer is worthy of his hire).

1470. [Ɔde-ne-man]/[Deɛ ɔde ne man] nsɛe no.
*[The Head of a State]/[He who controls the state] does not destroy it.*
(You don't destroy what gives you your power and position).

1471. Deɛ waba da koro, anom asɛm nsa da koro.
*He who comes on one day, his words don't get finished in that day.*
(You don't get easily bored with a stranger).

1472. Deɛ aba pɛn na yɛde kaakae mmɔfra, na nyɛ deɛ ɛyɛ afotosɛm ma wɔn.
*What has happened before is what we teach the children, and not what they themselves have experienced.*
(You don't have to tell people what they already know).

1473. Deɛ aba pɛn na ɛsan ba.
*What has happened before happens again.*
(History repeats itself).

1474. Deɛ ɔbarima pɛ na ɔyɔ.
*Whatever a courageous man desires to do, he does.*
(A determined man gets his way).

1475. Deɛ aberewa pɛ na ɔpotɔ die.
*Whatever an old woman likes, that is what she prepares and eats.*
(The older we get the more we rely on our own individual tastes).

1476. Deɛ obi de adaduasa anante aduro no, yɛ obi afikyire.
*What someone has taken thirty days to reach, is another person's back yard.*
(People's fortunes differ).

1477. Deɛ obi wɔ na obi nni bi, na ɛnyɛ deɛ obi nim.
*What someone has another may not have, but it not the same with what someone knows.*
(Knowledge can be shared).

1478. Deɛ obi ayɛ na yɛhwɛ ne so yɛ.
*What someone has done and we can see, we copy.*
(We learn by precept).

1479. Deɛ obiara pɛ na ɔnya a, anka kɔkɔsakyi di Nankwaasehene.
*If anybody could get what they wanted, then the vulture would be Chief of the Slaughterhouse.*
(If wishes were horses, beggars would ride).

1480. Deɛ wabɔ di bi.
*The one who has cooked takes a little.*
(The person who produces should have his share).

1481. Deɛ wabɔ fam na ɛdam butu n'ano.
*He who has been ruined, madness comes from his mouth.*
(When you have nothing to lose, you speak irresponsibly).

1482. Deɛ wabɔ fɛ na ne werɛ bɛfiri n'amumuyɔ a, nyɛ deɛ wɔabɔ no fɛ a.
*If the person who has wounded another forgets his offence, at least the one who has been harmed will not forget.*
(You forget your own sins but not those committed against you).

1483. Deɛ wabɔ ka awuo no, yɛmmisa n'akyiri adeɛ.
*He who has died through debt, we don't ask for his inheritance.*

1484. Deɛ wabɔ nsaa na yɛda no aseɛ na nyɛ deɛ wadi abuada ama yɛn.
*He who has given a funeral donation is the one whom we have to thank and not he who has fasted for us.*
(Practical support is more appreciated than sympathy).

1485. Deɛ abɔfra pɛ na ɔtotɔ.
*That which a child likes, he buys.*
(Everyone has their own taste).

1486. Deɛ yɛmmoro no, yɛnsum no.
*He who should not be beaten, we don't push him.*
(If you decide to respect someone, you do so wholeheartedly).

1487. Deɛ borɔfere abubu aguo no, yɛnkɔ hɔ anyina.
*Where the pawpaw has been felled, we do not go to look for firewood.*
(You can't get blood out of stone).

**1488. Deɛ wabrɛ ntɔ deɛ wabrɛ adeɛ.**
*An experienced person (lit. a tired person) does not buy another experienced person's goods.*
(Wise people cannot deceive each other).

**1489. Deɛ n'Aburowbaa kane na ɔde ayamuɔnwono baeɛ.**
*The person whose maize grew first, brought about meanness.*
(The first person to commit an offence is the one who is copied by others).

**1490. Deɛ woda a, ɔde ne nsa si wo soɔ no wonyane a, n'anim na wohwɛ.**
*The one who touches you with his hand while you sleep, is the one whose face you look at when you wake up.*
(You confide in those you know best).

**1491. Deɛ wada a, n'ani nkum na nnakorokoro nya no.**
*He who has gone to bed and does not feel sleepy, then sleeplessness takes him.*
(If you are not serious in your intentions, you attribute your shortcomings to another).

**1492. Deɛ ɔda adansini mu nsuro kurohyɛ.**
*He who sleeps in an uncompleted room does not fear the burning of the village.*
(If you have nothing to lose, you have nothing to fear).

**1493. Deɛ ɔda ne gya na ɔnim sɛdeɛ ɛsi hyehye no fa.**
*He who lies by the fire knows how it burns.*
(The man who is suffering alone knows the extent of his sufferings).

**1494. Deɛ ɔda nsuo mu nsuro awɔ.**
*One who stays in the water does not fear cold.*
(You don't fear what you are used to).

**1495. Deɛ ɔnna na ɔnim deɛ ɔnna.**
*He who does not sleep understands he who does not sleep.*
(Like understands like).

**1496. Deɛ ɔdasani pɛ ne nnim.**
*What human beings like is to be famous.*

**1497. Deɛ ɔde n'adeɛ de benkum na ɛgyeɛ.**
*The owner of a thing accepts it with the left hand.*
(It is very rude to use your left hand to give or accept a gift, to eat or to point the way with, as this hand is regarded as dirty. If however something is yours, you can collect it in any way you choose).

**1498. Deɛ wode bɛdi asɛmmɔne na woatete sika ama dibɛm no, fa di asɛmpa na wo sika ntena hɔ nnwen.**
*If you are going to do bad things to someone and to pacify them with money, far better to do good things and to save the money.*
(Do what is right the first time and you will not waste time and money).

**1499. Deɛ ɔde n'agosenewa regye a, wɔnse sɛ: "Me ngo wɔ mu".**
*If the owner of the small palm oil pot wants to have it, you don't say: "My oil is in it".*
(Remember when you borrow something it is not yours for keeps).

**1500. Deɛ ɔde ahwedeɛ baa fie na ɔde nwansena baa fie.**
*He who brought sugarcane into the house brought the fly into the house.*
(Something which is attractive may have inherent disadvantages).

**1501. Deɛ ɔde nkankammadeɛ baeɛ, na ɔde nwansena baeɛ.**
*He who brought the bad smell also brought the flies.*
(The person who causes trouble is responsible for what follows after).

**1502. Deɛ ɔde akokoɔduru hyia abɛbrɛsɛ kwan no, abɛbrɛsɛ ma no poma ma ɔde huri ɔno ara amena.**
*He who uses courage to meet hardship on the way, hardship gives him a stick for him to jump over fate's trench.*
(With courage you can face up to every adversity in life).

**1503. Deɛ ɔde ne kraman na ɔyi n'ano kaseɛ.**
*He who owns a dog takes a bone from his mouth.*
(The person who has authority over you is the person who can tell you what to do).

**1504. Deɛ ɔde n'amaneɛ nnyae faba.**
*The habitual criminal cannot leave off procuring.*
(Once a thief, always a thief).

**1505. Deɛ ɔde n'ani na ɔfee aseɛ.**
*He to whom the eye belongs can pull down the skin below it.*
(Certain intimate actions can best be performed by oneself).

**1506. Deɛ ɔde ne ti, na ɔnim mu asɛm.**
*He to whom the head belongs, knows what goes on inside.*
(Only you can know your own thoughts).

**1507. Deɛ adedie wɔ na, owuo wɔ.**
*Where there is inheritance, there is death.*
(Used where one thing implies another).

**1508. Deɛ adeɛ ahia no na ɔtu akwamfo.**
*It is the man who needs something who must search for it.*
(A man is most conscientious over the things which concern him personally).

**1509. Deɛ ɔresu su kɔso ara ne nsɔresm.**
*He who weeps cannot weep beyond the cemetery.*
(Even sorrow has its limits. Or; Death defeats sorrow).

**1510. Deɛ adeɛ atɔ n'ani no, nyɛ ɔno ara na ɔyie.**
*He who has got dust in his eyes cannot blow it out himself.*
(Some tasks you are unable to do yourself and you must have help to do them).

**1511. Deɛ adeɛ wɔ no, na ɔdie, na ɛnyɛ deɛ ɛkɔm de no.**
*He who owns a thing eats, not he who is hungry.*
(It is ownership and not need which counts).

**1512. Deɛ ɔdi bem nsoa odwan.**
*The one who is acquitted never carries the sheep.*
(The sheep in this case would be the fine on the one found guilty. Hence: An innocent man does not have to bear court expenses).

1513. Deε wadi dwiratwε dware mprεnsa ansa na wakɔ ahemfie.
*A person who has had intercourse on an Odwira day, bathes three times before he enters the chief's palace.*
(A person who has offended custom must pacify the elders before he is accepted back in society).

1514. Deε wadi fɔ na ɔkasa.
*He who is guilty is the one who has much to say.*
A guilty man will try and talk himself out of a situation.
(A warning against believing what a man you think is guilty, says).

1515. Deε ɔbεdi fufuo, yεnkame no apesie.
*The one who is going to eat fufuo, we don't keep other starch foods from him.*
(If someone is going to be given the best and he chooses the less good, we don't refuse him).

1516. Deε wadi "agyiratwe" dwa mmisa "ntakuo" nan.
*He that has traded agyiratwe does not turn back for ntakuo.*
(Agyiratwe is a large and ntakuo a small amount. Hence: A person who has flourished does not descend to a lower level of trade).

1517. Deε wadi kan na yεtu n'akyire gya.
*He who takes first place is the one whose fire we take.*
(We ask help from the most successful).

1518. Deε ɔdi kan pori a, deε odi akyire hwε yie.
*If the leader stumbles, the follower takes care.*

1519. Deε wadi akankyeε ka sε ɔbedi ɔkraman bini a, yεnnye no akyinnyeε.
*If the one who eats ripe-plantain kenkey says he will eat a dog's stools, don't doubt him.*
(The two things look much alike! Hence: Don't doubt someone who has proved themselves in similar circumstances).

1520. Deε ɔdi nkokɔ no, ɔnam a, na ɔso nkokɔbuo.
*He who eats chicken, when he is travelling he carries the coop.*
(You make provision for what is important to you).

1521. Deε ɔdi nkonkonte se ɔbedi samina a, yεnnye no akyinnye.
*If someone eats cassava dough and says they will eat soap, do not argue with them.*
(See Proverb 1519).

1522. Deε ɔdi kɔtɔkɔ akyiri mmisa ɔwea.
*The one who follows the porcupine does not ask for the tree bear.*
(You don't change allegiance from a stronger power to a weaker).

1523. Deε ɔdi akyire sua deε ɔdi kan nanteε.
*He that follows behind learns to imitate the walk of the one in front.*
(We copy those we follow).

1524. Deε wadi asono asono (ahodoɔ) mmiεnsa se ɔbεdi aduonu a, yεnnye no akyinnyeε.
*If he who has eaten seven times three says he will eat twenty, we don't doubt him.*
(If someone can do great things we know he can achieve anything less).

1525. Deε wadi asuo mu kan nnom nsufi.
*He who has gone to the river first, does not drink dirty water.*
(First come, first served).

1526. Deε ɔbedi wo ti, se ɔbεdi wo forɔ a, wonnye no akyinnye.
*If he who would eat your head says he will eat your bottom, don't contradict him.*
(If a person is capable of performing one important act, he can perform a lesser one).

1527. Deε ɔdi wo dabiara di wo a, εnyε ya.
*He who has sexual intercourse with you habitually, does not cause pain.*
(Familiarity makes things easy).

1528. Deε ɔredidi awuo no, yεnkame no aduane.
*He who eats before dying, we don't deny him food.*
(Even a dying man has his rights).

1529. Deε εdɔm rebo no aku no, na yεbɔ no bie, na nyε deε wɔrebo no agyae no.
*He who is being beaten to death by the mob, is the one who we beat a bit but not the one who is being beaten and let go.*
(Be careful in maltreating anyone who can retaliate).

1530. Deε εdɔm ako afa no nkyε agyapadeε.
*He who is a prisoner of war does not give away his heirlooms.*
(If you are confined away from home, you cannot dissipate your goods).

1531. Deε wodua, εno ara na woteε.
*What you sow you reap.*

1532. Deε odwan gyina na ne ba gyina.
*Where the sheep stands, her lamb stands.*
(Like father, like son).

1533. Deε ɔdwan pε na ɔde ne fufuo boɔ.
*Where the sheep likes, there he makes himself white.*
(You do as you please with yourself).

1534. Deε wadwane na ɔnim deε ɔhunta.
*He who has escaped knows where he hides.*
(You know your own intentions best).

1535. Deε ɔredwane na yεpamo no na nyε deε ɔte faako.
*We chase someone who is running away and not someone who stays in one place.*
(We persecute those who show weakness, not those who remain firm).

1536. Deε woafa aboa no, εhɔ ara na wodwa no.
*Where you have taken an animal is where you flay it.*
(You deal with a problem on the spot).

1537. Deε yεfa Tanɔ na yεgyae n'Amoa.
*Where we take the Tano fetish is where we leave his Amoa fetish (his wife).*
(You take something to its place of origin).

1538. Deε ɔfa owufoɔ tuo na ɔfa ne kunafoɔ.
*He who inherits a dead man's gun, also takes his widows.*
(A man who inherited someone's property in the old days, and sometimes today, took on responsibility

for or married the widows. Hence: One thing follows logically on another).

**1539. Deɛ womfɛre no ɔkoto deɛ wofɛre no akyi.**
*One you don't feel shy of hides behind the one you feel shy of.*
(You work to get what you want through people you know are respected by the person you want help from).

**1540. Deɛ ɔrefiri o, deɛ ɔrema amono o, deɛ ne dea se ɔnna ntɔn.**
*Whether it is to him who buys on credit or to him who pays on the spot, the owner says he will no longer sell.*
(Used when someone has decided not to do something and no amount of persuasion will change their mind).

**1541. Deɛ ngohina sie, yɛnto hɔ aboɔ.**
*Where an oil pot stands, you don't throw stones.*
(Or: Don't cause trouble in a delicate situation).

**1542. Deɛ agyan rewɔ no na ɔham.**
*He whom the arrow pierces draws in his breath.*
(The person who suffers reacts to his suffering).

**1543. Deɛ ɔregyeɛ amma a, deɛ ɔrema remma.**
*If the collector does not come, the donor does not come either.*
(It takes two to make a bargain).

**1544. Deɛ ɔgyegye mo no, ɔno ara na ɔkyɛ mo.**
*He that collects rice, it is he alone who shares it out.*
(The one who starts a job should finish it).

**1545. Deɛ yɛgyina gye adadeboɔ no, ɛhɔ na yɛfiri dwane.**
*Where we stand to receive bullets, it is there that we escape the danger.*
(If you stand firm, you can free yourself from trouble in the long run).

**1546. Deɛ ɔgyina hɔ na ɔde adefom ba.**
*One who is standing up is the one who initiates grabbing.*
(A person who is prepared for action initiates it).

**1547. Deɛ ɔgyina hɔ na ɔhwe aseɛ na nyɛ deɛ ɔda hɔ.**
*He who is standing is the one who can fall down, not he who lies on the ground.*
(He that is down needs fear no fall. The person who has most stands to lose most).

**1548. Deɛ ɔgyina akono nsuro owuo.**
*He who stands in the battle-front does not fear death.*
(A brave man does not fear death).

**1549. Deɛ yɛgyina we dwannam no, ɛhɔ ara na yɛgyina gye akoraboɔ.**
*The place you stand to chew mutton is the same place that you receive bullets.*
(There is a positive and a negative side to everything).

**1550. Deɛ ɛhia Dankyira Kyei na ɔdekɔ abeɛ mu.**
*What is necessary to Kyei (from) Dankyira is what he puts into his chanting.*
(Dankyira Kyei was a well-known singer at the court of Dankyirahene Ntim Gyakari. He was known for making new innovations in his songs. Hence: You use what seems good to you to achieve your aim).

**1551. Deɛ ne ho adwo no se: deɛ ɔresiripɛ yɛ anyɛn.**
*A person without problems says: the one who is sleepless is a devil.*
(Witches and devils fly by night. Some people who have trouble sleeping resent those who have none and make accusations against them).

**1552. Deɛ ahoɔden kyiri ne kɔm.**
*That which strength fears is hunger.*
(Everyone has a weak point).

**1553. Deɛ wahunu bi pɛn se: "Ɛmmra ma yɛnhwɛ."**
*One who has seen something before says: "Let it come and we shall see."*
(An experienced person is not afraid of what he knows).

**1554. Deɛ wahunu bi pɛn sɛ yɛkyiri.**
*He who has seen things before can say we taboo (something).*
(Experience allows you to judge a situation).

**1555. Deɛ wahunu nhunu mprenu.**
*The thing which you have once experienced does not happen twice.*
(One should not make the same mistake twice).

**1556. Deɛ wahunu apem nkamfo ɔha.**
*One who has seen a thousand does not praise a hundred.*
(A rich man does not appreciate a small gift).

**1557. "Deɛ yɛahunu ni!" ɛmpa ahennie mu da.**
*"Wonders will never cease!" never leaves chieftaincy.*
(People in authority hear many strange things).

**1558. Deɛ wahwɛ wo ama wo se afifiri no, wo nso wohwɛ no ma ne deɛ tutu.**
*The person who has reared you and made you grow teeth, you also must look after them when they lose their teeth.*
(You must care for those who have cared for you).

**1559. Deɛ wohwɛ n'anim a nisuo ba na wosu kyerɛ no.**
*A person in whose presence you are able to weep, you weep for them to see.*
(It is to the person who you believe will help you that you tell your sorrows).

**1560. Deɛ ɔhwehwɛ nyansa akyiri kwan na ɔhunu nyansa na, deɛ ɔgyae nyansa akyiri die yera ne nyansa.**
*He who searches for wisdom sees wisdom, but he who leaves wisdom behind, loses his wisdom.*
(If you are industrious you achieve something, but if you neglect things you fail).

**1561. Deɛ ɔrehwehwɛ yere nto mmaa ho pe.**
*One who is looking out for a wife does not speak contemptuously of women.*
(You don't talk against those you are hoping will help you).

**1562. Deɛ ɛhyɛ, woamfa anhyɛ a, ɛfiri tɔ.**
*If you don't fix it where it should be fixed, it comes unstuck.*
(If you don't do things properly, you don't succeed).

1563. Dɛ ɔhyɛ kyerɛ-kawa na ɔkyerɛ kwan.
*He who wears a ring on the forefinger points out the way.*
(The kyerɛ–kawa is a special kind of ring which is used for pointing out things. Hence: A person who is competent in doing something does it).

1564. Deɛ ɔbɛhyɛ nsa nka n'ano ansa.
*He who pours out the drink does not taste it first.*
(Visitors are served first. Hence: If someone knows they will get something they are not anxious to grasp their share).

1565. Deɛ wahyɛ wo tiri no, sɛ ɔno na ɔbɔ no.
*He who molds your head (like a waterpot) is the one who can break it.*
(Those who know most about you can harm you most).

1566. Deɛ ɔreka n'asɛm ho nyɛ ahi sɛ deɛ ɔredi ho adansewia.
*The person who is explaining his case is not disliked but he who bears false witness to it is.*
(The judge does not dislike the accused but the man who gives false witness).

1567. Deɛ aka asutifi na ɛdɔɔso na nyɛ asunaafoɔ.
*What remains in the source of the river is more than has flowed through its mouth.*
(More remains for the future than has already been expended).

1568. Deɛ ɔkaeɛ se ɔboa a, yɛnnye no akyinnye.
*If he who said something (true) says he is not speaking the truth, we don't argue with him.*
(If you are not a witness to an event you can't judge a situation but must take the word of one who is).

1569. Deɛ kasa wɔ no, adeɛ nkye ntɛm.
*Where there is quarreling, dawn does not come quickly.*
(Bickering inhibits progress).

1570. Deɛ ɔkɔhunu woɔ na ɔfua tɛne.
*He who discovered honey is the one who holds the torch.*
(The person who knows the place directs the way).

1571. Deɛ wakɔ Korɔmante akɔko agye ntam aba no ɔnhwere: "Meka wo se."
*He who has gone to Korɔmante to fight and take the oath is not denied: "I swear on your father".*
(A person who has committed himself fully is not denied a small thing).

1572. Deɛ wakɔ Mampɔn Dawuampɔn akɔfa ntam aba no, ɔnhwere "Ka me-se".
*He who has gone to Mampɔn Dawuampɔn to collect the oath and return, is not denied "Swear on-my-father".*
(See Proverb 1571).

1573. Deɛ ɔrekɔ na yɛbɔ nkɔntene hwɛ no, na ɛnyɛ deɛ ɔreba.
*It is he who is going that we stretch our necks to make an effort to see, not he who is coming.*
(Because he who is coming we shall see anyway. Hence: If you know something is on its way, you wait for it).

1574. Deɛ ɔkɔ anadwo-gorɔ na ɔnya ɛka na ɛnyɛ deɛ ɔda dan mu.
*He who goes out to dance all night is more likely to have trouble than the person who sleeps quietly at home.*
(Trouble troubles those who trouble trouble).

1575. Deɛ ɔkɔ anyina annya bi amma a, ofie mpa huhuhuhu.
*If someone who goes to collect wood does not bring it, there is always criticism in the house.*
(If people are not satisfied by someone's work, they grumble continually).

1576. Deɛ ɔkɔ-asuo na ɔbɔ ahina.
*The one who goes for water is the one who breaks the pot.*
(The person most closely involved in something is most likely to damage it).

1577. Deɛ ɔrekɔ atɛn, deɛ ɔreba atɛn, deɛ ɔte hɔ ne atɛn turodoo.
*He who is passing on his way is a witness, he who is coming back is a witness, but he who is on the spot is the true witness.*
(The person who has been there all the time makes the best witness).

1578. Deɛ ɛkɔm gyeɛ ara ne meeɛ.
*What hunger desires is satisfaction.*
(If someone really needs something, only getting it will satisfy them).

1579. Deɛ ɛkɔm aku no no, yɛmmisa n'adaka.
*If a man dies of hunger, you don't ask for his box.*
(It is no use looking for compensation from a penniless man).

1580. Deɛ ɔkɔsee sɛ ɔtorɔmo mmerɛbo yɛ dɛ no, wɔnni nnya no.
*He who announced that the bongo's liver is sweet, we don't eat without him.*
(Someone who has shared in procuring something should share in using it).

1581. Deɛ ɔkɔse ayie na ɔma yɛkum bayifoɔ.
*He who announces a funeral makes us kill the witch.*
(One man's action brings about the down fall of another).

1582. Deɛ ɔbɛku wo nne se ɔbɛku wo ɔkyena a, ma ɔnku wo nne prɛko na kɔ home.
*If he who is going to kill you today says he will kill you tomorrow, rather let him kill you at once today and get your rest.*
(It is better to suffer at once if you cannot avoid it than to put it off until the morrow and suffer in anticipation).

1583. Deɛ kukuo antumi annoa no, koraa ntumi nnoa.
*What the pot could not cook neither could the calabash.*
(If the expert cannot do a job, neither can the amateur).

1584. Deɛ wakum kwatani na ɔfa ne mpaboa.
*He who kills the leper takes his shoes.*
(If you get rid of someone who is doing a dangerous job, you may have to take it on yourself).

1585. Deɛ ɔkum nanka na ɔkan nansini.
*The one who kills the viper counts the lame.*
(If someone kills a tyrant, he knows best the extent of
the crimes the tyrant committed).

1586. Deɛ akuma wɔ ne nsam na ɔtumi butu nnua.
*He who has an axe in his hand is able to fell trees.*
(If you have the tools you can do the job).

1587. Deɛ ekuro wɔ, nwansena mpa hɔ da.
*From where there is a sore a fly never leaves.*
(People collect where it is profitable).

1588. Deɛ ɔkuta gyatɛn ara na ɔnim deɛ ɔrekɔ.
*It is the person who holds the flaming torch who sees
where he is going.*
(The well-prepared man knows what he is up to).

1589. Deɛ ɔkuta afena wɔ animuonyam sene baabi
hene.
*The sword-bearer has more respect than the chief of
some place or other.*
(If you follow an important person, you have more
respect than a small person on his own).

1590. Deɛ ɔkuta ntrama o! Deɛ ɔbɛfiri o! Ɔdedeɛ se:
ɔrentɔn bio.
*He who holds the string of cowries! He who wants to
take it away for credit! The owner says: he won't sell.*
(Cowries were used as money. Hence: If you quarrel
with someone over something, you lose it).

1591. Deɛ wakyekyere woɔ ne deɛ ɔbɛtoo woɔ a
wansane woɔ, wɔn mu biara nni ho a wo biribi a ɔwɔ
baabi ne no.
*He who has tied you up and he who came to see you
tied and did not release you, neither of them is any
use to you.*
(Hobson's choice–there is no distinction between two
evils).

1592. Deɛ wakyerɛ wo awiakwan a, woamfa soɔ no,
adeɛ sa wo a wommisa no tɛne.
*The person who has shown you the way in the daylight,
and you did not pay heed to them, you don't go to at
night and ask them for a torch.*
(If you advise someone and they take no notice, you
don't expect them to come to you for help when in
difficulty).

1593. Deɛ n'akyi apaeɛ no, nyɛ ɔno ara na ɔpam.
*If someone's back is broken it is not he who will mend
it.*
(If a man is in real trouble he needs someone to help
him out of it).

1594. Deɛ ɛkyini kɔwie ne aboboano.
*Where roaming about ends is at the doorway.*
(Wherever you go you return home).

1595. Deɛ kyiniiɛ si ne so na ɔyɛ ɔhene.
*Whoever is under the umbrella is the chief.*
(The chief is the only person entitled to use an umbrella
at a public ceremony. Hence: Status is attached to
position and not necessarily to talent).

1596. Deɛ ɔmaa wo aburow bɔɔ dɔkono no, woredi
dɔkono na wohunu ne ba a, wo werɛ mfiri no.
*The one who brought you the corn to make kenkey,
while you are eating, if you see his child you do not
forget him.*

(Don't forget to show gratitude to those who help you.
This can be done equally well through their children).

1597. Deɛ ɔman aduru no so, wototo no mu a, ɔbu wo
nan mu.
*If you interfere with the person who should inherit the
state, he breaks your leg.*
(If you get between a man and his just rights, then you
should not be surprised if you suffer for it).

1598. Deɛ mmorɔsa ahwie aguo no, ɛhwa mpa hɔ da.
*Where foreign drink is poured out, the smell never
leaves the place.*
(A great man's reputation lives after him).

1599. Deɛ ɔne wo didie na ɔwe wo nam.
*It is he who eats with you who eats your meat.*
(The person closest to you is the one who can take
most advantage of you).

1600. Deɛ yɛne no tu amu na yɛne no bɔ pɔ.
*A person with whom we exhume a dead body is the
one with whom we conspire.*
(You only do a dangerous job with someone you can
trust).

1601. Deɛ ɔni woɔ, na ɔsu wo a, nisuo ba.
*He who is familiar to you, if he weeps for you, he
weeps profusely.*
(Familiarity brings consideration).

1602. Deɛ n'ani baako abɔ se ɔne wo bɛhye a, ɔse:
"Dwɛɛ!"
*He who has lost one eye, if he says he will strive hard
against you, he means it (lit. he says: "Dwɛɛ").*
(Handicapped people are believed to be mean and
treacherous. You should be careful about quarrelling
with people who are malevolent).

1603. Deɛ w'ani nna no, ɛhɔ na wo funu da.
*Where you don't think of, is where your corpse lies.*
(You don't plan where to die).

1604. Deɛ n'ani akyea na ɔhwɛ toa mu.
*The one who has crooked eyes looks into a bottle.*
(Some disadvantages can be turned to advantage).

1605. Deɛ w'ani ateteɛ sene deɛ wɔwoo woɔ dɛ.
*Where you have lived is worth more to you than your
birth-place.*
(The place which you regard as home means more
than the place where you happened to be born).

1606. Deɛ anidasoɔ nnie na adeɛ firi ba.
*Where there is no hope it is there that you get profit.*
(You get help where you least expect it).

1607. Deɛ n'anim seɛ odwan no, wode akokɔ ka n'anim
asɛm a, w'ano fomfom.
*A person who deserves a sheep, if you give them a fowl
and are speaking to them, your speech is confused.*
(If you give inadequate thanks you are likely to be
embarrassed).

1608. Deɛ ɔnim ɔman asɛm ase na ɔdi ɔman mu
asɛm.
*He who knows the history of the State, becomes a
judge of it.*
(If you are conversant with the situation, you are in a
position to handle it).

**1609. Deε ɔnim nsaa na ɔtɔ n'ago.**
*He who knows the value of the nsaa blanket buys its rag.*
(The nsaa blanket is from the North of Ghana and much valued. Strips of blanket are sometimes used to tie round the head at funerals. Hence: If something is precious even the smallest part of it is so).

**1610. Deε ɔnim w'ase a, ɔbɛkyerε w'ase te ase a, womfrε wo ho ɔdehyeε.**
*He who knows your history and will narrate it, if he is alive, you don't call yourself a royal person.*
(You can't pretend in the presence of someone who knows the truth).

**1611. Deε ɔnim ɔware toɔ, na ɔtoɔ**
*He who knows the rules of the ware game, plays it.*
(If you don't know the rules, don't try and join in).

**1612. Deε ɔnipa pɛ, na owuo nso pɛ.**
*That which man likes, Death also likes.*
(Death takes what is dearest to you).

**1613. Deε onipa bεyε biara, wɔbεka ne ho asεm.**
*Whatever a person does, people will talk about him.*
(You cannot stop people gossiping!)

**1614. Deε nnipa nim yε dinseeε.**
*What human beings know is how to destroy reputation.*
(Said when someone exhibits the "pull-him-down syndrome"-resentment of others' successes).

**1615. Deε wanya nhunui na, ɔnya no nkaeε.**
*He who has seen something before, knows how to bear witness to it.*
(Experience counts).

**1616. Deε ɔnya ketewa a, ɔma woɔ na ɔnya kεseε a, ɔbεma woɔ.**
*The person who gets a little and gives you some, if he gets a lot he will also give you some.*
(Generosity is consistent).

**1617. Deε ɔnyaa sika de bɔɔ kɔnkɔsani bosea no, ɔte sε kwasea a, ɔde ne se bɔɔ adwe maa onyansafoɔ bεfa weeε.**
*The person who got money and gave it as a loan to a trouble-maker is like a fool who used his teeth to crack a palm kernel for a wise man to eat.*
(If you have sympathy for a known trouble-maker, you are considered a fool).

**1618. Deε wanya asɔmorɔdwe ato aweε nse deε ne yafunu mu da mpan sε: "Merenya wo mayɔ".**
*He who has eaten a palm beetle does not tell the one who has an empty stomach that: "If I were you, I would be happy").*
(Be content with what you have, however little it may be).

**1619. Deε yεbεnyini akɔduru no, yemfiri hɔ nyini bio.**
*Where we shall stop growing, we don't grow on from there.*
(Everyone has his limits).

**1620. Deε ɔrepam wo nsaneeε a, wonka se: "Mabrε".**
*If someone is chasing you and has not stopped, you don't say: "I am tired (of running").*
(You can't rest when you are in trouble).

**1621. Deε ɔrepε daberε nkyerε n'akyi sε: "Medwonsɔ kɛtɛ so".**
*He who wants a sleeping place does not reveal: "I am a bed wetter".*
(When you are in need you hide your weaknesses).

**1622. Deε ɔrepε adeε akɔ kɔtɔkɔ no, yεnyε no aborɔ.**
*The one who tries to get something to go to the porcupine, we do not hamper him.*
(The porcupine symbolizes Asante. Hence, when used in Asante: You don't stand in the way of someone working for the benefit of your society).

**1623. Deε ɔpε sika na ɔnya bi.**
*He who likes money, gets it.*
(If you want something badly enough, you find a way of getting it).

**1624. Deε yεmpε yεnsane nkɔfa.**
*What we do not like, we do not turn back for.*

**1625. Deε yεmpε, yεtena no hia.**
*If you don't like a place, you stay there reluctantly.*

**1626. Deε ɔmpε wo nsuo, na ɔmpε wo biribiara.**
*He who dislikes your water, dislikes everything else about you.*
(Someone who rejects everything to do with you, rejects you yourself).

**1627. Deε apem sε no na yεnkame no ɔha.**
*He who is worthy of a thousand, we don't deny him one hundred.*
(If someone deserves a lot we don't deny him a little).

**1628. Deε sasaborɔ abu ne sisi mu ama no awuo de atopa kɔ asamando.**
*The person whose waist has been crippled with rheumatism so that he dies has taken waist shaking to the after world.*
(If you don't deal with your problems in this world, you take them to the next).

**1629. Deε ɔse: "Ma yεnkɔ," se: "Ma yεnsan" a, nnye no akyinnye.**
*If he who says: "Let us go,"says: "Let us return", you don't refuse him.*
(If you accept someone's advice then you should carry it through).

**1630. Deε ɔse: "Nya biribi die no", womma ɔkɔm nku no.**
*He who says: "Get something to eat", you don't let him die of hunger.*
(Your help those who help you).

**1631. Medeε na mese onyina bεso kwadu sεε na atentirehuo.**
*As for me, I hoped the silk-cotton tree would produce bananas but it only produced kapok.*
(Said when you have expected the impossible from someone and have been disappointed).

**1632. Deε ɔse Apenten atuo yε apem se, emu ahanum deε, twerεhoɔ nhyε ano a, yεnnye no akyinnye.**
*If he who says that Apenten's guns are a thousand says five hundred of them lack flints, we don't argue with him.*
(An expert should know best).

1633. Deɛ waseɛ na yɛbua no.
*He who says something is the person we reply to.*
(It's the questioner who gets the answer).

1634. Deɛ ɔsee kɛtɛ wɔ [kwan]/[tempɔn] mu ne deɛ ɔkɔtiaa soɔ, hwan na ɔyɛɛ bɔne?
*He who spread his sleeping mat on the [path]/[track] or he who trod on it, which was the worse?*
(Is the man who invites harm or the person who responds to his invitation the more guilty)?

1635. Deɛ ɔsene wo afonkɛseɛ no, na ɔsene wo ntasukɛseɛ.
*He who has fatter cheeks than you has more saliva than you.*
(If someone is greater than you he also has more).

1636. Deɛ y'asensane no, n'abɔgye nyɛ paena.
*A person who has scarifications, his jaw is not difficult to remove.*
(A person who has once been a victim is easily victimized again).

1637. Deɛ wasi ne dan mu ɔnna, na anene bɛsi so a na ɔrehwan nkoromo.
*The person who built the house finds it difficult to sleep in, but when the crow comes to perch it starts snoring.*
(A man who labors much for something does not always gain what he hopes to on its achievement. A stranger may, however, benefit from it without having made any effort).

1638. Deɛ yɛsie akyakyafoɔ no, ɛhɔ na ɔkyakyani tena su ne ho.
*Where we bury the hunchbacks, there a hunchback stands to weep for himself.*
(No one likes to be reminded of his own mortality. Or: Everyone is mourned by his own kind).

1639. Deɛ w'asie na ɔyie.
*He who has kept something is he who finds it.*
(The person who keeps something knows where he has put it).

1640. Deɛ ɔso aburo-pae mmisa kankan-hyɛn.
*He who carries a load of maize does not need to ask for a Dutch ship.*
(The old name for Dutch Accra was Kankan and thus the Dutch were called Kankanfoɔ - Kankan-people - or Kankan brofoɔ - Kankan-Europeans. Hence: You don't look for people who don't appreciate what you have to give or sell).

1641. Deɛ ɔso ngo nni adwamusɛm.
*The one who carries palm oil does not take part in a crowded game.*
(People in glass houses should not throw stones).

1642. Deɛ ɔso na ɔmene ne yɔnko.
*The one who is larger swallows his companion.*
(The rich buy up the poor).

1643. Deɛ ɔso twene kɛseɛ nni biribi a, ɔwɔ awerɛkyekyerɛ.
*If he who carries the big drum has nothing else, he has condolences.*
(There is always some small reward for performing a public service).

1644. Deɛ aso teɛ na ano bua.
*What the ear hears the mouth reveals.*

1645. Deɛ ɔresu na [yɛsu boa no]/[yɛsu no abia].
*He who is weeping, we weep to help him.*
(We show sympathy to those who need it).

1646. Deɛ ɔresu su kɔso ara ne nsɔreɛm.
*He who weeps cannot weep beyond the cemetery.*
(Even sorrow has its limits).

1647. Deɛ ɔresua woɔ ma wo hwene bɔ.
*He who mimics you makes you talk through the nose.*
(A person who dislikes you, ridicules you).

1648. Deɛ asuhina [bodammɔ]/[agohina] sie no, yɛntoto aboɔ.
*Where the full [water pot]/[oil pot] stands we don't throw stones.*
(See Proverb 1641).

1649. Deɛ wasunti awuo, yɛmfa mmirika nkɔ n'ayie ase.
*He who stumbles and dies, we don't run to celebrate his funeral.*
(Once bitten, twice shy).

1650. Deɛ asuo afa no, yɛmmisa n'aduradeɛ.
*The person who is drowned, we don't ask for his garments.*
(If something important is lost, you don't bother about lesser things)

1651. Deɛ osuo yɛ na owia yɛ.
*What the water does is what the sun does.*
(Both bring growth to plants. Hence: Things may be very different but have similar effects).

1652. Deɛ atamfoɔ atɔn no ama aprɛmo no wɔnkamfo no bio.
*The person whose enemies have sold him to a cannon, is not praised again.*
(The Asantes always kept the best captives to work for them. They sold those they did not want to the Europeans on the Coast as slaves. Hence: You don't praise a person you do not value).

1653. Deɛ ɔtase afetewa no, di n'adeɛ.
*He who gathers the fruit of the vitex cienkowskii, eats what belongs to him (lit. his own thing).*
(This fruit is very sweet. Hence: If you take the trouble to obtain something good, you use it).

1654. Deɛ ɔte gya ho aduane na ɛbene kane.
*A person who sits near the fire's food cooks first.*
(You achieve most by staying near what you are doing).

1655. Deɛ ɔteeɛ ante, deɛ ɔteeɛ anhunu aseɛ kyerɛ.
*He who heard it did not hear, he who did hear could not explain it correctly.*
(Some people pretend not to hear what is said, so that they will not be implicated; others are unable or unwilling to interpret correctly what is said, even though they hear it).

1656. Deɛ watena aprɛmoso anom tawa no, yɛmfa akwadamma nyi no hu.
*He who has sat at the cannon's mouth to smoke cannot be scared by a shot-gun.*
(The tried warrior is fearless).

1657. Deɛ watiti ne ho awuo de ahoɔhyene kɔ asamando.
*He who has scratched himself to death has gone to the next world with itches.*
(If someone has suffered bitterly from something they never forget).

1658. Deɛ ɔtoo abɛ antɔ abɛ a, ɛnyɛ deɛ ɔtasee mmɛfua na ɔbetɔ.
*If the person who uprooted the palm tree did not buy the tree, how much less will the person who collected the nuts buy it.*
(If the main person concerned does not act correctly, why should someone less involved)?

1659. Deɛ watɔ adeɛ na ɔnim sɛ ɔde ka.
*He who has bought something knows how much he owes.*
(You know your own obligations best).

1660. Deɛ ɔtɔeɛ ammee a, ɔtɔ a, ɔde sie.
*If he who bought was not satisfied, when he buys again he puts it by.*
(If you are not given a fair share of what you produce, then you have to find a way to keep what you need).

1661. Deɛ wotɔ na wotua ho ka.
*What you buy you pay for.*
(You don't get anything in life for free).

1662. Deɛ watɔ nsansono mu awuo, ɔde ntidɛ kɔ asamando.
*He who dies amongst the nsansono plants has gone to the underworld with constant scratching.*
(Nsansono are poisonous plants that sting. Hence: A person who dies under unpleasant circumstances is never relieved of his problems).

1663. Deɛ ɔtɔ nsunam, nwe n'ani ase abɔn.
*The one who buys fish does not eat what comes out of its eyes.*
(When something belongs to you, you can make use of the best part of it and discard the rubbish).

1664. Deɛ wanto bennaa wɔ ne toberɛ.
*He who did not know (the use of) bennaa (a weight) has a day in the future to know it.*
(Even if you are not yet experienced you may learn in the future. Or: Everything has its own time).

1665. Deɛ ne ntoma ateteɛ na ɔnim sɛdeɛ ɔsi fura no.
*He whose cloth is torn knows how to put it on.*
(You know best how to deal with your own shortcomings).

1666. Deɛ ɔtɔn mɛnsa de butu, na deɛ ɔretɔ nso adane no.
*He who sells corn cake turns it over and the buyer also turns it over.*
(The seller turns it over to hide the burned area, the buyer to uncover what the seller has tried to hide. Hence: More than one person knows the tricks of a trade).

1667. Deɛ ɔreton yɛ na, na deɛ ɔretɔ nso yɛ na.
*He who is selling is scarce and he who is buying is scarce.*
(The success of one person depends on another).

1668. Deɛ ɔbetumi na ɔpagya.
*He who can do so lifts it up.*
(You only take on what you are able to perform).

1669. Deɛ tumi wɔ, akyinnyeɛ nni.
*Where there is power there is no opposition.*
(Power likes to be absolute).

1670. Deɛ ontumi dane deɛ ɔtumi.
*He who has no power depends on he who has it.*

1671. Deɛ watwa nkontompo ama ne kuro agyina yɛ sen deɛ waka nokorɛ ama ne kuro abɔ.
*He who uses dishonesty to enable his town to stand firm is better than he who speaks the truth and ruins his town.*

1672. Deɛ wobɛtwa no pɛpɛ no, wotwaa no pɛ a, na woawie.
*What you are going to cut more than once, if you had cut it properly the first time, you would have completed the job.*
(You don't need to spend unnecessary time over something you could have dealt with at once).

1673. Deɛ ɔretwa sa nnim sɛ n'akyi akyeaa.
*He who is cutting a path through the bush does not see its crookedness behind him.*
(The person doing a job cannot always tell where he goes wrong. A recommendation to take time over a difficult job).

1674. Deɛ ɔwaduro pɛ ne "tum tum".
*What the mortar likes is the sound of pounding (lit. tum tum).*
(Men enjoy what they can do well).

1675. Deɛ ɔwe nkokɔ-nam, na ɔsi nkokɔbuo.
*The one who enjoys chewing chicken builds his hen coop.*
(If something is important to you, you make sure you have it).

1676. Deɛ wawe akɔkono se ɔbɛwe kyiremirekuku a, yɛnnye no akyinnye.
*If he who chews the palm beetle grub says he will eat the white ant queen, we don't contradict him.*
(If you can do one thing, you are likely to be able to do something similar).

1677. Deɛ wawe kɔtɔ ka sɛ ɔbɛwe koraa a, yɛnnye no akyinnye.
*If the one who has chewed the crab tells you he will chew the calabash, don't doubt him.*
(Both have hard shells. Hence: Don't doubt someone who has proved himself in similar circumstances).

1678. Deɛ ɔwoo ɔbakwasea ammrɛ sɛ deɛ ɔtetee no.
*The person who gave birth to a stupid child did not toil as much as the one who brought him up.*
(It is harder to complete a difficult job than to start it).

1679. Deɛ owoo woɔ tease a, yemfrɛ wo "agya ba".
*If the person who gave birth to you is still alive, we don't call you "father's child".*
(While your mother is there, your first allegiance is to her).

1680. Deε wawo ato "Agyako" ntwa aboba.
*He who has named his child "Stop-fighting" does not prepare bullets.*
(A known pacifist should not prepare for war. Have the courage of your convictions).

1681. Deε ɔwo din na yεbɔ ne din.
*He who has a name has it mentioned.*
(An important person is talked about).

1682. Deε ewɔ ɔdɔ nsam na ɔde ma.
*That which love has is what it gives out.*
(Love is generous).

1683. Deε εwo ahenkwaa tirim no, na ɔso ho daeε.
*What is in the mind of the Chief's servant is what he dreams about.*
(You are influenced most by the things which most deeply concern you).

1684. Deε ɔwɔ aka no, suro sonsono.
*He who has been bitten by a snake fears a worm.*
(If you have been harmed by something, you fear anything which resembles it).

1685. Deε ɔwɔ akurofo nsεe ne yɔnko akurofo.
*He who has a deserted village should not spoil his companion's.*
(Try to avoid causing others the same troubles you have suffered. More generally: Do as you would be done by).

1686. Dee wawɔ n'ani sekan se obεwɔ ne serε mu a, yennye no akyinnye.
*He who has damaged his eye with a knife, if he says he is going to damage his thigh in a similar way, you don't contradict him.*
(If someone has once done something stupid, you don't doubt that he is able to do something similar again).

1687. Deε ɔwo piredwan na yede piredwan ma no sie.
*He who has a piredwan, we give him a piredwan to keep.*
(A piredwan is a large weight of gold. Hence: A man is treated according to his rank. Or: Honour to whom honour is due).

1688. Deε ɔwɔ yere na ɔnim sεdeε ɔteε.
*The man who has a wife knows what she is like.*
(No one knows the character of a person more intimately than those closest to them).

1689. Deε ɔnni bie kɔ ayie a, ɔmma adeε nsa so.
*If someone who has no relative goes to a funeral he does not wait until nightfall to leave.*
(A single person needs time to fend for himself).

1690. Deε ɔnni hɔ sene deε ɔwɔ hɔ adan-kekare.
*The one who is absent is better than the one who is present at building the house.*
(Adan-kekare is the first stage of house making, where you fix the sticks for walls and line the sides of a house. A person who is absent when a job is done always thinks he could have done it better himself).

1691. Dee ɔnni hɔ, yεgya no aboɔ.
*He who is absent, we leave stones for him.*
(If you are not present you can't expect people to give you what you want).

1692. Deε ɔnni Apea ne Boakye wɔ Kumase no, ɔnya n'asεm a, ɔno ara na ɔdie.
*He who has no Apea nor Boakye in Kumasi, if he gets a case, he alone has to tackle it.*
(Apea and Boakye are common names. Hence: You can't thrive in a community without connections there).

1693. Deε ɔnni nan dwane Ɔpεnimma na Ɔpεpɔn abεto no kwan mu.
*He who has no legs escapes in December and January meets him on the road.*
(Time catches up with someone who has constantly to delay. Hence: A warning against procrastination).

1694. Deε ɔnni ateasefoɔ pa, na ɔwɔ asamanfoɔ pa.
*He who has no good members of the family alive, has good departed ones.*
(A family cannot always thrive, but just as it has done well in the past, so it may do so in the future).

1695. Deε wawuo na ɔnim deε aku no.
*He who is dead knows the one who killed him.*
(Some problems can only be solved after death).

1696. Deε wawuo nnim "Katawoto".
*He who is dead does not know "Cover your behind".*
(The dead do not care about conventions).

1697. Deε wawuo nnim n'akyi asεm.
*He who has died does not know the problems which follow after.*
(Death frees you from all worries).

1698. Deε ɔyam aduhwan mpepa ne nsa ho kwa.
*The person who pounds sweet-smelling herbs never entirely wipes the scent from their hands.*
(If you perform well you continue to benefit from your actions).

1699. Deε yεrewura no sεpɔ mpo yεma no aduane di.
*Even the man they are preparing for executioner is given food to eat.*
(The sεpɔ is a knife placed through the cheeks of a condemned man to prevent him from swearing an oath. Hence: However great the trouble, man must eat).

1700. Deε yεreyε no aku no na yεdi dansεε tia no, na nyε dε yεreyε no agyae no.
*He that we harm so that he dies is the one we bear witness against and not the person we harm and let go.*
(Something we may be involved with in the future is more important than something which is over and done with).

1701. Deε εyε wo dε no, na eyε w'akoa dε.
*Something which is sweet to you is also sweet to your servant.*
(Like master, like man).

1702. Deε anyε yie, yεmfa nka asεm.
*What did not become useful, is not mentioned in conversation.*
(We don't bother with things which are of no use to us).

1703. Deε yεn nsa hyε n'anom no, yempae n'apampam.
*If we have our hand in someone's mouth, we don't hit him over the head.*
(If you are in someone's power you don't abuse him).

**1704.** Me deɛ, na mese onyina bɛso kwadu sɛɛ na atentirehuo.
*As for me, I said that the silk-cotton (Bombax buonopozense) tree would produce bananas, but it only produced silk-cotton.*
(I hoped for the impossible).

**1705.** "Wodeɛ wɔ mu, meremfa mma wo", na ɛmaa ɔdetɔnfoɔ di awuo.
*"You have a share in it but I won't give it to you," made the seller commit murder.*
(Too much argument leads to violence).

**1706.** Me deɛ mayɛ denkyɛnyinapa, ɛduru afe a, na memene boɔ.
*I am like an aged crocodile, at the end of each year I swallow a stone.*
(The crocodile is said to swallow a stone each year, so that if you open its stomach, you can tell its age. Hence: Misfortune comes to me regularly).

**1707.** Wo deɛ anyɛ yie a, wonkɔfa obi deɛ nyɛ wo deɛ.
*When what you have is not good, you don't go and take what belongs to someone else.*
(Be content with what you have).

**1708.** Adeɛ a obi mpɛ no, na obi nso pɛ.
*Something which one person does not like, another does.*
(It takes all sorts to make a world).

**1709.** Adeɛ a wode huna akɔdaa a, ɔbɛsuro no, wode huna panin a, ɔrensuro.
*A thing which, if you show it to a child, he will fear, if you show it to an elder, he does not fear.*
(You can't threaten an experienced person as you can an inexperienced one).

**1710.** Adeɛ a yɛde nsa yɛ no, yɛmfa nsuo nyɛ.
*What we perform with alcohol, we don't perform with water.*
(Everything has its right place).

**1711.** Adeɛ a yɛde yɛ wo a, ɛnyɛ wo dɛ no, mfa nyɛ wo yɔnko.
*If what we do to you is not liked by you, don't do the same to your companion.*
(Do as you would be done by).

**1712.** Adeɛ a ɔhene pɛ na yɛyɛ ma no.
*What the chief wishes, we do for him.*
(Obedience to the man in supreme authority must be absolute).

**1713.** Adeɛ a Onyame bɛma wo, biara ɛmpare wo da.
*If God gives you something, no one can take it from you.*

**1714.** Adeɛ a ɛwɔ wo kurom a, ɛnyɛ fɛ no na ɛte sɛ deɛ ɛwɔ obi kurom.
*A thing which is in your own town is not good for you, how much more so something which is in your neighbor's town.*
(If you do not value something which is your own, you don't put a greater value on the same thing elsewhere).

**1715.** Adeɛ a ɛwɔ akyiri na yede susu serɛ.
*What is far away is what we compare the thigh with.*
(If you cannot compare things in fact, you compare them through imagery).

**1716.** Adeɛ a ɛwɔ amansan no, nye baakofoɔ dea.
*Something which belongs to everyone does not belong to any individual.*
(You tend not to take care of communal property but only of your own).

**1717.** Adeɛ a ɛyɛ dɛ nhyia mmienu.
*Sweet things don't go together in twos.*
(Unique things seem better than those which are duplicated. Or: Like often does not go with like).

**1718.** Adeɛ a, ɛyɛ dɛ kum ɔkwasea.
*It is something sweet which kills a fool.*
(A thoughtless man does not consider the consequences of over-indulgence).

**1719.** Adeɛ a ɛyɛ dɛ se ɔne wo bewu a, wone no wu.
*If something sweet says it will die with you, you and it die together.*
(You are prepared to suffer for what you like best.

**1720.** Adeɛ a ɛyɛ fɛ, yɛ fɛ, na ɛnyɛ anibere.
*Something which is beautiful, is beautiful, but it is not to be coveted.*
(Covetousness is a sin).

**1721.** Adeɛ a ɛyɛ foɔ na ne boɔ yɛ den.
*A thing which is cheap is really expensive.*
(It does not pay to buy cheap).

**1722.** Adeɛ a ɛyɛ hyeɛ na yɛhuhuo.
*Something which is hot we blow on.*
(We endeavor to cool down a situation).

**1723.** Adeɛ a, ɛbɛyɛ mmusuo, wohunu a, wodwane.
*The thing which will bring bad luck, if you see it, you avoid it.*

**1724.** Adeɛ a ɛyɛ, na ɛyɛ.
*If something is good, then it is good.*

**1725.** Adeɛ-a-ɛyɛ-nini dwuma a ɛdi kan, yɛ mmusuo; deɛ ɛto so mmienu yɛ asoɔden; deɛ etia mmiɛnsa a, ɛyɛ hyɛbere.
*Misfortune which happens once, is accidental; if it happens twice, it is due to stubbornness; if it happens thrice, it is considered as fate.*
(A first offender is given the benefit of the doubt, a second needs punishment, but the third is beyond sympathy and must be dealt with ruthlessly. Hence: Continuous wrong-doing is inexcusable).

**1726.** Adeɛ a ɛbɛyɛ woɔ, ne adeɛ wobɛnya, emu biara mpare wo da.
*What will happen to you and what you will get, neither of them will by-pass you.*
(Predestination).

**1727.** Adeɛ a ɛbɛyɛ yie nsɛe.
*A thing that is going to be all right does not spoil.*
(A thing which is predestined to thrive, thrives).

**1728.** Adeɛ a ɛnyɛ na yɛyɛ no yie.
*If something is not good we make it good.*
(Used to encourage someone to do better).

**1729.** W'adeɛ bɔ yɛ den a, mfudeɛ bere gu.
*If you sell your things at too great a price, all your produce will ripen and fall.*
(If you are too grasping you lose, not gain, by it).

# Proverbs of the Akans

**1730. Adeɛ da hweamanini ani a, yɛyi to atekyɛ mu ansa na yɛahohoro ho.**
*If something is in the current of a river, we pull it into the mud before we clean it.*
(Concentrate on the main thing first, then you are in a position to take other actions later).

**1731. Adeɛ da pata ano a, yi no ntɛm, na mma ɛnkɔ akyiri ansa.**
*The thing lying near the entrance to the shed, pick it up quickly and do not let it get out of reach.*
(Take the opportunity when it comes, or you may lose it).

**1732. Adeɛ hia ɔdehyeɛ a, ɛhia no kakra ara bi.**
*If a royal person lacks something, it is something small he lacks.*
(Rich people or people with good connections are not bothered by great needs).

**1733. Adeɛ hia ɔdɛnkyɛm a, ɔdidi nsuom na ɔnnidi kwaeɛ mu.**
*When the crocodile is hard-pressed, it eats in the water and not in the forest.*
(However difficult the conditions are you don't act beyond your own domain).

**1734. Adeɛ hia [akyamfoɔ ba]/[ɔhene nana] a, ɔkuta tuo na ɔnsoa kɛtɛ.**
*However poor a [shield-bearer's son]/[chief's grandchild] is, he carries a gun and not a mat.*
(A man whose ancestors are respected will not stoop to menial tasks).

**1735. Adeɛ hia ɔsebɔ a, ɔwe wira.**
*When a leopard is in need, it chews leaves.*
(In time of need even the most powerful make do with what they can get).

**1736. Adeɛ ho adeɛ nyɛ na a, anka Krɔbofoɔ mfrɛ kora sɛ "kyemee".**
*If work done on something were not difficult the Krobo people would not call the calabash "kyemee" (something precious).*
(Working on a calabash, in particular carving on its back, is tedious. Hence: Something worked hard for is valued highly).

**1737. Adeɛ kye a, adeɛ sa.**
*If day breaks then evening comes.*
(One thing inevitably follows another. Life is full of ups and downs).

**1738. Adeɛ kye akokɔ a, na wadi afe.**
*If day breaks for the chicken, it has lived a year.*
(A day's reprieve is worth much for one who expects to suffer).

**1739. Adeɛ bɛkye a, yɛfrɛ no ɔkyena.**
*If dawn is going to break we say it is to-morrow.*
(Retribution will catch up with you).

**1740. Adeɛ kyeeɛ na woanhunu a, adeɛ saeɛ deɛ wohunuiɛ.**
*If day broke and you did not see (it breaking), when night fell that you saw.*
(Even if you don't know how something started, you know how it ended).

**1741. Adeɛ mmienu nyɛ kyɛna.**
*Two things are not difficult to share.*
(Used when the solution to a problem is easy to see).

**1742. Adeɛ sa a, kɔkɔɔ dane tumtum.**
*When day is spent red turns to black.*
(It is easier to cheat someone in the night).

**1743. Adeɛ sa a, na dunsini asoa kyɛ.**
*If evening comes then a tree stump carries a hat.*
(Bad people do their clandestine activities in the dark).

**1744. Adeɛ resa a, na yɛhunu deɛ ayie wɔ no.**
*If night falls, then we see the holders of the funeral rites.*
(At the appropriate time we can see who the chief actors are in a situation).

**1745. Adeɛ sa a, na asɛm asa.**
*When evening comes all activities cease.*
(There is an end to every trouble).

**1746. Adeɛ saeɛ na woanhunu a, adeɛ kyeɛ deɛ wohunieɛ.**
*If when it got dark you could not see, at daybreak you saw.*
(You can't deny that you know about something, once it has come to light).

**1747. Adeɛ nsaeɛ a, yɛmmɔ Nyame sobɔɔ.**
*If night has not come we do not reproach God.*
(One never knows when one's luck will change).

**1748. Adeɛ nsaeɛ a, nkwanta nyera.**
*If evening has not come, the path does not get lost.*
(When you are aware of the truth of a situation, another person cannot deceive you about it).

**1749. Adeɛ nsa ano.**
*Night does not affect the mouth.*
(At any time of day or night we may need food or to express ourselves).

**1750. Adeɛ sɛ wo na woanya bi a, yɛkyiri.**
*If something is due to you and you don't get it, we taboo it.*

**1751. Adeɛ rebɛtɔ na wɔakɔyi twene keseɛ a, ɔkyekye se: "Me tiri ho wɔ apɔ".**
*If the day of the big festival is coming and they are going to bring the State drums, the broad-fronted crocodile says: "I've got bumps all over my head".*
(Crocodile skin is used on the drums. Hence this is said when someone wants to avoid responsibility and finds a suitable excuse).

**1752. Adeɛ wɔ fie a, yɛnkɔto ntwene ha mu.**
*If something valuable is in the house, you don't throw it into the bush.*

**1753. Adeɛ wura ne panin.**
*The person who owns something is senior.*
(Ownership takes precedence).

**1754. Adeɛ yɛ pɛna.**
*Things possessions) are hard to come by.*
(Wealth is hard to achieve).

1755. Adeɛ yɛ yie bebrebe a, na ato ne sɛeɛ.
*If something flourishes too much, then it begins to spoil.*
(Overdoing something spoils it).

1756. Adeɛ yera a, yɛfiri fie na yɛpɛ.
*If something is lost we look for it first at home.*
(If you have a problem try and solve it at home first).

1757. Adeɛ yera a, yɛpɛ no akwansini.
*If a thing is lost we look for it in every corner.*

1758. Adeɛ yera dodoɔ mu a, yɛde tɛkrɛma na ɛpɛ.
*If one thing is lost among many, we use our tongues to find it out.*
(You use soft words to find out the truth).

1759. Adeɛ yera a, ɛwɔ onipa nsam.
*When a thing is lost, it is in someone's possession.*

1760. W'adeɛ yɛ fɛ a, obi na ɔkamfoɔ na ɛnyɛ wo ara na wokamfoɔ.
*If you have something beautiful, someone may congratulate you, but you don't praise it yourself.*

1761. W'adeɛ yera a, nnipa nyinaa yɛ wo akrɔmfoɔ.
*If your possession is lost, all men seem to you to be thieves.*
(If you can't find something, you tend to suspect everyone of stealing it).

1762. Ɔdeɛ kurom ne Manye.
*The yam's town is Manye.*
(Every family has its place of origin).

1763. Nneɛma nyinaa dane suahunu.
*All things follow on learning.*
(Experience is the best teacher).

1764. Nneɛma nyinaa nsɛe pɛ.
*All things do not spoil in the same way.*

1765. Ɔdeɛmmanii no ara na ɔkuta ne hyɛberɛ mu.
*A modern person holds their own destiny.*
(We should be self-sufficient).

1766. Nnɛmma se: "Tete asoeɛ wɔnsoɛ hɔ bio". Na adɛn nti na wɔntu tete mmokyea mu abusua baako na ɛnka mmienu?
*The younger generation say: "We no longer rest in the ancient resting place". Why then do they not throw away one of the three old hearthstones and leave two?*
(Used in warning people against discarding all old traditions as useless. They are so much a part of man that he cannot do without them. Three hearth stones are used to balance the cooking pot).

1767. Adefɛdɛfɛ na ɛmaa ɛkoɔ nyaa awiawuo.
*Because of flattery the bush-cow met a sudden death.*
(Beware of flattery; it lowers your defenses).

1768. Ɔdeɛfoɔ anim yɛfɛre.
*In front of a benevolent person we are easily embarrassed.*
(You are ashamed to seek favors from someone who is always helpful).

1769. Ɔdeɛfoɔ soa bɔtɔ a, yɛkyi.
*If your benefactor carries his own bag, we don't approve.*

(If someone has helped you, you should help him in return).

1770. Ɛdeɛn na ɛkum bayepa maa afaseɛ bɛnyaa kofie mu hyeeɛ?
*What killed the good yam so that the water yam got a chance to enter into the mound?*
(If the good is there and the less good is given preferential treatment, we wonder why).

1771. Ɛdeɛn na awareɛ rebɛyɛ Praa a, ɔrebɛdi afaseɛ ato, n'ano aduro?
*How is the marriage going to benefit Praa, if she is going to eat water yam to poison herself?*
(Life is more important than anything. The water yam is taboo to the Pra River and thus to the Praa family. You should not break a taboo for any reason).

1772. Adefoforɔ ho yɛ anigye sene dada.
*A new thing is more admired than an old one.*
(People like to keep up with the fashions).

1773. Adefoforɔ nyɛ fɛ a, anka Ɔhemmaa mmɔ abia.
*If something new were not good to look at, the Queen Mother would not wear seed beads.*
(Even those in high places follow fashion).

1774. Adehwɛsoɔ ho mfasoɔ ne hiada.
*The enjoyment of one's frugality comes in time of need.*
(We store up things for a rainy day).

1775. Adehyeɛ repere mfofo a, ɔkyeame nni gyinaberɛ.
*When royals are struggling for the land, the linguist has no place in the competition.*
(An outsider, however important, cannot compete with the family).

1776. Ɔdehyeɛ bɔ dam a, yɛfrɛ no asaborɔ.
*If a royal goes mad, we call him a drunkard.*
(A good position in society protects you from ridicule).

1777. Ɔdehyeɛ: yɛdi no nsuom-nam na yɛnni no sono.
*A royal: we eat it as fish and not as elephant.*
(The fish is small and it is the water that makes it great. It is not a man's stature that makes him great but his followers).

1778. Ɔdehyeɛ: yɛnni no yafunum.
*A royal: we do not act it in the womb.*
(It is environment, not nature, that makes people arrogant).

1779. Ɔdehyeɛ din nyera da.
*The name of a royal is never lost.*
(A significant person can always be found and his name lives on).

1780. Ɔdehyeɛ nhyehyɛ; sika na ɛhyehyeɛ.
*Royalty is not consumed; it is money that is consumed.*
(A good position in society is more permanent than wealth).

1781. Ɔdehyeɛ anko a, akoa dwane.
*If a royal does not go to battle, the slave runs away.*
(If a leader does not give a good example, his followers will desert him).

**1782. Ɔdehyeɛ wɔnnoa nni, na sika ne asɛm.**
*Royals, they don't cook and eat, but money is the real problem.*
(Its no good having a great name if you are poor).

**1783. Ɔdehyeɛ mu nni akɔdaa.**
*There is no child amongst royals.*
(All members of the royal family are treated with respect).

**1784. Ɔdehyeɛ, yempae.**
*Being royal, we don't advertise.*
(Modesty is one of the attributes of a good family).

**1785. Ɔdehyeɛ nsi hene.**
*A royal does not enstool a chief.*
(There is a right man for every job. Don't try and do what you are not entitled to do).

**1786. Ɔdehyeɛ te hɔ a, akoa nni adeɛ.**
*If a royal is available, a slave does not take charge (or inherit).*
(The person entitled to something takes precedence).

**1787. Ɔdehyeɛ nyɛ akoa na yɛabɔ ne din abɔ owuo din.**
*The royal is not a slave whose name we associate with death (lit. that we speak his name to speak death's name).*
(You do not refer directly to a chief's death. You must say something like "A great tree has fallen," if you wish to refer to it. Slaves were formerly killed to go to serve the chief in the afterlife. A member of the royal family would not be treated this way. Hence: Some people are immune to certain calamities).

**1788. Ɔdehyeɛ ayie, yɛyɛ no mfensa.**
*A royal's funeral we celebrate for three years.*
("Three years" is a conventional way of saying a very long time. If you are an important person your name is never lost).

**1789. Ɔdehyepanin nwuieɛ a, ɔdehyekuma mfa ahennie nhyehye ne ho.**
*If the senior royal is not dead, the junior royal does not boast of his future kingship.*
(Don't count your chickens before they're hatched).

**1790. Adehyesɛm, yenni no kookoo ahahan so.**
*Acting-like-a-royal, we do not do it on cocoa leaves.*
(You need something behind you before you throw your weight about).

**1791. Dekɔdeɛ a ɛkaa kɔkɔsakyi maa ne tiri ho paeɛ, ɛno are na ɛmaa akokɔhwedeɛ nan ase worɔeɛ.**
*Whatever made the vulture's head bald, the same thing made the bushfowl's legs sore.*
(One man's problem is shared by others great and small).

**1792. Adeketewa na ɛdane keseɛ.**
*A small affair grows into a great one.*
(Deal with problems at once or they will escalate).

**1793. Adekyɛ akatua ne aseda.**
*The reward of generosity is gratitude.*

**1794. Ɛdɛm da dwa a, yɛnkata so.**
*If a deformity comes into the open, we do not cover it up.*
(You can't hide your disabilities in public).

**1795. [Ɔdemmerefua]/[Ɔdompo] rekɔda ara ne nhema yi!**
*The marsh mongoose went to sleep as the day was breaking.*
(Said of a newly rich man who boasts of his wealth).

**1796. Ɔdemmerefua ho wɔ biribi a, anka ɔrennante nsuo ho mmɔ akɔto.**
*If the marsh mongoose were rich, he would not have walk on the river bank to dig for crabs.*
(Only a poor man does menial jobs willingly).

**1797. Ɔdemmerefua anya abɔfono dada.**
*The marsh mongoose has already had its carcass.*
(It is no use telling someone something he already knows).

**1798. Ɔdemmerefua nya biribi di a, ɔbu kankane kwasea.**
*If the marsh mongoose has had something to eat, it calls the African civet a fool.*
(If you are well off you can afford to insult others).

**1799. Ade-mono a atete hyɛ bɔtɔ mu no, na Oburoni na ɔnwonoeɛ.**
*If a new material tears as it is in the bale, then it is the European who wove it.*
(The cause of trouble is from its origins).

**1800. "Adɛn na watia me gyawa soɔ?" yɛ tɔkwa pɛ.**
*"Why have you stepped on my foot?" is a way of initiating a quarrel.*
(You don't quarrel over unimportant things unless you are actually seeking a quarrel).

**1801. Ɔdɛnkyɛm da nsuo mu, nso ɔhome mframa.**
*The crocodile lies in the water, but it also breathes air.*
(Refers to a talented person who has several different capabilities).

**1802. Ɔdɛnkyɛm ne pitire na ɛda, nso ɔfom no a, na waka no.**
*The crocodile and the cat fish sleep together, but when the latter offends the crocodile (lit. if it offends it), it bites it.*
(Living together does not mean you will always agree).

**1803. Ɔdɛnkyɛm se obi nko obi hɔ nkɔdidi. Ɔda nsuo mu nti, sɛ ɔkyere nsuo-nam di a, ɔnkɔ ahua.**
*The crocodile says no one goes to another person's place to eat. That is why he lies in the water, so that if he catches fish to eat, he has not gone to anyone to eat.*
(Everyone should care for himself and not go begging around for food).

**1804. Ɔdɛnkyɛm wedeɛ kyɛn wede-pa adeɛ.**
*The crocodile's skin is better to eat than any other.*
(Used when you want to indicate that what you have is as good as the best).

**1805. Ɔdɛnkyɛm nwu nsuo-ase mma yɛmmɛfrɛ kwakuo sɛ ɔbɛye no ayie.**
*A crocodile does not die under the water for us to call the monkey to celebrate its funeral rights.*
(People of different origins do not follow each other's customs).

1806. Dɛnkyɛmumu ɔse: "Me yafunu ne m'adeɛ nyinaa sa wo so".
*The denkyɛmumu plant says: "My belly and all my things are available for you".*
(A submissive person serves freely).

1807. Dɛnkyɛntire wonya twa a, na woawie no.
*The head of a crocodile, if you finish cutting it, that is its end.*
(If a leader is killed the army is defeated. Compare Proverb 6431).

1808. Adenoa ho nhia a, anka yɛwe abebeɛ mono.
*If cooking were not necessary, we would eat the river snail raw.*
(We act according to custom).

1809. Ade-pa na yɛtɔ abɔɔden.
*We buy a good thing at a high price.*

1810. Ade-pa na ɛtɔn ne ho.
*A good thing sells itself.*

1811. Ade-pa wɔ nyinkyɛre mu.
*Something good is in a long life.*

1812. Aderɛ bɔ boɔ a, ɛno ara na ɛtua.
*If a cutlass names a price, it pays it itself.*
(If things are valuable they are usually profitable).

1813. Aderɛ bu a, yebɔ foforɔ poma mu.
*When a cutlass breaks, we make another handle for it.*
(If someone man dies, another takes his place in the family).

1814. Aderɛ mpo anya ayɛ, na akɔwie asɔ.
*If the cutlass does not get gratitude, how much less the hoe.*
(Used when people show lack of gratitude for hard work and service).

1815. Aderɛ tumi kwaeɛ a, anka yɛankɔbɔ akuma.
*If the cutlass could clear the forest, we would not have made the axe.*
(If the ordinary man could do the job, we would not get someone special to do it).

1816. W'aderɛ twa wo a, wonto ntwene.
*If your cutlass cuts you, you don't throw it away.*
(You don't discard a disobedient child or servant just because they make a mistake).

1817. Adeseɛɛ nyɛ ahonya.
*Spoiling of a thing is not wealth.*
(Destructiveness is never productive).

1818. Adeseɛɛ nyɛ sɛena na ne yɔ.
*Spoiling of a thing is not harder than constructing it.*
(It is easier to destroy than to build).

1819. Yɛde yɛ wo na woamma yɛanhunu sɛ ɛyɛ wo ya a, yɛnnyae wo fayɛ.
*If we do something to you and you don't show us that you are affected, we don't stop doing it.*
(If you don't disagree openly, people will take it that you agree).

1820. Wodi mmaa akyi a, w'afuo ka adwooguo.
*If you follow after women too much, your farm becomes neglected.*

(A farmer was once helped to cultivate his farm by the duiker. Whenever he asked the duiker anything he replied as above. One day the man's wife found out about the duiker and made him promise to kill it for meat. When he lifted his cutlass to do so, the duiker ran away and he wounded himself so badly that he could not farm again. As it ran away the duiker repeated this proverb. Hence: If you listen to women too much, your work is spoilt).

1821. "Di bi ma menni bi" nyɛ aboadie.
*"Eat a bit and let me eat a bit", is not fraud.*
(Live and let live is just).

1822. "Madi bi" nyɛ ɔmeeɛ.
*"I have eaten a bit" is not satisfaction.*
(Enough is not a feast).

1823. "Adi-bi-pɛn," nyɛ dina.
*"To have eaten a bit before", is not difficult to eat (next time).*
(We can cope with what we are familiar with).

1824. "Madi, madi" na ɛde afuhyɛwa ba.
*"I have eaten, I have eaten" brings a protruding stomach.*
(Greed gives evidence of itself).

1825. "Madi, madi" ne "Mane, mane" na ɛnam.
*"I have eaten, I have eaten" results in diarrhea (lit. I have defecated, I have defecated).*
(Overdoing things leads to real trouble).

1826. "Di-bi-ma-yɛnkɔ" na amma batani anyɛ kɛseɛ.
*"Eat a little and let us go" made the traveller grow lean.*
(Don't hurry).

1827. Wodi obi deɛ a, ɔdi wo deɛ.
*If you consume someone's thing, then he consumes yours.*
(You scratch my back, I'll scratch yous).

1828. Yɛdi obi adeɛ a, na yɛfɛre no.
*If someone helps you (lit. you eat somebody's things), you respect them.*

1829. Wodi obi asɛm ma no a, woma ne ntoma ka ne mmati.
*If you involve yourself in arbitration in someone's place, you make him leave his cloth on his shoulder.*
(If you act in someone's place, you relieve them of all responsibility).

1830. Wodi abirekyie bɔne akyi a, w'ahina bɔ.
*If you follow a bad goat, your waterpot breaks.*
(If you let a troublesome person distract you, you suffer).

1831. Wobɛdi biribi a, wodi no prɛko.
*If you are going to eat something, you eat it at once.*
(Procrastination is the thief of time).

1832. Wodi bɔne akyi a, woyɛ bɔne.
*If you follow up on bad things, you offend.*

1833. Wodi mmɔnkɔ mmɔborɔ akyi a, anka worenkye nwe da.
*If you follow the pitiable life of the shrimp, you do not fry and eat it.*
(If you are too soft-hearted you cannot enjoy life).

**1834. Wobɛdi ɔbosom kosua ama wagye wo odwan deɛ, ɛneɛ nya di n'akokɔ.**
*If you are going to eat the fetish's eggs so that he demands a sheep of you, it is better to eat his chicken.*
(In for a penny, in for a pound).

**1835. Wodi oburoni adeɛ a, wɔko apremo ano.**
*If you accept a gift from a white man, you always fight with cannons.*
(If you allow yourself to be influenced by gifts and power, you are always under obligation to follow the powerful).

**1836. Yɛrebɛdi deɛ yɛkyiri na deɛ yɛmpɛ.**
*We are going to eat what we taboo, then what about what we dislike?*
(If we commit a great sin, other troubles become less important).

**1837. Wodi deɛ etuo ayɛ akyiri a, anka wonni honam da.**
*If you follow what a gun has done, then you will not ever eat fresh bush meat.*

**1838. Yɛredi adi bio na ɛma ɔhɔhoɔ sereɛ.**
*We are eating so that we may eat again, makes the visitor smile.*
(Present enjoyment is all that interests the passer-by).

**1839. Madi dɔkono mpo wɔse mawe nwira na mɛwe ahwedeɛ.**
*Even if I ate kenkey they say I ate leaves, how much more so if I chew sugar cane!*
(You blame me if I offend you a little, so you will blame me even more if I give greater offence).

**1840. Woredi adua a, wokae deɛ ɔnoaeɛ.**
*If you are eating beans, remember who has cooked them.*
(Be grateful for sharing with someone the results of their work).

**1841. Yɛdi aduro pe kyɛre.**
*We eat medicine so that we live longer (lit. remain).*
(You take precautions to survive).

**1842. Wodi dwa na ɛbɔ wo wɔ tɛkrɛma so a, ɛnyɛ ya.**
*If you trade and it goes well and you enjoy it (lit. it hits you on the tongue), you don't suffer.*
(If you are successful, you have nothing to complain about).

**1843. Wodi adwene dɛ akyi a, anka wobɛhwɛ asuo Firaw.**
*If you were to follow the sweetness of the fish, you would bail out all the water of the River Volta (in order to collect more fish).*
(If you like the good things of life too much, they lead to extreme actions).

**1844. Wodi afaseɛ a, na asɛm fa w'aseɛ.**
*If you eat water yam, then events overtake you.*
(Play on words. If you invite trouble you get it).

**1845. Woadi mferemferemmadeɛ, yerekɔku wo, woduruu nkwantia a, wose: "Masunti asikyire".**
*Because you have eaten tasty things, we are going to kill you, yet when you have reached the outskirts of the town you say: "I have stumbled over sugar".*

(Don't add insult to injury. If you have committed an offence and go on doing the same thing, it shows you have not repented).

**1846. Wodi fo a, na w'ano adwo.**
*If you become guilty, then you are no longer powerful.*
(People do not respect those who have been caught and found guilty).

**1847. Odi-afoofi na ɔtoto gya.**
*He who stays at home buys firewood.*
(If you don't work for things, you have to pay for them).

**1848. Yɛdi afompata na yenni afomkum.**
*We try and bring about reconciliation but we don't aim at bloody vengeance.*
(A peacemaker always tries to avoid violence).

**1849. Wodi funu akyi a, wogye funu yɔɔyɔɔyɔ.**
*If you follow a corpse (to the cemetery), you give the corpse sympathy.*
(If you decide to do something serious, you should put your whole self into it).

**1850. Yɛredi agorɔ foforɔ a, yenni amim.**
*If we are beginning a new game, we don't cheat.*
(It is only when things become serious that people show their true character).

**1851. Wodi hammusuo a, mmoa kyerɛ wo ahayɔ.**
*If you are unlucky in hunting, then the animals teach you how to hunt.*
(If you are unlucky you have to learn even from you enemies how to avoid ill-luck).

**1852. Wodi hia na worebɔ akora, wonhunu.**
*If you are in want and you are growing old, you don't realize it.*
(Old people have fewer needs).

**1853. Wodi w'ahoɔfɛ akyi a, worenwu w'akra wuo.**
*If you follow your own beauty, you won't die a natural death.*
(If you depend too much on good looks, you get into trouble).

**1854. Wodi hwinhwim adeɛ a, basabasa bisa wo.**
*If you act in a hurried way, confusion will seek for you.*
(Gently does it).

**1855. Wodi akokɔ bɔne akyi a, wo nsa si fam.**
*If you follow a bad fowl, your hand touches the ground.*
(If someone does you wrong, be careful it does not lead you into an even worse position).

**1856. Wodi w'akoma akyi a, woyera.**
*If you are arrogant, you get lost.*
(Pride goes before a fall).

**1857. Wobɛdi kooko amono a, anka wodii no afuo so.**
*If you were going to eat raw cocoyam, you would have eaten it on the farm.*
(You don't ask others to solve a problem which you can solve yourself).

1858.Wodi akorafoɔ baanu ntam a, wɔfrɛ wo konkɔnsani.
*If you owe allegiance to two fellow wives, they call you a traitor.*
(Double allegiance leads to abuse).

1859. Worebɛdi nkosua a, wonse sekan.
*If you are going to eat eggs, you don't sharpen a knife.*
(Don't make a great fuss over small things).

1860. Wodi akuokunisuo akyi a, nisuo ku wo.
*If you follow the flame tree (Spathodia campanulata), tears destroy you.*
(The seeds of this tree are used by children to simulate weeping when they are playing at funerals. Hence: If you are too sympathetic, you will suffer).

1861. Wodi ekuro nna a, na womia ɛyam.
*If you rarely have a sore then you dress your ring-worm.*
(It's only when you have nothing serious to worry about that you worry over trifles).

1862. Wodi kwasea akyi a, wobu wo dwetire abɔnten.
*If you follow after a fool, you show your money in a public place.*
(To avoid disgrace, we should not involve ourselves with an undesirable person).

1863. Yɛredi ɔkyekye no na asibe si egya so.
*While we are eating the broad-fronted crocodile's meat, the monkey's is on the fire.*
(A minor case is being tried but a greater is on the way).

1864. Adi amma wo ba, ɛbɛka wo nko.
*Eating and depriving your child of food, you will be left alone.*
(Selfishness brings loneliness).

1865. "Madi, mamma wo" nti na Kwaamanfoɔ nyinaa yɛ abɔfoɔ.
*"I have eaten, I did not give you any" made all the people of Kwaman become hunters.*
(Kwaaman, formerly Kwawman, was a dense forest region near Nsuta. The hunters there were known for their meanness in sharing their catch. It was a case of every man for himself. But: Selfish people do teach each other to be self-sufficient).

1866. Wodi ɔman ne ɔman ntam a, wɔfrɛ wo konkɔnsani.
*If you play one State off against another, they call you a traitor.*
(No man can follow two masters).

1867. Wodi amantrenu a, woyera.
*If you owe allegiance to more than one person you get lost.*
(The crested guinea fowl (asam) was much admired by the stone partridge (aboko) and out of kindness offered to paint her. When she had only painted the underside, the partridge became so arrogant that she stopped. When the partridge died, her own people, seeing the color of her chest, said she was a guinea fowl and that they could not bury her. Thus if you try and belong to two worlds, you lose both).

1868. "Mɛdi no animanim yi ara" yɛ amono.
*"I will eat straight away" brings raw food.*
(More haste less speed).

1869. Wodi nokorɛ daa a, ɛda a wobɛdi atorɔ no, yɛnhunu.
*If you tell the truth always, the day you will tell a lie, we don't detect it.*
(A reputation for truth is worth its weight in gold).

1870. Yɛdi panin anom asɛm so, na yɛnni ne tirim asɛm so.
*We follow what the elder has said but not what is in his head.*
(Don't invent motives for what your superiors have in mind, but pay attention to what they say).

1871. Wodi papa, wonyini kyɛ, na adeɛ na wannya.
*If you are kind you grow to old age, but you will not be rich.*
(Kindness brings happiness not riches).

1872. Wodi papa a, wonsuro nimo.
*If you are kind you don't fear slander.*

1873. Wodi peme a, wosoa peme.
*If you eat heavily, then you carry a heavy load.*
(If you commit a great crime then your punishment is great).

1874. Wodi apetebie akyi a, aboa teaa foro wo.
*If you chase the striped squirrel, then the snake climbs (and bites) you.*
(If you go after something and don't pay attention to where you are going, you suffer for it).

1875. Woredi aponkyerɛne akyi ama no dammirifua a, anka wobɛbrɛ.
*If you take time to console a frog, you get tired.*
(He is always falling and beating his breast. Hence: If someone is constantly in trouble you exhaust yourself with sympathy).

1876. Woadi nsamanfoɔ tɔ, wɔretoa wo asamando; yerekyɛ akunafoɔ a, wose: "Me deɛ ne kɔkɔɔ a ɔdi mu no".
*You have eaten the mashed yam of the spirits of the departed, they are chasing you to the under world; if we are sharing widows you say: "I want the fair-colored one!"*
(You have committed a taboo and are in real trouble and yet you ask for the best. Hence: If you have offended someone you can't demand a favor from them).

1877. Wodi nse a woanwu a, ɛmmɔ wo ka.
*If you swear an oath on a fetish and you don't die, you don't lose by it.*
(You don't lose anything by affirming the truth and clearing your name).

1878. Wodi asɛm na woanhunu ano a, na woahunu ano ara ne sa.
*If you are considering a problem and you can't get a result, then the result is what you have experienced.*
(If you can't solve a problem, you are stuck with it).

1879. Wodi asɛm na wokyea w'aso bua aten, na wodi mu abadwadeɛ a, wofe.
*If you judge a case with partial ears and you share the fine (make a profit), you vomit.*

(You cannot, in the long run, profit from getting someone else into trouble).

1880. **Wodi asɛmpa a, wonya animuonyam.**
*If you do a job well, you reap admiration.*

1881. **Wodi asɛmpa a, wonsuro ahemfie.**
*If you act according to custom, you don't fear the chief's palace.*
(If you lead a good life and obey the rules of the community, you don't fear authority).

1882. **Yɛdi asɛmpa de pɛ ɔtɔfoɔ.**
*We use consideration to attract a prospective buyer.*
(A good salesman needs tact).

1883. **Di asɛmpa na daakye bi yɛamfa praeɛ annya wo kwan.**
*Lead a good life and in future a broom may not be used to see you off.*
(When someone who is supposed to be bad or unlucky leaves a house, the inmates sweep after him. Thus the proverb means you should lead a good life so that people respect you).

1884. **Wodi Asiemmiri adeɛ a, woyɛ Asiemmire ayie.**
*If you inherit Asiemmiri you perform his funeral.*
(Asiemmire was a very famous hunter. If you inherit from someone you are expected to perform his funeral rights and take on his other duties and responsibilities).

1885. **Wodi sika bɔne a, wofe.**
*If you consume bad money, you vomit it up again.*
(In the long run you cannot profit from dishonesty).

1886. **Wodi ɛsono akyi a, wonyera.**
*If you follow an elephant, you don't lose your way.*
(If you follow a powerful man you are secure).

1887. **Wodi soro, di fam a, ɔtwe bɔ wo fɛ.**
*If you eat above and eat below the duiker damages you.*
(If you follow two masters you will get into trouble).

1888. **Wodi torɔ a, wobrɛ.**
*If you tell lies, you get tired.*
(Once you start telling lies you are liable to be caught out or have to go on and on producing new ones).

1889. **"Mɛdi wo, mɛdi wo", yɛmfrɛ no odie; ɛtua mu a, na yefrɛ no odie.**
*"I will have intercourse with you, I will have intercourse with you," we do not call it intercourse, if it is real then we call it intercourse.*
(Promise is not the same as performance).

1890. **Wodi wo fie asɛm na wohunu di a, ɛmfiri dwa.**
*If you arbitrate a case at home and you are successful, it does not become public.*
(Don't wash your dirty linen in public).

1891. **Wodi wo ho wo ho a, ɛyɛ mmusuo.**
*If you do everything on your own, it is taboo.*
(It is wrong to be solitary).

1892. **Woredi wo nkosua, na woredi wo nkokɔ mma.**
*As you are eating your eggs, you are eating your hen's baby chicks.*
(If you consume your capital you have nothing left).

1893. **Madi, madi, ne mane, mane, na ɛnam.**
*I have eaten, I have eaten, and I have defecated, I have defecated, go together.*
(If you are greedy, you suffer the consequences).

1894. **Yɛdi wo ni a, di wo ho ni.**
*If they respect you, respect yourself.*
(It is important to have self respect if you are a public figure).

1895. **Yɛbɛdi wo atɛm mprɛ ɔha, na woammua a, amaneɛ nni mu.**
*If we are going to abuse you a hundred times, and you don't reply, there is no case.*
(It takes two to make a quarrel).

1896. **Wodi wo to aborɔ a, wota wo yam.**
*If you hold in your wind, you fart in your stomach.*
(If you try to avoid small problems, you will let yourself in for big ones).

1897. **Wodi wo yɔnko ho nsɛm a, daakye ɔno nso bɛdi wo deɛ bi!**
*If you gossip about your companion, later he will also gossip about you.*

1898. **Yɛredi awu a, yɛnkum ɔmanni.**
*If we are killing someone, we don't kill a fellow citizen.*
(You don't damage those who have the same interests as yourself).

1899. **Yɛnni nam nnya ogya.**
*We don't eat meat and leave out the fire.*
(Certain people cannot be by-passed in deliberations).

1900. **Worenni ɔsaman aduane a, wɔmfa wonsa ntomu.**
*If you do not intend to eat the food of the spirits, you don't put your hands in it.*
(Said for instance of a man who makes a girl pregnant--he cannot plead that he has had no interest in her).

1901. **Adi bɛyɛ wo a, ɛnnim sɛ adeɛ asa.**
*If you will suffer, it does not matter if you are in the dark.*
(If you are predestined to suffer, it does not make any difference where you are, you will suffer just the same).

1902. **"Adi-nyɛ-wo" nte nokorɔ bi so.**
*"Woe betide you!" is not a one way affair.*
(Hate is reciprocal).

1903. **Adiama ne adiama ne agorɔ.**
*"(I) eat and give (you) some", and "(You) eat and give (me) some", is playing the game.*
(Share and share alike).

1904. **"Dibem" twa asɛm.**
*Pleading guilty shortens a case.*

1905. **Adidaa na ɛyɛ, na nyɛ [adidaako]/[adiprɛko].**
*Daily satisfaction is better than one day's indulgence.*

1906. **Wodidi bata anim a, edwa bɔ wo.**
*If you consume in advance, your marketing becomes unsuccessful.*
(If you live on credit you do not prosper).

**1907. Yɛdidi bata anim, na yɛnnidi bata akyi.**
*We accept money for future expenses and not for past expenses.*
(We should not earn to pay debts but to plan for the future).

**1908. Wodidi abɔntene so a, yɛbɛbɔ wo didiawuro.**
*If you eat (have sex) outside the house, we make you eat to the accompaniment of a gong-gong.*
(Having sex in the bush is a taboo, being an insult to Asaase Yaa, Mother Earth. Hence: If you commit a taboo, you will face public disgrace).

**1909. Wodidi afiduasa mu a, w'ano mmene bo.**
*If you eat in thirty houses, you cannot criticize.*
(You cannot criticize those who help you).

**1910. Wodidi wo fie na woamme a, na wokɔ ahua.**
*If you eat at home and you are not satisfied, then you go begging.*
(If you cannot be self-sufficient then you trouble others).

**1911. Didi kwan biara nware.**
*A journey in search of food is not a long one.*
(If something is important to you, you don't mind the time spent on it).

**1912. Wodidi mee a, na wogya nnuanfunu.**
*If you have eaten and are satisfied then you leave the residue.*
(It is only when you are satisfied that you think of what to do with what is left over).

**1913. Wodidi na woammeɛ a, na wo tɛkrɛma kɔ wo dodom atweeɛ.**
*If you eat and are not satisfied, then your tongue goes to lick the roof of your mouth.*
(If you are not satisfied you search for more).

**1914. Woredidi na woanto wo bo aseɛ a, ɛhia wo.**
*If you eat and you don't take time, you choke.*
(Too much haste brings disaster).

**1915. Woadidi wo nsa mu a, w'ahonya te kyɛre mu.**
*If you eat out of your hand, you will not obtain riches.*
(If you behave like a ne'er-do-well then you will remain one).

**1916. "Didi ntɛm, ma yɛnkɔ" bebrebe na amma awirakwaa anya honam.**
*Too much "eat quickly and let us go", led the servant to become lean.*
(Too much bullying and lack of consideration leads to discontent).

**1917. "Adidi-antɔ-wo-ho" na ɛde feɛ ba.**
*"Eating and working immediately after" brings vomiting.*
(If you make someone work unreasonably, they will act against you).

**1918. Adidibɔne na ɛde Twɛnwonsa ba.**
*Bad-eating brings about Slowdown.*
(Too much of anything is bad).

**1919. Adididodoɔ na ɛma kɛseyɛ a, anka adowa anya anantuo.**
*If greed were to lead to becoming fat, then the antelope would have got calves (on its legs).*

**1920. Adididodoɔ na ɛmma wowa ka penentoa mu.**
*Because of gluttony the bee was stuck in the bottle.*
(Greed leads to disaster).

**1921. Adidie-mmirika wɔ meneaseɛ.**
*Quick eating depends on the throat.*
(A person's ability to act depends on the help they get).

**1922. Adidie mu wo adanseɛ.**
*Even eating has a witness.*
(You need a witness in case of future trouble).

**1923. Adidie ne nna nyɛ akorɔkorɔ.**
*Eating and sleeping are not things you beg people to do.*
(Some things cannot be dispensed with).

**1924. Didimeɛ nyɛ adepɛ.**
*Eating to satisfaction is not craving for riches.*
(Wanting enough is not being greedy).

**1925. Didimeɛ na ɛyi ɔburoni nansin adie.**
*Greed showed up the European's wooden leg.*
(Overindulgence reveals your weaknesses).

**1926. Adidipakyie a, ɛdii fie kan, na apɔpee ku no.**
*The gourd food-container that entered the house first is the one which suffered from the splashing up of rain.*
(You may have the privilege of recounting your experiences and being a pioneer but none the less you had to suffer for it).

**1927. Didiwuo nyɛ animuonyam.**
*Dying on a full stomach is not an honor.*
(Death is death, however you meet it).

**1928. Digya ne muna na ɛnam.**
*Refusal to share food leads to annoyance.*
(Meanness makes people dislike you).

**1929. Odikuro ba pɛ n'ahohora a, ɔnya.**
*If the son of a small chief likes abuse, he gets it.*
(You maintain your position in society by self-respect or others will not respect you).

**1930. Odikuro yare abenkum a, ne mma ne ne nananom nyinaa yare abafam.**
*If the village chief is left-handed, his children and his grandchildren all suffer from inability to stretch the arms well.*
(It was taboo to use the left hand for many things in Akan society. Children were forced to use the right hand, even if born left-handed. Hence: If you are odd, so will your descendants be).

**1931. Edin bra.**
*A name determines a character.*
(The Akan believe that you take on the character of the person you are named after. Hence: Be careful in naming anyone as you are thus determining their character).

**1932. Edin ne din na ɛhyia, na nyɛ suban ne suban.**
*A name and a name can coincide, but not one character and another.*
(Names may be the same, but all men differ).

**1933.** Adinkra ba Apau se: "Mennim sɛdeɛ nnipa bewie",
*Adinkra the son of Apau says: "I do not know the destiny of man",*
(Adversity causes a man to think deeply).

**1934.** Din pa yɛ sene ahonya.
*A good name is better than riches.*

**1935.** Dɔ bi di a, nsamampɔ huu!
*Weed a portion to use, then the cemetery is cleared.*
(A cemetery is normally kept unweeded. To use it as a farm indicates greed, as it is taboo to do so. Hence: Don't do more than you should).

**1936.** Wodɔ afuo na sɛ Onyame anhunu mu a, ɛnyɛ yie.
*If you cultivate a farm but God does not watch over it, all does not go well.*
(Success depends on God's support).

**1937.** Ɔdɔ de bɔne kyɛ.
*Love forgives shortcomings.*

**1938.** Ɔdɔ de asetena pa ba fie.
*Love brings a good manner of living to the home.*

**1939.** Ɔdɔ nkɔ asuo, ɔnkɔ anyina, nso ɔdidi.
*Love does not go for water and does not go for firewood, but it eats.*
(Love is served by the loved one).

**1940.** Ɔdɔ mu nni nkekaawa.
*There is no stain in love.*
(Love is pure).

**1941.** Ɔdɔ ntie fa ntie dawuro.
*A lover does not listen to argument.*
(Love is blind).

**1942.** Ɔdɔ ntie yɛse-yɛse.
*Love does not listen to rumors (lit. we say, we say).*
(You don't take notice of criticisms of someone you love).

**1943.** Ɔdɔ, yɛnni no sika.
*True love is not based on wealth.*

**1944.** Ɔdɔ yare asobrakyeɛ.
*Love is ill with stubbornness.*
(Love does not yield to persuasion).

**1945.** Ɔdɔ yɛ wuo.
*Love is death.*

**1946.** Adɔbɛ-aba akwagyan na yɛde yɛ abɛbudeɛ.
*The raffia-palm seeds, we use them for remembrance.*
(Many different objects, including the adɔbɛ fibers and seeds were strung together on a string to remind people of proverbs and to teach them. Hence: Said of something which teaches you to remember).

**1947.** Adɔbɛ, gyae abubuo bɔ na bisa bɛtene sɛ ɛyɛɛ dɛn na ɔyɛɛ tenten.
*Raffia palm, stop grumbling and ask the tall palm-nut tree how it managed to grow tall.*
(Instead of grumbling, try and do something about the situation you are in).

**1948.** Adɔbɛ-nwam ne ɔwam pa nsɛ.
*The raffia-palm and the great hornbill are not the same.*
(People belonging to the same family may not all be alike in character).

**1949.** Dodoɔ di a, dodoɔ yɔ; dodoɔ yɔ a, dodoɔ di.
*If many people are to eat, many people must produce; if many people produce, then many people can eat.*
(Prosperity depends on hard work).

**1950.** Dodoɔ funu mmɔn.
*Many people's corpses do not smell.*
(If everyone suffers there is no discrimination).

**1951.** Dodoɔ kɔ agyina a, ɔbaako nni asɛm ka.
*If many people go to a meeting, a single person has nothing to say.*
(A minority is not considered by the majority).

**1952.** Dodoɔ kyɛ sakoraama.
*Plenty share a calabash of palm wine.*
(If something is to be shared, you share it, however small the amount).

**1953.** Dodoɔ kyiri ɔbaako.
*Many detest a single one.*
(The crowd hates an individualist; a lonely person is easily cheated).

**1954.** Dodoɔ mu mamfrani ne deɛ wɔbu no aboa.
*The odd-man-out is considered a beast.*
(A stranger or an eccentric is often victimized).

**1955.** Dodoɔ yɛ adeɛ.
*Numbers can achieve anything.*
(Many hands make light work).

**1956.** Wododomse tu a, ato amokomoko.
*When you lose your back teeth, you have to use your gums to chew.*
(In times of difficulty you have to use a substitute for the real thing).

**1957.** Adodowa nyem a, ɔno nko ara na ɔwoɔ.
*If the small black fly is pregnant, it delivers by itself.*
(However unimportant you are, you perform your own tasks in life).

**1958.** Adodowa yɔnko ne kwadu na Oburoni yɔnko ne Obibini!
*As the banana fly is a companion of the banana, so is the European a companion of the African.*
(All exploiters are alike).

**1959.** Ɔdɔfoɔ a ɔdɔ me no na ɔde ɔdɔ noa aduane ma me die.
*A lover who loves me, prepares food made with the Ɔdɔ fish.*
(A play on words. Someone who loves you gives you the best).

**1960.** Wo dɔfoɔ kyɛ wo yere a, na wakyɛ wo akasakasa.
*If your loved one gives you a wife, then they give you dissension.*
(A favor given by someone who is not interested in its being a success, is bound to bring trouble).

1961. Ɔdɔfoɔ wu a, na ɔtamfoɔ ani awu.
*If a beloved one dies then the one who hates them is ashamed.*
(Death leaves hatred without a target).

1962. Dɔkono a ɔfura ntoma mpo yɛkyɛ no dɛn na akɔwie aboodoo a ɔda adagya.
*Even kenkey which wears a cloth is not respected, how much less the Akuapem roasted kenkey which has no cover (lit. lies naked).*
(Ordinary kenkey is wrapped in leaves and tied up; but aboodoo, the Akuapem roasted kenkey, is only partly wrapped in leaves. Hence: If those who are protected are easily destroyed, how much more so the unprotected).

1963. Dɔkono bɔ dam a, ɛnenam sɛn mu.
*When kenkey becomes mad, it moves about inside the pot.*
(We are all bound by some restrictions in society, however much we dislike it).

1964. Dɔkono kankyeɛ annyae dɛ yɛ a, yɛnnyae no buweɛ.
*Kenkey made with ripe plantain, if it does not stop being sweet, then we do not stop breaking and devouring it.*
(If you are too helpful people abuse your kindness).

1965. Wodom aberewa a, ɔhoahoa wo.
*If you favor an old woman, she praises you.*
(If you are kind to someone they will do anything for you).

1966. Adom nyinaa firi Nyame hɔ.
*All good things are from God.*

1967. Adom–Batam soma; ontie fa ntie dawuro na wasi kwan so.
*Sending a foolish person on an errand; he does not listen to anything, and then he makes off.*
(If you chose an incompetent person to do a job, don't be surprised if he does not even listen to your instructions and then goes off without doing anything).

1968. Ɛdɔm gu a, yɛnhyɛn abɛn.
*If an army is defeated, we don't blow a horn in its honor.*
(You cannot show off if you are unsuccessful).

1969. Ɛdɔm gu a, kagya ɛsi n'anan.
*When the army departs, the kagya plant (Griffonia simplicafolia) takes over.*
(This plant is often found growing on deserted land. Hence: When an important person leaves, the unimportant take over authority).

1970. Ɛdɔm kum anoseseadeɛ, na wɔnkum dɔmmarima.
*The victorious army kills the person with a big mouth but does not kill the brave man.*
(The brave are always respected but if you talk too much you suffer for it).

1971. Ɛdɔm ani bere a, ɛnyɛ kɔreɛ ntakara mu a.
*If the army gets angry it is not at the eagle's feather.*
(The eagle stands for the general. Military anger is reserved for the enemy).

1972. Ɛdɔm ani sa odedeni.
*The masses (lit. the army) are always critical of a popular person.*
(Envy never ends).

1973. Ɛdɔm nim dɔm akyi.
*One army knows the movements of another.*
(One expert understands another).

1974. Ɛdɔm ano yɛkɔ no akokoɔduru, na yenkɔ no atɛnnie–so.
*We go to war with courage, but we do not go with mere abuse.*
(It is actions that count and not words).

1975. Ɛdɔm suro dɔm.
*An army fears an army.*
(You fear your enemies).

1976. Ɛdɔm nnwuiiɛ a, yenkan atɔfoɔ.
*If the army is not destroyed we do not count the slain.*
(It is only after a disaster that we count the cost).

1977. Ɛdɔm yɛ koro a, wɔdi nkonim.
*If an army becomes allied, it becomes victorious.*
(Unity brings strength).

1978. Ɔdom–Amansan mmua atɛn.
*A public–spirited person does not give a verdict.*
(A good public servant does not take sides).

1979. Ɔdomankoma a, ɔbɔɔ adeɛ na obɔɔ ahiafoɔ.
*God who created possessions, created the poor.*
(The world is as God created it, with both rich and poor).

1980. Ɔdomankoma bɔɔ adeɛ, Bɔrebɔre bɔɔ adeɛ, yenhunuu kotebɔ a wapam gyatahene da.
*The Creator created things, Almighty God created things, but we have never seen a time when the kusimanse chased the lion away.*
(Some things are totally impossible or improbable, such as a weak person defeating a very powerful one).

1981. Ɔdomankoma bɔɔ etwɛ bataa kɔteɛ ho.
*The Creator created the vagina alongside the penis.*
(God created desire and satisfaction at the same time).

1982. Ɔdomankoma bɔɔ owuo ansa na ɔrebɔ akɔm.
*The Creator created Death before he created possession (fetish possession).*
(No amount of trying can put you above your senior).

1983. Ɔdomankoma bɔ Owuo ma Owuo ku no.
*The Creator created Death for Death to kill him.*
(A good servant becomes a bad master).

1984. Ɔdomankoma kɔɔ wuo no, ɔde n'akyiri gyaa agyinaeɛ.
*When the Creator went to his death, he left behind him a symbol.*
(Nothing is completely lost, it becomes something else).

1985. Ɔdomankoma na ɔma Owuo di nkani.
*The Almighty makes Death go ahead.*
(God rules even Death).

**1986. Ɔdomankoma nsɛneɛhene ne sukɔnkɔn.**
*The Almighty's court crier is the heron.*
(A watchful person knows what is going to happen).

**1987. Ɔdomankoma Wuo Kontonkurowi da amansan kon mu.**
*Almighty Death the Halo lies round the neck of all mankind.*
("Kotonkurowi" means the halo around the sun or the moon. Hence: No one can avoid death).

**1988. Ɔdomankoma Wuo, wofrɛ no Agya o, wofrɛ no Ɛna o, ɔdewo bɛko.**
*Almighty Death, you call it Father, you call it Mother, it will still take you.*
(There are some situations you cannot talk yourself out of).

**1989. Ɔdomankoma Wuo, wofrɛ no nnɛ o, wofrɛ no ɔkyena o, ɔrennane n'akyi nkyere wo.**
*Almighty Death, you call it today, you call it tomorrow, it will not turn its back and leave you.*
(Death never refuses to take someone).

**1990. Ɔdomankoma Wuo suro soboɔ a, anka ɔremfa onipa.**
*If Almighty Death were to be afraid of blame, he would not have taken man.*
(If you are sure that what you are doing is right, you should do it, no matter how much you are criticized).

**1991. Ɔdomankoma Wuo nyɛ obi a, yɛne no di kamamenka.**
*Almighty Death is not a person we play with.*
(Someone once took Death to Court, saying he had not been given notice of his intent. Death replied that he had given it, but had been ignored. The person had had many illnesses and by going to the doctor, had got adjournments. Now the court would allow no more. Hence: Death's final judgement cannot be appealed against).

**1992. Ɔdomfoɔ nan, yɛtwa no nyaa.**
*A benefactor's leg, we cut it cautiously.*
(You treat gently those who help you).

**1993. Dompe a ɔkraman de hyira n'ano no, ɛyɛ agyinamoa aniso dadeɛ bi.**
*The bone that the dog cherishes is a bit of old iron to the cat.*
(One man's meat is another man's poison).

**1994. Dompe a kuntunu antumi ammɔ mu no, ɔkraman bɔ mu a, ɛnyɛ yie.**
*The bone which the hyena could not crack, if the dog tries to crack it, it is not successful.*
(When a strong man cannot succeed, neither can a weaker).

**1995. Dompe biara nyɛ den nsene adwonkubɛn.**
*No bone is harder than the hip bone.*
(You can't do more than your worst. A gesture of defiance).

**1996. Ɔdompiafoɔ na ɔma dɔm guo.**
*The commander of the army enables the defeat of the enemy.*
(It is leadership that counts).

**1997. Odompo nam anadwo a, ɔsi agyeren.**
*If the marsh mongoose walks in the dark, it staggers.*
(If the situation is obscure, even an expert can make mistakes).

**1998. Odompo nim asuomnu a, ɔkɔnu po mu.**
*If the marsh mongoose knows how to swim, let him swim in the sea!*
(If you boast you can do something, prove it publicly).

**1999. Odompo se: "Wobrɛ ansa na woadi dɛ".**
*The marsh mongoose says: "You toil before you live in luxury."*
(Labor brings its own reward).

**2000. Odompo tiri ye nam, yɛntwa wedeɛ nto so.**
*The marsh mongoose's head is meat; you don't need to cut skin to add to it.*
(Sufficient unto the day is the evil thereof).

**2001. Ɔdɔnkɔ de akokɔ na ɛbɔ ne ho asuo ɔmfa odwan.**
*A slave uses a chicken to wash himself but he does not use a sheep.*
(You act according to your position in society).

**2002. Ɔdɔnkɔ kyiri bɛdom.**
*A slave taboos the best palm nuts.*
(A pure orange palm nut, whose tree gives a very strong wine. A slave fears to take the best of anything).

**2003. Ɔdɔnkɔ pɔ bebrebe a, yɛde no kɔ ayie.**
*If a slave becomes too familiar we take him to a funeral custom.*
(In the old days slaves were sacrificed at funerals to go with the departed spirit into the next world. If someone abuses their position, they are removed).

**2004. Ɔdɔnkɔ nsiesie ne ho se ne wura.**
*A slave does not dress like his master.*
(You must show due decorum in your behavior and not try and act above yourself).

**2005. Ɔdɔnkɔ nya adeɛ a, ɔbɔ dam.**
*If a slave gains possessions, he goes mad.*
(If a poor man suddenly becomes rich, it unbalances him).

**2006. Ɔdɔnkɔ yera a, yɛkɔpɛ no no, na ɛfiri ɔdehyeɛ ntira.**
*If a slave is missing and we go and search for him, it is because of a royal.*
(If you are attached to an important person, people take trouble over you).

**2007. Nnɔnkɔfoɔ baanu hwɛ ɔnantwie a, ɛkɔm ku no.**
*If two slaves look after a cow, hunger kills it.*
(Said of something which falls between two stools).

**2008. Dɔnkɔrehene pɛ ne ho ano na ɔnnya a, ɔbisa ne man.**
*If the chief of Dɔnkɔre cannot do what he should do, he asks the citizens of his state (for advice).*
(If you are responsible to someone you make sure they know your difficulties).

**2009. Adonko-toɔ mu wɔ biribi a, anka apan da apakan mu.**
*If swinging backwards and forwards were worth something, then the bat would recline in a palanquin.*
(If wishes were horses, beggars would ride).

2010. Odonno: "Menyɛ dɛn? Wɔayere me to, ayere m'ano, ɔdorobɛn, ɔdorobɛn."
*The hour-glass drum says: "What shall I do? They have tied my head and my bottom, dum-dum-dum, dum-dum-dum."*
(I am not in control of my own destiny, but what can I do about it)?

2011. Odonno mu anyɛ dɛ a, na ɛfiri deɛ ɔbɔ mu.
*If the hour-glass drum does not sound good, it is because of the person who plays it.*
(Mismanagement comes from the manager, not from what he manages).

2012. Ɔdorobɛn na ɛgyegye ma [ɛbɔm]/[asuhina].
*It is the tapping reed which collects for the palm-wine pot.*
(Ɔdorobɛn is the hollow reed used for wine-tapping. Hence, this is used when someone apparently insignificant is essential to an important man).

2013. Ɔdorobɛn pae mmɔfra nsam na ɛmpae mpanin nsam.
*The tapping reed breaks in children's hands but not in the hands of elders.*
(What is a problem for a child is easy for an adult. See Proverb 2012).

2014. Ɔdorobɛn se waboro nsa na aketekyiwa nso nye dɛn?
*The tapping reed says it is drunk, then how much more so the palm-wine pot.*
(A servant cannot claim to outdo his master. See Proverb 2012).

2015. Doteɛ ka wo nantin a, ɛka wo to.
*If mud dirties your legs, it also dirties your bottom.*
(If your relative is involved in a dirty business, you, too, will be contaminated).

2016. Ɔdɔtɔ homa-korɔ mmua.
*One creeper does not make a thicket.*

2017. Ɔdotɔnoma se asan ne abusuasɛm nti na ɔhyɛ dɔtɔmu, ɛfiri woyera wɔ kwaeɛ mu a wo nhwehwɛ yɛ hwehwɛna.
*The nightjar says because of misfortunes and family matters it hides in the thicket, because if you get lost in the forest, it is difficult to be found.*
(A careful person takes precautions).

2018. Adowa a, ɔde ne nan te-ase a, kurotwiamansa mmɔ ntoa nkɔko.
*If the royal antelope is alive, the leopard does not wear a cartridge belt to go to war for him.*
(The royal antelope is considered king of the beasts, although it is so small. Hence: If the king is present, then the servant does not take command).

2019. Adowa nya owu a, bisa nsɛmma.
*If the royal antelope meets its death, ask the fibre trap.*
(A person is always victimized by his enemy).

2020. [Adowa]/[eyuo] nwo ba na ɔnkɔse ɔwansane.
*The [royal antelope]/[black duiker] does not give birth to its child for it to resemble a bushbuck.*
(Like father, like son).

2021. Adowafoɔ amma ntɛm, na ɛfiri mmɔkwaabɔ.
*If the adowa dancers did not perform in time, it was because of begging for cloth.*
(If you do not have what you need to do something, your time is wasted in searching for it).

2022. Adɔyeɛ nti na nsiammoa kaa nam mu.
*Because of benevolence the larvae of the meat fly remains in the meat.*
(If someone is good to you, you stick by them).

2023. Adu Takyi Bɔtɔnkuruwa: "Ɔkɔtɔ didi a, na ɛyɛ aponkyerɛne ya".
*The hero Adu Takyi Bɔtɔnkuruwa says: "If the crab eats, the frog is jealous".*
(Many people are jealous of the success of others).

2024. Dua a ebɛbere ama yɛate bi adie no, yɛnsoso ogya ngu aseɛ.
*The tree which will bear fruit and enable us to pick some and eat, we don't light a fire underneath.*
(You don't harm someone who helps you).

2025. Dua a aboa no pɛ, na ɔwu da aseɛ.
*An animal dies under the tree it loves.*
(If a person sticks to a job or action till his death, it is an indication that he had dedicated himself to it).

2026. Dua a ɛfifiri nyinaa na ɛnyini a, anka yɛrenya wiram kwan.
*If all the trees which sprout were to mature, then we would have no path through the forest.*
(If everyone were to succeed in life there would be no one to do the work).

2027. Dua a egya da mu ho, ahoma nsere no.
*The tree that catches fire, the lianas do not laugh at.*
(You don't laugh when misfortune attacks those on whom you depend).

2028. Dua a agye ntini mpo tutu, na ɛnte sɛ onipa na ɔtutu ne nan.
*If a tree that has roots can fall down, how much more a human being who walks on legs.*
(If a strong man can be defeated, how much more a weak one).

2029. Dua a ɛbɛkyene na wotwa so a, ɛtumi fɛfɛ.
*If a tree is going to live long and you cut it, it sprouts again.*
(Predestination).

2030. Dua kontonkyenkronkyi na ɛma yɛhunu dwumfoɔ.
*It is the crooked piece of wood which enables us to recognize a good craftsman.*
(A man's skill is measured by his ability to tackle difficult material).

2031. Dua a Ananse adi awuo a, Ntikuma nkɔtena aseɛ ntɔ nko.
*The tree under which the spider ate and was killed, Ntikuma does not go under to sleep.*
(Ntikuma was the son of Kwaku Ananse the spider. Once bitten, twice shy. Or: You learn from the misfortunes of others).

**2032. Dua a annya ntini pa, ɛtu.**
*It is the tree that does not have good roots, that is uprooted.*
(You need to be well-rooted in your society).

**2033. Dua a ɛrepɛ din na esi nsuo so.**
*It is the tree that wants fame that stands by the stream.*
(Water enables a tree to grow big. Hence: If you want fame you must go where it can be nourished).

**2034. Dua a ɛsi sie so nkyɛre nyini.**
*A tree which grows on an anthill does not delay in growing.*
(People thrive in the right environment).

**2035. Dua a ɛsi nsuo mu, nsuro awɔ.**
*A tree which grows in the water is not afraid of the cold.*
(You do not fear what you are used to).

**2036. Dua a ɛto nam na ano yɛ hyeɛ.**
*The stick which is used to roast meat is the one that burns fiercely.*
(If you are involved in a project, you cannot avoid the consequences).

**2037. Dua a atoto abɛ na ano hyeɛ.**
*It is the wood which has been used to smoke out a palm tree which has its mouth burnt.*
(It is the warrior who gets wounded).

**2038. Dua a ɛyɛ [den]/[fɛ] nkyɛre [afuo so]/[hahan mu].**
*The tree which is [hard]/[beautiful] does not stand long [on the farm]/[in the forest].*
(The brave die young).

**2039. Dua a ɛyɛ den na ɛbuo.**
*It is the tree which is strong that falls.*
(A powerful man is open to attack).

**2040. Dua a ɛyɛ den na yɛde [nantwie]/[aboa] mantam mu.**
*It is to the strong tree that we tie the [cow]/[animal].*
(You chose the best tool or person for the job).

**2041. Dua a awuo, na aporɔ no, yɛntwitwa mfa mma fie mmɛsɔ.**
*A tree which has died and rotted, we do not cut up to take home to burn.*
(You do not waste your time over a useless job).

**2042. Dua bata boɔ a, ne twe yɛ twana.**
*If a tree grows near a rock, it is difficult to cut.*
(You cannot easily get at a man who has a protector).

**2043. Dua bi ne dua bi mmɛn a, ɛntwi.**
*If two trees stand apart, they do not rub against each other.*
(Propinquity leads to strife, lack of contact prevents it).

**2044. Dua biara a anomaa pɛ no, na ɔwu da aseɛ.**
*Any tree the bird likes, death lies underneath.*
(You stand most risk of being attacked at the place you most frequent).

**2045. Dua biara nso nnya nhwiren da.**
*No tree ever bore fruit before flowering.*
(First things first).

**2046. Dua bɔ dua so ansa na awae.**
*One piece of wood strikes another before it splits.*
(Every disaster has a cause).

**2047. Dua bu a, ɛtɔ deɛ n'aban kɔduru.**
*If a tree falls, it falls to where its length reaches.*
(A person is no greater in death than in life).

**2048. Dua bu to dua ansa na aduru fam.**
*When a tree is uprooted it falls on another before it reaches the ground*
(An important man's downfall affects those around him directly. Or: One must observe the proper protocol before reaching the top person).

**2049. Dua mmu ntɔɔ fam a, yenni ho mmire.**
*If the tree does not fall to the ground, we don't gather mushrooms from it.*
(Mushrooms or toadstools grow on rotten wood. Hence: One action depends on another).

**2050. Dua-dumfrane nsi kuro-nkwantia, nnane ɔbosompɔn, nnyegye abɛtem, mma abotokura nni nnɔre sradeɛ wɔ berɛ a yɛnwe ne nam.**
*The odum tree does not stand at the outskirts of the town to become a great fetish and collect palm nuts, to let the striped mouse eat them and become fat without our eating it.*
(Farmers returning from their farms often left part of their produce under some particular tree which was the shrine of a spirit. Hence: We do not toil for some useless stranger to eat).

**2051. Dua dwamanfoɔ na ɛbu tɔ kwanmu.**
*It is the prostitute tree that falls across the road.*
(A prostitute makes her position obvious. Hence: When you come from the farm you have to climb over any tree which has fallen across the path).

**2052. Dua mfa mfeɛ aduasa nkyea na yɛmfa afe koro ntene no.**
*A tree does not take thirty years to bend for one to take a year to straighten it.*
(You cannot undo past wrongs quickly or by wishful thinking. Old wounds heal slowly).

**2053. Dua kantankyinanka wotumi twa a, ɛda wo so; woantumi antwa a, ɛda wo so.**
*If you are able to fell a powerful tree, it is your own affair; if you are unable to fell it, it is also your own affair.*
(You success depends on yourself).

**2054. Dua koro gye mframa a, ɛbu.**
*If one tree stands alone against the wind, it breaks.*
(There is strength in numbers).

**2055. Dua korɔ ntumi nye kwaeɛ.**
*One tree cannot make a forest.*

**2056. Dua kunkon na ammu a, na ɛwɔ deɛ asaase reka kyerɛ no.**
*If the bent tree did not fall, it was because of what the earth told it.*
(There must be a reason for an expected event not to take place).

**2057. Dua ma ne ho kwan a, na ɛwoɔ dɔre mu.**
*If the tree allows itself to be used for honey, then honey will be found there.*
(If you allow people to take advantage of you, they will do so).

**2058. Dua na ɛma homa hunu soro.**
*It is the tree which enables the creeper to reach the heights.*
(If you are helped by an influential man, you prosper).

**2059. Dua repɛ w'anim ahwɛ a, na ɛso wo ntoma mu.**
*If a tree wants to see your face, it catches hold of your cloth.*
(If someone wants to see you they attract your attention first).

**2060. Dua si akuraa a, ne ntini wɔ fie.**
*If a tree stands in the village, the roots are in a house.*
(A man's roots are in his family group).

**2061. Dua si nsuo mu a, ɛmpore.**
*If a tree grows in the water, it does not shed its leaves.*
(In the dry season in West Africa, many trees shed their leaves. Hence: You do not put yourself to a lot of trouble and suffering if you have all you need).

**2062. Dua so yɛkɔ no tipɛn.**
*We go to the latrine (lit. the tree) with our own age group.*
(This colloquial expression comes from the time when everyone went behind a tree! Such things you only did with your own age group. Hence: Some private things are only discussed between members of the same generation).

**2063. Dua tan wo a, na ɛbu bɔ woɔ.**
*The tree which hates you, crashes on top of you.*
(People must have a motive to harm or kill).

**2064. Dua tenten na ɛma kontromfi hunu ha mu.**
*A tall tree enables the baboon to see inside the forest.*
(With help, you can do what you need to do).

**2065. Dua yɛ den a, yɛde akuma na ɛtwa mu.**
*If the wood (lit. tree) is hard, we use an axe to cut it.*
(However difficult a problem, it can be solved).

**2066. Dua rebɛwu a, ɛfiri n'ase na ɛmfiri ne nkona.**
*If a tree is dying it is from its roots and not from its branches.*
(Whatever happens has a root cause. Or: If the children misbehave, it is because of the influence of their parents).

**2067. Nnua a ɛbɛn na ɛtwie.**
*Trees which grow near each other rub against each other.*
(It is with people near to you that you quarrel. Or: Proximity leads to intimacy).

**2068. Nnua nyinaa woso a, ɛka abɛ.**
*If all trees shake, only the palm-nut tree is unaffected.*
(There is exceptions to every rule).

**2069. Nnua nyina rebɛtene na yɛde deɛ ɛwɔ he ayɛ sɔduro?**
*Should all the trees grow straight, which one would we use for the handle of a hoe?*
(If we were all alike, how should we get the different jobs done?)

**2070. Nnua nyinaa yɛ aduro, na wonnim a, na wose: "Dua bɔne yi, montwa ntwene."**
*All trees are medicinal, but if you don't know, you say:*

*"This tree is bad, cut it down".*
(You disregard people if you don't know their virtues).

**2071. Nnua nsaeɛ na anomaa atu asi onipa apampam.**
*Trees are not finished so that birds land on the crowns of human heads.*
(The situation has not reached such a state that people should act out of order).

**2072. Wodua Aburow na woamma koterɛ bi anwe a, ɔsa bi we.**
*If you plant corn and refuse to give some to the lizard, it takes some.*
(However mean you are, those working for you will by all means take a share).

**2073. Wodua Aburowne abra a, abra na ɛfifiri.**
*If you plant corn and deceit, deceit will grow.*
(Once you start being deceitful it is difficult to stop, like corn, from small beginnings it grows to great size).

**2074. Wodua kɔnkɔnsa Aburowa, ɛfifiri wo nan ho.**
*If you plant false corn, it germinates by your feet.*
(If you start something bad, it will develop to your detriment).

**2075. Wodua nkontompo a, wotu abra.**
*If you plant falsehood, you reap deceit.*
(If you are a liar, people will always doubt you).

**2076. Nnua me aburow, dua me nkateɛ na m'ase akyene.**
*Don't plant me maize, plant me groundnuts so that I may continue to flourish in the ground where I am planted.*
(It is better to invest in something which continues to be productive than in something which brings quick profit once).

**2077. Adua bere gono ansa na ate atɔ.**
*The bean ripens properly before it falls.*
(A plan has to mature before it can be put into effect).

**2078. Adua apateram na ɔforo dupɔn.**
*It is the large bean which climbs the great tree.*
(It is the strong man who gets to the top).

**2079. W'adua anso yie a, wonte no yie.**
*If your beans don't bear well, you can't get a good harvest.*
(You cannot reap what you have not sown).

**2080. Duamani na yɛtu ne ntini anadwo.**
*It is a familiar tree which we uproot in the night.*
(If you know someone well, you know how to deal with them at all times).

**2081. Aduane a wobɛdi ama anya woɔ no, na ɛyɛ adeɛ a wokyiri.**
*If food that you eat purges you, then you taboo it.*
(You abstain from what harms you).

**2082. Aduane a onipa die na ɛbɔn ne ho.**
*It is the food which man eats that gives him a smell.*
(You can tell a man by his deeds).

**2083. Aduane a woto a, ɛbɛhyeɛ no, wonoa a, ɛbɛhye.**
*If the food that you bake is burnt, that which you boil will burn.*
(If something is predestined, you cannot avoid it).

2084. Aduane a woammɛto no wɔ w'akora ne w'aberewa bokyeaa soɔ no, na ɛyɛ w'akyiwadeɛ.
*The food which you have not taken from your old man's and your old woman's hearth is taboo to you.*
(People are conservative in their tastes and like what they are familiar with).

2085. Aduane bi a wonni no, wonnoa.
*The food you don't eat, you don't cook.*
(Don't embark on a profitless venture).

2086. Aduane biara bɛkwati waduro a, ɛnyɛ borodeɛ.
*If any food keeps out of the mortar, it is not the plantain.*
(Some people are never out of trouble).

2087. Aduane bɔne nkwati kɔm nkum onipa.
*Bad food does not avoid a hungry person, so that he dies.*
(However bad a situation, you should try and do what you can to get out of it).

2088. Aduane dɛ ne ne hyehyeɛm.
*Food's sweetness is when it is hot.*
(There is a moment of success).

2089. Aduane hyeɛ yɛ dina.
*Hot food is difficult to eat.*
(It is difficult to make quick decisions).

2090. Aduane kwati waduro a, na ato awesawesa.
*If food slips by the mortar, then it results in a great deal of chewing.*
(If you don't treat a thing properly, it gives you a lot of trouble).

2091. Aduane kwati tɛkrɛma a, na ɛnni boɔ.
*The food which slips past the tongue has no price.*
(There are some things you cannot do without).

2092. Aduane nyinaa nyɛ dɛ pɛ.
*Not all food is equally sweet.*
(Everyone has his preferences).

2093. Aduane panin ne aburow.
*The elder of all food is corn.*
(Said to praise someone for their special qualities).

2094. Aduane yɛ dɛ a, tɛkrɛma na ɛhunu.
*If the food is good, the tongue recognizes it.*
(Everything has its own judge).

2095. Duben Fosu kuta nantwie mu na ɔnte mpentenkwa a, na ɛwɔ ase.
*If Duben Fosu is carrying the cow but is not rejoicing, there is some good reason for it.*
(Not everyone who should rejoice does so. They may have reasons of their own
for not doing so).

2096. Dubena ankum ɛkuro a, ɛbere ani.
*If the tree bark does not heal a sore, it removes the scab.*
(Everything has some use, even if it does not live up to expectations).

2097. [Adubinsu kwakuo]/[osua] te we, na ɔnte mma ne ba.
*The [Adubinsu monkey]/[white-nosed monkey] picks and eats, but she does not pick for her child.*
(One usually caters for oneself first).

2098. Due, due mu wɔ due, nanso ɛwɔ deɛ ɛsi ne mmatire.
*Amongst many messages of condolence there are those which are received with bowed shoulders.*
(Amongst many mourners only a few are really emotionally involved).

2099. "Oduei!" yɛka no anoɔhare.
*"That's mine!" you say (it) quickly.*
(If you want to take something which is open for anyone to take, you must act quickly).

2100. Due nkum kuro.
*Condolences don't heal a sore.*
(Actions speak louder than words).

2101. Dufɔkyeɛ da nsuo ase kyɛre sɛn ara a, ɛrennane ɔdɛnkyɛm.
*Even if the rotten log lies a long time in the river, it will never turn into a crocodile.*
(You cannot change the essential nature of things).

2102. Dufɔkyeɛ rebedane ɔdɛnkyɛm na yɛaye no deɛn?
*The rotten log is going to turn into a crocodile, and what shall we do with it then?*
(If someone of lower class betters himself, how should he be treated)?

2103. Adufudeɛ adeɛ da owuo afa.
*Excess leads to death.*
(If you act out of greed, you will suffer).

2104. Adufudeɛ adeɛ te sɛ ɔnwam takara, ɛbɛwie aseɛ no na ɛte sɛ apem.
*Cheap things are like the feathers of a hornbill, the end result is a thousand.*
(Beware of seeking after things you can get cheaply as they may lead to a greater debt).

2105. Adufudepɛ nti na ɔbaa de nkyene gu nkwan mu ma ɛtware mu.
*Because of greed, when a woman puts salt in the soup, it is overdone.*
(If you're too anxious to excel, the results of your work may be ruined).

2106. Adufudepɛ nti na aboa kuntanu annya nim.
*Because of greed the hyena did not achieve respect.*
(Greedy people are never respected).

2107. Odufudepɛfoɔ nya wuo a, na ɛfiri ne dodoti. .
*If those who like sweet things die, then it is because of the inside of the mouth.*
(If you are too greedy, your greed leads to your downfall).

2108. Odum se: ɔwɔ ɔbosom a, ɔdi etɔ. Ɔdan se ɔwɔ ɔbosom a, ɔboa.
*The odum tree says: it has a spirit within it which eats mashed yam. If the ɔdan tree says it has a spirit, it lies.*
(The odum tree is believed to be a suitable residence for spirits; the ɔdan is not. Hence: You believe a powerful man when he boasts but not a weak one).

2109. Odum si hɔ dada a, yɛse ɔyɛ Ɔtanɔ, na abonsamfoɔ abɛsi soɔ.
*If the odum tree which stands there for along time, is, you think, the Tano fetish, how much more so if the devil perches on it!*
(If you already fear something, you will fear even more when there is really something fearful there).

**2110. Adunsinfoɔ nkyiri "Gyebihyɛho".**
*Herbalists don't taboo "Add more to it".*
("Add more to it" is the client asking for more medicine.
Hence: Everyone likes his work to be appreciated and
continued).

**2111. Dunsini a yɛkwatiri ho nni baabi te.**
*The tree stump from which we will take bits, has
nowhere else to stay.*
(Said of someone whom everyone takes advantage of,
who cannot hide away).

**2112. Dupɔn keseɛ si afuo mu, yɛnnu abɛ ngu
aworata.**
*If a great tree stands on the farm, we do not cut the
palm nuts and scatter them anywhere.*
(If the man in authority is present, you don't take your
case to anyone else).

**2113. Odupɔn atutu no, na boroferɛ na esi n'anan.**
*When a great tree is uprooted, pawpaw grows in its
place.*
(One powerful man does not necessarily inherit from
another, but the inheritor may be fruitful in his own
way).

**2114. Odupɔn atutu no, na kɔtɔkɔ hyɛ aseɛ.**
*When the great tree has been uprooted, the porcupine
is still underneath.*
("Odupɔn" is often used as a figure for a leader; the
porcupine is the symbol of the Asante nation. Hence: If
the leader is destroyed, the people remain).

**2115. Aduro a ɛfiri kɔmfoɔ nsam nyinaa yɛ adupa.**
*All medicine from the fetish priest's hand is good
medicine.*
(If you have a firm faith in someone or something, then
anything that comes from them is taken as good).

**2116. Aduro bɛgye wo a aterema.**
*If medicine is good for you only a spoonful will help.*
(If something is helpful, even small quantities will
help).

**2117. Aduro nka ɛse, nso nka kɛtrema, na ɛyɛ den na
yɛnom?**
*A medicine does not touch the teeth, nor the tongue,
then how do we drink it?*
(If you make things too complicated, you don't act at
all).

**2118. Aduro nyɛ nam a, nyɛ ne ntoaseɛ ara.**
*If medicine is not powerful at least you have to pay a
deposit.*
(You pay the workman whether his work is good or
not).

**2119. Ɛbɛduru berɛ a, akwatia bɛware aye tenten no,
na ɔtenten nkɔ dan ano.**
*If the time comes when a dwarf will grow to be tall, then
the tall person will not be able to enter a doorway.*
(If you climb in rank, so do those ahead of you).

**2120. Woduru nkwantanan so na wommisa a, woyera.**
*If you stop at the cross roads and you don't ask the
way, you get lost.*
(In changing circumstances, don't be afraid to ask for
advice).

**2121. Woduru ntɛm a, yɛgu wo so abɛ.**
*If you arrive in good time, we will pour your palm soup
for you.*
(The early bird catches the worm).

**2122. Ɛduru sɛ yede kooko bɛkɔ atweɛ a, anka nkamfoɔ
bɛdi mu bi.**
*If it comes to the time when we shall use soft cocoyam
for a hunting expedition, then the nkamfo yam will
also be used.*
(If one person who is little considered becomes useful,
so do his counterparts).

**2123. Wonnuruu sɛ wodware awowa mu ha wodware
mu a, yeyi wo tɔn.**
*If you have not reached the position of being able to
act as a surety and you try to do so, we sell you up.*
(Don't take on financial burdens which you are unable
to bear).

**2124. Yɛnnuruu sɛ yɛma ɔhene akye a, yɛmma no
akye.**
*If we have not reached the stage of saying good-
morning to the chief, we don't say good morning to
him.*
(We act according to our position in society).

**2125. Adusɛɛ Akyakya se: "Obi ntumi nsere m'akyakya
gye sɛ Ɔsɛɛ".**
*Edusei the hunchback says: "No one except the
Asantehene can laugh at my hump".*
(Hunchback dwarfs often become servants of the
important chiefs. Hence: The servant of a powerful
master is respected).

**2126. Dutan mmubu nyɛ ne mmaboa.**
*A big tree does not break and leave the branches
unbroken.*
(The downfall of a great man affects his dependents).

**2127. Dutan ne dupɔn tutu a, kokokyinaka bɔ
nyinyen.**
*If the big tree and the great tree are uprooted, the blue
plantain-eater wanders in vain.*
(Said when you lose all those on whom you depend).

**2128. Dutan tutu a, ɛho nhoma twetwe.**
*If the big tree falls, the lianas hanging from it tear.*
(See Proverb 2126).

**2129. Dutan nyɛ biribi a, ɛyɛ agyegyensuo.**
*If the big tree has nothing else, it has the ability to
collect rain water.*
(If the head of the family is regarded of little importance,
at least he has authority over certain family affairs
which benefit the whole family).

**2130. Adutwie nim twi a, ɔtwi kwaem na ɔntwi
serɛso.**
*If two trees know how to grind against each other,
they do so in the forest and not in the long grass.*
(The long grass country is the savannah to the north
of Asante. Hence: It is where competition is stiff that
you have to fight for your rights, not where there is
little or none).

**2131. Dwa so hantan, efie awerɛhoɔ; yɛkyiri.**
*Public pride, grief in the home; we abhor both.*

**2132. Ɛdwa bɛba a, ɛfiri anɔpa.**
*If there is going to be a market, it begins in the morning.*
(An early bird catches the worm).

**2133. Dwabum bɔ a, ohiani adeɛ na ɛyera.**
*If an uproar occurs in the market, the poor man's thing goes astray.*
(It is always the poor who suffer first).

**2134. Adwadie mu wɔ amanneɛ.**
*Trading has its customs.*
(Every profession has its own rules and regulations, even if they are not written ones).

**2135. Dwaebofoɔ nnim sɛ ɔyɛ Nim-sɛ-meteɛ ba.**
*An arrogant person does not know he is a humble man's child.*
(If you are arrogant, you think you are too good to mix with ordinary people, even if your own antecedents are humble).

**2136. Adwafoɔ mma na wɔdwa wɔn aboɔ.**
*A stone breaker's children break their own stones.*
(People who share like interests do the same things. Or: Talents are inherited).

**2137. Dwaha ahoma nyɛ ahoma pa a, anka yɛmfa no mmɔ nyansapɔ mmiɛnsa.**
*If the dwaha string were not good string, it would not be used for making wisdom knots.*
(A wisdom knot consists of three reef knots and symbolizes wisdom, because it requires skill to undo. Hence: A wise man works with good material).

**2138. Dwaman so wɔ mmara.**
*A city has laws.*
(Everywhere has its own laws and regulations).

**2139. Adwan a wɔkɔɔ adidie mmaeɛ a, yennae afoforɔ ngu mu.**
*If the sheep which have gone to graze have not returned, we do not allow new ones to follow them.*
(Once bitten, twice shy).

**2140. Odwan a ɔnam abɔntenso na yɛtwe ne so abaa, na nyɛ deɛ ɔda buom.**
*It is the sheep which wanders on the streets that we beat and not the one in the fold.*
(A disobedient person gets into trouble easily, not the obedient).

**2141. Odwan a ɔbɛyɛ asisie na Onyame ma ɔyɛ dwantorɔ.**
*It is the sheep that will be troublesome that God makes lame.*
(Judgement is with the Lord! God denies advantages to those who do evil).

**2142. Odwan ba nsuro nnwahoma.**
*The lamb does not fear the sheep's rope.*
(You do not question what you are accustomed to).

**2143. Odwan abɔfono, yɛfa no ohia.**
*A sheep's carcass, we use in times of hunger.*
(Beggars can't be choosers).

**2144. Odwan dabere ne bamma ho; woanom nsa aboro a, kɔ fie kɔda.**
*The sheep's sleeping place is on the stoop; if you have drunk wine and become drunk, go home to bed.*
(Don't behave like an animal).

**2145. Odwan dii-dii na ɔbɔ ahina.**
*A tame sheep breaks the pot.*
(A person who knows you well is in a position to do you the most damage).

**2146. [Odwan]/[Aboa] firi fifire na ne ho nwii na yenhunuu.**
*The [sheep]/[animal] sweats but it is because of its fleece (lit. hairs) that we don't notice it.*
(The sufferings of some are not always visible to others).

**2147. Odwan gyina okurompɔn ho a, na ne wuo na aduru hɔ.**
*If a sheep stops to watch the insect, then it has reached its time of death.*
(This insect which looks like a mantis is reputed to kill sheep by mesmerizing them with its swaying movements so that they themselves sway with it and finally fall dead. Hence: If you are attracted by something dangerous, you should expect the worst).

**2148. Odwan ho baabi de berɛboɔ.**
*Part of the body of a sheep is the liver.*
(It takes all sorts to make a world; and you must learn to deal with all of them).

**2149. [Odwan Kwaatemaa]/[Odwantem] se: "Merehwɛ ɔsebɔ na mawo no so."**
*The [sheep Kwaatemaa]/[long-legged sheep] says: "I am going to look at the leopard so that I shall give birth to a baby like it".*
(There is an Akan theory that things the pregnant woman experiences can impress themselves on her child's character. Hence: Pre-natal influence! Or: If you do well, people try and imitate you).

**2150. Odwan ano ka nkyene a, ɔnnyae weɛ.**
*When a sheep's mouth touches salt, it does not stop nibbling.*
(When a weak man finds something pleasant to do, he finds it difficult to stop).

**2151. Odwan nyini wie a, yɛmfrɛ no adwammoa.**
*If a sheep has finished growing, we don't call it a lamb.*
(If a person is mature, you treat them as such).

**2152. Odwan pupua na ɔwo ahenasa.**
*It is the small stocky sheep that gives birth to triplets.*
(Said when someone apparently insignificant achieves great things).

**2153. Odwan bɛwu na ɔnya nwuiɛ a, yɛmfrɛ no ɔdwanfunu.**
*When a sheep is going to die but is not yet dead, we do not call it a dead sheep.*
(Do not prejudge a situation).

**2154. Odwan wuda yɛ ɔdasani wuda.**
*The day a sheep dies is the day a man dies.*
(All deaths are the same).

**2155. Yɛdwane bɔne na yɛnnwane papa.**
*We flee from bad but we don't flee from good.*

**2156. Wodwane Nyame a, wohyɛ n'ase.**
*If you run away from God, you are still under Him.*
(You cannot escape from the hand of God).

**2157. Odwanfunu nsuro sekan.**
*A dead sheep does not fear the knife.*
(There is an end to all suffering).

**2158. Odwanini de ne korona na ɛdi asie, na nyɛ ne mmɛn.**
*A ram fights with its heart and not with its horns.*
(Bravery comes from within a man and not from his physique).

**2159. Ɔdwanten nwo abirekyie.**
*A sheep does not give birth to a goat.*
(Characteristics are inherited not acquired).

**2160. Dwantire se: "Me tirimu fitaa; ɔkwasea bobonya, menni fɔ nti na mebɔ hyire".**
*The head of the sheep says: "My conscience is free; the righteous fool, I never taste of guilt, hence I am always in white".*
(Said of someone who suffers unjustly).

**2161. Wodware prako a, wosɛe wo nsuo kwa.**
*If you bath a pig, you spoil your water in vain.*
(Don't waste time trying to do something which will be of no use).

**2162. Adwareɛ foeɛ ansa na osuo retɔ.**
*The bathroom became wet before it rained.*
(You came and found an already existing situation).

**2163. Adwe, yɛwe no nkoro-nkoro.**
*Palm kernels, we chew them one by one.*
(Difficult problems are best tackled singly).

**2164. Adwen te sɛ ngo, ɛda a, yɛnane no.**
*The mind is like palm oil, when it lies still we heat it up.*
(A mind needs stimulation if it is to work to full capacity).

**2165. Adwen te sɛ kwaeɛnoma, nyɛ ɔbaakofoɔ na ɔnya.**
*Knowledge (lit. the mind) is like a forest bird, one person alone cannot catch it.*
(You learn from others. Or: Wisdom is not the possession of one person).

**2166. Ɔdwen redwen na Ɔdwendwere redwen.**
*Camwood (Baphia nitada) is thinking, then so is the bush.*
(Play on words. A reply to someone boasting that they alone can think out a solution to a problem).

**2167. Adwendwen nua ne: "Me ampa ara me ni?"**
*Much thinking is the brother of: "Is this what I have become?"*
(Too much reflection leads to self-doubt).

**2168. Ɔdwendwenfoɔ na yɛdwene asɛm kyerɛ no na nyɛ ɔkwasea.**
*It is a thoughtful person we ask advice from, not from a fool.*

**2169. Wodwene bɔne a, na bɔne toa wo.**
*If you think bad thoughts, then evil entangles you.*

**2170. Wodwene adwene pa a, wonya adepa.**
*If you think good thoughts, you will achieve good things.*
(The power of positive thinking!)

**2171. "Medwene sɛ", adwene yɛ asunsumabotoɔ; ammɔ mu a, ɛfom.**
*"I think that" is a thought thrown at random, if it does not hit the target, it misses.*
(Man's judgement is fallible).

**2172. Adwene a ɔda nsuo mu mpo ɔpɛ aba ama sukom de no, na ɔkwakuo a ɔsi dua soɔ?**
*If even the fish in the river, when the harmattan comes, is thirsty, then how much more so the monkey that sits on a tree.*
(The harmattan is the dry season. Hence: If the person in a privileged position suffers, how much more so the outsider. Or: If you are entitled to inherit something and you do not get it, how much less will someone who has no right to it).

**2173. Adwene da nsuo mu nso ɔdidi kokoso.**
*The fish lies in the water but gets its food from rocks above the surface of the pond.*
(Kokoso means literally: on top of a thing that sticks out above the surface of the water. It might be a rock or it might be organic material. Hence: You may live at home, but your income comes from outside).

**2174. Adwene da bunu mu ɔnnya nsuo a, ɔkɔtɔ a ɔda bɔn mu nnware nsra.**
*If a fish in the pond has no water, the crab that lies in its hole does not wash and oil itself.*
(See Proverb 2172).

**2175. Adwene da nsuo mu nso osukɔm tumi de no.**
*Though the fish lies in the water, yet it can become thirsty.*
(The fact that you have access to something does not mean you have all you need).

**2176. Adwene nna nsuo mu na ɔnse sɛ sukɔm de no.**
*The fish lying in the river does not need to say that it is thirsty.*
(If you live in conditions of plenty, don't say you are in need. Compare Proverb 2175).

**2177. Adwene: "Meredwene me man ho."**
*The fish: "I am constantly thinking of (the welfare of) my state."*
(Said of someone who cares what is happening to his town or state and tries to plan to help it).

**2178. Adwene di adwene a, na ɔdore.**
*If fish eats fish, then it grows fat.*
(We climb by pushing down others).

**2179. Adwene nkoara nnɔre.**
*A fish does not grow fat on its own.*
(Everyone needs help in prospering).

**2180. Adwene su, na nsuo mu a ɔda nti na obi nhunu ne nisuo.**
*When a fish weeps it is only the water in which it is lying that prevents you from seeing its tears.*
(People rarely appreciate the sufferings of those in positions of power).

**2181. Adwene nkɔ nsuo mu Kwasiada na yɛnhwe nyi no Dwoada.**
*The fish does not go into the river on Sunday for us to fish and catch it on Monday.*
(Plans take time to mature).

**2182. Adwennimmoa se ɔpɛ su a, na ɛnkyerɛ sɛ ɛsɛ sɛ ɔkyini kɔpɛ deɛ obi awuo.**
*If a lamb says it likes weeping, it does not mean it should go about asking for a place where someone has died.*
(Just because you like doing something, it does not mean that you have to overdo it).

**2183. Odwennini ahoɔden ne ne mmɛn. Wopane a, na woayɛ no awie no.**
*The rams strength is in its horns. If you pull them out, then it is powerless.*
(If you remove a man's main defence, he is powerless).

**2184. Odwennini kɔ n'akyi ansa na wapam.**
*The ram withdraws before it attacks.*
(A clever man plans before attacking a problem).

**2185. Odwennini yɛ asisie a, ɛfiri n'akoma na ɛmmfiri ne mmɛn.**
*If a ram is troublesome, it is so from its heart and not from its horns.*
(A bully is one by character and not by physique).

**2186. Adwetakyi anomaa werɛmfoɔ a, ɔkɔ asuo a, ɔde n'ano.**
*The Adwetakyi bird goes to fetch water with its beak alone.*
(Said of one who does great things with little support).

**2187. Adwetakyi anomaa werɛmfoɔ se: ɔrensi dan kwan nkyɛn na obi abɛfa ne ba.**
*The Adwetakyi bird says: it will not build its house by the roadside so that someone can take its chicks.*
(Said of someone who keeps their private life private so that their family should not be troubled by outsiders. In this case the bird's name is probably the appellation of the nightjar).

**2188. Dwetire a ahweteɛ yɛ hwehwɛna.**
*If the capital is squandered it is hard to get it again.*

**2189. Edwie wɔ ne kankuaa.**
*Even a louse has its cupping-glass.*
(However insignificant you are, you have some gift or talent).

**2190. Odwiratwa-nantwie se: "Mede m'ani mehwɛ wo".**
*The cow fattened for the Odwira festival says: I am looking at you with my eyes".*
(Said when someone begs for mercy from another).

**2191. Wodwo bayerɛ na ammɔ a, nnunu no.**
*If you dig yam and it has not flourished, don't blame it.*
(If someone doesn't flourish, it is because of their environment).

**2192. Wodwo w'ani dwa tɛtia a, wohunu ne nsono.**
*If you work slowly and carefully skinning the ant, you see its intestines.*
(Patience brings its reward).

**2193. Wonnwo a, wodwo obi sɛn mu.**
*If you don't calm down, you cool down in someone's cooking pot.*
(If you lose your temper and don't act reasonably, you will be made to suffer for it).

**2194. "Ɛnnwoeɛ, ɛnnwoeɛ" dwo wo yɔnko anom.**
*"It has not cooled, it has not cooled" cools in your companion's mouth.*
(The image is presumably of someone delaying eating to wait for the food to cool and allowing someone else to eat it as a result. Hence: If you neglect your chances, someone else profits from them).

**2195. Dwodwurodwo dwan, obiara twa bi di.**
*A foolish man's sheep, everyone can cut their share and eat.*
(If you are foolish everyone takes advantage of you).

**2196. Dwokorɔ nti na (emma) Abotakyi kuro bɔeɛ.**
*It was a piece of roasted yam which ruined the town of Abotakyi.*
(A piece of yam, fought over by two children, caused the citizens of this town to take sides and so led to civil war. Hence: Little quarrels can lead to big ones and so to ruin).

**2197. Nnwom nyinaa ne "haa-ho".**
*All songs are jolly.*
(Songs are made to cheer you up).

**2198. Wodwonsɔ gu faako a, na ɛfiri ahuro.**
*If you urinate in one place, it produces foam.*
(If you concentrate on one thing at a time you get a good result).

**2199. Woredwonsɔ na wota, na wotwa w'ani na obi ne hɔ a, wonya mfaso-prenu.**
*If you are urinating and you fart, and you look around and no one is there, you have gained doubly.*
(Certain indulgences which are socially undesirable give much pleasure when practiced privately).

**2200. Ɔdwontofoɔ nkɔeɛ a, yɛnsua ne nne.**
*If the singer has not departed, we should not imitate his voice.*
(You don't criticize a bad performer in his presence).

**2201. Adwotwa ho adeɛ yɛ abusudeɛ.**
*Deception breeds ill-luck.*
(Things got by dishonesty turn sour on you).

**2202. Adwuma bɔne nte sɛ korɔnobɔ.**
*Bad work is not worse than (lit. is not like) stealing.*
(It is better to do any kind of work than to steal).

**2203. Adwuma sini nni akatua.**
*Work half-done attracts no pay.*
(You pay by results).

**2204. Adwuma bɛyɛ yie a, ɛnnim sika ketewa.**
*If work is going to be successful it does not matter if there is little money.*
(What is predestined to succeed, will succeed).

**2205. Odwumayɛni di ahomasin.**
*The workman is entitled to take some of the hide for himself.*
(Used as justification for taking what is left over after a job is finished).

- F -

**2206. Wofa ɔbaa yɔnkoɔ a, ɛhia wo.**
*If you take a woman for a companion, you will be in want.*

**2207. Wofa ɔbarima kwan mu a, wo sekan yera.**
*If you get up against a real man on the road, your knife goes astray.*
(A warning against offending those stronger than yourself, even if armed).

**2208. Wofa abirekyie adamfoɔ a, wogya abɔdwesɛ.**
*If you make friends with a goat, you grow a beard.*
(A man tends to copy his friends or to become like them).

**2209. Wofa abofu twa dunsini a ɛsi wo nkwanseɛ a, wohwere wo soafoɔ.**
*If, out of anger, you cut the tree stump on your farm, you lose your carrier.*
(You put your load on the stump before lifting it onto your head. Hence: You should not lose your temper and get rid of something which helps you)

**2210. "Mafa madi" na ɛda hɔ retwɛn wo.**
*"I have taken and eaten," it is waiting for you.*
(If you misuse something, in the long run you will have to take the blame for it).

**2211. "Fa ha hyia me!" nyɛ akwankɔ.**
*"Go and meet me there," is not a good beginning for a journey.*
(Start with someone you would travel with, don't arrange to meet them somewhere on the way and so miss them).

**2212. Wofa kunafoɔ bɔne a, wotwa wo saman pa powa.**
*If you marry a bad widow, you defy your departed spirits.*
(This proverb is about marrying a woman you "inherit" from a dead kinsman. Hence: Don't involve yourself with something known to be dangerous).

**2213. "Fa wo nsa to me kotokuo mu yi nimdeɛ yi no nimdeɛ mu" nyɛ nimdeɛ.**
*"Put your hand into my bag to take out wisdom, but do it wisely", is not wisdom.*
(Misusing wisdom is not wise).

**2214. Wofa nwansena abofu a, wobere wo kuro.**
*If you become annoyed with the fly, your sore is opened.*
(If you allow yourself to be irritated, you act unwisely).

**2215. Wofa asaasedeɛ bebrebe a, wobɔ korɔno.**
*If you lay hold on too many earthly treasures, you become a thief.*
(Too much greed corrupts).

**2216. Wofa [ɔsebɔ]/[gyahene] yɔnkoɔ a, wonsuro ham bio.**
*If you keep company with a leopard, you no longer fear anything in the bush.*
(If you are friends with a powerful man, you don't need to fear anyone).

**2217. "Fa wo sɛn" na ɛde tokwa ba.**
*"Take your cooking bowl away", brings about quarrels.*
(Rejection of normal services causes resentment).

**2218. Wofa wo so ne w'akonnwa a, yɛnnye wo nsam.**
*If you occupy a stool which you are equal to, it is not taken from you.*
(If you use authority well, you keep it).

**2219. Wofa Tafo a, wosi Boɔkurom.**
*If you pass through Tafo, you enter Boɔkurom.*
(There is more than one solution to any problem).

**2220. "Fa tom, fa tom", na ɛyɛ adesoa.**
*"Add to it, add to it", makes a burden.*
(Small things add up to big ones).

**2221. Wofa tope na woanwe a, na ɛfiri deɛ wofaa no.**
*If you take the big snail and do not eat it, it is because of the place you took it from.*
(If you don't use something you have taken trouble to acquire, it is because you doubt its origins).

**2222. "Fa twa w'ani so" ne "fato w'ani so" nyinaa ye baako.**
*"Look about you," and "Cast your eyes about," is the same thing.*
(It is difficult to distinguish between similar things. Or: Don't squabble over details).

**2223. Wofa yafummɔne a, wodi wo ho kyeame.**
*If you are born with a bad stomach, you become your own linguist.*
(If your stomach makes noises, you have to explain it yourself. Hence: You have to explain your own shortcomings).

**2224. Woremfa a, wonkuta mu den.**
*If you won't take it, you don't hold it fast.*
(You don't hold onto something you do not want).

**2225. Yɛmfa obi asɛm ho a, yɛmfa mmu ntɔdie.**
*If someone's affair does not concern us, we don't involve ourselves in expenses over it.*
(Don't poke your nose into other people's affairs).

**2226. "Yɛmfa mmɔ, mfa mmɔ", nso ɛhɔ ara na yɛdebɔ.**
*"We don't knock against, we don't knock against," but it is there that we knock.*
(Constant denial does not stop a thing from happening).

**2227. Yɛmfa abɔdwesɛ-hunu na ɛkɔ Sraha.**
*Just because you have a beard, you don't go to Salaga.*
(Salaga is a northern town. Many Northerners were bearded. Hence: You don't go to a place just because you resemble the people there).

**2228. Yɛmfa bɔne ntua bone ka.**
*We don't use evil to pay the debt of evil.*

**2229. Yɛmfa deɛ wawuo adeɛ mmoa ayie.**
*We don't take the possessions of the deceased to help (pay for) the funeral.*
(Certain people have certain responsibilities, which cannot be borne by others).

**2230. Yɛmfa adeɛ num nto aduonum ho.**
*We don't compare five things with fifty.*
(We don't compare the small with the big).

**2231. Yɛmfa nnompe hunu nyɛ nkwan na yempɛ ne dɛ.**
*We don't take only bones to prepare soup, and expect it to be sweet.*
(You get out of life what you put into it).

**2232. Yɛmfa nnwoa dada nyɛ nkwan.**
*We don't use old palm kernels to make soup.*
(Forget and forgive).

**2233. Yɛmfa efie adeɛ nkɔdi no ɛha mu.**
*We don't take something belonging to the home to eat outside.*
(What belongs to the family, should be kept in the family).

**2234. Yɛmfa fie nyɛ ɛham.**
*We don't take the home to be the bush.*
(You should behave with decorum in the home).

**2235. Yɛmfa [agyan]/[bɛn] dada nto foforɔ ho.**
*We don't compare an old [arrow]/[catapult] with a new one.*
(You can't compare the old with the new. New brooms sweep cleanest).

**2236. Yɛmfa hia ntwetwe sankuo.**
*Whilst we are poor we don't pluck the lute strings.*
(The poor must work not play).

**2237. Yɛmfa ahummɔbɔ nyɛ ɔpe.**
*We do not use sympathy as an excuse for sexual relationships.*
(Sympathy is one thing and sexual relationships another. Don't confuse them).

**2238. Yɛmfa ahurihurie nsisi fɛnfɛm.**
*You don't use jumping about to cheat a jumper.*
(You cannot trick a person at his own game).

**2239. Yɛmfa akokɔ korɔ ntwa abosom mmienu so.**
*We don't take one fowl and sacrifice it to two fetishes.*
(You cannot serve two masters at one time).

**2240. Yɛmfa kokuroko nni amin.**
*We don't use mere bulk to cheat.*
(It is intelligence, not bulk, that counts).

**2241. Yɛmfa akraa nto sono tuo.**
*We don't use a wax bullet to shoot an elephant.*
(A serious situation needs a drastic solution).

**2242. Yɛmfa mani-dorowa nto panneɛ pa ho.**
*We don't compare a needle of local manufacture with an imported one.*
(Don't equate inferior with superior).

**2243. Woamfa Memeneda ansra kwan a, wode Kwasiada dwane.**
*If you don't spy out the road on a Saturday, you will flee on Sunday.*
(If you don't plan ahead in fighting a battle, you will lose).

**2244. Yɛmfa mmirika nkɔto ɔtwe.**
*We don't use running to reach the duiker.*
(You do not compete with the expert in his own field).

**2245. Yɛmfa nam mma akɔdaa na yɛatete ho sradeɛ.**
*We don't give a piece of meat to a child from which we have taken the fat.*
(If you give, give generously: don't be stingy).

**2246. Yɛmfa ananse mma ho nsuo nnware funu.**
*We don't take boiling water to wash a corpse.*
(When water bubbles you say that father Ananse the spider is washing his children. Extremely hot, but not boiling, water is used to wash and soften a corpse. Hence: You must treat a person with consideration whether dead or alive.

**2247. Yɛmfa yen ani na ɛka nkwan hwɛ.**
*We don't use our eyes to taste the soup.*
(Don't judge by appearances).

**2248. Yɛmfa anihahane nkɔ aperenkensema kurom.**
*We don't go with big eyes to the bush-baby's town.*
(This animal has very large eyes. Hence: Don't carry coals to Newcastle).

**2249. Yɛmfa anohunu na ɛpamo obusuyɛfoɔ.**
*We don't use wanton talk to drive away an evil man.*
(You have to sacrifice to get rid of evil).

**2250. Yɛmfa anoteɛ nkɔgu obi apɛsire.**
*We don't take fluent speech to flow at someone else's wake-keeping.*
(You should not throw your weight about in another person's sphere of influence).

**2251. Yɛmfa ɔnopɔnhunu na ɛkɔ Basel asɔre.**
*We don't take empty boasting to the Presbyterian church.*
(The main Presbyterian missionaries in Ghana were the Basel mission. Originally, only those who dressed "respectably" in European suits were allowed to officiate in the Presbyterian church. Therefore you had to have some wealth before you could participate. Hence: Before you can obtain something valuable you have to be in a position to do so).

**2252. Yɛmfa "Woanya me nyɛɛ" mmu ɔman.**
*We don't use "I have been a victim of yours" to run a State.*
(A statesman should not be vengeful).

**2253. Yɛmfa nyansa nkɔ aburokyire.**
*We don't take wisdom to go overseas.*
(Don't carry coals to Newcastle).

**2254. Yɛmfa nyanyankyerɛ nni mmɔfra-gorɔ.**
*We don't use the scorpion to take part in a children's game.*
(Some things are not to be played about with but to be taken seriously).

**2255. Yɛmfa mpaboa korɔ nkɔ ahemfie.**
*We don't go to the chief's palace with only one sandal.*
(You take off your sandals in the presence of the chief. Hence: You should always show respect to those in authority).

2256. Yɛmfa sekantia nnwa esono nwie na yɛde adwa nanka.
*We don't use the short cutlass to skin an elephant and when we have finished use it to skin a puff-adder.*
(You don't use the same things to deal with important people as you do with ragamuffins. For instance you entertain honored guests with your best drinks but not the beggar who comes to the door).

2257. Yɛmfa asɛnhia nni agorɔ.
*We don't take important matters to play with.*

2258. Yɛmfa asɛnhia nsoma ɔbatan.
*We don't give a serious message to a nursing mother.*
(You don't give an urgent task to someone who has other important obligations).

2259. Yɛmfa sika kɔkɔɔ nto anomaa kɔn mu mma ɔmfa ntu nkɔ wiramu.
*We don't put a gold nugget round the neck of a bird and let it fly away into the forest.*
(You don't leave your precious things with those who cannot care for them).

2260. Yɛmfa srɛsuo na ɛnoa kowedeɛ.
*We do not use water from a stagnant puddle to cook bush-cow's skin.*
(You should make adequate preparations for a big job).

2261. Woamfa anto deɛ ɛda a, ɛfiritɔ.
*If you don't put it in its proper place, it gets missing.*
(Keep things tidy and you won't lose them).

2262. Ma yɛmfa nto wo so, na mma no nnyɛ hɔ.
*Accept their accusations, but don't let them prove true.*
(If you are slandered, don't argue, but act so as to prove your accuser wrong).

2263. Mfa tua kuro anim a, yɛnnyae mmisa sɛ: "Aboa bɛn ni?"
*If a guinea worm is in the sore, we don't ask:"What kind of animal is this?"*
(If something is obvious, you don't question it).

2264. Mfa nyɛ biribi a, ɔyɛ asaaseboa.
*If guinea worm is nothing else, it is a ground insect.*
(Everything can be identified by some characteristic or quality).

2265. Yɛmfa yɛn ano hunu mpamo busuyɛfoɔ.
*We don't use our mouth to drive away witchcraft.*
(You must use adequate means to ward off danger. Mere talking is not enough).

2266. Afa na ɛboa ɔtomfoɔ ma ɔtono.
*It is the bellows that help the blacksmith to forge.*
(Everyone depends on someone else for his success in life).

2267. Faako a yɛgyina dua adeɛ, ɛhɔ ara na yɛgyina teɛ.
*Where we stand to plant something, there we stop to reap.*
(What we sow we reap).

2268. Faako a yɛkum onanka, ne yɛfiri aseɛ kan ne sini anim.
*The place where we kill the adder is where we start to count the slices cut (from it).*
(One act follows directly on another).

2269. Faako a ɛsono awu atɔ, ɛhɔ nhahan nyinaa pore.
*Wherever the elephant dies, all the leaves are destroyed.*
(When a big man is in trouble, so are those around him).

2270. Afafantɔ: "Nsa ni ho! Na aka sika".
*The butterfly: "Drink is here! But money is short".*
(Said when poverty restricts your pleasures and plans).

2271. Afena bi da bi so.
*One sword is senior to another.*
(There is rank in everything).

2272. Famfa di hene wɔ sika so.
*The scoop reigns over your money affairs.*
(The brass scoop was usually placed over gold weights, when packing them up, to protect them. Hence: Said of someone who protects and controls the household).

2273. Fantefoɔ yɛ Akanfoɔ a, na nyɛ ɛne Akompifoɔ.
*If the Fantes are Akan, then you don't include the Akompi people.*
(If you are talking of important matters, you don't bother over trifles).

2274. Ɔfarebae, yɛnyi no agorɔ mu.
*The creator of a dance should not be excluded from it.*
(Do not despise or get rid of the person to whom you owe your position).

2275. Afaseɛ nye "Baye-pa" nso ɛno na obi de hyira n'ano.
*The water yam is not a true yam, but it is that which someone uses for*
soul-washing.
(If you can't get the best, then you find a substitute).

2276. Mfasoɔ nti na yɛdi dwa.
*We trade because of profit.*
(We work to earn).

2277. Mfatoho na ɛde mpoatwa ba.
*Comparison brings defiance.*
(Comparisons are odious).

2278. Ɔfatuo na ɔdi aninsɛm.
*One who takes hold of a gun acts in a manly fashion.*
(If you have the means to do something, you should have the courage to do it).

2279. Ɔfatwa te amaneɛbɔ mu.
*Gossiping grows out of saying what your mission is.*
(When you arrive anywhere you are asked what your mission is. Hence: One thing leads to another).

2280. Ɔfatwafoɔ! Ɛbɛka wo nko.
*Sycophant! You will be left alone.*
(The sycophant ends up being rejected by everybody).

2281. Fawohodie ne yera na ɛnam.
*Freedom results in getting lost.*
(Too much freedom leads to lack of direction).

2282. "Fawohodie" nyɛ duabɔ, nanso akyire wɔ asɛm.
*"Take your freedom", is not a curse, but it has its repercussions.*
(Freedom entails responsibility).

2283. Afe bi yɛ asiane.
*Some years are full of trouble.*

2284. Afe nkyɛre ba, nanso ɛnto nnipa nyinaa.
*A year comes quickly but not all people can survive it.*
(People can't live for ever).

2285. Afe so a na yɛma afenenhyiaboa "Yaakɔ!"
*At the end of the year we give the chameleon condolences.*
(The chameleon is supposed to appear once a year and also to die when giving birth. Hence: Some people are never without trouble and need our sympathy).

2286. Ɔfe ho nnua no ebi ara ne [mpampuro]/ [nkampuro].
*One of the trees along the Offin river is the bamboo.*
(However insignificant one is, one is still a member of the family).

2287. Ɛfeɛ akyi nni abofono.
*After vomiting there should be no nausea.*
(When a problem is settled it should be forgotten).

2288. Afeefeɛ de akaekaeɛ ba.
*Too much investigation brings too many memories.*
(Let sleeping dogs lie).

2289. Wofeefee efunu ani a, wohunu ɔsaman.
*If you study a corpse's eyes, you see a ghost.*
(Too much probing brings unpleasant consequences).

2290. Wofeefee asɛm mu a, wohunu mu yie.
*If you look into a problem closely, you can see it clearly.*

2291. Fɛfɛ na ɛyɛ fɛ na akokɔ wura dan mu a, ɔkoto na ɛnyɛ sɛ ne tiri bɛpem.
*It is because of courtesy (lit. beauty that is beautiful) that, if a chicken enters the room, it bows its head, and not because it would knock its head.*
("Fɛ" means beautiful or handsome in appearance; but it is also used to describe well-mannered behavior. Hence: We act sometimes out of good manners and not self-interest).

2292. Fɛfɛ na ɛyɛ fɛ na ɛma yɛyɛ owufoɔ ayie, na nyɛ sɛ ɔbɛsorɛ amfiri amenamu aba fie ntira.
*It is because of courtesy (lit. beauty that is beautiful) that we celebrate a funeral for the dead, but not so that they can get up out of the tomb and return home.*
(Not all actions have ulterior motives. See Proverb 2291).

2293. Fɛfɛ na ɛyɛ fɛ nti na ɔdamani tu mmirika a, ɔsɔ ne nufu mu, na ɛnyɛ se ɛbɛte atɔ ntira.
*It is because of beauty (lit. beauty that is beautiful) that the young girl holds her breasts when running and not because they may fall off.*
(Said when someone makes a fuss in order to draw attention to themselves. See Proverb 2291).

2294. Wo mfɛfoɔ redane atwe a, dane bi.
*If your contemporaries are turning into duikers, turn too.*
(When in Rome do as Rome does).

2295. Wo mfɛfoɔ regye asra na woannye bi, yɛse wo mmɔwerɛ awu.
*If your intimate friends take snuff and you don't take*

some, we say that your finger nails have died.
(If you refuse to share something with your friends they think your friendship is dying).

2296. M'afɛfoɔ nyinaa kɔ anadwo-ha, me nko mekɔɔ bi a, makɔto pɛtɛ tuo.
*All my friends go hunting at night, but when I alone went I only shot a vulture.*
(Said when someone has consistent bad luck).

2297. Wo mfɛfoɔ tan wo a, wɔfrɛ wo "Saara".
*If your contemporaries dislike you, they call you "Always the same".*
(Give a dog a bad name and hang it).

2298. Afɛkubɔ nti na kɔtɔkɔ nyaa awia wuo.
*Because of fellowship the porcupine had an afternoon death.*
(Staying by a friend may be costly).

2299. Afɛkubɔ te sɛ asanom, woanhwɛ wo ho so yie a, ɛma wosopa.
*Companionship is like drinking too much palm wine, if you are not careful, it leads to disgrace.*
(Too much enjoyment of good company can lead to unwise actions and so to disgrace).

2300. Fɛmfɛm ne Hɔnhɔn hyia mu a, na mmirika asa.
*When the two fastest runners (Fɛmfɛm and Hɔnhɔn) meet for competition, then all (other) running ceases.*
(Fɛmfɛm means nimble. Hence: In the presence of professionals, amateurs become insignificant).

2301. Wofɛm opepeni sika a, wotɔn w'asomdwoeɛ.
*If you borrow a Northerner's money, you sell your peace.*
(Don't put yourself in the power of a difficult person).

2302. Afenawa a ɔkɔɔ anyina anya bi amma fie a, yɛfrɛ no ɔkwadwofoɔ.
*If the maid-servant went to look for firewood and did not bring some to the house, we call her an idler.*
(When someone does not succeed in life they attract criticism).

2303. Afenawa Kraa, susu ma dwanam nyɛ wo dɛ, ɛfiri sɛ obi deɛ aba na obi deɛ nam kwan so.
*Maid-servant Kraa, try not to let mutton be too sweet to you, because someone's case has come and someone else's is on the way.*
(Don't be too satisfied with present pleasure as your turn may come to suffer).

2304. Fenni da me so, Aberɛkwasi da me so. Adeɛ nkɔkye Kwasiada a, na matwa ntoma ama me kora ba?
*I am responsible for Fenni, am responsible for Aberɛkwasi. When we reach Sunday am I expected to buy my fellow wife's child a piece of cloth?*
(When you have your specific responsibilities you should not be asked to take on more than you can cope with).

2305. Wofɛre a, wofɔn.
*If you are shy, you grow thin.*
(If you are shy to complain, you have to do without things).

2306. Wofɛre w'afenawa a, wodi nnuane fi.
*If you fear your maid servant, you eat stale food.*
(Unless you maintain discipline amongst those who work for you, you suffer).

**2307. Woferɛ onipa bi a, ɛnkyere sɛ wosuro no.**
*If you respect a person, it is not that you fear them.*
(Respect is not the same as fear).

**2308. Woferɛ w'ase a, woyere nhunu wo aware.**
*If you fear your in-law, your wife won't make your marriage a success.*
(Good relations with an in-law are important but you should not do everything they say if you want a good marriage. Stick to your guns).

**2309. Woferɛ wo yɔnko ba a, ɔtete wo kyɛ.**
*If you are shy to chide your companion's child, he will tear up your hat.*
(Don't be afraid to stop someone who is doing wrong, whoever he may be).

**2310. Efere da faako a, ɛbere.**
*If the pumpkin lies undisturbed, it ripens.*
(If a person's life is not upset they continue to flourish and produce).

**2311. Eferɛ, yɛdi no butaa-butaa.**
*The pumpkin, we eat it without enjoying it.*
(We do some things because we have to and not because we want to).

**2312. Eferɛ firi n'ase na ebum.**
*Pumpkin blossoms from its roots.*
(A person grows out of their inherited background and flourishes accordingly).

**2313. Fɛreɛ ne wuo, fanyinam wuo.**
*Shame and death, death is preferable.*

**2314. Fɛreɛ nti na Agya Ananse de ɔtwe kyɛ hyɛ srɛ adɔ.**
*Because of shame Father Spider wears an antelope skin hat to beg for help in weeding his farm.*
(Kwaku Ananse went to his mother-in-law's house and stole some of her very hot cooked beans. He put them under his hat to hide them and burnt himself bald. Hence: Said of someone who tries to hide what he is like because he wants to get something out of you).

**2315. Wo fɛrefoɔ fere a, wofɛre.**
*If those you respect become ashamed, you too become ashamed.*
(The problems and ideas of those you respect become your own).

**2316. Wo fɛrefoɔ hunu w'atabɔeɛ a, ɔgyae wo fɛreɛ.**
*If those who respect you see through your dealings, they stop respecting you.*
(If people get to know your shortcomings, they cease to respect you).

**2317. Efiada anto Ata a, ɔnnware Abamo.**
*If Ata did not live until Friday, he was unable to wash Abamo.*
(Ata is a twin; Abamo the fetish that protects twins. Hence: Used when some unavoidable circumstance makes one break a promise or give up a plan).

**2318. Afiase yɛ fe sɛ deɛn ara a, ɛnyɛ ahotɔ na wɔde da hɔ.**
*Even if the prison is beautiful, you don't stay there at peace.*
(There is no relaxing in slavery).

**2319. Afidiboa wɔ fie a, yɛnkum ayɛmmoa.**
*If you have caught a bush animal in a trap, you don't kill a tame one.*
(Use what you can get from outside now and keep what you have at home for a rainy day).

**2320. Fidie hwan a, ɛkɔ ne nkyi.**
*If the trap is sprung, it goes back to its original position.*
(There is no place like home).

**2321. Fidie nsiane ketebɔ ho nyi nhahamma.**
*The trap does not by-pass a leopard to trap leaves.*
(You do the job you are meant to, not a lesser one).

**2322. Efie a nkwadaa nni mu no, na mpanimfoɔ bɔ nkɔnkɔn.**
*If there are no children in a house, then the elders get whooping cough.*
(If there is no one else to do a job then you have to do it yourself).

**2323. Efie abosea twa wo a, ɛsene sekan.**
*If the gravel at home cuts you, it is more painful than a knife.*
(If someone intimate hurts you, it is worse than if a stranger does).

**2324. Efie dwo a, na ɛha mu dwoɔ.**
*If the home is calm then the bush becomes calm too.*
(Peace spreads from the home).

**2325. Efie kata asɛm so.**
*The house covers up problems.*
(Don't wash your dirty linen in public)

**2326. Efie akokoɔduru nyɛ akokoɔduru.**
*Bravery in the house is no bravery.*
(You get a good reputation from public actions not private ones).

**2327. Efie mu nsɛm, yɛka no deɛ onim.**
*A matter for the home is broached by the one who knows best.*
(Only those intimately concerned know what goes on in the home and knows how to discuss it).

**2328. Efie ne fie.**
*Home is home.*
(There is no place like home).

**2329. Efie panin na ɔdidi, didi pono so.**
*When the head of the family eats, he eats at a table.*
(Normally people sit around the compound to eat their meals, but the head of the family has his special table. Hence: Privileges are for the privileged).

**2330. Wo fiefoɔ ma wo so a, abɔntensofoɔ hwɛ wo to.**
*If the people in your house lift you up, those outside see your bottom.*
(If those close to you show you up, then strangers hear about it).

**2331. Ofie nwansena ka onipa a, yɛma ohurie dibem.**
*If the housefly bites someone, we apologize to the tsetse fly.*
(If a friend turns against you, you stop chasing the enemy).

2332. Ofie nwansena nkeka onipa kwa.
*A housefly does not bite a man without reason.*
(It is through our own actions that we invite trouble).

2333. Fifire mu wɔ sadeɛ.
*There is profit in sweat.*
(Hard work brings its own reward).

2334. Afikyi-borɔdeɛ, yɛmmu no [anikyie]/[anikyeɛ].
*The plantain in the back yard, we don't [despise it]/*
*[blink at it].*
(Blinking at someone is a way of expressing dislike.
Hence: You don't treat your intimate helper rudely).

2335. Wofura "anya-wo-ho" a, na wonnya wo ho.
*If you put on a rich cloth, it does not mean you are*
*rich.*
(Do not judge by appearances).

2336. Wofura ntomago a wonni apiripiragorɔ.
*If you put on an old cloth you don't play a violent*
*game.*
(You act within your means).

2337. Wofiri fie bobɔ nkukuo na wode firi adi a,
yɛnkyiri.
*If you begin at home to break pots and you go outside*
*and continue doing so, it is nothing new.*
(If you are the same kind of person inside the family
and out, people cannot blame you).

2338. Yɛfiri [ko]/[baako] na ɛkɔ [no]/[mmienu].
*We count one before we count two.*
(First things first).

2339. Wofiri Nsaba dwa so baeɛ a, wose wotoɔ onipa
taku, nso wo nko na wonam.
*If you come from Nsaba market and you say you bought*
*a person for five pesewas, you alone went there.*
(You need a witness to prove your case).

2340. Wofiri ntɛm boro asuo a, na wotumi twa.
*If you begin swimming early, you cross in time.*
(An early bird catches the worm).

2341. Yɛfiri tete na yɛfrɛ Twumasi Ankra.
*From the times of our ancestors, we have called on the*
*name of Twumasi Ankra.*
(Our customs are ancient).

2342. Afirifiriwa si hɔ a, ɛpo mpɛn aduasa.
*If the salt and oil tree (cleistopholes patens) stands*
*there, it sheds its leaves thirty times.*
(Anything useful is never left alone).

2343. Afisɛm nyɛ ntomago na yɛasi ahata abɔnten.
*Domestic affairs are not like dirty clothes, that we lay*
*them to dry in public.*

2344. Wofiti kurotia a, yɛdɔ wo; di nnansa hwɛ.
*When you are on the outskirts of the village, we love*
*you; but see what happens after three days!*
(Familiarity breeds contempt).

2345. Wofiti kurotia na nkɔdaa pa wo aboɔ a, kɔma
mpanimfoɔ dibem.
*If you are entering the village and the children throw*
*stones at you, go and apologize to the elders.*
(Deal with the root cause of the trouble).

2346. Wofiti prɛko to "huu" a, ɔsaman gye wo so.
*If you suddenly hoot, a ghost responds.*
(If you shout, you may only hear the echo of your own
voice. Hence: Think before you act or you may be
shocked at what happens).

2347. Fituo da mpan, fanyinam sɛ bɔne te ano.
*An empty house lies open; it is better if even an evil*
*person lives there.*
(A deserted place is open to abuse. Hence: Any human
being is better than none).

2348. Ɛfɔ nne wo a, na wose: "Ɛnne merenkɔ duaso".
*If you don't need to defecate you say: "Today I won't*
*visit the latrine."*
(You refrain from normal activities only when you don't
need to involve yourself in them).

2349. Afoanima Aburow-Ahahan, ɔse: "Magye nim
ama kankuaa".
*Afoanima Maize-leaf says: "I have worked laboriously*
*for other people to enjoy".*
(A person should be allowed to share the fruits of their
own labor).

2350. Afodeɛ nyɛ biribi a, ɛyɛ osafohenneɛ.
*If the sash is nothing else, at least it is part of the*
*warrior's paraphernalia.*
(The afodeɛ is a sash girded round the waist. Hence:
Everything has some use).

2351. Fofie anto Ata a, Abamo ka dan mu.
*If Ata does not survive the holy day (Fofie, Friday), then*
*Abamo is kept (unregarded) in the room.*
(If something ceases to be effective it is disregarded.
See Proverb 2317).

2352. Fofonoma hu wo, na nkwaɛnoma hu wo na,
wosum fidie a, ɛyi ahum-ne-aham-ne-ahahan-hunu.
*If the birds in the clearing notice you and the birds of*
*the forest notice you, if you set a trap it catches mere*
*empty leaves.*
(If a treacherous person becomes well-known he
cannot function).

2353. Wofom wo fukwan a, obiara nhu wo mmɔbɔ.
*If you lose your way on the path to your farm, no one*
*will have sympathy for you.*
(If you act stupidly people have no sympathy for you).

2354. Ɔfom ba a, na mpata aba.
*When an offence comes, then pacification comes.*
(Everything has its antidote).

2355. Fompata nti na oburoni yɛɛ nsa.
*Because of reconciliation the white man made drinks.*
(Anything that is valuable has been created for a
purpose).

2356. Fompata nni hɔ a, anka ɔbɛtwani ntwa abɛ.
*If there is no attempt to bring about a reconciliation,*
*then the palm-wine tapper will not tap the palm tree.*
(Palm wine is used for pacification. Hence: If you don't
take one action the resulting one will not follow).

2357. Mfomsoɔ mpa onipa ho.
*To err is human.*

2358. Afonfanu we adeɛ a, ɛde ntɛm.
*If two cheeks chew something, the job is quickly done.*
(Two can do better than one).

2359. Fɔntomfrɔm da Mosini kɔn ho a, wose ɛda bankye ankorɛ mu.
*If the talking-drums are on a Moshie man's shoulders (neck) you say they hang in the forks of a cassava plant.*
(You don't have feeling for people you despise).

2360. Ɛfoɔ din mpa adebɔ mu.
*The name of the colobus monkey is never absent from appellations.*
(Ɛfoɔ also means the people from a certain place - Asante-foɔ, Nta-foɔ, and so on - and is thus used often. Hence: If you are popular, your name is never lost).

2361. Ɛfoɔ se: "Deɛ ɛwɔ m'afonomu nyɛ me dea, deɛ ɛwɔ me yafunu mu na ɛyɛ me dea".
*The Colobus monkey says: "What is in my mouth is not mine, but what I have in my belly is my own".*
(A bird in the hand is worth two in the bush).

2362. Ɔforeɛ se ɔretie deɛ ɛbɛba nanso nsuo na ɔrehwehwɛ.
*The Ɔforeɛ says it is listening to what will happen, but really it is expecting rainfall.*
(Ɔforeɛ is a river fish. Some people hide their motives for doing things).

2363. Ofori Akantankanawa a ne ho nyɛ den no, onua ne Ofori Kwabrane a ne ho yɛ den.
*Ofori-the-willowy, who is not strong, has a brother, Ofori-the-stout, who is strong.*
(Every weak person has a protector, every family has its week and strong).

2364. Ofori nkoa Akuapem! Wɔnsom bi, wɔnnan bi, nanso wɔnne wɔn ho.
*Akuapem, the subjects of Ofori! They serve no one, they depend on no one, but they are not independent.*
(Akuapem is the state to the south of Asante. He is neither flesh nor fish nor fowl).

2365. Worebɛforo dua pa a, wofiri n'ase na womfiri soro.
*If you are going to climb a tree, you start from below and not from above.*
(Begin at the beginning and do things the right way).

2366. Woforo dua a, foro tenten na wote hwe a, atumpan ama wo dammirifua.
*If you climb a tree, climb the tall one so that if you fall down, the talking drums will play condolences for you.*
(If you have ambitions, let them be big ones so at least if anything happens to you, you will have the merit of being known).

2367. Woforo dua na wote hwe a, woasi fam ara ne no.
*If you climb a tree and you fall down, you have come down at any rate.*
(You have arrived at a certain position however you have done it).

2368. Woforo dua a, yɛpia woɔ.
*If you climb a tree, we support you.*
(If a man is onto something good, he will get support).

2369. Mfɔteɛ a wowu a, wɔbedi wo nam no, se wotease na wɔrewe wo ntoma a, na woafa no saa ara.
*The white ants that will eat your corpse when you die, if you are alive and they are eating your cloth, you accept it.*
(If someone is going to inherit from you when you die, don't bother if they take small things when you are alive).

2370. Mfɔteɛ nim adeɛ we a, wɔnkɔwe apakyie ma yɛnhwɛ.
*If the white ants know how to chew something, then let them eat the gourd for us to see.*
(If you boast you can do something, you will asked to give evidence of it by tackling something hard first).

2371. Mfɔteɛ we nneɛma nyinaa, nanso wɔnwe penentoa.
*White ants can chew up all things, but they can't chew up a bottle.*
(There are limits to everyone's potentialities and not everything is vulnerable to the same means of attack).

2372. Fotoɔ a yɛkan mu piredwan no, asia mpa mu.
*The gold-weight bag, if we weigh out a piredwan, an asia always remains.*
(A piredwan is a small weight; an asia is a small weight. Hence: If you are dealing in large quantities a small amount is always available).

2373. Fotoɔ mu ne anim nsɛ.
*The treasury bag's inside and outside are not the same.*
(The bags, which contained gold and other valuables, were often wrapped up on the outside with an old piece of cloth or skin. Hence: Don't judge by outside appearances).

2374. Afotuo dodoɔ sɛe ɔdeyɔfoɔ.
*Too much advice spoils a good worker.*
(If someone knows their job, let them get on with it).

2375. Afotuo te amanneɛbɔ mu.
*Advice is derived from the story narrated.*
(You can only advise on the facts you are given).

2376. Mframa a ɛbɔ tu ɛboɔ no, aburow-hono te nka a, ɛdwane.
*The wind that blows to remove a stone, when the maize husk feels it, it flees.*
(Something which defeats a strong person is automatically avoided by the weak).

2377. Mframa mmaeɛ a, na hwedeɛ mu yɛ krana.
*If the wind does not come, the long grass is motionless.*
(If there is no one to trouble you, you can remain at peace).

2378. Mframa de huu-huu pe adeɛ a, ɔnnya.
*If the wind blusters a lot to get things, it does not succeed.*
(Blustering does not get you anywhere).

2379. Mframa fa boɔ a, na apakyie ada ne ho so.
*If the wind takes a stone, the gourd takes precautions.*
(If the strong man suffers, the weak takes precautions).

**2380. Mframa mfa nnipa nkɔɔ da.**
*The wind has never blown away a man.*
(Everything has its own limits).

**2381. Mframa mpusu dunsini.**
*The wind does not shake a tree stump.*
(There are some things that even a strong man cannot influence).

**2382. Mframa sɛɛ dua, ɛka sɛɛ aberanteɛ.**
*The wind destroys the tree, (as) debt (also) destroys the young man.*
(A warning against getting into debt).

**2383. Mframa resen a, yɛmma no akonnwa.**
*If the wind is passing by, we don't give it a stool.*
(Don't give too much importance to a passing event).

**2384. Frampɔn se ɔremfa ayan ho hwee. Nanso wɔyan atumpan a, wɔse: Frampɔn dammirifua".**
*Frampɔn says he won't have anything to do with the drums. Yet, when they beat the talking-drums they say:"Condolences Frampɔn".*
(You cannot always avoid being involved in something by just saying you don't want to be. Other people may have different ideas about it).

**2385. Afranimaa kɔ ayie a, ɔda ɔkwasea afa.**
*If a foolish woman goes to a funeral, she sleeps with a foolish man.*
(Birds of a feather flock together).

**2386. Wofrɛ ɔbaa "Gye-wo-ho-gyaeɛ" a, ɔno ara nim berɛ a ɛhia sɛ ɔba.**
*If you call a woman "Go your own way", she alone knows the time she will reply to your invitation.*
(An expert knows when to act. Or: You get what you, yourself, have asked for).

**2387. Wofrɛ obi na wannye so a, na ɛwɔ deɛ wahunu.**
*If you call someone and they do not respond, then it is because of what they have seen.*
(Once bitten, twice shy).

**2388. Wofrɛ adwaman a, na ne nsa da n'ano so.**
*If you call a prostitute, then her hand is on her vagina.*
(You judge people by their actions).

**2389. Wɔfrɛ wo ahemfie a, wobisa wo nsa, w'ano ne wo kɔte.**
*If you are called to the palace, you question your hand, your mouth and your penis.*
(If you are called before authority, you wonder what you have done).

**2390. Afɛduane na ɛyɛ dɛ, na ɛnyɛ menko meyam.**
*A meal to which one is invited is better than eating by oneself.*
(Good company is better than being alone).

**2391. Frɔmfrɔm nte hɔ da.**
*Freshness does not remain always.*
(Situations change).

**2392. Wofua "bebrebe ne booboo" a, na woawie amaneɛ hunu.**
*When you bury "a great deal" (your father) and "sobbing" (your mother), that is the end of your suffering.*
(This is a very idiomatic and almost untranslatable proverb. After experiencing the worst someone becomes immune to suffering).

**2393. Wofua onipa nsa na ɔse: "Gyae me kɔn" a, gyae no, na ebia na ɛhɔ na ne kɔn wɔ.**
*If you are holding someone's hand and he says "leave my neck", do so, because it may be that his neck is there.*
(If someone rejects you, leave them alone, whatever reason they may give).

**2394. Wofua Yanehene ba a, wose: "Merepɛ Kramohene madi?"**
*If you are carrying the Yanehene's child, you say "I would like to be installed Kramohene?"*
(The Yanehene is one of the most famous chiefs in Northern Ghana; the Kramohene is just the elected head of the Moslem community in any town. Hence: It is more honorable to serve an important man than to have an unimportant job somewhere else).

**2395. Fufuo nko ara nnante.**
*Fufuo does not walk alone.*
(Fufu is eaten with soup or stew and not alone. Hence: Everyone needs a companion).

**2396. Fufuo akontaa, yɛbu no waduro mu.**
*Fufu's arithmetic, we work it out in the mortar.*
(We plan distribution before we produce).

**2397. Fufuo nni hɔ a, yɛdi adua.**
*In the absence of fufuo we eat beans.*
(You only take the second best when you can't get the best).

**2398. Fufuo tum tum, akyire ne yɛhunu.**
*Pounding fufuo you only see the results.*
(You only see the results of a man's labor).

**2399. Fufurantu, Brofurantu, kɔtɔ bɔ peme a, ɔsan n'akyi. Obi mpɛ wo agorɔ a, tena w'ase.**
*Fufurantu, Brofurantu (just sounds), if a crab falls backwards, it returns to base. If someone does not like to play with you, stay in your own place.*
(Don't try and move with people who do not like you).

**2400. Fukwan tenten ma nkuruma sene.**
*A long farm road makes the okro become hard to use.*
(Distance makes family contact difficult).

**2401. Ofuntum asaase nka nkyerɛ akyenkyena sɛ ɔnnyae akɔm na atɛmmuda aba.**
*The one who churns the earth should not tell the allied hornbill to stop administering fetish because the judgement day has come.*
(He who indulges in one vice, should not criticize someone indulging in another).

**2402. Funtumfunafu ne Dɛnkyɛmfunafu baanu yafunu yɛ yafunkorɔ; nanso wɔredidi a na wɔreko no, na firi atwimenemudɛ ntira.**
*Stomachs mixed up, crocodiles' stomachs mixed up, they both have one stomach but when they eat they fight because of the sweetness of the swallowing.*
(There are several versions of this proverb, some of which have slightly different meanings. It represents the dilemmas of the Akan family system. Anything which is acquired for the family is good for the whole family, but the pleasure of enjoying it is an individual thing; and this fact often causes quarrels. Compare Proverbs 2403, 2418 and 2422).

**2403.** Funtumfuramfu ne dɛnkyɛmfuramfu, wɔn nyinaa afuru bafua, nso wɔredidi a, na wɔrefom. Ɛfiri sɛ, yɛdi aduane menemutwitwi.
*Stomachs mixed up, crocodiles mixed up, both of them have one belly, but when they are eating, they struggle over it (the food). This is because we swallow food because of the taste in the throat.*
(Compare Proverbs 2402, 2418 and 2422).

**2404.** Efunu a ɛbɛsie nnim sudɛ.
*A corpse that is going to indicate a guilty person does not appreciate proper weeping.*
(When a corpse is carried to the cemetery it sometimes knocks against the door-or leads its carriers to the house-of someone who is then believed to have been responsible for the death. Such activities cannot be put off by the beautiful celebration of the funeral. Hence: Justice cannot be by-passed).

**2405.** Efunu a ɛyɛ fɛ nka dan mu.
*A corpse which is beautiful does not remain in the room.*
(Beauty does not survive death).

**2406.** Efunu di fɔ.
*A corpse is guilty.*
(A dead man cannot defend his reputation).

**2407.** Efunu nya ɔsoafoɔ a, ɔsi.
*If the corpse gets a good carrier, it can point out (its enemies).*
(If something is in good hands it prospers. See Proverb 2404).

**2408.** Efunu nyɛ nna, na yɛasosɔ nkɔdaa funu so.
*Corpses are not scarce so that we value a child's corpse.*
(Said when it is easy to get a replacement for someone without taking someone who is not suitable).

**2409.** Afunumu ho ha ɛnyɛ fɛ, na nyɛ n'ahoɔden.
*The donkey is not beautiful to look at, but it is strong.*
(Put not faith in appearances).

**2410.** Afunumu wu a, na ɛta asa.
*If the donkey dies, flatulence finishes.*
(If something is no more, any attendant problems cease to exist. Or: If a talented performer dies, others cannot imitate him).

**2411.** Afuo mu panin ne ɛhyeɛ.
*The elder of the farm is the boundary.*
(There are some people without whom we cannot have peace).

**2412.** Afuo mu nni biribi a, ɛwɔ kranana.
*If a farm has nothing else, it has perfect quietness.*
(Nothing is without some quality).

**2413.** Afuo te sɛ adɔsoa, yɛnhwehwɛ mu nhunu mu da koro.
*A farm is like a bundle you carry (a funeral donation), you cannot look at everything there at one time.*
(Patience does it).

**2414.** Afuo, ɛyɛ me deɛ, asaase ɛyɛ ɔhene deɛ.
*The farm is mine but the land belongs to the chief.*
(In Asante a citizen does not own the land absolutely but is allocated it by the chief who is the overall owner. A citizen has absolute right to his farm and its produce and it is inherited by his family. He cannot lose it unless he commits a major offence against the state. Thus the proverb means that as well as his rights every citizen has an obligation to the state).

**2415.** Wo mfuo dɔɔso a, woyɛ ne nyinaa.
*If you have many farms, you cultivate them all.*
(However great your responsibilities, you must live up to them).

**2416.** Wofura kuntunkuni, me nso mefura kɔbene a, wommisa me sɛ: "Efie yɛ?"
*You are wearing a brown funeral cloth and I also am wearing an orange colored funeral cloth, then you should not ask: "Is all well at home?"*
(A funeral cloth indicates that someone has died. Hence: Don't ask stupid questions when you know the answer).

**2417.** Ofuruntum wuo sae mmatatwene.
*The death of the rubber tree (Funtumia) spoils the liana (Cercertis afselii).*
(If a person on whom you depend, falls, you, too, come down).

**2418.** Afutu-afutu dɛnkyɛmmerefunu, wɔn nyinaa afurubaako, nso wɔkuta aboa a, wɔperɛ no so.
*All mixed up crocodile with one stomach, they all have one stomach but if they hold an animal, they struggle over it.*
(This is one of the proverbs referring to a crocodile with two heads and two tails. In this case, one half holds a fish or animal. Hence: Everything which is acquired by individual members of the family is to its benefit, but taste and enjoyment is individual. Compare Proverbs 2402, 2403 and 2422).

**2419.** Futukokɔnini agya Kwaa awia bɔ no a, wadi afe.
*The little ground beetle, Father Kwaa, every day means a year to it.*
(Said of someone whose expectation in life is small).

**2420.** Futukokɔnini ne kɔtɔ nom nsa a, wɔ boro safoɔ.
*If the small beetle and the crab drink, they beat up the owner of the drinks.*
(Apparently harmless people, when drunk, can be very aggressive. Don't be surprised at the results of drink).

**2421.** Futukokɔnini pɛ daberɛ na ɔkɔfa ɔsebɔ yɔnkoɔ.
*The little beetle likes a sleeping place, so that is why he became the leopard's companion.*
(Said when a weak person goes to a strong for protection).

**2422.** Futumereku ne denkyɛmereku (wɔn tiri yɛ mmienu na wɔn yafunu baako) se: "Ma kakra ntwi wo mene mu, na ma kakra ntwi me deɛ mu, na ne nyinaa nkɔhyia yafunu-korɔ mu."
*Stomach mixed up and crocodile mixed up, (their heads are two but their stomach is one) say: "Let a little slip down your throat, and let a little slip down mine, and it will all meet in one stomach".*
(Compare Proverbs 2402, 2403, and 2418).

- G -

**2423. Ngo die ne ne hua.**
*The desire to eat palm oil comes from its scent.*
(Advertising makes a thing popular. Not all things attract for the same reason).

**2424. Agofaako na ɛde kwaseabuo ba.**
*Discrimination in playing a game brings about cheating.*
(Don't focus all your attention on one other player in a game or you will be considered a cheat).

**2425. Agofɛɛfɛ mu nni abosonnom.**
*If a game goes on smoothly, we don't swear oaths about it.*
(We do not quarrel over success).

**2426. Agohia sene hia pa.**
*Having no one to play with is worse than poverty (lit. Game-poverty is worse than real poverty).*
(Loneliness is one of the worst forms of suffering).

**2427. Agohunu nkyiri "Mesa bi."**
*A game which is played for fun does not taboo "I will dance too".*
(Everyone can take part in a free entertainment).

**2428. Agopa tua ne ho ka.**
*A good game pays for itself.*

**2429. Wogoro Bosom Po ne Ayesu ntam a, boba si wo.**
*If you play between the Sea God Po and the River God Aye's oath, the grinding stone will crush you.*
(If you play off two important people you will get into trouble).

**2430. Wogoro doko ho a, ɛdane wo doɔ.**
*If you play with diarrhea, it turns into something worse.*
(If you neglect the first symptoms of trouble, it becomes more difficult to deal with).

**2431. Yɛregoro foforo a, amim nni mu.**
*If we are going to play something new, undue advantage is not in question.*
(No one has advantage at the beginning of a new experience).

**2432. Agorɔ a ɛreba wo ni ne wo se fie no, wompɛ ntɛm nkɔhwe.**
*The dance which is coming to your mother and father's house, you don't hurry out to see.*
(If something is coming to you, don't be impatient for it).

**2433. Agorɔ a ɛyɛ dɛ, yɛnko aseɛ.**
*If the game is good, we don't fight at the place.*
(If something pleases, you don't spoil it).

**2434. Agorɔ a ɛyɛ dɛ na ɛkum Fɔdwoɔ.**
*An enjoyable game kills Fɔdwoɔ.*
(Adwoa Fɔdwoɔ was an old lady who enjoyed the drumming game of sikyi, but in old age could no longer dance. One day she passed a dance with her grand-daughter and could not resist the temptation and joined the young people, and was pushed over and accidentally killed. Hence: Too much indulgence in what you enjoy leads to disaster).

**2435. Agorɔ a ɛyɛ de na ɔwea su aseɛ.**
*If the dance is good, the tree hyrax sings at it.*
(What is enjoyable is enjoyed by all. This animal has a cry like a child in the night).

**2436. Agorɔ mfitiaseɛ nyɛ anibereɛ.**
*The beginning of the game is not provocative.*
(Problems don't arise at the beginning of a project, but later on).

**2437. Agorɔ, yɛgoro no atipɛn.**
*Games, we play in our own age groups.*
(People tend to amuse themselves with their contemporaries).

**2438. Agorɔ bɛsɔ a, ɛfiri anɔpa.**
*If the game (dance) will be successful, it will be so from the morning.*
(Good things show their quality from the outset).

**2439. Agorɔ ansɔ a, egu.**
*If a game does not prosper, it finishes.*
(An unprofitable enterprise soon comes to an end).

**2440. Agorɔ nnwu mpanin anim.**
*A game does not break up in the presence of elders.*
(Elders are able to maintain discipline and see things run properly).

**2441. Agorɔ reyɛ dɛ no na adeɛ resa akwantufoɔ.**
*If a game is amusing then by and by night overtakes you.*
(Something good makes you forget time).

**2442. Agorɔ yɛ fɛ a, na yɛwea kɔhwɛ.**
*If the dance is pleasing, we crawl to see it.*
(A good thing is worth any effort to reach it).

**2443. Agorɔfɛ nko, na ntam nko.**
*A good game is one thing but an oath is another.*
(If you are playing or joking, that's fine, but don't overdo it or it may lead you into court).

**2444. Agradaa nyɛ biribi a, ɛdwa pono mu.**
*If lightening does nothing else, it can split the door.*
(Everything has its own talent).

**2445. Wogu apem gu abrane a, gye sɛ wode kɔ kuro-kɛseɛ mu.**
*Whatever great things you do, unless you go to the big city (you can't really be a great man).*
(Wealth is meant to be made use of and only through activities in the city can you become really powerful!)

**2446. Wogya wo din hɔ a, yɛbɔ ma wo.**
*If you leave your name behind we mention it for you.*
(Whatever you do, good or bad, people will comment on it).

**2447. Wogya kɔnkɔnsa puaa a, wohyɛ wo ho nso.**
*If you cut your hair one-sidedly, you make yourself open to easy identification.*
(If you act badly in society, you lay yourself open to suspicion).

**2448. Agya mma nya a, mepɛ, ɛna mma nya a, mepɛ papaapa.**
*When my father's children make a fortune, I am pleased, but when my mother's children make a fortune I like it even better.*
(You belong to your mother's family; so anything to their benefit benefits you too. Hence: Blood is thicker than water).

**2449. Agya bi awu a, agya bi te aseɛ.**
*If some father dies, another remains alive.*
(When your father dies, the persons who inherits from him should look after you. However this often does not happen so there is some bitterness in this proverb. Hence: There should always be someone to whom you can look for advice and protection).

**2450. Agya bɔfoɔ a ɔhunta dua akyiri, obi anhu wo a, Onyame ahu wo.**
*Father hunter who hides behind a tree, if no one else has seen you, God has done so.*
(Nothing is completely secret. God sees all).

**2451. "Agya, gyae na menka," yɛkyiri.**
*"Father, let me say it", we taboo.*
(A young person should not speak for his father or elder if the latter is present).

**2452. W'agya akoa twa dua a, wose: "Ɛyɛ mmerɛ".**
*When your father's slave cuts down a tree you say: "The wood is soft".*
(You tend to underrate the achievements of those inferior to you).

**2453. Agya Kra ne Agya Kwakyerɛmɛ, emu biara mu nni animuonyam.**
*Father Soul and Father Slave Kyerɛmɛ, none of them has any significance.*
(Whatever you call him, a slave is always a slave. Hence: You can't change someone's nature or status by giving them a fancy name).

**2454. "Agya Kwadwo, wonsa nwunu!" Ɔse: "Ɛfiri wo nkwammɔne."**
*"Father Kwadwo, the palm of your hand leaks." He says: "It is because of your bad soup!"*
(People eat with their hands traditionally so the insult would mean "you are a dirty feeder." Hence: If you deliberately accuse or insult someone they return the insult).

**2455. Agya Ananse nwoo ne ba Ntikuma na ɔwɔ deɛ ɔsoa ne bɔtɔ.**
*Before Father Spider begat his son Ntikuma, he had someone to carry his bag.*
(I managed quite well before you came, thank you!)

**2456. Agya, yɛnnya no mmienu.**
*A father, we don't have two.*
(Some things are unique).

**2457. Ogya a ɛbedere no, ne wisie nko.**
*A fire which is going to blaze up, has a different smoke.*
(Evidence of success comes before the fact).

**2458. Ogya a ɛyɛ nam nkyɛre hi.**
*A log which fires quickly, finishes quickly.*
(If you are too clever, you are easily dispensed with).

**2459. Ogya a ɛyɛ nam na yɛtwa so bi da.**
*If firewood is durable, then we cut a bit to sleep with.*
(In the villages, fires are used in the room at night for warmth. Hence: If a woman is beautiful, she is never without an admirer).

**2460. Ogya bɛhi ato anyinaboaa.**
*The firewood will be consumed until it reaches the wood insect.*
(However well you think you are concealed, your turn to suffer will come).

**2461. Ogya hye akɔdaa a, ɔto twene.**
*If a firebrand burns a child, he throws it away.*
(We learn from experience to dispense with what is harmful to us).

**2462. Ogya hye wo a, woprɛ to wo ba so ansa na woayi afiri ne so.**
*If a spark from the fire burns you, you shake it off onto your child before you take it off him too.*
(What affects a senior person in the family, affects the juniors too).

**2463. Ogya na ɛfiri wisie.**
*Fire-wood gives off smoke.*
(There is no smoke without fire).

**2464. Ogya na ɛma ɔkɔtɔ dane broni.**
*The fire makes the crab go pink (lit. change into a European).*
(Suffering may change a man's nature).

**2465. Ogya ne atuduro nhyia.**
*Fire and gunpowder do not agree.*
(Used when two people always spark each other off).

**2466. Ogya, yɛto no ahuahua.**
*A fire, we warm ourselves at it bit by bit.*
(Anything dangerous we attend to carefully).

**2467. Ogya nyɛ dɛ nso ɛhye wo nsa a, gye sɛ wotafere.**
*Fire is not sweet but if it burns your hand, all the same you lick it.*
(You have to accept adversity whether you like it or not).

**2468. Agyaakwaa se: ɔnni koraa, nti na ɔde ne to hwe asuo.**
*The dragon-fly says: it has no calabash, so it uses its tail to drain water.*
(If you can't do a thing one way, do it another).

**2469. Agyaakwaa wɔ ntakuo nnum a ɔde bɛtɔ kodoɔ a, anka ɔremfa ne to nhwe asuo.**
*If the dragon-fly had twenty-five pesewas to buy a canoe, he would not be using his bottom to skim the water.*
(Beggars can't be choosers).

**2470. Ogya-hurenhuren ma mmarima boto.**
*An intense fire makes men enervated.*
(A big case inhibits action, through confusion).

**2471. Ogya-hurenhuren atwene, yɛnto no yampeaa.**
*The drum Ogya-hurenhuren (which warns of fire and other serious matters), is not played calmly.*
(Serious matters demand a sense of urgency).

2472. Wogyae deɛ woreyɛ a, adaagyeɛ nyɛ nna.
*If you stop what you are doing, you have leisure.*
(You have to give up one thing for another).

2473. Yɛgyae ɔkafoɔ nan a, yɛnnyae ne ti.
*Even if we let go of a creditor's leg, we don't let go of his head.*
(You let a man go and find money to pay a debt, but you don't forgive him the debt).

2474. "Gyae kasa" yɛ kasa.
*"Stop talking" is talking.*
(You don't correct a mistake by making one).

2475. Wo gyae wo nkwadaa-gorɔ a, wonkyɛre wu.
*If you stop your childish games, you die soon.*
(Man needs to be able to enjoy himself to thrive).

2476. "Gyae ma ɛnka" na ewɔ baabi, na nyɛ "Yi firi wo tirim".
*"Leave the matter as it is" is in existence, but not "Clear it from your mind".*
(Forgiving is not forgetting).

2477. "Gyae apinsie." Ɔse: "Menhunu biribi a, anka merensi apini".
*"Stop groaning." He says: "If I did not see anything then I would not be groaning".*
(No one does anything without a good reason).

2478. "Gyae-saa-yɔ," annyae saa yɔ a, "Gyae-akyiredie," nso nnyae akyire die.
*"Stop acting in that way" does not stop acting, then "Stop reacting" also does not stop reacting.*
(If you do not stop provocation, then people will not stop reaction).

2479. Ɛnyaee wo hia a, wonnyae mmɔbɔ yɛ.
*If you have not overcome your poverty, you have not got rid of misery.*
(If circumstances do not change, neither does your emotional state).

2480. Woannyae apatapata a, yɛnnyae wo abisabisa.
*If you don't stop making up quarrels, we don't leave off asking questions.*
(If you meddle in other people's affairs, they will meddle in yours).

2481. Yɛnnyae su a, ɛnyɛ kunafoɔ.
*Even if we should stop crying, this does not mean the widow.*
(There is an exception to every rule).

2482. Yɛnnyae asutene na yɛkɔnom ɔtareɛ.
*We don't leave a flowing stream to drink at a (stagnant) pool.*
(You don't change better for worse).

2483. Woannyae atono a, wotono aboa bi se.
*If you don't stop forging, you forge a strange animal's tooth.*
(Forge, in the sense of work with metal. Constant overwork brings disaster).

2484. Gyahene ho nyɛ den a, kankane deɛ ɔtumi no.
*Even if the leopard is not strong, it is stronger than a civet cat.*

(Even if a powerful man is old or sick, he still has more power than a lesser man).

2485. Gyamanhene se ɔbɛkɔ Komɔagya a, ɔne ne pɔnkɔ nansini.
*If the Gyaman chief says he will go to Komɔagya, he does so with a three-legged horse.*
(The three-legged horse represents a not necessarily important but indispensable person or object which always accompanies someone wherever they go. It could be used of a personal servant or of something like a special pen. The proverb is used in this sense. Hence: There he goes with what he always takes with him).

2486. Agyan nti na yɛyɔ ɛkyɛm.
*Because of the arrow we make the shield.*
(If it were not for aggression, defensive weapons would not be necessary).

2487. Agyanka dane korɔmfoɔ.
*An orphan turns into a thief.*
(If you have nothing, then you are forced to steal).

2488. [Gyankura]/[Agyinamoa] nni fie a, na [gyampraka]/[akura] de ahurisie.
*If the cat's away the mice will enjoy themselves.*

2489. Ogyasrama te gya a, ɛhye deɛ ɔbɛn no.
*If the charcoal fire sparks, it burns the person near it.*
(If you are near danger, you may be embroiled).

2490. Agyata dɔɔso wo wiram a, anka nnipa rennya baabi ntena.
*If there were too many lions in the bush, men would have nowhere to live.*
(God plans everything with a reason).

2491. Ogyatanaa, wokɔ ho na woannwene wo se a, wokyea wo ti.
*A flaming fire, if you go near it you either show your teeth or turn your head.*
(You have violent reaction to a dangerous situation).

2492. "Gye bi" na wanto no a, ɛso wo ara.
*"Take some" if you don't reach him, you yourself carry it.*
(You should learn to share in life).

2493. "Bɛgye-a-gye," yɛde biribi na ɛseɛ.
*"If you are willing, take it", we say it with something.*
(You don't offer to do something for someone unless you have the means of doing it).

2494. Meregye wo ban ama wo a, womfa homa nhunta me?
*If I am helping you to make a fence, surely you won't take the rope and hide it from me?*
(If someone is trying to help you, you don't deprive them of the means of doing so).

2495. Yɛgye obi adeɛ yɛ no yie na yɛnnte nsɛɛ no.
*We receive someone's thing to take good care of it and not to spoil it.*
(If you are entrusted with something, look after it well).

**2496.** "Gye biribi hyɛ w'ano pipiripie mu" nyɛ atɛnnidie.
*"Take something and put it in your big mouth," is not an insult.*
(If someone is helping you, it does not matter much what they say. Actions speak louder than words).

**2497.** Wogye abɔfra nsam [asɔmorɔdwe]/[nwa] we a, wommee, ɔsan su dwan wo ho.
*If you take the [palm beetle]/[snail] from a child's hand and eat it, you are not satisfied and he will trouble you with his weeping.*
(Don't be mean to no purpose nor to your own detriment).

**2498.** Gye mmɔfra kɔtena patom a, womfa nyɛ ahenie.
*If you are given some children to sit with in the alcove, you don't turn it into chieftaincy.*
(Don't act above yourself, nor make too much of a trivial responsibility or occasion).

**2499.** Wogye bɔdamfoɔ akyinnye a, na ɔbɔ wo abaa.
*If you dispute with a madman, he uses a stick to beat you up.*
(Don't argue with someone who cannot see reason).

**2500.** Yɛgye deɛ ɔbɛkɔ kyena adeɛ ma deɛ ɔbɛkɔ nnɛ.
*We take the things belonging to the person who is going tomorrow to give to him who is going today.*
(First things first).

**2501.** Wogye di sɛ oburoni pɛ w'asɛm a, hwɛ kwantenten a watwa aduru ha.
*If you think a whiteman likes you, see the long journey he has taken to get here.*
(People only make great efforts for personal gain and not because they like you).

**2502.** Yɛgye yen ho a, yɛgye no dwaso.
*If we decide to sell ourselves, we do so in a public place.*
(We keep our treachery outside the home).

**2503.** Yɛgye nkokɔ a, yɛgye no Boronfoɔ no.
*When we need fowls, we get them from Brong.*
(This is an insult and means take small matters to small people. An arrogant attitude of paramount power).

**2504.** "Gye kɔtɔprɛ we, nanso mmɔ mu", yɛntee bi da.
*"Take the crab's claw to eat, but don't crack it", we have never heard of.*
(Don't ask someone to do something impossible).

**2505.** "Gye sika kɔ dwam kɔtɔ nkyene berɛ me!" Nkyene amma, sika amma, na worebɛka ama no ayɛ dɛ tesɛ sika?
*"Take money and go to the market to buy salt for me!" Salt did not come, money did not come either, so what can you tell me to make it as delicious as money?*
(If your offence is unpardonable, no amount of talk can exonerate you).

**2506.** Yɛgye wo yokɔ a, wogye wo ho yɔsan.
*If we lead you into trouble, you find a way to get out of it.*
(Problems are made to be solved).

**2507.** Wogyegye ɔhene pa ma wo wura a, wo nso wonya akoa pa yɔ.

*If you take a good chief to be your master, you also make a good slave.*
(Like master, like man).

**2508.** Ɔgyegye korɔntan sene deɛ ɔbɔ.
*He who urges people to steal is worse than the one who does it.*
(The instigator of a crime is worse than its perpetrator).

**2509.** Agyegyemmerewa se: sɛ wodi mmerewa akyi a, wokɔ deɛ yɛnkɔ.
*An old woman's guide (aide) says: if you take notice of old women's idiosyncrasies, you will do something which is "not done" (lit. you will go where we do not go).*
(Age should be respected; but don't go too far in doing what the aged tell you to do).

**2510.** Ɔgyegyefoɔ se n'ano yɛ nam a, ɔde kum Aburifoɔ na ɔmfa nkum Adukuromfoɔ.
*If the tempter says his mouth is poisonous, he uses it to kill the people of Aburi and not those of Adukrom.*
(This is an Akuapem proverb, but names of other towns may be substituted. There is a limit to a man's capacity to do evil).

**2511.** Agyekum te ase dada a, yɛse ɔyɛ ɔsaman na ɛntee ne sɛ yɛde no akɔto nsamampɔ mu.
*Even when Agyekum was alive we said he was a ghost, how much more so now that he lies in the cemetery.*
(If an amateur is considered as a professional, how much more the real professional).

**2512.** Agyekum wuo na ɛhia na ɛnyɛ deɛ ɔbɛdi n'adeɛ.
*We are more concerned with Agyekum's death than with the person who will inherit him.*
(We should tackle things in the order of their importance).

**2513.** Agyenegyenensuo se "Meregyene nsuo ansa na mahono no".
*The clear and limpid water says: "I am cleaning the water so that I can dirty it again".*
(Sometimes we feel it necessary to mend something in order that we may break it again).

**2514.** Agyenkwa nim nkwa gye a, anka ɔnsi ne wura nna so resu.
*If the Savior knows how to save life, he would not sit on his master's grave and weep.*
(If someone were good at something he would not have failed and then be boasting of his talent).

**2515.** Agyensu pɔn ne Nyankopɔn.
*The well of a person who collects its water is God.*
(The relationship of the giver to the receiver of essentials is one of complete dependence).

**2516.** Gyentia dada ano nyɛ sɔna.
*The old fire-brand's end is not difficult to light.*
(It is easy to rekindle an old flame, or an old love).

**2517.** Wogyimi a, na wɔku woɔ.
*If you are stupid, they kill you.*
(i.e they execute you! Hence: Stupidity is worse than crime).

**2518. Gyimi gyegye buro gu nnipa so.**
*Folly brings blame onto people.*
(If a foolish person leads you to do something wrong, you will have to take the blame for it).

**2519. Gyimi nyɛ adepa na yɛasua.**
*Folly is not a good thing for us to learn.*
(Used generally to mean: Don't follow bad examples).

**2520. Yɛgyina dua kontonkyi so na yɛtwa dua pa.**
*We stand on a crooked tree to cut a good one.*
(You must pass through difficulties to achieve success).

**2521. Magyina nkansannkansan so ato pɛtɛ tuo, m'ase anyi me ayɛ; na nyɛ akorɔma rebɛkyere n'akokɔ a, meyɛ "Hie, hie" na m'ase bɛyi me ayɛ.**
*I had to stand on something prickly to shoot at a vulture; my in-law was not grateful. How much less when a hawk is going to catch the chicken, and I shout "Hi, hi", will my in-law be grateful.*
(If someone is ungrateful for a major favor, you don't feel like performing a lesser one).

**2522. Magyina Kasampire bepɔ so ato ɔbɔpɔn topɛn korɔ ama ɔbɔpɔn ada n'asokorɔ so, ama amansan atwe nkuma akɔdwa adi, mannya ayɛ; na mekɔgyina Kusa bepɔ ayaase huroo ketebɔ na mɛnya ayɛ?**
*I have stood on Kasampire hill to shoot a great animal (elephant) to death with one shot, for the citizens to use an axe to chop it up and eat it, and did not receive any gratitude; how much less if I stand in the valley below Kusa hill and shout at a leopard, shall I receive thanks.*
(If people are ungrateful in great things, how much more so in small things).

**2523. Yɛgyina akyenkyena "asɔkwaa-mmɔ-me-so" na yɛbɔ ɔnwam anom akɔkono.**
*We use the allied hornbill's "white-crested-hornbill-tell-me-it", to get the palm-beetle grub out of the great hornbill's mouth.*
(We depend on our knowledge of one person's actions to find out about a related one's).

**2524. Yɛgyina nsa sini so na ɛbɔ kaseɛ.**
*We depend on part of a bottle of alcohol to narrate our mission.*
(If you take a message and libations are poured, you should return with a little in the bottle to prove you have been there. Hence: Any serious matter demands evidence of participation).

**2525. Yɛgyina asɛmpa akyi na nyɛ asemmɔne.**
*We back (lit. stand behind) a good affair but not a bad one.*
(Be discriminating and only support what you know to be good).

**2526. Woagyina ntentene, woanhunu dwam, na wotena ase a, na wobɛhunu dwam?**
*If you stand upright you don't see the gathering, how much less so if you sit down.*
(If you can't do something by making a major effort, how much less can you do so if you relax).

**2527. Yɛnnyina nkrane mu ntete nkrane.**
*We don't stand still among driver ants to pull the ants off.*
(You get out of the way of danger before you deal with its side-effects).

**2528. Yɛnnyina Kwakuo anim nnye no "Yaa aku".**
*Wo don't stand before a monkey and give him the Bosomuru clan response.*
(There is a proper response for each ntorɔ group, "Yaa aku" is the Bosomuru response, and the monkey is taboo to the Bosomuru ntorɔ. Hence: You do not deliberately offend someone in their presence).

**2529. Yɛnnyina akono nnwono ɛkyɛm.**
*We do not stand to weave a shield on the battle field.*
(We should prepare in advance).

**2530. Yɛnnyina nkwanta mpɛ manni, nanso ɛhɔ ara na yɛgyina pɛ.**
*We do not stand at the junction to look for someone we know, but none the less it is there that we look for him.*
(Said at a subsequent meeting when people have already met casually and are not complete strangers).

**2531. Yɛnnyina mpoano nnom asra.**
*We do not stand on the seashore and take snuff.*
(Not every place is suitable for all actions).

**2532. Yɛnnyina eyuo anim nwɔ nsemma.**
*We don't set the trap in front of the black duiker.*
(You do not let people see how you are going to catch them out).

**2533. Agyinamoa akoa ne abotokura.**
*The slave of the cat is the striped mouse.*
(Everyone has their victim).

**2534. Agyinamoa Kyeiwaa se: obi nkyerɛ katakyie nto dɔm ano.**
*The cat Kyeiwaa says: no one has to make the warrior stand at the war front.*
(A professional does not need instructions as to what to do; he does it).

## - H -

**2535. "Eha yɛ dɛ, eha yɛ dɛ", na amma prako annya nwoma.**
*"It is sweet here, it is sweet here", led the pig not to get a skin.*
(If something is very enjoyable, it is difficult to stop doing it).

**2536. Ɔha da apem so.**
*A hundred lies on top of a thousand.*
(When you have finished a big job, there are always the ends to be tidied up and minor expenses to be paid).

**2537. Ɔha na ɔnim ha-tokuru mu.**
*The flying-squirrel knows the tree's hole.*
(The one who lives in a place knows its nature).

**2538. Ɔha nti na woregu adwaa a, tutu; na ɔtu a, ɔfa soro.**
*If it's because of the flying-squirrel that you are setting a ground trap, then dismantle it; because when it flies, it flies above.*
(If you want to catch someone, it is no good trying to do so in the wrong place).

**2539. Ɔha tu a, ɔfam; ɔda hɔ a, ɔfam.**
*If the flying-squirrel flies, it sticks to something; if it stays still, it sticks to something.*
(Whatever you do, you don't change your nature).

**2540. Ahabayerɛ ammɔ a, obi nnwo.**
*If the wild yam is not productive, no one digs it up.*
(No one troubles about something unproductive).

**2541. Ahabayerɛ bum nti na yɛsi no pam.**
*The wild yam produces leaves in profusion, that is why we support it with a stick.*
(All talk and no action sometimes takes people in).

**2542. Ahabayerɛ nso di a, yenhohoro ngu.**
*If the wild yam is not sufficient, we don't wash part of it away.*
(Waste not, want not).

**2543. Wohaahaa w'ani bebrebe a, ɛtuatua wo tiri ho.**
*If you stare too much, they (your eyes) are still attached to your head.*
(It is up to you if you want to harm yourself).

**2544. Ahahamma pae a, ɛpae gu kwaem na ɛmpae ngu mpoano.**
*If leaves fall, they fall into the forest and not into the sea.*
(You die where you have lived).

**2545. Ahahan-dwane sɛn hɔ a, ahahammono te tɔ fam.**
*If the dry leaves hang there, the green leaves are falling to the ground.*
(The young die while the old live on).

**2546. Nhahan-ata mmienu kabɔm a, ɛyɛ pepe.**
*When two leaves are placed together, they are hard to break.*
(This stands for the importance of cooperation. United we stand, divided we fall. The emblem is often used at the top of stool umbrellas).

**2547. Ɔhantanni na ɔkyiri nnipa.**
*A haughty person dislikes people.*
(If you are stand-offish, you don't make friends).

**2548. Aharawa nyɛ nam pa bi, nanso yɛde frafra nkwan.**
*The lung is not good meat, but we take it to scatter in the soup.*
(It takes all sorts to make up a society. Everyone has some use).

**2549. Wohare faako a, wobutu.**
*If you paddle on one side (of a canoe), you capsize.*
(If you are too one-sided, you don't thrive).

**2550. "Hei, hei" na amma akorɔma anyɛ keseɛ.**
*"Hi, hi", that is why the hawk does not grow fat.*
(Too much criticism and chasing about stops a man from being successful).

**2551. Ɔhemma tena ase a, papa nni adaagye.**
*When the Queen Mother sits in state, the fan has no rest.*
(A Queen Mother is fanned when she is in public. Hence: A servant cannot rest while his master or mistress works).

**2552. Ɔhemmɔne nni baabi, na ɔsafohene bɔne na ɔwɔ baabi.**
*There is no such thing as a bad chief, though a bad war captain can be found.*
(The man at the top can never be said to be wrong, so we blame people below him).

**2553. Ɔhemmɔne tena adwa so a, n'akyidifoɔ brɛ.**
*If a bad chief is enstooled, his followers grow weary.*
(A bad leader exhausts his people).

**2554. Ahemfoɔ baanu bɔ didiwa a, ɔbaako yi ayowa hɔ.**
*When two chiefs eat together, one of them picks up the dishes.*
(There is seniority in every situation).

**2555. Ɔhene a yɛmmɔ ne kyɛm soɔ na ɔde nantin-bini kɔ adwabɔ.**
*A chief whom we dare not advise is the one whose faeces drop on his heel when he goes to a durbar.*
(If you resent honest criticism, you let yourself in for ridicule).

**2556. Ɔhene a ɔda apakan mu se kaseɛ awɔ no na wɔn a wɔso no nso ɛ?**
*A chief who is reclining in a palanquin is complaining that he has been pricked by a thorn, how much more so his carriers?*
(If a protected person suffers, how much more the general public).

**2557. Ɔhene a yɛnka n'anim asem na ɔwe atakraboa a ɔnni tiri.**
*A chief before whom we fear to express an opinion is the one who eats the bird without a head.*
(There is a story of a chief who was given a vulture to eat because his hunters feared to tell him they could get nothing else. Hence: Listen to someone's reasons for not being able to comply with your requests, before you rebuke them).

2558. Ɔhene a ɔbɛku wo mmaeɛ a, wose woanyini akyerɛ.
*If the chief who is going to kill you has not yet come, you think you have attained old age.*
(Pride comes before a fall).

2559. Ɔhene a yɛntu no adwa so ani wu a, ɔwu ne menem.
*If a paramount chief who is above destoolment becomes ashamed, he dies through his throat (i.e he takes poison).*
(A paramount chief cannot abdicate; he can only commit suicide if he wants to leave the stool. Hence: A great man prefers death to shame).

2560. Ɔhene a ɔwɔ kuro mu yɛ abɛnkum a, ne nkoa nyinaa sua no.
*If a chief who is in the town uses the left hand, all his servants copy him.*
(Using the left hand is taboo in most respects. Hence: If you are an important person, those around you imitate whatever you do).

2561. Ɔhene a ɔnni bie na ɔsoa n'apakan.
*It is a poor chief who carries his own travelling basket.*
(A poor man has no choice).

2562. Ɔhene ba ne deɛ ɔse te adwa soɔ.
*The child of a chief is he whose father is on the stool.*
(If a man is important his children will be treated with respect. They do not, however, inherit).

2563. Ɔhene ba ntutu mmirika nkɔhwɛ tiri.
*A chief's child does not run to see heads.*
(The heads of important defeated enemies used to be brought to the chief. Hence: You don't get excited over what you see often).

2564. Ɔhene ba, yɛntwa no powa.
*The child of a chief, we do not insult him.*
(You don't insult the relatives of those in power).

2565. Ɔhene bi berɛ so wɔhu, na obi berɛ so wɔayere.
*In one chief's reign skins are singed and in another's they are spread in the sun.*
(Customs change with rulers).

2566. Ɔhene da apakan mu a, ɛyɛ no sɛ ɔrensi fam da.
*If a chief is lying in his palanquin, it seems good to him that he should never descend from it.*
(The moment a person reaches a comfortable and important position in society, he forgets he is fallible).

2567. Ɔhene dɔ wo a, ɔmma wo nto ntam.
*If a chief likes you, he does not lead you into swearing an oath.*
(Swearing an oath begins legal proceedings. So this means he does not lead you into litigation. Hence: If you are well-liked, you are protected from making mistakes).

2568. Ɔhene nko (ara) nnante.
*A chief does not travel alone.*
(Whatever happens to an important man affects his followers. He always has support).

2569. Ɔhene bɛkum wo a, ɛnnim ahamatwe.
*When a chief is going to kill you, it is no use casting lots.*
(Some fates are impossible to avoid, whoever's advice you ask).

2570. Ɔhene kyiniiɛ: ebi da ebi akyi.
*The chief's umbrella: someone is on top of someone.*
(Every man has his superior. Paramount chiefs sometimes have a double umbrella, one on top of the other, which symbolizes this idea).

2571. Ɔhene na ɔyi ɔdansefoɔ adie.
*It is the chief who identifies a witness.*
(In front of a chief or in court, everything hidden comes to light).

2572. Ɔhene ne wo ka a, na ɔku woɔ.
*If a chief and you are on (too) intimate terms, he kills you.*
(If you know too much, you suffer for it).

2573. Ɔhene anim na obi nka, na n'akyi deɛ obi ka.
*No one speaks their mind in the presence of a chief, but behind his back they talk.*
(You don't criticize authority openly, but it is nonetheless criticized in private).

2574. Ɔhene nufo dɔɔsɔ a, amansan na wɔnum.
*If a chief's breast is full, all the people of the state drink from it.*
(The wealth and well-being of the ruler is to the benefit of the people).

2575. Ɔhene nya [dɔm]/[ahotrafoɔ] pa a, na ɔse: "Me berɛ so dwo".
*If a chief has [a good army]/[good advisers] then he says "My reign brings peace".*
(A strong defence or wise counsel enables you to live in peace).

2576. Ɔhene nya nnipa pa a, na ɔse: "Menim amammuo".
*If a chief has good followers he says: "I know how to conduct affairs".*
(Good servants make a good master).

2577. Ɔhene asɛm yɛ akyekyereɛ-korona, ɔde yan no a, amaneɛ.
*A chief's affairs are like his special necklace, if he puts it on, there is trouble.*
(If an important man brings a case against you, you are in trouble).

2578. Ɔhene aso te sɛ sɔneɛ, ɛmu akwan boro apem.
*A chief's ears are like a sieve, there are more than one thousand ways to them.*
(The man at the top has many ways of hearing the truth or getting to know things).

2579. Ɔhene aso te se ɛsono aso.
*The ears of a chief are as big as an elephant's.*
(see above).

2580. Ɔhene suae prɛko na ɔnsuae mprɛnu.
*A chief is sworn in once, he is not sworn in twice.*
(A man of integrity does not break his word. Or: Once you get to the top, you can go no further).

2581. Ɔhene tamfo ne deɛ ɔne no firi mmɔfraase.
*A chief's enemy is the one who has grown up with him from childhood.*
(It is the people who grow up with you who do not show you respect, as they know too much about you).

2582. Ɔhene bɛtan wo a, na ɛfiri nhenkwaafoɔ.
*If a chief is going to hate you, it is because of his followers.*
(It is those who surround a chief, who can misinterpret your actions and turn the chief against you. Hence: It is the people nearest a person that make him your enemy).

2583. Ɔhene te sɛ bɛmu. Woto tuo bɔ no a, woseɛ w'akoraboɔ.
*A chief is like a bunch of palm nuts. If you fire a gun into it, you waste your bullets.*
(The removal of a leader does not necessarily mean the downfall of the state).

2584. Ɔhene te sɛ ɔdum, ɔnni anim nni akyire.
*A chief is like the odum tree, he has no front nor back.*
(A chief should be impartial in his judgements).

2585. Ɔhene nni awaresɛm.
*A chief does not arbitrate in marriage cases.*
(Personal affairs are not matters for the state).

2586. Ɔhene wu a, na mmɛntia di ahim.
*When a chief dies, the state horns swing around continuously.*
(When an important person dies there is a great deal of noise and ceremony).

2587. Ɔhen-kɔkorawa na yɛsisi no na nyɛ ababunu.
*An ancient chief is the one whom we cheat and not the young one.*
(If you are weak people take advantage of you).

2588. Ahenkwaa bɔne gyegye buro gu ne wura so.
*A bad royal slave brings blame upon his master*

2589. Ahenkwaa di adwene na wadwene asɛm.
*The royal slave eats fish to become thoughtful.*
(Play on words. Used of people who associate with the wise and learn from them).

2590. Ahenkwaa dufudepɛni ne sika bɔ nsaaho.
*A royal slave who is greedy is deprived of money.*
(If you are too greedy for present pleasure, you don't achieve great things in the long run).

2591. Nhenkwaa dodoɔ de atorodie ba.
*Too many royal slaves bring about tale-bearing.*
(Too many cooks spoil the broth).

2592. Nhenkwaafoɔ na wɔmma ɔhene ho yɛ hu.
*The royal slaves make the chief a person to be feared.*
(It is a person's followers that build up his position and thus their own. Without them he is but an ordinary man).

2593. Ahennwa fata wo a, yɛde gye woɔ.
*If the stool is suitable for you, we give it to you.*
(You get what you are entitled to).

2594. Ahennwa nyɛ babaayɛnten na yɛatena so mmienu.
*A chief's stool is not like a log on which two people can sit at the same time.*
(Only one man can rule at a time).

2595. "Ahia me na hwɛ me," nti na obi yɛ akoa.
*"I'm in need, so look after me", that is how someone becomes a slave.*
(If you are too subservient, people will abuse you).

2596. Ɛhia ɔbarima a, ne yere bɔ ne so mpekua.
*If a man is in need, his wife despises him.*
(Poverty leads to lack of respect).

2597. Ɛhia ɔbarima a, na ɔnwuiɛ.
*If a man becomes poor, it does not mean he has died.*
(Poverty does not mean death).

2598. Ɛhia barima a, ɔsɔ ne barima mu.
*If a man is in need, he has his manhood.*
(As a last resort, a man may have to sell himself to live).

2599. Ɛhia batani hia paani.
*If the employer is in want so is the employee.*

2600. Ɛhia bɔmmɔfoɔ a, ɛhia no ne n'apiretwaa.
*If poverty strikes the hunter, it strikes him and his bag.*
(A servant is affected by the fate of his master).

2601. Ɛhia oburoni a, ɔdi mankani.
*If a European is in need, he eats cocoyam.*
(Europeans seldom eat the cocoyam as they prefer the real yam, which is much more expensive. Hence: In times of need we are all alike).

2602. Ɛhia oburoni a, ɔka Twi.
*If a European is in need, he speaks Twi.*
(In times of need a proud man learns to compromise).

2603. Ɛhia oburoni a, ɔsane po.
*If a European is in need, he walks on the shore.*
(When in need you come down from your pedestal and think of home).

2604. Ɛhia wo hwɛfoɔ a, na ahia wo.
*If your guardian is poor then so are you.*
(Like master, like man).

2605. Ɛhia Ɔkanni a, ɔdi nse.
*If an Akan person is in want, he swears on something.*
(In some circumstances an apparently reliable person will tell lies).

2606. Ɛhia Ɔkanni a, Ɔkanni na ɔhwɛ no.
*When an Akan person becomes poor, an Akan person looks after him.*
(People belonging to the same group, should have sympathy for each other).

2607. Ɛhia kɔmfoɔ a ɔdi braduane, na ɔnya baabi si a, wabɔ ne ho asu.
*If the fetish priest is in want he eats food prepared by a menstruating woman and then, when his condition improves, he cleanses himself.*
(It was traditionally taboo to eat such food. In times of need you may have to do something wrong, but when better times come, you repair the wrong).

2608. Ɛhia kɔmfoɔ, hia yarefoɔ.
*The priest is in need, so is the sick man.*
(The priests needs money and the sick man needs medicine. We all need something from someone else).

2609. Ɛhia kramo a, na ɔhyɛ kyekye batakari.
*If the Moslem is in need, he wears an inferior smock.*
(You dress according to your means).

2610. Ɛhia [kurotwiamansa]/[ɔsebo] a, ɔwe [atwa]/
[wira].
*If the leopard is hungry it eats [the prickly yam plant]/
[leaves].*
(Beggars can't be choosers).

2611. Ɛhia onipa a, ɔda wiram.
*If a man is in need, he sleeps in the forest.*
(A poor man has no choice).

2612. Ɛhia opuro Kwasi wɔ papa so a, ɔdane ne ho hyɛ
mmerɛkɛnsono mu.
*When squirrel Kwasi gets into trouble on the palm
branch, it goes amongst the young palm fronds.*
(If the adult cannot help you, you seek help from the
young).

2613. Ɛhia two, hia pieto.
*If the hydrocele is troubled, so are the pants (shorts).*
(Used when something is to mutual disadvantage).

2614. Ɛhia wo a, ma nnipa nhunu.
*If you are in need, let people know of it.*

2615. Ɛhia wo a, na wɔrewe sumina-dwe.
*If you are in want, you eat palm nuts from the refuse
heap.*
(Beggars can't be choosers).

2616. Ɛhia wo a, na wo nsa deda wo nsa yam.
*If you are in need, then you go on begging (lit. one
hand lies on the belly of another).*
(When you beg you put the back of one hand on the
palm of the other and move it up and down. Hence:
The poor cannot afford pride).

2617. Ɛhia wo a, nwu.
*If you are in need, don't die.*
(Do not despair in adversity).

2618. Ɛhia wo na woka asem pa a, ɔmanfoɔ bu no
nhurudunhweaa.
*If you are poor and you give good advice, society calls
it all lies.*
(A poor man is not respected).

2619. Ohia da mu na wohunu nnipa suban.
*Poverty teaches you the nature of people.*
(A friend in need is a friend indeed).

2620. Ohia de wo na ɛmfaa wo nnuruu deɛ ɛbɛduru a,
ɔnnyae wo.
*If poverty has overcome you but it has not taken you to
where it is going to take you, it won't leave you.*
(What is predestined must be fulfilled).

2621. Ohia, yɛdi no fie, na yɛnni no dwa so.
*Poverty, we suffer at home, but not in public.*
(You hide your suffering within the family group).

2622. Ohia hia wo a, ɔba kwasea tu wo fo.
*If want troubles you, a foolish child advises you.*
(If you are in need, you take advice from anywhere you
can get it).

2623. Ohia hia wo a, na woto nsuonwunu mu a, ɛhye
wo.
*If you are suffering from poverty and you fall into cold
water, it scalds you.*
(If you are unfortunate, everything goes against you).

2624. Ohia hia wo a, wowe abirekyinwoma.
*If you are in need, you chew the skin of a goat.*
(Beggars can't be choosers).

2625. Ohia wo na wote abeteɛ a, ɛdane [ɛfan]/[ɛferɛ].
*If you are in want and you get corn porridge, it turns
into [ɛfan]/[a pumpkin].*
(Ɛfan is a herb used like cocoa-yam leaf to make stew.
Ɛferɛ is a pumpkin. Both are regarded as inferior to
corn porridge. Hence: If you are poor, everything acts
to your disadvantage).

2626. Ohia ma adwendwene.
*Poverty leads to planning.*
(If you are poor, you are forced to think of ways to
make a living).

2627. Ohia ma awiɛmfoɔ nyansa yera.
*Poverty makes a humble person's wisdom vanish.*
(Poverty destroys one's standards).

2628. Ohia na ɛde patapaa ba.
*Want leads to dissension.*
(A poor person argues over every pesewa).

2629. Ohia na ɛma yɛde bɔwereɛ twa borɔdeɛ.
*Want makes us use our nails to cut plantain.*
(Want is a hard taskmaster).

2630. Ohia na ɛma ɔdehyeɛ yɛ akoa.
*Poverty causes a royal to become a slave.*
(However important you may think you are, if you are
in want, you have to do what you are told).

2631. Ohia na ɛma adwe we mako.
*Want makes the monkey chew pepper.*
(A poor man eats what he can get).

2632. Ohia na ɛma ohiani tɔn ne nyansa ma osikani.
*Poverty makes the poor man sell his wisdom to the
rich man.*
(If you are poor, you are easily deceived).

2633. Ohia na ɛma ɔkanni yɛ aboa.
*Poverty leads the Akan to become a beast.*
(In times of need even the best people become
unscrupulous).

2634. Ohia na ɛma ɔtwea kɔ anɔpa-bɛ soɔ.
*Poverty makes the worthless man go in the very early
morning to tap palm wine.*
(Poverty leads you to being more enterprising).

2635. Ohia ne gyimi.
*Poverty is stupidity.*
(Only fools are poor!)

2636. Ohia nua ne adwoodwoo.
*The brother of want is peacefulness.*
(If you are known to be poor, you must avoid getting
into trouble).

2637. Ohia panin nyɛ panin pa.
*An impoverished elder is not a real elder.*
(If you have no means you wield no power).

2638. Ohia asoma woɔ, ɛbɛyɛ dɛn na worenkɔ.
*When poverty sends you, how can you refuse to go?*

2639. Ohia te sɛ ɛwoɔ, ɛnnɔre faako.
*Poverty is like honey, it does not mature in one place.*

**2640. Ohia nte bokɔro so.**
*Poverty does not reside in one place alone.*

**2641. Ohia nti na aserewa sisi aburobia sɔɔ.**
*Because of poverty the sunbirds perch on the canna.*
(The birds eat the canna seeds. Hence: A humble person keeps to a humble place, where he can at least eat).

**2642. Ohia tua akɔnnɔdeɛ.**
*Want spoils our appetite for precious things.*
(You don't bother about what you cannot afford).

**2643. Ohia tumi nye tumi pa.**
*The power of a poor man is not real power.*
(You have no power without possessions).

**2644. Ohia nni aburokyire a, anka Oburoni ammɛhata ne ntoma Abibirem.**
*If there had been no poverty overseas, then the European would not have come to spread his cloths in Africa.*
(Poverty leads men to act).

**2645. Ohia yɛ [adammɔ]/[animguaseɛ].**
*Poverty is [madness]/[a disgrace].*

**2646. Ohia yɛ ya a, ɛfiri fie, na ɛmfiri abɔntenso.**
*If poverty is bitter, it is so from the home and not from outside.*
(Unless your family is poor, you are not really poor).

**2647. Ohiada mu nti na onipa didi a, ɔgya bie.**
*Because of future famine (lit. the day of need), a man leaves part of the food he eats.*
(We plan against future want).

**2648. Ahiafoɔ nim asɛm di, na mmom ɛho abadwadeɛ na ɛsua.**
*Poor people know how to settle a case, but the price coming out of it is small.*
(A poor person has a poor reward).

**2649. Ɔhiani ba ne osikani ba goro a, ne ho tu.**
*If a poor man's child and a rich man's child are playing together, the former enjoys it.*
(Everyone gets something out of contact with riches).

**2650. Ohiani abaawa korɔ nkyere brɛ.**
*The poor man's only slave girl soon gets tired.*
(Overwork and poverty exhaust).

**2651. Ohiani bu bɛ a, yɛmfa.**
*If a poor man makes a proverb, it does not spread.*
(No one takes notice of what the poor say).

**2652. Ohiani di pɔwadeɛ a, ɛte sɛ wadi dwan.**
*If a poor man eats a small coin's worth of something, it is as if he eats a sheep.*
(If you are poor, a little is as good as a feast).

**2653. Ohiani didi abraa-abraa.**
*A poor man eats without discrimination.*
(Good taste is a luxury).

**2654. Ohiani mfa abofu.**
*A poor man does not become angry.*
(A poor man suffers in silence).

**2655. Ohiani fura kente a, yɛse ɔfura kyɛnkyɛn.**
*If a poor man puts on kente cloth, we say he is wearing black cloth.*
(A poor man is not respected, however he tries to gain face).

**2656. Ohiani funu nkyɛre fie.**
*A poor man's corpse does not remain long in the house.*
(A poor man is buried cheaply and quickly).

**2657. [Ohiani]/[ɔhɔhoɔ] funu, yɛsie no [nkwankyen]/[anɔpa].**
*A [poor man's]/[stranger's] corpse, we bury it [by the roadside]/[in the morning].*
(You don't spend time and money over something you don't value).

**2658. Ohiani gyaaseni ne nwansena.**
*The poor man's attendant is the fly.*
(A poor man has to put up with dirt and discomfort).

**2659. Ohiani hyɛ pɛtea a, yɛbu no awowa.**
*If a poor man wears a ring, we regard it as something in pawn.*
(If a poor person shows off, it leads people to suspect them).

**2660. Ohiani ka asɛm a, ɛdane asɛmmɔne.**
*If a poor man says something, it changes into bad news.*
(If you are poor, people misinterpret you).

**2661. Ohiani nka aberempɔn-tam.**
*A poor man does not swear the oath of a paramount chief.*
(If you swear a chief's oath, he must hear your case. It can cost a good deal to take a case before a big chief. Hence: You don't let yourself in for something you cannot afford).

**2662. Ohiani kanea ne ayerɛmo.**
*A poor man's lantern is the lightening.*

**2663. Ohiani kyerɛ kwaeɛ a, yɛnno.**
*If a poor man shows an area of forest, we don't cultivate it.*
(Kwaeɛ means virgin forest, here: that is, land where you could start a farm. Hence: You are suspicious of the advice of the poor however good it may seem).

**2664. Ohiani nkyiri asisirape.**
*A poor man does not taboo the flying white ant.*
(This insect is edible but not a delicacy. Hence: A poor man eats what he can get).

**2665. Ohiani na ɔwe nantwie aharawa.**
*A poor man eats the cow's lungs.*
(If you are poor, you are satisfied with what others reject).

**2666. Ohiani ne ɔdefoɔ ngoro.**
*The poor and the rich do not play together.*
(People of different classes do not relax together).

**2667. Ohiani nim nyansa a, ɛka ne tirim.**
*If a poor man knows wisdom, it is kept in his head.*
(A poor man keeps his thoughts to himself).

**2668. Ohiani anim yɛ ɔdefoɔ tan.**
*A poor man's face is ugly to a wealthy person.*
(A rich man finds everything to do with the poor disagreeable).

**2669. Ohiani nom tawa-pa a, ɛyɛ no sɛ taasɛnfi.**
*When a poor man smokes good tobacco, it is to him like his dirty old pipe.*
(If what you already have something that satisfies you, you don't look elsewhere).

**2670. Ohiani nya adeɛ a, ɔman bɔ.**
*If a poor man becomes rich, the state is ruined.*
(Quick acquisition of wealth results in dissension).

**2671. Ohiani bɛnya ne ho na batakwan asi.**
*Before a poor man becomes rich, the way to acquire wealth through trade is closed.*
(It is hard for an unlucky person to succeed even if the way appears to be there).

**2672. Ohiani nyansa hyɛ osikani nsam.**
*A poor man's wisdom is in the hands of a wealthy person.*
(A poor man's intelligence is of little use unless he is backed by a wealthy man).

**2673. Ohiani nyansa nnuru dwam.**
*A poor man's wisdom does not come into public places.*
(The wisdom of the poor is disregarded).

**2674. Ohiani pam akoroɔ a, na ɛyɛ no sɛ ɔdidi sanyaa.**
*When a poor man mends his broken wooden bowl, it serves him just as well as if he ate off a tin plate.*
(A tin plate is much valued. Hence: In poverty, you make do with what you can get and don't bother about the niceties of life).

**2675. Ohiani mpo daberɛ.**
*A poor man does not refuse a sleeping place.*
(The poor sleep wherever they can get shelter).

**2676. Ohiani asem hwehwe nnipa aso.**
*A poor man's problem, people wonder about it.*
(People don't trust the explanations of the poor).

**2677. Ohiani asommɛn ne batafoɔ se.**
*The poor man's short horn is the bush-pig's tooth.*
(If you are poor, you make use of poor substitutes).

**2678. Ohiani ntankɛseɛ ne: "Haado".**
*The poor man's great oath is: "If it were not for..."*
(If you are poor, regrets are in vain).

**2679. Ohiani ntɔn adeɛ mma ohiani ntɔ.**
*A poor man does not sell something for a poor man to buy.*
(If you have nothing, you can do nothing with it).

**2680. Ohiani tuo hwehwe sikani aso.**
*A poor man's gunfire passes over a rich man's ears.*
(A rich man does not fear a poor one).

**2681. Ohiani nni biribi a, ɔwɔ tɛkrɛma a ɔde tutu ka.**
*If a poor man has nothing else, he has a tongue with which to delay paying his debts.*

**2682. Ohiana nni adwemsɛm.**
*A poor man does not make a public donation.*
(If you can't make a good impression, you keep quiet).

**2683. Ohiani nni asem nni bem.**
*A poor man who has a case is never innocent.*
(Prejudice is against the poor).

**2684. Ohiani nni yɔnkoɔ.**
*A poor man has no friend.*

**2685. Ohiani yane gorɔ a, yɛse ɔyane nnwahoma.**
*If a poor man wears a silver chain, we say he is wearing a sheep's rope.*
(Poor man no friend).

**2686. Ahihi nsere ahaha.**
*Hihi does not laugh at Haha.*
(One fool should not laugh at another's folly).

**2687. Ahina bɔ a, na n'abɔmena mu trɛ.**
*If the water pot breaks, then the hole in it is widened.*
(If someone is in difficulty, then all his other troubles increase).

**2688. Ahina abɔ, na kuruwa reyɛ dɛn akɔ asuo?**
*The water pot is broken, how then is the cup going for water?*
(The one who supports you has died, then how can you fend for yourself?)

**2689. Ahina firi pataso hwe ase a, na n'awieɛ mu ara ne no.**
*If the water pot falls from the roof beam, then that is the end of it.*
(What is destroyed can never be renewed).

**2690. Ahina nni hɔ a, na yɛde ntoa suae abɛ.**
*If the water pot is not there, we take a gourd to collect palm wine.*
(When you don't have the right thing for a job, you have to use a substitute).

**2691. Ahisɛm nti na yɛkum nsonkuronsuo a, yɛhua hwɛ.**
*Because of provocation when we kill the bed bug, we sniff at it.*
(If you get rid of a nuisance, you make quite sure that it has gone).

**2692. Wo ho bɔn a, wonteta ngu mu.**
*If your body smells, you don't fart as well.*
(Don't make things worse).

**2693. "Wo ho deɛ ɛyɛ fɛ, nanso w'asem nyɛ fɛ." nyɛ animuonyam.**
*"You are beautiful, but your manners are not," is not a cause for respect.*
(Mere beauty is a thing of no merit; good manners are what matters).

**2694. Wo ho yɛ den a, wonsene boɔ.**
*Even if you are strong, you are not stronger than a stone.*
(There are limits to everyone's capabilities).

**2695. Wo ho yɛ den a, wonyɛ baanu adwuma.**
*However strong you are, you cannot do the work of two.*
(Two are always better than one).

2696. Wo ho yɛ den a, nyɛ sɛ abrane dodoɔ anya woɔ.
*If you are tough, it is not so when many strong people seize you.*
(All things are relative).

2697. Wo ho yɛ den pii a, wohwere tɔkwakofoɔ.
*If you are too tough, you cannot get someone to fight.*
(If you are too strong and determined, people avoid quarreling with you).

2698. Yɛn ho yɛn ho mu yɛnni nnɔmmata.
*Among ourselves we don't have to be at loggerheads.*
(There is no cause for friends to quarrel).

2699. Wo ho yɛ hu a, yɛnyi wo hu.
*If you are a person to be feared, you cannot be scared.*
(A person in a position to create fear, is not afraid of others).

2700. Wo ho yɛ tan a, yɛnku wo.
*If you are ugly, we don't kill you.*
(Ugliness is not a crime).

2701. Wo ho yɛ tan, na wosrɛ adeɛ a, na yɛmma woɔ, na sɛ wokari wo sika tɔ a, enneɛ wo dea.
*If you are ugly and you beg for something and we don't give it to you, if you weigh out your gold to buy something, it belongs to you alone.*
(Whatever happens, what you pay for is yours).

2702. Ahodasoɔ ne barima.
*Readiness is manly.*
(It is good to be prepared).

2703. Ahɔduane yɛ wo dɛ a, w'animuonyam yɛ ketewa.
*If a stranger's food is sweet to you, your dignity becomes small.*
(Greed makes you act in an undignified way).

2704. Ɔhɔhoɔ a ɔbaeɛ anhunu ɔmanni a, ɔmanni nso nhunu ɔhɔhoɔ.
*If a stranger who came did not recognize a citizen, then the citizen also did not recognize a stranger.*
(Tit for tat).

2705. Ɔhɔhoɔ a ɔma wo nya adeɛ na ɔma wonya ɛka.
*A stranger who causes you to get something, also causes you to get into debt.*
(Everything has a good and bad side).

2706. Ɔhɔhoɔ di nsekuro a, ne dwan te yera.
*If a stranger takes to rumor-mongering, it is his sheep that is untethered and gets lost.*
(People will not stand for a stranger who stirs up trouble and meddles in their affairs. He will get into trouble for it).

2707. Ɔhɔhoɔ nni abɛnkwan.
*A stranger does not eat palm soup.*
(A stranger is not given the best).

2708. "Ɔhɔhoɔ nni nkɔ," yɛ ɔmanifɔneɛ.
*"Let the stranger eat and go," makes the citizen lean.*
(Too much generosity leads to poverty).

2709. Ɔhɔhoɔ bɛhunu kuro mu asem a, na ɛfiri ɔmanni.

*If a stranger understands a town's affairs, it is because of a citizen.*
(You only get intimate information from an insider).

2710. Ɔhɔhoɔ [hunu adeɛ]/[nnim] a, ɔmanni akyerɛ.
*If a stranger understands the situation, a citizen has explained it.*
(You should not reveal inside information about family affairs to a stranger).

2711. Ɔhɔhoɔ kyɛre fie a, n'akokɔ nkwan dane nkuruma nkwan.
*If a stranger remains in the home, his chicken soup turns into okro soup.*
(Do not overstay your welcome).

2712. Ɔhɔhoɔ nkyere bomukwan.
*A stranger does not show someone a short-cut.*
(If you are not familiar with a place you should not pretend to know it).

2713. Ɔhɔhoɔ nkyere ɔhɔhoɔ.
*A stranger does not arrest a stranger.*
(You need experience to detect a crime).

2714. Ɔhɔhoɔ akyi mpa asɛm.
*If a stranger leaves, there is always something to be said about him.*
(Once a person has gone, we talk about them).

2715. Ɔhɔhoɔ na ɔdi akokɔ, n'ani abɔ.
*It is the stranger that eats the fowl whose eyes have failed.*
(You can easily deceive someone who is not familiar with a place).

2716. Ɔhɔhhoɔ na ɔsunti aponnwa.
*It is the stranger who trips over the threshold.*
(If you are unfamiliar with something, you must be careful nto to make mistakes in dealing with it).

2717. Ɔhɔhoɔ ne kuromani nsɛ.
*A stranger and a citizen are not alike.*
(You don't treat a stranger in the same way as someone you know well).

2718. Ɔhɔhoɔ ani akɛse-akɛse, nanso ɔmfa nhunu kuro mu asɛm.
*The stranger's eyes are very big, but he still cannot understand the town's affairs.*
(A stranger can never really understand the customs and culture of a place).

2719. Ɔhɔhoɔ pɛ wo yere a, na ɔfrɛ no "M'ase".
*If a stranger likes your wife, then he calls her "My mother-in-law".*
(Be careful of people who show too much intimacy in your home).

2720. Ɔhɔhoɔ nsene kuromani.
*A stranger is not better than a fellow citizen.*
(Consider your own people first).

2721. Ɔhɔhoɔ nsoa funu ti.
*A stranger does not carry the head of a corpse.*
(This is reserved for the family. A stranger should not interfere in the internal affairs of a state, nor the personal affairs of a family group).

2722. Ɔhɔhoɔ bɛsoeɛ wo na wannya wo adeɛ a, ɔgya wo ka.
*When a stranger stops at your house and does not leave you anything, he leaves you debts.*
(A mean visitor is a menace. Or: People can either be grateful or ungrateful).

2723. Ɔhɔhoɔ te sɛ abɔfra.
*A stranger is like a child.*
(A stranger, like a child, is ignorant of local laws and customs).

2724. Ɔhɔhoɔ te sɛ susuansuo, ɔresene a, ɔnsia.
*A stranger is like flood water, when he is moving, he is not impeded.*
(A stranger passes by quickly, so no one cares too much how he behaves. It is presumed that he is ignorant).

2725. Ɔhɔhoɔ ante asem a, ne bɔtɔ bete.
*If a stranger does not hear something, his bag will hear.*
(Don't gossip about a person if you can't say something to their face, or someone else will report you back to them).

2726. Ɔhɔhoɔ nto mmara.
*A stranger does not break laws.*
(A stranger does not know the customs and laws of the land and so is excused if he accidentally breaks them and makes mistakes).

2727. Ɔhɔhoɔ nto ɔware.
*A stranger does not play ɔware.*
(Ɔware is a game played among friends. Hence: A warning against poking your nose into other people's affairs).

2728. Hɔhopa na yebɔ no din.
*A virtuous foreigner, we mention his name.*
(Virtue brings its own reward).

2729. Hohoro w'ano ntɔtorɔ ansa na waka obi deɛ.
*Wash the mark from your cheek (made by dribble) before you draw the attention of another to his own.*
(Remove the beam from your own eye before seeking to remove the mote from your brother's).

2730. Hohoro wo nsa bɛdidi nyɛ mmusuo.
*Wash your hands and come and eat is not an offence.*
(It is no harm in asking someone to do something if it is for their own benefit).

2731. Ɔhɔhoranfoɔ de n'ahohoran firi ne kurom.
*A boaster: his boasting starts in his own town.*
(Your vices grow out of your own background).

2732. Ɔhɔho-sekufoɔ na odwan we ne borɔdeɛ.
*An inquisitive stranger gets his ripe plantain eaten by sheep.*
(If you are too inquisitive, you get into trouble).

2733. Nhohowa tare bese ho; ɔrente nwe, ɔrente ntɔn. Na ɔbɛyɛ bese dɛn?
*The red ant clings to the cola; it is unable to pick and chew it, it is unable to pick and sell it. What then does it want with the cola?*
(Don't be a dog in the manger).

2734. Ɔhohwini, wɔwo no.
*A n'er-do-well was born.*
(It takes all kinds to make a world).

2735. Ahoma da boɔ so a, yɛntwa.
*If a rope lies on a stone, we don't cut it.*
(If someone is well-protected, you don't harm them).

2736. Homa tentene na ɛte kokɔbini.
*It is the long rope that picks up the fowl's excrement.*
(Too much of anything breeds trouble).

2737. Homa toto a, yɛde nsa mmienu na ɛsane.
*If the rope tangles, we take two hands to unravel it.*
(Two hands are better than one).

2738. Homa ware a, ɛtoa.
*If the string is too long, it tangles.*
(Don't bite off more than you can chew).

2739. Homa-homa kyere ketebɔ.
*Many strings together catch the leopard.*
(Many unimportant people together can defeat a powerful man).

2740. Ahomasoɔ mu nni biribiara sɛ amaneɛ.
*There is nothing more in pride than getting involved in trouble.*
(Pride comes before a fall).

2741. Honam dadaa adwareɛ nyɛ dwarena.
*An old body is not hard to wash.*
(You deal more easily with what is familiar to you).

2742. Honam fufuo na ɛta sɛ no.
*It is a light-skinned person who we accuse of farting.*
(During the harmattan some African skins turn scaly white, unless they are cared for. People who allow their skins to become ashy are derided and are likely to be accused of any minor misdemeanor. Hence: If you are not considered important, you will be blamed for any misdemeanors taking place around you).

2743. Honam kankan, yɛde wo.
*Body odor is natural.*
(Every one is born with their own characteristics).

2744. Honam akwaa mu panin ne tiri.
*The elder of the body is the head.*
(The man who uses his head gets to the top).

2745. Honam mu nni nhanoa.
*There are no boundaries in the body.*
(What affects one part of the body affects it all. Or: What affects one person affects the whole community).

2746. Honam te sɛ asaase, ɛgu ahodoɔ.
*A body is like land, there are different kinds.*
(We cannot all be alike).

2747. Honam tete a, ɛka kaseɛ.
*When the body wears away, only the bones remain.*
(However much an important man has lost, something still remains to him).

2748. Honam yɛntɔ.
*We do not buy our body.*
(Your body is irreplaceable. Hence: Treat it with respect).

**2749. Honam-kuro, yɛmia no atirimuɔden.**
*A sore on the skin, we dress with cruelty.*
(You must be cruel to be kind).

**2750. Honam-kuro anwu a, ɛporɔ.**
*If a flesh-wound does not heal, it rots.*
(There is only one alternative – you either gain or lose).

**2751. Ɔhonankani fie gye hwa.**
*The home of a selfish person gives off a smell.*
(If you are selfish, you have no one to help you keep things in good order).

**2752. Ahonu ntu kuro.**
*Repentance does not create a sore.*
(If you repent your action, there is no longer a cause for friction).

**2753. Ɔhonyafoɔ na ɔse sika sekan a, ɔde twitwa nkontommire.**
*If a wealthy person whets a cutlass made of gold, he uses it to cut coco-yam leaves.*
(A wealthy person is careless of his things as he can replace them).

**2754. Ahoɔden bebrebe yɛ mmusuo.**
*Too much strength is a misfortune.*
(A strong man is expected to perform feats of courage and may be the first to suffer).

**2755. Ɔhoɔdenfoɔ soa ɛbeɛ-nam a, ɛporɔ**
*If a strong man carries the meat of a forest hog, it rots.*
(One man, however strong, cannot do the work of many).

**2756. Ɔhoɔdenfoɔ soa ɛtoɔ a, ɛbu.**
*If a strong man carries the end of something, it breaks.*
(If you don't take responsibility according to your position, there is trouble).

**2757. Ahoɔfɛ ntua ka.**
*Beauty does not pay debts.*

**2758. Ahoɔfɛ nyɛ adepa a, anka yɛn ani mmereho mpɛ bi.**
*If beauty were not a good thing, then we would not be seeking for it.*
(Everyone seeks for the best).

**2759. Ahoɔhene nti na yɛgya bowerɛ.**
*Because of itching we grow our nails.*
(We plan ahead for the future and have reason for our actions).

**2760. Wohoro wɔ asuwa mu na amfi a, wode kɔ asutene mu.**
*If you clean something in a small stream and you are not successful, you take it to a big stretch of water.*
(If a case is judged and you are not satisfied with the result, you appeal to higher authority).

**2761. "Hu m'ani so ma me", nti na atwe nam mmienu-mmienu.**
*"Blow in my eyes for me", makes duikers walk in pairs.*
(Everyone needs a companion to help him on in life).

**2762. Yɛhu wo ɛdwa nyinaa ase a, wotɔn adeɛ a, yɛntɔ.**
*If you have a bad reputation in all markets, if you sell anything, we don't buy.*
(If you have a bad name, people avoid you at any cost).

**2763. "Yɛahu wo ha a, mma yɛnhu wo do", yɛka kyerɛ ɔmammɔfoɔ.**
*"We have seen you here, don't let us see you over there," is what we say to a turn-coat.*

**2764. Yɛnhuu ɛban ho a, yɛnsɛ kɛtɛ.**
*If we have not seen the wall of the room, we do not spread the sleeping mat.*
(First things first).

**2765. Ɛhu a yede yi atɔfoɔ akwa no, ɛno ara na yɛde bɔ yen ho ban.**
*Fear that makes you run away from bad events is the same fear that you use to defend yourself.*
(You can't always run away, there are times when you have to face up to the situation with courage).

**2766. Ɛhu nsuro ɔmani.**
*Fear does not fear a fellow citizen.*
(No one fears what he is used to).

**2767. "Hua na wobɛte", yɛdi no abusua mu.**
*"Sniff and you will be able to catch the scent", we say amongst the family.*
(If you belong to a family it is easier to smell out what is happening inside it).

**2768. Wo huahua tɔkwa bebrebe a, wohwere patafoɔ.**
*If you try and start quarrels too often, you lose your peacemaker.*
(A constant trouble-maker does not go on getting help in solving his problems).

**2769. Huam, yɛmpɛ no dadaso.**
*Glamour, we don't find it in old matters.*
(Old and well-known things do not excite you).

**2770. Ohuammɔ sen "Merenkɔ koraa".**
*Disappointment is worse than "I am not going at all".*
(Unmet expectations are worse than no promises at all).

**2771. Ɛhuboa ɔbaako nhunu.**
*A single person does not see a frightening beast.*
(No one believes a strange story unless there is a witness).

**2772. Ohufoɔ na ɔbɔ akosɛm.**
*A coward puts about rumors of war.*
(A coward always fears the worst).

**2773. Ohufoɔ na ɔka mmarimasɛm akokyire.**
*A coward talks bravely while retreating.*

**2774. Ohufoɔ na ɔyɛ bogya pamu.**
*A coward discriminates amongst members of his family.*
(A coward gives way to pressure and avoids involvement in family quarrels).

**2775. Ohufoɔ suro dɔm nti na ɔtwa aborɔdɔɔ.**
*A coward fears the army, therefore he feigns inability to fight.*
(If you fear to do so, you make any excuse not to act).

2776. Yɛhuhu akɔdaa twɛ so na yɛaka.
*If we blow air on a young girl's vagina, we have sexual relations with her.*
(You need tact to get what you want from somebody).

2777. Ahuhuboɔ fra abrammoɔ-pa a, woyi no twene.
*If a false weight is mixed up with the real weights, you put it aside.*
(False weights are easily rejected. You can reject falseness if you wish to).

2778. Huhu-huhu nyɛ hu a na ɛfiri deɛ wonyɛeɛ.
*If a rumor is not frightening to someone it is because of what they have not done.*
(An innocent man does not have a bad conscience).

2779. Ahuhusɛm mpa abranteɛ akyi.
*A young man is prone to vanity.*
(Youth is arrogant).

2780. Ahunatesa annya animuonyam mpo a, owɔ nkwa.
*If a person who maintains his youthfulness has no dignity, at least he has long life.*
(Everything has its compensations).

2781. Wohunta yɛ a, yɛhunta hu wo.
*What you do in secret, we see in secret.*
(Nothing is really hidden).

2782. "Mehunuiɛ a anka", na aseɛ awie.
*"Had I known", is always too late.*
(Vain regrets).

2783. «Mehunuiɛ a anka,» nni aduro.
*«Had I known», has no medicine.*
(Once you have missed your chance, it does not come again).

2784. Wohunu ɔbaa na ntoma mfura no a, na ɛfiri ne mma ntira.
*If you see a woman who does not wear a good cloth, then it is because of her children.*
(A woman sacrifices all for her children. When they are grown it is up to them to see she has everything she wants).

2785. Yɛnhunu ɔbaa anim a, yɛnsɛ kɛtɛ.
*If we have not seen a woman's face, we don't spread the sleeping mat.*
(Until you've seen her, you don't know if she is willing to sleep with you. Hence: Be sure you know what you are doing, before you take action).

2786. Wohunu aberewa a, wose ɔnii awia-kɔteɛ da.
*If you see an old lady, you say she has never had intercourse in the afternoon.*
(You cannot judge how people behaved in their youth from how they act in old age. More generally: Appearances are deceptive).

2787. Wohunu aberewa a, ɛsɛ ɔnnii bere da.
*If you see an old lady, it is as if she has never lived well.*
(However well they are cared for, the old deteriorate).

2788. Wohunu obi a ɔyɛ kitikiti wɔ abɔnten so a, hwɛ no komm, na sɛ ɔyɛ ɔbarima a, ɛdɔm bɛba ama woahunu no.
*If you see someone who throws their weight about in public, look at them carefully and if he is a real man, if the crowd attacks him, he will show you.*
(A boaster is shown up when he has to prove his boasting).

2789. Wohunu obi adeɛ so hwɛ a, ɛka wo hɔ.
*If you take care of someone's property well, it becomes your own.*
(If you are trustworthy, people will help you).

2790. Mahunu ɔbomokyikyie a wakum dɛnkyɛm pen.
*I have seen a river fish which killed a crocodile before now!*
(There are some wonders which, even if true, you cannot prove easily. This fish can reputedly kill a crocodile by biting the liver, lungs and heart. It has serrated spines on the pectoral fins which can be locked in an extended position and are very sharp).

2791. Wohunu abusudeɛ a, wofee w'ani hwɛ.
*If you see an abomination, you look at it well.*
(People are fascinated by horrors).

2792. Wohunu damma so hwe a, ɛdane taku.
*If you take care of damma, it changes into taku.*
(Damma is a small weight; taku, a larger one. Hence: What you care for, flourishes).

2793. Wohunu deɛ wabɔ awuo na n'anim da hɔ a, ma no due, na wahunu amane.
*If you see a person who has coughed to death (almost) and his face is normal, condole him, for he has suffered.*
(You should show sympathy for those who have suffered and passed through difficulties).

2794. Wohunu deɛ woadie na w'ano yɛpɔ a, ɛnyɛ ya.
*If you know what you have consumed to make your mouth swell, it is not painful.*
(If you now what you have done to entail punishment, you can't complain).

2795. Wohunu adeɛ a, fa w'ani hwɛ na ɛmma w'ano nka bi.
*If you see something, look at it well, but don't make your mouth say it.*
(Keep your eyes open, but don't interfere with what does not concern you).

2796. Yɛhunu adidie ansa na yɛhunu adepɛ.
*We know how to eat before we know how to search for a fortune.*
(First things first).

2797. Yehunu dua a ɛbɛwɔ yɛn a, yɛtwa so na yɛnsene ano.
*If we see a stick that will injure us, we cut it, we don't sharpen its end.*
(Prevention is better than cure. Or: Don't make matters worse than they are).

2798. Wohunu odwan to a, bu no sɛ ɛyɛ nam, ɛfirisɛ, wɔtɔɔn no no, na ɛka ho na wɔtɔ tuaa ka.
*If you see the anus of a sheep, consider it as meat, because, when they bought it, it was part of what they paid for.*
(No part of the body is valueless. Or: No member of the family is valueless).

**2799. Wohunu ofikɛse mu abaawa a, ma no due na ɔbrɛ.**
*If you see a young servant girl from a large house, condole her, because she must be tired.*
(Just because you come from a wealthy place, it does not mean you don't suffer there).

**2800. Wobehunu ka a, na yede soma woɔ.**
*If you will know how to say it, then we send you (with a message).*
(If you are qualified you will get the job).

**2801. Wobɛhunu aka na asɛntifoɔ na ɛyɛ na.**
*You will know how to tell something, but the listeners are hard to find.*
(It is hard to get someone to take advice).

**2802. "Mɛhunu-mɛka", ne ɔbrɛ na ɛnam.**
*"I will see it and comment on it," leads to suffering.*
(This expression is associated with someone who is constantly pointing to faults that he sees. Hence: If you have high standards, you suffer for them).

**2803. Wohunu wo ka tutu a, yɛnyi wo adwo.**
*If you know how to postpone a debt, we don't take you as a pawn.*
(In the old days, if you could not pay a debt, either you or a member of your family had to go and work it off for the creditor as a "pawn". Hence: Said of a man who can talk himself out of most difficult situations).

**2804. Wohunu woka tutu a, woho asɛm nkɔ abanmu.**
*If you know how to postpone a debt, you are not taken before the government.*
(It is possible to talk yourself out of a difficult situation).

**2805. Wohunu "Ma-yɛnkɔhwɛ" a, wonna nhwɛ bio.**
*If you see "Let's-go-and-see", you do not look at it again.*
(Once you have seen something, you are no longer interested in seeing it).

**2806. Wohunu akɔdaa twɛ a, hwe no yie na ɛbɛtɔ da bi na woretua sika na woanya ahwɛ.**
*If you see a child's vagina, look at it well, because the day will come when you will be paying money to see it.*
(When opportunity strikes, grasp it).

**2807. Wohunu nkɔnkonsa di a, na woahunu tugya.**
*If you know treachery, then you know desertion.*
(A treacherous man loses his friends).

**2808. Wobɛhunu nkontompo nyinaa akyi a, ɛnyɛ: "Gyina hɔ na merekɔ aba".**
*If you know how to detect all sorts of lies, this does not include: "Stand there and I will come soon".*
(Simple lies are the most difficult to detect).

**2809. Mahunu kontromfi a ne yere awuo na wasi atimum, na wo, wansane deɛ, ɛfa wo ho bɛn?**
*I have seen a baboon who has grown long hair because of his wife's death, but you, antelope, how does it concern you?*
(Don't copy blindly and without reason the action of others).

**2810. Wohunu korɔno bɔ a, wohunu brɛbrɛ-wo-mu-ase.**

*If you know how to steal, you know how to bend your body.*
(If you do wrong, you must know how to wriggle out of trouble).

**2811. Mahunu okusie a ɔsene ɛsono kɛseɛ pɛn.**
*I have seen a rat bigger than an elephant before now!*
(You are telling a tall story!)

**2812. Wohunu akyekyedeɛ a, wose wada, nanso ebia na ɔrebɔ mpaeɛ.**
*If you see a tortoise, you say it is sleeping, but perhaps it is praying.*
(Someone may appear to you to be inactive about a situation when in fact he is working on it).

**2813. "Mehunu wo akyɛre". Ɔse: "Ɛne nnɛ".**
*"I've not seen you for a long time." He says: "Its to-day".*
(The time has now come for you to fulfill your obligations).

**2814. Wohunu ɔmanni a, sɔ wo tuo mu, na ɔmanni nyɛ.**
*If you see a fellow citizen, get hold of your gun, because a fellow citizen is wicked.*
(The person nearest to you is the one most likely to damage you).

**2815. "Mehunuiɛ na mamfa", ne "manhunu", nsɛ.**
*"I saw it, but did not take it", and "I did not see it", are not alike.*
(A witness is more likely to be accused than a person who was not there).

**2816. Wohunu na woanka a, ɛfa wo so.**
*If you see (something bad) and you say nothing about it, it will overcome you.*
(If you connive at evil, it will affect you too).

**2817. Wohunu ananse a, ku no, anyɛ saa a, ɔbɛdane kyɛmfoɔ abɛka wo.**
*When you see a spider, kill it; if not, it will change into a bird-spider and bite you.*
(The bird spider has a poisonous bite. A warning in a situation when one is suspected of being an enemy but has not yet shown oneself up. Hence: Don't deal with those you don't trust).

**2818. Wohunu nnɛ deɛ a, na wohunu ɔkyena deɛ.**
*If you see to-day's thing, then you have also seen to-morrow's thing.*
(There is nothing new in the world).

**2819. Wohunu anene a, wose asɔkwa. Wohunu asɔkwa a, wose anene. Anene akratoma gu ne kɔn mu; asɔkwa akratoma gu ne tiri so, wɔn nyinaa bafua.**
*If you see a crow, you say it is a white-crested hornbill. If you see the hornbill, you think it is a crow. The crow has a white cloth round its neck; the hornbill has a white cloth on its head. They are both equal.*
(There is no point in fighting for supremacy amongst equals).

**2820. Yenhunu onipa dakoro nse no sɛ: "Woafɔn".**
*If we see a person one day only, we should not say to them: "You have grown lean."*
(Don't judge too quickly. We judge by comparisons).

2821. Wonhunu onipa tebea mu a, womma no mmaawareɛ.
*If you have not seen how a man lives, you don't give him a woman to marry.*
(You need to know all about something or someone before you get irrevocably involved in the situation).

2822. Wohunu no si a, wohunu no sɔne.
*If you know how to pound (palm nuts), you know how to sieve.*
(If you know one part of a job, you should be able to finish it).

2823. Wohunu nwamma aba a, na woahunu bamporɔsuo.
*If you see the fruit of the ricinordendron neualotii, then you know the season of heavy rains has come.*
(Said when some sign, generally well-recognized, means that trouble is coming).

2824. Wohunu nyansa bebrebe a, woma odwan akye.
*If you become too wise, you say good-morning to a sheep.*
(If you try to be too clever, you will make a fool of yourself).

2825. Wobɛhunu nyansa nyinaa a, nkwasea nyansa deɛ worenhunu bi.
*If you were to be able to know all wisdom, a fool's wisdom you would not be able to know anything about.*
(You can't be one hundred per cent wise. Folly also has its place).

2826. Mahunu apetebie a ɔse awu ama watwitwa ntwoma, na wo, amoakua, nso a w'ano bese yiɛ.
*I have seen a squirrel whose father died rub himself with red earth, but you, ground squirrel, why is your mouth red with cola.*
(If something does not concern you, don't poke your nose into it).

2827. Wohunu Praa na ɔso yaawa-dwanta a, wommisa no·deɛ aba.
*If you see Praa (a forceful woman) carrying a big pan containing funeral paraphernalia, you do not ask what has happened.*
(If it is obvious what someone is doing, it only annoys them to ask about it).

2828. Wohunu prako mmɔbo a, wo nsa mpa boɔ so da.
*If you have sympathy with a pig, your hand will never be free of a stone.*
(The stone is to scare off the pig. Hence: If you spoil a troublesome person, they will continue to trouble you).

2829. Ohunu mprenu nti na yɛnni ɔkoterɛ nam.
*Because of seeing twice we do not eat lizard's meat.*
(It is the experienced man who warns the inexperienced of danger).

2830. Wohunu sɛ akwagyinamoa ada fotoɔ mu a, nka sɛ wada.
*If you find a cat amongst the treasury bags, don't say that it has gone to sleep.*
(Appearances can be deceptive).

2831. Woahunu sɛ nsoromma firi soro abɛbisa ɛpo sɛ dabɛn na nsuo bɛto da?
*Did you ever see the stars come down from above to ask the sea when it would rain?*
(If the man on the spot does not know, why ask a stranger?)

2832. Wohunu sɛ Otumfoɔ te hwɛdɔm so a, na ato no abeseweɛ.
*If you see that the Asantehene sits of the hwɛdom chair, then he is chewing cola.*
(This is one of the chairs of state and is used on serious occasions. Some things are only reserved for very serious occasions and must not be dealt with lightly).

2833. Wohunu sɛ wo yɔnko abɔdwesɛ rehye a, sa nsuo si wo deɛ ho.
*If you see a friend's beard on fire, fetch water for yours.*
(One man's calamity is another man's warning).

2834. Wohunu asosini na ɔsi akɔnkɔn a, na wagyae ne [tebea]/[hyɛbea].
*If you see a person with amputated ears sitting on someone's shoulders, then you know he has stopped his bad behavior.*
(In the past people had their ears cut off for certain crimes. Hence: We do not acclaim a known transgressor unless he is known to have changed his ways).

2835. Yehunuu nsuo ansa na yɛrehunu nsa.
*We saw water before we saw alcohol.*
(Seniority does not indicate quality).

2836. Wohunu takyiako a, wose osua, nso ne panin mu ara ne no.
*If you see the black ant, you think it is very young, but it is in its old age.*
(If you do not have the knowledge to judge, don't do so. Appearances can be deceptive).

2837. Wohunu atofo a, na wokɔn dɔ ɛtwɛ.
*If you see a woman's bustle, then you feel like having sex with her.*
(The atofo is a piece of cloth worn in a kind of roll at the back, where they may keep their money and other valuables, and on which it is easy to carry a child. This bustle stands for her femininity. Hence: You are stimulated by something provocative).

2838. Wohunu tu a, wohunu sɔne.
*If you know how to fly, then you know how to land.*
(If you are proficient in one part of a job, you must be proficient in the whole).

2839. Wohunu atwewa mmɔbɔ a, wodi nkwan hunu.
*If you feel for the young duiker, you eat your soup without meat.*
(If you are too sympathetic, you suffer for it).

2840. Wohunu wo wura som a, wofa wo ho di.
*If you know how to serve your master well, you become independent.*
(Good service enables you to progress in life).

2841. Wonhunu biribi da a, na wopɛ bi hwɛ.
*If you have never seen it before, then you say you would like to see something of it.*
(Everyone likes experiencing something new).

2842. Woanhunu deɛ wokɔtoo no a, deɛ wokɔtoo no nso nhunu wo a wobaeɛ.
*If you don't acknowledge the person you approach, he too will not acknowledge you if you come to him.*
(Do as you would be done by).

2843. Yɛrehunu sɛ dua Dumfrane bɛsi kurotia adane bosom agyegye abɛtem ama abotokura akɔdi adɔre sradeɛ wɔ berɛ a yɛnwe ne nam.
*We shall not sit idly by for the mighty odum tree to grow at the outskirts of the town to become an obosom to collect sticks of plantain for the striped mouse to grow fat on, while we don't even eat its meat.*
(When you placate a fetish you expect to benefit yourself; you don't expect the profit to go to an outsider who contributes nothing to society. Hence: It is no good condoning practices which are unprofitable to you).

2844. Woanhunu wo fie asɛm di a, na ɛfiri dwa so.
*If you are unable to settle your case at home, then it is heard of outside.*
(Don't wash your dirty linen in public).

2845. Wonhunuu ɔwɔ ti a, wommɔ no abaa.
*Unless you have seen a snake's head, you do not strike it.*
(You have to assess a situation before dealing with it).

2846. Wonhunu wo yere tirim a, bisa wo nso wo tirim hwɛ.
*If you don't know the mind of your wife, ask your own mind to see.*
(Be careful an accusation does not grow out of a guilty conscience).

2847. Hunuamaneɛ bra yɛmmɔ.
*We don't strive for suffering.*
(We don't look for difficulties in life).

2848. Wohuri wo ho a, na yesɔ woɔ.
*If you jump down, we catch you.*
(When you are ready to act, people support you).

2849. Yɛrebɛhuri asafo a, yɛnkuru ngu so.
*If we are going to jump in asafo dances, we don't dress up.*
(You prepare according to what the occasions demands).

2850. Wohuri tra panin a, wosa ne mɛn mu.
*If you jump over an elder, you get stuck in his crutch.*
(If you behave badly towards an elder, you suffer for it).

2851. Wohuri twa a, nwira gu w'ani.
*If you jump up and cut it, particles fall in your eyes.*
(If you try and do more than you are able to, you suffer for it).

2852. Yɛrehuri wo, wose: "M'ani so biri me".
*We are tossing you up and you say: "I'm feeling dizzy".*
(You should not be surprised at an expected happening).

2853. Huriiɛ si adwa mu.
*The tsetse fly sits on the stool!*
(If authority is vicious you keep quiet. The tsetse fly has a nasty sting and carries sleeping-sickness).

2854. Ohuriiɛ si akyekyedeɛ akyi a, ɔsi hɔ kwa.
*If the tsetse fly sits on the back of a tortoise, he sits there in vain.*
(The fly can't bite through the shell. Hence: You can't get blood out of stone).

2855. Ehuro ma onipa bere.
*Teasing makes people angry.*

2856. Ohurukutu Akwasi Poku se: dademintim mpo mframa fa no na ɛnte sɛ kookoo-ahahan.
*Windbag Akwasi Poku says: even heavy iron is carried away by the wind, how much more the leaves of cocoa.*
(Even the strong are defeated, how much more the weak).

2857. "Ahu-yuu," na ɛma ɔkɔmfoɔ nya kwan kaekae nsɛm.
*"I mean, I mean," makes the priest find a way to think of what he is going to say.*
(If you need time to think of what to say, you find a way of delaying conversation).

2858. Hwan na ɔbɔ ne wura donno a, ɔmpusu n'awan?
*Who is it that beats his master's hour-glass drum and does not shake his shoulder?*
(You play the drum under the armpit. When you release the shoulder, it both relaxes it and alters the tone. Hence: However hard you work, you must be allowed to relax sometimes).

2859. Wohwe aberanteɛ yere a, woko tɔkwa-prɛnu.
*If you beat a young man's wife, you fight twice.*
(Be careful whom you insult; you may bite off more than you can chew).

2860. Yɛrehwe w'ani so a, wonka sɛ: "Mekyiri nkasadwaa".
*If you are being slapped, you don't say: "I taboo insinuation".*
(If you are facing a serious situation, you don't bother about trifles).

2861. "Hwe ase, nhwe ase," yɛ nkontompo suman.
*"Fall down, don't fall down," is a liar's talisman.*
(You cannot follow two opposite things at the same time. Inconsistency is the characteristic of a liar).

2862. Yɛrehwe, yɛntumi nhwe a, yɛnnwonsɔ ngu mu.
*We are collecting water, if we can't do it, we don't urinate into it.*
(You don't add insult to injury).

2863. Hwɛ me bosom so ma me a, womfa nyɛ akɔm.
*If I ask you to take care of my fetish for me, you don't use it for possession.*
("Akɔm" refers to the activities of the priest possessed by his fetish, including, particularly, the twirling dance. Hence: Don't presume to take actions you are not entitled to).

2864. "Hwɛ di ma me," nti na ani sɔ panin.
*"Go and plead for me," is why one should respect an elder.*
(Honor the elders, as you may need them to protect you).

2865. Yɛhwɛ agyan dada so na yɛyɛ foforɔ.
*We look at an old arrow in order to make a new one.*
(The old provides a model for the new).

2866. "Hwɛ wo ha! Hwɛ wo ha!", nyɛ agorɔ.
*"Look at this part of you. Look at that", is not a game.*
(Unnecessary criticism only causes harm).

2867. "Hwɛ ha ma mennidi" nti na atwe mmienu nam.
*Because of "watch while I am eating", two duikers move together.*
(There is safety in numbers).

2868. "Hwɛ wo ho! Hwɛ wo ho", nyɛ amanyɔ.
*"Look at yourself! Look at yourself!" is not good politics.*
(It is wiser not to indulge in open criticism).

2869. Worehwɛ apɛ akorosee na wonya aponkyerɛne a, ɛnam no biara ne no.
*If you are collecting the small frog and you get the big one, then it is all the same kind of thing.*
(If you are looking for something and you find something better, you can't complain).

2870. Yɛhwɛ Kuruni anim na yɛama no ɛmo.
*We look at the Kru man's face before we give him his rice.*
(You have to make a judgement before you discriminate. The Kru people eat rice).

2871. Yɛhwɛ onipa anim na yɛsene dua-nipa.
*We study the face of a man before we make a carving of him.*
(It is by studying the nature of something that we copy it).

2872. Yɛhwɛ onipa anim na yɛsoa no twene.
*We look into someone's face before we give him a drum to carry.*
(You judge a man's capabilities before you give him a job).

2873. Yɛhwɛ yɛn awan-so ansa na yɛaka abɔntentɔkwa.
*We consider our backs before we indulge in public fighting.*
(You make sure you have backing up support before you become aggressive).

2874. Yɛhwɛ yɛn yere twɛ so na yɛatɔ ho tam.
*We see what size a wife's vagina is before we buy a loin-cloth for her.*
(We measure a situation before we act on it).

2875. Monhwɛ Sao, na monhwɛ kyɛm.
*Keep an eye on Sao, but don't look at the shield.*
(Don't be put off by a man's protective covering).

2876. Yenhwɛ osuo anim nhwie ahina mu nsuo go.
*We don't expect the rain and pour away the water in the pot.*
(Don't prejudge a situation. Hang on to what you have until you get a replacement).

2877. Ahweaa de brɛbrɛ na ɛtware kwan mu.
*The kusimanse crosses the road with caution.*
(With care you can achieve what you want).

2878. Ɔhweamo na ɛma asuo ho yɛ hu.
*The current makes the stream excite fear.*
(It is power that makes us fear someone with an important relation).

2879. Hweasuo wɔ ntakuo num a, ɔde betɔ koraa a, anka ɔremfa ne to nhwe asuo.
*If the dragonfly had twenty-five pesewas to buy a gourd, it would not be using its bottom to skim the water.*
(Beggars can't be choosers).

2880. Hwedeɛ so bebrebe a, yɛde no gye ban.
*If the elephant grass grows big, we use it for a fence.*
(If you get above yourself, you are made use of).

2881. Ahwedeɛ yi biara ne obonto.
*Amongst the creatures caught in the dam-pond is the tadpole.*
(See Proverb 503. Do not discriminate amongst family members, even if some are apparently unimportant).

2882. Wohwehwɛ mma akyekyere kuro na woanya a, wonkum apemfoɔ.
*If you are looking for children to build up the town and you do not get them, you do not kill those who are pregnant.*
(You do not deliberately destroy the thing you need).

2883. Wohwehwɛ opuro na woannya a, wowe apetebie.
*If you look for the small forest squirrel and you don't get it, you eat the striped-squirrel.*
(If you can't get what you want, you take the nearest thing to it).

2884. Mehwehwɛ Ɔsaben makra no, na ɛnte sɛ n'ankasa nam.
*I look for Ɔsaben to give him a message, but that is not better than if he himself comes.*
(Presence is better than messages).

2885. Wohwehwɛ asɛm mu a, wohunu n'ase.
*If you consider a matter properly, you see its solution.*
(If you study a problem well, it can be resolved).

2886. Wo hwene bu a, na w'anim akyea.
*If your nose is broken, your face is distorted.*
(Don't cut off your nose to spite your face).

2887. Wo hwene yɛ a, enyɛ abɔfono nyinaa na ɛfa.
*If you can smell, it is not all carcasses you have to smell.*
(However able you think you are, you don't have to involve yourself in all unpleasant situations).

2888. Ahwennee pa nkasa, gye awuruwuro.
*Good beads don't make a noise, rather the valueless ones.*
(Empty barrels make most noise).

2889. Ahwenneɛ te mpanin anim a, ebi nyera.
*If the beads break before the elders, they do not get lost.*
(Elders know how to respect confidences, therefore it is safe to speak freely in front of them and not hide anything).

**2890. Anwenhema pɛ adanseɛ nti na hyire si ne hwene sɔɔ.**
*The white-nosed monkey likes witnessing, that is why white clay is on its nose.*
(White clay is sprinkled on people found innocent in a case and who are rejoicing. The monkey would share in the celebrations, being witness for the defence. Hence: If you perform well, you will be acclaimed).

**2891. Hwennorɔ yɛ aduane a, anka akɔdaa rempene kɔm da.**
*If mucus were to be food then a child would never feel hunger.*
(If wishes were horses, beggars would ride).

**2892. Hwennua mpo, ɛhyee da ntamu na ɛnte sɛ ani ne ani.**
*Even between the nostrils there is a barrier, how much more so between the eyes.*
(Even those who are relatives are divided, how much more so those who are independent).

**2893. Hwenteaa se: ɔno deɛ ɔbɛyɛɛ fie yie na wammɛsɛe fie.**
*The spice tree (Xylopia aetheopica) says: it came to put the house in order and not to destroy the house.*
(Said of someone anxious to help improve conditions).

**2894. Hwento mmɔ kyim mu kwa.**
*A noseless person does not crack a bone for nothing.*
(Before you do something which is painful, you must make sure it is beneficial to you. It hurts a noseless person to bite hard).

**2895. Hwento mmɔ ose.**
*A broken nosed person should not sing in jubilation.*
(A person should realize their limitations).

**2896. Hwerɛma na ɛtewtwe dwom ba.**
*Whistling leads into song.*
(Certain actions lead on to others).

**2897. Hwerɛmo de bereberɛ na ɛtware kwan mu.**
*The big thorn creeper (Combretum) slowly crosses the road.*
(A dangerous man acts cautiously).

**2898. Ahwɛwo-da-bi ba na wɔhwɛ no.**
*"He-has-cared-for-you-once's" child, you look after him.*
(You help those who have helped you in life).

**2899. Hwimhwim adeɛ kɔ sorɔsorɔ.**
*A thing easily gained goes quickly.*
(Easy come, easy go).

**2900. Yɛnhwinti prɛko mmɔ ahina.**
*We don't stumble once and break a pot.*
(You often have a warning before an accident happens).

**2901. Ohwintimpraku agorɔ, wokɔhwɛ a, worewu; woankɔhwɛ a, wo yere ne wo mma rewu.**
*The game of spring the trap, if you go and see, you are dying; if you don't go and see, your wife and children are dying.*
(Hobson's choice. Someone is going to suffer and your only choice is between yourself and those you are responsible for).

**2902. Wohyɛ aba faako a, ɛda adi.**
*If you hide the seed in one place, it becomes detected.*
(This refers to a game played with two closed fists. You are asked to guess in which one an object is hidden. If you play for a while, you learn to anticipate the other person's choices. Hence: If you continue one act too long, you are found out).

**2903. Wohyɛ babɔne a, yɛku no kyere wo.**
*If you train a child badly, we kill it in your presence.*
(If you don't educate your children well, you will live to regret it).

**2904. Wohyɛ Aburowawia a, awifoɔ tu.**
*If you stack your corn in the daytime, thieves remove it.*
(If you publicize your wealth, you may get it stolen).

**2905. Wohyɛ fidie mu, wonwu agyan ano.**
*If you fall into a trap, you don't die from an arrow wound.*
(A choice of two equally bad alternatives).

**2906. Wohyɛ akɔdaa asoeɛ, na woduru hɔ, na woansoeɛ no a, ɔsu gu ne yam.**
*If you (usually) unload a child's headload at a certain spot and you fail to do it, when he reaches that point, he weeps internally (lit. he cries into his stomach).*
(You should always keep your promises to children or they will be very hurt).

**2907. Wohyɛ kunafoɔ a, wohyɛ wo ho.**
*If you make the widow suffer, you also suffer.*
(When you do evil, you are affected by it).

**2908. Yɛhyɛ nsa si hɔ na yɛnom no akyire yi.**
*We collect palm wine and store it so that we drink it later on.*
(We provide for the future).

**2909. "Hyɛ wo sapɔ mu nsuo", yɛka kyerɛ deɛ yɛpɛ no yiye.**
*"Put water on your sponge", we say to someone we like very much.*
("Put water on your sponge", means "prepare yourself." Hence: If we like someone we take trouble over them and encourage them when necessary).

**2910. Yɛnhyɛ habɔdɔm na yɛantu yen nan nka n'ano.**
*We do not tame the wild hunting dog and then kick him in the mouth.*
(If you are teaching someone manners, then you must behave well yourself).

**2911. Ɛhyeɛso aduane amee wo a, na ɛfiri hɔ manso.**
*If food grown on the boundary does not satisfy you, then it is because of litigation.*
(If you are fighting over something, you don't get full satisfaction from it).

**2912. Ɛhyeɛso aduane nyɛ mmeɛ na mmom, kwaseabuo nti na ɛma yɛpere hyeɛ.**
*The foodstuff at the boundary does not satisfy, but because of cheating that is where we litigate over the boundary.*
(Some people act from spite rather than from profit. It is not worth quarrelling over something which is valueless).

2913. Ahyehyɛeɛ Mmorodewa ɔse: "Nwaenwaeho amma me anyɛ yie".
*The burnt stalk of the plantain says: "Stripping has made me unfortunate".*
(Said of someone whose financial obligations are greater than his means).

2914. Ahyehyɛmpɛtea de n'ahoɔfɛ sisi ɔman.
*A wearer of rings uses his beauty to cheat the state.*
(People are deceived by a grand appearance).

2915. Nhyehyɛwoakyire nti na yɛsa koterɛ bɛn a, ɔnka ne ho.
*It is only pride which causes a lizard not to move when you shoot an arrow at it.*
(Pride may lead to bravado).

2916. Ɛhyɛn tu a, na apolisifoɔ afɛre.
*When the train takes off, the police are ashamed.*
(A bully is shamed when there is no one there to bully).

2917. Hyɛn kɛse si hɔ a, abonto fam ho.
*If a great ship lies there, small boats are attached to it.*
(A great leader has many followers).

2918. Woahyia odikuro ɔda fam yɛretwe no ase, wonse: "Nana, efie yɛ?"
*If you have seen the village chief lying on the ground and being dragged along, you don't say: "Nana, how is all at home?"*
(Don't kick a man when he is down).

2919. Yɛhyira yen ano pɛ adepa na yɛmfa mpɛ owuo.
*We bless our mouth for something good, but not for death.*
(We pray for good living and not for destruction).

2920. Yɛhyira yɛn ano pɛ asɛm pa na nyɛ amaneɛ.
*We bless our mouth to say good things, but not for litigation.*
(See Previous Proverb. If you pray, you pray for something good and not for trouble).

2921. Wohyira w'ano a, wose: "M'adeɛ mmoro me na ɔnnkɔboro obi".
*If you pray, you say: "My own relative should beat me and not beat an outsider".*
(You pray that trouble should be kept inside the family).

## - K -

**2922. "Maka a maka," na ɛyɛ ahi; na nyɛ "Menkaeɛ".**
*"I have told you, I have told you", is annoying; but "I have not told you", does not annoy.*
(A humble reply avoids trouble).

**2923. "Maka a maka", ne "Mase a mase", na ɛde amaniko ba.**
*"I have told you, I have told you", and "I have spoken, I have spoken", bring about quarrels with your intimates.*
(Constant criticism and bickering with your friends leads to a real fight).

**2924. "Maka a maka", ne nua ne "Ma yɛnkɔgya me, na monkɔtutu me ka."**
*"I have told you, I have told you", has a brother "Accompany me so that I go and excuse myself from my debts".*
(If you boast of a wrong deed you have to talk yourself out of punishment for it).

**2925. Woka deɛ yɛnka a, wohunu deɛ yɛnhunu.**
*If you say what we don't say, you see what we don't see.*
(If you disregard conventions, you get into trouble).

**2926. Woka afanu a, woka w'ano.**
*If you speak on two sides, you get into trouble.*
(You cannot serve two masters at the same time).

**2927. Yeka ɔhene anom asɛm, na yɛnka ne tirim asɛm.**
*We say what a chief has said, but we cannot tell what is in his head.*
(You cannot judge a man only by what he says).

**2928. Woka hwɛ a, na wohunu ne dɛ.**
*It is only when you taste it that you can see how good it is.*
(You cannot judge a thing without trying it).

**2929. Woreka akɔ wo yere ho, na ɔdane n'akyi kyerɛ wo a, ɛmma no nyɛ wo ahomete, ɛfiri sɛ, n'akyiri kwan mpo na ɛyɛ tia.**
*If you are approaching your wife and she turns her back on you, don't be upset, because that is the shortest way in.*
(Disadvantages can be turned into advantages).

**2930. Woka wo kurom asɛm na woboa a, wo ntoma na ɛdi wo adanseɛ.**
*If you talk about your home town's affairs and you are lying, your cloth (which you are wearing) is your witness.*
(Whatever you do, good or bad, something is there to witness it, even if only your conscience).

**2931. Woka kyerɛ prako sɛ: "Mɛne w'anom", a, ɔse: "Ka mese".**
*If you tell a pig: "I will defecate in your mouth," he replies: "Swear on my father".*
(Its no good threatening someone with what he likes. Pigs are supposed to like dirt).

**2932. Woka ɛkyim na woammua so a, aboɔ gu mu.**
*If you cook the blood of an animal and you don't cover it, gravel gets inside.*
(If you do something important and you don't take care, the work spoils).

**2933. Yɛbɛka ama wo a, ɛnnim sɛ adeɛ asa.**
*If we are going to defend you, it does not matter if night falls.*
(If someone is prepared to stand by you, he will do so at any time).

**2934. Woreka ama wo bo adwoɔ no, na obi nso bo afu.**
*When you are going to say something to cool down your temper, then at the same time someone else is getting angry.*
(What may have a good effect on you, may have a bad effect on another person).

**2935. "Ka me fituo mu" nyɛ ntam pa.**
*"Swear on my deserted village," is not a real oath.*
(Don't try and make jokes about serious matters).

**2936. "Aka me nko," yɛmfa ntutu ka.**
*"I am the only one left," we don't use in postponement of paying debts.*
(Flimsy excuses are not acceptable).

**2937. Woka mogya gu a, mogya na ɛtene no.**
*If you spill blood, blood alone can straighten it.*
(An eye for an eye and a tooth for a tooth).

**2938. Woaka na yɛyi wo ano: "Yɛnyɛ no dɛn?", na yɛrempɛ atie.**
*If you say something and we retort: "Does it concern us?," then it means we don't want to listen.*
(Inattentiveness means lack of interest).

**2939. "Woaka na ka bio", nye ya; na "Woakari na kari bio", na ɛyɛ ya.**
*"You have said it, but say it again", is not bitter; but "You have weighed it out, but weigh it out again", is bitter.*
(To ask someone to repeat themselves is harmless, but to ask them to repeat an action implies distrust).

**2940. Woka na wonya obi to wo so a, na yɛgye wo die.**
*If you speak and you get a seconder, then we believe you.*
(If a statement is confirmed by someone else, then you believe it).

**2941. Woka na anyɛ hɔ a, na yɛfrɛ wo se ntoatoa.**
*If you promise and you fail, we call you an idle boaster.*
(Keep your promises or you will be despised).

**2942. Woka nna-kyiri a, wote mmoadoma su.**
*If you go to bed late, you hear the birds singing.*
(If you suffer as a result of being late, it is your own fault).

**2943. Woka wo ni a, woka wo se bi.**
*When you swear the oath of you mother, you should also swear the oath of your father.*
(Don't rely on one way of doing things only).

**2944. "Meka nnipa nyinaa" nti na ohuriɛ annya ogyamfoɔ.**
*"I bite all people," that is why the tsetse fly has no supporters.*
(A vicious man has no friends).

**2945. Woka nokorɛ a, wo ho nyɛ ahi.**
*If you speak the truth, you will not provoke indignation.*
(People who always speak the truth do not antagonize others).

**2946. Eka wo nsa a, ɛgyae fɛ-yɛ.**
*As soon as you obtain it, it ceases to be beautiful.*
(Familiarity breeds contempt).

**2947. Woka asakyire a, mmaabasia hwe wo.**
*If you are the last person to dance, women beat you up.*
(If you are lazy or uncooperative, you are punished for it).

**2948. Yɛka sɛ: "Gyae me nnan", na yɛnse sɛ: "Gyae me ti".**
*We say: "Let go my legs", but we don't say: "Leave my head alone".*
(When someone is in your power, you can control them physically, but you cannot control their thoughts).

**2949. Yɛka sɛ: "Mahyɛ wo bosome", na yɛnka sɛ: "Mahyɛ wo nsoromma".**
*We say: "I have given you a month", but we do not say: "I have given you the stars!"*
(We have given you a certain time to pay up, but not eternity).

**2950. Woka asɛm bi na woto sɛbe a, yɛnkyi.**
*If you say something unpleasant and you apologize first, it is not a taboo.*
(The word sɛbe is used in conversation to indicate you are about to say something that might offend the person you are speaking to and wish to apologize first. It means, thus, that no offence is intended. Hence: It is the way you say things that matters, not what you say).

**2951. Woka asɛm na ansi asɛm so a, yɛfrɛ no "nkorɔdɔkyerede".**
*If you say something and it does not have a bearing on the problem under consideration, we call it "prattling".*
(Try and be relevant when something serious is being discussed).

**2952. Yeka w'asem na woante a, wokɔ Anteade.**
*If we advise you and you don't pay heed, you go to Anteade.*
(There's a peace of wordplay here. "Anteade" sounds like "Hasn't heard anything". So it's a suitable place for people who don't listen. Hence: If you don't take advice then no one will advise you).

**2953. Woka nsowa ho ntam a, wode kɔtɔ na ɛma abadwadeɛ.**
*If you swear an oath about a fish trap, you use the crab to pay your fine.*
(Swearing an oath begins legal proceedings. Hence: Reparation for a sin should be appropriate).

**2954. Woka ntam gu amena mu a, ɛpue fi.**
*If you swear an oath into a hole, it will come to light by and by.*
(There is a story of a man who wanted to test this saying. He swore an oath into a trench and after many years went to tell the Chief that he had done so and no one had discovered his action. The Chief immediately

ordered his arrest and execution. No secret is safe, for one day it may be revealed. Hence: Truth will out).

**2955. Wobɛka ntam ama yɛaku wo deɛ, fa ɔhene yere ma yɛnku wo.**
*If you are going to swear an oath to let us kill you, take the chief's wife and let us kill you.*
(In for a penny, in for a pound).

**2956. Woka toɔ ka ano a, wotwa koowa dwan.**
*If you say the bottom (in one place) and say the mouth (in another) you kill the sheep (as a fine) for slander.*
(If you are inconsistent in what you say or do, you will get into trouble).

**2957. Woka wo twene tosee-tosee a, yɛsa no fosee-fosee.**
*If you play your drum anyhow, we dance to it anyhow.*
(The kind of question you ask, indicates the kind of answer you will be given).

**2958. Yɛnka nni w'akyi a, wose ɛyɛ dɛ.**
*If we don't follow you, you say it is good.*
(You don't know the real situation unless you're involved).

**2959. "Ɛnka, Ɛnka", ɛka mmɔfra so.**
*"Don't worry, don't worry", then it remains with the children.*
(If one generation does not tackle a problem, the next has to).

**2960. "Nka, nka", yɛte no amannɔneɛ.**
*"Don't say it, don't say it", we hear it abroad.*
(People cannot resist repeating secrets, particularly when constantly warned not to!)

**2961. Yɛnka nkyerɛ kunafoɔ sɛ: "Da ma menna bi".**
*We don't tell a widow: "Come and sleep so that I can sleep".*
(You don't ask someone to do what you know they cannot).

**2962. Woanka sɛ wonie a, obi nka sɛ wowɔ hɔ.**
*If you don't say you are here, no one will say you are there.*
(If you don't stand up for yourself, no one else will).

**2963. Yenka asɛm pa nkyerɛ tibɔnkoso.**
*We don't say something good to a blockhead.*
(Don't waste good advice on fools).

**2964. Ɛka a ɛnsene woɔ, ɛnsene wo yɔnko.**
*A debt you could not stand, neither can your companion.*
(If something is beyond your means, don't implicate others).

**2965. Ɛka dada dom ne wura.**
*An old debt blesses the creditor.*
(If you are repaid after a long time, it comes as a bonus).

**2966. Ɛka, yɛdan no anibereɛ.**
*A debt, we demand it in anger.*
(By the time you have to demand repayment, you have become frustrated and angry).

**2967. Ɛka ho aduro ara ne "Gye wo sika".**
*The antidote for debt is: "Take your money".*

2968. Ɛka kyɛ a, ɛmporɔ.
*If a debt delays, it does not rot.*
(A debt is always a debt, however old).

2969. Ɛka kyɛre a, ɛkyɛre mpemanim.
*If a debt endures a long time, it doubles.*

2970. Ɛka te sɛ nsuohyeɛ, wonu mu, nu mu a, ɛdwo.
*A debt is like hot water, if you stir it constantly (lit. stir it, stir it), it cools.*
(In the long run, if you work hard at it, you will be able to pay your debts).

2971. Ɛka tɔ kurom na ɛnni wura a, ɔhene fa; adedie nso ba kurom na ɛnni wura a, ɔhene dea.
*If there is a debt in town which has no owner, the chief takes it; if there is something good in town which has no owner, the chief takes that, too.*
(The person at the top has to take final responsibility – good or bad).

2972. Ɛka nni agorɔ.
*A debt is not to be played with.*
(Take your debts seriously).

2973. Ɛka nni "ka wo nsa pɛ!"
*Debt has no "use your hand to collect".*
(If you are in debt you have nothing to spare).

2974. Ɛka yɛ adepa a, anka ɔkaa a nna nsuo mu.
*If a debt (ɛka) were valuable, then the small fish (ɔkaa) would not lie in the water.*
(Play on words. Debts never got anyone anywhere).

2975. Ɛka nyɛ nku na yɛate sra.
*A debt is not grease that we take to oil ourselves.*
(Don't show off your debts).

2976. Ɛka nyɛ ntoma na yɛapam afura.
*Debt is not a cloth to be sewn and worn.*
(See Proverb 2975).

2977. Ɛkaa ɔbaa a sugyani nko a, anka yɛbɔ mmɔguo a, yɛmpɔn.
*If it were for a woman without a husband alone to decide, then we would go on singing songs and telling tales endlessly.*
(If you are poor or have no responsibilities, you would like there to be constant free entertainment).

2978. Ɛkaa deɛ ɔnni ntoma nko a, anka yɛgorɔ asafo daa.
*If it were for the man without a cloth alone, then we would play asafo music daily.*
(A poor man would like all to be as poor as himself. You dance asafo dances without a cloth, which costs money).

2979. Ɛkaa odwumfoɔ a, ɔsene funnaka nko ara a, anka nnipa wu daa.
*If it was left just to the carpenter who makes coffins, people would die daily.*
(What is good for one person is bad for another).

2980. Ɛkaa ahodaadane nko a, anka akyemfrakatakyi di hene.
*If it were for swooping about alone, the swallow would be a chief.*
(Being a good specialist at one thing, does not mean that one is a leader).

2981. Ɛkaa akyeame nko a, anka wɔsɔ akyeamepoma mu na wɔabu atɛn.
*If it were left to the linguists alone, holding the linguist's staff qualifies you to give judgement.*
(Every group would like to use its position to exercise power).

2982. Ɛkaa akyemfrakatakyi nko a, anka nnua so apore.
*If it were for the swallow alone, all trees would shed their leaves.*
(Swallows do not nest in trees. This proverb indicates selfishness leading to the detriment of the community as a whole).

2983. Ɛkaa nkokɔ nko a, anka tɛfrɛ ada ayeya.
*If the chickens were to have their own way, then the cockroach would fall on its back.*
(If a cockroach falls on its back, it cannot right itself. Hence: Your enemy always wants to have you at his mercy).

2984. Ɛkaa me nko a, anka adua so sɛ ntɛ.
*If it were for me alone, the beans would bear fruit like the marble plant seeds.*
(The seeds of the marble plant (dioclea reflexa – ntɛ or ntɛw) are much bigger than beans. These seeds are used to play games like oware. Hence: If wishes were horses, beggars would ride).

2985. Ɛkaa ano-hunu nko ara a, anka ɔkraman sene ɔsebɔ.
*If it were for vocal expression alone, then the dog would excel the leopard.*
(Don't judge a man for one quality alone).

2986. Ɛkaa nsee nko a, anka onyina awu.
*Left to the woodpeckers alone, the onyina tree would die.*
(The bird builds its nest inside holes in, and gets insects from, a rotten tree. Someone's downfall is to someone else's benefit).

2987. Ɛkaa ɔtamfoɔ nko a, anka wawie wo.
*Left to the enemy alone, you would have ceased to exist.*
(The enemy wants only one thing, your destruction!)

2988. Ɛkaa ntesihɔ nko a, anka ɛda abɛ ase.
*If it were just a matter of moving the palm winepot, it would be better to leave it under the palm tree.*
(You only make a change if it is profitable to do so).

2989. Ɛkaa nwa ne akyekyedeɛ nko a, anka etuo rento wiram da.
*If there were only the snail and the tortoise, there would be no firing in the forest.*
(Violence is only necessary to obtain what you cannot get by peaceful means).

2990. "Kaakaagyan", yɛka kyerɛ huuhu-nipa.
*"It seems to be good", is said to a person who acts without thinking.*
(We don't take much notice of someone irresponsible).

2991. Ɔkaakyire na ɔsoa akuma.
*The last-born carries the axe.*
(Every man has his specific job to do).

2992. Akaatia-nini Agyabena, ɔnni mfofo mu, na ɔnni kwaeɛ mu, na yɛpɛ no he a na yɛhu no?
*The male chimpanzee Agyabena, it is not in the clearing, nor in the forest, then where shall we find it?*
(Said of a problem to which there is no apparent solution).

2993. Okabɔfoɔ nni man mu a, anka yerenhunu sikani da.
*If there are no contractors of debts in the state, then we do not ever see a rich man.*
(Positive goes with negative).

2994. Kabom ma nkonim.
*Union brings victory.*

2995. Kabɔnaa na ɛde adwoyie ba.
*A vagrant makes enslavement come.*
(In the days of slavery, unattached people could easily be captured and sold. Hence: Wandering aimlessly about leads you into trouble).

2996. Oka-nna-akyire na ɔte mmoadoma nyinaa su.
*The last to go to bed hears the cries of all the animals.*
(If you want to know what happens, you must be patient).

2997. Kadwam nyɛ awerɛhoɔ.
*Part payment is not a grievance.*
(A little is better than none).

2998. Kae wo Bɔfoɔ wɔ wo mmeranteberɛm ansa na nnabɔne aba.
*Remember your Creator in the days of your youth, before the bad times come.*
(Always be grateful to your benefactor and he will continue to help you).

2999. "Kae da bi!" yɛde se bonniayɛfoɔ.
*"Remember the past", we say to those who are ungrateful.*
(You should always show gratitude for past favors).

3000. "Yɛbekae wo daa", yɛnka no kwa; nyɛ wo papayɔ a na ɛyɛ wo bɔneyɔ.
*"We will remember you always," we don't say it for nothing; it may be either because of your good deeds or your bad ones.*
(Whatever you do, some people will remember and talk about it).

3001. Yɛkae gyefoɔ na yɛnkae ɔpɔsobɔni.
*We remember a person who has defended us but not the one who has prosecuted us.*
(If you are generous, you are remembered).

3002. Wokae ɔhene dadaa a, na ɔhene foforɔ nyɛ.
*If you remember the old chief, the new chief is no good.*
(A man is admired most after his death, when his replacement seems inferior).

3003. Woankae ansere a, wokae su.
*If you do not remember and smile, you remember and weep.*
(Memories are either sweet or sour).

3004. Ɔkaekaefoɔ na ɔma ɔdwendwenfoɔ di nim.
*A person with a good memory makes a deep thinker succeed.*
(If you have an intelligent helper, you succeed).

3005. Ɔkafɔ didi.
*A debtor eats.*
(However difficult circumstances are you must have something in life).

3006. Ɔkafoɔ na ɔhwe anɔpa bosuo.
*A debtor gets wet with the morning dew.*
(If a man is in debt and does not want to meet his creditors, he must leave the house very early in the morning. Hence: If you are in trouble, you suffer for it).

3007. Ɔkafoni adeɛ kɔ amoamu amoamu.
*A debtor's goods are dissipated.*
(If you owe money, it is difficult to get your finances straight again).

3008. Kafra nkum kuromanso, ɛdwo asɛm ano.
*Apologies don't kill litigation in a town but they cool down the situation.*
(Apologies don't solve a situation but they ease tempers).

3009. Kaka bu ɛsono se.
*Toothache breaks the elephant's tusk.*
(All men suffer alike, be they great or small).

3010. Kaka ne ɛka ne ayafunka fanyinam ɛka.
*Toothache and indebtedness and stomach ache, debt is preferable.*
(Play on words. Choose the best of several bad things).

3011. Kakapeaka: wopɛ no, wompɛ no, wakɔka abɛka wo.
*A cantankerous person: whether you like it or not, he has involved you (in a case, quarrel or problem).*
(However self-respecting you are, you can't avoid some troubles).

3012. Yɛrekame wo awareɛ, wose: "Merepere yɛyɛre madi".
*We are depriving you of marriage and you say: "I desire the best of women".*
(If you are refused something it is no good asking for anything connected with it).

3013. Nkamfena nyɛ nam bi a, anka apofoɔ din mforoo po.
*If the small dried fish were not good meat, then the fishermen's names would not be widespread by the ocean.*
(A man's reputation depends on the value given to what he does).

3014. Nkamfena nyɛ atomdeɛ pa mpo a, yɛde no frafra nam.
*If the small dried fish is not good meat, at least we mix it with other meat.*
(If someone is not themselves important, they at least mix with important people).

3015. Yɛrekamfo wo danta wɔ badwam no, na yɛrehunu w'adwonkubɛn.
*As we are praising your loin cloth in a public place, then we are seeing your hipbone.*
(Flattery leads people to reveal secrets).

3016. Yɛrekamfo wo duaforɔ no, na yɛrekamfo w'akyakya.
*As we admire you way of climbing a tree, we also admire your hump.*
(The hump is acquired as a result of falling. Pride comes before a fall).

3017. Wokamfo kuraaseni a, ɔma wo ma no dibem.
*If you praise an uncultured person, he makes you apologize.*
(If you do good to an ignorant person, he does not recognize it).

3018. Yɛrekamfo wo tutoɔ no na yɛrekamfo wo nsasini.
*We are praising your shooting, we are also praising your amputated arm.*
(Too much acclamation brings about a person's downfall).

3019. Kampesɛkwakye se: sɛ ɔnim sɛ abɛ rebɛbere a, anka wankɔware adɔbɛ nkonto.
*The drongo says: if he had known that the palm nuts were going to ripen, then he would not have married the raffia palm with a twisted leg.*
(Vain regrets. If you had known that someone would prosper, you would not have followed a less successful person).

3020. Nkamfoɔ se: "Mempere ɔwaduro bi".
*The Nkamfo yam says: "I will never struggle for the mortar".*
(Someone will not struggle for something with which he has no connection).

3021. Wokan nantwie a, wokan ne dua.
*If you count the cow, you count its tail.*
(You count a complete object, not just part of it).

3022. Kanea yɛde nwera ahyɛ mu ne deɛ yɛde birisi ahyɛ mu, nhyerɛn pɛ.
*The light that we cover with a light cloth and that which we cover with a dark one, do not shine in the same way.*
(Circumstances change potentials).

3023. Nkanka repɛ wo tiri awe a, na wɔwe wo kyɛ.
*If termites want to eat your head, they eat your hat.*
(If someone want to harm you he will harm what you value first).

3024. Nkanka nwe aboɔ.
*The white ants do not eat stones.*
(There is a limit to any man's capabilities).

3025. Kankan-hyɛn butu a, baako nni aku.
*When the Dutch boat upsets, one person does not struggle alone.*
(The old name for Dutch Accra was Kankan and thus the Dutch were called Kankanfoɔ - Kankan-people - or Kankan brɔfoɔ - Kankan-Europeans. Hence: A big disaster involves many people).

3026. Kankane a wasi so foforɔ no na ɔte sɛ ɔkyɛm a waporɔ ateteɛ.
*The civet cat which has recently come of age is like a leopard which is rotten and torn.*
(An important man who has a great reputation, even when his power goes, is greater than a lesser man at his prime).

3027. Ɔkankabi se sɛ enyɛ ne busuani ne aketekyire a, anka ne kawa nna ne kɔn mu.
*The millipede says if the cricket were not its relative then its ring would not be around its neck.*
(It is relatives who share the family property, not strangers).

3028. Ɔkanni ba de ne tɛkrɛma na ɛpra ne ho.
*An Akan uses his tongue to cleanse his body.*
(A soft tongue gets you out of trouble).

3029. Ɔkanni ba nnante nkɔwu.
*An Akan should not walk to his death.*
(A person who is well thought of should not act carelessly).

3030. Akantamakuro rebɛguo a, obi annunu obi no, na ɛfiri sɛ obiara nsa wɔ mu bi.
*If Akantama village is going to ruin, no one blames another, because everyone's hand is in it.*
(When everyone shares in something happening, all must bear the responsibility for it).

3031. Kantankrankyi Ayɛboafo, ɔpimpini n'akyi ansa na wagyam.
*Kantankrankyi Ayɛboafo, the great executioner's sword, retreats before it acts.*
(You recoil before you attack).

3032. Ɔkanto-gyasi mpa mono.
*The candle wood tree (Farara xanthoxyloides) does not fail to remain fresh.*
(A symbol of longevity and toughness. This wood is very strong and not easily destroyed. It is used for torches).

3033. Wokari wo sika tɔ aboa na ɛnyɛ a, wowe.
*If you weigh out your gold to buy an animal and if it is not good, you eat it.*
(Waste not, want not).

3034. Wokari wo sika tɔ aboɔ a, wowe no.
*If you weigh out your gold to buy a stone, you are entitled to chew it.*
(What you do with your own things is your own business).

3035. Woankari damma a, taku yera.
*If you don't weigh out a damma, you lose a taku.*
(Damma is a small weight of gold-dust; taku is a larger weight. Hence: If you are mean in small things, you lose big ones).

3036. Wokasa a, wohwɛ wo mmati.
*If you are talking you look over your shoulder.*
(Be careful what you say, someone may be listening in).

3037. Kasa dodoɔ yɛ nuho dodoɔ.
*Talking too much results in regretting.*
(Think before you speak, or you may regret it).

**3038. Wokasa nkwasea-kasa a, yɛbua wo nkwasea mu.**
*If you talk foolish talk, we reply to you foolishly.*
(If you play the fool you will be treated as such).

**3039. Woankasa wo tiri ho a, yɛyi wo ayibɔne.**
*If you don't say how you want your hair styled, they will give you a bad haircut.*
(You must express your wants clearly, or mistakes will be made).

**3040. Kasabodin nti na kɔkɔsakyi yam tuiɛ.**
*Owing to constant slander the vulture had constant diarrhea.*
(Constant slander causes distress).

**3041. Kasadɛ nti na amma ɛkoɔ yam antuo.**
*Because of compliments the bush cow did not get frightened.*
(Beware of flattery, it may lead to disaster).

**3042. Wokasakasa a, w'ano pa.**
*If you talk too much, your mouth slips.*
(If you are too talkative, you say things which will lead you into trouble).

**3043. Ɔkasamɛɛ yɛ mmusuo.**
*Loquacity is a misfortune.*

**3044. Akasanoma kasa yɛ obi ahi.**
*The African sparrow's chirruping is hated by someone.*
(We all have our likes and dislikes).

**3045. Ɔkasa-pa pam abofuo.**
*A soft answer drives away wrath.*

**3046. Kasasie sene pɔtɔ de.**
*Decisions previously taken are preferable to using an alien language.*
(It is better to settle what you are going to say behind closed doors, in your own language, than to take the matter to a public court where you have to speak a foreign one (English)).

**3047. Kaseɛ yɛmmɔ no mprɛnu.**
*The reason for a visit we don't give it twice.*
(Don't waste your time in repetition).

**3048. Kasu ne kagya nni aseda.**
*Say-and-weep and promise-and-fail, have no thanks.*

**3049. Ɔkatakyie bɛko a, ɛwɔ ne tirim.**
*If a valiant man is going to fight, it is in his mind (i.e. he keeps it secret).*

**3050. Akatakyie asuo Puupuu, ɛnyɛ dɛ na nso ɛnyɛ hwam, nanso yɛde aprɛmo na ɛwɛn no.**
*The Akatakyie River Puupuu is not sweet nor sweet-smelling, nonetheless we protect it with cannons.*
(The river was not far from Cape Coast and so was protected by its guns. Hence: Said when something of little apparent value is zealously guarded or fought for).

**3051. Kataman kuta adeɛ a, obi nnye.**
*If the Creator holds something, no one can deny Him.*
(God possesses all).

**3052. Kataso-muamuaso, ma ade pa yera.**
*Condoling and conniving makes a good thing go astray.*
(If you don't point out a person's misdeeds, society becomes corrupted).

**3053. Yɛrekeka ma Mfemfena no, na Yɛne Awurade.**
*As we are telling Mfemfena, then in effect we are telling Awurade.*
(Mfemfena was the first linguist of Awurade Basa, first Adansehene: hence, if you want to make a case known to a superior, you inform a subordinate, who will pass the information on).

**3054. Yɛrekeka ma funu, na yɛrekeka ma dampan.**
*We are preparing the corpse, then we are preparing the empty alcove.*
(The dampan is an open-sided room in a chief's compound, where a body can be laid in state. Hence: We prepare for things stage by stage).

**3055. Akekakeka nyɛ kana na akyire asɛm.**
*Mere repetition of things is not difficult but the aftermath is the problem.*
(It is more easily said than done).

**3056. Kentɛn mmiɛnsa sisi hɔ a, yɛde ahoboa na ɛsoa.**
*Three baskets stand there, we need preparation to carry them.*
(You need to prepare well to succeed in a tough job).

**3057. Kɛntɛn annwono yie a, na ɛfiri n'ahyeaseɛ.**
*If the basket was not well woven, it is because of its beginning.*
(Failure starts from the beginning).

**3058. Akentɛnnwa nyɛ biribi a, na ɛnyɛ mu atenatena.**
*If an easy chair is not worth anything, it is good for stretching out in.*
(Everything has its value).

**3059. Ɔkeseɛ nnim biribi a, ɔnim sunsumbiguo.**
*If a strong man does not know anything else he knows how to push people around.*
(A person uses his distinctive gifts, whatever they are).

**3060. "Akɛsesɛm" na ɛde ohia ba.**
*"Showing off" beyond your means brings poverty.*
(If you pretend to have more than you do, you lose what you have).

**3061. Kɛsrɛkɛsrɛ dɔ krɔbene, ɔdwene dɔ ne deɛ.**
*The Kɛsrɛkɛsrɛ tree (Dracaena manii) loves his heartwood and the ɔdwene tree (Baphia nitidia) loves his too.*
(The wood of these two trees is used to make dyes. Hence: If you are of service to others, you have a good opinion of yourself).

**3062. Kete-soafoɔ nni adwamsɛm.**
*The carrier of the Kete drum does not show off.*
(If you have nothing to boast of, don't boast).

**3063. Ɔketebɔ gye porɔporɔ a, ɔsɔ ne dadeɛ mu.**
*If the leopard flees, it carries its tools with it.*
(A warrior always carries his weapons, even in defeat).

3064. Aketekyire se: sɛ enyɛ ne biribi ne kankabi a, anka ɔwu a, ne kawa nna ne kɔn-mu.
*The cricket says: if the millipede were not his relation he would not have worn the millipedes rings after his death.*
(Inheritance is only for relations).

3065. Aketekyire-nini bɔ fɛ a, ebi ka n'ani.
*If the male cricket gives a fatal blow, some of it gets in its eyes.*
(A warning against fighting or litigation. You will suffer even if you win).

3066. Aketekyiwa ho nyɛ fɛ, nso ɔne mpanimfoɔ na ɛnam.
*The palm wine pot is not beautiful, but it keeps company with the elders.*
(It is usefulness and not beauty that count).

3067. Akitiriku amoadudu, w'akyiri wɔ bi a, na yɛdi wo ni.
*Cow pea (nicknamed Amoadudu) it is only when you have something behind you that we respect you.*
(The cow pea, Vigna unguiculata, is one of the most widely distributed local beans. They can be mixed with corn and cooked in balls, which are generally eaten with something else, hence the proverb. Every man needs a supporter).

3068. Kitiriku rekɔpɛ ɛtwe adi na wannya ɛtwe anni a, ne kuro mmere.
*If a person full of sores wants to enjoy sex and he has no vagina to use, his sores do not get opened.*
(Every cloud has a silver lining).

3069. Meko a, meto, medwane a, meto; kampesɛ menkɔtɔ dɔm ano, ɛfirisɛ manwu a mɛnya sadeɛ.
*If I go to war, I am guilty; if I run away, I am guilty; I had better go and fight on the battle front, because if I don't die then I may succeed in capturing a fortune.*
(It is better to face great odds where you may achieve success, than to avoid them and suffer at any rate).

3070. Woko kɔ w'anim a, na woyi dɔm.
*When you fight and press onwards, then you will conquer.*

3071. Ɔreko ko n'ano.
*He who is fighting, fights for his mouth.*
(We struggle for our daily bread).

3072. Woko kobɔne a, ntoa mpa w'asene mu.
*If you fight an unprofitable war, you never take the belt from your waist.*
(Don't indulge in useless squabbles).

3073. Woko nkodene a, na wonya abɔdin.
*If you fight a good fight, then you achieve an appellation (a good name).*

3074. Woko nkrane na wɔnkɔ a, wontwɛre abɛ ngu mu.
*When you are fighting soldier ants and they don't go away, you don't peel palm nuts and drop them among them.*
(Don't wage war in kid gloves).

3075. Woko na woanyi dɔm a, womfa nnomum.
*When you fight and don't win, you don't take captives.*
(You don't benefit from a lost battle).

3076. Woko aniani a, wohwere tire.
*If you fight carelessly, you don't capture (lit. you lose) heads.*
(In the old days warriors would cut off the heads of important men killed in battle, to present to their chief. Hence: If you don't strive hard you won't succeed).

3077. Yɛrenko nso yɛrennwane, na yɛgina akodɔm ano reyɛ dɛɛn?
*We are not going to fight and we are not going to run away either, then why are we standing on the battlefield?*
(Don't involve yourself if you aren't willing to see the project through).

3078. Yɛko yere no yɛnko ba.
*We fight for a wife but not for a child.*
(A man struggles to get a wife and then the children follow. Hence: One thing automatically follows from another).

3079. "Mekɔ a meremma (bio)", yɛka no nkwantia.
*"If I go, I won't return (again)", we say it at the outskirts.*
(If you intend to do something unpopular you keep it a secret until the last moment).

3080. "Wokɔ a, ɛnkyɛ", ɛnte sɛ wo ara wonam.
*"If you go, don't stay long", is not like when you go yourself.*
(If you are not sure of something being properly done by others, do it yourself).

3081. "Wokɔ a, mekyea no", na ɛfiri nkaeɛ ne papayɛ.
*"If you go, I greet him", is because of his good reputation and good deeds).*
(You recognize a person who has done something you remember warmly).

3082. Wokɔ baabi na nokorɛ resua a, na nkontompo na wabo no.
*If you go somewhere and truth is weeping, it is falsehood that has beaten it.*
(Those who speak the truth suffer more than liars).

3083. Wokɔ bata na woantwa w'ani a, yɛfrɛ wo "ɔkabɔnaani".
*If you are going on a trading trip and you don't return, we call you a "person swallowed by debt".*
(If someone who travels to gain something does not succeed, then he is shy about returning).

3084. Wokɔ bata pa a, na lɔre de wo besi w'aboboano.
*If you travel for trade successfully, the lorry brings you to the gate of your house.*
(A successful person is treated with respect).

3085. "Mekɔ bi," yɛnka no kwa.
*"I will accompany you", we never say it gratuitously.*
(If you decide to share in someone's actions, you must be prepared to share their expenses).

3086. Wokɔ obi kurom na ɔkum akokɔ ma wo di a, ɛnyɛ ne deɛ na woaweɛ, na wo deɛ a ɔwɔ fie no na woadie.
*If you go to someone's town and he kills a fowl for you to eat, it is not his fowl that you have eaten but your own which is at home).*
(If you accept hospitality, you must return it too).

**3087. Wobɛkɔ aburokyire na woannya nkɔeɛ a, wonka hɔ asɛm.**
*If you want to go abroad and have not succeeded in going, you don't talk about it.*
(You don't boast of what you are unable to achieve).

**3088. Wokɔ ɛdwa mmienu a, na wohunu deɛ ɛba**
*If you go to two markets, you see which one is better.*
(If you have a choice, you can judge which is best).

**3089. Woreкɔ afidihwɛ na aserewa sere dwa mu: "Hwee! hwee!" a, wodi wo tirim awerɛhoɔ; sɛ nso ɔyɛ "Sere! sere!" a, wodi wo tirim ahurisie, ɛfirisɛ anyɛ nwono a ɛyɛ dɛ.**
*If you are going to look at traps and the sunbird jeers at you "Hwee! hwee!" you become sorrowful; but if it says "Sere! sere!" (lit. "Smile! smile!"), you are delighted; because if failure does not come success does.*
(Life is full of ups and downs and you have to accept whatever comes your way).

**3090. Wokɔ afunsie na woamma ntɛm a, na ɛbo na ɛwɔm.**
*If you go to the burial and you don't come back quickly, then it is because of drink.*
(Funerals are occasions at which much alcohol is consumed. Hence: If you linger over an unpleasant job, it must be for some good reason).

**3091. Wokɔ agorɔ na yɛgye wo nkonta firi wo nsam a, na yeagu w'agorɔ.**
*If you go and play and they take your drumsticks from your hand, then your play is brought to an end.*
(You can't do a job without the right tools).

**3092. Wokɔ ahayɔ na woannya aboa anku no, na enti woreba fie, na wotia akyekyedeɛ so a, wonnyae no hɔ nkɔ.**
*If you go hunting and you cannot find an animal to kill and so return home, and you step on a tortoise, you don't leave it behind.*
(You must sometimes accept the second best).

**3093. "Mekɔɔ hɔ akyɛre" ne "mekɔ hɔ daa" ntumi nnye akyinne.**
*"I have not been there for a long time", and "I go there often" cannot argue.*
(A person who is familiar with something knows it best).

**3094. "Mekɔɔ hɔ nso mamfa" ne "Mankɔ hɔ"; "Mankɔ hɔ" na ɛyɛ nokorɛ.**
*"I went there but I did not take it" and "I did not go there"; it is "I did not go there" which is the truth.*
(Absence is the best alibi).

**3095. "Kɔ ahua" mmɔ koraa.**
*"Go begging" does not break the calabash.*
(You don't bite the hand that helps you)

**3096. "Kɔ ahua turu ba", yɛkyiri.**
*"Go begging with your child on your back", we don't approve of it.*
(Don't exploit your family and friends).

**3097. Woakɔ Hwimase, wɔrehwim adeɛ, woanhwim bi, wokɔɔ Hwedeɛm a wɔrehwere adeɛ a, ɛhɔ na worekɔpɛ adeɛ ahwim?**
*If you have gone to Hwimase and they were snatching things, you did not snatch any, if you went to Hwedeɛm,*

*where people lose things, it is there that you want to snatch something.*
(There's a play on the names of the places. Hwimase might be translated "Snatch–town", and Hwedeɛm "Losers". Hence: Don't be a square peg in a round hole).

**3098. Wokɔ Kankan dwa so kɔtɔ adeɛ na woannya be a, wɔpata wo ka.**
*If you go to Kankan to buy something and you don't get it, you are kept from debt.*
(The old name for Dutch Accra was Kankan and thus the Dutch were called Kankanfoɔ – Kankan–people – or Kankan brɔfoɔ – Kankan–Europeans. Hence: If you don't buy, you can't get into debt).

**3099. Wokɔ kuro bi so na ɛhɔfoɔ yɛ nkwaseafoɔ a, yɛ wo ho kwasea bi, na wɔdane anyansafoɔ a, woadane bi.**
*If you go to a certain town and its people are foolish, act foolish too, and when they change to wise, you also change to it.*
(When in Rome, do as Rome does).

**3100. Wokɔ kuro bi so na wohunu sɛ akɔdaa te akonnwa so na ɔpanin te fam a, mma ɛnyɛ wo nwanwo, na ebia na akɔdaa no yɛ hɔ hene.**
*If you go to a certain town and you see that a child is sitting on a stool, and an elder sits on the ground; don't let it surprise you, for perhaps the child is the chief there.*
(Don't prejudge a situation until you know all the facts).

**3101. Wokɔ kuro bi so na wohunu sɛ atwenenoo gu nkwan tia a, nka sɛ ɛhɔfoɔ agyimi; ebia na wɔnnwe hɔ nam.**
*If you go to some town and you see the spoor of animals on the outskirts, don't say the inhabitants are foolish; it may be that they taboo the eating of those animals' meat.*
(See Proverb 3100).

**3102. Woreкɔ kuro bi so na wote akokɔbɔneeɛ a, nka sɛ woaduru; ebia na ɔsi ɔbatani nnooma so.**
*If you are going to a certain town and you hear the cock crow, don't think you have arrived yet; for it may be that it is perching on the load of a traveller.*
(See Proverb 3100).

**3103. Wokɔ kuro mu na ɔhene bom fam a, wommisa adwa.**
*If you go to a town and find its chief sitting on the ground, you do not ask for a stool.*
(When in Rome do as Rome does).

**3104. Wokɔ kurom na wohunu sɛ ntakara fufuo si onipa tirim a, wommisa ne mpasua.**
*If you go to a town and you see white feathers on a person's head, do not ask of his rank.*
(Don't ask what you should know).

**3105. Wokɔ kurom na ɛhɔfoɔ de nkosua redi abototoɔ a, di bi, na ebia na ɛhɔ mmara ne no.**
*If you go to a town and its people are throwing eggs at each other, do it too, for perhaps it is the custom there.*
(When in Rome do as Rome does).

3106. Wokɔ kurom na sɛ ɛhɔ odikro mantam dedua mu a, yɛmmisa sɛ mu hɔ yɛ.
*If you go to a town and its small chief is tied to one of the trees (in the street), then you don't ask if all is well in the place.*
(If there is obvious evidence of trouble, you don't ask if all is well!)

3107. Wokɔ okusie kurom na ɔrewe nnwoa a, wowe bi.
*If you go to the rat's town and it eats palm kernels, you chew some too.*
(When in Rome do as Rome does).

3108. "Mekɔɔ kwa" ne "Mebaa kwa", ne nyinaa yɛ kwa.
*"I went in vain" and "I came in vain," both are in vain.*
(Two negatives don't make a positive).

3109. Wokɔ Akwam sa na sɛ woannya biribi a, wote sapɔ.
*If you go to fight in the Akwam area, if you don't get anything else, you can pluck sponge.*
(Akwam, in the Eastern Region of Ghana, used to be known for the high quality of its sponges. Hence: However poor people are, you can get something from them).

3110. Woakɔ Akyease, wɔrekyea, woankyea bi. Wokɔɔ Abirem a wɔrebirim nkurafoɔ a, ɛhɔ na worekɔkyea?
*You went to Akyease, they were marching there, and you did not take part. You went to Abirem where people whipped people, is it there that you are going to march?*
(See Proverb 3097).

3111. Wokɔ akyekyedeɛ kurom na ɔdi nnɔteɛ a, wodi bi.
*I you go to the tortoise's town and he eats earth, you eat some too.*
(When in Rome do as Rome does).

3112. Kɔ Akyemfo kɔtɔ nkyene bra; nkyene amma, sika nso amma, na worebɛka ama no ayɛ sɛ nkyene?
*Go to Saltpond to buy salt and come back; salt did not come back, money also did not come; and are you going to say that in that respect it is like salt?*
(There are some situations you cannot talk your way out of).

3113. "Kɔɔ akyirikyiri" ne "Kɔɔ dadaada", hwan na oyɛ panin? Ɔpanin ne "Kɔɔ dadaada.
*"Went far away" and "Went long ago", who is the elder? The senior is "Went long ago".*
(Time takes precedence over distance).

3114. Wokɔ na obi yere reko a, mpɛ ntɛm mmua bi, na ɛwɔ deɛ waye no.
*If you go to meet someone quarrelling with his wife, don't involve yourself hurriedly, for there is something she has done.*
(Don't interfere in something without knowing the facts).

3115. Ɔreko na ɔkɔ.
*He who is going is the one who goes.*
(If you are ready, you will be sent).

3116. "Ɔkɔ" ne "ɔba" nsɛ.
*"He goes" and "he comes" are not the same.*
(One action differs from another).

3117. "Merekɔ sɛn ni?" na ɛde akobɔ baeɛ.
*"How am I going back?" brings lack of desire to return.*
(If you have not the means to do something and getting it would be too difficult, then you avoid doing it).

3118. Yɛrekɔ nnomaanomaa a, yɛnyi pirebuo kwan mu.
*If we are going to the land of birds, we don't collect nests on the way.*
(You don't carry coals to Newcastle).

3119. Wokɔ anɔpasuo na woannya bi a, na wosa apitiri-apɔtɔe.
*If you are going to collect water from the stream in the early morning and you do not get any, you collect muddy water.*
(Necessity makes one accept what one can get).

3120. Wokɔ mponkyerɛne kurom kɔto sɛ mponkyerɛne nyinaa tete fam a, wotena fam bi.
*If you go the frogs' town and see that all the frogs are on the ground, you, too, sit on the ground.*
(When in Rome do as Rome does).

3121. Wokɔ ɔsa na woannya sadeɛ a, wonhwere anammɔntutuo.
*If you go to war and you don't get loot, you at least get foot pains.*
(Whatever you do there is some result, good or bad).

3122. Wokɔ asansakyerɛ na woba no nsansa a, yɛde nsansa hyia wo.
*If you go to capture a hawk and you return empty handed, you are received with empty hands.*
(You are only rewarded after you prove your success).

3123. Wokɔ so nsuo anɔpa a, ɛboa wo anwumerɛ.
*If you go for your water in the morning, it will help you in the evening.*
(Early work is beneficial).

3124. Wokɔ tɛkrɛma-sa a, wonyi dɔm.
*If you fight with your tongue only, you lose the battle.*
(Words don't win a war).

3125. Wokɔ ntɛm a na yɛgu wo so abɛ.
*If you go early, we serve you palm soup.*
(The early bird catches the worm).

3126. Wokɔ awareɛ a, bisa.
*If you are going to get married, make enquiries first.*
(Make enquiries before you commit yourself).

3127. Wokɔ wiram kɔbɔ ntɔn na ɛtoto a, wode ba fie bɛnwono kɛtɛ a, ɛtoto.
*If you go to the forest to collect reeds for weaving mats and it is tangled, when you bring it home to weave, it remains tangled.*
(Something does not change its nature by being moved from one place to another).

3128. "Ɔrekɔ" nyɛ ɔgofoɔ.
*"He is going" is not a player.*
(You do not rely on someone who is due to leave for good).

3129. Woakɔɔ ayie, woannom nsa, woanka twenee, woansa woammɔ nsaa, na afei wokɔɔ ayie kɔyeɛ dɛn?
*When you went to the funeral, you did not drink, you*

*did not play the drum, you did not dance, you did not donate, then what did you go to the funeral to do?*
(There is no use being present if you do not participate).

**3130. Wokɔ wo yɔnko nkyɛn agorɔ na oni pam no a, na ɔne wo.**
*If you go to your neighbor's house to play and his mother drives him away, it refers to you.*
(Take notice of an indirect warning).

**3131. Woankɔ (baabi) amma a, yɛmma wo akwaaba.**
*If you haven't gone (somewhere) and returned, we do not welcome you.*

**3132. Yɛnkɔ, yɛmma, na ɛbɛyɛ dɛn na yɛahunu sɛ yɛaka kwan mu.**
*We don't go, we don't come, then how can we know that we are stranded.*
(Unless you have had experience, you can't judge the realities of a situation).

**3133. Woankɔ bi a, wose yɛanko.**
*If you did not go (with us), you say we did not fight.*
(People who don't take part in something denigrate it).

**3134. Wonkɔɔ obi abɛ so a, wonnye no sa-kane.**
*If you have not gone to someone's palm wine-tapping area, you do not take the first wine tappings.*
(You can't experience in absentia).

**3135. Wonkɔɔ obi afuom da a, wose wo nko ara na woyɛ akuafoɔ.**
*If you never went to anyone else's farm, you say you alone are a farmer.*
(If you are ignorant of other's achievements you become conceited).

**3136. Ankɔ-ayie ne soboɔ.**
*One who does not go to a funeral is the person we reproach.*
(You can only be reproached if you are at fault).

**3137. Ako reka sɛ "kaa-kaa" no na ɔse "yɛpere di, na yɛmpere mma yɛn yɔnko".**
*When the parrot says "kaa-kaa" it means (lit. then it says) "we struggle to eat, but we don't struggle for the benefit of our companions".*
(Every man is out for himself).

**3138. Ako ano yɛ den nti na obi nkye no nnie.**
*Because the parrot has a loud voice no one catches it to eat.*
(Some people avoid trouble by making a lot of fuss).

**3139. Ako mpɛ sɛ obi ha no nti na ɔto ne nkosua gu dua mu.**
*The parrot does not want anyone to trouble it and therefore it lays its eggs inside a tree.*
(Said when someone wishes to keep their family life private).

**3140. Ako mpo na yɛretɔn no agye ntakuo num yi na ɔnwam?**
*If even the parrot is being sold for a trifle, what about the hornbill?*
(If something more valuable is sold for a trifle, then the price of a trifle is nothing).

**3141. [Ako]/[akokɔ] se: ɔrefiri nnɛ agyina ne nan-korɔ so, ɛfiri sɛ, ebia na ɔhene bi rebɛba a, ɔbɛma obiara agyina ne nan-korɔ soɔ.**
*The [parrot]/[fowl] says: if from today it will stand on one leg, because perhaps a chief is going to come, who will make everyone stand on one leg.*
(Your time may come too. Prepare for the future).

**3142. Ako se: "Ɛnnɛ ni, na ɔkyena".**
*The parrot says: "Even today is hard, what of the morrow?"*
(Sufficient unto the day is the evil thereof).

**3143. Wo nko wodidi a, wo nko wone.**
*If you eat alone, you defecate alone.*
(Village latrines are outside the village and particularly at night, people like company to go there. Hence: If you don't share what you have, people will not keep company with you).

**3144. Ɔko ba a, na asisie aba.**
*When war comes, rumors have come.*
(Strife breeds rumors).

**3145. Ɔko bi a yɛanko bi no, yɛmfa mu sadeɛ.**
*The war we don't take part in, we don't take booty from.*
(You must earn something before you get it).

**3146. Ɔko, yɛko no agya mma.**
*War, we go in a group of father's children.*
(Your father's child by a different mother cannot inherit from you and therefore has no motive for killing you. Hence: You move with those with whom you can have a disinterested relationship).

**3147. Ɔko na ɛkyerɛ nsese.**
*A war leads to planning.*
(In difficult times, you are careful how you act).

**3148. Akoa a ɔnim som di ne wura adeɛ.**
*A slave who knows how to serve inherits his master's property.*
(Good service brings its rewards).

**3149. Akoa bi de kaka resɛe dwanam.**
*Someone with a toothache is spoiling mutton.*
(Don't be a dog in the manger).

**3150. Akoa di dwan a, ne ho dwan no.**
*If a slave eats mutton, he becomes sad.*
(In the old days, slaves like sheep were sacrificed, in particular to accompany their masters into the next world. Thus if you are in an inferior position even good things may remind you of you position).

**3151. Akoa nni awu na yɛnkum ne wura.**
*When a slave commits murder, we don't kill his master.*
(A man suffers the consequence of his own deeds).

**3152. Akoa nni mpɔ kwa.**
*A slave does not eat the second yam crop without reason.*
(If you give your servants the best, it means you appreciate what they have done).

3153. Akoa didi mee na sɛ ɛkɔm de ne wura a, ne deɛ no yɛ afuhyɛ.
*If a slave eats his fill while his master is hungry, his is mere wind in the stomach.*
(A servant cannot prosper unless his master does).

3154. Akoa didi ne wura ho.
*A slave exploits his master.*

3155. Akoa hantani na yɛde no sie funu.
*A proud slave is taken and buried with the corpse (of his master).*
(If you are arrogant you are likely to suffer from your superiors).

3156. Akoa hunu na akoa nkyerɛ.
*A slave sees but does not reveal.*
(If you are working for someone and you show what needs doing, you will be asked to do the work yourself. Don't bring unnecessary suffering on yourself).

3157. Akoa nhye ne ho ntu sa.
*A slave does not make up his own mind about going to war.*
(A slave has no right to views of his own).

3158. Akoa korɔ Gyammi, ɔnni wo ho a, wo ho nye.
*Only one slave Gyammi, if he is away from you, you are not happy.*
(It is painful to lose one's only help).

3159. Akoa koro Kwagyei!
*One slave is a Jack of All Trades.*
(A single servant must do all kinds of work. Or: A person without help has to cope with everything).

3160. Akoa kyerɛ agyapadeɛ na omfa bi.
*A slave indicates inheritable property, but he cannot inherit it.*
(You be unable to benefit from what you know).

3161. Akoa kyerɛ nyansa a, yɛnfa, nanso ɛka ba a, ɔno na ɔyɔ adwuma ma yɛde tua.
*If a slave shows wisdom, we don't take (any notice), but if we get into debt, it is he who has to work in order to pay it off.*
(If you are dependent on someone, however wise you may be, you have to suffer from their misjudgments).

3162. Akoa nkyere dadua.
*A slave does not arrest a person who has committed an oath-offence.*
(If you are not qualified, you cannot deal with serious cases).

3163. Akoa nkyerɛ nnannua.
*A slave does not point out where good sticks for building are to be found.*
(See Proverb 3156).

3164. Akoa nim ne wura.
*A slave knows his master.*

3165. Akoa nya ne ho a, ɔfrɛ ne ho Sonani.
*When a slave becomes rich (and free), he calls himself one of the Asona family.*
(The Asona are one of the main Akan clans. Hence: If you have achieved great things, you get a great name).

3166. Akoa nya ne ho a, ɔnom nyankonsuo.
*If a slave becomes a free man, he drinks rainwater.*
(In the old days, rainwater was considered a drink fit for kings. Hence: If you are independent you can make your own choice).

3167. Akoa nyansa wɔ ne wura tirim.
*A slave's wisdom is in his master's head.*
(A slave makes no decisions for himself but does what his master says).

3168. Akoa pa na ɔka ne wura aduane hwɛ.
*A good slave tastes his master's food to see if it is good.*
(A good servant thinks first of his master).

3169. Akoa mpa ne wura.
*A slave does not choose his master.*

3170. Akoa ampɔ a, na ɛfiri wura.
*When a slave is not well-behaved, it is because of his master.*
(Like master, like man).

3171. Akoa sane asukɔ na yɛma ɔkɔ a, ɔdwane.
*When a slave has ceased to go for water and you force him to go, he runs away.*
(A privilege once granted is difficult to withdraw).

3172. Akoa som sompa a, ɔfa ne ho di.
*If a slave serves his master very well, his purchase-price is discharged.*
(If a slave served his master particularly well, he was sometimes freed. Hence: If you work hard and are loyal, you will be rewarded).

3173. W'akoa sene wo ahoɔden a, na ɔsene wo tumi.
*If your slave is stronger than you, then he has more power than you.*
(Don't let those who work for you dominate you).

3174. Akoa som ne wura animia.
*A slave serves his master with all his might.*
(A person in authority excites veneration).

3175. Akoa te se kyekyire; wode nsuo kakra gu ne so a, na wahono.
*A slave is like corn-flour; when you pour a little water on it, it becomes soft.*
(A servant is easily influenced by kind treatment).

3176. Akoa te sɛ twerɛboɔ, ɛnni etuo ano a, ɛnyɛ yie.
*The slave is like the flint, if it is not attached to the lock of a gun, things can't go well.*
(A good master makes effective use of a servant and has his loyalty).

3177. W'akoa nyɛ a, wosoma no afie nyinaa mu.
*If your slave is no good, you send him on errands to many different houses.*
(You waste time in correcting a stupid person's mistakes).

3178. Ɔkɔ-asua amma a, wommisa ahina.
*If the one who goes for water does not return, you don't ask for the pot.*
(If one who has to bring something disappears, you have to accept that the thing has gone too).

3179. Kɔayie ammɔ nsaa ɛnneɛ, fanyinam sɛ woankɔ.
*To go to a funeral and not to donate, it is better that you don't go.*
(If you don't contribute to something you might as well not be there).

3180. "Kɔba-kɔba' na ɔkɔ a ɔmma.
*"Gocome-gocome", then he goes and does not come.*
(If you trust people too much, one day they will let you down).

3181. Ankɔbea nnim gyata.
*A stay at home does not know a lion.*
(He who has never had cause to fear, does not recognize its source).

3182. Akobɛn de asɛm nam.
*The war horn means trouble is on the way.*
(You only give a serious warning when really necessary).

3183. Kɔbere mfamfa: "Aban nhyeeɛ a, menhyeeɛ".
*The copper scoop: "If the palace is not burnt down, neither am I burnt".*
(The copper scoop was used for removing the dust from gold dust and was kept with the gold-weights. Hence: If a master is not destroyed, neither is his servant).

3184. Yɛrekɔbɔ dɔm asu a, ɔpanin ho mpa mu.
*If we are going to purify the people, an elder is never absent.*
(Serious matters cannot be attended to without the presence of the elders).

3185. Akɔbo yɛ animguase.
*Self-exile is a disgrace.*
(You don't gain anything by staying permanently away from home).

3186. Ɔkobɔni, baabiara yɛ no baabi.
*A vagabond, anywhere is somewhere to him.*
(A wanderer has no feeling for home).

3187. Ɔkobɔni firi adi a, yɛmmisa n'akyiri akwan.
*If a vagabond leaves home, we don't go after him.*
(You don't take trouble over a useless person).

3188. Kɔbɔnsɔ se: ɔrebɛyɛ adwuma, na aka kakra sɛ adwumayɛ aduru so.
*The blue butterfly says: it is coming to work and in a little time, work will come.*
(Some moths and butterflies migrate in April of just before the main planting season. It is time to prepare for work ahead).

3189. Kɔbɔnsɔ Adwoa se: "Me na medii kan maa ɔmanfoɔ tee sɛ osua reba, nanso nsuo baeɛ a, m'aduadeɛ anyɛ yie.
*The Blue Butterfly Adwoa says: I first informed the people of the state about the approach of rain, the rain came but my garden did not benefit from it."*
(Good deeds do not necessarily bring the reward you hoped for).

3190. Ɔrekɔbra owuo nsoa mpafe.
*He who is going to bring death does not carry pains in the side.*
(If you intend to do something about a difficult situation, you must free yourself from all impediments).

3191. Akɔdaa a wammɛbɔ bra na yɛde abonkuruwa sie no.
*A child who does not come to stay, we use the castor oil plant to bury him.*
(It is believed that if a child dies very young it does not wish to stay. The leaves of this plant are wrapped around its body. Hence: If you know someone does not want to be with you, you don't treat them with respect).

3192. Akɔdaa a ɔbɛda ama yɛada bie, na yɛdeda no.
*If a child is going to sleep to allow us to sleep a little, then we coax him to sleep.*
(You should help the person who is willing to be helped).

3193. Akɔdaa a ɔdidi mpaninfoɔ atɛm, ɔse: "Madidi wo ni anaa wo se atem?"
*If a child insults the elders he says: "Have I abused your mother or your father?"*
(A person who is bad cannot help showing his badness wherever he is).

3194. Akɔdaa a ɔbɛhyɛ ne ho yie wɔ hɔ a, obi nkyerɛ wo.
*A child who will educate himself well, if he is there, no one shows you.*
(You can recognize inborn talent).

3195. Akɔdaa a ɔbɛnyini bɔne na ɔbɔ borɔdedwo bosea.
*If a child will grow up bad, then he borrows roast plantain.*
(A thief starts thieving early).

3196. Akɔdaa a ɔbɛnyini ayɛ ɔpanin a, agyinaeɛ ne ɔsetie.
*A child who will grow to becomes a good elder, his bearing is respectful.*
(A person shows his character young in life).

3197. Akɔdaa a wantie oni ne ɔse kasa no na ɔbono bra Kurudapaakuo.
*If a child does not listen to her mother and father's advice, she has her menstrual period at Kurudapaakuo.*
(Kurudapaakuo is a holy day for tending to the stools. The child would have to keep away from the celebrations. Hence: If you are disobedient, you suffer for it).

3198. Akɔdaa a ɔnni hwɛsofoɔ na asɛmmɔne kotokuo sɛn n'aboboano.
*A child who has no guardian has a bag of troubles hanging at his doorway.*
(The unprotected suffer).

3199. Akɔdaa a ɔse ɔremma oni nna no, ɔno nso renya nna.
*A child who says it would not let its mother sleep, does not sleep itself.*
(If you prevent others from doing what they want, then you yourself will suffer for it).

3200. Akɔdaa bɔ mmusuo nkron a, ɔfa mu num.
*If a child breaks nine taboos, he is punished for five.*
(Don't think your supporter will support you one hundred percent. Or: Whatever happens you must take punishment for some of your misdemeanors).

3201. Akɔdaa bɔ mpanin bɛdɛ a, yɛsoa no mpanin-nesoa.
*If a child makes an adult's farm-container, you load it with an adult's load.*
(If you are too precocious, you must bear the consequences).

3202. Akɔdaa boapa wu a, wɔboapa sie no.
*When a child pretends to be dying, you must pretend to bury him.*
(You play along with the child's imagination).

3203. Akɔdaa bɔne na ɔnyini (yɛ) ɔpanin bɔne.
*A bad child grows into a bad elder.*
(A bad character begins in youth).

3204. Akɔdaa de osuaa na ɛdi dwa na ɔmfa piredwan na ɛdie.
*A child takes osuaa to the market but not a piredwan.*
(Osuaa is a small weight; a piredwan is a large one. Hence: People should only be given what they are capable of using).

3205. Akɔdaa dwo, yɛhunu so na yɛaka.
*A child's baked food, we blow on it before we bite.*
(You train someone to be careful by showing them the dangers).

3206. Akɔdaa fotoɔ kɛseɛ yɛ ka.
*A child's big treasure bag is a debt.*
(A child cannot buy anything. It is his family that has to incur debts, if he has expensive needs).

3207. Akɔdaa fura ntoma kɛseɛ a, ɔtwetwe no ase.
*If a child puts on a big cloth, he drags it along.*
(If you have no experience, don't try to do more than you can).

3208. Akɔdaa hunu ne nsa hohoro a, ɔne mpaninfoɔ didi.
*If a child knows how to wash his hands, he eats with the elders.*
(If you act responsibly, you will share privileges).

3209. Akɔdaa anhunu adwadie a, n'asia nyera.
*If a child does not know how to trade, then the asia is not lost.*
(Asia is a small weight. Hence: If someone is not in a position to use a thing, he is unlikely to spoil it).

3210. Akɔdaa nhwɛ kwansɛn mu kwa.
*A child does not look at a soup pot for nothing.*
(If a child wants something, he shows it).

3211. Akɔdaa ka deɛ yɛnka a, ɔhunu deɛ yɛnhunu.
*If a child speaks what we do not speak of, then he sees what we do not see.*
(If you attempt to do what you are not supposed to, you get into trouble).

3212. Akɔdaa kawa na ɛnkɔ panin na nyɛ n'aduane.
*A child's ring will not fit an elder but its food will.*
(A child may help an elder in some ways but not in others).

3213. Akɔdaa kɔda gya na ɔpere ho a, ne ntoma hye.
*If a child goes to lie by the fire and is restless, its cloth catches fire.*
(Don't let an unexperienced person take risks or they will get hurt. Also: Don't play with fire!)

3214. Akɔdaa kɔtɔ panin nkyɛn a, ɔte mpaninsɛm.
*A child who crouches by an elder hears wise talk.*
(If you stay with wise people, you learn wisdom).

3215. Akɔdaa kyerɛ mmusuo a, yɛnyi.
*If a child reveals an omen, we do not act on it.*
(We do not trust a child's judgement).

3216. Akɔdaa mo tam kɛseɛ a, ɛtu no hwe.
*If a girl wears a big loin cloth, it makes her fall.*
(Don't bite off more than you can chew).

3217. Akɔdaa mmɔborɔ te sɛ taawisie.
*A child's misery is like tobacco smoke.*
(A child's sorrow evaporates quickly).

3218. Akɔdaa na wodeɛ nti na wohunu kɔtɔ ani a, wose abaa.
*Because you are a child, if you see the eyes of a crab, you say (they are) sticks.*
(Appearances are deceptive; but experience teaches you to distinguish one thing from another).

3219. Akɔdaa ani ansɔ ɔpanin a, ofrɛ mpapa sɛ nhaha.
*If a child does not respect his elders, he pronounces the name of the palm branch nasally.*
(A disrespectful person learns nothing from the elders).

3220. Akɔdaa nim adidi na ɔnnim asɛm ka.
*A child knows how to eat but not how to express itself.*
(Doing is one thing, being articulate is another).

3221. Akɔdaa nim wa bɔ na ɔnnim ahorɔ to.
*A small child knows how to cough but does not know how to spit.*
(People's ability is limited by their age).

3222. Akɔdaa nnim adware a, nyɛ n'afuru soa.
*If a child does not know how to bath, it does not mean washing its belly.*
(No matter how ignorant a person is, there is something he can do well).

3223. Akɔdaa nnim gyata a, [ɔbu no sɛ aboa bi]/[ɔse ɔyɛ ɔdwan].
*If the child does not know a lion, [he says it is some animal]/[he says it is a sheep].*
(Innocence may lead you into trouble).

3224. Akɔdaa nya sika a, ɛda ɔpanin kotokuo mu.
*If a child has any money, it lies in an elder's pocket.*
(You are not given responsibility until you are ready for it).

3225. Akɔdaa nya tirim-kam a, ɔnsoa dadeɛ kyɛ.
*If a child gets a sore on the head, it does not wear a helmet.*
(You don't do something to make a situation worse than it is).

3226. Akɔdaa nyansa ne ɔpanin deɛ nsɛ.
*A child's wisdom and an elder's are not alike.*
(True wisdom comes with age).

3227. Akɔdaa nyini ne se fie na ɔnka ne se pato mu.
*A child grows up in his father's house but he does not remain in his father's care.*

(Ultimately you return to your mother's family, wherever you grow up).

3228. Akɔdaa pa na ɔnya adeɛ.
*A good child gets what it wants.*
(Virtue is rewarded).

3229. Akɔdaa repɛ adekɔkɔɔ ahwɛ a, yɛte damenama ahahan kyerɛ no.
*A girl who says she wants to see red things, we take the leaves of the Ashanti blood shrub (Mussaenda erythrophylla) to show her.*
(Used for instance of a stubborn child gets into the hands of the police or if a girl has sexual relations before puberty. The plant is used in the kyiribra ceremonies connected with the latter).

3230. Akɔdaa aperɛwa to borɔdeɛ a, ɔde akuma na ɛhwa.
*The troublesome child, when he toasts plantain, scrapes it with an axe.*
(A naughty child betrays his character through his actions).

3231. Akɔdaa se ɔbɛtete mako a, gyae no ma ɔntete, na ɛkɔ n'ani a, ɔbɛgyae.
*If a child says it will pick pepper, let it pick, for if it goes in its eyes it will stop.*
(Allow a stubborn person to learn from their own mistakes).

3232. Akɔdaa sika te sɛ anyankoma-gya, wotwa so a, ɛdum.
*A child's money is like the wood of the myrianthus (God's heart) tree, if you light it, it goes out quickly.*
(Certain things are always ephemeral).

3233. Akɔdaa som kɔteɛ bebrebe a, ɔhyia deɛ ɔntumi nnie.
*If a girl has sex (lit. holds a penis) a lot, she meets what she cannot cope with.*
(Don't concentrate too much on one thing).

3234. Akɔdaa su a, yɛmmɔ no duam.
*If a child cries, we don't tie him to a log.*
(You don't meet distress with violence).

3235. Akɔdaa su mpanin-su a, ɔtua ayiaseka.
*If a child weeps like an adult, he contributes to the funeral expenses.*
(If you act as a responsible person you share responsibility, good or bad).

3236. Akɔdaa sua a, ɔse ɔyɛ ɔdehyeɛ.
*If a child is small, he says he is a royal.*
(Some dependent people take their privileges for granted).

3237. Akɔdaa te ne ho firi oni ne ɔse ho ntɛm a, ɔhunu n'adwe bɔ.
*If a child leaves his mother and father early, he knows how to crack his own palm kernels.*
(If a child is independent, he learns early how to behave like an adult).

3238. Akɔdaa tɔɔ baha so ansa na ɔrehunu kɛtɛ.
*A child lay on plantain fibers before he saw a mat.*
(The kɛtɛ is the best sleeping mat. Hence: You have to pass progressively through ranks in life).

3239. Akɔdaa twa fufuo a, ɛtwa deɛ ɛbɛkɔ n'ano.
*If a child cuts fufuo, he cuts what he can put in his mouth.*
(Used when someone has spoken above his station in life and causes offence. A person should obey custom).

3240. Akɔdaa twa kɔntɔmoa kɛseɛ a, ɛhia no.
*If a child cuts a big lump of fufuo, it gets stuck.*
(Don't bite off more than you can chew). ·

3241. Akɔdaa twa kɔntɔmoa kɛseɛ, na ɔnka asɛnkɛseɛ.
*A child cuts off a big portion of fufuo, but he does not take part in important discussions.*
(A person can consume a lot without making serious contributions).

3242. Akɔdaa twɛ, wohwɛ a, ɛnhwɛ, woyi w'ani a, ɛnyi.
*A child's vagina, if you look at it, you are embarrassed, at the same time you can't take you eyes away (lit. if you look at it, it does not look, if you take your eye off it, it does not come off).*
(People are fascinated at seeing what they should not see).

3243. Akɔdaa bɛwu a, ɛnnim sɛ suman da ne kɔn mu.
*If a child is going to die, it matters not if a charm hangs round its neck.*
(What is predestined to happen, will happen).

3244. Akɔdaa yɛ mpaninsɛm a, akyɛdɛ hwere no.
*If a child acts as an adult (i.e. throws his weight about), he is deprived of gifts.*
(It is humble people who are given things, not those who act aggressively).

3245. Akɔdaa yɛ somakorɔ a, ɔdi n'akɔnnɔdeɛ.
*If a child likes going on errands, it eats its favorite food.*
(If you are amenable, people treat you well).

3246. Akɔdaa nyem a, ɔno ara na ɔwoɔ.
*If a child becomes pregnant, she delivers by herself.*
(If you do something unexpected, you have to cope with the results yourself).

3247. Nkɔdaa hunu ɔkɔreɛ a osuo ahwe no a, wɔse ɔyɛ ɔpɛtɛ.
*If children see an eagle which has been beaten by the rain, they say it is a vulture.*
(An inexperienced person will misjudge a situation).

3248. Nkɔdaa pɛ nam nso wɔsuro nantwie.
*Children like meat but fear the cow.*
(Said of someone who fears to take the necessary steps to achieve what he wants).

3249. Kodiabɛ ne kɔtwaabɛ, ɛmu biara mu nni akyamfoɔ.
*Go-and-eat-palm-nuts and Go-and-tap-palm-trees, neither of them are well regarded.*
(Some jobs are not respected even if productive).

3250. Kodoɔ yɛ ma a, odwan nya bi di.
*When the big wooden bowl is full, the sheep has a chance of a bite.*
(When there is plenty, everyone benefits).

**3251. Kodoɔ yɛ ma a, tantia ka bi.**
*If the big wooden bowl is full, the lid eats a little.*
(Everyone benefits in times of prosperity).

**3252. Ɔkodoɔ, yɛhare no afanu.**
*The canoe, we paddle it on both sides.*
(You should consider both sides of a question if you
want to give a balanced judgement).

**3253. Ɔkɔeɛ amma ntɛm a, na ɛfiri nsɛkuro.**
*If someone who has gone does not come back soon,
then it is because of gossip.*
(An evil tongue drives people away).

**3254. Koekoeɛ kɔ Aburowmu, kɔ nkuruma mu, na ɔnkɔ
ɔboɔmu.**
*A little beetle can get into corn, or into okra but it
cannot penetrate a stone.*
(Everyone has his limitations).

**3255. Wokɔfa obi atɔpɛ kɔyɛ adwuma a, wohohoro so
kɔto deɛ ɛda.**
*If you go and take someone's hoe and work with it,
wash it and take it back to where it belongs.*
(If you borrow something, be careful of it and replace
it).

**3256. Wonkɔfaa kontromfi asɔ na ɔredi wo mfudeɛ yi,
na wobɛfa n'aderɛ.**
*You have not gone to collect the baboon's hoe but it
is eating your crops, and yet you will go and get his
cutlass.*
(Don't put yourself under obligation to a grasping
person).

**3257. Kofi Amoako se: "Ɛnyɛ me na mepɛ aduane, na
me yafunu na ɛha me.".**
*Kofi Amoako says: "I don't want to eat much, but my
stomach troubles me".*
(Real necessity forces a man to do something he would
not otherwise do).

**3258. "Kofi, wo nsa nwunu". Ose:"Efiri wo nkwammɔne".
"Kofi, w'ano yɛ hare." Ose: "Wotwaa no sɛ wo ba deɛ a,
anka menni nwieeɛ".**
*"Kofi, your hand leaks!" He says: "It is because of your
bad soup." "Kofi, your mouth is too quick!" He says:
"If you had given me a big ball of fufu as you did to
your child, then I would not have been able to finish
eating it".*
(Don't give preferential treatment to your own family
in the presence of a stranger. Or: Treat strangers with
respect. Compar 2454).

**3259. Kofirikwansoɔ na ɔware Temanmuhunu.**
*An inexperienced stranger marries a good-for-
nothing.*
(Lack of experience leads to a bad choice).

**3260. Ɔkofoɔ ko kɔ n'anim na ɔnko nkɔ n'akyi.**
*A warrior fights to advance but does not retreat.*
(A brave man does not give way).

**3261. "[Kɔhyɛ]/[Kɔtena] ɔhyen mu" nyɛ awerɛhoɔ.**
*"Go and sit in the moonlight" is not an affliction.*
(You should not be troubled by a situation whose end
is in sight).

**3262. Worekɔhwɛ wo fidie na wohunu aberɛbeɛ a
wahyɛ akɔmfo a, wonnane no nnya.**
*If you are going to inspect your trap and you see a
two-spotted palm civet which has committed suicide,
you don't go on and leave it.*
(Don't refuse a free gift).

**3263. Woakɔka kurokurokoko ntɔkwa, wokakyerɛ
ɔpetɛ sɛ ne tiri ho apa; kurokuro te fie a, na ne bo afu.**
*If you have invited a turkey to fight, you taunt the
vulture with its baldness; the turkey sits at home and
becomes offended.*
(An insult to one man is also an insult to another
similar to him).

**3264. Wo koko yɛ duru a, na woto ɛsono tuo.**
*If you are courageous, you shoot an elephant.*
(A man needs courage to face a powerful man – and in
doing so he shows his courage is real).

**3265. Wo koko yɛ duru a, wonnwura ogya mu.**
*Even if you are brave, you can't enter a fire.*
(There are limits even to bravery).

**3266. Akokɔ a wagyimi na ɔne akorɔma kɔ agyina.**
*A chicken which is foolish confers with the hawk.*
(Only a fool trusts his enemy).

**3267. Akokɔ a ɔbɛkyɛ no, akorɔma nkye no.**
*If the chicken is destined to live long, it will not be
taken by the hawk.*
(Predestination).

**3268. Akokɔ a wo ne no da no, wompɛ no ntɛm.**
*The fowl with which you sleep, you don't need to hurry
to search for.*
(If you look after your servants of family, they will be
there when you want them).

**3269. Akokɔ a ɔnni wura na akorɔma kye no wiɛ.**
*If a hen has no master, the hawk takes it to eat.*
(Everyone needs a protector).

**3270. Akokɔ ba a ɔbɛn oni na ɔdi abɛbɛ srɛ.**
*The chick that is found near its mother eats the
grasshopper's thigh.*
(If you stay near the one on whom you depend, you get
the best of everything).

**3271. Akokɔ bɔne na ɔpo aburow.**
*A bad chicken rejects the corn.*
(A contrary person does not thrive).

**3272. Akokɔ boro nsa a, na ne werɛ afiri akorɔma.**
*When the fowl is drunk, he forgets the hawk.*
(A drunk man does not heed danger, or some people
ignore danger when they are enjoying themselves).

**3273. Akokɔ da ntɛm a, ɔmfa ka (mma ne wura).**
*If the fowl goes early to bed, it does not bring debt (to
its master).*
(If you stay in the house, you don't get into trouble).

**3274. Akokɔ de mfɔteɛ na ɛhyira n'ano.**
*If a chicken takes a termite, then it blesses its mouth.*
(Chicken and eggs are used for soul-purifying purposes,
after accidents or misfortune. The idea is that the
termite is for the chicken what the chicken is for us.
Hence: Every creature has its own special food).

3275. Akɔkɔ redi wo yɔnko Aburowa, pamo no, na da bi ɔbɛdi wo deɛ.
*If a fowl eats your neighbor's corn, drive it away, for someday it will eat yours.*
(Help others that they may help you in the future).

3276. Akɔkɔ fufuo kyɛre fie a, ne ho bere.
*If a white chicken stays long in the house, it becomes red.*
(If conditions improve, so do people's character and appearance).

3277. Akɔkɔ gye ne ho gye a, akorɔma kye no.
*When a chicken separates itself from the others, a hawk takes it.*
(If you try to act alone you will suffer for it).

3278. Akɔkɔ ho ntakara mpensa, ne nyinaa tuatua ne wedeɛm.
*The fowl has thousands of feathers, but they are all attached to its skin.*
(Whatever your condition you have to care for those you are responsible for, however many they are).

3279. Akɔkɔ ho tɛ no a, akorɔma kye no.
*If the chicken is too happy, the hawk grabs it.*
(If you overstep the mark you get into trouble).

3280. Akɔkɔ hwɛ aberewa, na aberewa nso hwɛ akokɔ.
*The fowl looks after the old woman and the old woman looks after the fowl.*
(Said of an arrangement which suits both participants).

3281. Akɔkɔ hwete mfuturo a, ɔhwete ma ne mma.
*If the hen scratches in the dust, she scratches for her children.*
(A woman works primarily for her family).

3282. Akɔkɔ hwetehwete a, ɔhunu gyansakyi boapea.
*If a fowl scratches too much (lit. scratches, scratches), it will see the ape.*
(If you poke your nose into too many places, you will get into trouble).

3283. Akɔkɔ nkwa sɔ ne wura nsam.
*The life of the chicken is in its master's hands.*
(If you depend completely on someone you are at their mercy).

3284. Akɔkɔ nan tia ba na ɛnkum ba.
*The fowl's foot steps on the chicken but does not kill it.*
(A parent chastises a child but does not harm him).

3285. Akɔkɔ ne Aburownna.
*The fowl and corn do not sleep together.*
(Enemies keep apart).

3286. Akɔkɔ nni aso, nanso ɔnya n'asotorɔ a, yɛde ma no.
*The fowl has no ears, but when they should be boxed, it gets slapped just the same.*
(A poor man must pay his debts, even if he has not the means of doing so).

3287. Akɔkɔ ani sa Aburowfua (korɔ).
*A fowl's eye is always ready to attack a (single) grain of corn.*
(Every man pays extra attention to his own needs).

3288. Akɔkɔ nom nsuo a, ɔde kyerɛ Nyame.
*When a fowl drinks water, it shows it first to the sky–God.*
(You should show gratitude to God before anything else).

3289. Akɔkɔ mmerantua, sradeɛ nni mu.
*The boastful chicken has no fat.*
(An empty barrel makes most noise).

3290. Akɔkɔ na ɔyɛ aboa, na ɔdidi a, ɔde n'ano twitwiri fam.
*Because the fowl is a foolish creature (lit. an animal), when it eats, it rubs its beak on the ground.*
(Some people seem to excel in demonstrating their folly).

3291. Akɔkɔ ne sekan mmɔ nkuro.
*A chicken and a knife do not litigate.*
(You do not challenge a powerful person).

3292. Akɔkɔ pa butu aduasa nanso ɔtumi hwane ne nyinaa.
*A good hen sits on her eggs thirty times and still she is able to hatch them all out.*
(A fruitful woman can raise many children successfully).

3293. Akɔkɔ pa na yɛbua no.
*A good hen we put a basket on top of it.*
(i.e we keep it indoors to lay eggs. Hence: An obedient person is easy to control).

3294. Akɔkɔ pa na ɔwo asɛnsɛ. Asɛnsɛ: "Me nko me firi he?"
*A good hen gives birth to the one with curled feathers. It in turn says: "Where do I alone come from?"*
(This proverb expresses the feelings of the odd man out who questions his origins. Fowls with curiously reversed feathers which always look tattered are sometimes born to a normal hen).

3295. Akɔkɔ sa kyee a, ɛnyɛ akorɔma fɛ.
*No matter how well a fowl dances, it does not please the hawk.*
(You can do nothing to please your enemy).

3296. Akɔkɔ se: "Adeɛ ansa a anka mɛmeeɛ".
*The chicken says: "If darkness had not fallen, I would have had my fill".*
(Said of someone very greedy who is frustrated).

3297. Akɔkɔ se ɔbɛmene aponkyerɛne a, ma ɔmmene na ɔbɛhunu akyire.
*If the fowl says it will swallow a frog, allow it to swallow, for it will see the result.*
(If people insist on doing something foolish, let them, they will then realize the consequences).

3298. Akɔkɔ se: "Menim me tirim asɛm na mennim me kosua mu asɛm".
*The hen says: "I know what is in my own head but not what is in my eggs".*
(You know your own thoughts, but not those of your children).

3299. Akɔkɔ se: animguaseɛ nyɛ dɛ nti na wahyɛ n'ano nso.
*The fowl says: because disgrace is not pleasant, that is why it has made its mouth a different shape.*
(To avoid controversy you need to stress your individual identity).

3300. Akɔkɔ se: "Asɛmpɛ nti na mayɛ m'ano feafea".
*The fowl says: "It is because of being a busybody that I have a pointed beak".*
(Certain characteristics arise out of a person's character and certain situations require certain equipment).

3301. Akɔkɔ ntakara na ɛma akokɔ yɛ kɛseɛ.
*It is the feathers of a fowl which make it look big.*
(Fine feathers make a fine bird).

3302. Akɔkɔ ntakara nyini a, ɛtuatua ne honam mu.
*If the feathers on a fowl grow old, they remain attached to it.*
(Even if a chief's subjects grow rich or old, they are still his subjects. Or: People belong to a family, whatever their condition).

3303. Akɔkɔ tena fie kyɛ a, ɔdɔre sradeɛ.
*If a fowl stays long in the house, it grows fat.*
(If you take care of something, it thrives).

3304. Akɔkɔ ti yɛ mmeɛhe a yɛrebɔ mu?
*How big is a chicken's head that we should strike at it (with a stick)?*
(Don't bully the poor man).

3305. Akɔkɔ tire a ɛda nkwanta: ɔpanin yare a, ɛda nkwanta; abɔfra yare a, ɛda nkwanta.
*Chicken's head that lies at the cross-roads: an elder is sick, it lies at the cross-roads; a child is sick, it lies at the cross-roads.*
(A fowl is sacrificed on many occasions. Some people suffer whatever happens).

3306. Akɔkɔ nto badwam.
*A chicken does not lay eggs in public.*
(Certain actions should be kept private).

3307. Akɔkɔ wɔ nkwa aduro a, anka yɛmfa no ntwa abosom so.
*If a fowl possessed life-giving medicine, we would not take it to sacrifice over fetishes.*
(If a man can cure illness he does not die from it).

3308. Akɔkɔ nni fie a, na nkosua nni fie.
*If there is no hen in the house, there are no eggs.*
(First things first).

3309. Nkokɔ de borɔ dɛkum ako.
*Fowls use beating to kill the parrot.*
(A person separated from his family is open to abuse).

3310. Nkokɔ yɛ aduasa a, wɔn nyinaa tiri pɛ.
*Even if the chickens are thirty, all their heads are alike.*
(You can't change a man's nature).

3311. Kokoam asɛm, yɛka no "ɔnni hɔ".
*Things done in a corner, we call them "he is not there".*
(Keep secrets from those who shouldn't hear them).

3312. Akokɔba firi kosua mu.
*A chicken comes out of an egg.*
(Everything originates from something else).

3313. Akokɔbaatan a ɔdɔ ne mma no na ɔbutu ne mma soɔ.
*It is a good hen who loves her chickens and broods over them.*
(Used as a symbol for a good ruler who looks after the people well).

3314. Akokɔbereɛ nim adekyeeɛ nanso ɔhwɛ onini ano.
*The hen knows when it is dawn but leaves it to the cock to announce (lit. she looks to the cock's mouth).*
(A wise woman leaves it to her husband to make public announcements).

3315. Kɔkɔbo aduro ne ten.
*The medicine for the dwarf mongoose is one stroke.*
(If you want to get rid of a troublesome person, you should do it hurriedly).

3316. Kɔkɔbo ne akokɔ nni adamfofa.
*The dwarf mongoose and the chicken have no friendship between them.*
(Said of traditional enemies).

3317. Kɔkɔbo se: "Akokɔ, ma yɛnkɔ duaso yi." Akokɔ se: "Me ne wo kɔɔ duaso awia mpo, na menyaa me tiri didii mu, meɛhene na anawdo?"
*The dwarf mongoose says: "Chicken, let us go to the latrine in the evening." The chicken says: "Even if I were to go to the latrine with you in the daytime, it would not be safe, how much less at night?"*
(The animal is know for attacking chickens. Hence: You don't willingly run into danger).

3318. Kɔkɔbo se: ɔnne sika nti na ɔde ne nyansa kyere mmoa weɛ.
*The dwarf mongoose says: it has no money and therefore it uses its intelligence to catch and eat animals.*
(An intelligent person can survive without riches).

3319. Kokobɔne de ne wura kɔ ahemfie na ɔmfa no mma.
*Bad temper takes its owner to the palace (chief's court) but it does not make him return.*
(It does not pay to lose your temper).

3320. Kokobɔne ma ne wura di hia.
*A bad temper makes its owner poor.*

3321. Kokoɔ a ɛse wo sɛ "Kwaha wo ntoma kɔko" no, eno ara na ɛse wo sɛ "Kɔ ma dibem".
*The temper which commands you "Fold your cloth down to go and fight" is the same as the one which tells you: "Go and apologize."*
(The same force which makes you act foolishly, also leads you to repent).

3322. Akokɔduedue se: "Ohiani tena hwerɛmo so a, ɛyɛ no sɛ ɔte akentennwa so".
*The wagtail says: "When a poor man sits on a thorny liana, he feels as if he is sitting on a low chair".*
(A man used to adversity does not fear it).

3323. Akokɔduedue ayirefasɛm yɛkyiri.
*The wagtail denying the charge of adultery is a taboo.*
(The wagtail's movements suggest sexual intercourse.
Hence: If everyone knows you are guilty, it is foolish
to deny it).

3324. Akokɔhwedeɛ da Firaw ho nso ɔdware mfuturo.
*The francolin lives near the Volta River, yet it bathes
in the sand.*
(You may have plenty of something and yet not chose
to use it).

3325. "Akokɔhwedeɛ, gyae pene!" Ɔse: "Ohia ntira!"
*"Francolin, stop worrying!" It says: "It is due to
poverty."*
(A man does not complain without reason).

3326. Akokɔhwedeɛ kɔgye nwa ho abotɔ-ase suman,
na wanhu no sɔre no, ɔde n'adeɛ sane kɔmaa no.
*The francolin went to take a charm for patience from
the snail, but since he could not look after it well, he
took it back to him.*
(If you know you can't cope with a situation, it is no
good pretending to be what you are not).

3327. Akokɔhwedeɛ pensɛmako ɔse: wowɔ ahoɔden a,
na woto nkosua dodoo.
*The busybody bushfowl says: if you have good health,
then you can lay many eggs.*
(With good health you can achieve much).

3328. Akokɔhwedeɛ pensɛmako: "Deɛ ɔreyɛ me te me
nan ase".
*The quarrelsome bushfowl (says): "Someone who is
seeking my downfall, sits at my feet".*
(An enemy inside the family can be a source of constant
suffering, since they are not so easy to deal with as
enemies from outside).

3329. Akokɔhwedeɛ se: adeɛ akye ato ntwɛtwɛdɛ.
*The francolin says: it is daybreak again and it is left
to struggle.*
(Each day brings its battle for existence).

3330. Akokɔhwedeɛ awo auoson-nson, nanso ɔnnya
obi nsoma no, na efiri abawuo.
*The francolin has given birth to seventy seven (chicks),
but she has no one to send on an errand, because of
the death of chicks.*
(You appear to prosper, but the time may come when
misfortune makes you lose all you have gained).

3331. Nkokɔhwedeɛ mmienu nkɔko obi afuo ase.
*Two francolins do not fight together over someone's
farm.*
(Two people should not fight over something they
both steal from).

3332. Kokokyinaka Asamoa, ɔdi ne hene wɔ ne
kwaeɛm.
*Asamoa the blue plantain eater, he is king in his own
forest.*
(Every man is king of his own castle).

3333. Kokokyinaka se: ɔredi n'awereɛhoɔ a, na
Onyankopɔn se wanya ne kyerɛma.
*When the blue plantain eater laments, God Almighty
says he has a drummer.*
(God appreciates the supreme performer. The blue-
plantain eater taught the drummers to drum).

3334. Akokɔ-mmrɛntowa, sradeɛ nni mu.
*An arrogant fowl lacks fat.*
(If you show off you don't prosper).

3335. Akokɔnini a kuntunakuntun-kantann, ɔfiri kosua
mu.
*However great he thinks he is, the cock comes out of
an egg.*
(Everyone starts from small beginnings. A warning
against idle boasts).

3336. Akokɔnini Abankwaa, ne yerenom mpensa-
ahasa, nso ɔdware mfuturo mu.
*The worthy cock has three thousand three hundred
wives, but he bathes in the dust.*
(Good management is one thing and a big family is
another!)

3337. Akokɔnini biara nni hɔ a ne ba di n'akyi.
*There is no such thing as a cock which is followed by
the chicks.*
(A man does not look after his children).

3338. Akokɔnini ho yɛ den a, ɔyɛ no ne mmaa so na
ɛnyɛ onipa so.
*If a cock is strong, he is so for the hens and not for
man.*
(A man's qualities are essentially for his own people
and not for strangers).

3339. Akokɔnini kraa ne obirekuo kraa nsɛ.
*The soul of the cock and the clock bird's differ.*
(People may do the same job but be quite
different. The clock bird is supposed to announce
the hours, just as the cock announces the arrival of
the day).

3340. Akokɔnini nweweɛ yɛ bi nom ani so sɛɛ akɔm.
*The cock's courtship seems to certain people like
fetish possession.*
("Akɔm" refers to the activities of the priest possessed
by his fetish, including, particularly, the twirling dance.
Hence: Appearances can be deceptive).

3341. Akokɔnini pa firi kosua mu.
*Even the greatest cock came from an egg.*
(All men came into the world the same way).

3342. Akokɔnini se: ɔrenni akokɔberee akye nwura ka
mu.
*The cock says: it will not follow the hen for it to lead
him into the drain.*
(There is a point beyond which a man won't go, even
for a woman).

3343. Akokɔnini se: "Ɛkaa ɔtamfoɔ a, anka mabɔn
anadwo na wɔaku me".
*The cock says: "If the enemy had his way, then I should
crow at midnight and be killed".*
(A cock crowing in the middle of the night is a taboo.
Hence: An enemy is always looking for you to make a
slip-up and so get caught).

3344. Akokɔnini se ɔnim adekyeeɛ nanso ne yere na
ɔka kyerɛ no.
*The cock says he knows when it is morning but it is his
wife who tells him so.*
(Indicating the power of women behind the scenes.
Compar 3314).

**3345. Kokoniwa na amma dɔteɛ ansɔ.**
*The sore on the toe did not make the building clay malleable.*
(If work does not go well, it is due to some hinderance).

**3346. Akɔkono de bɛtɛbɛtɛ na ɛwe abɛ.**
*The palm beetle grub eats the palm tree bit by bit.*
(Slow but sure).

**3347. Akɔkono nkɔdi n'ase yere na ɔnnyae, nkɔto ne pa nkyerɛ n'ase no.**
*The palm-beetle grub should not have sex with its in-law's wife and then later on go and shake his waist before his in-law.*
(The insect moves as though having sex. Hence: Don't add insult to injury).

**3348. Akɔkono nua ne asɔmorɔdwe.**
*The palm grub's brother is the beetle.*
(The grub evolves into the beetle, which looks very different. Hence: Appearances may be deceptive. Or: The grub is still the same creature as the beetle. Hence: A man's nature is what is inside him, not his outward appearance).

**3349. Akɔkono se: "Wosɔ me to a, ne wohunu m'asa".**
*The palm beetle grub says: "When you hold my bottom, you see my dance".*
(If you want someone to do his best, give him the necessary support and incentive).

**3350. Kokoɔ a yɛde kɔ ɔko no, yɛmfa nkɔ awareɛ.**
*The temper which we use to go to war, we don't take it to go and marry.*
(Emotions vary according to the needs of the occasion).

**3351. Kokoɔ nnim ne wura ba.**
*Temper does not know his master's child.*
(If you lose your temper you can do anything to anyone).

**3352. Kɔkɔɔ kata mumu so.**
*Red skin covers up ugliness.*
(One good quality makes people forget a blemish).

**3353. Kokora nnim bamfoɔ.**
*The wild yam (Dioscorea minutiflora) does not know the thorny climber.*
(The plants look alike. Hence: People may look alike but not be related in any way).

**3354. Akɔkoraa a wammɔ ne bra yie, na ɔsoa ne kɛntɛn.**
*The old man who has nothing carries his own basket.*
(Keep your friends in life or you may live to regret it).

**3355. Akɔkoraa nua ne dua-wuiɛ.**
*The old man's brother is a dying tree.*
(Death hovers over the old age of man and God's other creations, alike).

**3356. Akɔkoraa to gu a, ɛkɔ ababunu deɛ mu.**
*If an old man throws it away, it goes into the hands of a young man.*
(The strength of the old man is taken up by the young in a family).

**3357. Akɔkoraa wɔ nkwa a, ɔnni mfensa.**
*If an old man has life, he does not stay for three years.*
("Three years" is a conventional way of saying a very long time. Hence: There is a limit to everything).

**3358. Kokoram bu hwene na aprefa nso di ani.**
*Scrofula spoils the nose and pink-eye spoils the eye.*
(Everything is prey to something).

**3359. Kokoram amfɛre wo sɛ ɔbɛtɔ wo hwene so a, woremfɛre sɛ wode ahahan bɛtare ne so.**
*If scrofula does not mind attacking your nose, you do not mind placing a leaf (medicine) on it.*
(If people take undue advantage and act to your detriment, you too take action to protect yourself).

**3360. Kokoram nam wo tiri ho a, na wo hwene na ɔrepɛ.**
*If scrofula walks around your head, it means it is looking for your nose.*
(No one embarks on anything without knowing what their final aim is).

**3361. Kokoramni a ɔregye asekannuro, yɛse "Mentwa hene?" Ɔse "Twa baabiara", na ɛwu a, etwa da etwa so.**
*A man with scrofula who goes to get medicine against knife wounds is asked "Where shall I cut?" He replies "Cut anywhere", because when the wound heals, it will form a scar amongst many.*
(A man with a load of troubles does not worry about one more).

**3362. Kɔkɔsakyi a me yɔnko a; kwakuo a, m'adamfo a.**
*Vulture is my companion; monkey is my friend.*
(I have the support of two people, and so have no problems).

**3363. Kɔkɔsakyi, obi nhunu ne mmrantebɛrɛ mu, nhunu ne nkɔkoraa-bɛrɛ mu.**
*A vulture, no one sees his young days, neither does anyone know his old age.*
(Because a dead vulture is seldom seen people believe that the vulture has medicine for rejuvenation. Hence: Some people never seem to alter).

**3364. Kɔkɔsakyi rebɛdidi a, ɔbisa sumina.**
*If the vulture is going to eat, it consults the rubbish heap.*
(The person who provides for you is the person you consult before acting).

**3365. Kɔkɔsakyi aduasa nkron wɔ hɔ a, nyiyimu biara nni mu.**
*If there are thirty-nine vultures there, there is no difference between them.*
(Human nature is the same everywhere).

**3366. Kɔkɔsakyi reka ɔsoro nsɛm kyerɛ wo a, nnye no akyinnye.**
*If the vulture tells you what is in the air, don't argue with him.*
(Don't argue with the expert).

**3367. Kɔkɔsakyi ɔkrampa, ne din nyɛ dɛ, ne ho nso nyɛ hwam.**
*The vulture's name is not sweet and its body is not sweet-smelling.*
(Said of someone of whom nothing good can be said).

**3368. Kɔkɔsakyi Ampomaa se: sɛ ɔda abusua mu a, anka nyɛ ɛne sɛ otu nkurɔfoɔ funu na odie yi.**
*The vulture Ampomaa says: if he had belonged to a (good) family, then it would not have dug up people's corpses to eat.*
(A poor man has no choice).

**3369. Kɔkɔsakyi mmranteberɛm mpo wannya tirinwi nyɛ ne nkɔkorawaberɛm na ɔbɛnya tirinwi.**
*If the youthful vulture did not grow hair on his head, then it is not now that he is old that he will get it.*
(What the young cannot achieve, nor can the aged).

**3370. Kɔkɔsakyi rempɛ fie aba a, anka ɔrensisi sumina so.**
*If the vulture did not wish to come into the house, it would not stand on the rubbish heap.*
(A person who wants to join a certain group of people keeps as near them as possible).

**3371. Kɔkɔsakyi se: "Mede me kwasea pɛ nyinkyɛre".**
*The vulture says: "I make myself a fool to reach old age".*
(Said by someone who acts foolish to avoid trouble).

**3372. Kɔkɔsakyi se odompɔ ho bɔn.**
*The vulture says the marsh-mongoose stinks!*
(The pot calls the kettle black).

**3373. Kɔkɔsakyi se nnipa tirim yɛ sum nti na ɔto ne nkosua gu onyina nkɔn mu.**
*The vulture says people are wicked and that is why it lays its eggs on the top of the silk-cotton (Bombax buonopozense) tree.*
(Said of, or to, someone who has been persecuted for no reason, to urge they take precautions).

**3374. Kɔkɔsakyi se: sɛ ɔbeba abɛsrɛ wo biribi ade ama wabu no animtia deɛ, ɔbɛdidi sumina so.**
*The vulture says: rather than having to beg you for anything to eat and to be ridiculed, he will eat on the midden.*
(It is better to be poor than to be despised).

**3375. Kokotako Kɔtɛmbrantɛm Yirikayiri. Ɔbarima rebɛwu a, na ne yere suro.**
*Parasite, Go-quickly-come-quickly, Frightening fellow. If a man is going to die, than his wife is afraid.*
(The first part of the proverb is repeated by two people in alternation. The point is in the last phrase. At certain times we become afraid of those we are close to).

**3376. Kɔkɔte Asamoa se: "Wonni yɔnkoɔ a, wode wo mma yɛ yɔnkoɔ".**
*The bush pig Asamoa says: "If you have no companions, you make companions of your children".*
(If you have children, you are never without company).

**3377. Kokotiako a ɔte Bɛkwae, ɔrensom ɔhene, obi a ɔbɛsom ɔhene nso ɔmma no nsom no.**
*"Invincible" from Bekwai does not serve the chief, and also the person who will serve the chief he does not let him serve.*
(There was once a lazy drunkard at Bekwai whom people feared and who was so abusive that he drove others away from serving the Chief, so that the Bekwaihene was left without service. Hence: A dog in the manger destroy's other people's opportunities).

**3378. Kokurobotie nnye asra kwa.**
*The thumb does not receive snuff for nothing.*
(There is a reason for every action).

**3379. Okokuroko gyina akono no, na biribi hyɛ ne mfono mu.**
*(When) a warrior stands at the war front, there is something in his cheeks.*
(An experienced person knows how to provide for himself).

**3380. Wokɔkyere obirebe ba fie na wowɔ bayerɛ fufuo ma no, ma ɔdi a, ɔne dwuma aba.**
*If you ask the grey plantain eater to come to the house and you are pounding fufu and give it some, and it eats it, it defecates the seeds of the trumpet tree.*
(This bird eats the seeds of the trumpet-tree. A man does not change his nature according to how you treat him).

**3381. Akɔm nhyɛaseɛ ne adammɔ.**
*The beginning of fetish possession is madness.*
("Akɔm" refers to the activities of the priest possessed by his fetish, including, particularly, the twirling dance. Hence: There is method in some people's madness).

**3382. Akɔm kɔ, aka ntwaho.**
*Being possessed goes, twirling around is left.*
(See Proverb 3381. One of the activities of the priest possessed by his fetish, is the twirling dance. Hence: Sometimes we must make do with second-best).

**3383. Akɔm mu abrebrekuro pam akɔmfoo-ninko.**
*Knocking against sores during possession drives away the good fetish priest.*
(See Proverb 3381. If you continually harass someone, they desert you).

**3384. Akɔm ne nkyerɛmu.**
*Prophesy (lit. possession) amounts to explanation.*
(See Proverb 3381. In this context, it is the predictions that priests make with their second sight that is most relevant. Hence: What has been said enables one to have an insight into the situation).

**3385. Akɔm nyansa bi ne "Mekɔm odwan-funu ti".**
*Some of possession's wisdom is: "I foretell a dead sheep's head".*
(See Proverb 3381. This expression was once used by a fetish priest to tell that the Asantehene was dead. To reveal the plain truth would have been taboo, so he put it that he was working to protect a dead sheep. Hence: A wise man speaks in proverbs).

**3386. Akɔm nyansa na ɛwɔ ɔbaakofoɔ ani so, na ɛnyɛ asɛm nyansa.**
*The wisdom of possession is on one person but not wisdom of solving problems.*
(See Proverb 3381. Some talents are restricted, others are universal).

**3387. Akɔm yɛ asisie a, ɛfiri Ɔkɔmfo [Anɔkye]/[Frempɔn Manso] berɛ so.**
*If the administration of possession was a fraud it was so from the time of the great priest [Anɔkye]/[Frempɔn Manso].*
(See Proverb 3381. Fraud is not the possession of one generation alone. Or: Customs can be bad even if they have been held for many generations).

**3388. Akɔm nyɛ; Krakye Dɛnte nyɛ.**
*(If) possession is no good, neither is the Krakye Dɛnte fetish.*
(See Proverb 3381. Krakye Dɛnte is a major Asante shrine. Hence: If something is bad, then the source of it must be bad too).

**3389. Ɛkɔm ba a, na yɛhunu deɛ ɔwɔ aduane.**
*If famine comes, then we see who has food.*
(In time of real trouble, we can recognize those who have the means to survive).

**3390. Ɛkɔm aba na sɛ worekɔsrɛ borɔdeɛ bɛtem na yɛma wo duro a, na yɛaku wo.**
*If hunger comes and you ask for one plantain and they give you a bunch, it kills you.*
(If someone gives you a very generous gift you say; "you are killing me", meaning I can never thank you enough. Hence: Killing with too much kindness).

**3391. Ɛkɔm ba a, na anene di aburow.**
*If hunger comes, the crow eats corn.*
(Hunger makes a man change his habits).

**3392. Ɛkɔm de aberewa a, ɔsu ne nana.**
*If the old woman is hungry, she demands on the behalf of her grandchildren.*
(People are often ashamed to ask for themselves and will pretend to ask for others).

**3393. Ɛkɔm de akɔdaa a, na ɔsu.**
*If a child becomes hungry, it weeps.*
(Deprivation makes you emotional).

**3394. Ɛkɔm de akura a, ɔsu pɛ aduane na ɔnsu mpɛ mma.**
*If the mouse is hungry, it cries for food and not children.*
(First needs should be satisfied first, the rest can wait).

**3395. Ɛkɔm de ɔhɔhoo a, ɔda; na odidi mee a, wabisabisa nkurɔfoɔ yerenom nsɛm.**
*If a stranger is hungry, he sleeps; but if he is full, he tries to find out about the wives of the townspeople.*
(If you are well off, you indulge yourself).

**3396. Ɛkɔm de ɔhɔhoo a, ɔdefiri ne kurom.**
*When a stranger is hungry, he brought it from his own town.*
(If a man is poor it is because of his origins).

**3397. Ɛkɔm de ɔsebɔ a, ɔmfɛre aboa biara.**
*If it is hungry, a leopard is not shy of catching any animal.*
(In time of need even a powerful man will eat anything).

**3398. Ɛkɔm de wo a, ɛde wo nko.**
*If you are hungry, it is only you who feel it.*
(You alone have to bear your own suffering).

**3399. Ɛkɔm de wo a, womfa wo nsa mmienu nnidi.**
*Just because you are hungry, you don't eat with both hands.*
(Be content with what you actually need and don't be over-greedy).

**3400. Ɛkɔm ma onipa ani bere.**
*Hunger makes people angry.*
(In times of real need people react violently out of frustration).

**3401. Ɛkɔm ne ka: fanyinam ka.**
*Hunger and debt: debt is preferable.*
(It is better to owe than to suffer).

**3402. Ɛkɔm-pa nko na sukɔm nko.**
*Real hunger is one thing and thirst is another.*
(No two things, even forms of suffering, are alike).

**3403. "Komm" nua ne "foo".**
*Calm's brother is silence.*
(Birds of a feather flock together).

**3404. Wokɔma odompo akye a, hwɛ deɛ ɔsam.**
*If you go and say good-morning to the marsh mongoose, note where he lurks.*
(You can judge a person from his circumstances).

**3405. Kɔmabɔne kum owura.**
*Bad temper kills its possessor.*

**3406. Akɔmboafoɔ yɛ na.**
*Assistant priests are rare.*
(Efficient helpers are difficult to find).

**3407. Akɔmfɛm di aponkyerɛne akyi a, ɔbɛdi no kɔm.**
*If a guinea fowl chases a frog, it will only become hungrier.*
(It cannot swallow it. Hence: Don't waste time in chasing after unprofitable things).

**3408. Nkomena mu na sika hyɛ.**
*Inside a mine is where gold is found*
(You must seek for a thing in the proper place).

**3409. Komfoɔ a ɔkaa se osuo bɛtɔ na osuo antɔ, ne deɛ ɔkaa sɛ osuo rentɔ na osuo tɔeɛ; wɔn nyinaa yɛ adɔmfo-torofoɔ.**
*The priest who predicted that it would rain and it did not rain, and he who said that the rain would not fall, but it fell; both are lying priests.*
(All liars are equally bad).

**3410. Kɔmfoɔ ba wu a, yɛse wafom bosom.**
*If the priest's child dies, we say the priest has offended the fetish.*
(You claim to have the ability to solve problems for others, but you can't solve your own).

**3411. Kɔmfoɔ ba yare a, ɔnkyɛre wu.**
*When a priest's child is ill, it dies quickly.*
(Physician heal thyself).

**3412. Kɔmfoɔ aboadeɛ na ɛkaa ka mu; na ne ntoaseɛ deɛ ɔgyae ansa na deɛ ɛbɛ ba rebu.**
*A fetish-priest's promised reward was left unpaid; but at least he retained the deposit he collected before his failure.*
(even if you fail at your job, at least you get something for trying).

**3413. Kɔmfoɔ anna a, na ɔhunu akɔm.**
*When a priest does not sleep, he becomes proficient (lit. he sees possession).*
(An assiduous worker becomes proficient).

3414. Komfoɔ de ne ti pem dua so a, na ɛyɛ sikanibereɛ ntira.
*The priest who hits his head against a tree does so out of lust for money.*
(People will do anything for money).

3415. Komfoɔ dwa deɛ ɔni no.
*The fetish priest shakes hands with the one he knows very well.*
(People in high places tend to practice nepotism).

3416. Komfoɔ Dwamena ankɔgye ntakuo mmiɛnsa a, anka Kwabena Tenten ankɔforo bofunu ante antɔ.
*If the priest Dwamena had not gone to collect three five pesewa pieces, then Kwabena Tenten would not have gone to climb, and have fallen down.*
(If someone had not commissioned a job, then the person performing it would not have suffered).

3417. Komfoɔ Adwoa kɔ akɔm na wanya biribi a, n'atikopuaa deɛ yɛnti ho.
*Adwoa the priestess, if she goes to be possessed and does not get anything, her hair-do is never interfered with.*
(If you do not succeed in a venture, at least your life is safe).

3418. Komfoɔ gyimi a, na ne bosom nso gyimi.
*If the fetish priest becomes stupid, so does his fetish.*
(A man is judged by the actions of his servants).

3419. Komfoɔ ka nim na ɔnka ntwo.
*The fetish priest says something to get fame, but he doesn't say it to get disgrace.*
(We act for profit not for loss).

3420. Komfoɔ kɔm kuro ti kwa; kuro wura wo hɔ.
*A fetish priest gets possessed and foresees the fate of the town; the town's owner is (still) there.*
(You may be respected in a place but not necessarily be the top man).

3421. Ɔkomfoɔ akɔm te kɔ a, na ato nyansakɔm.
*If the fetish priest loses his power, then he begins to rely on his imagination.*
(If you don't have the real thing, you pretend you have).

3422. Komfoɔ kɔm wo a, wokɔm wo ho bi.
*If the priest prophesies to you, you prophesy to yourself also.*
(If you find something working against you, you must find your own way out of the situation).

3423. Komfo Anɔkye boaa Ɔseɛ Tutu no, aboadeɛ na ɔgyeeɛ na wannye Asanteman.
*When Komfo Anɔkye came to help (Asantehene) Osei Tutu, he collected his fees, but he did not collect the Asante nation.*
(If I am helping you, it does not mean I should make a slave of you).

3424. Komfo Anɔkye de mpaboa foro onyina.
*Kɔmfo Anɔkye climbed the silk-cotton (Bombax buonopozense) tree with sandals.*
(There is a story of how the famous priest climbed a tree at Agona and left the imprint of his sandals on it. Hence: To a remarkable person, anything is possible).

3425. Komfoɔ annya sunkwani a, ɔbrɛ.
*If a fetish priest does not get fetish servants, he becomes helpless.*
(There are some things which you cannot do without aid).

3426. Komfoɔ se gyedua a ɛsi abɔnten mmu a, ɔbɛkyerɛ deɛ ɔbɛkɔm aseɛ.
*If the fetish priest prophesies that the nim tree will fall, then he will tell which one he will practice under.*
(Some people wish for bad times to profit from them but in the long run it will make them, themselves, suffer).

3427. Komfoɔ se ɔsrɛ Onyame sɛ ɔmmoa no akɔm.
*The priest says he is praying to God to help him in his possession.*
(With God's help, anything is possible).

3428. Komfoɔ nsuro anisobirie.
*A fetish priest does not fear giddiness.*
(Priests spin when they dance. Hence: You don't fear what your training has accustomed you to).

3429. Komfoɔ nni nkɔntorɔ mma yɛntwa ɔbosonsoafoɔ ti.
*The priest does not give false predictions for you to cut off the head of the fetish carrier.*
(You don't punish a slave for his master's mistakes).

3430. Akɔmfoɔ aduasa hwɛ oyarefoɔ a, wɔdi kɔntorɔ.
*When thirty fetish priests look after a sick man, they are lying.*
(If you depend on too many people, you are bound to get some bad advice).

3431. Komfo-barima nhunu biribi a, ɔmfa ne tiri mpem dan mu.
*If a powerful priest has not foreseen something, he does not knock his head against a wall.*
(You don't punish yourself for no reason).

3432. Komfo-barima se ɔbɛsɛn wiem wɔ afigya a, ma ɔnnsɛn fie mma yɛnhwɛ.
*If the powerful priest says he will hang in the sky outside the home, let him hang in the house to let us see.*
(If you want to do something spectacular in public, practice at home first).

3433. Komfo-bɔne a watena yarefoɔ ho ama komfo-pa abɛto no, ayɛ bi.
*The bad priest who cared for a sick man until the good priest came has also done well.*
(Anyone who has been able to help, even in a small way, should be congratulated).

3434. Komfo-bɔne kyerɛ mmusuo a, yɛde n'akokɔ na ɛyie.
*When a bad fetish priest points out a taboo, we sacrifice his chicken.*
(If you cheat, you will pay for it in the end).

3435. Komfo-bɔne se ɔman bɛbɔ a, ɔte mu bi.
*If a bad priest says the state will be destroyed, he is among its people.*
(If you endanger your community, you endanger yourself).

**3436. Kɔmfo-daban a ɔkɔm wiem tumi kɔm fam.**
*A fetish priest who dances and is possessed from above can also be possessed from below.*
(A good priest can foresee the future–with help from the fetish "above"–but he can even more easily tell what is going on in his community, and thus "prophesy" based on his own knowledge of what is going on here "below". Hence: If you can do something difficult, you can also do something easier).

**3437. Kɔmfo-daban hyɛ nkɔm a, mfeɛ mmiɛnsa na ɛba mu.**
*If a fetish priest who dances, foretells something, it takes three years before it materializes.*
(Even if you have to wait a long time, the truth will out).

**3438. Kɔmfoɔ-Ninko mmrɛeɛ a, bɛhwɛadefoɔ nse sɛ wɔaberɛ.**
*If a powerful fetish priest is not tired out, onlookers should not say that they are exhausted.*
(If a heavy worker is not tired nor should the onlooker be).

**3439. Kɔmfo-pa biara nnyaa nim ne kurom da.**
*No good priest has ever been famous in his own town.*
(A prophet is not without honour save in his own land).

**3440. Akɔmfo-twene, woworo no woro no a, deɛ ɛka ara ne sɛ: "Ɛwɔ do wɔdo, wɔde bɛba".**
*The fetish drum, if you beat it and beat it, what it says in the end is: "It is there, it is there they will bring it".*
(If you are efficient, in the end people will patronize you).

**3441. Nkɔmmɔ a ɛyɛ dɛ sene sika domma.**
*Interesting conversation is worth more than riches (lit. a domma of gold dust).*
(Good conversation is priceless).

**3442. Nkɔmmo tenten ma asɛm ani te yera.**
*Lengthy conversation leads to losing the thread of the argument.*

**3443. Wo nkɔmmoa yɛ den a, wonhwere abisafoɔ.**
*If you are successful as a consultant, you don't lose your clients.*

**3444. Nkɔmmodie bebrebe ma onipa yera.**
*Too much gossiping makes a man become lost.*
(If you are too talkative, you don't pay attention to what you are doing).

**3445. Wo nkɔmmɔdifoɔ ho yɛ so ahi a, na wose: "Menni adaagye".**
*If you don't want to take notice of a gossip, then you say: "I have no time to spare".*

**3446. Wo kɔn yɛ tiatia a, wokɔfa saworowa nto mu?**
*If you have a short neck, do you wear a long cowrie necklace?*
(It is no good acquiring what you are not equipped to use).

**3447. Akɔneaba ne anwono.**
*Going and coming is the way to weave.*
(It is by hard work that we achieve success).

**3448. Nkɔnkɔnsa bare kuro hyia a, na ano adwo.**
*If treachery encircles the town, then it loses power.*
(Traitors destroy a state).

**3449. Kɔnkɔnsani ho yɛ hu sene aboa ɔwɔ.**
*The treacherous person is more terrible than a snake.*

**3450. Kɔnkɔnsani ankɔ ɔko a, ɔdɔmmarima nkɔ ntɔ.**
*If a treacherous man does not go to war, a great warrior does not fall.*
(Where there is no treachery, there is no defeat).

**3451. Kɔnkɔnsani apakyie, yɛde nnabraba na ɛbue.**
*The treacherous man's gourd, we use cunning to open it.*
(If a man is known to be tricky, be careful whenever you have dealings with him).

**3452. Kɔnkɔnsani repɛ ɔhene adi na wannya anni a, ɔsuae ɔman fidie.**
*If a treacherous person wants to become a chief and he is unable to do so, he sets a trap against the state.*
(An unsuccessful contender for power causes trouble).

**3453. Kɔnkɔnsani tena kurom a, kuro bɔ.**
*If a treacherous person stays in the town, the town spoils.*
(One man can spoil a community).

**3454. Ɔkɔnkɔnsani ntoma nyɛɛ mmienu da.**
*A treacherous person never has two cloths.*
(If you make yourself unpopular, you don't thrive).

**3455. Konkontimaa Gyesi Apere nya wuo a, na ɛfiri adwene.**
*When the tadpole Gyesi Apere dies, the fish must be the cause of that.*
(If you mix with a crowd you will be treated as one of them. The tadpole is eaten by larger fish which are its natural enemies so the proverb could also refer to when a powerful man destroys an insignificant one).

**3456. Konkontimaa se: anka ɔyɛ ahwedeɛ na din pa na wannya.**
*The tadpole says: formerly he was a fish but he could not get a good name.*
(A person would have done better were it not for unfavorable circumstances).

**3457. Akonkuromfi ani soso sene no a, na ɔyɛ ɔmumu.**
*If the eyes of the preying mantis are bigger than his body, then it becomes ugly.*
(The mantis has prominent eyes which are very noticeable when it turns its head from side to side. Pride is degrading).

**3458. Akonkuromfi se ɔbɛforo boɔ a, ɔne ne sɛkyerɛampɔmfi.**
*The preying mantis says he can climb stones, then he does so with his own help (lit. with his preying mantis).*
(Sɛkyerɛampɔmfi is another name for the mantis. Hence: You need to be self-sufficient).

**3459. Akonkuromfi yɛɛ ɔbrane a, anka ɔnnyae tɔkwako da.**
*If the mantis had been a giant, then it would never have stopped fighting.*

(The mantis will attack most other insects with a view to consuming them. Hence: Said of a small but aggressive person).

### 3460. Akɔnnɔ bɛkum hiani.
*Longing will kill the poor man.*
(A poor man's dreams can never be satisfied).

### 3461. Akonnwa nyɛ babaa yantarie yɛatena so mmienu.
*A stool is not a log that two people can sit on side by side.*
(You cannot share leadership).

### 3462. Akonnwa fufuo, yɛntena so kwa.
*A white stool, we don't sit on it for nothing.*
(You cannot be installed on a white stool unless you are qualified to be so. You are not given privileges unless people think you are worthy of them).

### 3463. W'akonnwaboaa mpo to wo so a, woyi w'ano.
*If even the creature in the stool accuses you, you defend yourself.*
(Even if someone whose evidence is authentic accuses you, you must put up a defense).

### 3464. W'akonnwaboaa se woata a, wonnye no akyinnye.
*If the creature in the stool says you passed wind, you don't argue with it.*
(If a person who knows everything about you says something about you, you don't deny it).

### 3465. Wokono ɔdeɛ gya ɔpanin a, ɛkɔ asam.
*If you by-pass an elder in placing the yam where it will best germinate, it will go bad.*
(You cannot do without an elder's advice).

### 3466. Nkonsa asomfo koraa yɛwo wɔn.
*The unimportant people who serve in the palace, we give birth to them.*
(Some experiences are common to all).

### 3467. W'akonta ne wo ka a, na ɛfiri ɛka a wonne no ntira.
*If you and your brother-in-law are intimate, then it is because you don't owe him anything.*
(Debts make enemies).

### 3468. Nkonta pan a, na agorɔ agu.
*If the drum sticks break, the playing finishes.*
(If your tools spoil, you can no longer perform your task).

### 3469. Kontihene mpere ɔmanhene.
*The Kontihene does not struggle to become a paramount chief.*
(The Kontihene is the chief next to the paramount chief and deals with the youth and the common people. Hence: Everyone has his own sphere of influence).

### 3470. Kontire ne Akwamu kum adowa a, ɛwɔdeɛ ɔmee mu.
*If the Kontire and Akwamu chiefs kill the antelope, there is one who was satisfied (by the meat).*
(These chiefs were commander and second-in-command of the Asante armies when the chief himself was not there. The antelope is small. Hence: Even in a bad situation, someone is satisfied).

### 3471. Kɔntoa na ɔpɛ na homa hyɛ ne kɔn.
*The gourd has a string round its neck because it wants it so.*
(Said when someone is oppressed or overworked because they are willing to be treated badly).

### 3472. Kɔntoa mpɛ ahohoahoa nti na ɔsen dɔtɔ mu.
*Because the gourd does not like ostentation it hangs in the thicket.*
(Said of a modest person).

### 3473. Nkontompo bare hyia kuro a, na sennifoɔ to ate.
*If lying goes right round a town, then the liar is found out.*
(Dishonesty shows itself up in time).

### 3474. Nkontompo bunkum nokorɛ so.
*Falsehood overshadows the truth.*
(Lies go further than the truth).

### 3475. Nkontompo na ɛma nokorɛ boɔ yɛ den.
*Falsehood makes the price of truth high.*
(We value what is made rare by its opposite).

### 3476. Nkontompo ne berɛ na ɛnam.
*Falsehood and fatigue go together.*
(It becomes exhausting keeping up the process of lying).

### 3477. Nkontompo ne nnabraba hia a, na abea.
*If falsehood and double-dealing meet, it is difficult to judge between them.*
(It is difficult to compare the merits of two equally bad things).

### 3478. Nkontompo asa a, na ɛnyɛ "gyina hɔ na mereba a".
*Even if lies are finished, that does not include "just wait here and I'll be back".*
(The dishonest will always find excuses).

### 3479. Nkontompo ne nnabraba sɛe ɔman.
*Treachery and double-dealing spoil the state.*

### 3480. Nkontompo, yɛntwa no kwa.
*We do not tell lies for no reason.*

### 3481. Okontomponi bɔ birim daa.
*A liar is always starting.*
(A dishonest man is a nervous man).

### 3482. Okontomponi dan, yɛpa so, na yɛnhye ho.
*A liar's house, we deroof it, we don't burn it down.*
(The best way of punishing a deceitful man is to bring his deceit into the open).

### 3483. Okontomponi ma yɛkum ɔnokwafoɔ, nanso nokorɛ da adi da bi.
*A liar makes us kill a trustworthy man, but truth will inherit one day.*

### 3484. Okontomponi na ɔse: "Me danseni wɔ akyirikyiri".
*A liar says: "My witness is in a far country".*

### 3485. Okontomponi se ɔne wo bɛforo duna a, ma ɔnni kan na di n'akyi.
*If a liar says he and you will climb a tree, let him go first and you follow after.*
(Never turn your back on a treacherous man).

**3486. Okontomponi se wo sɛ "Hwɛ soro" a, wohwɛ fam.**
*If a liar tells you: "Look up", you look down.*
(You don't trust the instructions of a liar).

**3487. Kontromfi a ɔsi boɔ soɔ na aboa kɛseɛ su a, ɔka sɛ "ooh hoo".**
*The baboon that sits on the top of a rock, when the lion (lit. great animal) roars, he says "ooh hoo".*
(You can afford to answer back when out of reach of a powerful man).

**3488. Kontromfi kɔ apam a, ɔno ara na ɔnim deɛ ɔpam kɔso.**
*If the baboon goes to clear the bush, he knows up to where he has to work.*
(An expert knows what he is after).

**3489. Kontromfi akɔkorawa na ɔware kontromfi aberewa.**
*The ancient baboon marries the old lady baboon.*
(Like seeks out like).

**3490. Kontromfi kyea sɛdeɛ akyeamfoɔ kyea, nanso ne to kɔɔ.**
*Even if the baboon walks with a linguist's gait, his bottom is red.*
(A linguist is an important figure at court and walks in a dignified manner. Hence: You cannot hide your true character).

**3491. Kontromfi na kunasuman fata ne nsa, nso kwafea na ne yere awuo.**
*The bracelet charm fits the baboon's wrist but it is the red monkey's wife who died.*
(A thing belongs to the person who has a right to it, not to the one who would like it most).

**3492. Kontromfi se: "Ɔbrane wu ne koko".**
*The baboon says: "The brave man dies because of his boldness".*

**3493. Kontromfi se ɔde ne ho rekɔtwitwiri esie na ɔne ɔfrote ayɛ pɛ, nanso ɔyɛ kwa.**
*The baboon says it is going to rub itself against the anthill so that it will be like the kob, but it will come to nothing.*
(You cannot change your essential nature by wishful thinking or by imitating someone else's behavior).

**3494. Kontromfi se: "Afei ne ampa".**
*The baboon says: "The game is on".*
(Now I shall really reveal the truth. Said when the climax of a situation is reached).

**3495. Kontromfi se: "Ohia na ɛma akyenfoɔ ka ɛha mu".**
*The baboon says: "Poverty is what makes a distinguished person stay in the forest".*
(Full many a flower is born to blush unseen).

**3496. Kontromfi se: "Wohyɛ m'afonom a, na mɛnya asɛmpa maka makyerɛ woɔ".**
*The baboon says: "If you fill my cheeks with food, I shall reveal the truth and tell it to you".*
(Said when people ask for money before doing a favor).

**3497. Kontromfi se: "Me suman ne m'ani".**
*The baboon says: "My amulet is my eyes".*

(Said by someone who wants to see something physically before believing).

**3498. Kontromfi se: "Yɛturu ɔba wɔ yɛn anim na yɛnturu no wɔ yɛn akyi".**
*The baboon says: "We carry our young in front of us and not on our backs."*
(Everyone believes their own customs to be the best).

**3499. Kontromfi ntoma atete a, n'akyea deɛ ɛwɔ hɔ daa.**
*If the baboon's cloth is torn, its gait is there always.*
(The baboon is supposed to have a particularly stylish gait. Hence: Everyone has something to be proud of).

**3500. Ɛkoɔ de aniberɛ na ɛkyere bɔfoɔ.**
*The bush cow kills the hunter out of rage.*
(If you do not annoy a person, he will not harm you).

**3501. Ɛkoɔ kum Nkranni a, merenkɔ n'ayie; na Nkranni kum ɛkoɔ a, merenwe ne nam.**
*If the bush cow kills an Accra man, I won't go to his funeral; and if the Accra man kills a bush cow, I won't eat it.*
(The quarrel is a real one).

**3502. Ɛkoɔ pusupusu nunum a, na ɔte ne hua.**
*If the bush cow shakes the (aromatic) onunum plant, then it smells its scent.*
(You need to disturb something to know its real nature).

**3503. Ɛkoɔ se: ɛsono nni man mu a, anka ɔyɛ bɔpɔn.**
*The bush cow says: if the elephant is not around, he is the great creature.*
(If a more important man were not around, then I would be the greatest!)

**3504. Kooko kyɛre pata so a, ɛgyae hene yɛ.**
*The riverside cocoyam, if it is kept in the roof beams long, loses its ability to make you itch.*
(The fresh skin of the cocoyam causes skin irritation, but after a period it becomes harmless. Hence: If a man holds a position of responsibility for a long time, he tends to become less strict in his discipline).

**3505. Kookoohene se ɔsene wo a, ɔsene wo wɔ kookoberɛ, na ɔnsense wo fupɛberɛ.**
*If the Cocoa king says he is greater than you, he is greater than you in the cocoa season, but he is not greater than you in the off-season.*
(Cocoa is a seasonal crop and brings in money twice a year. At those times farmers can afford extravagance. In the off-season they may be poor. Fupɛberɛ is the season between the rainy and the dry seasons. Hence: Your position depends on achievements over the years, not on "quick come, quick go" money).

**3506. Kooko nyɛ aduane bi na yɛabɔ ne din akɔ atɔ.**
*Cocoyam which grows by water is not such a food that we should think of it to buy.*
(A worthless thing does not occupy the mind).

**3507. Kookoase bayerɛ, yɛde ne soɔ na ɛhunu ne bɔ.**
*Yam beneath the cocoa trees, we consider its blooms to see if it is mature.*
(When a girl reaches puberty you know she is ready to have children).

**3508. Kookoo mmaeɛ a na akuafoɔ yɛ ahobrɛaseɛ adie.**
*It is when the cocoa has not come (i.e. in the off-season) that the farmers become humble.*
(The poor cannot afford to be haughty. See Proverb 3505).

**3509. Kookootonturawa ɔse "Oho!"**
*An empty cocoa pod says: "I don't care!"*
(A person who has nothing to lose does not care what he does or says).

**3510. "Merekɔpɛ biribi abɛdi", ne "Mebɛyɛɛ deɛn?" na ɛnam.**
*"I am going to look for something to eat", goes with "What did I come here for?"*
(If circumstances force you to go into the forest on a forbidden day (daabɔne), you might see something terrible to make you regret your action. Need forces a man to do many unwise things).

**3511. Worekɔpɛ Ɔnyame ahwɛ na wohyia Oburoni a, na woasan.**
*If you wish to see God and you meet a European, you return.*
(Europeans are expected to be able to achieve almost anything. If you find someone to help you, you stop asking God for help).

**3512. Wokora obi sika a, wotete wo ntoma.**
*If you keep someone's money, you tear your cloth.*
(Money used to be tied up in the corner of a cloth. There is no profit in caring for what is not yours).

**3513. Koraa a abɔ nsa nsa.**
*A calabash that is cracked can't collect palm wine.*
(If you are sick, you can't work properly).

**3514. Koraa a ɛda nsuo mu nsuro awɔ.**
*The calabash lying in the water, does not fear the cold.*
(If you are already in trouble, you don't fear it).

**3515. Koraakurafoɔ nhwere nsa.**
*A calabash holder is not deprived of drink.*
(If you are prepared, you get what you want).

**3516. Akoraboɔ nnim ɔmanni.**
*Bullets don't recognize comrades.*
(Shoot carefully. Be sure your violent action does not damage your fellow citizens).

**3517. Korafoɔ fufuo nsɔ wɔ korafoɔ ani so da.**
*A co-wife always criticizes another wife's fufuo.*
(You criticize the work of those you are jealous of).

**3518. Korafoɔ te wo ho asɛm a, ɔsi no atofo.**
*If a co-wife hears something about another, she carries it on her bustle (i.e. she carries it around like a child).*
(Women sometimes wear their cloth in a kind of roll-a bustle-at the back where they may keep their money and other valuables, and on which it is easy to carry a child. Hence: We spread and elaborate stories against those we don't like).

**3519. Korankyewa abɛ: wɔn ara nu na wɔn ara ayɛ.**
*Korankyewa's palm tree: they cut nuts and prepare them themselves.*
(You know how to use your own things best).

**3520. Ɔkoreɛ se: anisodeɛ na wɔhunu na ɔnnim adwene mu asɛm.**
*The eagle says: he has a wide vision but he does not know matters of the mind.*
(You can judge what you see but not what is in the mind of man).

**3521. Korɔboni baa nnwane nkɔ bata nkɔka batam kwa.**
*A Krobo woman does not normally travel to trade and remain there for no reason.*
(Because of strict puberty rites, some Krobo women leave the area young, because they have already had sexual relations and are afraid of being shamed. People who stay from home and endure hardship do so out of necessity).

**3522. "Korɔdɔ-Korɔdo" nyinaa si asɛm so.**
*It may seem to you double Dutch, but it is very much to the point.*
(Some people appear to speak rubbish but it is sometimes very much to the point).

**3523. Wokorɔkorɔ aboa no bebrebe a, wodi nkosua hunu.**
*If you are too kind to an animal, you eat plain eggs.*
(If you are to soft-hearted you have to do without things).

**3524. Akorɔkorɔ na yɛde gye ɔdamfoɔ nsam adeɛ.**
*It is through coaxing that we are able to get something from a madman.*
(Tact is the best way of obtaining something from a difficult person).

**3525. Akorɔma fa me fa, na ɔdidi a, menni bi.**
*The hawk takes my half, but when it eats, I don't get anything.*
(A mean or grasping person takes but does not give).

**3526. Akorɔma se: "Fakɔntɛm adeɛ biara yɛ akorɔneɛ".**
*The hawk says: "Every take-it-away-quickly is stealing".*
(If you act suspiciously, you will be suspected).

**3527. Ɔkorɔmfoɔ wia ɔkorɔmfoɔ adeɛ a, Onyankopɔn sere.**
*If a thief steals from a thief, God smiles.*
(No one minds if a bad man is paid in his own coin. God likes to see justice done).

**3528. Ɔkorɔmfoɔ wu a, na ne nsa na aku no.**
*If a thief dies, it is his own hand that killed him.*
(He who lives by the sword shall die by the sword).

**3529. Korɔmante Agyinamoa, woretu ne fo no, na ne dua da Kramfoa bɛdɛ mu.**
*While you advise the cat of Koromantin, its tail lies in Kramfoa's palm basket.*
(Kramfoa was an important Chief who did not take advice and lost his life for this reason. The proverb is used of people who will not take advice).

**3530. Korɔnobɔ na ɛyɛ aniwuo na nyɛ ohia.**
*Stealing is shameful but not poverty.*

**3531. Ɔkoropatuo ani soso nanso, nyɛ nnoɔma nyinaa na ɔde hunu.**
*The eagle-owl's eyes are big, but it is not everything that it is able to see.*
(However talented you are, there are still things you cannot do).

3532. Ɔkoropatuo se: nyɛ afei na ɔrekɔ gye ahoɔdennuro de manso abɛto ɛfie.
*The eagle-owl says: it is not now that it is going to collect power-medicine for litigation to come to its home.*
(Power-medicine builds your strength, which suggests you are preparing for a struggle. Hence: If you want peace, don't initiate trouble).

3533. Ɔkoropatuo se: ɛnyɛ sɛ ahoɔden na ɔnni na mmom anuadɔ na ɛyɛ no nti na nnomaa tu gu ne so da biara no.
*The eagle-owl says: it is not because of the strength that it lacks but because of its benevolence that the birds fly after it every day.*
(Some people mistake the benevolence of others for weakness).

3534. Ɔkoropatuo asisi ne ti ase ama ɔkoropɔn agye ne nsam hene adi.
*The eagle-owl bows his head for the eagle to destool him.*
(Said when a man is succeeded by one stronger than himself).

3535. Kɔsankɔbi, yɛhyɛ no ma ɔkɔsoa atuduru.
*A man who fears war is made to carry gunpowder to the battle.*
(If you try and avoid trouble, you often find yourself in the thick of it).

3536. Kosɛ nkum kuro, nanso ɛdwodwo yea ano.
*Pity does not cure a sore, but it cools it down.*
(Sympathy is no cure, but it helps).

3537. Ɔkɔse-ayie na ɔma wɔkum bayifoɔ.
*A funeral announcer causes them to kill a witch.*
(One action unwittingly leads to another person's suffering).

3538. Yɛrekɔsene, wodi mu a, yɛde bɔ wo mmrane a, na wompɛ?
*When we are going to carve it, you are with us, then if we are drumming your appellations, you do not like it?*
(If you involve yourself with something, then you can't avoid what comes out of it).

3539. "Kɔsi" a nkɔsi; "Kɔda" a nkɔda.
*"Sit awake" does not sit awake, "Go and sleep" does not go and sleep.*
(Said of a person who does not react to any command).

3540. Ɔkɔsoa nisuo Animanam: "Mehunu a, mɛka, nti deɛ ɛni me soɔ, wɔde ma me."
*The carrier of fetish water Ignorant-of-criticism: "Because, if I see it, I say it, even what I am not responsible for, they hold me responsible for" (lit. they give it to me).*
(People who point out others' faults are likely to be criticized themselves).

3541. Worekɔsrɛ obi ntwoma a, hwɛ ne bamma ho.
*If you are going to ask someone for red clay, look at his swish seat.*
(If someone does not use something himself he is unlikely to be able to help you. In this case red clay is used to put a polish on the floors and seats in a house).

3542. Kosua bɔne baako sɛɛ nkosua pem.
*One bad egg spoils a thousand eggs.*
(One bad person can corrupt many).

3543. Kosua mpo nnwanam sɔ ho.
*Even the egg has its extras.*
(Whatever you do, you get some extraneous benefits from it).

3544. Kosua se: "Mete sɛ tumi, womia me a mebɔ, wogyae me mu a, mebɔ fam".
*The egg says: "I am like authority, if you crush me, I break; if you let me go I fall and break to pieces on the ground".*
(Power needs to be handled carefully).

3545. Nkosua nyinaa mpata asuo.
*All eggs do not pacify the river.*
(Not everyone values the same things).

3546. Akosua mmɔ mmusuo na Akua mfa.
*Akosua should not invite a curse and leave it for Akua to bear.*
(You should not be made to suffer for another's misdeeds).

3547. Kosuamua, ɔse: "Me nsɛm nyinaa aka me tirim".
*The unbroken egg says: "All my affairs are in my head".*
(A reserved or inhibited person is unable to express themselves).

3548. Yɛnkɔte aduro a ɛne ahahan.
*If we say we are going to collect herbs, they are nothing but leaves.*
(Whatever we do, we need something to achieve our ends).

3549. Kotebɔ bɔ bum a, na ɛwɔ deɛ ɛrepam no.
*If the leopard rushes away, then it means there is something chasing it.*
(If a great man retreats, then there is something radically wrong).

3550. Kotebɔ bɔ bum a, ɔkɔ n'anim, na ɔnkɔ n'akyi.
*If the leopard rushes, it rushes forwards not backwards.*
(A brave man does not retreat).

3551. Kotebɔ fom [ne tweneno]/[n'ammɔn so] a, ɔyera.
*If the big animal [misses its own path]/[deviates from its footprints], it gets lost.*
(If you don't stick to your own traditions, you go astray).

3552. Kotebɔ ne koterɛ sɛ din, nanso wɔnsɛ honam.
*The names of the leopard and the lizard are similar, but not their bodies.*
(A man cannot be judged by his name alone).

3553. Kɔtebɔtɔ hwe ase a, ɛmpae.
*An uncircumcised penis, when it falls, does not break.*
(Well-protected things don't spoil easily).

3554. Kɔtedie mu nni biribi a, ɛyɛ nkwahaduro.
*If sexual affairs are not at all profitable, they are (at least) a medicine for curing the vagina.*
(Everything has some real value. You must suffer to be healthy).

3555. Kɔtedie nyɛ din na emu awoden.
*It is easy to have sexual intercourse but it is not easy to give birth.*
(You should consider the results of your actions before acting).

3556. Wo kɔte abenem, wokuta baa de gyina me so, wobaa me die anaasɛ wobaa me kum?
*Your penis is erected, you are holding a club at me, did you come to have sexual relations with me or to kill me?*
(You cannot be hostile and make demands at the same time).

3557. Kɔte denden ne ɛtwe denden hyia a, ɛwo ɔba sɛmmerɛden.
*If a strong penis meets a strong vagina, they produce a hard-headed child.*
(Two positives can't make a negative).

3558. Kɔteɛ fe a, ɛfe gu ɛtwe mu.
*If the penis vomits, it does so into the vagina.*
(Every action has its appropriate place).

3559. Kɔteɛ ano tae a, ɛnte sɛ wɔmma.
*If the tip of the penis were to become blunt, it could not be as blunt as a mortar.*
(If a strong man becomes weak, he is still stronger than a weak man).

3560. Kɔteɛ nni ani nso ɛhunu ɛtwe di.
*The penis has no eyes but it can see how to use the vagina.*
(Every specialist has his own skills at doing things).

3561. Kɔteɛ wu a, yɛdwonsɔ mu.
*If the penis becomes impotent, it can still be used for urinating.*
(If an important person loses power, at least there are some things that he can still do).

3562. Ɔkotehunuiɛ nti na obi anni ne nam.
*Because of people's knowledge of the lizard, no one eats its meat.*
(People used to defecate in the bush and when they went there they often met lizards and therefore regarded them as unclean. Hence: You don't involve yourself with something you deem to be impure).

3563. Kɔtekɛse na ɛwo ahenemma.
*A big penis produces kingly children.*
(Fine cocks make fine chicks).

3564. "Kɔtena ɛhyɛn mu", nyɛ awerehɔɔ.
*"Go sit in the moonlight", is not misery.*
(If something you are asked to do is not unpleasant, don't complain).

3565. Kɔtekrawa ma dwannam yɛ no dɛ bebrebe a, yɛde nnompe boro no da bi.
*If an infertile man enjoys mutton too much, one day we will take the bones to beat him.*
(In the old days, if a couple did not have children, the man would be publicly castigated. Hence: If you neglect the most important things for self-indulgence, you are punished by society).

3566. Ɔkotepomponini ne ɔprammire nsɛ.
*The agama lizard and the cobra are not alike.*
(Things which are different, remain different in all circumstances).

3567. Ɔkotepomponini mpɛ bɔtɔ kuta nti na ne bɔtɔ sa ne mene ase.
*The agama lizard does not like holding a bag, that is why its bag hangs under its chin.*
(This lizard has a large bag of loose skin beneath its chin. Hence: Different people like different things, but none the less they may be forced to take what they do not like).

3568. Kɔtepɔɔsen se: sɛ woyɛ ɔbaa a, ɛnyɛ kɔteɛ nyinaa na ɛsɛ sɛ wodie, efiri sɛ yɛdi kɔteɛ de pɛ adeɛ.
*The long-tailed whydah bird says: if you are a woman, it is not all penises that you allow entry to, because we accept penises in order to receive inheritances.*
(People act for gain).

3569. Ɔkoterɛ a ɔfiri duaso tenten so bɛsi fam se: sɛ obiara renkamfo no a, ɔbɛkamfo no ho.
*The lizard that fell from the tall tree to the ground says: if no one will praise it, it will praise itself.*
(If others do not recognize your achievements, you may have to boast of them yourself).

3570. Koterɛ a ɔtare ahina ho botoɔ yɛ tuna.
*The lizard which clings to the water pot is difficult to throw a stone at.*
(It is difficult to get at a person who is attached to an influential man).

3571. Koterɛ ba nim sɛ oni nni nufoɔ nti na owo no a ɔnum mframa de nyini no.
*The lizard's child knows that its mother has no breasts to suckle it so it sucks in air to grow.*
(You adapt yourself to things as they are).

3572. Koterɛ di hia nti na ɔkyere ananse.
*Because the lizard is poor, it catches spiders.*
(A poor man has no choice).

3573. Ɔkoterɛ fam dan ho, na ɔmmu ngu fam.
*The lizard stays on the wall but it does not demolish it.*
(You do not destroy what is of use to you).

3574. Koterɛ nnua bayerɛ.
*A lizard does not plant yams.*
(You don't waste time doing something which is of no use to you).

3575. Koterɛ firi soro bɛhwe fam a, ɔse: "Asaase, w'ani so biri wo anaa?"
*The lizard falls from above and says: "Earth, are you feeling dizzy?"*
(Said when someone who should be suffering inquires rather from someone else if they are doing so).

3576. Koterɛ nim sɛ yafunuyareɛ bɛba, nti na ɔbutu ne yafunu soɔ.
*Because the lizard knew its belly would ache, it lies on it.*
(Prevention is better than cure).

3577. Koterɛ nya nkwa a, na ɔto aduosia.
*If the lizard survives, then it lays sixty eggs.*
(The longer one lives the more one can produce).

3578. Koterɛ nsa nhyia onyina, nso ɔforo da biara.
*The lizard's hands cannot go round the silk-cotton (Bombax buonopozense) tree, but he climbs it daily.*
(Size is irrelevant to skill).

**3579. Kotereɛ nsa nkete-nkete nso ɛno ara na ɔde hyɛ ne yerenom nkyene.**
*The lizard may have tiny fingers, but it is able to give salt to his wives.*
(Everyone uses their natural gifts, however modest they may seem).

**3580. Kotereɛ se: deɛ ɔtoo boɔ bɔɔ no ho nyɛ no ahi, sɛ deɛ ɔgyina nkyɛn na ɔse: "Saa deɛ, w'ani gyene".**
*The lizard says: it does not abhor the person who takes a stone to throw at it as much as he who stands by and says: "In fact, you aim well".*
(Worse than the person who acts against you is the person who urges him on).

**3581. Kotereɛ se: ɔnim sɛ ɛkɔm bɛba, nti na ɔkutiri akitereku ho.**
*The lizard says: it knows that hunger will come, that is why he scrapes beans and saves them.*
(It is good to provide for the future).

**3582. Kotereɛ nsi ne dan mma akura nkɔgye nkɛntɛn so.**
*The lizard does not build its house for the mouse to rule over it.*
(One person does not work for another to benefit).

**3583. Kotereɛ nsuro awu asie.**
*A lizard does not fear to feign death.*
(You will do anything to save yourself in a difficult situation).

**3584. Kotereɛ nwe mako mma fifire mfiri aponkyerɛne.**
*The lizard does not chew pepper for the frog to sweat for it.*
(Eating pepper causes sweating. Hence: A man does not suffer for another's sins).

**3585. Kotereɛ wɔ dasuo mu a, ɔnhwere ban.**
*At midnight the lizard does not lack a wall.*
(Said of someone who can always find shelter).

**3586. [Koterɛ]/[ɔkotepomponini] wɔ yam aduro a, anka yam rensi no ataadeɛ.**
*If the [lizard]/[agama lizard] had medicine for skin infections, then its body would not be clothed in spots.*
("Yam", the skin disease in question, is probably ring worm. Hence: If we had the cure for something, we obviously would not suffer from it).

**3587. Kɔtie bɛse me a, wonka sɛ: "Mawie di".**
*If I ask you to go and listen and report back to me, you don't say: "I have finished settling it".*
(You don't do more than you are asked).

**3588. Yɛnkoto a, yɛnna.**
*If we don't bend, we don't lie down.*
(One thing can only follow another).

**3589. Wokɔto abasin na ɔte adwa so a, ɛmma no nyɛ wo nwanwa, ɛfiri sɛ ebia na ɔdii dɛm wɔ ɔko ano.**
*If you find a one-armed person on the stool, don't be surprised, because perhaps he was wounded in the battle-front.*
(A Chief once ordered all his subjects to use their left hands - a taboo - because the chief of the next-door state did so and was highly thought of. The reason was that this chief had lost his right arm in fighting a leopard and so was forced to use his left, not that it

was better to do so. Hence: You should not copy an action until you know the reason for it).

**3590. Wokɔto obi na ɔte gya ho, na sɛ ɛnyɛ awɔ na ɛde no a, na ɛkɔm na ɛde no.**
*You are going to meet someone and he is sitting by the fire, then if he is not cold, he must be hungry.*
(One action may have several possible explanations).

**3591. Wokɔto obi na ɔrene ahuro a, wonse no sɛ: "Ma me kyereboa na gye ahuro".**
*If you go and meet someone who is excreting foam, you don't say to them: "Give me hard faeces and take this foam".*
(Don't add insult to injury).

**3592. Wokɔto kontromfi na ɔsɛn hɔ a, wommisa no adwa.**
*If you go and see a baboon crouching there, then you don't ask it for a stool.*
(Don't ask someone for what they have not got).

**3593. Wokɔto onihafoɔ wɔ afuom a, ma no amo, na ɛnyɛ biribi mpo a, owia rehye no.**
*If you meet a lazy person on the farm, congratulate them, and if they do nothing, at least the sun is burning them.*
(A lazy person should be encouraged in any activity, rather than being left idle).

**3594. Worekɔtɔ nnipa na wannya bi a, wosan akyi.**
*If you are going to buy a man and you don't get one, you have to return.*
(If you are not successful, you still have to return home).

**3595. Wokɔto sabokwani na wadi ɔhene a, na wagyae ne nneyɛeɛ.**
*If you go and see a drunkard and he has been made a chief, it means he has given up his wrong-doing.*
(If someone is successful it means they are reformed).

**3596. Wokɔto sɛ obi ne wo yere gyina kokom a, nka sɛ ɔrentumi mpɛ no ɛfiri sɛ wɔn kɔte ne ɛtwɛ no nni fie na wɔahyɛ da akɔfa aba.**
*If you see that a man and your wife are conversing in private, don't say that he cannot go into her because the penis and vagina are not left in the house so that they can go and get them.*
(You never know when someone will succumb to temptation, even if you believe that they will not do so).

**3597. Wokɔto sɛ akɔdaa retu ɔpanin fo, na sɛ deɛ ɔretie afotuo no nyɛ ɔyarefoɔ a, na ɔyɛ ɔpanin hiani.**
*If you come across a child that is giving an elder advice, if the one listening is not a sick person, then he is a poor elder.*
(Only poverty or sickness can make someone listen to an inferior's advice).

**3598. Yɛnkoto ntwene a, yɛmfa nkɔsie adaka mu.**
*If we should throw it away, we don't keep it in a box.*
(You don't keep rubbish with precious things. If you don't need something get rid of it).

**3599. Ɔkɔtɔ a ɔda sika ho mpo, ɔtwere abɛ.**
*The crab, although it lies on gold, chews palm nuts.*
(Even if you have something precious it does not mean that it is of primary importance to you. Or: A man must eat to live).

**3600. Ɔkɔtɔ bɛn asuo nti na ɔte asuo kasa.**
*Because the crab lives near the river, he knows the language of the river.*
(You know the ways of the place you live).

**3601. Ɔkɔtɔ bɔ peme a, ɔsan n'akyi.**
*When the crab falls on its back, it turns back.*
(When you escape from danger, you recoil).

**3602. Ɔkɔtɔ deɛ ne bo dwɛ, nyanyankerɛ deɛ ɔnkɔ.**
*The crab's destiny is destruction, the scorpion goes free.*
(You should not show favoritism between two people whose actions and customs are similar).

**3603. Ɔkɔtɔ redwa wo no, na ɔredwa wo aka wo.**
*The crab is shaking hands with you, but he is shaking hands in order to bite you.*
(When a bad man approaches you in a friendly way, be careful you don't know what he plans).

**3604. Ɔkɔtɔ mfiri nsuo ase nkɔbisa owuo sɛ: "Yɛahyia mprɛ sɛn?"**
*The crab does not come from beneath the water to ask death: "How many times have we met?"*
(You don't associate yourself with something which will cause your death).

**3605. Ɔkɔtɔ foforɔ aprɛ mu nni nam.**
*A young crab has no meat in its claws.*
(The young lack maturity).

**3606. Ɔkɔtɔ ne futukokonini nsere afe korɔ mu.**
*The crab and the ground beetle do not rejoice in the same year.*
(The crab likes rain and the beetle likes it dry. People's needs differ).

**3607. Ɔkɔtɔ ne aponkyerɛne se: obi mpɛ w'agorɔ a, wosan w'akyi.**
*The crab and the frog say: if no one likes your game, you retreat.*
(Don't approach someone who hates you. The frog avoids the crab which grips it with its claws).

**3608. Ɔkɔtɔ nsuo, animinam: "Mehunu a mɛka nti, deɛ ɛnni me sɔɔ, wɔde ma me".**
*The crab's hole full of water called "I know": "Because whatever I see, I will say, but as to the allegations which are made against me, I am innocent (lit. things which are not due to me they give to me)".*
(Someone who points out faults is liable to be accused themselves).

**3609. Ɔkɔtɔ annya baabi pa anna, nti na ɔda amena mu.**
*Because the crab does not have a good sleeping place, it sleeps in a hole.*
(People often act from necessity, not choice).

**3610. Ɔkɔtɔ mpo di sukɔm, na ɛnte sɛ ɔkwakuo a ɔte soro?**
*Even the crab gets thirsty, not to speak of the monkey that lives above.*
(If the person in the know goes short, so will the outsider).

**3611. "Ɔkɔtɔ, wosi anwea yi so reyɛ deɛn?" Ɔse: "Merehwɛ deɛ opitire ne mma reyɔ".**
*"Crab, why do you sit on the sand?" It replies: "I am watching what the fish and its children are doing".*
(Said when someone has no ulterior motives for what they are doing).

**3612. Ɔkɔtɔ nwo anomaa.**
*The crab does not give birth to a bird.*
(You take after you own family).

**3613. Kotodwe bɔ dua, ɔyea mpa mu da.**
*If the knee hits wood, it never stops hurting.*
(A sensitive person does not cease to feel hurt, even after some time).

**3614. Kotodwe nsɔre nkɔboro hasuo kwa.**
*The knee does not get up to go and fight the dew for no reason.*
(One has to have a good reason for going out very early in the morning).

**3615. Kɔtɔkɔ a ne mpea gu n'aso soɔ, hwan na ɔbɛtumi ne no adi asie?**
*The porcupine with its quills on its back, who will be able to challenge it?*
(The porcupine is the symbol of the Asante nation. Hence: Who can challenge Asante? Or: You don't challenge a powerful man unless you know you can beat him).

**3616. Kɔtɔkɔ rekɔ kɔtɔkɔ fie a, ɔmfa adidideɛ.**
*If one porcupine visits another's home, he does not take food.*
(When clansman visits clansman, he is provided for).

**3617. Kɔtɔkɔ renko a, hwɛ n'amiadeɛ.**
*If the porcupine is not about to fight, look at what it is wearing.*
(The porcupine's quills look like a battle-dress. Hence: If you see an armed man, you presume he will fight).

**3618. Kɔtɔkɔ ne gyahene nni atohyia.**
*The porcupine and the leopard do not play catch together.*
(It is dangerous to play with one's enemies).

**3619. Kɔtɔkɔ nni hɔ a, apɛsɛ yi mmusuo.**
*If the porcupine is not there, the brush-tailed porcupine pours libation (on his behalf).*
(When the commander is absent the second in command takes over).

**3620. Kotɔkorɔ a akɔte aduaba a, abereɛ ato fam no, sɛ woredi a, wamma no abunu.**
*Bent stick which plucks ripe fruit and brings them down, if you are eating, you don't give it unripe fruit.*
(A man should not be denied the fruit of his own labor).

**3621. Kotoku-saabobe, ɔnkasa nso ɔhome.**
*The cocoon does not talk but it breathes.*
(A stranger's character is not easily determined).

**3622. Kɔtokɔsamanakwa a ɔnim adekyeɛɛ mu asɛm, adeɛ rebɛkye a ɔse: "Asaase rebue, asaase rebue". Adeɛ resa nso a ɔse: "Asaase remuna, asaase remuna". Anim rebae a, na ɔbirekuo nso agye so: "Duuu, duuu, duuu, duuu".**
*The drongo knows what problems the morning brings. At daybreak it says: "The earth is opening, the earth is opening." When evening comes it also says: "The earth is frowning (getting dark), the earth is frowning." When light comes the coucal also adds: "Duuu, duuu, duuu, duuu".*
(A person who has foresight is respected by those who know his talents).

**3623. Kɔtɔkɔsamanakwa kasa ntɛm nso aprawa da gya no.**
*The drongo sings early but the giant pangolin sleeps earlier than it does.*
(We each have our own special talents).

**3624. Kɔtɔkɔsamanakwa a ɔse ɔnim adekyeɛ my asɛm, adeɛ rebɛkyea, ɔse: "Asaase reboeɛ, asaase reboeɛ". Adeɛ rebɛsa a, ɔse: "Asaase remuna, asaase remuna". Na sɛ afei obirekuo gye ne so sɛ: "Duu, duu, duu!" a, na kɔtokɔsamanakwa na ɔhunu adekyeɛ ne adesaeɛ mu nsɛm, anaasɛ obirekuo?**
*The drongo that says it knows what problems the morning brings, at daybreak it says: "The earth is opening, the earth is opening!" When evening comes, it says: "The earth is frowning (i.e. becoming gloomy), the earth is frowning". But now if the coucal adds to it: "True, true, true," then was it the drongo that actually detected when the morning and the evening arrived, or was it the coucal?*
(See Proverb 3622. These sayings represent the birds' songs. Hence: The one that makes the most noise is not necessarily the best informed).

**3625. Kɔtokɔsamanakwa yɛɛ ɔkɔreɛ a, anka ɔde mmɔgyeɛ besi aborɔsan.**
*If the drongo were to be an eagle, it would take jawbones to build a store house.*
(Said of a troublesome man who, if he gets enough power could be very dangerous).

**3626. Kotokuo te a, na batire ho adwo no.**
*If the shoulder bag tears, then the shoulder is free.*
(If someone you are responsible for is not there, you are relieved of you responsibility).

**3627. Kotokurodu yɛ nnam a, ma ɔntwa owuo ho.**
*If the mason-wasp is brave, he should revolve round death.*
(Bravery has its limits).

**3628. Akotokyiwa na ɛnni hɔ nti na yɛde ntoa resuae abɛ.**
*It is because there are no pots that bottle gourds are used to tap palm-wine.*
(If you can't get the best you have to use what you can get).

**3629. Kɔtɔprɛ na ɛma ɔkɔtɔ ho yɛ hu.**
*It is for its claws that the crab is feared.*
(A man is feared because of his power).

**3630. Kotorobankye na worebɛdie? Afei na worebɛwuo!**
*Are you about to eat poisonous cassava? Be careful for you are about to die.*

("Kotorobankye" is a poisonous cassava sometimes mistaken for the edible one. Hence: A warning to keep off dangerous pursuits).

**3631. Kotorobankye nyɛ a, egya na ɔnim.**
*If poisonous cassava is not good, the fire detects it.*
(See Proverb 3630. Only the expert can detect if something is no good).

**3632. Kotorobankye ɔbɛkyene bo, na ɔhyɛɛ fam, hyɛɛ fam no, ɔporɔeɛ.**
*The poisonous cassava (says) it will grow old like the stone, so it has remained long in the ground (lit. stayed in the ground, stayed in the ground) and grown rotten.*
(See Proverb 3630. Don't delay too long or you may achieve nothing. Or: Mere age is not achievement).

**3633. Yɛrekɔtwa wo ti a, wose: "Me kyɛ!"**
*If we are going to behead you, you say: "My hat!"*
(Said to people who face great trials yet worry over small things).

**3634. "Kɔtwe si ho na bɛse me" a, wonka sɛ: "Mawie di".**
*If (I say) "Go and take it and put it down and tell me," you don't say: "I have finished eating it".*
(The initial invitation is a request to take something from the kithcen. Hence: Don't exceed what you are asked to do).

**3635. Woakɔtwe wene abɛto wo ho so. Ma memfa wo nkɔte a, wose: "Mebɔ wa". Ma memfa wo nwane a, wose: "Me dwonku yɛ me ya". Ma memfa wo nsi akɔnkɔn a, wose: "Woabɔ mmusuo enti kɔpɛ odwan bɛtwa". Mekɔpɛ odwan no ba a, mɛtwa ama onipa anaa sɛ osaman?**
*You have brought trouble on yourself. Let me take you somewhere to hide, you say: "I cough". Let me run away with you, you say: "My hip-bone hurts". Let me take you and put you on my shoulders, you say: "You have committed a taboo which demands the slaughtering of a sheep". If I go and bring a sheep, will it be for a living person or a ghost?*
(If you are too difficult in accepting help, you may die before it reaches you).

**3636. "Kowu-anya-ntoma", yɛde dadaa funu.**
*"Die in order to get a cloth", we use it to trick the corpse.*
(It is no good waiting until someone is dead to help them).

**3637. Yɛnkɔyi mmusuo a, ɛda kɔmfoɔ akɔmman mu.**
*If we are going to sacrifice (lit. to ward off mischief), it is in the fetish-priest's shrine.*
(There is an appropriate place for everything).

**3638. Wo [kra]/[tiri] nyɛ a, na wonya asafo nsam amaneɛ.**
*If you [soul]/[head] is not a lucky one, you fall into the hands of an asafo company.*
(If you are unlucky, you find the whole community against you).

**3639. Wonkra nkɔsiiɛ a, yɛmma wo due-ne-wia.**
*If you have not said goodbye properly, we don't say good-afternoon when you go.*
(If you are not polite, you won't be treated politely).

**3640. Nkra nyɛ akɔmmuo.**
*Giving a message is not a neck-ache.*
(It is not a hard thing to deliver a message).

**3641. Ɔkra nam fie na ɔse ne bɔtɔ a, anadwoboa mfa ne nsa nto mu.**
*If a cat hangs its bag in the house, the nocturnal animal (i.e. the mouse) does not dip its hands into it.*
(A slave does not challenge his master).

**3642. Ɔkra se: awerɛkyekyerɛ nti na ɔde ne ho twitwiri nnipa ho.**
*The cat says: it is for consolation that it rubs itself against man.*
(You make friends because you need sympathy).

**3643. Ɔkra wɔ piafoɔ a, anka ɔbɛyɛ nam asene ɔkraman.**
*If the cat were to have a patron, then it would become a better hunter than the dog.*
(Without patronage even the ablest cannot achieve success).

**3644. Nkrabea nyinaa nsɛ.**
*Not all destinies are alike.*

**3645. Nkrabea nni kwatibea.**
*Destiny cannot be evaded.*

**3646. Krakɔhwɛ na ɛyɛ fɛ na nyɛ krakɔsu.**
*Sending word that one should go and look is fine, but not that one should go and weep.*
(A person going to another place anticipates something good, not bad).

**3647. Krakɔseɛ Nana, wokra no a, na ɔseɛ.**
*The grandson of the deliverer of a message, when you give him a message, he delivers it.*
(The children of a professional know how to act in a professional way).

**3648. Worekraakraa w'ani apɛ boɔ ato abɔ anomaa no, na ɔno nso rekraakraa n'ani apɛ deɛ ɔbɛtu afa.**
*When you are searching for a stone to throw at a bird, then it is also looking round to find a place to escape to.*
(While you plan to catch someone out, they also plan their escape).

**3649. Ɔkraman a ɔkɔcɔ ahayɔ anhunu yɔ, na ɔkra na ɔbɛyɛ deɛn?**
*The dog which went hunting did not achieve anything, so the cat, what can it hope to do?*
(What the expert cannot achieve, neither can the amateur).

**3650. Ɔkraman a ɔkɔɔ n'ase kurom kɔfaa nam weeɛ na ɔse: "Mede me din agya dada".**
*The dog that went to his in-law's town to steal meat to chew says: "I left my name behind long ago".*
(Said by the criminal who has nothing to lose).

**3651. Ɔkraman a ɔte borɔde-hono so, ɔno a ɔnwe, nso ɔmma obi nwe.**
*The dog which lies on the plantain skin does not chew it and does not let anyone else chew.*
(Don't be a dog in a manger).

**3652. Ɔkraman bɔ ka a, ɔde ne wedeɛ na ɛtua.**
*If the dog gets into debt, it can only pay with its skin.*
(A poor man who gets into trouble must bear the consequences).

**3653. Ɔkraman fa kosua a, ɛbɔ wɔ n'anom.**
*If a dog takes an egg, it breaks in its mouth.*
(A difficult situation needs tactful handling. Don't let fools step in where angels fear to tread).

**3654. Ɔkraman fa samina a, ɛkura no kwa; ɔnni ntoma ma ɔde asi.**
*If a dog takes a piece of soap, it is holding it for nothing; it has no cloth to wash.*
(Don't be a dog in the manger).

**3655. Ɔkraman hyɛ bɔ sɛ ɔbɛfa akyekyedeɛ abɔfono a, ɛkɔm ku no.**
*If a dog boasts it will take the tortoise's carcass, it will starve to death.*
(The dog can't break the tortoise's shell with its teeth. Hence: If you boast of doing the impossible, you will achieve nothing).

**3656. Ɔkraman akannie yɛ kwa.**
*A dog's going ahead means nothing.*
(Rushing about to do something without proper authority is pointless).

**3657. Ɔkraman kɔ obɔmmɔfoɔ fie a, ɛyɛ dɛn ara a ɔbɛkɔ ne wura fie.**
*If the dog goes to the hunter's house, whatever happens it will return to its master's house.*
(You may go elsewhere to eat or to work but by all means you will, in the end, return home).

**3658. Ɔkraman mmusuo da n'apampam.**
*The dog's misfortune lies on its head.*
(A dog cannot lick its own head. Hence: If you can't deal with your own troubles, you continue to suffer from them).

**3659. Ɔkraman na ɔbu ne bɛ sɛ: "Adekɛseɛ nyera".**
*It's the dog that makes a proverb saying: "Big things don't get lost".*
(An important thing is not forgotten altogether).

**3660. Ɔkraman ne a, Onyame na ɔpopa ne toɔ.**
*If a dog defecates, God wipes its bottom.*
(God cares for the needy).

**3661. Ɔkraman anom yɛ no dɛ a, ɔnwe ne [kɔnmu nnawa]/[nkɔnsɔn kɔnsɔn].**
*Even if a dog's mouth is watering, it does not chew the bells round its neck.*
(However great the desire, some things are impossible to achieve).

**3662. Ɔkraman nyiniiɛ a, na yɛfrɛ no "kukua".**
*If a dog is not full grown, then we call it "little pot".*
(You don't expect people to take on responsibilities above their age or station in life).

**3663. Ɔkraman se ahwehwɛahwehwɛ na ɛma agorɔ yɛ dɛ.**
*The dog says gazing at each other makes playing pleasurable.*
(Watchers stimulate players as well as enjoying the game, but it is sharing that makes playing enjoyable).

**3664. Wo kraman se obɛkyere sono ama wo a, na ɔredaadaa wo.**
*If your dog says he will catch you an elephant, then he deceives you.*
(Don't believe idle boasting).

**3665. Ɔkraman se: sɛ ɔnim sɛ ne ba rebɛwu a, anka ɔtɔnee no gyae dompe.**
*The dog says: if he had known that his puppy was going to die, then he would have sold it to get a bone.*
(Vain regrets).

**3666. Ɔkraman se: "Sɛ anka anadwo na yɛdi dwa a, anka yɛbɛhunu ɔbarima a ɔtɔ nam".**
*The dog says: "If we did the marketing at night, we would see who is the best buyer of meat".*
(In different circumstances, different people are best qualified).

**3667. Ɔkraman te hɔ dada a, ɔse ɔrepɛ mmirika-hunu atu, na yɛabɛse no sɛ n'ase dwan ayera.**
*If the dog stays long in one place, he says he wants to run around and see what is going on, how much more so if we inform him that his in-laws sheep is lost.*
(Someone who wants to do something will be inclined to do it more if they find a good excuse).

**3668. Ɔkraman te pataso na sɛ ɛnyɛ ɔno na ɔforoe a, na obi na ɔmaa no so sii hɔ.**
*If a dog is on the ceiling storage rack and if it did not climb there itself, then someone must have lifted it up there.*
(If you are caught doing something and say you are not responsible, then someone else must be).

**3669. Ɔkraman atirimusɛm da ne koko, na ɛnna ne tirim.**
*A dog's secret thoughts lie in its chest and not in its head.*
(Some people act without thinking).

**3670. "Kramo, daakena". Ɔse "Aba sa".**
*"Moslem, condolences." He says "It has happened so".*
(However sad, fate must be accepted).

**3671. Kramo mmusuyie ne sraha.**
*A Moslem's warding off mischief is in the giving of gifts (to the needy).*
(Some charitable acts are done for self-interest).

**3672. Kramo nnim biribi a, nyɛ "Ku-no-ma-me".**
*If the Moslem knows nothing, it is not "Kill him for me" (i.e this is one thing he does know).*
(Muslim's in Asante are associated with the practice of sorcery directed both to the welfare and to the disadvantage of others. Hence: Even if a practitioner is not skilled, he knows the elements of his trade).

**3673. Kramo torofoɔ amma yɛanhunu kramo pa.**
*A moslem liar does not allow us to know the true moslem.*
(It is the bad members of a community who damage its reputation).

**3674. Nkrampaa se: ɔreyɛ bese, ama bese animguase; sɛɛ ɔnnim sɛ ne daakye aduane na ɔresɛe no.**
*The African mistletoe (Loranthaceae) says it is disturbing the cola so that the cola may be disgraced (lit. its shameful deeds are spoiled); but it does not realize it is in fact spoiling its own future daily bread.*

(This semi-parasitic plant sometimes ends up by killing the host tree. Hence: If someone is kind to you and helps you, don't abuse their trust and ruin them or in future you will be without help).

**3675. Nkran Takyi se: "Medane sɛ me man ayɛ [yie]/[adɔre]".**
*Takyi from Accra (Ga Mantse) says: "All that I want to see is that my town flourishes".*
(The Ga Mantse is the senior Ga chief. A leader wants his state to flourish).

**3676. Nkrane hwete a na wɔnyerae.**
*The soldier ants disperse but they don't get lost.*
(If an intelligent person is distracted from doing something, it does not mean they will not do it later).

**3677. Nkrane ka wo a, wode kɔse Agyekum.**
*If the soldier ant bites you, you complain to the Queen Ant.*
(You complain to the person at the top if a servant misbehaves).

**3678. Nkrane nam a, atibire wɔ mu.**
*If the soldier ants are on the move, there are leaders.*
(In any society there are natural leaders).

**3679. Nkrannyedua mu Asieduwaa kɔmfoɔ: "Ɔsikani hunu ohiani a, ɔse wabɔ dam".**
*The Priestess Asieduwaa who is in the physic nut (Jatropha curcas) grove says: "When a rich man sees a poor man, he says he is a madman".*
(Poverty makes a person look miserable and sometimes unkempt).

**3680. Nkrantɛ nkɔ baabi nnya ne nam.**
*The cutlass does not go and leave its sharpness behind.*
(Wherever a man finds himself, he is there with his natural talents).

**3681. Ɔkrawa-nini te hɔ a, ɔkrawa-bereɛ mmɔ adwe.**
*If the male white-crowned mangabe is there, the female white-crowned mangabe does not crack palm kernels.*
(If a man is there, he does the hard work for his family).

**3682. Nkrawiri se: "Merebɛyɛ biribi ama ɔmanfoɔ ahwɛ".**
*The Nkrawiri drum says: "I am going to perform something for those present to see".*
(Said when someone is boasting of what he will do, implying "Let us see if he can do it").

**3683. Krobea Asante Kɔtɔkɔ Yirifianwama: wɔrepe wo ahwɛ no, na wɔrepe wo asere wo.**
*Crow-like Asante Kɔtɔkɔ Powerful and Cunning: they want to see you, they also want to laugh at you.*
(Krobea is another name for Anene the black and white crow which is a totem of the Asona clan. Once an Asante farmer found that his crops were being stolen by bush-pigs, but the crow warned the pigs any time he neared them. The pigs promised the crow food, but did not keep their promise. When the man saw what the crow was doing, he asked it to keep quiet as he and the crow belonged to the same clan. He, too, said that he would give it food. The crow kept silent and some of the pigs were caught. The crow was given his share. The bush-pigs accused the crow

before the other animals, but it replied that it only kept faith with those who kept faith with it. The appellation Krobea is used to express this side of the character of the porcupine. The appellation Yirifianwama indicates cunning. Hence: People may want to see you for many reasons – bad as well as good).

### 3684. Krobonko gyegye nnipa kɔma Pra.
*A trouble maker lures people into the Pra River.*
(i.e. to drown. Krobonko was a stool servant in Dankyira who used to get people into trouble by trickery. Hence: A trouble maker leads people to despair).

### 3685. Nkromma te ase a, Badu nni adeɛ.
*If the ninth-born son is alive, the tenth-born does not inherit.*
(Nkromma is the ninth child; Badu is the tenth male child of a woman. Hence: Seniority matters).

### 3686. Ɔkromantan hyɛ ne ho sɛ ɔbɛkum ananse a, ɔboa.
*If the large mantis says he will kill the spider, he lies.*
(Vain boasting).

### 3687. Ɔkromantan bɛkɔ wuo na biribi hyɛ n'afono mu.
*Before the large mantis goes to the grave, it must have something in its mouth.*
(No great man dies in vain).

### 3688. Krɔmante annwo dodoɔ no, na ɛfiri Kofi Krampo.
*Krɔmante has not had many children because of Kofi Krampo.*
(One man suffers from another man's acts).

### 3689. Ɔkromfoɔ ba fie a, na yɛhunu deɛ mmusuo wo ne ho.
*If a thief comes to the house, then we see who is the unlucky person.*
(It is only when something happens that we can judge who is prone to bad luck).

### 3690. Ɔkrɔmfoɔ nni daberɛ.
*A thief does not have a sleeping-place.*
(If you are anti-social, no one wants to house you).

### 3691. Ɔkrɔmfoɔ nsene afuo wura.
*The thief is not braver than the owner of the farm.*
(If something is not yours, you hesitate in taking it).

### 3692. Ɔkrɔmfo wu a, na ne nsa na aku no.
*If a thief dies, it is his hand that killed him.*
(It is a man's way of life that leads to his death).

### 3693. Krufihene se: "Ɔhene de ɔhene".
*The Krufi drum says: "A chief is a chief".*
(Krufihene is the nickname for the master drum of the Kete-kwadum drum ensemble, which plays in the presence of the chief; and this is what it says. Hence: If you hold a position of respect, however small, you are respected).

### 3694. "Krukru-krukru", nka bɔn mu.
*"Scrabbling" does not remain in a hole.*
(Whatever is done secretly finally comes into the open).

### 3695. Yɛreku wo a, wonse sɛ: "Morebere me kuro".
*If we are going to kill you, you don't say: "You are*

hurting my sore".
(You don't worry over small things when a major disaster confronts you).

### 3696. "Mɛku-wo-mawu" nyɛ abaninsɛm.
*"I will kill you and commit suicide", is not a manly action.*
(If you have courage to do something, you should have courage to face up to the consequences).

### 3697. Nku me fie na woakɔsu me abɔnten.
*Don't kill me in the house and then go and weep for me in the street.*
(If you cause trouble for someone in private, do not pretend you have not done so when in public).

### 3698. "Eku-gyeɛ!", eku agye. "Eku ma me ɛ", eku kyee.
*"Monkey take", monkey takes. "Monkey give me", monkey refuses.*
(Said of a mean and grabbing person who takes but does not give).

### 3699. Akua nhwinti na yɛamma Akosua due.
*Akua should not stumble for us to condole Akosua.*
(You suffer as a result of your own actions, not someone else's).

### 3700. Akua mpo, woantumi no, na Kwaku.
*Even Akua you could not stand, how much less Kwaku.*
(If you cannot tackle an easy job, don't try a hard one).

### 3701. Okuafoɔ bankye ammɔ a, na kɔtɔkɔ afɛre.
*If the farmer's cassava does not thrive, then the porcupine is ashamed.*
(If someone benefits from another's work, and the work does not succeed, the parasite becomes ashamed).

### 3702. Okuafoɔ yɛ adwuma a, ɔgye n'ahome.
*After work the farmer must rest.*
(All work and no play makes Jack a dull boy).

### 3703. Akuama yɛ aduru a, anka ɔtwe nam ntenten wɔ wiram.
*If the akuama fruit were to be a medicine, the duiker would have walked upright in the bush.*
(If what you need is always available you get on in life. The duiker walks delicately on its feet, suggesting it has a sore).

### 3704. Akuapem Abibifoɔ hunuu atono nanso obi ntonoo aprɛmo da.
*The Akuapem Africans knew how to forge guns but not one forged a cannon.*
(Said of someone who knows how to do something but fails ever to make full use of his knowledge).

### 3705. Akuapem tuo nya akyigyinafoɔ a, na ɛkum aboa.
*If the Danish musket gets a good handler, it kills game.*
(A man works successfully with a good tool).

### 3706. Okuapenni se ɔbɛka Akyem a, ma ɔnka, na abofuo bɛba da bi.
*If the Akuapem person wishes to speak in the Akyem dialect, let him, but anger will betray him.*
(When a man is angry, he betrays his true origins).

3707. Kube si apemfoɔ kurom a, ɛpore gu.
*If the coconut stands in a pregnant woman's town, it let's its nuts fall and waste.*
(Pregnant women cannot climb trees. Hence: If you are unable to make use of something, it goes to waste).

3708. Okufoɔ mmɔ afɛ.
*A person full of sores does not enter into fellowship (with anyone).*
(If you know you are vulnerable, you avoid those who may hurt you).

3709. Kukuban mpɛ ntɛm nsoa adwerɛwa a ne dua wareɛ.
*The giant squirrel does not rush to support the ground-squirrel whose tail is long.*
(These two kinds of squirrels are prized for the beauty of their tails. Hence: A man does not promote a rival).

3710. Kukuban su abrempɔn–su a, yɛto no aberempɔn tuo.
*If the giant forest squirrel cries in a powerful voice, we shoot it with a powerful gun.*
(If you pretend to be greater than you are, great will be your downfall).

3711. Okunkuwonfoɔ didi nkukuhena mu.
*A potter eats from broken pots.*
(A professional tends to neglect his own home).

3712. Kukuo a ɛsi amamfo so se: wakyɛre na deɛ ɔnwonoo no nso ɛ?
*The pot that stands in a ruined town says: it has waited long, then what about its maker?*
(Said of someone who complains unnecessarily when others have more reason to do so).

3713. Kukuo hena a ɛsi anaafoɔ eyɛ biribi a, ɛkora nkurabini.
*The damaged pot which is put at the foot of the bed, if it does nothing more, it stores the pellets of mice.*
(Even apparently useless people have some use).

3714. Kukuo mu nsa se moka mo tiri bɔ mu a, na ɛma kuro no yɛ kɛseɛ.
*The pot of palm wine says if you bring your heads together the town grows bigger.*
(Strength through unity).

3715. Kukurubini rekukuru bini a, wose ɔyɛ kwasea nanso deɛ ɔresoɛ no deɛ obu no mpensa.
*When the dung beetle carries excrement you say it is a fool, but the one who is helping him to take the load down thinks that it is worth three thousand.*
(Value is in the eye of the beholder).

3716. Kukurubini se: ɔnim deɛ ɔde bini kɔ a yɛbetɔ, nti na ɔprɛ.
*The dung beetle says: it knows where to take dung to where they will buy it, that is why it rolls it.*
(This beetle makes large balls of dung which it rolls to its hole in a very skilled way. No one constantly performs an action which is not to his profit).

3717. Wokum birekuo, kum akokɔ a, adekyeɛ fa w'ase.
*If you kill the coucal and kill the chicken, morning will take you by surprise.*
(These two birds both announce the dawn. Hence: If you kill those who help you to do a job, you will have to rely on yourself).

3718. Wokum adekyeɛ a, esum duru wo.
*If you kill daylight, darkness overcomes you.*
(If you destroy what is good, you suffer from the bad that is left).

3719. Wokum dɔm a, na wodi dɔm adeɛ.
*If you kill the hostile army, you inherit its property.*
(You have to finish a job successfully to profit from it).

3720. Woakum odwan ama onifrani adi, wanyi wo ayɛ, na wokɔsi ne ntoma de buruu go so a, na ɔbɛyi wo ayɛ?
*If you have killed a sheep to give a blind man to eat, he was not grateful to you, then when you wash his cloth and add blue, will he then be grateful?*
("Adding blue"–i.e. a blue whitener–indicates that this is a recent coinage. If someone is not grateful for a big favor, he will not be grateful for one he cannot see and appreciate).

3721. Wokum "mafa madi" a, wokum "mpanin-mmɛtie."
*If you kill "I have taken and eaten it," you kill "elders-come-and-listen".*
(If you get rid of unwillingness to share, you also get rid of the necessity to report to the elders).

3722. Yɛkum akagyawa hyɛ oni yam.
*We kill the ground squirrel and put it on its mother's stomach.*
(When a child commits an offence and is punished, the mother is blamed).

3723. Wokum akagyawa wɛ nkatekwan a, na ɔkɔ n'abusua mu.
*If you kill the ground squirrel to make ground-nut soup, it goes into its own family.*
(You don't harm someone by handing them over to their own people).

3724. Wokum ɔkom kum pɛtɛ a, wo dufa ka wo nsam.
*If you kill the palm-nut vulture and kill the hooded vulture, your lump of medicine remains in your hand.*
(Both birds are used in making medicines. Hence: If you don't have the ingredients to complete something important, it is useless).

3725. Wokum akura a, wosoa brefi.
*If you kill the mouse, you carry the palm basket.*
(If a mouse gets into the storage basket you have to take the basket outside and upset it before you catch the mouse. Hence: You have to work to free yourself from trouble).

3726. Ɔkum–akyekyedeɛ nna ne nwoma.
*The one who kills the tortoise does not flay it.*
(One action does not necessarily follow another).

3727. Ɔrekum nkyiri "Mayɛ dɛn?"
*A killer does not taboo "What have I done?"*
(If you decide to harm someone, you are not put off by their pleas).

3728. Wokum manifoɔ na woankata n'ani a, ne sasa nya wo.
*If you kill a fellow citizen and you don't cover his eyes, his bad spirit gets you.*
(You cannot trick people who are known to you with impunity).

3729. Wokum ananse, kum okramantan kum odwan a, nyansa nni hɔ bio.
*If you kill the spider and kill the insect which kills sheep, there is no wisdom there any longer.*
(If you get rid of wise people, you will miss their advice).

3730. "Wokum no a, anka wodii no aboa", yɛ ɛka.
*"If you had killed him, then you would have eaten him as an animal", is a debt.*
(The words in quotes are those used in a chief's court when you are found guilty. The judgement of "guilty" means you pay a fine. Hence: However small the case you have to pay).

3731. Wokum anomaa a, ɔto asia na woyi ne yam asia a, na asia asa.
*If you kill a bird that lays a golden egg (lit. asia) and remove the golden egg, you get no more golden eggs.*
(Asia is a large amount of gold dust. Hence: If you destroy your capital, you cease to get interest).

3732. Wokum nyansafoɔ a, na woasɛe adeɛ; na wotɔn no de a, wonyɛɛ hwee.
*If you kill a wise man, you have spoiled something; if you sell him though, you have not done anything great.*
(If a wise man lives, he will find a way to thrive).

3733. Wokum ɔpanin ma wo dɔfo bɛdi adeɛ a, wohwere nyansa.
*If you kill an elder to let your sweetheart inherit, you lose wisdom.*
(It is an advantage to have an elder in the house to consult. Hence: You can't have it both ways).

3734. Yɛkum ɔsebɔ a yɛmfrɛ no asabontwe.
*If we kill a leopard, we do not call it a golden cat.*
(If you achieve great things, you don't claim to have done lesser ones).

3735. Yɛkum ɔwɔ a, yɛtwa ne ti.
*If we kill a snake, we cut off its head.*
(You must finish a job once begun. Don't do things by halves).

3736. Yɛankum aboa a, yɛnni n'ayamdeɛ.
*If we don't kill an animal, we do not eat its internal organs.*
(First things first).

3737. Yɛn kum bi a, yɛmpam bi.
*If we don't kill some, we don't drive away some.*
(Finish one thing before you begin another).

3738. Wonkum mmarima a, womfa mmaa.
*If the men are not killed the women are not carried off.*
(If you want to take something you must first deal with its owner).

3739. Monkum Kuntuankama na ne nkapo nhyehye mo.
*Until you had killed Kuntuankama you could not wear his bracelets.*
(It is only when a great man falls that you can take his precious things. Death conquers all).

3740. Akuma da Kwaku Manu kɔn ho a, wose ɛda bankye akorɛm.
*If the axe lies on Kwaku Manu's shoulder, you say it lies in the fork of a cassava plant.*
(We treat some people without feeling).

3741. Nkumaa-nkumaa na yɛhwɛ wɔn ma wɔnyini.
*It is the young that we look after to allow them to grow up.*
(Big things grow out of small).

3742. Kumase abrabɔ te sɛ apakyie, woammua so yie a, nkura goro mu.
*Existence in Kumasi is like a gourd, if you don't cover it well, the mice play in it.*
(If you are not careful in a city, you get into trouble).

3743. Okunafoɔ, yɛfa no kuna dan mu.
*A widow, we take her in the mourning room.*
(As soon as a woman loses a husband, those interested show their interest. If you are interested in something you should decide quickly).

3744. Okunafoɔ na wamma adwareɛ anwoɔ.
*A widow did not make the bathroom dry.*
(A widow has to bathe three times a day. Unusual circumstances lead to unusual results).

3745. Okunafoɔ su yɛ mmiɛnsa: "Agya, fa me dɔ", "Agya na wogyaa me sɛn ni?" na "Agya se ɔde me gya wo-o!"
*The widow has three forms of lament: "Husband, take me with you", "Husband, how did you leave me?" and "Husband says he has given me to you".*
(There is a practical aspect to every complaint).

3746. Okunini su abua mu.
*A great man weeps through his pipe.*
(He suffers in silence).

3747. [Kunkumaboɔ]/[aseboɔ] se: nsuo antɔ a, anka ɔne ɛboɔ pɛ.
*The dried mud used for building says: if it did not rain it would have been as strong as a real stone.*
(If it were not for circumstances, I would be as good as you).

3748. Nkunkyire na ɛma Buruwaa dware asukɔkyeaa.
*Going to sleep with her husband makes Buruwaa bathe in icy water.*
(If you want something enough, you are prepared to suffer for it).

3749. Akuntun kuntun nkɔdaa na ɔnkuntun mpanimfoɔ.
*A stick subdues the child but it does not subdue the elder.*
(You need an appropriate means of controlling different groups of people).

3750. Akuntun-akuntun mu wɔ biribi a, anka ɔsebɔ afiri abɛn.
*If arrogant movement were profitable, it would have given the leopard a horn.*
(If pure arrogance got a man anywhere, then it would make him a chief).

3751. Akuntun-ankuntun, yɛyɛ no dɔm ano na yɛnyɛ no mmaa so.
*Blustering you use at the war front, you don't do it to show off before women.*
(Fit the action to the occasion).

3752. Okuntunkununku nni abusua nti na ɔde ne ho bɔɔ [Duedu Akwaban]/[ntɛtia] na ɔwu wasie no.
*The great silk-cotton (Ceiba pentandra) tree has no family, therefore he joined [Duedu who has plenty of family]/[the ant] so that when he dies, he will bury him.*
(However strong you may be, you need a family to support you or you must find a substitute for it).

3753. Okuntunkununku Kunkunamoa firi pato kurom bɛhwease a, ɔse asaase yɛ tratra.
*If the cockroach from the ceiling falls to the ground, it says that the ground is flat.*
(A person's mind is limited by environment and he cannot judge beyond his knowledge. Beware of quick judgments on insufficient information).

3754. Wokunu pɛ wo a, ɛnnim sɛ woyɛ kwadwofoɔ.
*If your husband loves you, he does not care if you are a lazy person.*
(Love glosses over shortcomings).

3755. Akura huhu ansa na waka.
*The mouse blows on it before it bites it.*
(One thing leads to another).

3756. Akura akoa ne abotokura.
*The mouse's slave is the striped mouse.*
(Everyone has someone who serves him).

3757. Akura kɔsi koserɛ so a, ɔwe n'afuru ma, gya deɛ aka hɔ.
*If the mouse gets onto the thigh of the carcass of the bush cow, it eats its fill and leaves what remains.*
(If you unexpectedly find yourself in clover, you make the most of it).

3758. Akura ne agyinamoa wɔ fie a, wompae deɛ wawia atomdeɛ.
*If the mouse and the cat are in the house, you do not ask who has stolen the meat.*
(If people are notorious for something, they always get blamed for it).

3759. Akura se: "Deɛ ɔkum me nyɛ me ya, sɛ deɛ ɔde me hwee fam".
*The mouse says: "He who kills me does not hurt me as much as the one who throws me on the ground".*
(You dislike a straightforward enemy less than one who backs him up).

3760. Akura se: "Maka na menweeɛ."
*The mouse says: "I have bitten but I have not eaten".*
(Said when you intended to do something, but someone inhibited your action).

3761. Akura susu asusubɔne a, ɔtɔ mmɛsuo mu.
*If a mouse thinks bad thoughts, it falls into the pot used to refine palm oil.*
(If you intend mischief, you run into trouble).

3762. Akura te sɛ nantwie mpo a, [agyinamoa akoa ne no]/[ɔkra ne ne wura].
*Even if the mouse were to be as big as a cow, [it would still be the cat's slave]/[the cat would still be its master].*
(It is not size alone that makes authority but also custom and inheritance).

3763. Nkura dodoɔ tu bɔn a, ɛnnɔ.
*If many mice dig a hole, it does not go deep.*
(Too many cooks spoil the broth).

3764. Akura-temaa a ɔdo adeɛ wɔ fie a, yɛmfa bɛn mpamo koterɛ.
*If the quick little house mouse eats things in your house, you don't take a catapult to shoot at the innocent lizard.*
(The small grey, yellow-chested mouse is a menace in the house and chews up many things, but it is hard to catch. If someone troublesome is about, you don't waste time attacking an innocent person).

3765. Nkuraasefoɔ nim asɛm di na emu abadwadeɛ na wɔnnim kyɛ.
*Villagers know how to settle a matter but they don't know how to share the fees.*
(Settling a dispute is easier than sharing money).

3766. Kuro a ɛdi mu na pusuban si mu.
*An important town has a central tower.*
(You can tell the standing of the town by its buildings).

3767. Kuro a ɔhene nni mu no, wodi mu asɛm a, ɛntwa da.
*If there is no chief in a town, if you get involved in a case there, you can't get out of it easily.*
(It is difficult to solve problems without authority).

3768. Kuro a, mmirikatufoɔ nni mu no, ɔkyakyani tu mu mmirika a, yɛse ɔresɛn.
*If there are no runners in a town, if a hunchback runs in it, we say he excels.*
(If we don't have a specialist we appreciate the amateur who tries).

3769. Kuro a anifirafoɔ nko ara na wɔte mu no, akɔniabɔ baako a ɔwɔ mu na ɔdi so hene.
*A town which contains only blind people, if a one-eyed person is there, he becomes the chief.*
(A one-eyed man is king in the city of the blind).

3770. Kuro a wopɛ mu bosea a, wonya no, wopɛ mu mma anso a, wontɔ ka.
*If you want to take a loan in a town and you get one, if you also like its women, you don't pay the debt.*
(If people can be taken advantage of in one way, they can be taken advantage of in another).

3771. Kuro mma na wɔdua boɔ.
*Citizen's plant a stone.*
(A stone, unlike a seed, does not grow quickly! Hence: Those who live permanently in a place can afford to wait for slow development. A stranger wants everything to happen quickly).

3772. Kuro bi mu wɔ dɔm a, kuro no so mmokyea nsa.
*As long as there are people in a town, hearths will remain.*
(As long as there are people cooking and leading a normal existence there is life in the community).

**3773. Kuro bi mufoo kyiri ɔmanni abɛn.**
*Some people in a town dislike their local horn.*
(A prophet is not without honour save in his own land).

**3774. Kuro biara, mmarinsɛm wo mu.**
*In every town there are men of action.*

**3775. Kuro biara [Mɛnsa]/[Aborɔmpa] wɔ mu.**
*In every town there is a [Mɛnsa]/[Aborɔmpa].*
(The third child of one sex–Mɛnsa, for a boy; Mansa for a girl–is expected to be troublesome. There is a saying: "Aborɔ mpa Mɛnsa tirim" or "Evil things are never out of Mensa's head," and thus Aborɔmpa has become a by-name of Mɛnsa. The proverb means that there is a trouble-maker in every town).

**3776. Kuro biara wɔ ne wura.**
*Every town has its leader.*

**3777. Kuro biara nni hɔ a kwasea nni mu.**
*There is no town in existence in which there is no fool.*

**3778. Kuro rebɛbɔ a, ɛmfiri anonomsafoɔ brono so.**
*If the town is going to be destroyed, it does not come from the district of drunkards.*
(It is those in a responsible position who cause a town to thrive or fall, not those who are not interested in power).

**3779. Kuro kɛseɛ nyera ɔmanni.**
*(Even) a great town does not lose its citizens.*
(You know your way about your own area).

**3780. Kuro korɔ mu nni nyansa.**
*In a single town there is no wisdom.*
(Someone who travels gains more experience than a stay-at-home).

**3781. Kuro mpo bɔ na ɛnte sɛ fie.**
*If even a town is destroyed, how much more the home.*
(If the whole is destroyed, so are its parts).

**3782. Kuro mu dwo a, na ɔhɔhoɔ si ne ntoma hata abɔnten.**
*Is a town is peaceful, then a stranger can wash his cloth and hang it outside to dry.*
(In times of peace, you can lead an open life, whoever you are).

**3783. Kuro mu yɛ din na, na asɛm wɔ mu.**
*If a town becomes quiet, something is happening there.*
(There is calm before a storm).

**3784. Nkuro dɔɔso a, woyi bi ayɛ.**
*Of several towns one must be praised above the others.*
(All things are not equal. There is always one who excels).

**3785. Ekuro a ɛhia na yɛbɔ no dudo.**
*If a sore worries you, you dress it.*
(When a situation needs dealing with, you deal with it).

**3786. Ekuro a ɛbɛkum ɔkraman na ɛtɔ n'apampam.**
*The sore which will kill the dog is found on the top of its head.*

(Where he cannot lick it. Said when the solution to a problem is beyond your reach).

**3787. Ekuro a ɛso na ne sasa so.**
*If a sore gets bigger, so does its dressing.*
(The dressing is made of soft plantain fibre. Hence: If something becomes more serious, so do the means of dealing with it).

**3788. Ekuro bu dompe mu a, yɛmmia bio.**
*If a wound breaks out in a major bone, we do not dress it any more.*
(If the worst has occurred, you can't do any more about it).

**3789. Ekuro bɔn baanu, na ɛntutu baanu.**
*A sore may be smelled by two people, but it does not pain them both (lit. it doesn't pain two).*
(You suffer for your own sins, not others').

**3790. Ekuro amamfo ne etwa.**
*The sore's deserted town is a scar.*
(Some things are never entirely lost from view).

**3791. Ekuro ntuu wo da a, wose nwansena ne wo ka.**
*If you've never suffered from a sore, then you say that the fly is a good friend.*
(If your friends have never been tempted, you don't know their real nature).

**3792. Ekuro wɔ hwene mu a, nna mmɔn bio.**
*If you have a sore in your nose, it does not stink any more to you.*
(If you get accustomed to something, you no longer notice it).

**3793. Ekuro wu a na dwoa ahwete.**
*If a sore heals, the inflammation in the gland disappears.*
(If a major event is settled, the smaller problems cease to exist).

**3794. Akurofoso abosea se: "Owuo na wamma yɛn ano ammoa".**
*The deserted towns small stones say: "It is because of Death that we have been scattered".*
(People suffer from circumstances beyond their control).

**3795. Akurofoso apakyie se: "Gyae me dane-dane na deɛ ɔduaa me awu".**
*The gourd of the deserted town says: "Stop fiddling with me, for the one who planted me is dead".*
(Don't interfere with people over whom you have no authority).

**3796. Kurom kwasea ne odikuro.**
*The town-fool is a sub-chief.*
(A leader takes responsibility for dealing with all manner of tiresome problems and is constantly facing trouble. The sub-chief does not have the privileges and perks of a chief; but he still has all the problems. Hence: Said of someone who accepts burdens without adequate recompense).

**3797. Wo kurom pɛtɛ di wo nam a, ebi ka.**
*If your town's vulture eats your carcass, a part remains.*
(People you know well show more consideration than strangers).

**3798. "Kurom yɛ dɛ, kurom yɛ dɛ", na ɛde akobɔ ba.**
*"The town is nice, the town is nice", brings inability to return home.*
(If you wait too long, you fail to act at all).

**3799. Kuromani na ɔnim kurom asɛm.**
*It is the citizen of a town who knows the town's affairs.*
(A person who belongs to a group knows its affairs best).

**3800. Okurompɔn rekum n'adwan na mfefena nso rehunu ne nwa.**
*As the okurompɔn insect kills the sheep, so the grub destroys the dried snail.*
(The okurompɔn is an insect that looks like a mantis. It is reputed to kill sheep by mesmerizing them with its swaying movements, so that they themselves sway with it and finally fall dead. Hence: Everyone has enemies who are less important than he is).

**3801. Okurompɔn rehwe nnwa no, na odwan so refa ho wu.**
*While the insect is looking at the snail, the sheep is also dying through that.*
(See Proverb 3800. The idea is that the insect does not kill the sheep deliberately. Hence: People's downfall may be caused unintentionally).

**3802. Akuropɔn mmaa, wɔayɛ aboko, wɔnhwete faako.**
*Akropong women are like stone partridges, they don't scratch in only one place.*
(This proverb is said about the women of many towns. It appears to be a prejudiced statement about the infidelity of women. But it could also mean that they can do two or three things successfully at the same time!)

**3803. Akuropɔnfoo te sɛ apakyie, woammɔ wɔn a, wommue.**
*The people of Akropong are like gourds, you must beat them before they budge.*
(This is an Akuapem proverb. The people are reportedly reserved and need prodding into action).

**3804. Kurotwiamansa a wayare afɔn no, ne ho dɛn te sɛ kankane mmiɛnsa a aka abom.**
*Even the leopard which is sick and has grown thin is as strong as three civet cats together.*
(Even if a powerful man is weak or sick, he still has more power than a lesser man).

**3805. Kurotwiamansa ba nsuro bogyanam.**
*The young leopard does not fear bloody meat.*
(You don't fear what you are used to).

**3806. Kurotwiamansa da hahan mu a, ɔyɛ yerɛyerɛ, nanso etuo de no ba fie a, na n'ano retwa ahuro.**
*If the leopard stays amongst the leaves, he rustles them, but when the gun takes him home, then his mouth foams.*
(A man may be king of his own castle, but elsewhere he is powerless).

**3807. Kurotwiamansa hunuu nifa to a, anka aboa biara nka wiram.**
*If the leopard knew how to spring upon its prey from the right then no other animal would survive in the bush.*

(A leopard is supposed always to strike from the left. If a man were to be equally good at all things, he would be supreme).

**3808. Kurotwiamansa Kwadwo, ne mfemfem yɛ du pɛ, nanso hwan na ɔbɛtumi agyina n'anim akan?**
*The leopard Kwadwo has ten whiskers, but who will be able to stand in front of him and count them?*
(No one dare question a strong and fearless man).

**3809. Kurotwiamansa kyere akyekyedeɛ a, ɔdane dane no kwa.**
*If the leopard catches a tortoise, it turns it over and over in vain.*
(The tortoise stays within its shell and cannot be got out. Hence: It's no good attempting the impossible).

**3810. Kurotwiamansa na wamma adowa ayie amma.**
*It was the leopard who made the antelope's funeral a failure.*
(Fear isolates).

**3811. Kurotwiamansa nante sese ase a, sese woso biribiri.**
*If the leopard prowls in the thicket, the thicket shakes a great deal.*
(The presence of a powerful man is always felt).

**3812. Kurotwiamansa se: ɔnam ha mu kwa, akyekyedeɛ na ɔde ne ha.**
*The leopard says: he prowls in the forest in vain, the tortoise owns it.*
(Mere brute force cannot achieve everything).

**3813. Kurotwiamansa se: ɔne wo bɛfa adamfoɔ a, mfa n'anum nyɛ kwan.**
*The leopard says: if he and you are going to be friends, don't use his mouth as a passage.*
(Don't presume on friendship with a powerful man).

**3814. Kurotwiamansa se wawu a, ɔboa, ɔdaadaa wo.**
*If the leopard says it is dead, it is lying, it is deceiving you.*
(If a dangerous man appears to be weak, beware).

**3815. Kurotwiamansa tɔ fam a, Damfo Adu bɔ no se.**
*If the leopard falls, then the big flies (Damfo Adu) rejoice.*
(One man's downfall is to another man's advantage).

**3816. Kurotwiamansa wɔ hɔ yi, ɛmmu no akora.**
*The leopard as it is, we don't regard it as old.*
(A powerful man retains his power, regardless of age).

**3817. Kurotwiamansa wɔ padua, nanso obi ntumi ntwa so nwe.**
*The leopard has a long tail, but no one can cut it off to eat.*
(Some tasks are too dangerous to be performed).

**3818. Kurotwiamansa wura dwammuom firi a, yɛmmisa sɛ: "Ebi aka?"**
*If the leopard enters the sheep-fold and returns, we don't ask: "Does something remain?"*
(Don't ask the obvious. Or: You cannot expect mercy from an enemy).

**3819. Nkurukutie se ɔnim sɛ ɛkɔm bɛba nti na ɔkutirii dua ho sieɛ.**
*The tree ant says he knew that famine would come and*

*that is why he scraped the tree and kept it.*
(You should prepare in advance for a rainy day).

3820. Nkuruma se ɔbɛdi ahurisie wɔ nkwan mu a, na ɔnim deɛ nkyene aka akyerɛ no.
*If the okro says it will enjoy itself in the soup, then it is because of what the salt has told it.*
(If someone who is already involved says something is good, then you take their word for it).

3821. Nkuruma-kesɛ se: "M'abɔ me yeaa agu me yam."
*The ripe okro says: "I keep all my seeds in my belly."*
(If someone near you hurts you, you may say nothing, but your stomach aches over it).

3822. Wokusa bayerɛ bebrebe a, ɛpinim.
*If you keep turning yam which is being roasted, it becomes black.*
(Something which is overworked is spoilt).

3823. Kusibɛdɔ, wosa, mesa.
*A fat rat, you eat, I eat.*
(You share the profits of what you work for).

3824. Okusie a ɔda bɔnnuasa mpo yɛkyɛ no, na ɛnte sɛ ɔkɔtɔ a ɔda bɔn korɔ.
*A rat who has thirty holes we manage to catch, how much more the crab which lies in one hole.*
(If you achieve something hard, then why can't you achieve something easy?)

3825. Kusie a ɔnni famafoɔ na apa bo no.
*The rat which does not have a protector is the one which is caught in the trap.*
(Everyone needs someone to protect them in life).

3826. Okusie bankam ne adwe.
*The rat's amber beads are palm kernels.*
(Everyone has something he thinks most beautiful).

3827. Okusie bɔ bɔn tu gya hɔ a, amoakua kɔfa.
*If the rat digs a hole and leaves it, the ground squirrel takes possession of it.*
(Said when one man works for another's benefit).

3828. Okusie bɔn mu nni biribi a, ɛwɔ mmadwoa.
*Even if there is nothing else in a rat's hole, it holds palm kernels.*
(A man's means of livelihood are the last thing he gives up).

3829. Okusie dane ahweaa a, ne dua poma no.
*If the rat tries to turn into a kusimanse, its tail gives it away.*
(You can't change your nature by just trying).

3830. Okusie kɔfa adwe na Onyame te ayerɛmo a, ɔdane twene.
*If the rat goes to take a palm kernel and God sends lightning, it throws it away.*
(Fear is the supreme emotion).

3831. Okusie-aku, yɛgye no aku. Akranteɛ-aku, yɛgye no aku. Abotokura-aku, yɛgye no aku. Nanso wɔn nyinaa san kɔsom akrantee-aku.
*Rat who responds aku, we reply aku. Grass-cutter who responds aku, we reply aku. Striped mouse who responds aku, we reply aku. But they all go back to serve the grass-cutter whose response is aku.*

(There is an order of precedence in every place. If a man is first in his own community he will come under someone else outside).

3832. Okusi-kwasea na sɛ ɔhunu agyinamoa ba a, ɔde no kɔyɛ n'abaawa.
*A stupid rat, if it sees a kitten come, goes and takes it for a maid-servant.*
(An enemy is an enemy, however young).

3833. Okusie se: mmadwoa yɛ sika a, anka wanya adeɛ so.
*The rat says: if palm kernels were money, it would be very rich.*
(If wishes were horses, beggars would ride).

3834. Okusinini annɔre sradeɛ a, na ɛfiri mpaprɛbɔ.
*If the male rat does not grow fat, it is from clearing the bush.*
(You can't thrive on over-work).

3835. Okusinini anhunu adwebɔ, na ɔbereɛ bɔ a, ɔwe bi.
*If a male rat does not crack a palm nut but his wife does, he will still eat some.*
(It is not a disgrace for a man to get help from his wife).

3836. Wokuta ahwetehweteɛ a, wommisa dua.
*If your cutlass is blunt, you do not ask for a tree.*
(If you don't have the tools for a job, you don't try and get it).

3837. Mekuta sekan, kuta afena; na sɛ mehyia ntɔkwa a, deɛ ɛwɔ he na memfa nto [fam]/[nkyɛn].
*I carry a knife and a cutlass; but if I run into a fight, which one of them should I [put aside]/[throw away].*
(A choice of two weapons).

3838. Yɛkuta wo ti a, wommisa w'anom asɛm.
*If we grasp your head, you don't ask about your mouth.*
(If you are in real danger, you don't concern yourself with lesser problems).

3839. Wokuta ɔtuo a, womfa abaa.
*If you carry a gun, you don't need to take a stick.*
(If you have the best, you don't need the second best as well).

3840. Wokuta wo yere a, na wokuta wo ba.
*If you hug your wife, you hug your child.*
(Treat members of the family equally).

3841. Yɛnkuta abaa mma ɔwɔ nkeka yɛn.
*We don't carry a stick for a snake to bite us.*
(If we have the means of preventing something happening, we use it).

3842. Yɛnkuta "nankana" nnyae "nankana" na yɛnka sɛ: "Mehunuiɛ a, anka".
*We don't hold "had I known," release "had I known" and later say: "If only I had known".*
(It's no good having vain regrets).

3843. Kutiruku se: ɔnni biribi a, ɔreda ɔnwono ase.
*The bitter bean says: if it has nothing else, it gives thanks to its bitterness.*
(Something may appear to be a disadvantage but at the same time protect you from molestation).

**3844. Nkuto, yɛsra no hiada.**
*Shea butter, we use it (lit. we grease (ourselves with) it) in time of poverty.*
(Shea butter is the cheapest skin-cream available in Ghana and is made locally from the shea-nut. If you can't get the best from "over there", you take what you can afford.

**3845. Kutukwaku ammɛto wo a, na ɛfiri adekyeɛ.**
*If the hyena did not meet you, it is because of daybreak.*
(If someone does not succeed in his bad activities it is because they come to light).

**3846. Kutukwaku sere anadwo a, na ɛwɔ deɛ wanya.**
*If the hyena laughs in the night, then he knows what he has.*
(If a secretive person acts publicly, something serious must have happened).

**3847. Nkwa nyɛ dɛ a, anka owuo nyɛ ya.**
*If living were not sweet, then death would not be bitter.*

**3848. Wonkwaa wo dan mu mmaa ɛmmeree yie a, wonkɔkwa wo yɔnko deɛ mu.**
*If you have not polished the floor of your room with a mixture of red clay and chaff to make it shine well, you do not go to smooth your companion's floor.*
(You attend to your own affairs first).

**3849. Kwaakwaadabi a wanya ato pa bi antoɔ na ɔkɔtogu ɛkoɔ mmɛn mu.**
*The crow which was unable to lay eggs in a proper place, laid its eggs in the horns of a bush cow.*
(Improvidence leads to unwise action).

**3850. Kwaakwaadabi baako ntu ne yɔnko ani.**
*One crow does not take out his companion's eyes.*
(Brother does not harm brother).

**3851. Kwaakwaadabi dɔfo ne kɔkɔsakyi a na ɛyɛ ne yɔnko a.**
*If the crow's lover is the vulture, then he must be its companion.*
(If you say you love someone who is universally rejected, then he must be a real friend).

**3852. [Kwaa-kwaa-wuo]/[abotokuro] wamma akwannya anyɛ no fo.**
*Striped mouse, you did not let the opposite side of the path find him guilty.*
(Be satisfied with what you have or you will suffer).

**3853. Kwaakye adeɛ yɛ fɛ a, yɛde sika na ɛtɔ.**
*If Kwaakye's things are beautiful, we take money to buy them.*
(Things worth paying for are never free).

**3854. Kwaasansa se: sɛ wopɛ din pa a wonya, wopɛ nimomu nso a wonya.**
*The buzzard says: if you want a good name you get it, if you want a bad name you get it too.*
(You get the reputation you work for).

**3855. Kwaata adwasum, yɛdii no da koro.**
*Kwaata town's night time market was held only once.*
(The people of Kwaata once planned to hold markets at night so that they could cheat people. They wrapped up balls of sand in leaves and cooked them as kenkey.

However, visitors from a nearby village had also taken the opportunity to use counterfeit money. The experiment was discontinued! Hence: As you plan to trick someone, so will he plan to trick you).

**3856. Kwabena Asante ankoto sebɔ tuo a, anka asɛm amma fie.**
*If Kwabena Asante had not gone to shoot a leopard, trouble would not have come to the house.*
(One thing leads to another).

**3857. Kwabena Tumpɔ akɔm: wokɔhwɛ a, wo ni awu; woankɔhwɛ a, wo se awu.**
*Kwabena Tumpɔ's priestly dance: if you go and watch it, your mother dies; if you don't go and watch it, your father dies.*
(Hobson's choice).

**3858. Kwabɛtene akuntun-akuntun sɛ ɛbɛbuo, sɛ ɛmmuo, okuafoɔ yam hyehye no.**
*If the tall palm tree bends, whether it breaks or not, the farmer's stomach pains him.*
(i.e. he worries. Hence: Some situations are worrying, whether you know the final outcome or not).

**3859. Ɔkwabrane di awu a, na ɛfiri kakyerɛ.**
*If the strong man kills another person, it is because of gossiping.*
(If you believe all the tales you are told, it leads to violence).

**3860. Ɔkwabrane na ɔso ne ngo; sɛ ɔbɛbɔ no o, sɛ ɔbɛton o, ɔno ara na ɔnim.**
*If a strong man is carrying his oil; if he breaks it or if he is going to sell it, he alone knows.*
(A man can do what he likes with his own possessions).

**3861. Kwadwo Akɔre nya nkɔdɔɔ Boa no na ɛhɔ nkɔnsɔn didi.**
*Before Kwadwo Akɔre went to make a farm at Boa, the monkeys fed themselves.*
(Life goes on. Or: Even without modern amenities, man survives).

**3862. Kwadwo Anɔkwa a ne ni awuo, ɔse: "Ɛnyɛ biribi ɛfirisɛ ɛba saa daa.!"**
*Kwadwo Anɔkwa whose mother has died says "It isn't anything much, because such things happen daily".*
(If you are accustomed to hardship, you become immune to it. Or: Death is inevitable).

**3863. Ɔkwaduo kɔ Nyedu a, ɔbɛba abɛto n'afirifoɔ.**
*If the yellow-backed duiker goes to Nyedu, he will return to meet the trapper.*
(However much you run from it, you will still be exposed to danger).

**3864. Ɔkwaduo se: "Woammrɛ na wodidi a, ɛnyɛ dɛ".**
*The yellow-backed duiker says: "If you don't struggle before you eat, it does not taste good".*
(You appreciate more what you have worked for).

**3865. Ɔkwadwofoɔ bini nketenkete.**
*A sluggard's faeces are very small.*
(If you don't work, you don't produce).

**3866. Ɔkwadwofoɔ afenawa ne ɔdeyɔfoɔ.**
*The lazy person's female servant is a hard worker.*
(Lazy masters make their servants work hard).

3867. Ɔkwadwofoɔ afuo nyɛɛ kɛseɛ da.
*A sluggard's farm never becomes big.*
(A lazy person never becomes rich).

3868. Kwaeɛ a agye yɛn no, yɛmfrɛ no kwaeɛwa.
*The forest that has adopted us, we do not call it a small forest.*
(You do not insult your benefactor).

3869. Kwaeɛ mu akrukyirɛboa: me nua ne wo, anka me ne wo bɛgoro, na wo ho huu nti na mesuro woɔ.
*Puff adder in the forest: you are my brother, normally I would play with you, but because of your frightfulness I fear you.*
(You fear even your friends, if they are dangerous).

3870. Kwaeɛ mu yɛ dinn a, na ɛfiri sɛ mmoadoma kɔ adidi.
*If the forest is quiet, then it is because all the creatures have gone to eat.*
(If a situation changes from the normal, there must be a reason for it).

3871. Kwaeɛ mu yɛ hu a, onipa na ɔka.
*If the forest is frightening, then a person tells you.*
(If something gets a bad reputation, it is because people have talked about it).

3872. Kwaagyebi anomaa se: ɔnim ewiem asem.
*The Kingfisher says: it knows what is in the air.*
(Said of someone who always knows what is going on in his or her environment).

3873. Akwagyinamoa da mfofom a, asɛ wawu.
*If a cat is sleeping in the mfofom plants (Aspilia latifolia), it seems to be dead.*
(Do not judge by appearances).

3874. Akwagyinamoa da suka mu a, wose wawu, wode abaa ka no a, na wohunu ne teberɛ.
*If the cat is lying in the roof gutter, you say it is dead, but if you take a stick and touch it you see how it is.*
(When someone is troubled you see their true nature. Or: See Proverb 3873).

3875. Kwaku Ananse se: "Adeɛ mmienu yɛ kyɛna".
*Kwaku Ananse says: "It is difficult to share two things".*
(Kwaku Ananse or a cheater says this: it is difficult to cheat if the solution is obvious).

3876. Kwaku Antwi a ɔwɔ se-waworawa mpo se ɔrentumi nwe dompeden; na akɔwie sɛ asɔkwa a ɔnni se.
*Even Kwaku Antwi who has strong and broad teeth says he can't chew hard bones; how much less the hornbill that has no teeth.*
(If the expert cannot solve a problem, how can the layman?)

3877. Kwakunini amponku kasa yɛ ɔbɔfoɔ ahi.
*The great male monkey's talking annoys the hunter.*
(If someone dislikes you, he dislikes everything about you).

3878. Kwakuo ba a, yɛkum abirekyie, ɔkwakuo amma a, yɛkum abirekyie.
*If the monkey comes, we kill the goat, if the monkey does not come, we kill the goat.*
(No matter what happens we will stick to our decision).

3879. Kwakuo mfiri wura mu mmɛwansi mma ɛnyɛ sɛ onipa.
*The monkey cannot come from the bush and sneeze like a man.*
(A servant cannot be above his master).

3880. Kwakuo nam nyɛ dɛ a, ɛnte sɛ mmire.
*If a monkey's meat is not sweet, it is better than mushrooms.*
(You take the best you can get, failing a better).

3881. Kwakuo nam tweapea so na ɔkɔda, nanso ne se aporɔ.
*The monkey walks on the false chewing stick tree (Garcinia) to sleep, but it has rotten teeth.*
(You do not necessarily benefit from what is available to you).

3882. Kwakuo se dɔtɔ mfa no nsie a, na ɔnkyerɛ se ɔmfa no koraa.
*When the monkey told the thicket to hide it, it did not ask it to take it as a possession.*
(If someone asks for help, don't take advantage of him).

3883. Kwakuo se: ɔremfa mumu prɛnu nti na ne nkwan fremfrem no.
*The monkey says: it can't have two defects, so it makes good soup.*
(Everybody knows the monkey is ugly, so that's one defect. Hence: Everyone has some usefulness).

3884. Kwakuo se ɔrekɔte abotoɔ na ɔhunu ɔbɔfoɔ a, ɔdane ne ho brakasimane.
*If the monkey is going to pluck fruit and sees a hunter, it slips away stealthily.*
(If you see your enemy before he sees you, you find a way of avoiding him).

3885. Kwakuo suro ɔbɔfoɔ, nti na ɔredidi a, ɔte bi sie n'afono mu.
*The monkey fears the hunter, that is why when it's eating, it stores some (food) in its pouch.*
(Said of a careful person who provides against the future).

3886. [Kwaku-ntakuo-nnum]/[abirekyie] se: anowesa mpoma awerɛkyekyerɛ.
*[Kwaku-five-sixpenny-pieces]/[the goat] says: even chewing brings about satisfaction.*
(Even simple pleasure satisfy).

3887. Kwaku-tire a ɛnyɛ dɛ no, yɛntwa ntɔn yɛn yɔnko.
*If the monkey's head were not sweet, you would not cut it and sell it to your companion.*
(You can only make profit from the profitable).

3888. Kwaakye adeɛ yɛ fɛ a, yɛde sika na ɛtɔ.
*If Kwaakye's things are beautiful, we take money to buy them.*
(Valuable things for are never free).

3889. Nkwamafoɔ na ɔbɔ ɔman.
*He who gives life is the same person who spoils the state.*
(A man who has power for good also has power for bad).

3890. Kwame Fofie Dadeɛ se: "Obi to boɔ na amfa soro a, ɛfa fam".
*Kwame Fofie Dadeɛ says: "If someone throws a stone and it does not go above, it falls onto the ground".*
(There are only two alternatives).

3891. Kwame Tua te a, na Aban ate.
*If Kwame Tua hears of it, then the Government knows.*
(Kwame Tua was an Asante traitor who passed on to the British information about the Asantes during the Asante wars. Hence: If a tell-tale hears something, you know he will pass it on).

3892. Kwamenaa mpɛ ne ho asɛm nti na ɔte adukuro mu.
*The ant-hill does not like trouble, that is why it stands in the buttress of a tree.*
(If you have a protector, you are not so likely to get into trouble).

3893. Kwamenaa si adukuro mu a, na ne fie ne hɔ.
*If the ant-hill stands in the buttress of a tree, then that is its home.*
(If someone is seen regularly in a place then they must have some permanent connection with it).

3894. Ɔkwamuni se: wowɔ asau a, na wohata tabono.
*A person from Akwamu (or a member of the Asafo Akwamu company) says: if you have a large fishing net, you let the paddle dry out.*
(If you have the necessary equipment, then you prepare for action).

3895. Ɛkwan a odompo awu mu no yɛmfa mu akwagyansa fo.
*On the road where the marsh mongoose has died, you do not catch the leopard easily.*
(Fore-warned is fore-armed).

3896. Ɛkwan a emu yɛ hu no, yɛnko no ntiantia so.
*A road that is fearful to travel by, we do not walk there slowly.*
(We hurry to avoid trouble).

3897. Ɛkwan a yɛnnim soɔ na yɛyera ne nkwanta-nan soɔ.
*The path which we don't know at all, we get lost at its cross-roads.*
(When you do not know the circumstances and you have to come to a decision, you make a mistake).

3898. Ɛkwan a wonsuro mu na aboa kye wo weɛ.
*It is the path you do not fear that the wild beast catches you on to eat.*
(You are more easily caught unawares).

3899. Ɛkwan a ɛyɛ wo kwan na wotuo.
*If the journey is yours, you make it (lit. The journey that is your journey is the one you make).*
(If you are predestined to do something, that is what you must do).

3900. Ɛkwan nnuruu ne kɔda a yɛnkɔ.
*If the time to travel has not arrived (lit. the journey has not reached its going-day), we don't go.*
(You should act at the right time).

3901. Ɛkwan nnuruu ne kɔda na wokɔ a, wonnuru.
*If a journey is not due and you go, you will not reach your destination.*
(If you don't do things at the right time, you fail).

3902. Ɛkwan ho bintuo nhua ɔbaakofoɔ.
*The faeces along the path do not stink to only one person.*
(Some unpleasantness affect all alike).

3903. Ɛkwan mu yɛ hu , na onipa wɔ hɔ.
*If the road is dangerous, it is because a man is there.*
(It is, above all, man who is to be feared).

3904. Ɛkwan nsi anomaa.
*The road does not stop a bird.*
(You are not held up by what does not concern you).

3905. Ɛkwan ware a, yɛde yɛn nan na ɛtwa, na ɛnyɛ akuma.
*If the road is long, we take our legs to cut (follow) it, but not an axe.*
(No matter how long a case, it should be settled peaceably).

3906. Ɛkwan wɔ hɔ yi, yɛgya no deɛ ɔwɔ din.
*We give a seeing-off party to someone who has a name.*
(A good name is better than riches).

3907. Ɛkwan wɔ aso.
*The road has ears.*
(Be careful where you talk as someone may always be listening).

3908. Nkwan a ɛyɛ dɛ na ɛtwe adwa.
*Soup which is good attracts people.*
(A good thing sells itself).

3909. Nkwan dwo a anosini ka bi hwɛ.
*If the soup cools the one without lips tastes a bit.*
(When something is generally known even the most handicapped can discuss it).

3910. Nkwan pa na ɛtwetwe adwa.
*A good soup attracts seats.*
(A talented and helpful person draws others to them).

3911. Nkwan bɛyɛ dɛ a, ɛfiri fam.
*If the soup is going to be good, it is from the earth.*

3912. Nkwan bɛyɛ dɛ a na ɛfiri ɔbarima.
*If the soup will be good, it is because of a man.*
(Man inspires woman).

3913. Nkwan yɛ dɛ a, ɛta sa bi nom.
*If the soup is good a spoon also takes some.*
(You benefit from the good quality of your own work).

3914. Nkwan yɛ dɛ a, Tanɔ sa bi nom.
*If the soup is good, then Tano (fetish) will drink a bit.*
(If you achieve success the gods should be thanked by offering them a share).

3915. Nkwan nyɛ dɛ a, ne kahwɛ deɛ, empa.
*If the soup is not good, at least we taste it.*
(We must try something before we can judge it).

3916. Nkwan nyɛ dɛ a, nkyene na ɛka.
*If the soup is not good, the salt reveals it.*
(Those intimately concerned can tell the quality of something best).

3917. Ɔkwan-fanu a ɔde ne kwan te ase a, hwerɛmo nnye kwan.
*If the herb (Desmodium adscendens) who is the owner of the road is alive, then the shrub (Combretum) does not take over the road.*
(Desmodium adscendens is a small herb with trifoliate leaves and pink pea flowers which often grows on both sides of forest paths. Combretum is a thorny climbing shrub, several varieties of which have the same name – hwerɛmo. Hence: If the owner is present, no one else can take authority).

3918. Kwankora-kutafoɔ na ɔtwa nkontompo, na ɛnyɛ kwankora.
*The one who holds the wooden ladle tells lies, but not the ladle itself.*
(A servant merely does his work, he does not decide policy).

3919. Nkwankorɔ sɛe nkwampem.
*One type of soup spoils a thousand pots.*
(A bad person spoils the whole society).

3920. Akwankwaa hiani de aniberee na ɔsoa taa-si.
*The poor young man out of desperation carries the heavy load of tobacco.*
(Adversity makes you take on any work).

3921. Nkwannkyɛn mako se: "Wobɛbubu me a, bubu me, na gyae me anikyibuo".
*The wayside pepper says: "If you will break me, break me, but stop scolding me".*
(It is better to be killed than disgraced).

3922. Nkwannkyɛn borɔdeɛ se: "Nwaawaeho amma me anyɛ yie".
*The roadside plantain says: "The stripping off of my leaves does not allow me to flourish".*
(Said of someone whom everyone takes advantage of).

3923. Ɔkwannua na ɛyɛ dɛ.
*Companionship is sweet.*

3924. Akwanso-sɛm dɛ nti na wote ntasuo gu nsuo ani a, ɔkaa bɛsɔ.
*A traveller's good news makes the fish jump to pick what you spit into the river.*
(Everyone appreciates good news).

3925. Nkwanta dodoɔ yera kwan.
*Too many cross-roads lead one astray.*
(Too much advice or too much choice confuses one).

3926. Nkwantanan, ka nokorɛ.
*Cross-roads, tell the truth.*
(The cross-roads represent the point at which all views coincide, giving material for decision. You must know all the facts before you decide).

3927. Akwantimfi baa, yɛdi no ahoɔhare.
*A wayside woman, we take her swiftly.*
(If you feel guilty about something, you hurry over it).

3928. Akwantimfi firikyiwa, ankɔ wo a, ɛhenhane wo.
*The wayside castanet, if it does not fit you, it gets loose.*
(You need to become familiar with something before you know if it suits you. For instance: Don't marry someone you don't know well).

3929. Akwantimfi atwirepe: ɔbaa a ɔnni barima na yɛbo no yi akyea.
*The condition of a isolated road: if a woman has no man, then we beat her and swagger.*
(If someone has no defense, they are treated roughly).

3930. Ɔkwantempɔn a ɛsi ma yɛyi no akwa, na yɛfrɛ no kwatikwan.
*The main road that is blocked so that we bypass it, we call it a by-pass.*
(If you don't tell the truth in a case, we accuse you of being devious).

3931. Ɔkwantempɔn mu kusie, ɔnni mmirika a, na ɔwɔ akokoɔduru.
*The rat by the roadside, if it cannot run well, then at least it is brave.*
(It is a courageous person who takes risks).

3932. Ɔkwantempɔn mu sahoma: "Me na mepɛ m'adonko na wɔreto me adonko".
*Liana on the main road: "As for me, I allow swinging and that is why they are swinging on me".*
(If you make yourself available to all, your help will be abused).

3933. Ɔkwantempɔn si a, na yɛyi no akwa.
*If the main road is closed, we bypass it.*
(If you are stopped from doing things one way, then you will do them another).

3934. Ɔkwantenni nim asɛm ka na ɔnnim asee kyerɛ.
*A traveller knows how to tell tales but he does not know how to explain them.*
(Seeing is one thing and interpreting what you see is another).

3935. Ɔkwantentene akwaaba na ɛyɛ.
*It is good to be welcomed from afar.*
(If you have succeeded in returning from a difficult journey, you are respected).

3936. Ɔkwantia yɛ mmusuo.
*A shortcut is a misfortune.*
(If you try to get something cheap or easily, you may have to pay heavily for it later).

3937. Nkwantia abesesu-abesesu, asɛnkɛseɛ reba a, frankaa nsi so.
*The outskirts of a town are full of spat-out cola; when a case is on the way, there is no flag to indicate it.*
(You must look for evidence where you can find it. You will not always get formal notice of a serious event).

3938. Akwantuo abɔsoɔ ne dan mu.
*The tying of the girdle to begin a journey takes place in the room.*
(Plans start at home).

3939. Ɔkwarifa bankyiniɛ ne sie.
*The rat's umbrella is the anthill.*
(We all have something to protect us from adversity).

**3940. Kwasea bu aboterɛ sɛ ade fo.**
*The fool regards patience as undesirable.*
(A stupid person does not take the time to do things right).

**3941. Kwasea redi ne sika a, ɔse ne nsania yɛ mmerɛ.**
*A fool who has used up all his money says his scales are out of order.*
(No one likes to admit to foolishness and any excuse will be given to hide it).

**3942. Kwasea didi nkwasea mu na onyansafoɔ didi nyansa mu.**
*A foolish person eats foolishly, and a wise person eats wisely.*
(Everyone performs according to their character).

**3943. Kwasea dua, yɛntia so mprɛnu.**
*A foolish tail, we don't tread on it twice.*
(Once bitten, twice shy).

**3944. Kwasea mantam odwan a, ɔnte: wu na awuo.**
*If the fool ties a sheep, it cannot free itself: its only choice is to die (lit. death is what it dies).*
(A foolish person's excess of zeal may have disastrous results).

**3945. Kwasea na yɛkyerɛ no adeɛ soro a, ɔnhunu.**
*A fool, if we show him what is above, he does not see it.*
(Foolishness is blind).

**3946. Kwasea na ne dwan te mprɛnu.**
*It is a fool's sheep which breaks loose twice.*
(Only a stupid man makes the same mistake twice).

**3947. Kwasea na wanya ne tuo: sɛ ɔgyina hɔ na ɔbɛto o, sɛ ote hɔ na ɔbɛto o, anaasɛ ɔbɛda ayeya na wato a, ɛmfa obi ho.**
*The fool that has a gun: if he stands and fires, if he sits and fires, or if he lies on his back and fires, it is his own business.*
(You can do what you like with your own things as long as you do not harm anyone).

**3948. Kwasea na ɔse: "Wode me yɔnko na wonne me".**
*The fool says: "You mean my companion but not me".*
(If you are friends with someone you will be judged with them. You cannot avoid this by denying friendship in times of adversity).

**3949. Kwasea na yɛte ne nnuadewa tɔne no.**
*A fool is the one whose garden eggs we pick and sell to him.*
(It is easy to bamboozle a fool).

**3950. Kwasea ani te a, na agorɔ agu.**
*If a fool becomes clever, then the game spoils.*
(If a person refuses to be taken advantage of any more, you cannot do anything about it).

**3951. Kwasea nnim biribi a, ɔnim ne fufuo tɔ.**
*If a fool knows nothing else, he knows about his lump of fufu.*
(Even a fool knows how to eat).

**3952. Kwasea nnim biribi a, ɔnim merentie.**
*If a fool does not know anything else, he knows "I am not going to listen".*
(Even the worm turns).

**3953. Kwasea nya ne funu a, deɛ na ɔde yɔ.**
*If a fool gets his corpse, he does what he likes with it.*
(You have authority over what is yours whatever your character).

**3954. Kwaseabuo nti na yɛpɛ sika.**
*It is because of treachery that we earn money.*
(If you have no money, you may be obliged to cheat to get it).

**3955. Kwaseabuo nti na yɛsi ɔhene.**
*It is because of treachery that we enstool a chief.*
(Men choose rulers in order to have an ordered community).

**3956. Kwasiada a mekɔduaeɛ na menyaa, deɛbɛn na Ɛdwoada a mesoaa apampa kɔɔ afuom.**
*If on a Sunday I went to cultivate but I did not manage to get anything, then why should I take a head pad and go to the farm on Monday?*
(If the main project does not succeed you cannot get a profit from the follow-up).

**3957. Kwatani a ɔrekɔ dwa se: "Mekɔ a, merenkyea obiara", nanso obi na ɔrenkyea no.**
*A leper who is going to the market says: "When I go I will not greet anyone", but no one dares to greet him.*
(You may have decided not to work with someone, but perhaps they have already decided not to work with you).

**3958. Kwatani bɔ wo twɛdeɛ na sɛ ampae a, ne kuro bere.**
*If the leper gives you a blow and you are not wounded, his sore is opened.*
(If someone takes up a project from which he stands to lose, it is he who suffers).

**3959. Ɔkwatani ɔse: "Ntoma pofa yi ara bɛso me fura, ɛfirisɛ mawie kɔ awie ba".**
*The leper says: "Only this half piece of cloth will be enough for me to wear, because I have no position in society (lit. I have finished going and coming)".*
(The outcast cannot afford to care how he lives).

**3960. Nkwatenten nti na Ɔdomankoma bɔɔ aduro bataa nnipa ho.**
*Because of a long life Almighty God created medicine to be used by human beings.*
(God created what was essential to mankind).

**3961. Kwaterekwa se ɔbɛma wo ntoma a, tie ne din.**
*If Nudity says he will give you a cloth, listen to his name.*
(Don't trust idle boasting).

**3962. Wokwati aberewa a, wonhunu ntwan.**
*If you by-pass an old lady, you cannot know the nature of a wrinkled skin.*
(Certain signs bear witness to the nature of a situation).

**3963. Ɔkwati-Akuro amfa abɔnten no, na ɛfiri ne ka.**
*If a by-passer of towns did not pass through the street, it was because of his debt.*
(If someone fails to do the obvious he must have a good reason for it).

**3964. Wokwati, kwati a, wokwati wo ti.**
*If you take a round about way all the time (lit. by-pass and by-pass), you by-pass your head.*
(You miss your good luck. Hence: If you avoid people, you also avoid profit).

**3965. Yɛnkwati Firaw nkɔ Nta.**
*We cannot go to Gonja without crossing the Volta (lit. by-pass the Volta to go to Gonja).*
(If you are to achieve something, certain obstacles must be overcome).

**3966. Akwatia di ɔtenten akyi a, ɔdi no kwa.**
*If a short person follows a tall person, he follow him in vain.*
(Don't try and compete with those who are better equipped than you).

**3967. Akwatia hiani na ɔfura ntoma pofa.**
*It is a short poor man who wears a half-piece of cloth.*
(A normal man's cloth is made from a full eight to ten yards: a half-piece would be six yards. Hence: Poverty makes people accept what they can get).

**3968. Kyakom-kyakom-kyakom, fufuo akonta, yɛbu no waduro mu.**
*Chew, chew, chew, fufu mathematics, we work it in the mortar.*
(Every activity has its own area of planning).

**3969. Akyakya adwa tɔ a, ɔdi.**
*If the hunchback's stool reaches its turn, he inherits.*
(If something is predestined to happen, it happens).

**3970. Akyakya, ɛsi w'akyi a, wogye, ɛsi w'anim a, wogye.**
*If the hump is behind you, you take it, if it is in front of you, you take it.*
(You accept what life brings you).

**3971. Akyakya si w'akyi a, na wɔhu so mmɔbɔ na ɛsi wo koko a, na wo ara na wobo gyeeɛ.**
*If the hump is on your back, then they sympathize with you, but if it is on your chest, it is because you like it so.*
(You will be pitied for trouble you could not foresee, but not for something you could have prevented).

**3972. Akyakyafoɔ nam apem a, wɔn nyinaa yɛ yɛpɛ.**
*If a thousand hunchbacks are lined up, they will have the same shape of buttocks.*
(People of the same family share the same characteristics).

**3973. Akyampɔmaa nwoo ne ba Yaw Dɔnkɔ no, na ɛwɔ deɛ ɔsoa Dankyira Amoako Ata.**
*When Akyampɔmaa had not yet given birth to her son Yaw Dɔnkɔ, there was already someone who carried the Dankyirahene Amoako Ata.*
(Yaw Dɔnkɔ was the servant of Dankyirahene Amoako Ata. Hence: Some things have been done since time immemorial. Or: You need not think that you are the only person capable of doing something).

**3974. Wokyɛ Kwaku Ananse adekyɛ a, berɛ mpa wo so.**
*If you share in the way Kwaku Ananse shares, you will never cease to be weary.*
(Cheating is exhausting).

**3975. Yɛkyɛ animuonyam na woannya bi a, animguaseɛ ba a, ɛnka wo bi.**
*If we are sharing out dignity and you get none, if disgrace comes you are not affected.*
(Every positive has a negative).

**3976. Ɛkyɛ butu anaasɛ ɛda ne nkyɛn mu a, sɛdeɛ ɛteɛ biara ne wura dea.**
*Whether the hat turns over or turns on its side, whatever the case may be, it belongs to the owner.*
(Something which belongs to you, is yours wherever it is).

**3977. Wo kyɛ tu tɔ a, na wo tiri nte{e}ɛ.**
*If your hat falls from your head, then your head remains intact.*
(Losing something does not alter your nature).

**3978. Ɔkye-ani mfa torɔ.**
*He who shares eyes does not take a blind one.*
(A distributor makes sure he is satisfied first).

**3979. "Akyea na ɛmmuiɛ", ɛsene abɛbuo nyinaa dɛ.**
*"It has bent but it has not fallen down", is better than all proverbs.*
(While there is life there is hope).

**3980. Wokyea no a, ɛhwie gu.**
*If you tip it, it pours out.*
(If you don't take care in performing a task, you'll make a mess of it).

**3981. Ɔkyeame a ɔnnim asɛm ka, ɔse: "Nana, w'asom a".**
*The linguist who does not know how to express himself well says: "Nana (Chief), take it as you heard it".*
(The linguist speaks for the chief, but also repeats what others have said in a more formal way. This expression ("w'asom" literally is "your ears") means, in effect: "I don't need to repeat what you've heard, because you've already understood it." Hence: If you are not good at something, you try to dodge it).

**3982. Ɔkyeame dane ɔhene pa a, yɛkyi.**
*If the linguist turns into a proper chief, we taboo it.*
(Do the work you are chosen for and don't try and be something you are not).

**3983. Ɔkyeame a wasiesie ɔman ama ayɛ yiye na yɛfrɛ no kontomponi.**
*The linguist who has put things in order in the state is called a liar.*
(A prophet is not without honour save in his own land).

**3984. Ɔkyeame Anim ka asɛm a, ɔse no mpanimfoɔ mu.**
*If the linguist Anim talks about a serious matter he does so amongst the elders.*
(The linguist uses the language of the learned. Serious matters should be discussed with serious people).

**3985. Ɔkyeame pata abɔnten so ntɔkwa a, ɔbuada.**
*If a linguist involves himself in street quarrels, he goes hungry.*
(The linguist gets his share of court fees for cases taken before the chief but would not be paid for interfering in outside quarrels. Hence: If you involve yourself in business that does not concern you, you suffer for it).

3986. Akyekyedeɛ a ɔrepɛ ne yere amaneɛ na ɔse: "Wɔ m'akyi mmɛsa ma me".
*When the tortoise wants to quarrel with his wife, he says: "Plait my hair for me and let me go".*
(An excuse, however ridiculous, can always be found if you want to quarrel).

3987. Akyekyedeɛ a ne tiri hyɛ abena mu koraa yɛtwitwa, na ɛnte sɛ ɔprammire [a ne tiri gya soro]/[a ɔnya wo a ɔbɛka woɔ].
*Even the tortoise whose head is entirely in its shell is being cut up; how much more the black cobra [whose head shows conspicuously]/[who, if he catches you, will bite you].*
(If a well protected person is in trouble, how much more a feared one who has nowhere to hide).

3988. Akyekyedeɛ butu hɔ a, ɔbutu n'ayamkeka so.
*When the tortoise lies down, it lies on its stomach troubles.*
(Its own problems. If a man is pensive and quiet it is probably because he is thinking about his own problems).

3989. Akyekyedeɛ hunu amane wɔ n'abena mu.
*The tortoise, too, has discomfort in its shell.*
(You can't always judge how a man is by his appearance).

3990. Akyekyedeɛ rekɔ sere-sere no, na ɔredwane ara ne no.
*The tortoise goes smiling along but it is actually fleeing.*
(You can't always judge from a man's looks what he is doing).

3991. Akyekyedeɛ na ɔka n'asɛm se: "Asɛm mpɛ nnipa, nnipa na wɔpɛ asɛm".
*The tortoise says: "Trouble does not look for men, it is men who look for trouble".*
(If you trouble trouble, trouble troubles you!)

3992. Akyekyedeɛ na ɔkyerɛ ne bɔberɛ.
*The tortoise itself show its vulnerable spot.*
(Don't stick your neck out).

3993. Akyekyedeɛ sa n'abena mu.
*The tortoise dances in its shell.*
(Said of a self-sufficient person).

3994. Akyekyedeɛ se: "Ɔbarima mfɛre adwane".
*The tortoise says: "Man is not ashamed to run away".*
(Discretion is the better part of valor).

3995. Akyekyedeɛ se borɔdehono weɛ yɛ wena.
*The tortoise says the chewing of plantain skin is hard.*
(Said when someone is asked to do something they do not normally do but because of poverty may be forced to do).

3996. Akyekyedeɛ se: "Ɛhia ma adwene".
*The tortoise says: "Need makes one think".*
(Deliberation is necessary for survival).

3997. Akyekyedeɛ se: ahoɔden na ɔnni bie na anɔpasɔreɛ deɛ ɔnne ho ka.
*The tortoise says: he has no great strength but he is able to get up in the morning.*
(Weakness does not stop you doing everything).

3998. Akyekyedeɛ se ne ho akɔ a, ɔnsene bayerɛ a ɛda gya mu.
*If the tortoise says he is hot, he is not hotter than a piece of yam in the fire.*
(Said when you are hot, thirsty and dying for a drink but are still able to continue).

3999. Akyekyedeɛ se: ɔne ɔbɔfoɔ redi mafa mafa a, anka ɔno na ɔfaa ɔbɔfoɔ kane.
*The tortoise says: if it and the hunter were to enter into the business of picking each other, then it would have taken the hunter first.*
(Although rights belong to the first-comer, some people ignore the fact and usurp these rights. The tortoise was in the forest before man).

4000. Akyekyedeɛ se: ɔnnim faako a ɔbɛwu ada nti na wapam n'adaka da mu.
*The tortoise says: it does not know where it will die, therefore it carries its coffin about and sleeps in it.*
(Always be prepared).

4001. Akyekyedeɛ se: "Nsa kɔ na nsa aba".
*The tortoise says: "Hand go, hand come".*
(Give and take; sometimes used of taking a bribe).

4002. [Akyekyedeɛ]/[ɔkɔto] rewea, ne ba rewea, hwan na ɔbɛgye ne yɔnko taataa?
*The [tortoise]/[crab] crawls, its child crawls, but which will teach the other to walk upright?*
(You cannot change your essential nature, young or old).

4003. Akyekyedeɛ nni nufoɔ nso ɔwo a, ɔnim ɔkwan a ɔfa so yɛne ne ba.
*The tortoise has no breasts but if it gives birth, it knows how to rear its child.*
(God provides us all with the means of developing).

4004. Akyekyedeɛ yɛ bonyaa-bonyaa firi ne bɔ mu.
*The tortoise has been slow since creation.*
(You are as God made you).

4005. Ɔkyekyefoɔ adeɛ, nkura na wɔdie.
*The miser's goods, it is the mice that eat them.*
(If you store up goods you do not need, they go to waste).

4006. Kyɛkyɛrɛawareɛ nti na ɔbatabata ɔsrane da biara.
*The evening-star-who-is-desirous-of-being-married always keeps near the moon.*
(If a woman is after a man to marry, she will try and keep near him as much as possible).

4007. Wokyekyere a, na wonsoae.
*You tie up (your load) but you don't carry it.*
(One action does not automatically follow on another).

4008. Wokyekyere funu soa ɔbayifoɔ a, na ɛte sɛ deɛ wode kotorobankye abɔ ngo mu.
*If you tie up a corpse and make a witch carry it, it is like dipping poor cassava into palm oil.*
(See Proverb 3643. You cannot punish a person by giving them what they like).

4009. Wokyekyere mprenkensema sɛ wode rekɔsoa Gyebi na woanto no a, ɛyere wo ara.
*If you tie up a load of junk and carry it to hand over to Gyebi to carry and you do not meet him, you must carry it yourself.*

(If you try and get someone else into trouble you may end up in it yourself).

**4010. Yɛnkyekyere aboa no mfensa na ɛda a, adeɛ rebɛkye ama yɛansane no no, ɔnse sɛ: "Ɛnnɛ deɛ, homa no mu amia".**
*We don't tie up an animal for three years for it to say on the eve of the day we release it: "Today the rope is too tight".*
(If you have endured long, it is foolish to complain at the moment of release).

**4011. Nkyɛkyere ho annwo no a, na ɛfiri akranteɛ.**
*If the wild plants do not thrive, it is because of the grass-cutter.*
(If the exploited do not thrive it is because of their exploiter).

**4012. Yɛnkyekyere nyansa nkɔhyerɛ Ananse.**
*You don't tie up wisdom and show it to Ananse.*
(It was through Ananse's failure to climb a tree with the bundle of wisdom that it fell and spread throughout the world. Hence: Don't deliberately taunt someone).

**4013. Ɔkyekyere-osuo nim kyekyere a, ɔnkyekyere adesaeɛ ma yɛnhwɛ.**
*The one who prevents the rain from falling, if he really knows how to do it, should prevent darkness from coming and let us see.*
(If you are efficient then you should be efficient all round).

**4014. Akyem [prosi]/[polisi] se: sɛ ahoɔfɛ tua ka a, anka wanya ne ho.**
*The red-headed weaver bird says: if beauty were profitable, then he would become rich.*
(Natural gifts do not necessarily bring profit).

**4015. Akyem se: "Meyɛ me pirebuo a, meyɛ no wese wese wesee; meyɛ me yere deɛ a, meyɛ no basa, basa, basaa; na ɛduru anwummerɛ a, wabɛda me hɔ".**
*The weaver bird says: "I build my nest and build it in an orderly manner, I build my wife's and I make it in an untidy way; so that when evening comes she will sleep with me".*
(An Akan woman often lives in her own home and visits her husband from time to time. Hence: If you depend on someone to plan for you, you will find their plans work out to their own advantage).

**4016. Ɛkyɛm a emu atwitwa no, yɛnnwono bio.**
*A shield which has been cut to pieces, we do not weave again.*
(You cannot restore a ruined reputation).

**4017. Ɛkyɛm tete a, ɛka ne brɛmo.**
*When a shield wears out, its framework remains.*
(If a person loses his wealth or position, signs of them still remain).

**4018. Ɛkyɛm wɔ wo na sɛ wodebɛhwe wo ho mperɛ aduasa a, yɛnkame wo.**
*If you have a shield and if you strike yourself with it thirty times, we don't blame you.*
(You can do what you like with your own things).

**4019. Ɔkyɛmfoɔ se kɔwae abena a, ehu biara nni mu.**
*If the bird spider says go and cut the bark of a tree, you need have no fear (lit. there is no fear in it).*
(You do not fear the tyrant for whom you work).

**4020. Akyemfra katakyi de ahodanedane firi Nyame so, nanso ɔmfa nkyere ne ho.**
*The brave swallow has been given agility by God, but it does not sue it to show off.*
(God-given gifts are to be used for their proper purposes).

**4021. Akyemfra katakyi se: "Ahodanedane ne asɛm".**
*The brave swallow says: "Agility is the thing".*
(You have to get around to succeed in life).

**4022. Akyemfra katakyi se: "Srane ne anɔpa".**
*The brave swallow says: "My real business is in the morning".*
(A warning against procrastination).

**4023. "Ɔkyena mɛsi dan," na amma ɔpɛtɛ anya dan.**
*"Tomorrow I will build a house," made the vulture homeless.*
(Procrastination leads to inaction).

**4024. "Ɔkyena mɛkɔ, adekyeeɛ mɛkɔ" ma obusuyɛfoɔ di kan.**
*"Tomorrow I will go, the next day I will go" makes the evil-doer take the lead.*
(Delays are dangerous).

**4025. Ɔkyenebene se: "Onipa-mama yɛnhu no prɛko".**
*The green mamba says: "A handsome man, we don't see him only once".*
(If you admire something, you notice it whenever it appears or you look for it again).

**4026. Kyenekye ankye a, na kye ara na ɔrenkye.**
*If Kyenekye (Survival) does not survive, then he is destined not to survive.*
(Not everyone lives up to expectations).

**4027. Nkyenkwaakyensɛm, yɛdi no fotoɔ mu.**
*Ostentation comes out of a full treasury bag.*
(Showing off comes from possessing riches).

**4028. Nkyɛnkyɛma se ɔnim kwan si a, ɔnkɔsi nsamankwan ma yɛnhwɛ.**
*If the elephant grass says it knows how to block the path, it should go and block the way leading to the land of the dead for us to see.*
(An idle boaster should have his bluff called).

**4029. Akyenkyena wɔ tonsuom a, Asɔkwaa nhwere aderɛ.**
*If the allied hornbill is in the blacksmith's forge, the white crested hornbill does not lose his cutlass.*
(If you have a relation in a place, you are never without help of that kind).

**4030. Akyenkyena nya dua a, ɛso sie nyɛ no sina.**
*If the allied hornbill gets a tree it is easy for him to perch.*
(If you have the right implements or surroundings your work is easy).

**4031. Akyɛnkyɛn-bɛmu firi soro bɛhwe ase a, wahunu biribi.**
*If the cluster of palm nuts falls from above, then it has suffered (lit. seen something).*
(Those that fall from high positions suffer greatly).

**4032. Kyenkyentakyi kuro biara nyεε kεse da.**
*A town where people are difficult or quarrelsome never grows big.*
(People need peace to prosper).

**4033. Wokyεre badwa ase a na wodi abadwadeε.**
*If you keep long at a function, you take part in the sharing of the fees.*
(If you participate fully in something you share any profit from it).

**4034. Wokyεre dampɔn mu a, wofa mumfufuatrε.**
*If you stay long in the room you collect good white beads.*
(When you come into the dark windowless room you see nothing. Gradually your eyes become accustomed to the dark and you can see about you. Hence: If you are patient you can find what you want).

**4035. Wokyεre adowa na woma no aduane pa na wogyae no a, ɔsan kɔmene duaba.**
*If you catch an antelope and you give it good food, if you let it go it will go back to chewing fruit.*
(You cannot change a person's essential nature unless they are under your immediate control).

**4036. Wokyere akokɔbaatan a, wasesa ne mma kwa.**
*If you catch the good mother hen you catch its chicks easily.*
(If you capture the leader, you can easily take his followers).

**4037. Yεkyere kɔkɔbo a, akokɔ bɔ hyire.**
*If we catch the kusimanse, the chickens rejoice.*
(If an enemy is defeated, his victims are happy).

**4038. Wokyere ɔkɔtɔ a, wosɔ n'aprε.**
*If you catch a crab, you hold its claws.*
(If you capture a dangerous man, you make sure to disarm him).

**4039. Yεnkyere akorɔma nto afiase ma atwakwaa nsu nwu.**
*We do not catch a hawk and imprison it for the chickens to weep themselves to death.*
(Once the persecutor is gone, the persecuted can enjoy their freedom).

**4040. "Kyere akyekyedeε tutu no", ɔse: "Akokɔ woate?"**
*"Catch the tortoise and pluck it," he says, "Chicken have you heard that?"*
(Indirect warning. It is an Akan way of warning someone to do it indirectly by appearing to refer to a third person).

**4041. Wokyεre kuraaseni duaa we a, ɔda a, na εtua n'ano.**
*If you teach an uneducated person how to clean teeth with a chewing stick, if they sleep, then it is still in their mouth.*
(A foolish person overdoes what he is asked to do).

**4042. Wokyεre onipa akunseε na woku no a, εnyε no ya.**
*If you tell someone they ar going to be killed, it is not painful.*
(A guilty person cannot complain of just punishment).

**4043. Kyerε me wo yɔnko na mεnkyerε wo wo suban.**
*Show me you companion and let me show you your character.*
(A person's character is judged by his friends).

**4044. Wokyerε wo ho akwan nyinaa na εhia wo a, εdene wo.**
*If you boast in every way and are in want, things will be difficult for you.*
(A warning to be reticent).

**4045. Woankyere akokɔnini anhyε buo mu a, worenhunu adekyeeε.**
*If they don't catch the cock and put it in the coop, they will never see daybreak.*
(Take care of those who serve you, or you may suffer).

**4046. Yεnkyere korɔmfoɔ kwan so.**
*We don't arrest a thief on the road.*
(You need evidence to show your case is genuine).

**4047. Woankyerε sε wowɔ hɔ a, obi renhunu sε wowɔ hɔ.**
*If you don't show people you are there, no one will know you are there.*
(You must make yourself known or no one can know you).

**4048. Akyerε se ɔbεko a, ɔne n'akɔmfodeε.**
*If a condemned man says he will fight, it is left to him and his Asafo company (to decide).*
(The Asafo Company will accompany him to execution. You may want something very much but it is improbable you will get it).

**4049. [Akyerε]/[owifoɔ] mpo daberε.**
*A person about to be killed (a thief) does not refuse a sleeping-place.*
(If the worst is to happen, you are grateful for any help).

**4050. Ɔkyere se ɔtumi kyere ntoma a, ɔnkyere ne ho mma εnhwε.**
*If the comb says it can weave cloth, then let it show us how.*
(Reply to idle boasting).

**4051. Nkyerεaseε bebrebe bɔ kuro.**
*Much tracing of origins spoils a town.*
(It is considered very impolite to inquire into the ancestry of people outside your own family. Hence: If you question about people's ancestors too much you will end up in strife).

**4052. Ɔkyerefo Baakuma da fam a, yεnnyae nkɔdi nsεmma.**
*If Ɔkyerefo Baakuma lies on the earth (i.e he is dead but not yet buried), we don't leave (the ceremony) to try petty cases.*
(Ɔkyerefo Baakuma was a popular Asante chief. When he died, a holiday was made in his honor and no cases were taken to arbitration until he was buried. Hence: Don't desert something important to do petty things. Or: First things first).

**4053. Ɔkyerefo kaa baabi nti na ne kunafoɔ twee mpena.**
*Because a wealthy man died, his widow indulged in prostitution.*

(In Akan society the maternal family inherit and not the wives. Hence: A spoiled person who has not had to work, if faced with destitution must do anything to survive. )

**4054. Akyerekyeɛ amma borɔdeɛ ammere.**
*The small squirrel did not make the plantain ripe.*
(A parasite does not make something prosper).

**4055. Ɔkyerema Nyannɔ nim ayan a, ɔyane ma Ɔsɛe na ɔnyane mma awiɛmfoɔ.**
*If the drummer Nyannɔ is skillful in drumming, he drums for Osei (the Asantehene) not ordinary people.*
(A man who is really skilled at his job will be working for the most important people in the state).

**4056. Ɔkyɛwpafoɔ, yɛmpae n'apampam.**
*A supplicant, we do not hit him on the head.*
(You do not abuse those who show you respect).

**4057. Ɔkyifoɔ kyiri ne sɛn mu.**
*A person who has taboos, taboos from his own pot.*
(Taboos are personal and apply only to those who accept them).

**4058. Akyini-Akyini sene Anyini-Anyini.**
*A man seeking experience does better than a sedentary elder.*
(Active interest gets you further than passive knowledge).

**4059. Okyinnyefoɔ na aduro kye no.**
*It is the skeptic who is caught by the fetish (lit. medicine).*
(If you have to be exorcised by a fetish, you go through many humiliating experiences. Hence: If you have no faith in anything you lay yourself open to humiliation).

**4060. Okyinnyefoɔ na ɔtɔ asosini.**
*A skeptic buys a person with amputated ears.*
(If you are too critical, you will be left with something which is not good).

**4061. Akyinnyeɛ na ɛde ntankɛseɛ ba.**
*Argument results in the swearing of the Great Oath.*
(The Great Oath of Asante was the most serious oath that could be sworn and necessitated the case being brought before the Asantehene himself. An unsuccessful action meant death. Hence: Unwise actions result from fierce argument).

**4062. Kyirefua mpo nnwanam wɔ ho.**
*Even a single egg has some meat in it.*
(Everything is of some use).

**4063. Okyiremirekuku wu a, ɛsie dwiri.**
*If the ant-hill dies, the mound breaks up.*
(If the leader is no more, society disintegrates).

**4064. Wokyiri aniyɛnan a, wonkɔ ahennwareɛ.**
*If you taboo more than one person, then you don't marry a chief.*
(If you don't like rivals, you don't involve yourself in a situation where they are inevitable).

**4065. Wokyiri nsuo a, wo ne nsa nto kɛsɛ.**
*If you taboo water, you and alcohol don't become friends.*
(You must be consistent in your likes and dislikes).

**4066. Yɛnkyiri sɛ nsɔ mmienu gu apampa mu.**
*It is not a taboo for two hoes to be in one headpan.*
(Having extra is not a sin).

**4067. W'akyiri dua bu a, yɛmmu wo bi.**
*If the one who supports you falls victim to us, we don't make you suffer too.*
(We don't make you suffer for the sins of those you depend on).

**4068. W'akyiri kuro, wo yam kuro, ɛhe na wobɛda ahwɛ wiem?**
*You have a sore on your back, you have a sore on your front, then where will you lie so that you can see the sky?*
(If your problems are too many, then it is hard to find a solution to them).

**4069. Akyire nyɛn ɔba.**
*Absence does not bring up a child.*
(Used to chide someone who leaves their child to grow up without them).

**4070. Yɛnkyiri kooko nni ne mma.**
*We don't taboo cocoa and eat its products (lit. its children).*
(If you dislike one member of a family, you should be prepared to keep away from the rest).

**4071. Okyiri-awareɛ nni awaresɛm.**
*A person who taboos marriage does not settle a marriage case.*
(If you have nothing to do with something, you have nothing to say about it).

**4072. Akyiriwia mu wɔ biribi a, nka kusie ne ɔha na wɔyɛ panin.**
*If there were to be something special in daytime fasting, then the rat and the flying squirrel would be elders.*
(Not all actions lead to prosperity).

– L –

**4073. Lɔre foro nyɛ forona na ne sie.**
*It is not difficult to board a lorry but it is difficult to alight.*
(It is easy to get into trouble but hard to get out of it).

- M -

**4074. Woma ɔbakwasea kwan sɛ ɔnnɔ mfikyifuo a, ɔdɔ osamanpɔ huu.**
*If you give a fool permission to cultivate a back-yard farm, he clears the clan burial ground completely.*
(An irresponsible person misuses privilege).

**4075. Woma w'abɔfotwene yɛ wo dɛ pii a, w'apiretwaa te yera.**
*If you enjoy the acclamation of the hunter's drums too much your hunting bag tears and gets lost.*
(If you allow yourself to be distracted by praise or pleasure too much you lose sight of essentials).

**4076. Ma ɔdabɔ nkɔ ansa na woafrɛ no agyabonti.**
*Let the bay duiker go before you call it agyabonti.*
(Don't call a person by a bad name while he is around. Don't do anything intentionally to offend others).

**4077. Woma adeɛ a ɛyɛ hu yɛ wo hu a, wo kuro gyina.**
*If you allow a frightening thing to frighten you, your town flourishes.*
(If you treat a powerful man with respect, he does not trouble you).

**4078. Ma ɔdɔ ntɔ nkyɛ wo.**
*Let love buy for you.*
(Don't always buy things for people to show your love, love itself is more precious than gifts).

**4079. "Ma memfa me nsa nto wo kɔn mu kakra", na ɛde adwaman ba.**
*"Let me put my hand around your neck a bit", brings adultery.*
(One action intentionally or unintentionally brings about another).

**4080. Woma ahurihurie yɛ wo dɛ a, woto fɛmfɛɛm.**
*If you enjoy jumping, you catch up with the nimble.*
(If you practice a lot, you achieve success).

**4081. Woma akɔdaa akye a, oni na ɔgye so ma no.**
*If you say good-morning to a child, its mother responds for it.*
(If you try to take advantage of a weak person, a stronger member of the family will act to protect them).

**4082. Woma w'akoma ha wo a, woha wo ho.**
*If you allow your heart to trouble you, you distress yourself.*
(If you are too emotional, you suffer).

**4083. "Ma me ba nna!" nyɛ ayɔnkofa.**
*"Let my child sleep!" is not companionship.*
(A good friendship is not conditional).

**4084. "Ma me aduro seesei ara!" nyɛ aduro.**
*"Give me medicine just now", is not medicine.*
(Haste makes waste).

**4085. "Ma no mfa nkɔ na ɔde bɛba", na ɛyɛ fɛ.**
*"Let him take it away and he will return it," is fine.*
(It's good to be trusting).

**4086. Woma onyansafoɔ diberɛ na wanhwɛ so yie a, woto ɔbakwasea fanyinam.**
*If you give a clever person a good job and he does*

*not fulfill his obligations, it were better that you had taken a fool.*
(A bad clever person can do more harm than a fool).

**4087. Woma atetekwaa gyawurusie a, ɔbobɔ hyɛ ne mɔtoam.**
*If you give a simpleton a big cloth, he folds it and puts it in his armpit.*
(Some people are natural non-conformists).

**4088. Mema wo a, wogye na, "ma me" a, woyi wo nsa dwane?**
*If I give you, you take, but "give me" and you hide your hand and run.*
(Used of a grasping person who does not reciprocate).

**4089. Woma wo ba fufuo a, woma no nam ka ho.**
*If you give your child fufu, add meat to it.*
(If you want to help someone, do it wholeheartedly).

**4090. Yɛama wo ɔbaa sɛ, ɛne no nna nnawɔtwe, woantumi ne no anna, adeɛ kɔkyeeɛ na ɔrekɔ ne baabi a, wose: "Ma memfam wo".**
*We have given you a woman to sleep with for a week and you could not, when the morning came and she was about to go home, you say: "Let me embrace you".*
(If you can't do a thing at the proper time, don't try and do it at the last moment).

**4091. Yɛma wo kontihene na w'ani ansɔ a, bonsuahene bɔ wo.**
*If we offer you a paramount chieftaincy and you refuse it, you are denied a small chieftaincy.*
(If you refuse big responsibilities, you will not be offered small ones).

**4092. "Mema wo ni akye", ne "Mema w'aberewa akye", nsɛ.**
*"I bid your mother good-morning," and "I bid your old lady good-morning", are not the same thing.*
(The first expression with a certain emphasis indicates insult, the other is normal. Hence: If you want a quarrel you provoke it. Or: There's all the difference between politeness and provocation).

**4093. Woma wo panin fɛre da koro a, ɔma wo fɛre da biara.**
*If you make your elder ashamed one day, he makes you ashamed every day.*
(If you offend a person in authority even once, they make life miserable for you).

**4094. Woma wo werɛ firi wo kuromhene mmɛntia a, woyera dwabɔ ase.**
*If you allow yourself to forget the sound of your town's horn, you get lost in the gathering.*
(If you disregard your origins, you will suffer for it).

**4095. Woma ɛwoɔ yɛ wo dɛ dodo a, ɛnyane wo yam.**
*If you let honey be too sweet to you, you get a runny stomach.*
(Over-indulgence brings suffering).

**4096. Woammma obi anhunu bi a, obi renkyerɛ wo bi.**
*If you don't let anyone see some, no one shows you any.*
(Give and take).

**4097. Amma-me-ho-annwoɔ kuro nyɛɛ kɛse da.**
*Those-who-don't-want-people-to-be-free town never grows big.*
(See Proverb 4033).

**4098. Womma me nnidi a, meremma wo nna.**
*If you don't let me eat, I won't let you sleep.*
(Tit for tat).

**4099. Woamma w'ani ansɔ deɛ wowɔ a, ɛhwere wo.**
*If you don't respect what you already have, you lose everything.*
(If you don't look after your possessions, you lose them).

**4100. Woamma yɛansere wo a, yɛsu wo.**
*If you don't let us laugh at you, we weep for you.*
(We are sorry for those who lack a sense of humor).

**4101. "Meremma wo, meremma wɔn mma wo", yɛkyi.**
*"I won't give you! I will not let them give you!" we do not like it.*
(Depriving someone of something for no reason is bad).

**4102. Woamma wo yɔnko antwa nkron a, wo nso worentwa du.**
*If you don't let your companion eat nine portions, you also won't get ten.*
(If you don't share, you don't prosper).

**4103. Maade hyɛɛ aseɛ ansa na ɔreforɔ.**
*The maade yam had to grow before it could climb.*
(You must walk before you can run).

**4104. "Maakye, maakye!" nkum aberewa.**
*"Good-morning, good-morning!" doesn't kill the old lady.*
(A lonely person appreciates attention).

**4105. Wo maame bo wo a, wosu, wo papa bo wo a, wosu, wo mpena bo wo a wosere.**
*When your mother beats you, you weep, when your father beats you, you weep, but when your lover beats you, you smile.*
(Within the family, love and anger are close together).

**4106. Mako bere ɛse a, nkyene hoa no.**
*If pepper reddens the teeth, salt cleans them.*
(Each person to his own job).

**4107. Mako nyinaa mpatu mmere pɛ.**
*Not all pepper ripens at the same time.*
(Not all people mature at the same age).

**4108. Mako mpo ɛyɛ a, ɛdɔre mmoaa.**
*Even if the pepper plant is all right, it gathers creatures (grubs).*
(If you prosper, you collect dependents).

**4109. Mako se: "Biribi kɔ me ba ani".**
*Pepper says: "Something has gone into my child's eye".*
(If you are guilty of doing something, don't blame others who do it).

**4110. Mako yɛ aduro a, anka apatuprɛ nne mfa.**
*If pepper were medicine, the bulbul would not defecate thread worms.*
(Said to someone using the wrong remedy).

**4111. Mako yerawa se: "Biribi na aba ntira, anka metɔ ani a anka biribiara ne no nsɛ".**
*The mashed pepper says: "Because circumstances have changed, if I fall in the eye it is not as powerful as it was".*
(People's position in society change with changing circumstances).

**4112. Amamfrafoɔ na ɛsɛe ɔman.**
*Settlers from another town spoil the state.*
(Divided loyalties cause trouble).

**4113. Ɔmamfrani nnyini kronkron.**
*The stranger never grows to perfection.*
(However hard he may try the stranger in another land can never become completely assimilated).

**4114. Ɔmampam se: "Me deɛ ne sɛ mepam me man nyɛ mammɔeɛ".**
*The monitor lizard says: "Mine is to help build and not to destroy my state".*
(Said of a peacemaker).

**4115. Mampɔn Safo se: "Ohia na ɛma Ɔkanni anim gu aseɛ".**
*Safo from Mampɔn says: "It is poverty that brings disgrace to an Akan person".*
(Safo was a well-know proverb-maker from Mampong in the nineteenth century. Poverty ruins a person's reputation).

**4116. Mampɔnten hiani nni biribi a, ɔwɔ kamafoɔ.**
*If a poor person from Mampɔnten has nothing else, he has a defender.*
(A poor man from Mampɔnten-Asante-about 12 kilometers from Kumasi-was once in trouble, but to the surprise of those who were troubling him, some citizens supported hi,. Thus people realized that even if poor, you may have supporters. Hence: Even the poor have someone to stand up for them).

**4117. Ɔman ba, yɛnto no bradɛ.**
*A citizen, we do not trick him.*
(It is difficult to cheat someone who is familiar with the situation).

**4118. Ɔman ba yɛ Adanseni a, ɛnte sɛ Adansehene awo ba.**
*If a citizen is a citizen of Adanse, it is not as if the Adansehene has had a child.*
(A blood relationship is stronger than any other).

**4119. Ɔman bi so dehyeɛ yɛ ɔman bi [akoa]/[akyerɛ].**
*One state's royal is another state's [slave]/[condemned man].*
(One person's slave is another person's master).

**4120. Ɔman rebɛbɔ a, ɛfiri afie mu.**
*If the state is going to collapse, it is from its homes it does so.*
(The well-being of the nation depends on the well-being of its individual homes and citizens).

**4121. Ɔman rebɛbɔ a, ɔmampam na ɔkuta poma.**
*When the nation is about to come to ruin, it is the monitor lizard which should hold the staff.*
(There's a play on words here. "Ɔman-pam" would mean "put together the nation"; "ɔmampam" is the monitor lizrd. Hence: Only unity can save the nation).

**4122. Ɔman bɛbɔ a, na ɛfiri ɔkyeame.**
*If the state is going to fall, it is because of the linguist.*
(Used of an important person whose unwise words destroy his community).

**4123. Ɔman mpo bɔ na nyɛ ɛnne ofiboboɔ.**
*A nation can be destroyed, how much more one house.*
(If the powerful have fallen, how much more the weak).

**4124. Ɔman, yɛmmu no anibuo.**
*The state, we don't govern it lazily.*
(Government needs constant attention).

**4125. Ɔman gya wo kam a, wompopa.**
*If the state gives you a mark of identification, you do not do away with it.*
(Whatever the customs of your state are, you obey them).

**4126. Ɔman ku wo a, na ɔhene ku woɔ.**
*When the people of the state (want to) kill you, then the chief kills you.*
(The chief is the mouthpiece of his people. If they want something badly enough, he performs it).

**4127. Ɔman mu yɛ dɛ a, ene wo fie.**
*If there is something good (lit. sweet) in the state, then it is (because) your house (is in good order).*
(Happiness begins at home).

**4128. Ɔman mu yɛ dɛ a, nnipa nyinaa te mu bi.**
*If there is something good (lit. sweet) in the state, all the people stay in it.*
(Prosperity is shared by all).

**4129. Ɔman nyinaa safoa yɛ baako.**
*To all the state there is just one key.*
(The Asantehene - in Asante - or other Amanhene in their own states are the key to everything there).

**4130. [Ɔman]/[Amammuo] te sɛ kosua, woanhwɛ so yie a, ɛfiri bɔ.**
*[The state]/[governing] is like an egg, if you don't look after it well, it falls and breaks.*
(Power needs careful handling).

**4131. Ɔman ti ne abadwafoɔ.**
*The head of the state is its councilors.*
(The elders are those who rule the state).

**4132. Ɔman twa wo sama a, wompopa.**
*If the people of the state dress their hair in a certain way, you do not deviate.*
(Most people follow the current fashion).

**4133. Womane obi a, wo nan mu na ɛdwo woɔ, na wo bo nnwo.**
*If you send someone, your legs don't trouble you, but you are not satisfied.*
(It is better to do a job yourself).

**4134. "Amane a mahunu", yɛmfa ntutu ka.**
*"How I have suffered", we don't use to ward off a debt.*
(You should not play on people's emotions to avoid responsibility).

**4135. Amaneɛ hyɛɛ aseɛ ansa na ɛreforo.**
*A case began from its roots before it climbed up.*
(You can't always tell when a small case is going to develop into a big one).

**4136. Amaneɛ nyɛ nyana, na ɛnyɛ ne fakɔberɛ.**
*Trouble is not hard to get, but the trouble is to find a way out.*
(It is easy to get into trouble but not so easy to get out).

**4137. Ɔmanni ba mmua nna.**
*A citizen's child does not go hungry to bed.*
(A community cares for its own people).

**4138. Ɔmanni, yɛku no sum mu.**
*A citizen, we kill him in the dark.*
(If you want to destroy someone in your own community, you try and do it surreptitiously).

**4139. Ɔmanni kyiri ɔmanni abɛn.**
*The citizens dislike their own horn.*
(A prophet is not without honour save in his own land).

**4140. Ɔmanni na ɔkum ɔmanni.**
*It is a citizen who kills citizen.*
(if someone knows you well they can hurt you easily).

**4141. Ɔmanni yera a, yɛde ɔmanni abɛn na ɛhwehwɛ no.**
*When a local man is missing, they use his state horn to recall him.*
(You need to know a man's origins to know how he can be approached).

**4142. Amanika, yɛdan no fotoɔ.**
*A debt amongst friends, we ask for it at the right time.*
(You only ask a friend to repay a debt when you know he has the money).

**4143. Amaniko, yɛko a, yɛkeka nwi so (na) yɛntutu ase.**
*If we join in a family squabble, we bite off hair but we don't pull it out.*
(A family quarrel is not a cut-throat affair).

**4144. Amankuo nim huri a, ɔhuri tɔ ntoma mu na ɔntwa adaban mu.**
*If the rhinoceros beetle knew how to jump, it would jump into cloth but not to cut an iron rod.*
(Even with talent and knowledge possibilities are limited).

**4145. Amankuo [Kuturuku] se: ɔnim sɛ ɛkɔm bɛba, nti na ɔkutirii adɔbɛ nkɔn mu sieeɛ.**
*The rhinoceros beetle says he knew that famine would come, that is why he cut the young raffia palm leaves to store.*
(Said of someone who provides ahead).

**4146. Ɔmanmu mpo, ɛbɔ na ɛnte sɛ kukuo.**
*Even the state can be destroyed, how much more a clay vessel.*
(If a strong person falls, how much more easily a weak one may fall).

**4147. Amansan adwuma nyɛ ɔbaakofoɔ adwuma.**
*Everyone's work is no one's work.*
(People normally pay little attention to community work).

**4148. Amansiesie nti na akyɛm-nini kyini mpirebuo aduasa nkron ano.**
*Because of putting things in order, the male weaver bird goes round thirty-nine nests.*
(A person who is patriotic helps the community).

**4149. Manso nyɛ aduane na yeadi amee.**
*Litigation is not food that we can eat and be satisfied.*
(Litigation never brings real satisfaction, it just creates appetite for more).

**4150. Mansoboafoɔ yɛna.**
*A promoter of rebellion is rare.*
(A good leader of opposition is difficult to find).

**4151. Ɔmansofoɔ ntoma nhyiaa no da.**
*A litigant's cloth is never sufficient.*
(A warning against the waste of money in litigation).

**4152. Mansotwe te sɛ bayerɛ amena; obi ntɔɔ mu mfaa ne ho sɔnn mfirii da.**
*Litigation is like the yam-pit; no one ever came out of it scot free.*
(If you indulge in lawsuits, even if you win, it is bound to cost you a lot. It is always better to keep free of the law).

**4153. Ɔmansotwefoɔ didi anadwo.**
*A litigant eats in the night.*
(A constant litigant has no time for anything else).

**4154. Ɔmannyɔfoɔ nyɛ anem.**
*A statesman should not be vindictive.*
(A real statesman does not resent criticism nor want to victimize those who disagree with him).

**4155. Mmatatwene nya amane a ofuruntum fa mu asia.**
*If the liana (Cercertis afzelii) gets into trouble, the rubber tree takes an asia worth of it.*
(An asia is a weight of gold dust. Hence: If you are involved with someone you share their troubles).

**4156. Me a meda ayeya menhunu Nyame, na wo a wobutu hɔ?**
*If I who lie on my back cannot see God, how can you who lie on your stomach?*
(If a person who sees a problem cannot solve it, how can one who can't even understand it).

**4157. Me a mede me yafunu mennya mma, na merekra me yere ne me mma abɛka me ho?**
*Even I cannot fill my stomach, so how do I invite my wife and children to join me?*
(If you are too hard up, you cannot provide for others, let alone the family).

**4158. Me a mesii me dan, meda a, menna, na aboa kɔkɔsakyi bɛsi so da ma n'ani kom sɛn?**
*I who have built my room, I go to bed but cannot sleep, but how is it that the vulture can come and perch on it and begin dozing?*
(The owner of a place should be able to enjoy it more than a stranger).

**4159. Ɔmeeɛ ne akɔnnɔ nni twaka.**
*Satisfaction and desire to eat something don't go together.*
(If you are content with what you have, you don't go about looking for more).

**4160. Ɔmeeɛ nyɛ akyakyayɛ.**
*Repletion is not a protuberance.*
(It is not wrong to be satisfied, but overeating is wrong).

**4161. Memene-Ahene nantwie a, yɛmfa no mfa afikyire, na yɛmfa no mfa abɔnten, nanso yɛne no nna no, na ɛyɛ abusudeɛ.**
*A young woman who has passed puberty but was not officially shown to the Queen Mother (and therefore has committed the taboo of kyiribra) we don't take her across the back yard, we don't take her in the street, neither do we sleep with her, for it is a curse.*
(Anything which is taboo to the community should be rejected completely).

**4162. "Me ne wo bɛkɔ", yɛde daadaa funu.**
*"You and I will go (to the underworld)" we say to delude the corpse.*
(Don't be misled by insincerity).

**4163. "Me ne wo pɛm", yɛnka no kwa.**
*"You are I are alike", we don't say it in vain.*
(The proof of the pudding is in the eating).

**4164. Mmerɛsa se: wɔannya nsuo anom a, na wɔnom wɔn woɔ.**
*A swarm of bees says: if they do not get water to drink, they will drink their honey.*
(If the worst comes to the worst, we have to live on capital).

**4165. Amfɔ abɔ aboa a, fidie mia aboa, ma aboa mia asaase.**
*If the big trap catches the animal, the trap presses the animal which makes the animal press the earth.*
(Cause and effect; chain reaction).

**4166. Amfɔ di mfensa a, ɛbɔ.**
*If the big trap is three years old, it functions better.*
(Age brings skill and endurance).

**4167. Amfɔ na ɛkyerɛ ne ntoasoɔ.**
*It is the big trap that indicates its own length.*
(Time will tell how immediate achievement promotes further success).

**4168. Womia w'ani a, wofiri fufuo mu.**
*If you persevere, you will put on white.*
(If you stand up to adversity you will triumph. Wearing white is a sign of victory and joy).

**4169. Womia na amfata wo a, na yɛfrɛ wo dapaafoɔ.**
*If you adorn yourself and it does not suit you, then we call you a good-for-nothing.*
(If you try and do not succeed, people criticize you).

**4170. Womia fidie mu pii a, ɛgyae aboa.**
*If you tighten the trap too much, it lets loose the animal.*
(You lose by over-doing things).

**4171. Mmienu se: "Wofa baako a na asɛm asa",**
*Two say: "You take one then our problem is over".*
(Share and share alike).

**4172. Mmiɛnsa se: "W'adeɛ nsa da!"**
*Three says: "You will never become destitute."*
(Used for instance as a wish when giving a gift of three, which is a lucky number to the Akans as it is elsewhere).

**4173. Amim nnim atida.**
*Cheating does not know contentment.*
(A cheat has no peace of mind).

**4174. Amire kum kuro, na ekuro ku no.**
*The shingle wood (Terminalia glaucescens) cures a sore, but a sore kills it.*
(The bark of this tree is used to heal sores. Everything has something to which it is vulnerable).

**4175. Amma na wawuo ama adeɛ ahia Kwame, na anka dɔkono kɛntɛmma, nyɛ ho ham ne koobi sini.**
*Amma died and left Kwame in want, or else a basket full of kenkey would not attract only a small piece of koobi fish.*
(Necessity forces you to make do with what you can get).

**4176. Amma Sɛɛwaa amfɛre sɛ ɔbɛgu wo ho fi a, wo nso womfɛre sɛ wobɛbɔ no adagya.**
*If Amma Sɛɛwaa does not regard you and talks against you, you too do not regard her and strip her naked.*
(Once a woman of the royal family was very spoilt and disgraced all other women; knowing they could not attack her. One day one of the women with impunity stripped her naked and cured her of her arrogance. Hence: Tit for tat).

**4177. Mmire firi a, ɛnya tufoɔ.**
*If a mushroom grows, it gets a picker.*
(Something which is appreciated always has someone who wants it).

**4178. Mmire-mmiraa funu, yɛmfa mfa afikyire, nso yɛmfa mfa abɔntene. Dɛɛ ɔde ne dan nso regye.**
*A corpse which has committed suicide in the bush, we do not carry it through the back yard, we do not carry it in the main street. The owner of his room is also taking it back.*
(i.e the owner of the room refuses to let the body be laid in state there. Hence: A matter which is taboo should be forgotten as soon as possible).

**4179. Mmirika mu wɔ biribi a, anka ɔkraman di hene.**
*If there was something special in running, a dog would be a chief.*
(If wishes were horses, beggars would ride).

**4180. Mmirika annuru da a, brɛbrɛ nnuru da.**
*If running does not reach a destination, then slowness won't.*
(If the best does not succeed, nor will anything else).

**4181. Mmirika so kokoam a, na asa.**
*If running reaches its goal, it is finished.*
(Everything has its appropriate end).

**4182. Mmirikisie a yɛantumi annɔ, na yɛfrɛ no nsamampɔ.**
*Virgin forest which we could not cultivate, we call it a spirit grove.*
(You fear what you are unable to face up to).

**4183. Amo Akwasi ba ne wo a, wokyiri ntakraboa.**
*If you are Amo Akwasi's child, you taboo birds.*
(Taboos go in families. If you belong to a family you accept its norms).

**4184. "Mo! Mo!" kum aberewa.**
*"Well done, well done", kills the old woman.*
(You can congratulate a person too much!)

**4185. Amoakua na yɛde ne dua tu aduro, nso ɔyare a, ɔnnya aduro.**
*It is the ground squirrel whose tail is used for medicine, but when it gets ill, it has no medicine.*
(Physician heal thyself).

**4186. Amoakua nim sɛ nsuo bɛtɔ nti na ɔkɔdaa fam.**
*The ground squirrel is aware that there will be rain, so it has found shelter in the ground.*
(Foreknowledge leads to an adequate provision for the future).

**4187. Amoakua anom dɛ nti na ɔdua nkateɛ a, ɛnyɛ yie.**
*Because of sweet mouth of the ground squirrel, when it grows ground nuts, they do not flourish.*
(Said of someone who dissipates the result of their work on good living).

**4188. Amoakua se: "Medua nti m'ayɔnkofoɔ kyiri me".**
*The ground squirrel says: "It is my tail that makes my companions jealous of me".*
(The squirrel's tail is much prized. Hence: Said when someone is trying to find a reason for jealousy or unkindness).

**4189. Mmɔbɔnsɛ Agyewaa ne opitire ntumi mpere kwansɛn mu.**
*The young shrimp Agyewaa does not compete with the mudfish in the soup pot.*
(Said for example of an orphan who cannot compete with the children of the house).

**4190. Mmɔbɔnsɛ nyɛ nam bi nanso ɛtere nkwan.**
*The shrimps are not meat but they flavor the soup.*
(No one is without their use in society).

**4191. Mmɔborɔ bɔ wo a, na ɛfiri w'anamɔn.**
*If a wasp stings you, it is because of your footsteps.*
(If you do not disturb a person, he does not harm you).

**4192. Mmɔborɔwɔ koobi wɔ nsuo mu a, na nnam wɔ mu.**
*If the fish Koobi is in the river, then there is plenty of fish there.*
(Said of something the presence of which indicates that the place is suitable for exploitation or development of that kind).

**4193. Mmɔdemmɔ bu mmusuo abaso.**
*Concentrated effort defeats hindrances.*

**4194. Mofoɔ de twɔɔtwɔɔ na ɛbu wɔn man.**
*The Mo people talk double-dutch (lit. use twɔɔtwɔɔ-a meaningless sound) to run their state.*
(To the Asante, the Mo people's language is double-dutch. Hence: Everyone is content with their own way of doing things).

**4195. Mogya mpa huriiɛ tirim da.**
*There is always blood in the head of a tsetse fly.*
(An evil person is never without evil thoughts).

**4196. Mmɔkwaabɔ amma yɛanhunu ohiani.**
*Borrowing clothes to wear, saves a poor person from exposure (lit. does not allow us to see the poor person).*
(Keep up appearances).

**4197. Momono te, na dwane teɛ.**
*The green leaf falls, the withered one also falls.*
(Adversity strikes old and young alike).

**4198. Mmɔnka mu na asuo nam.**
*It is in a ditch that the water runs.*
(Everything has its appropriate place).

**4199. "Mo-ne-awɔɔ" mpa da.**
*Congratulations for giving birth can never end.*
(People are always pleased at success).

**4200. Mmrɛntowasɛm na ɛmaa ɔwea hweree ne dua.**
*Showing off made the hyrax lose its tail.*
(At the time of the great flood, Noah chose the hyrax to be amongst the first animals to be brought onto the ark. It started showing off its tail, which was very beautiful, in the door of the ark. When Noah closed the door the tail was cut off and to this day the hyrax screams: "Noah, Noah!" Hence: Pride comes before a fall).

**4201. Mmɔnkyi-mmɔnka firi asaase mu.**
*Crooked ditches come from the land.*
(Whatever you are like, you still belong to the family).

**4202. Mmɔre mmɔn fa nnya fa.**
*Dough does not smell bad on only one side.*
(If a thing is bad, it is bad all through).

**4203. Mmoseaa kokwa ntɛm a, yɛde wɔn kɔ anwan.**
*If small stones become polished, we use them for playing marbles.*
(If people gain experience in life, they are made use of by others).

**4204. Ampasakyi se: "Mewɔ ni a, anka mente sɛɛ".**
*The vulture says: "If I had a mother then I would not be like this".*
(An orphan suffers).

**4205. Ampem so daeɛ a, ɔnsuo mma ɔhene.**
*If Ampem (a man who owes allegiance to no one) dreams, he does not dream for the paramount chief.*
(This refers to Bɔna who was chief of Bekwai who quarreled with the Asantehene and broke off relations with him. One day he dreamt a terrible dream which he should have referred to the Asantehene, but he failed, and disaster followed for Bekwai. Hence: If you disown a person you serve, you suffer).

**4206. Emum daeɛ ka ne tirim.**
*A deaf and dumb person's dream remains in his head.*
(An inarticulate person cannot explain their needs).

**4207. Emum mfa mumu prenu.**
*A deaf and dumb person does not take on a further disadvantage.*
(You don't willingly add to your own problems).

**4208. Mumokyire na ɛhyeɛ na mumokane deɛ ɛnhye.**
*Adversity in later life is painful (lit. hot) but adversity at its beginning is not painful.*
(It is better to be poor and young than old and poor).

**4209. Womuna tena sum mu a, obi renhunu w'anim.**
*If you make a face and sit in the darkness, no one sees your face.*
(It's no good complaining to yourself).

**4210. Omununkum Sakyi, ɔnni ani, nso ɔforo Nyame.**
*The cloud Sakyi has no eyes yet it climbs to God.*
(If you are destined to prosper you will do so whatever your disadvantages).

**4211. Mmusuo ba fie a, yɛyi.**
*If misfortune comes to the home, we drive it away.*

**4212. Mmusuo bɔ fie.**
*Adversity destroys the home.*

**4213. Mmusuo di adwini.**
*Adversity practices a trade.*
(Misfortune molds man).

**4214. Mmusuo di w'akyi a, na woware ɔbaa tiatia.**
*If you are pursued by a bad omen, you marry a short woman.*
(If you are unlucky, you get a bad choice).

**4215. Mmusuo ankɔ a, sadeɛ mma.**
*If calamity does not give way, fortune does not come.*
(You cannot be lucky and unlucky at the same time).

**4216. Mmusuo wɔ wo ho a, na [ɔwɔ]/[nwa] ka woɔ.**
*If you are under a curse, a [snake]/[snail] bites you.*
(If you have been cursed, something unfortunate is bound to happen).

- N -

**4217. Na anka asantrofie de takyiaforoboɔ na asɛm tɔɔ ne fie a wanhunu di, nti na yɛfrɛɛ no asantrofie.**
*Formerly the night jar was called Takyi-has-climbed-a-stone, but trouble came to the house and it could not see a solution, so we call it "A-case-remained-in-your-house."*
(A play on words. Some people lose their position as a result of their inability to cope with their problems).

**4218. Ana ka wo yayaaya a, woku no yayaaya.**
*If the scorpion stings you mercilessly, then you have to kill it mercilessly.*
(An eye for and eye and a tooth for a tooth).

**4219. Ana konkɔnkyea anafia atworodo, ɔka ɔbaatan ba a, gye sɛ asomorofi adwo.**
*The scorpion, when it bites a good mother's child, the pain lasts until the hearth grows cold.*
("Konkɔnkyea anafia atworodo" are bynames of the scorpion. Hence: If there is a troublesome person in the house, you will never have peace until he leaves).

**4220. "Ɛna dea, merefa, agya dea, merefa", na ɛde korɔno ba.**
*"Mothers things, I am taking them, father's things, I am taking them," makes one become a thief.*
(Thieving begins with bad habits at home).

**4221. Ɛna ne agya a wɔnnyɛ, yɛ sene awisiaa.**
*A bad mother and father are better than being an orphan.*
(Any parents are better than none!)

**4222. Anabo bankye ɛbo o, annɔ o, wɔde gye ɔban.**
*Poor quality cassava, if it grows big, if it does not grow big, we sell it for a single string of cowries.*
(Poor quality things, however big are worth little).

**4223. Anadwo gyatoɔ mu nni biribi a, ɛwɔ: "Da bi na meteee".**
*If the warming of oneself at night has nothing else, at least it has: "I heard it one day".*
(Story-telling and conversation have their own merits. Such things are exchanged round a fire in the evening. Hence: Every situation therefore brings its own advantages).

**4224. Anadwoboa nnɔre sradeɛ.**
*The gecko (lit. night animal) does not become fat.*
(You cannot alter your inherited characteristics).

**4225. Anadwosɛm na ɛyɛ ahometeɛ na anka ntontom ne hwan na yɛrebɔ no bɔprɛnu?**
*Evening affairs are vexatious or else who is the mosquito that we hit it twice?*
(At times the strong become weak and the weak take over).

**4226. Anafranku nsɔre aborɔdeɛ ase mma odwennini nwo ahenasa.**
*If the anafranku plant (Hilleria latifolia) was not under the plantain tree, even a ram would bear triplets.*
(The red fruit of this plant are poisonous to sheep or goats who eat its leaves. Hence: If there were no obstacles, we should all thrive).

**4227. Nnakofie na ahia no.**
*The grave mound is always poor.*
(It is not until you are dead that you can give up hope).

**4228. Anakurampɔn nkasadwaa: ɔse ɔnne wo, na wokɔgye so a, woadi fɔ.**
*Anakurampɔn's diatribe: he says it without mentioning your name, if you respond, you are guilty.*
(Anakurampɔn's name suggests a cantankerous person. If someone is being very insulting but they do not mention your name, it is better to keep quiet. If you react, it is admitting that the accusation refers to you and you may be thought guilty).

**4229. Yɛnam baanu (mmienu) sum fidie a, yɛnam baanu na ɛhwɛ.**
*If we go together to set a trap, the two of us go to inspect it.*
(In a joint undertaking you should share honestly).

**4230. Ɛnam obi batri so na yɛde hunu dwa mu.**
*It is over someone's shoulder that we see the crowd.*
(We gain our experience through others).

**4231. Ɛnam obi so na obi yɛ yie.**
*It is through one person that another person prospers.*
(We all help each other).

**4232. Yɛnam dufa mu na yɛdi ɔwɔ ti.**
*It is in medicine that we eat the snake's head.*
(Snakes are not normally eaten by the Akan. The heads of snakes are used in some local medicines, which are ground on a stone and molded into a lump. Hence: By cleverness you can get something out of even a difficult man).

**4233. Mena me kɔka sɛ akwagyinamoa ata? Ɔno na ɔwɔ aburopata?**
*Where shall I go to say that the cat has farted? Is it he who owns the corn barn?*
(The owner of a place is entitled to do what he likes there).

**4234. Yɛnam onipa tɛkrɛma so na ɛkɔ n'anom.**
*It is through a person's tongue that we enter his mouth.*
(It is by means of an intermediary who knows the situation that we achieve things).

**4235. Yɛnam onipa [anom]/[tɛkrɛma so] a, na ɛhunu ne tirim asɛm.**
*If we follow a person's [mouth]/[tongue], it shows us what his thoughts are.*
(By their words shall you know them).

**4236. Wonam nsansa kɔ kwan a, wonam nsansa ba.**
*If you start out on the road empty-handed, you return empty-handed.*
(You can't get anything for nothing).

**4237. "Wonam sɛ menam yi na woawia Mampɔn dwan", nyɛ duabɔ.**
*"You walk as I do but you steal the Mampong sheep", is not a curse.*
(If you warn someone of their behavior, you are not harming them).

**4238. Ɛnam ho yɛ na a, na yɛfe abebeɛ.**
*If meat is scarce, then we use the water-snail.*
(You only choose the inferior in times of need).

**4239. Ɛnam nni hɔ a, ne yɛde mmire yɛ nkwan.**
*If there is no meat, then we take mushrooms to make soup.*
(When we can't get the best, we take what we can get).

**4240. Ɛnam nyɛ dɛ a, ɛnyɛ nkekabɔsoɔ.**
*If the meat is not sweet, at least the eating of it with other things is good.*
(Even if work is of little profit, it is better than being idle).

**4241. Namkɔm na ɛma yɛwe asisirapɛ.**
*It is out of hunger for meat that we chew the flying white ant.*
(Those in need take the nearest thing to what they really want).

**4242. Namɔn a adi kan toɔ yɛ tona.**
*The legs which have taken the lead are difficult to catch up with.*
(It is hard to compete with the best).

**4243. Anammɔn nsia da hɔ ma obiara.**
*The six feet (coffin) awaits everyone.*
(Death is inevitable).

**4244. Ɔnammɔn mmutu kwa.**
*The sole of the foot does not turn over for no reason.*
(There is a cause for any unusual action).

**4245. Ɔnammɔn fa tire kwan.**
*The feet go the way of the head.*
(A person's behavior is controlled by his thoughts).

**4246. Ɔnammɔn ne asɛm.**
*A step is the problem.*
(The difficulty is to start a project).

**4247. Ɔnam-Pomaho nhuri asafo.**
*Cripple-with-a-stick does not take part in asafo dances.*
(Don't attempt what you aren't fit to do).

**4248. [Ɛnan bɔne]/[nan-kontonkyi] na ɔtia dɔteɛ mu bɔ nan pa ho.**
*A [wicked]/[crooked] leg collects dirt and smears it on the good leg.*
(No matter how careful you are you cannot keep free of other's trouble).

**4249. Ɛnan bu a, ɛkyerɛ ne tiabea.**
*If the leg breaks, it shows up in walking.*
(You cannot hide your faults).

**4250. Wo nan tia aderɛ so a, na wodi dwuma harehare soɔ (nti na yɛyɛ adeɛ a, yɛyɛ no ntɛm).**
*When your foot is on the cutlass, you do your work in a hurry (that is why when we make things, we do it quickly).*
(In an emergency you must work fast).

**4251. Anan ne anan goro a, ntoto mma; ano ne ano goro a, na ntoto ba.**
*If leg and leg play, there will be no fight; if mouth and mouth play, then a fight comes.*
(Talk can be dangerous).

**4252. Nana aberewa se ɔwɔ ɔbra pa ho suman a, anka obɔɔ bi too ne ba Tufoanteɛ asene mu.**
*The old grandmother says if she had had a good education talisman, then she would have made one for her child Disobedience's neck.*
(If you could make provision for keeping out of trouble, you would do so).

**4253. Nana aberewa tɔ akokɔ a, ɔde no to: "Mahunu be pɛn".**
*If the old woman buys a chicken she calls it: "I have experienced this before".*
(Age has learnt wisdom through experience).

**4254. Wo nana reka asɛm kyerɛ wo a, wonse sɛ: "Merekɔbisa eni".**
*If your grandparent is explaining something to you, you don't say: "I am going to ask my mother".*
(You accept the advice of the most experienced person).

**4255. Nananom a wɔkɔɔ ɛsa na obi anko anto wɔn, na nyɛ nsamampɔ mu nna.**
*The elders who went to war, no one can achieve what they achieved, but this does not mean being able to lie in the cemetery.*
(However great people are, some things we all share alike).

**4256. Ɔnanka bobonini dane asaase anya ɔnwam.**
*The horned viper, lying on the ground has caught the hornbill.*
(Patience has been rewarded).

**4257. Ɔnanka tiri yɛtwa no mmarima.**
*Only a real man can cut off the head of a viper.*
(It takes real courage to do a dangerous job).

**4258. Ananse a ɔgyina nsuo mu mpo adwene nka ne nan, na opuro a ɔda dua soɔ.**
*The spider who stays on the water has not had its leg bitten by the fish, how much less so the squirrel who lives up a tree.*
(If someone near has not suffered, why should someone far from trouble).

**4259. Ananse ka kyerɛɛ asantrofie sɛ: "Sɛ wobɛhwɛ asɛdua so a, hwɛ adua so, sɛ nso wobɛdi nkorowahene a, hwɛ nkorowahene so di!"**
*The spider told the nightjar: "If you are going to look after the lentils, look after them, but if you are going to be leader in the nkorowa dance, lead in the nkorowa dance!"*
(You should make up your mind which of two things you want to do. Don't be indecisive).

**4260. Ananse nkoa mmieɛhe na ebi rekɔ asuo ama ebi adɔ anyina?**
*How many servants has the spider so that some go for water and others go and fetch firewood?*
(A person who has no helpers must do everything themselves).

**4261. Ananse se adeɛ mmiɛnsa nyɛ kyɛna: "Mayi baako, yi baako na menyi baako".**
*Ananse says three things are not hard to deal with: "I have taken one, take one and let me take one".*
(The trickster's way of sharing. Said of someone who tries to get out of sharing fairly).

**4262. Ananse se ɔrenyɛ n'ano pankoo sɛ ɔpɔnkɔnini anim na yɛakeka ne ho nsɛm.**
*The spider says he will not make his mouth as long as a stallion's for people to gossip about him.*
(It is an insult in Akan societies to say someone's face looks like a stallion's. Hence: A cunning person does not want to attract attention).

**4263. Ananse antɔn kasa.**
*The spider did not sell speech.*
(People can talk as much as they like and it costs nothing).

**4264. Ananse nwoo ne ba Ntikuma na ɔde adesoa tu kwan.**
*Ananse had not given birth to his son Ntikuma when he took headloads on the road.*
(Indicating something which has been done since time immemorial).

**4265. Nanteankasa hya wuo a, na ɛfiri apetebie.**
*If the tree snake dies, it is because of the striped squirrel.*
(If you chase something continually, you court disaster).

**4266. Nanteɛ na ɛkyerɛ ne daberɛ.**
*Walking leads the way to the sleeping place.*
(Your ability to reach a position determines the position you reach).

**4267. Ɔnantefoɔ hunu amane.**
*A traveller suffers.*

**4268. Ɔnantefoɔ na ɔdi adɔdɔdeɛ.**
*A traveller eats sweet things.*
(When you travel, you enjoy new things. Contrast Proverb 4267).

**4269. Ɔnantefoɔ nya amaneɛ a, na ɔteasefoɔ bo adwo.**
*If a traveller gets into trouble, a stay-at-home becomes happy.*
(One person's trouble is another person's joy).

**4270. Ɔnantefoɔ nya sika a, ɔde brɛ okuafoɔ.**
*If a traveller acquires money, he brings it back to the farmer.*
(Wealth is to everyone's benefit, but we need food in order to live).

**4271. Ɔnantefoɔ see oni asɛm.**
*A traveller told his mother a tale.*
(Where there are no witnesses, tall stories can be told with impunity).

**4272. Ɔnantefoɔ sene oni ne ɔse asɛm.**
*A traveller is more experienced than his mother and his father.*
(Travel broadens the mind).

**4273. Ananteananteɛ na ɛde asesabɔ ba.**
*Wandering about brings idleness.*
(Work needs concentration).

**4274. Nantuo kɔsene serɛ a, na yareɛ wɔ mu.**
*If the calf is bigger than the thigh, then it is sick.*
(If the servant tries to make himself out to be greater than his master, there is something wrong with him).

**4275. Nantwie nko ara nnante mfiri serɛm mma Asante.**
*The cow alone does not walk from the North to arrive in Asante.*
(You have to be forced to do something to your disadvantage. See Proverb 818).

**4276. Nantwie mmɛn, ani awo nso aseɛ yɛ mono.**
*The outside of a cow's horns are dry but the insides are quick.*
(People may be less tough than they seem. More generally: Appearances can be deceptive).

**4277. Nantwie te a, ɔnim ne wura fie kwan.**
*If the cow gets free, it knows the road to its master's house.*
(A servant knows the whereabouts of his master).

**4278. Nantwihɔhoɔ na ɔtɔ amena mu.**
*A strange cow falls into a ditch.*
(It is the stranger who gets into trouble).

**4279. Wone hwan na worekɔse sɛ Yaw Kɔko atwe hama ata?**
*Who are you to say that Yaw the Red has pulled a rope and farted.*
(Don't cretaceous your superiors whatever they do).

**4280. "Ne nyinaa, ɛne me ara", na woafa mmusuo.**
*"Everything depends on me", then you have taken the bad omen.*
(If you accept responsibility you must be prepared to accept blame).

**4281. Ɛnnɛ na nsuo agyae tɔ, ama [mmire]/[sibire] agyae firi, ama nkwan pa agyae dɛ yɔ. Anka kɔkono ne nsuom nam nyinaa boɔ sempowa.**
*It is today that it has stopped raining and the [mushrooms]/[reeds] have stopped growing, as a result the soup has ceased to be sweet. Otherwise Kenkey and fish to go with it would have cost threepence.*
(An elaborate excuse for not providing what you cannot afford to provide).

**4282. Nneɛma mmiɛnsa na mmaa pereɛ: "Wonyɛ me hwee", "Wonyɛ me huu", ne "Wonyɛ me biribi", nanso emu ɛyɛ ade pa?**
*Women struggle over three things: "You don't do anything for me", "You don't give me anything", and "You do nothing for me," but none is good fortune.*
(It is unprofitable to have a negative attitude).

**4283. Nnɛmmafoɔ mpo se wɔnim amamfoso na ɛnte sɛ atetefoɔ.**
*Even the youth of today say they know the deserted settlement, how much more the people of ancient times.*
(An eyewitness account is better than hearsay).

**4284. Nnɛmmafoɔ se: "Tete asoeɛɛ, wɔnsoɛ hɔ bio". Na adɛn nti na wɔntu tete mmokyea mu abusua baako na ɛnka mmienu?**
*The younger generation say: "We no longer rest in the ancient resting place." Why then do they not throw away one of the three ancient hearth stones and leave two?*
(Whether we like it or not our habits, behavior and customs are based on the traditions of the past, and we cannot function without them).

**4285. Anene anyε somakɔɔ amma Onyankopɔn nti na wakwan akwan no.**
*It is because the crow failed to fulfill the errand given to him by God that he laments aloud.*
(The crow was sent on an errand by God and did not fulfill it and so lost his chance of preferment. Hence: A permanent warning to the disobedient).

**4286. Anene: "Meyε ɔkwasea a, anka nwera gu me kɔn mu?"**
*The crow (says): "Were I a fool, would I have had a white cloth round my neck?"*
(A white cloth is worn to celebrate victory, success or for rejoicing. Hence: If a man has an award, he must have merited it).

**4287. Anene-mmea-mmea wɔ ne nkaeda.**
*Even a person who defecates here and there has his time for remembrance.*
(No person is totally despicable).

**4288. Nenkyemɔnɔ amma yεahunu ɔbaa bɔne.**
*Tomatoes have made it impossible to tell an incompetent woman.*
(Tomatoes are now a staple of Akan cooking, but they were originally introduced from abroad. Hence: A good helper hides his master's weakness).

**4289. Wo ni a ɔnyε no, na εte sε obi ni [ɔbaatan biara dɔ ne ba].**
*If your mother is no good, she is better than some other person's mother [every good woman loves her child].*
(Your family is your family whatever happens).

**4290. Wo ni ba ne Kobuobi a, anka wonkamfo no sε twene kεseε fata ne ti.**
*If Kobuobi were to be your mother's son, then you would not flatter him that the big drum was a fit thing for him to carry (lit.: it would suit his head).*
(Kobuobi is a slave's name. Most drums are carried on the head. Hence: Just because someone is not a relative you should not bully him).

**4291. Wo ni ba wo nwonkorɔ mu a, wo din nyera.**
*If your sister is in the group of singing girls, your name will not be lost.*
(If your relation is in a good position, then your reputation will be enhanced).

**4292. Wo ni di hia a, wonnya no hɔ nkɔfa obi ni nyε ni.**
*If your mother is poor, you don't forsake her and take another person's mother to be your mother.*
(Do not despise your parents however poor they may be - they are still your parents).

**4293. Wo ni ankɔ dwa a, na womane wo ni kora.**
*If your mother does not go to market, then you send your mother's co-wife is sent.*
(If you can't get the best, accept the second best).

**4294. Wo ni te Abibirem na wo se te Aburokyire na wopε adeε a, wonkyεre nya.**
*If your mother lives in Africa and your father lives overseas and you need something, you don't keep long before you get it.*
(See Proverb 597. People who have good connections get what they want).

**4295. Wo ni te hɔ, wo se te ho a, womfrε wo ho ɔdehyewa.**
*If your mother is alive and your father is alive, you should not belittle yourself (lit. call yourself a small royal).*
(Whilst your parents live you should have a sense of security).

**4296. Εni yεntɔ.**
*We do not buy a mother.*
(Your mother is irreplaceable).

**4297. Wo ni wu a, w'abusua asa.**
*When your mother dies, your family group is finished.*
(The death of a mother is the worst that can happen to you).

**4298. Wo ni wu a, su mmɔbɔsu , na obi ahu wo mmɔbɔ.**
*If your mother dies, weep piteously, so that someone pities you.*
(When you are in difficulty, show it, so that someone may take pity on you).

**4299. Wo ni wu a, wonwu bi; na ɔfεre a, na wofεre bi.**
*If your mother dies, you don't die; but if she is shamed, you also are shamed.*
(Shame is worse than death).

**4300. Wo ni wu na wobɔ ka na woantua a, wo se wu ayie da.**
*Your mother dies and you incur debts, if you don't pay, your father dies on the funeral day.*
(If you refuse to honour your obligations, you may be faced with greater ones).

**4301. Wo ni wu na worebεyε ayie a, didi wie ansa; nkɔtɔ piti mma w'ani nkɔwu mpanimfoɔ anim.**
*When your mother has died and you are about to celebrate the funeral, finish eating first, so that you do not faint from hunger and disgrace yourself in front of the elders.*
(However bad a situation is, you have to keep yourself fit or you are a nuisance to others).

**4302. Wo ni nyε a, wo ni ara ne no.**
*Even if your mother behaves badly, she is still your mother.*
(Family obligations are sacrosanct).

**4303. Ani a εtoo tetehɔ na εbi ni hɔ na εnyε aso a εtoo tetehɔ.**
*The eyes that saw ancient things are not there now but this does not mean the ears which heard ancient things.*
(Memories remain for ears to hear).

**4304. W'ani bere a, deε woka nyε na.**
*If you are desperate, you say anything.*

**4305. W'ani bere a, wofa abirekyie bowerε we.**
*If you desire something (urgently to eat) you take a goat's hoof to eat.*
(Beggars can't be choosers).

**4306. W'ani bere a, wofa ogya mu.**
*If you are determined, you take risks (lit. fire).*

**4307. W'ani bere wo yɔnko adeɛ a, woyɔ bi na wonwia.**
*When you covet something belonging to your companion, you work for it but you don't steal it.*
(What is worth having is worth working for).

**4308. Ani bɔ a, ɛkɔ tire mu.**
*If your eye is damaged, it goes into the head.*
(What is yours stays with you, whatever happens to it).

**4309. W'ani rebɔ na ɛtɛ si wo so a, wofa no saa ara.**
*If you are going blind and you find it is only a cataract, you are content.*
(A cataract can be operated on. Hence: If you are faced with a major disaster, any small hope helps).

**4310. Ani hunu adeɛ a, ɛdi bi.**
*If the eyes see something, they eat a bit.*
(When something attracts us, we can't take our eyes from it).

**4311. Ani hunu na ano anka bi a ɛnyɛ asɛm.**
*If the eyes have seen but the mouth has not revealed anything, it is not a case.*
(You cannot get charged for seeing something, if you keep quiet about it).

**4312. W'ani ahunu nanso wo nsa renka, ɛsene mako yea yɛ.**
*What your eye has seen your hand is unable to touch, is more painful than pepper.*
(Said when although you have seen what is going on, you are unable or unwilling to interfere).

**4313. Ani anhunu adeɛ bi a, ɛnyɛ tan.**
*If the eyes have not seen something, it does not offend.*
(You cannot cretaceous what you have not seen).

**4314. Ani ahunu yea yɛ ya sene mako yayɔ.**
*A bitter experience is more painful than when pepper gets in your eyes.*
(Mental pain is worse than physical suffering).

**4315. W'ani kom na wanna a, wotɔ nkɔsi hwe ase.**
*If you are very sleepy and you don't sleep, you doze and fall over.*
(If you disobey nature, you suffer).

**4316. W'ani nkum a, na wose: "Mennya daberɛ".**
*If you are not sleepy, then you say: "I have no place to sleep".*
(If you are really tired, you can sleep anywhere).

**4317. [Ani ne ani][/[ano ne ano] hyia a, ntoto mma.**
*If [eye meets eye]/[mouth meets mouth], then no trouble comes.*
(If you can discuss things face to face you avoid trouble).

**4318. Ani nya a, na ɛhwene anya.**
*If the eye gets it, then the nose gets it.*
(Trouble which affects one person, affects their whole family).

**4319. W'ani sɛ mu a, yɛnni nnya wo.**
*If you are present, we do not eat and leave you out.*
(A person who is on the spot shares in whatever happens there).

**4320. W'ani ansɔ deɛ wowɔ a, ɛhwere wo.**
*If you are not pleased with what you have, then you lose it.*
(Be content with what you have, little be it or much).

**4321. W'ani te bebrebe a, wama apɔnkye akye.**
*If you are too clever, then you say "good-morning" to a he-goat.*
(Where ignorance is bliss, 'tis folly to be wise).

**4322. W'ani bɛtɛ na w'adeɛ asa.**
*Before your eyes open your goods are finished.*
(A generous person is easily ruined).

**4323. W'ani tra w'anintɔn a, woyera.**
*If you look beyond your eyebrows (are supercilious), you get lost.*
(Pride comes before a fall).

**4324. W'ani tua kete, wose agorɔ bɛn ni?**
*Your eyes see people dancing to the kete orchestra, yet you ask what kind of dance it is?*
(If you can see something for yourself, don't bother others about it).

**4325. W'ani tua kuro a, wommisa ne nkwantia.**
*If your eyes see the town, you don't ask the way.*
(If you can see what to do, don't ask for advice about it).

**4326. Ani wu a, ɛsi deɛ ɛsie.**
*If you become ashamed, you stay as you are.*
(Shame does not alter your essential character).

**4327. W'ani anwu dwabirem a, na ɛnwuu bɔne.**
*If you do not feel ashamed at the place of assembly, then your shame is not serious.*
(If your suffering is not public it does not affect your standing in society).

**4328. W'ani nnye a, na wose: "Merekɔ Dawu asanom".**
*If you are unhappy, you say: "I am going to Dawu to drink".*
(If you are unhappy, you look for happiness outside your own community).

**4329. W'ani annye wo kurom a, na ɛfiri dan [a wonnie ntira].**
*If you do not feel happy in your town it is because of the house [that you do not have].*
(If you have no security, you cannot be happy).

**4330. "Ɔni me da bi a, ɔnni me bio", yɛ ya.**
*"He knew me once, but he does not know me any more", is bitter.*
(The loss of an old friendship is bitter).

**4331. "Woni o!" yɛgye no komfoɔ anom.**
*"Attention," we hear it from the priest's mouth.*
(If the person concerned is present, you don't act on their behalf).

**4332. Onibie biribi a ɔwɔ baabi ne Onyame.**
*Someone who has no family has God as his family.*
(God cares for the lonely).

**4333. Anidasoɔ na ɛmma awirakwaa yɛ ahantan.**
*The act of anticipation makes the servant show off.*
(Pampering encourages arrogance).

**4334. Anidedawiem mfa saasedeɛ.**
*"Eye in the sky", does not take anything from the ground.*
(If you are not practical, you do not prosper).

**4335. Anidie nti na dabodabo na ma ɔkotokotoɔ na ɛnyɛ tumi na ɔntumi ntene ne mu.**
*It is because of respect that the duck bows as it walks and not because it cannot walk upright.*
(Don't think that because people show respect they are stupid).

**4336. Onifirafoɔ ntumi nnyegye onifirafoɔ taataa.**
*The blind cannot lead the blind.*

**4337. Onifirani mfa abofu wɔ kwaeɛ ase.**
*A blind person should not become angry whilst in a forest.*
(When in a difficult situation, you suffer in silence).

**4338. Onifirani se ɔbɛbɔ so boɔ a, na ne [nsa]/[nan] si bi so.**
*If a blind person says he will hit you with a stone, then his [hand]/[leg] is already on one.*
(If someone who has a disadvantage threatens you, you know he is already prepared for battle).

**4339. Anigyeɛ da nko na awerɛhoɔ da nko.**
*Happiness is for one day and sadness for another.*
(Life has its ups and downs).

**4340. Anigyebea sen awobea.**
*A place of joy is better than a birthplace.*
(The place where you are happy is more important to you than the place where you happen to have been born).

**4341. Aniha mu nni biribi sɛ ohia.**
*Laziness brings nothing but poverty.*

**4342. Onihafoɔ na ɛhia no a, ɔde wuo kyekyerɛ ne werɛ.**
*If the sluggard is in need, he takes death to cheer himself up with.*
(For a poor or lazy person, death is preferable to hard work).

**4343. Onihafoɔ na ɔse: "Ɔkyena mɛyɔ".**
*The sluggard says: "Tomorrow I will act".*

**4344. Onihafoɔ se ɔdefoɔ yɛ ɔkontomponi.**
*A lazy person says a worthy person is a liar.*
(The lazy are envious of hard workers).

**4345. Onihafoɔ ntoma nhyiaa no da.**
*A lazy person's cloth is never enough.*
(Laziness leads to poverty).

**4346. Anikɔkɔ yɛ adeɛ a, anka obi nsene ayeremire agyapadeɛ.**
*If the red eye were the thing, then no one would have more wealth than the red-eyed turtle dove.*
(Appearance does not qualify you for anything).

**4347. Anikorɔ nhwɛ karawa, nhwɛ asibe.**
*You can't keep an eye on the mangabey and the colobus monkey at the same time (lit. one eye does not look at the mangabey and look at the colobus monkey).*
(You can't do two jobs at once).

**4348. Anikyeɛ no ɛfiri tete, anikyeɛ firi Odomankoma ɔboa adeɛ.**
*Dishonesty is from long ago, dishonesty is from the time when the Creator created the world.*
(Man has always been dishonest).

**4349. Anikyie nkum ɔkorafoɔ ba.**
*An insulting look does not kill a fellow-wife's child.*
(Mere dislike does not damage the enemy).

**4350. Yɛnim odwanhwɛfoɔ na yɛnnim ne wura.**
*We know the person who looks after the sheep but not the owner.*
(You only know for sure what you see. Many wealthy men hide their wealth behind others).

**4351. Wonim gya bubu, na woware aberewa nana a, w'awareɛ sɔ.**
*If you know how to collect firewood and you marry an old lady's grandchild, your marriage becomes fruitful.*
(If you know how to please people, you succeed in life).

**4352. "Menim ha, menim ha", nyɛ abatadie.**
*"I know here, I know here", is not commerce.*
(Mere knowledge of places is not enough).

**4353. Wonim ho a, nka wo serɛ mporɔeɛ.**
*If you know how to roast (to preserve), you should not have left your thigh to rot.*
(If you can't do something in your own surroundings, you are not believed if you say you can do it elsewhere).

**4354. Menim ko a, anka me ni din nne Kraa.**
*If I knew how to fight, then my mother's name would not be "Slave."*
(If you are strong, your family is independent).

**4355. Wonim w'anomee a, wonkɔ asuo nnya wo koraa.**
*If you know where to drink, you don't go to the water and leave your calabash behind.*
(You don't forget what is essential to your enterprise).

**4356. Wonim wo pa to a, wonyɛ sɛ akorokorowa.**
*If you know how to shake your waist, you still cannot be as good as the shuttle.*
(The weaver's shuttle passes swiftly back and forth across the loom in a motion that suggests the gyrations of a dancer. Hence: You may be good, but others are better).

**4357. Wonim papa yɛ na wonyɛ a, ɛyɛ bɔne.**
*If you know how to do good and you don't do it, then that is bad.*

**4358. "Nim saa" biara nnii kan da; "Nim saa" ka akyire.**
*"Had I known", has never been realized beforehand; "Had I known", is always too late.*
(Vain regrets).

**4359. Yɛnim sɛ bɔmmɔne tere nkwan, nanso yɛhyɛ no afikyire ansa na yɛde abɛto nsania so.**
*We know that the fermented fish flavors the soup, but we ferment it outside the house before we bring it in for weighing.*
(The fish has a pungent odor. Hence: Some people are kept out of the way most of the time, but they are essential to society).

4360. Yɛnim sɛ yɛde ogya bɛkɔ sumina so, nanso yɛde
firi wiram ba fie a, yede wura fie ansa.
*We know that we throw firewood on the rubbish heap,
but when we first brought it home from the forest, it
was taken into the owner's house.*
(There is a right place for everything).

4361. Wonim sɛ ɔhwento nkuruma-nkwan yɛ wo tan,
na wokɔfaa no waree yɛɛ dɛn?
*If you knew the nose-less woman's okro soup was
unpleasant, why did you marry her?*
(In the old days they cut off a person's nose as a
punishment. If you marry someone who you know
has one defect, you only do so if she has other merits.
Hence: You only have yourself to blame if you make a
foolish choice).

4362. Yɛnim sɛ kontromfi kɔn wɔ hɔ nso yɛde homa
sɔ n'asene.
*We know that the baboon has a neck yet we choose to
tie it at the waist.*
(You have a choice. You don't need always to do the
obvious).

4363. Yɛnim sɛ Korɔmante bɛbere a, anka yɛantete no
abunu ansɛe no.
*If we knew that Korɔmante would become "ripe", we
would not have eaten it green.*
(The oath of Korɔmante is one of the most serious
in Asante. The Asante army toiled hard to beat the
Korɔmante people but finally found them submissive.
Hence: If you had known that something would end
up being easy, you would not have put so much effort
into it).

4364. Yɛnim sɛ nkyene yɛ dɛ; na yɛkɔ dwa so a, yɛtɔ
mako.
*We know that salt is sweet; yet if we go to the market,
we buy pepper.*
(Functions are different and so are needs).

4365. Wonim sɛ yɛbɛma wo adi kraman bini a, ɔne to
hɔ a, na woafa adi ntɛm.
*If you know that we are going to make you eat dog's
stools, as soon as it defecates, you must eat them at
once.*
(It is best to get over an unpleasant task as quickly as
possible).

4366. Menim sɛ me se rebɛwu ama ne wɔfaase afa
n'akyiri adeɛ a, anka ɔte aseɛ no, meyeree no gyee me
kyɛfa.
*If I had known that my father was going to die to allow
his nephew to inherit his things, then when he was
alive, I would have attacked him for my share.*
(If you get no reward from life, you regret not having
been tougher in your demands).

4367. Yɛnim sɛ mogya wɔ yɛn anom na yɛte ntaso.
*We know that blood is in our mouths but we spit out
saliva.*
(If you act in anger you may be justified but you may
also regret it).

4368. Yɛnim sɛ nnomaa dɔɔso, na anomaa werɛmfoɔ
na yɛpɛ no.
*We know that there are many birds, but it is the eagle
that we seek.*
(We seek the greatest and the best).

4369. Yɛnim sɛ ɛpo so, nanso nsuo tene gu mu.
*We know the sea is large, but just the same the rain
pours into it.*
(He who has much will be given more).

4370. Wonim seperewa bo a, wohunu [asɛm ka]/
[mpaninsɛm].
*If you know how to play the lute, you know [how to
talk]/[the business of the elders].*
(This instrument is played at court. Hence: If you know
how to do something which pleases the elders, you
learn wisdom from them).

4371. Wonim su a, nyɛ ayie nyinaa na wosu asɛɛ.
*If you know how to weep, it is not at every funeral that
you go to weep.*
(However good you are at something, you don't do it
everywhere).

4372. Wonim to a, na yɛma wo gyina kyenenoo soɔ.
*If you know how to shoot, then we let you stand on the
spores of an animal.*
(If you know how to do a job, then you will be chosen
to do it).

4373. Wonim tu a, tu wo dwono.
*If you know how to pull, pull out your own grey hair.*
(Before you remove the mote from your brother's eye,
consider the beam in you own).

4374. Wonim ɛtwe di a, wonkyɛne w'ase.
*If you know how to have sex, you are not better than
your father-in-law.*
(An experienced person has proved his capability).

4375. "Menim ayie yɔ", ene dampan.
*"I know how to organize a funeral", brings about an
empty house.*
(It's possible to be too enthusiastic).

4376. Wonnim adeɛ mmiɛnsa a, hwɛ bokyea.
*If you don't know three things, look at the hearth
stones.*
(The traditional hearth had three pots or stones on
which the cooking pot was put over the wooden fire.
Hence: Make note of the obvious).

4377. Wonnim dɔkono a aben a, deɛ ɛtoɔ ahyeɛ na
kyerɛ woɔ.
*If you do not know the well-cooked kenkey, that which
has had a part burnt will point it out.*
(Even a foolish person can make simple judgements).

4378. Wonnim w'akontagye mmɔfram a, hwɛ wo
wɔfaase.
*If you don't know what the child-hood of you brother-
in-law was like, look at his sisters' children.*
(Since the Akan family is matrilineal, the maternal uncle
rather than the father is the senior male relative in the
parental generation. Hence: Like father like son).

4379. Wonnim kuntunu a, wonhunu ne mma.
*If you don't know the hyena, then you don't know its
pups (lit. children).*
(If you don't know the important members of a family,
you are unlikely to know its lesser members).

4380. Wonnim kuro bi mu a, wonka mu asɛm.
*If you don't know a town, you don't talk about its
affairs.*

(Don't talk about something about which you are ignorant).

**4381. Wonnim nipa a, wo ne no nsi koso.**
*If you don't know someone, you do not make a partnership with them.*

**4382. Wonnim onipa tirim asɛm a, ɛnyɛ wo ne Ɔtu a ɔte Datɛ.**
*If you don't know what is in a person's head, it is not you and Otu who stays at Larteh.*
(Some people are noted to be trustworthy).

**4383. Wonnim asa a, na wose atwene nyɛ dɛ.**
*If you don't know how to dance, you say the drums are not good.*
(Sour grapes).

**4384. Wonnim sɛdeɛ wote a, hwɛ ahwehwɛ mu.**
*If you don't know how you look, look into the mirror.*
(Examine yourself before you reject criticism).

**4385. Wonnim wiram a, na yɛde asɔkwaa dane wo akyenkyena.**
*If you don't know the forest, then we exchange the white crested hornbill for the allied hornbill.*
(The inexpert person is always liable to be cheated).

**4386. Wonnim wuo a, hwɛ nna.**
*If you don't know death, then look at sleep.*
(If you can't see the original, then you can at least study something similar).

**4387. Yennim obi a, yɛmmɔ no mmrane.**
*If we don't know someone, we don't sing their praises.*
(You must know someone before vouching for them).

**4388. "Nim-Nim" nnim.**
*"Know-all" knows nothing.*
(If you pride yourself on your wisdom, it is a sign of ignorance).

**4389. Anim nkyene, [atiko wisa]/[akyire mako]: yɛkyiri.**
*Salt to your face, behind your back [guinea grains]/[pepper]: we taboo.*
(It is bad to cretaceous a person behind his back, if you can't do it to his face).

**4390. M'anim na ɛsɛ akorɔma, nanso menkyere nkokɔ mma.**
*My face is like a hawk's, but I don't catch chickens.*
(You may resemble a bad person but nonetheless be harmless).

**4391. W'anim sɛ kwasea a, na yɛbu wo kwasea.**
*If your face is like a fool's, we treat you as such.*
(You are judged by your appearance).

**4392. Anim nyɛ nyam a, ɛnte sɛ nammon mu.**
*If a face is not attractive, at least it is not like the sole of the foot.*
(A thing may be bad, but not that bad!)

**4393. Nimbayɔ se ɔni wo a, ɛnte sɛ wo bogya.**
*If the foster parent says they can care for you, it is not like your own blood.*
(Blood is thicker than water).

**4394. Onim-bebrebe se ɔni wo a, ɛnte sɛ w'adɔɔdɔɔwɛ.**
*If someone who knows a great deal says he knows you, it won't be as well as your intimate.*
(A wise person cannot know everything. Your intimates know you best).

**4395. Nimdeɛ firi obi ano.**
*Knowledge (or understanding) are from someone's mouth.*
(We learn from others as well as from experience).

**4396. Nimfi-nimfi akɔfrɛ nanka-nanka.**
*The small snake has gone to call the viper.*
(Small troubles lead to big ones).

**4397. Animguaseɛ mfata Ɔkanni ba.**
*Shame does not become an Akan child.*
(Shame is worse than death. The Akans say they fear being disgraced more than dying).

**4398. Animguaseɛ nyɛ batakari na yɛapam ahyɛ.**
*Shame is not a northern smock that we sew and wear.*
(We do not advertise our shame).

**4399. Nnimmo-nnimmo yɛ owuo.**
*Slander-slander is death.*
(If you're accused all the time, you die of shame).

**4400. Nnimmo antumi wo a, ɛtete wo ntoma.**
*If slander cannot do anything to you, it tears your cloth.*
(Slander damages your reputation, whether or not it's true).

**4401. Animu nte sɛ fotoɔ mu na yɛahwɛ mu ayi sika dabiara.**
*The face of man is not like the gold weight container from which we remove money often.*
(You should avoid frequent criticism in the presence of others. Criticism takes away a person's good opinion of himself).

**4402. Animu nyɛ bonsua na yɛahohoro mu dabiara.**
*The face is not like a cup that we clean inside every day.*
(A person who is conscientious does not attract insults).

**4403. "Menimyɛ-menimyɛ", ne amma apatuperɛ anhunu pirebuo nwono.**
*"I know how to do it, I know how to do it", made the bulbul unable to weave a proper nest.*
(If you are too sure of yourself and unwilling to learn, you don't do a job well).

**4404. Nimyɔ di bi.**
*He who knows how to do it is entitled to his share.*
(The laborer is worthy of his hire).

**4405. Nimyɔ di bi na ɔnni ne nyinaa.**
*He who knows how to do it takes a little, but he doesn't take all.*
(If you help in a job you are entitled to some of its proceeds but not all of them).

**4406. Nimyɔhunu nyɛ hwee, ɛwɔ wo ne asɛm.**
*To know how to do something is worthless, how to obtain what you want is the (important) thing.*
(Knowledge alone is useless, unless it leads to achievement).

**4407. Onini nya a, na ɔbereɛ anya.**
*If the male comes by something, the female has also acquired it.*
(Man provides but woman shares).

**4408. Anini mmienu nna bɔnkorɔ.**
*Two pythons do not sleep in the same hole.*
(Two powerful men cannot run the same house-hold or state).

**4409. Oninkumfoɔ ngoro asɔnkɔ.**
*A jealous person does not join in the activities of the Asɔnko Asafo Company.*
(A jealous person does not prosper in group activities).

**4410. Ninkunu yɛ kɔm a, ɛde mmarima nyinaa.**
*If jealousy were hunger, all men would be infected with it.*
(All men are jealous).

**4411. Aninyanneɛ, wɔnhunu no mprɛnu.**
*Severe suffering, it is not experienced twice.*
(Once you have been through a bad experience, a second one can never be as bad).

**4412. Onipa a wabɔ dam ateɛ no, deɛ ɔde hunahuna nkɔdaa deɛ ɛmpa.**
*If someone has gone mad and has been cured, at least what he uses to frighten children remains.*
(A mad person can never be completely cured).

**4413. Onipa a yɛde sanya mu aduane ayɛn no no, ɔhunu asanka mu aduane a, na ne werɛ aho.**
*A person who has eaten from a tin plate, if he sees food in an earthen dish, he is grieved.*
(If you have achieved a certain position in society, you are sad when you are forced to lower your standards).

**4414. Onipa a ɔde sasabonsam ba baa fie no na ɔde mpuhwɛ baeɛ.**
*The person who takes a forest devil's child home brings a curious crowd.*
(If you do something extraordinary, you expect a like reaction).

**4415. Onipa a ɔnhunu ne mfomsoɔ, nnim nsakra ne bɔnefakye.**
*A person who does not see his faults, does not know reform and forgiveness.*
(You must recognize your faults before you can be forgiven).

**4416. Onipa a ɔmpɛ wo no, ɔmpɛ wo ho hwee.**
*If a person does not like you, he does not like anything about you.*
(Hatred is absolute).

**4417. Onipa a ne sunsum yɛ duru na ɔbayifoɔ ntumi no.**
*A person who has a strong spirit cannot be affected by witchcraft.*
(A powerful person cannot be defeated).

**4418. Onipa a ne yere awuo na ɔnsu, nanso ɔnyɛ no ayie no, wogye di sɛ ɔnya wo a, ɔbɛyɛ wo dɛn?**
*A person whose wife dies and he does not weep and he does not hold a funeral, if he gets hold of you, what will he do to you then?*
(If a person is without feeling in intimate matters, he will treat a stranger even worse).

**4419. Onipa a yɛni no awia no, yɛnsɔ kanea nhwɛ n'anim anadwo.**
*If we know a person in the daytime, we don't light a lamp to look at his face in the night.*
(If you know someone, you should be able to recognize them at any time without making a fuss about it).

**4420. Onipa a ɔnnyaa amaneɛ da, nhyiaa ne gyegefoɔ a, na ɔse: "M'asom dwo me".**
*If a person who has never experienced trouble has not met his tempter, he says: "I am at peace".*
(If you don't know temptation, then you cannot claim to be virtuous).

**4421. Onipa a wanyini sene oduefoɔ.**
*The experienced elder knows better than the magician.*
(Real experience is worth more than any trickery. Used to warn the young).

**4422. Onipa a ɔmpɛ sɛ ne yɔnko yɛ yie no, ɔnyɛ yie.**
*If a person does not like his companion to do well, he will not himself do well.*
(If you don't want others to prosper you won't prosper yourself).

**4423. Onipa a ɔse nya biribi die no, womma ɔkɔm nku no.**
*If someone wishes you good living, you don't make him die of hunger.*
(You don't make those who wish you well, suffer).

**4424. Onipa a asɛm da ne soɔ nkɔ adwabɔ.**
*A person who has a case against him does not take part in an assembly.*
(You can't handle two problems at once).

**4425. Onipa a asɛmmɔne ato no na yɛma no daakena.**
*If someone falls on bad times, we express our sympathies to them.*
(It is right to sympathize with the unfortunate).

**4426. Onipa a ɔntɔɔ nam da kɔto brɛboɔ a, ɔde akuma na ɛtwitwa mu.**
*If a person who has never bought meat buys liver, he uses an axe to chop it.*
(If you don't know something you don't know how to treat it).

**4427. Onipa a awoɔ sɛ no na Onyame ma no awoɔ.**
*If someone deserves to give birth, God provides for it.*
(God provides for all).

**4428. Onipa a wayɛ bayie-awuo no, yɛnsu n'ayie ase.**
*If someone has died through witchcraft, we don't weep at his funeral.*
(If people have committed a taboo against society we do not regret their passing. Someone who confesses to having been involved in witchcraft is not given a proper funeral).

**4429. Onipa a ɔnyɛ, ɔwu a, ne saman nyɛ.**
*If someone is bad, if he dies, his spirit is bad.*
(If you are bad in life, you are bad in death).

**4430. Onipa reba a, wonse no sɛ: "Bra!"**
*If someone is coming, you don't say to him: "Come on".*
(You don't need to encourage someone who's already doing what you want).

4431. Onipa baakofoɔ se ɔbɛgye nyinkyɛre aduro a, ɔka amamfoɔ so.
*If a single person says he is going to get medicine for old age, then he remains in a deserted town.*
(There used to be a hard round medicine to preserve people in old age. It was said that until the medicine was excreted they could not die. Hence: If you act different from your contemporaries you are finally isolated).

4432. Onipa baakofoɔ te sɛ akokɔfunu.
*A single person is like a dead chicken.*
(One person alone does not thrive).

4433. Onipa biara nkyiri: "Fa w'asɛm pa kɔ do".
*No one dislikes: "Take your good news and then go".*
(We all welcome good news).

4434. Onipa biara nni hɔ a ɔnii dɛ da.
*There is not a single person who has never enjoyed life.*
(We all have our good times).

4435. Onipa bɔne yɛnkora no.
*We do not conceal a wicked person.*
(Don't protect the wicked).

4436. Onipa de adeɛ sie a, ɔde sie deɛ ɔpɛ a ɔbɛhunu.
*If a person takes something to hide, he hides it where he can find it.*
(There's no point in hiding something from others so well that you can't find it yourself. Hence: Don't cut off your nose to spite your face).

4437. Onipa de ne din nam.
*A person takes his name about with him.*
(Your reputation travels with you).

4438. Onipa de ne tɛkrɛma na ɛpra ne ho.
*A person uses his tongue to clean himself.*
(You talk yourself out of trouble).

4439. Onipa de ne kotokuo se a, ɔde se deɛ ne nsa beso.
*If a person hangs his bag up, he hangs it where his hand can reach.*
(You keep your possessions where you can make use of them).

4440. Onipa bɛdidi a, ɔbisa ne kotokuo.
*If a person wants to eat, he asks his pocket.*
(We need money to live).

4441. Onipa didi wie, na ɔnkasa nwie.
*A person finishes eating but he never finishes talking.*

4442. Onipa din anyera a, na ɛfiri ne nokorɛ.
*If someone's name is not lost, it is because of his truthfulness.*
(People respect those who are truthful).

4443. Onipa dɔ wo a, ɔdɔ wo ne wo nkwaseasɛm.
4444. Onipa dɔ wo a, ɔdɔ wo ne wo nkwaseasɛm.
*If a person loves you, he loves you with all your nonsense.*
(You don't judge those you love, but love everything about them).

4445. Onipa dɔ wo a, ɛnnim sɛ ɛbini wɔ wo ho.
*If someone loves you, it does not matter if there are faeces on your body.*
(Love accepts and conquers all).

4446. Onipa dɔre nkannerɛ gye nnakye a, ɔsene dadeɛ.
*If a person gets rusty, he is worse than iron.*
(A person who has lost his talents, is useless in the field of action).

4447. Onipa Dum gyina ho a, yɛnnyae mmisa dua dum.
*If the human Dum is standing there, we don't ask for the Odum tree.*
(If the person who can help is right here, we don't go looking for help elsewhere).

4448. Onipa dware a, na ɛmfiri kɔkoo a ɔrepɛ ayɔ ntira.
*When a person bathes, it is not because he wants to become light-skinned.*
(We don't only observe hygiene because of beauty).

4449. Onipa adwene nyɛ Onyame adwene.
*A person's mind is not the mind of God.*
(We are not infallible).

4450. Onipa fidie, yɛsuae no tempɔn mu, na yɛnsuae no kwannkyɛn.
*A human trap, we set it on the highway, but we do not set it by the wayside.*
(If you want to catch someone, you do it where you know they will go).

4451. Onipa fidie, yɛsum a, yɛkata so.
*A human trap, if we set it, we cover it up.*
(If one person wants to damage another he does it by hidden means).

4452. Onipa firi soro bɛsi a, ɔbɛsi nnipa kuro mu.
*If a person from above will come down, he will come into a human town.*
(Human beings live as members of a community and people join one community or another).

4453. Onipa mfiti prɛko mma n'ani nte.
*A person does not suddenly become wise.*
(Wisdom comes gradually).

4454. Onipa mfɔn kwa [ɛkɔm nne no a, na ɔde ka].
*A person does not lose weight without reason [if hunger does not overcome him, he gets into debt].*
(There is a reason for everything).

4455. Onipa mfoni ne ne ba.
*A person's image is his own child.*
(You can be judged through the behavior of your children).

4456. Onipa nnyae mmɔbɔ yɔ a, yɛnnyae no mmɔbo hunu.
*If a person does not stop being miserable, we do not stop showing him sympathy.*
(Sympathy continues as long as suffering).

4457. Onipa nnyimi nsi aseɛ.
*A person is never entirely foolish.*
(No man is a complete fool).

4458. Onipa ho hia sene sika.
*Man is more important than money.*

**4459. Onipa ho antɔ no a, na ɛfiri ɔno ara.**
*If a person is unhappy, it is his own fault.*
(We are often the cause of our own discontent).

**4460. Onipa ho yɛ den a, ɛfiri ne kotodwe.**
*If a person is strong, it may be due to his knee.*
(Strength depends on good foundations).

**4461. Onipa ho nyɛ fɛ nkɔsi aseɛ.**
*A person can never be entirely beautiful.*
(No one can be perfect).

**4462. Onipa honam na yɛde hunu n'asetena mu nsɛm.**
*A person's personal appearance shows the state of his personal affairs.*
(Your looks show how you are getting on in life).

**4463. Onipa anhyia serɛ a, anka ne kotodwe ka ne koko.**
*If a person did not have a thigh, then his knee would touch his chest.*
(We are all interdependent).

**4464. Onipa tɛkrɛma nyɛ bondua na ɔde ahugya ne ho.**
*A person's tongue is not a cow's tail that he uses for fanning himself.*
(You should not need to justify yourself if you lead a good life).

**4465. Onipa bɛkye a, ɔnni mfɛnsa.**
*If a person is going to live a long time, he cannot live forever.*
(There are limits to everything. Death is inevitable).

**4466. Onipa mee daa a, anka ote sɛ ɛsono.**
*If a person were always to eat until satisfied, he would be as big as an elephant.*
(If we had all we wanted all the time, it would be great!)

**4467. Onipa mu dua ne aduane.**
*A person's staff of life (lit. tree) is food.*

**4468. Onipa na ɔma onipa sɛeɛ.**
*It is one person who spoils another person.*

**4469. Onipa nam a, na ɔresiane amena.**
*As a person travels around, he skirts the edge of a pit.*
(A person who has to travel much is in constant danger).

**4470. Onipa nnante nkɔgye animguaseɛ.**
*A person does not walk to go and face disgrace.*
(You do not consciously court trouble).

**4471. Onipa ne asɛm. [Mefrɛ sika a, sika nnye so; me frɛ ntoma a, ntoma nnye so].**
*Man is the thing. [If I call money, money does not respond; if I call "cloth", cloth does not respond].*
(Poeple are more valuable than worldly riches).

**4472. Onipa nim adeɛ a, ɛbɛyɛ mmusuo ama no a, anka ɔrenka nkɔ ho.**
*If a person knew what would be a calamity for him, he would not go near it.*
(You avoid what you know to be dangerous, but you cannot avoid danger you cannot foresee).

**4473. Onipa anim te sɛ owia anim, wohunu a, na wobo adwo.**
*A human face is like the sun's face, when you see it, you calm down.*
(You may think you will complain to an important person, but when they are there, you keep quiet).

**4474. Onipa anim nyɛ bonsua na yɛahoro mu da biara.**
*The human face is not an oil pot which should be washed all the time.*
(A person should not always be scolded before he does the right thing).

**4475. Onipa anim nyɛ burodua na ɔde agye [ahohora]/ [animguaseɛ].**
*A person's face is not like a husk of maize, that he takes and uses for [cleaning]/[shameful purposes].*
(The maize-husk was used as toilet-paper. Hence: You should maintain self-respect as once it is lost it is difficult to regain).

**4476. Onipa animuonyam te sɛ kosua, sɛ woansɔ mu yie, na ɛfiri hwe a na abɔ.**
*A person's honour is like an egg, if it is not held properly, it falls and breaks.*

**4477. Onipa nokorɛ ne "Mamee".**
*A person's truth is "I am satisfied".*
(Say the truth and nothing but the truth).

**4478. Onipa anom asɛm na yɛgyina so bua no atɛm.**
*We depend on a person's statement to judge them.*
(We judge a person's words as much as their actions).

**4479. Onipa nyini wu na ɔnnyini ntu.**
*A person grows in order to die but does not grow in order to fly.*
(You cannot alter the nature of things. We all proceed towards death).

**4480. Onipa pa, na yɛto no badin.**
*A good person is the one we name a child after.*
(An Akan child is supposed to take on the character of the person it is named after. Therefore, naming is very important. If you chose someone to name you child after, it means you really respect them).

**4481. Onipa pa se ɔni wo a, ɛnte sɛ wo deɛɛdwɛɛwa.**
*If a good person says he knows you, it is not as well as your windpipe.*
(You are best known by your intimates).

**4482. Onipa pa nti na yɛda a, yɛto pono mu na ɛnyɛ ɔkrɔmfoɔ ntira.**
*Because of a good person, if we sleep, we shut the door, but not because of a thief.*
(Unlike the good person, the thief will open an unlocked door. Hence: A bad person is bad whatever happens, a good one may succumb to temptation).

**4483. Onipa mpatu mpɔ.**
*A person does not hurry to become civilized.*
(It takes time to learn correct behavior).

**4484. Onipa se ɔbɛsɛe wo a, ɛnnim sɛ woyɛ onipa pa.**
*If someone is determined to spoil your name, it does not matter if you are a good person.*
(Hatred does not depend on the quality of the hated).

4485. Onipa si bɔne kwan mu a, afotuo yɛ no sɛ sɛmɔdɛ.
*If a person sets out on a bad road, advice seems to him to be a joke.*
(You can't advise an obstinate person).

4486. Onipa soa adeɛ a ɔbɛtumi na nyɛ deɛ ɛbɛdɛn no.
*A person carries what he is able to, and not what is too heavy for him.*
(You only take on the responsibility you can cope with).

4487. Onipa nsu kwa.
*Man does not weep for no reason.*

4488. Onipa suro deɛ ɔbɛn no.
*A person fears the person who is near him.*
(It is the people closest to you who are in the best position to do you harm).

4489. Onipa tan wo a, da wo ho so.
*If a person hates you, take note of it.*
(Beware of hatred, it is dangerous).

4490. Onipa te sɛ serɛ, woyɛ no yie a, ɛyɛ yie, woanyɛ no yie a, ɛseɛ.
*A person is like the long grass, if you treat it well, it grows well, if you do not, it spoils.*
(Man thrives when well cared for).

4491. Onipa te ase a, na ɔyɛ onipa; na sɛ ɔwu ma yɛsie no a, na ato nkasɛɛ.
*When a person lives, he is a human being; but when he dies and is buried, only bones remain.*
(Alive, you are respected; dead, you are as nothing).

4492. Onipa tene ne nsa a, na yɛdwa no.
*If a person holds out his hand, we salute him.*
(You accept friendship when it is offered to you).

4493. Onipa nni hɔ a, na ne Nyame wɔ hɔ.
*If a person is not there, his God is there.*
(However bad a person is, we must praise what is good in him).

4494. Onipa wu a, yɛde ne papa na ɛsu no na nyɛ ne bɔne.
*If a person dies, we consider his good deeds and weep for him and not his bad deeds.*
(We remember what good a person does, not what bad).

4495. Onipa wu a, na wohunu n'adɔfoɔ.
*If someone dies, then you get to know those who love them.*
(It is at a funeral that we can see if a person had many friends or few).

4496. Onipa wu a ne tɛkrɛma ɛmporɔ no, na ɛfiri teasefoɔ.
*If a person dies and his tongue does not rot, it is because of living people.*
(The words that worthy people speak, live after them).

4497. Onipa wu a, na ne nam wɔ hɔ.
*If a person dies, his flesh remains.*
(A person's appearance lives on in his family).

4498. Onipa rebɛwu a, pampansorɔdɔ su hyia no.
*If a person is going to die, the fiscal shrike cries to meet it (the spirit).*
(Pampansorɔdɔ, the fiscal shrike, is also known as obayinomaa. Every action has its fore-runner. This bird's cry is supposed to presage death).

4499. Onipa wu a, na wawu.
*If a person dies, then he has died.*
(Once you are dead, you are dead. A dead person has no power).

4500. Onipa rebɛwu a, ɔpere.
*If a person is going to die, he struggles.*
(A person fights for his life).

4501. Onipa bɛwu ama n'akyiri aseɛ, eneɛ, fanyinam sɛ wammɔ ɔbra koraa.
*If a person is going to die and let their property be dissipated, then it is better that they did not achieve anything when alive.*
(If all your life's work is wasted by your successors, you have toiled in vain).

4502. Onipa bɛwu na sika tease.
*Man may die but his riches remain on earth.*
(You can't take it with you!)

4503. Onipa wu nsamampɔ mu a, yɛnsan mfa no nkɔ fie.
*If a person dies in the graveyard, we don't take him back home.*
(If you are in the right place, you don't miss your chance).

4504. Onipa yɛ deɛ ne ho bɛtɔ no na ɔnyɛ deɛ yɛbɛpene no.
*A person does what he is capable of doing and not what we would admire him for.*
(A person can only do his best).

4505. Onipa yɛ adeɛ gye ayɛyie.
*A person acts for reward.*

4506. Onipa yɛ wo yie a, mfa bɔne ntua ne so ka.
*If someone does good to you, do not repay the debt with evil.*
(One good deed deserves another).

4507. Onipa nyɛ abɛ na ne ho ahyia ne ho.
*A person is not a palm tree that has all it wants.*
(Human beings can never be self-sufficient).

4508. Onipa nyɛ dua na yɛabɔ no akam.
*A person is not a tree that we scar him.*
(You can't force a person to help you. Trees' bark is cut for medicine).

4509. Onipa nyɛ ɔpɔnkɔ na yɛde homa ahyɛ ne hwene mu.
*A person is not a horse that we should take a rope and put it round his nose.*
(You should treat a person with dignity and not try and boss them about).

4510. Onipa nyɛ prako na wawo ba adi.
*A person is not a pig to give birth to a child and eat it.*
(A pig sometimes eats its newborn piglets. Hence: A person should treat his children with respect and not exploit them).

**4511. Onipa ayɛyie sua.**
*A person's gratitude is small.*
(People are ungrateful).

**4512. Nnipa baanu bɔ mu tua mpatadeɛ a, ɛnyɛ tuana.**
*When two people together pay pacification fees, it is not hard to pay.*
(If you offend someone and are proved guilty, you may have to pay pacification fees; compensation to those you have wronged. Hence: Many hands make light work).

**4513. Nnipa baanu gyimi a, efie bɔ.**
*If two people are out of tune, the home breaks up.*

**4514. Nnipa baanu nti na yɛgye amanedeɛ.**
*It is because of two people that a third receives a parcel.*
(If someone asks you to take a parcel to a friend or to do something for them, you can't refuse because you know them both).

**4515. Nnipa bone yɛnkora no.**
*We do not preserve wicked people.*

**4516. Nnipa bɔne nti na mpire wɔ hɔ.**
*It is because of bad people that the whip exists.*
(It is only because people are bad that we need force to restrain or punish them).

**4517. Nnipa bonniayɛ nti na yɛma anomaa su na ɔnsereɛ.**
*Because of man's ungratefulness we say a bird cries and not that it laughs.*
(If you do not appreciate something, you disparage it).

**4518. Nnipa dodoɔ soa Nyankopɔn a, ɔbaako mmu akyakya.**
*If many people carry God, not one of them will develop a hunchback.*
(If we all pull together, none of us will suffer).

**4519. Nnipa dɔm gyina ho a, wommisa dua dom.**
*If the human army is stationed there, you don't ask the ordeal tree (Erythropheleum guineense) to act for you.*
(The bark of this tree was used in trial by ordeal. The innocent would vomit it up and the guilty die. Hence: If you intend to fight it out, you don't need other methods of finding the truth).

**4520. Nnipa gu ahodoɔ mmiɛnsa nanso obiara wo n'akyiwadeɛ: Ɔhene, ɔdɛhyeɛ na akoa. Ɔhene akyiwadeɛ ne akyinnyeɛ; ɔdehyeɛ deɛ ne nsamu, na akoa deɛ ne nkyeraseɛ.**
*People are classified into three categories, but everyone has his own taboo: the chief, the royal and the slave. The chief's taboo is argument, the royal's is discrimination and the slave's is the revealing of origins.*
(We all have our special dislikes).

**4521. Nnipa kyiri aponkyerɛne nso wɔnom ne ho nsuo.**
*People dislike the frog but drink the water it is in.*
(You may have to spend time with someone you dislike).

**4522. Nnipa na ɛma Ahennwa yɛ kɛseɛ.**
*It is people that make a chief's stool great.*
(It is the followers who maintain institutions and make them important).

**4523. Nnipa nti na yɛbɔ afena.**
*It is because of people that the sword is forged.*
(Because of man's quarrelsome nature, we need weapons of war and defence).

**4524. Nnipa nyinaa redane mmoa a, dane bi.**
*If all people turn into beasts, do likewise.*
(Follow the fashion!)

**4525. Nnipa nyinaa dɔ wo a, due.**
*If all people love you, condolences!*
(A popular person is bound to suffer, sooner or later).

**4526. Nnipa nyinaa mpatu nyɛ bɔne.**
*Men are not all bad at the same time.*
(We have our ups and downs and are sometimes good and sometimes bad).

**4527. Nnipa nyinaa pɛ Aburokyi-korɔ na nya na wɔnnya.**
*Everyone wishes to go overseas but the opportunity does not come to all.*
(See Proverb 597. All people desire good things but not all attain them).

**4528. Nnipa nyinaa pɛ ɔhene ayɛ, na woannya a, na wɔse mpo ahennie yɛ ya.**
*All people would like to be chiefs, but when they cannot get what they want, they say that even to rule as a chief is troublesome.*
(Sour grapes).

**4529. Nnipa nyinaa pɛ "Maakye-medaase" no, na ɛfiri biribi ntira.**
*All people like "Good-morning, thank-you", but there is a reason for it.*
(People like politeness and gratitude because it makes them feel good).

**4530. Nnipa nyinaa suro Ɔseɛ.**
*All people fear the Asantehene.*
(Supreme power is respected by all).

**4531. Nnipa nyinaa tirim adwene nsɛ.**
*All men's thoughts are not alike.*
(Each person is an individual).

**4532. Nnipa nyinaa wɔ ti, nso wontiri nsɛ.**
*All people have heads, but their heads are not alike.*
(Our fortunes and characters differ).

**4533. Nnipa nyinaa bɛwu, na owu pa na yɛrepɛ.**
*All people will die, but we wish for a good death.*
(All people hope to die in peace and dignity).

**4534. Nnipa nyinaa nyɛ, nanso wogye wo hwene so a, yɛse wo nko ara na wonyɛ.**
*All people are bad, but if you become notorious, we say you alone are bad.*
(If you excel others in vice, people single you out to blame).

**4535. Nnipa nyinaa yɛ Onyame mma, obiara nyɛ asaase ba.**
*All people are God's children, no one is a child of the earth.*
(We are all made in the image of God).

**4536. Nnipa papa bi kɔ ɛsa a, wɔmma na ahwen-totoa.**
*If a really good person goes to war, they don't return, how much less a broken-nosed person.*
(If the best does not succeed, how can others?)

**4537. Nnipa sa a, na mmoatia di adeɛ.**
*If people are no more, then the little people inherit.*
(See Proverb 461. If your family is finished it does not matter who inherits).

**4538. Nnipa bɛsɛe na ewiase wɔ hɔ.**
*Men will be spoilt but the world will remain.*
(All of us will die, but the earth remains).

**4539. Nnipa tirim asɛm yɛ mmaako-mmaako.**
*People's thoughts come one by one.*
(You cannot concentrate on two things at the same time).

**4540. Onipabɔne dwane akwaapono mu.**
*A guilty person takes the crooked path.*
(A person with a bad conscience cannot act straightforwardly).

**4541. Onipabɔnefoɔ ho nkrabea aduasa.**
*A bad person has thirty fates.*
(There are many ways in which a bad person may come to a bad end).

**4542. Onipabɔnefoɔ na yɛwɔ no sɛpɔ.**
*It's a bad person who gets the executioner's knife.*
(Punishment is for the wicked).

**4543. Onipabɔnefoɔ asatena yɛ ya.**
*It is hard to stay with a bad person.*

**4544. Onipabɔnefoɔ suro ne sunsum.**
*A bad person fears his own shadow.*

**4545. Onipabɔnefoɔ te kurom a, ne nkoa ne nnipa nyinaa.**
*If there is one bad person in town, his slaves are all the people.*
(The wicked person affects all the citizens of a state badly, whether they are good or bad).

**4546. Onipabɔnefoɔ wuo nyɛ nnipa ya.**
*The death of a bad person does not pain people.*

**4547. Onipakɛseɛ fɔn a, obi nhunu.**
*If a stout person becomes thin, no one notices it.*
(Someone who has much can afford to lose some of it).

**4548. Anitefoɔ kuro fu nsensan.**
*A cunning people's town grows into grass.*
(Too much cunning leads to neglect of responsibility).

**4549. Nnitire mmɔ nkuro.**
*The head which is cut off has no case to present.*
(It's no good being so aggressive in pursuing your rights that you lose your head in the process).

**4550. Anitorɔ se ɔbɛda a, yɛnnye no akyinnye.**
*If a blind person says he will sleep, you do not argue with him.*
(Blindness suggests closed eyes and, therefore, sleep. Hence: If a person is deeply involved in something, you should take his word for it).

**4551. Aniwa fufuo nkum anomaa.**
*The whites of the eyes do not kill a bird.*
(You see through the center of your eye not the whites. Hence: An incompetent person cannot do a job).

**4552. Aniwa na ɛtan onipa, na nyɛ aso.**
*The eye hates a person but not the ear.*
(It is only when something is seen that it excites negative comment).

**4553. Aniwa nnim awerɛhoɔ.**
*The eye does not know grief.*
(The ordinary functions of life must be performed, whatever the situation. Or: Feeling is in the mind and heart, not in the eye).

**4554. Aniwa tease a, na yɛ dɛn na kampɛsɛ nsuo agu soɔ.**
*If in normal times your eyes water, how much more so when you pour liquid into them.*
(If you usually perform well, how much more so when stimulated).

**4555. Aniwa nyɛ abura, nso ɛmu nsuo nsa da.**
*The eye is not a spring but its water is never exhausted.*
(There is no end to sorrow).

**4556. Wo niwaa ba sɔ ahyɛn-gorɔ ase a, wo din nyera.**
*If the child of your relative on the mother's side takes part in moonlight games, your name is not lost.*
(Your reputation is safe amongst blood relatives).

**4557. Niwaa, niwaa na ɛyɛ nwa mmienu.**
*Two small snails (lit. small snail, small snail) become two big snails.*
(Plans and people mature with time).

**4558. Niwaamma baanu redi abeteɛ a, wɔnkyea kodoɔ.**
*If two relatives on your mother's side are eating maize porridge, you do not tip up the bowl.*
(You do not cheat relatives).

**4559. Niwaamma nsae a, wɔfaaseɛ nni adeɛ.**
*If the relatives on your mother's side are not finished your sister's son does not inherit.*
(In normal Akan succession, property passes to other senior members of the matriclan. If no one of your own generation survives, this means one of your sisters' children; but before they can be considered, there are your own mother's children and her sisters' children. Hence: It is the people who have rights to something who get it, not the person who desires it).

**4560. Anka nsa nyɛ nwono na ɔkɔwensani ntasuo na ɛma nsa yɛ nwono.**
*Normally alcohol is not bitter but a drunkard's spittle makes it bitter.*
(A good thing is spoilt by association with bad).

**4561. Ankaadudwane, ɔse: "M'ayɛyie ne mmaa".**
*The lime says: "My praisers are sticks".*
(Used when ingratitude rewards kindness).

**4562. Ankamawaframoa nunum: "Obi anka me a, memmɔn".**
*The fever plant (Ocimum viride) says: "If no one pushes me, I don't give out my smell".*
(This plant is much used as medicine. It contains 23 percent of thymol, which gives it a strong smell. Hence, depending on context: Let sleeping dogs lie. Or: A person needs stimulation to give of his best).

**4563. Ankama nkɔtua ɛka a, ɔde ɛka aba fie.**
*If Ankama has been told to pay a debt, he brings back (more) debt to the house.*
(Said of someone who has been asked to help but makes the situation worse).

**4564. Nkateɛ nyɛ dɛ a, tie ne bɔ.**
*If the groundnut is not sweet, listen to how it cracks.*
(You can judge a person by his performance).

**4565. Nkekaboa, ebi ara ne ntontom.**
*The mosquito is one kind of beast of prey.*
(It is character, not size, that you judge people by).

**4566. Ankɔbi-na-ɔhunuiɛ bɔ kuro.**
*Someone-who-has-not-been-but-pretends-to-know –about-it spoils the town.*
(An uninformed gossip causes endless trouble).

**4567. [Ankonam di]/[Ɔbaako nam a, ɔdi] torɔ wɔ dom anim.**
*[A lone traveller]/[If a single person travels, he] becomes a liar before a crowd.*
(You need a witness to prove your case).

**4568. Ankora a nsuo nni mu na ɛyɛ dede.**
*An empty barrel (lit. a barrel that the water is not in) makes most noise.*
(An ignorant person causes most trouble).

**4569. Nkwa wɔ hɔ a, na anidasoɔ wɔ hɔ.**
*If there is life, then there is hope.*

**4570. Nkyene gu aboɔ mu a, yɛnsesa bio.**
*If the salt falls among the stones, we don't pick it up again.*
(Some things are irretrievable).

**4571. Nkyene nkamfo ne ho sɛ: "Meyɛ dɛ".**
*Salt should not praise itself saying: "I am sweet".*
(It is not good to be arrogant nor to praise yourself to others).

**4572. Nkyene [na ɛma]/[dɛ nti na] mako kum nnipa.**
*It is due to salt that pepper kills people.*
(We are encouraged to take pepper because it is mixed with salt. Hence: There is some joy with our suffering).

**4573. Nkyene tere nkwan mu a, tɛkrɛma na ɔka, na nyɛ ani.**
*If the salt flavors the soup, the tongue will tell you but not the eye.*
(The person with inside knowledge can judge, but not the outsider).

**4574. Nkyene antere abomu mu a, na nyɛ ɛta to a.**
*If salt does not flavor a broth, the same is not true of the bottom of the pestle spoon.*
(If you don't have enough for everyone, at least you help one person).

**4575. Nkyene wɔ hɔ a, bɔnam mporɔ.**
*If the salt is there, the meat does not rot.*
(If you have means of preserving, you preserve).

**4576. Ano a yɛde abu wo bem no, yɛde ma wo dibem a, wo bo nkyɛre dwo.**
*The mouth that has been used to find you innocent, if we use it to apologize to you, you easily calm down.*
(You listen to those who help and believe in you).

**4577. Ano a ɛfiri kane na ɛfa abɔfono.**
*The mouth that first mentions it, appropriates the carcass.*
(The first person to claim something gets it).

**4578. W'ano aba a, na wo nsa aba.**
*If your mouth can say something, then your hand must be able to fight.*
(A person who uses abuse must be prepared for a fight).

**4579. Ano berɛberɛ ma [aderɛ]/[abaa] tɔ.**
*A soft tongue makes the [cutlass]/[stick] fall.*
(Persuasion avoids violence).

**4580. W'ano anna a, yɛfrɛ wo mpaninnim.**
*If your mouth does not sleep, we call you before the elders.*
(A talkative person gets into trouble).

**4581. Ano kurokuro twa ne ho adafi.**
*A blabbermouth turns around and reveals (his secrets).*
(Just as a restless person talks in their sleep at night. Hence: If you talk too much, you are bound to let people know all about yourself).

**4582. Ano patiri a, ɛsene nammɔn.**
*If the mouth slips, it is worse than the foot slipping.*
(A wrong word can do great harm).

**4583. W'ano so a, wode hyɛn abɛn, na womfa nka asenkɛseɛ.**
*Even if your mouth is big, you use it for blowing a horn, but you don't use it to swear the great oath.*
(You may be strong but not strong enough to challenge final authority).

**4584. W'ano so a, womfa nhyɛn waduro na wode hyɛn abɛn.**
*If you have a big mouth, you don't blow a mortar, you blow a horn.*
(See Proverb 4583).

**4585. W'ano antumi w'abɛ a, ɛdɔre akɔkono.**
*If you don't blow hard enough into your palm tree, it accumulates grubs.*
(Akɔkono is the larva of the palm-beetle – asamanadwo – which breeds in palm trees. You blow heat into the tree to cauterize it, so that it does not rot before the wine is tapped. Hence: If you do not persist, your work may spoil).

**4586. Anobesebesa na εma yεtɔn akoa.**
*Mumbling enables us to sell a slave.*
(You find a roundabout way to hide your intentions).

**4587. Wonoa a, εbene, woto a, εbene.**
*If you boil it, it becomes cooked, if you roast it, it becomes cooked.*
(Whatever you do, you get the same result).

**4588. Wonoa aduane a εnyε wo dea a, deε ne dea gye ho nim fa.**
*If you cook food and it is not yours, the person to whom it belongs is praised for it.*
(It is the master who gets the credit, not the servant).

**4589. Wonoa ɔsa na wode nkontompo gya hyε aseε a, εmmene.**
*If you are cooking war medicine and there is the fire of untruth under it, it does not cook.*
(Honesty is the best policy).

**4590. Yεnoa ntwuropo di, na yemmene n'aba.**
*We cook the big garden egg to eat, but we don't eat its seeds.*
(However much you are in need, you should use discrimination).

**4591. "Noa-prenu", yε nkyenseeε.**
*"Boil it twice", makes the salt spoil.*
(Overworking something, spoils it).

**4592. Nobi Na se: ɔrenware pɔnkɔ, na funumu pɔnkɔ!**
*The Nobi Na says he won't marry a horse, how much less a donkey.*
(If you don't like something good, you are not likely to like something less good).

**4593. Anofanu twa benkum, twa nifa.**
*A two-sided knife cuts to the left, (and) cuts to the right.*
(Signifies impartiality and justice).

**4594. Ano-kεseε na εka nsεnkεseε.**
*It is the big mouth that says big things.*
(It is better to leave the announcement of grave or important events to those in power).

**4595. Εnne na tete atete ama Aborɔfo apempam, anka nyε ɔtwea yɔnko ne prako.**
*In these days the old has got tattered for whitemen to mend, otherwise the bitch would not be co-equal with the pig.*
(Things have changed from the old days, so that now people with different backgrounds are forced to work together).

**4596. Annɔ-Ampam na ɔwe akwankwaman.**
*A lazy person eats the biggest of the produce.*
(Some people always take advantage of the work of others).

**4597. Anokorampɔn ase firi soro, nti na obi nnim n'ase.**
*African mistletoe's roots come from the sky, therefore no one knows their origin.*
(The African mistletoe is also called Krampaa or dua-mu-dua. The origins of some things are clothed in mystery).

**4598. Nokorε di tuo.**
*Truth earns the gun.*
(Tell the truth and be damned!)

**4599. Nokorε kwan kɔ tee.**
*Truth's road is straight.*
(To tell the truth is simple).

**4600. Nokorε akyiwadeε ne akyinnyeε.**
*The abomination of truth is disbelief.*
(A person speaking the truth expects to be believed).

**4601. Nokorε mu nni abra.**
*In truth there is no deceit.*
(Truth is straight forward).

**4602. Nokorε nam ɔkwantiawa so bεduru fie, na nkontompo da so te kwan so.**
*Truth travels by a short route to reach home, but lies keep on along the road.*
(Truth is more direct than lying).

**4603. Nokorε ne nkontompo nnante.**
*Truth and falsehood do not walk hand in hand.*

**4604. Nokorε tam, yεmo no akwan-akwan.**
*Truth's loincloth, we tuck it in cautiously.*
(If you want to say the truth, be careful how you do it).

**4605. Anoku te ase dada a, n'ano repram nsuo, na Tεpa Baaneε ada sε ɔnhyira n'ano.**
*If the pig lives a long time, it produces saliva from its mouth, how much more when Tεpa Baaneε has instructed it to bless its soul.*
(Tεpa Baaneε is a powerful fetish. If someone normally does something he likes, he gets double enjoyment, if he is actually commissioned to do it).

**4606. Ɔnokwafoo ho yε ahi.**
*A truthful person is hated.*
(People do not like to hear the truth about themselves).

**4607. Ɔnokwafoo mo ne tam a, ɔmo no akwan-akwan.**
*If a truthful person puts on his cloth, he puts it on straight.*
(An honest person acts straightforwardly).

**4608. Wonom abua fa wo hwene mu a, wo ara na worekyerε wo ho akwan.**
*If you smoke the pipe and let the smoke go through the nose, it is you own nose that you are blocking.*
(If you are stupid enough to do something to your own detriment, we can't stop you).

**4609. Wonom ahina korɔ mu a, wonom fam.**
*If you drink from a single pot, you drink from the ground.*
(Don't put all your eggs in one basket. Make alternative provision).

**4610. Yεrenom nsuo a, yεhwε ne nkwammanoa.**
*If we are going to drink water, we look at its surroundings.*
(You consider the circumstances well before taking action).

**4611. Yɛnom nsuo twɛn pɛ.**
*We drink water to prepare for the harmattan.*
(A warning to make provision for the future).

**4612. W'anom asɛm asa a, na wose: "Ɔhene a ɔwɔ Aburokyire yɛ ɔhene".**
*If you have nothing to say, you say: "The king who is overseas is a king indeed".*
(See Proverb 597. If you have nothing good to say, you speak commonplaces).

**4613. W'anom yɛ wo dɛ a, wontwa wo tɛkrɛma nto nwe.**
*If you mouth is sweet to you, you don't cut off your tongue and roast and eat it.*
(There should be moderation in all things).

**4614. Anomaa a ɔda fidie mu nko ne ne su.**
*The bird that is caught in the trap, has a different song.*
(If you are in trouble, you use a different vocabulary from the usual one).

**4615. Anomaa a ɔredware nsuo se: "Hwan na ɔbɛdware n'akyi ama me?"**
*The bird that bathes in the river asks: "Who will wash my back for me?"*
(Said when someone has no help at all).

**4616. Anomaa ba hwɛ oni atuo so na watu.**
*The bird's chick watches its mother fly before it can fly.*
(We learn by example).

**4617. Anomaa biara wɔ n'aduaba a ɔdie.**
*Every single bird has its special fruit to eat.*
(God provides for all in one way or another).

**4618. Anomaa biara wu wɔ soro a, ne ntakara ba fam.**
*Whatever bird dies in the sky, its feathers fall to earth.*
(Some things are inevitable).

**4619. Anomaa, yɛmmɔ no pɔ.**
*We don't tie a bird in a knot.*
(You cannot trick a wise person).

**4620. Anomaa bɔne na ɔsɛe ne pirebuo.**
*A bad bird fouls its own nest.*
(If you are bad, it affects your own family first and foremost).

**4621. Anomaa de akɔneaba na ɛnwono ne pirebuo.**
*A bird uses coming and going to weave its nest.*
(It takes work to build up a home).

**4622. Anomaa mfa dua abufu.**
*A bird should not become angry with a tree.*
(You don't get annoyed with a person on whom you depend).

**4623. Anomaa fidie: "Me rekopɛ biribi abɛdi" ne "Mebɛyɛɛ dɛɛn?" na ɛnam.**
*A bird trap: "I am going to find something to eat" goes hand in hand with "Why did I come here?"*
(When you go to search for a livelihood you have to take risks).

**4624. Anomaa fie, ɛne ne pirebuo.**
*A bird's home is its nest.*
(If you want to be happy, you need your own home. Or: every creature has its own home).

**4625. Anomaa ho bɛyɛ fɛ a, na ɛfiri ne ntakara.**
*If a bird is beautiful, it is so because of its feathers.*
(Fine feathers make a fine bird).

**4626. Anomaa ahoɔden ne ne ntaban.**
*The bird's strength is in its wings.*
(Everyone has their strongest point).

**4627. Anomaa anka wo fidie mu a, ɔnha wo brɛ.**
*If a bird does not fall into your trap, it does not give you any problem to worry about.*
(If someone is not in your hands, it is no good worrying what to do about them).

**4628. Anomaa kɔ asuo a, ɔde n'ano na ɛsa.**
*If a bird goes for water, he uses his beak to collect it.*
(We use the implements God has given us in life).

**4629. Anomaa kokonekone, ɔkɔ nsutifi kɔhono nsuo na wakɔ anaafoɔ akɔbisa sɛ: "Hwan na ɔhonoo nsuo yi?"**
*The bird Kokonekone, goes to the source of the river and makes the water dirty and then he goes to the mouth and asks: "Who has dirtied this water?"*
(Said when someone has themselves caused trouble and then goes and asks elsewhere, who is causing the trouble pretending ignorance).

**4630. Anomaa koro di ayuo a, ɔtiatia so.**
*If one bird alone eats millet, it treads it under foot.*
(To work alone is wasteful).

**4631. Anomaa koreɛ anni nammono a, ɔnna.**
*If the eagle does not eat fresh meat, it does not sleep.*
(A person needs what he is accustomed to, to thrive).

**4632. Anomaa korɔnte kasa we esia, na onipa korɔnte nso kasa we nsa.**
*If the singing bird's reward is the caterpillar, then a clever person's reward is palm wine.*
(Each person should be rewarded with what he likes best).

**4633. Anoma kyɛre dua so a ɔgye boɔ.**
*If the bird stays long in one tree, it has a stone thrown at it.*
(If someone makes a constant nuisance of himself, he will be punished).

**4634. Anomaa na ɛsu sɛ no.**
*The cry suits the bird.*
(Our complaints arise from our own characters and circumstances).

**4635. Anomaa nantabo-ta-bo Tanoa, ɔno a, ɔnyɛ ɔha, ɔno nsoa ɔnyɛ kokokyinaka, nso ɔtu.**
*The bird spider, it is not a flying-squirrel, it is not a plantain eater, but it flies.*
(The spider travels from place to place "flying" (i.e swinging) at the end of its web. Hence: Said when an outsider achieves success as for instance when you have not been to a famous school but succeed where its scholars do not).

**4636. Anomaa nam nkɔso kyɛ.**
*There is not enough meat on a bird to be worth sharing out.*
(Said of some inconsiderable trifle which is not worth quarreling over).

4637. Anomaa nini antu a, [ne yere ne ne mma buada] / [ɔbuada].
*If the cock bird does not fly, [its hen and chicks go to bed hungry]/[it goes hungry].*
(Man must work to keep his family alive).

4638. Anomaa nitefoɔ, baha na ɛyi no.
*The cunning bird is caught with plantain fibers.*
(A clever person is caught with small things).

4639. Anomaa nitefoɔ, fidie yi ho ntɛntɛnoa.
*A cunning bird is caught on the tip of a tree.*
(If you are trying to be too clever, you will be caught out).

4640. Anomaa ano ware a, ɔde didi asuogya na ɔmfa ntware asuo.
*If a bird has a long bill, it uses it to eat on its own side of the stream, but it does not use it for stretching across the water.*
(A warning against interfering with other people's land or an indication of limit to the power of ownership).

4641. Anomaa ano yɛ den a, aboa biara nkye no nwe.
*If a bird can screech (lit.: if its mouth is strong), no wild beast can catch and eat it.*
(A vociferous person cannot be easily victimized).

4642. Anomaa nua ne deɛ ɔne no da dua korɔ.
*A bird's brother is the one with whom he sleeps on the same tree.*
(Birds of a feather flock together).

4643. Anomaa nni nsa, nso ɔde n'ano nwene ne pirebuo.
*A bird has no hands, but it uses its beak to weave its nest.*
(God provides everyone with a way of doing things).

4644. Anomaa nte sɛ akyekyedeɛ na wasoa ne pirebuo.
*A bird is not like a tortoise to carry its nest on its back.*
(You do not try and emulate those different from yourself).

4645. Anomaa nnwono pirebuo na ɔnna fam.
*A bird does not weave its nest and sleep on the ground.*
(If you have made provision for something, you make use of it).

4646. Nnomaa nnomaa ni ne abawɛre.
*The mother of all the birds is the Rainbow bird.*
(This is an imaginary bird. Hence: We all come from one origin).

4647. Anomua ne Tanɔ ho hu.
*The act of keeping silent about what goes on, is what makes the Tano fetish fearful.*
(A silent or reticent person is respected).

4648. Anomuɔdɛ na ɛmaa odufudepɛfoɔ bɔɔ ne ho tuo.
*Love of eating meat made a greedy person shoot himself.*
(If you are too greedy, you get yourself into trouble).

4649. Ɔnomuɔdefoɔ na kasɛɛ hia no.
*A person who likes a great deal of meat is troubled by the bone.*
(It is things associated with what you like best, that bring about your downfall).

4650. Ɔno-na-ɔredi-ama-woɔ, ɔwɔ mu bi na ɔyɛ woɔ.
*He-who-acts-on-your-behalf-in-a-case is amongst those who can damage you.*
(It is those who are most intimate with you who can do you the most harm).

4651. Yɛnnɔn nwoma nkɔ ahemfie.
*We don't soak a skin and take it to the palace.*
(You must finish a job before it can be judged. A skin is used to cover a drum and you would take the finished drum, not just the skin, as a gift to the chief).

4652. Anopa hyira ne ho.
*A good mouth blesses itself.*
(A careful speaker keeps peace with the world and himself).

4653. Anɔpa bosuo mmoro ɔbaakofoɔ.
*The morning dew does not wet one person alone.*
(Troubles come to many people alike).

4654. Anopa-dwuma ankɔ so na bɔnnɔɔ?
*Work done in the morning did not progress, how much more the leisure time work?*
(The morning is considered the best time for work. If you don't prosper when things are good, how can you at other times).

4655. Anɔpa-nom bɔn, nanso asɛmpa wɔ mu.
*One's mouth stinks in the morning, but good news comes from it.*
(Good can come out of bad).

4656. Anosɛmfoɔ biara nni ahoɔden.
*No vain boaster is powerful.*
(People boast to cover their weaknesses. A strong man has no need of boasting).

4657. Anosɛmfoɔ biara nnyaa ɔyerɛ da.
*No braggart ever gets a wife.*
(Women are not impressed by a boaster).

4658. Anoseseadefoɔ na yɛku no.
*A person who says whatever he sees, we kill him.*
(Indiscretion brings disaster).

4659. Anosini pɛ nsa na wanya nsa a, na ɛfiri n'ano.
*If a person whose lips have been cut off wants to drink and cannot do so, it is because of his mouth.*
(In the old days a dangerous rumor-monger might have his lips cut off. Hence: You pay the penalty for your arms).

4660. Anowedeɛ ka yɛ tuana.
*A debt from careless talk is hard to pay.*
(It is easier to talk yourself into trouble than out of it).

4661. Nsa na yɛde hyɛ nku no, ɛno ara na yɛde teɛ.
*The hand that you use in collecting the shea-butter, you use to smear it on.*
(The person who starts something carries it through).

4662. Nsa a ɛfata sɛ yɛbɔ kawa hyɛ, na yɛbɔ hyɛ.
*The finger that a ring suits is what we wear it on.*
(There is a fitting place for everything).

4663. Nsa brɛ dwa, ano na ɛdie.
*The hand gets tired in vain, it is the mouth which eats.*
(Said of someone who works hard for another to benefit).

4664. Wo nsa da ɔbɔn mu a, ɛmmra wo.
*If you hand is in the hole, it does not deceive you.*
(You trust your own evidence).

4665. Wo nsa da mu a, yɛnni nnya wo.
*If your hand is in the dish, we do not eat and leave you out.*
(If you are already involved in something, people let you get on with it).

4666. Nsa ankɔ nsuo mu a, nsuo nso nkɔ nsa mu.
*If palm wine does not go into the water, water also does not go into palm wine.*
(You scratch my back, I'll scratch yours).

4667. Wo nsa akyi bɛyɛ wo dɛ a, ɛnte sɛ wo nsa yam.
*If the back of your hand is sweet, it won't be as sweet as the palm.*
(Those inside the family are bound to care more for you than those outside).

4668. Nsa mu wɔ biribi a, anka asɔmorɔdwe nhome mfa n'akyi.
*If there were anything good in wine, the beetle would not breathe through its back.*
(Which it does! Said of someone who takes an unproductive action, to discourage him).

4669. Nsa nnuru yafunu mu nti na emu yɛ fi a, yɛde bɛntoa yie.
*Because the hand cannot reach into the stomach, if the stomach becomes dirty, we use an enema to ease it.*
(What one cannot do oneself one uses a tool to achieve).

4670. Nsa nwo ɔba pa.
*Liquor does not bring forth a good child.*
(Qualities are inherited, and a drunkard's child starts with a disadvantage).

4671. Ansa na ɔbaa bɛhoa afigya aduane no, na n'ani da ɔbarima so.
*Before a woman cooks food to be eaten outside the home, her eyes are on a man.*
(No one does anything special without a motive).

4672. Ansa na aborɔbɛ bɛfifiri no na nkasɛe afifiri dada.
*Before the pineapple fruited, its thorns had long been in existence.*
(The thorns protect the fruit. Hence: It is necessary to plan ahead for your protection).

4673. Ansa na obubuafoɔ bɛpam ne nua afiri adidiyowa ho no, na ɔrepɛ ayowa no mu na atafere.
*Before a lame person drives his brother from the food dish, he is wanting to lick the inside of the dish.*
(If a weak person takes action against someone he must have a strong motive).

4674. Ansa na burodua bɛkɔ yaane mu no, na ɛwɔ deɛ ntumɔn-nwi aka akyerɛ no.
*When the corn-cob enters the pit-latrine, it is because of what the hair around the anus has said to it.*
(The dry corn-cob is used as toilet paper in the villages. Hence: If someone accepts an unpleasant job, they know what they are after).

4675. Ansa na odwanten bɛwe dufunu no, na wahunu deɛ ɛserɛ nso wɔ.
*Before the ram chews the rotten log, he has seen where the grass grew.*
(You may know what is good, but for one reason or other not use it).

4676. Ansa na tɛkrɛma bɛdi dwanam no, na sekan adi bi.
*Before the tongue will eat mutton the knife, has already eaten a little.*
(Every one takes their cut).

4677. Ansa na akokɔ ne kurokurokoko bɛko no, na ɛfiri deɛ efiri.
*Before the chicken and the turkey have a fight, there is some reason for it (lit. it is caused by what causes it).*
(No one quarrels without reason).

4678. Ansa na mpire bɛkɔ nnipa nam mu no, na ɛfiri deɛ wayɛ.
*If the whip penetrates a person's flesh, then it is because of what he has done.*
(There is no smoke without fire).

4679. Nsadua nnum, ebi sene bi.
*Among five fingers, some are greater than others.*
(There is precedence in society).

4680. Wo nsam nni biribi a, wɔfrɛ wo "Yeinom nyinaa yɛ asɛm".
*If you have nothing in your hands, they call you "What is all this about?"*
(People do not respect the poor nor those who ask a favor without a gift).

4681. Wo nsam yɛ den a, na yɛbu mu.
*If you make your hand stiff, we break it.*
(You should learn to be flexible).

4682. Nsam bɛyɛ fi a, ɛrenyɛ sɛ ɔnammɔn mu.
*Even if your palm will get dirty, it will not be as dirty as the sole of your foot.*
(Some people's capacity for bad will always be greater than others).

4683. Nsateaa baako nkukuru adeɛ.
*One finger does not lift things up.*
(Man should not be asked to bear responsibility alone).

4684. Nsateaa baako na ɛte nku ma ɔde sra honam nyinaa.
*It is one finger which goes into the shea-butter, letting it grease the whole body.*
(One person makes a major contribution to society).

4685. Nsateaa du, nyinaa nyɛ pɛ.
*Of the ten fingers, not all are alike.*
(Not all the members of a family resemble each other).

**4686. Nsateaa kɔrɔ na ɛsa ngo wɔ ahina nkɔn ase.**
*One finger clears the oil from round the pot's neck.*
(A small thing is sometimes sufficient to do an efficient job).

**4687. Nsateaa num, ɛwɔ deɛ yɛde kye abebeɛ.**
*Amongst the five fingers is one that can be used for winkling out the water snail from its shell.*
(A family is made up of many different talents).

**4688. Nsateaa yɛ kuri a, wontwa ntwene.**
*If your finger is stumpy, you don't cut it off.*
(You don't get rid of a disabled member of the family).

**4689. Wo nsateaa yɛ tia a, wonni ntentenemu.**
*If your fingers are short, you don't play at stretching out.*
(You only do what is within your capacity).

**4690. Nsateaa nyɛ ponona, na ɛnyɛ tenena.**
*The fingers are not hard to close, but they are (also) not hard to open.*
(It is up to you whether you are mean or generous).

**4691. Nsɔkɔ nni abɛn bi na wahyɛn.**
*Nsɔkɔ has no horn to blow.*
(Said of someone who has no position in society but lives by pleasing others).

**4692. Nsɔkɔ nyɛ abɛn na yɛ abɔ.**
*Nsɔkɔ is not a horn that we should blow it.*
(Because one thing has the same name as another it does not mean you should treat it in the same way. Nsɔkɔbɛn are small horns).

**4693. Nsuo no ɛkɔ nsa mu, na ɛnyɛ nsa na ɛkɔ nsuo mu.**
*Water goes into palm wine, but it is not wine that goes into water.*
(Compare Proverb 4666. Precious things can be diluted but you don't waste them by getting rid of them).

**4694. Ntim Gyakari soaa ne man kɔbɔɔ no Feyiase.**
*Ntim Gyakari carried his nation to destruction at Feyiase.*
(Ntim Gyakari was the famous Dankyirahene who was defeated by Osei Tutu the Asantehene in about 1701. Recalcitrant people lead their followers to disaster).

**4695. Worenu w'aso mu, woreto wo pa, deɛ ɛwɔ hene ha ɛyɛ wo dɛ?**
*You are cleaning your ear, you are shaking your waist, which of them do you like the better?*
(You can't do two important things at the same time, so you must choose one).

**4696. Wo nua a ɔtane woɔ no, na ɔte sɛ obi nua a ɔdɔ woɔ.**
*If your brother hates you, then it is as if someone else's brother loves you.*
(Family ties are stronger than any individual emotions).

**4697. Wo nua ba ne ɔserɛbene a, w'adeɛ nka dɔtɔ mu.**
*If your brother's child were a red-legged squirrel, your goods would not be stranded in a thicket.*
(If your relative is working for something, you can get what you need from it).

**4698. Wo nua-baa ba nyiniiɛ a, wose ɔne wo ka.**
*If your sister's child has not grown, you say she (your sister) likes you.*
(People are friendly with those who are useful to them, but when the use is gone the situation may change).

**4699. Wo nua-baa serɛ so a, ɛnna wo so.**
*Your sister's thigh may be plump, but it does not lie on you.*
(There are some things you can never share, however good they are).

**4700. Nuanom nsae a, wɔfaase nni adeɛ.**
*If brothers are not exhausted, nephews don't inherit.*
(When a man dies his brothers are entitled to inherit from him. It is only when they are not there that inheritance passes to the nephews. Things must follow the correct procedure).

**4701. Onua-panin yɛ owura.**
*The eldest brother is the master.*
(Seniority must be maintained).

**4702. Nnuadewa-boaa a, yɛfrɛ no memiremfi, yɛdi ne sradeɛ nso yɛnni ne nam.**
*Maggot in the garden egg, which we call memiremfi, we eat its juice but we don't eat its meat.*
(Said of a troublesome member of the family who is despised but whose advice is nevertheless sometimes taken).

**4703. Onumtutufoɔ aduane ne [ɛfan]/[ɛferɛ].**
*The toothless man's meat is [ɛfan]/[a pumpkin].*
(Ɛfan is a herb used like cocoa-yam leaf to make stew and is soft and easy to eat. Ɛferɛ is a pumpkin which when cooked also becomes soft. Hence: If you are weak you are compelled to accept whatever you are given).

**4704. Wonunu kokora a, nunu nkamfo bi.**
*If you censure the wild yam, censure the nkamfo yam as well.*
(Both are bitter. Hence: If you blame one man for something you must blame another who does the same).

**4705. Wonunu akura a, na woanunu nkankama.**
*If you blame the mouse, you blame the source of the smell.*
(If you blame someone for something, you must also blame the cause of the trouble).

**4706. Onunum ho annwo no a, na ɛfiri ɔmanni.**
*If the fever plant (Ocimum viride) is not happy, it is because of a fellow citizen.*
(This plant is much used as medicine and neighbors come and ask for its leaves, if you have it in your yard. It contains 23 percent of thymol. Hence: If you are much in demand, you never have any peace).

**4707. Nisuo yɛ abura a, anka obi nsa obi deɛ da.**
*If tears were to be a well, then no one would ever collect water from another person's place.*
(If we had all the sympathy we needed we would not seek for more. Or: If supplies were infinite, we would not need to go elsewhere).

**4708. Nwa a woahu no na woretwe ne so tuo yi, na ɔwansane na wohunuu no a, anka wobɛyɛ dɛn?**
*Even a snail you have seen you have taken a gun to, then what are you going to do to the bush buck when you see it?*
(Reserve your strength for where it is necessary).

**4709. Nwa hunu ne ho so hwɛ a, ɔdane tope.**
*If a snail looks after itself well it grows into a big one.*
(If you are careful, you prosper).

**4710. Nwa nam nyinaa ne deɛ ɛtua n'ano.**
*The whole of a snail's meat is what is drawn out.*
(Said of someone whose only possessions are what they stand up in).

**4711. Nwa se: ahisɛm nti na wote na a, ɔbɔ apee.**
*The snail says: because of vexation, when you take it, it makes contemptuous noises.*
(A snail makes a kind of sucking noise when it is picked up. This sound is similar to one used as an expression of contempt in Asante. Hence: A helpless victim is unable to protect himself, but may none the less show contempt by his looks or actions).

**4712. Nwa retene na woka no a, ɔka kɔ mu.**
*If you touch the horns of the snail while it is crawling, it withdraws (into its shell).*
(If you disturb people while they are working, they will stop work).

**4713. Nwa wu nkwan mu a, ɔmporɔ.**
*If the snail dies in the soup, it does not rot.*
(When a soldier, for instance, dies in a just cause, it is not in vain).

**4714. Nwa-kyɛm mu mpa tabiraa.**
*On a stick of dried snails you cannot avoid a black one.*
(There is a black sheep in every family).

**4715. Ɔnwam didi a, opuro nso di bi.**
*If the hornbill eats some, the squirrel also eats some.*
(Share and share alike).

**4716. Ɔnwam ho wɔ adeɛ a, anka ɔrentu.**
*If the hornbill had all he needed, he would not fly.*
(No one goes anywhere without a reason).

**4717. Ɔnwam kɛsɛbirekuo Ata ma ne homene so a, na anwenhema agu ase.**
*When the great hornbill Ata rises up, the smaller hornbills bow down in respect.*
(You can tell an important man by the way people treat him).

**4718. Ɔnwam kɛsɛbirekuo Ata se: ɔnya obi ama wakɔse Tanɔ komfoɔ sɛ ɔnnyae tannuro no waewaeɛ, na ɔno a ɔdi n'aba mpo kokoram atɔ ne tirim.**
*The great hornbill Ata says: he would like someone to tell Tano's priest to stop cutting the bark of the tannuro tree, for even he, who eats the seeds, has scrofula on his head.*
(When a man of experience knows something is no good, he will warn others who are using it to desist).

**4719. Ɔnwam kɛsɛbirekuo Ata se, sɛ ɔnim sɛ abɛ bebere a anka wankɔdi adɔbɛ-aba.**
*The great hornbill Ata says, if he knew that the palm nuts would ripen he would not have gone and eaten*
*the raffia-palm nuts.*
(If a man knows good fortune is one the way, he does not chase after lesser things).

**4720. Ɔnwam kɛsɛbirekuo Ata se: "Mewo kokoram aduro a, anka mesu [kama]/[yie]".**
*The great hornbill Ata says: "If I had medicine for scrofula, I would sing nicely".*
(Said of someone who gives irrelevant excuses for not doing something properly).

**4721. Ɔnwam kɛsɛbirekuo Ata si dutan so a, ɔhunu Aburokyire, nanso sɛ sommorɔ si n'ani ase a, ɔnhunu ntu.**
*The great hornbill Ata perches on the great tree, it can see far and wide but if it gets a jigger under its eye, it cannot see how to pull it out.*
(See Proverb 597. Said of someone who can settle a big arbitration but is unable to deal with his own house problems).

**4722. Ɔnwam kɛsɛbirekuo, ɔse: "Adeɛ akye, na deɛben na yɛbɛdie?"**
*The great hornbill says: "It is daybreak, what are we going to feed on?"*
(You have to plan daily to eat).

**4723. Ɔnwam kɛsɛbirekuo su a, ɔse "Ɔpɛtɛ wokae o! Ɔpɛtɛ wokae o!"**
*If the great hornbill cries he says: "Vulture you've said it, vulture you've said it."*
(There is a folktale in which the hornbill ignores the vulture's warning to hurry up and make a nest. Hence: Said when someone disregards a warning).

**4724. Ɔnwam nim ne to nti na ɔmene adɔbɛ aba.**
*The hornbill knows how its bottom is, that is why it eats the fruit of the raffia palm.*
(The hornbill has a big anus. The seeds of the raffia palm are large. Hence: A person does not take on tasks he is not equipped to perform).

**4725. Ɔnwam se: ɔde n'asonterɛm na ɛhwɛ adeɛ.**
*The hornbill says: it looks at things sideways but does not comment.*
(Said of someone who knows what is going on but just lets things happen without interfering).

**4726. Ɔnwam tu na wansu a, ɔdane akyenkyena.**
*If the hornbill flies and does not sing, it is taken for (lit. it changes into) an allied hornbill.*
(If a man does not show his qualities openly, then he is taken for a lesser person).

**4727. Ɔnwamma: "Wose menyɛ nso sɛ metɔ a, na mmoa rebɛwe".**
*The Ɔnwamma (Richodendron heualotii) says: "You say I am no good and yet when my seeds fall, animals will eat them".*
(Said when a man's importance is only recognized when the situation is critical).

**4728. Nwammasuo te a, na ɔpɛ asi.**
*When the squall which brings down the fruit of the richodendron heualotii ceases, it is the time of the harmattan.*
(One thing presages another).

**4729. Nwansena de ne nsa gu n'akyi a, ɔse: "Deɛ aka akyire ɛdɔɔɔso!"**

*When the fly stretches its arms behind it, it says: "What remains is a great deal".*
(Used in the sense of: "I have done a great deal for you but you can still hope for more").

### 4730. Nwansena di atusie a, sisi a, ɔnsi gya mu.
*If the fly goes from place to place, it does not fly into the fire.*
(A person who is always on the move still avoids dangers).

### 4731. Nwasena si ayowa mu a, ɔtafere mu.
*If the fly is in the pot, he is licking in it.*
(People don't go somewhere without a reason).

### 4732. Nwansena mfa mmorɔsa ho bɛn.
*The fly has nothing to do with foreign drink.*
(Flies prefer palm wine. Hence: You are not interested in what does not concern you).

### 4733. Nwansena nni biribi a, ɔposa ne nsam.
*If the fly has nothing else, at least it rubs its hands.*
(Everyone has some gift).

### 4734. Nwansena yɔnko ne nwansenampobire, na enyɛ ne yɔnko ne ɔsebɔ.
*The companion of the ordinary fly is the flesh-fly, but it's not the case that its companion is the leopard.*
(Like moves with lie. Or: An inferior person does not accompany a great one).

### 4735. Nwansenampobire ampa funu ho a, yɛde no sie.
*If the blow fly does not leave the corpse, we bury it.*
(If you put yourself in a dangerous situation and don't watch out, you suffer).

### 4736. Nwansenampobire nni ano, nso ɔtwɛre abɛ.
*The big fly has no mouth, but it chews palm nut.*
(Even weak things can achieve success with patience).

### 4737. Anwenhema pɛ adanseɛ, nti na hyire si ne nwene soɔ.
*Because the white-nosed monkey likes to have a witness, white clay is on its nose.*
(White clay is used for celebrating. Hence: If you are supporting someone, you show it in a public way).

### 4738. Anwenhema-kwakuo: "Adeɛ bɛkye me sɛn ni?"
*The white-nosed monkey says: "How will the next day take me?"*
(We cannot foresee the future).

### 4739. Nwera nyɛ biribi a, ɛyɛ asunsuaneɛ.
*If calico is nothing else, it is good for tearing into strips.*
(Strips of white calico, usually tied round the head, are used for celebrating a victory in court, or at any joyous celebration. Hence: Everything has a use).

### 4740. Ɛnwerɛ ani sa ntomago.
*The thorn of the thorny shrub (Acacia pennata) is always against an old cloth.*
(A weak person is always victimized).

### 4741. Ɛnwerɛ suane deɛ ɛyɛ hare.
*The thorny shrub (Acacia pennata) tears a place that is thin.*
(A bully bullies the weak).

### 4742. Ɛnwerɛ nyɛ nnam a, nyɛ onipa honam.
*If the thorn of the thorny shrub (Acacia pennata) is not sharp, this does not apply to the human body.*
(i.e. it can still hurt a person. Hence: No matter how weak a powerful thing is, there is something it can damage).

### 4743. Nwerɛwerɛboa di adeɛ hyɛ akura.
*If the cockroach nibbles something, the mouse is blamed.*
(Two household pests. Hence: One rascal is often blamed for the deeds of another).

### 4744. Nwerɛwerɛboa na ɔte anadwoboa kasa.
*The cockroach understands the language of the gecko.*
(Both creatures are found in similar places and come out at night. Hence: People with similar habits understand each other).

### 4745. Nwi nyɛ na a, anka akyekyedeɛ wɔ bi.
*If hair was not difficult to grow then the tortoise would have some.*
(You cannot have what you want just by wishful thinking).

### 4746. Nwoma hunu nkɔ Aburokyire.
*Academic education (lit.: knowing how to use books) alone does not go overseas.*
(See Proverb 597. You need money and backing to make use of your qualifications).

### 4747. Nwoma suane deɛ ɛyɛ hare.
*The skin splits where it is softest.*
(Every thing or society has its vulnerable point).

### 4748. Wonwono a, na yɛbua soɔ.
*If you mould (a pot), we cover it for you.*
(If you provoke someone, they react).

### 4749. Yɛnya a, yɛnwia.
*If we have, we don't need to steal.*

### 4750. Wonya baabi gyinaa a, wohuro prammire.
*When you have somewhere (safe) to stand, you hoot at the black cobra.*
(You don't criticize a powerful man in his presence).

### 4751. Wonya baabi gyina a, na wose ɔnanka yi so.
*When you are out of its way you say the adder is gross.*
(See above).

### 4752. Wonya bi a, wopere ntosoɔ.
*If you get some, you ask for more to be added.*
(Once you have something, you become more demanding).

### 4753. Wonya deɛ ɔnni hɔ na wɔreyɛ no a, susu ka bi na wobirekyi a, saa ara na wɔde bɛyɛ woɔ.
*If someone is not there and people are abusing them, minimize your involvement in it, because when you are away, they will do the same to you.*
(Don't join in malicious gossip or you yourself will suffer from it).

### 4754. Wonya adeɛ a, di bi.
*If you amass wealth, enjoy a bit yourself.*

4755. Yɛnya adeɛ a, na bi yera.
*If we become wealthy, then a little goes astray.*
(Rich people can afford to be careless).

4756. Yɛnya adeɛ a, na yɛde bi kyɛ.
*If we become wealthy then we give some away.*
(Rich people can afford to be generous).

4757. Wonya ngo a, wodi ɛtɔ.
*If you have oil, then you eat mashed yam.*
(A delicacy. Hence: If you get a good position in life, you show off).

4758. Yɛnya kɔ a, na yɛnya ba.
*If we have been able to go, then we are able to come.*
(If there is free passage, we make use of it).

4759. Wobɛnya nko ara na yɛbɛgye wo a, anka ohia nyɛ ya.
*If you are able to pay and we ask you to, then poverty is not hard.*
(Life would be simple if we could easily fulfill all our obligations).

4760. Wonya kokoɔ so gyina a, na wose ɔdɛnkyɛm sɛ n'ano pɔ.
*If you are safe on the bank, then you tell the crocodile that it has a lump on its snout.*
(Don't make rude remarks about someone powerful unless you are sure you are out of their reach).

4761. Yɛnya nkwa, na yɛnya akwahosan.
*If we live a long life, then we are free from accidents.*
(If you are predestined to thrive, then you will thrive).

4762. Wonya no nhunuiɛ a, na wonya no nkaeɛ.
*If you are experienced in something, then you know how to talk about it.*
(The expert can explain his experiences).

4763. Wonya no kwa a, ɛkɔ kwa.
*What comes freely goes freely.*
(Easy come easy go).

4764. "Manya asɔ mu yi, sɛ wode abaa-o! dadeɛ-o!, merennyae mu da", yɛ nsensensɛm.
*"Once I have held it, if you use a stick or an iron rod, I'll never let go," is insubordination.*
(Said by someone determined by all means to hang on to an idea or a thing).

4765. Wonya wupa wu a, na wose: "Mmomfa me nto me ni yam".
*If you succeed in dying a normal death, you say: "Put me into my mother's womb".*
(If things are going your way, you make maximum advantage of it).

4766. Wonya ɔyɔnko pa a, worenhwehwɛ foforɔ.
*If you have gained a good companion, you don't look around for a new one.*
(If you are satisfied with something, don't change it for something new).

4767. Woannya adaagye amfa pono anto wo dan ano da koro a, wode mfeɛ mmiɛnsa hwehwɛ w'agyapadeɛ.
*If you don't ever find time to make a door for your doorway, it will take you three years to find your property.*
(A stitch in time saves nine).

4768. Woannya adaagye anyare a, wonya adaagye wu.
*If you don't have time to attend to your illness, then you have time to die.*
(Look after your health as a first priority or it may be too late).

4769. Woannya egya a, na wowe Aburowdɛbo amono.
*If you have no fire, then you eat the dry corn raw.*
(In times of need you are forced to do hard things).

4770. Woannya ɔhene anni a, na wose: "Mesɛ ɔbrafoɔ".
*If you do not achieve becoming a chief, then you say: "I am fit to be an executioner".*
(If you cannot get the best, you take the second best).

4771. Yɛnnya akyekyedeɛ a, yɛnte ne so homa.
*If we have not caught the tortoise we don't tie a rope on it.*
(Don't put the cart before the horse).

4772. Wonnya sɛ woretwa abɛ na asan abere aka ho.
*There is nothing more enjoyable than if you are going to tap a palm tree and you get palm fruit from it.*
(A bonus is always appreciated).

4773. Woannya suban pa wɔ fie a, wonya no fituo mu.
*If you don't acquire a good character in the home, then you have it in the deserted house.*
(If you don't take advice and behave properly, you end up in solitude).

4774. Annya antɔ a, annya antua.
*If a thing is not bought, it is not paid for.*
(Call it quits).

4775. Nyama na ɛdi ayɛyie na nyɛ kyɛma.
*Sharing entails thankfulness but not giving to strangers.*
(You should be generous with your intimates but not expect a return if you give to outsiders).

4776. Onyame a ɔbɔɔ me anyɛ me bɔne sɛ ɔtan a ɔwoo me a ɔde fɛreɛ hyɛɛ me mu sɛ menkɔ ahua mmra ma yɛnni.
*God who created me did not make me bad like my mother who bore me and who kept me in disgrace so that I should go and collect food from other people so that we could eat.*
(No one is born a beggar, circumstances make them so).

4777. Onyame mmuaa wo fɔ a, nka sɛ wo werɛ aho.
*If God has not passed judgment against you, don't say you are sorrowful.*
(Where there is life, there is hope).

4778. Onyame fa ne boɔ a, ɔnto no ntɛm.
*If God takes his stone, he does not throw it quickly.*
(The wheels of God grind slowly, but they grind exceedingly small).

4779. Onyame hwɛ nantwinini kɔte so na ɔbɔ nantwibereɛ twɛ.
*The creator considers a bull's penis before creating a cow's vagina.*
(God creates everything in an orderly manner).

4780. Onyame nkum wo a, ɔteasefoɔ brɛ kwa.
*If God is not going to kill you, a human being toils for nothing.*
(God alone decides your fate).

**4781. Onyame ma wo kabɔne a, wotua.**
*If God gives you a bad debt, you pay.*
(You cannot avoid God's judgment).

**4782. Onyame bɛma woamee a, ɛnnim sɛ woatua kɔntɔmoa kɛseɛ.**
*If God is going to satisfy you, it does not matter if you take a big portion of fufu.*
(Be content with what you have).

**4783. Nyame ma wo ɛsono kotokuo a, ɔmma wo deɛ wode bɛhyɛ mu.**
*If God gives you a bag made of elephant hide, He gives you something to fill it with.*
(There is no limit to God's generosity. He can fulfill all your needs).

**4784. Onyame ma wo yareɛ a, ɔma wo ano aduro.**
*If God gives you an illness, he also gives you medicine.*
(God provides for all contingencies).

**4785. Onyame amma wo ba a, mma no nyɛ wo ya, na ɛbua na ne papa mu a.**
*If God does not give you a child, don't be unhappy, for perhaps there is an especially good reason.*
(God knows best).

**4786. Onyame na ɔwɔ basin fufuo ma no.**
*It is God who pounds fufu for the armless one.*
(God helps the helpless).

**4787. Onyame ani wɔ ne mma pa so.**
*God keeps his eye on his true children.*

**4788. Onyame pɛ sɛ Asanteman yɛ yie, ɛnti na ɔmaa Nana Ɔsee Tutu ne Kɔmfo Anɔkye hyiaeɛ.**
*God wishes the Asantes well, therefore he sent Chief Osei Tutu to come together with Priest Anɔkye.*
(Kɔmfo Anɔkye was the famous Asante priest who brought down the Golden Stool, whose first occupant was Asantehene Osei Tutu. Hence: If God wishes us to do well, he gives us the means of doing it).

**4789. Onyame ampɔ wo se amma wo a, wopɔ wo se a, ɛmfi.**
*If God did not clean your teeth properly for you and you want to do it yourself, it is not successful.*
(People's teeth are naturally different colors. Hence: Without God's help you cannot succeed).

**4790. Onyame sɛbɛ da wo kɔn mu a, w'animuonyam mpepa da.**
*If you have God's talisman round your neck, you never lose your honor.*
(Some people have an innate protection from God).

**4791. Onyame soma wo a, ɔma wo fa monkyimɔnka kwan so.**
*If God sends you on an errand, he makes you walk on a difficult (lit.: smelly and dirty) road.*
(It is hard to do God's will).

**4792. Onyame ntɔn n'adeɛ mfa mmɔ apoo.**
*God does not sell his thing at an exorbitant price.*
(Unlike human beings, God does not cheat).

**4793. Onyame nwono serekye kente ma wo na woanhwɛ so yie a, ɛdane kyɛnkyɛn.**
*If God weaves a silk kente cloth to give you and you don't look after it well, it changes into an (inferior) bark cloth.*
(The silk kente cloth is the most prized of all Akan clothing. Hence: If you are given a position of trust and you don't live up to it, it is taken from you).

**4794. Nyamedua repɛ din pa nti na Anɔkye kɔ kɔm no.**
*The Nyamedua likes a good reputation and that is why (the priest) Anɔkye went to administer to it.*
(The Nyamedua is a three or four pointed stick which used to be found inside most Asante houses, holding a bowl for offerings to the gods and forming a family shrine used to bless the house and family. Hence: If you want respect you keep good company).

**4795. Nyamedua, yempae mu.**
*We do not split Nyamedua in two.*
(See Proverb 4794. You can't worship by halves).

**4796. Onyamehyɛberɛ nni adaneɛ.**
*God's destiny cannot be changed.*

**4797. Nyamesuro ne nyansa ahyɛseɛ.**
*Fear of God is the beginning of all wisdom.*

**4798. Anyamenyɔeɛ twɛdeɛ, woto no a, ɛpae.**
*A constant offender, if you hit him, you injure him.*
(If you get a chance to break your enemy's power, you make sure you do it effectively).

**4799. Nyankommiremire nka ahunumu da.**
*The sound of the approach of falling rain never hangs in the sky without its falling.*
(Every hidden action comes to light).

**4800. [Onyankompasakyie]/[Kɔkɔsakyi] kasa kyerɛ obonukyerefoɔ a, ɔte, nanso ɔte no abɛbuo mu.**
*If the vulture talks to the hyena, he hears, but he hears him in proverbs.*
(This refers to any two people who share a secret which enables them to communicate in code).

**4801. Nyankonnuro mmono pɔ mu da.**
*The parasitic plant on the tree never disappears into the forest.*
(Everybody knows their own place, even if they are dependent on others).

**4802. Nyankonsoromma: ɔman wɔ no daa. Ɔsrane deɛ ɛnnɛ-nnansa pɛ na wawu.**
*The stars: the state belongs to them for ever. As for the moon, three days from today it dies.*
(Referring to something which is dependable and warning against transitory relationships).

**4803. Nyankonsoromma: menne wɔn ka, ɔsrane na ɛfiri a, na ahia me.**
*The stars: I don't owe them, it is the appearance of the moon that impoverishes me.*
(Debts become due at the end of the month (moon-die). A warning to debtors).

**4804. Nyankonsoromma nkɔbisa opitire sɛ: "Dabɛn na ɔsrane bɛfiri?" mma opitire nse no sɛ: "Sukom de me".**
*The star went to ask the fish: "What day will the moon rise?" and caused the fish to reply to it: "I am thirsty".*
(A fuller version of the proverb continues: "Na nyɛ nsuo mu na wo da yi?" ("But isn't that water that you are lying in?"). To which the fish replies: "Sɛ wo a wofiri Nyame hɔ wonnim da a bosome bɛfiri, na me, sɛ meka sɛ sukom de me a, wontee bi da?" ("If you that come from God's place do not know the day when the moon will rise, then I, if I say that I am, thirsty, is that something that you have never heard?" – i.e. that surprises you). This second part is more an explanation than an essential part of the proverb. Hence: If someone who should know the answer does not, then it is no good asking a stranger).

**4805. Nyankonsoromma na ɔman wɔ no na nyɛ ɔsrane.**
*The stars possess the world but not the moon.*
(You rely on a consistent person, not an erratic one).

**4806. Nyankonsoromma se: wɔnne obi ka, na mmom ɔsrane na ɛfiri a, na wanya amane.**
*The stars say: they don't owe anyone a debt, however when the moon appears, they are not respected.*
(If the great man is away, the servants are in charge; but when he returns, they are disregarded).

**4807. Nyankonsoromma te Nyame so, na ɔnte ne ho so.**
*The stars depend on the sky, they are not independent.*
(Everything depends on something else).

**4808. Nyankontɔn kɔ nyaa: "Mehwɛ deɛ Onyame bɛyɛ me".**
*The rainbow passes away slowly (and says): "I am waiting for what God will do to me".*
(We all have to accept our fate).

**4809. Ɔnyankopɔn ba Kwasi Kɔtɔ ɔse: "Deɛ ɔbɛdi me nam ɔbɛnya mpre".**
*God's child, Kwasi Crab, says: "He who will eat my meat will get the pincers".*
(You may overcome someone but it will not be an easy job).

**4810. Onyankopɔn ba de ɔpatuwuo.**
*The Almighty's child dies a sudden death.*
(If God loves you, he does not let you suffer).

**4811. Onyankopɔn bɔɔ onifrani a, ɔbɔɔ deɛ ɔbɛsɔ no poma mu.**
*When the Almighty created the blind, he also created the person who would guide his stick.*
(God provides for all).

**4812. Onyankopɔn amma akyemfrakatakyi biribi mpo a, ɔmmaa no ahodaa–dane.**
*If God did not give the swallow anything else, he gave it agility.*
(Everyone has some gift, nimbleness of mind or body is such a gift).

**4813. Onyankopɔn hyɛ wo nsa koraa ma na ɔteasefoɔ ka gu a, ɔhyira wo so.**
*If God gives you a full cup and a human being spills it, he will top it up for you (lit. he blesses you more).*
(No one can interfere with God's plans).

**4814. Onyankopɔn na ɔgu ahina hunu mu nsuo.**
*It is God who fills the empty pot with water.*
(God helps the helpless).

**4815. Onyankopɔn na ɔhohoro ɔkraman twɛ.**
*It is God who cleans the bitch's vagina.*
(God helps the poor and helpless).

**4816. Onyankopɔn se: ɛne no nni nnɔboa a, di kan kɔdɔ no.**
*If the Almighty says: you should help each other in weeding, go to their farm first.*
(The little you do for a worthy man will be repaid a hundred fold).

**4817. Nyansa bebrebe ma ɔman bɔ.**
*Too much wisdom spoils the state.*
(If you are too clever, you fail).

**4818. Nyansa dodoɔ gyae aboa.**
*Too much wisdom lets the animal go.*
(If you are too clever, you may defeat your own purpose).

**4819. Anyansafoɔ baanu goro a, ntoto ba.**
*If two wise people play together, discord arises.*
(Two opinionated people can never agree).

**4820. Anyansafoɔ baanu hyia a, na yɛhunu onitefoɔ.**
*If two wise people meet, then we can see which is the wiser.*
(We judge by comparison).

**4821. Anyansafoɔ baanu kyɛ nwa mmiɛnsa a, asisie ba.**
*If two wise people share three snails, there is bound to be cheating.*
(Even wise people can't solve some problems).

**4822. Anyansafoɔ baanu twa abɛ a, ɛwu ntɛm.**
*If two clever men tap a palm tree, it dies quickly.*
(It is difficult for two people of equal authority to work together. Or: Too many cooks spoil the broth).

**4823. Anyansafoɔ nko ara kyekyere kuro a, ɛgu.**
*If only wise people build up the town, it spoils.*
(It takes all kinds to make a world. A community needs variety to succeed).

**4824. Onyansafoɔ, yɛmmɔ no pɔ.**
*A wise man, we do not tie him a knot.*
(You do not try and trick a wise man).

**4825. Onyansafoɔ de kwasea ti na esua ayie.**
*A wise man uses a fool's head to study barbering.*
(You take advantage of stupid people to get on in life).

**4826. Onyansafoɔ kasa tiawa.**
*A wise man speaks shortly.*
(Verbosity obscures the truth).

**4827. Onyansafoɔ nko na ɔdwendwenfoɔ nko.**
*A wise man is one thing and a thinker another.*

**4828. Onyansafoɔ kuta damma a, ɔtumi de gye kwasea nsam piredwan.**
*A wise man who has a small amount can take a large amount from a fool.*

# Proverbs of the Akans

217

(Damma is a small weight; piredwan a large one. Hence: Wisdom can do with a little what a fool can't do with a lot).

4829. Onyansafoɔ na ɔkɔm.
*It is a wise man who foresees the future.*
(Vision is one of the qualities of wisdom).

4830. Onyansafoɔ na ɔtumi bɔ dua pɔ.
*It is a wise man who can tie a tree in a knot.*
(As Ɔkɔmfo Anɔkye did. Only a very clever man can bring off the apparently impossible).

4831. Onyansafoɔ na ɔtwa akwammeɛ.
*It is a wise man who cuts the roots across the path (or: gets around an obstacle).*
(A clever person knows how to avoid trouble).

4832. Onyansafoɔ na ɔwɛn ɔhene yere panin.
*It is a wise man who keeps watch on the chief's senior wife.*
(A wise person takes care of and respects the key person in a household or situation).

4833. Onyansafoɔ na ɔyi ne ho ayiduane.
*A wise man isolates himself.*
(If you are wise, you keep your distance from people).

4834. Onyansafoɔ ne deɛ ɔwɔ aboterɛ ne ɛntoboaseɛ.
*A wise man is the one who is good-tempered and slow to anger.*
(Patience is a virtue).

4835. Onyansafoɔ na asɛm to ne fie a, ɔbɔ no pɔ.
*When there is trouble in a wise man's house, he ties it into a knot.*
(Wisdom is needed to solve a difficult problem).

4836. Nyansapɔ, kwasea ntumi nsane gye sɛ nyansafoɔ.
*The knot of wisdom, a fool cannot untie it, it takes a wise man.*
(Only a wise man can solve a difficult problem).

4837. Nnyansin ne panin nanso mmabaa na ɛma ogya dɛre.
*The log is senior but the kindling makes the fire burn.*
(Young people bring energy to a situation, although the old may have influence and power).

4838. Anyansini kɔte na ɛkɔ anyansini twɛ mu.
*The penis of a person who is too familiar goes into a too receptive vagina.*
(If you behave loosely, you make an opportunity for loose living).

4839. Nyanyamforowa na ɔdii kwaeɛm kan, nso wanya adukuro.
*The Nyanyamforowa tree (Mallotus oppositifolius) first settled in the forest, but it did not have a buttress root.*
(Mallotus oppositifolius, also called satadua, is a highly medicinal shrub whose leaves and other parts are used to cure dysentery, for poultices, etc. Hence: Seniority does not necessarily mean superiority).

4840. Nyanyankyerɛ Nyameba Kofi Kɔtɔ, ɔde ne to na ɛka na ɔmfa n'ano.

*The scorpion Kofi son of God, he takes his tail to bite but he does not take his mouth.*
(The enemy may not fight you openly but by other means. Don't expect your enemy to do the obvious).

4841. Nnyegyesoɔ na ɛma ɔbosom yɛ nnam.
*Adulation makes a fetish powerful.*
(Everything responds to praise and encouragement).

4842. Anyemforɔ fata kwakuo.
*Early pregnancy suits the monkey.*
(Everyone has some period of beauty).

843. Onyina de ne nkasɛɛ firi tete.
*The silk-cotton tree (Bombax buonopozense) and its thorns are very ancient.*
(Said of a custom which has been kept ever since man can remember).

4844. Onyina kuntann kwa, satadua na ɔdii kwae ase kan.
*The silk-cotton (Bombax buonopozense) tree is huge for nothing, the satadua (Mallotus oppositifolius) grew in the forest first.*
(See Proverb 4839. Seniority is more important than mere bulk).

4845. Onyina na ɔma asansa di bamee.
*It is the silk-cotton (Bombax buonopozense) tree which enables the hawk to behave with insolence.*
(The tree is very large and protects the hawk from molestation. Hence: The followers of an important man can act insolently).

4846. Onyina se ɔrekɔso nkuruma, afei ɔkɔpaeɛ a atentirehuo.
*The silk-cotton (Bombax buonopozense) tree said it was going to produce okro but when the fruit matured, it produced kapok.*
(Wishful thinking does not get you anywhere).

4847. Onyina se, sɛ ne so nni mfasoɔ a, na ɛnyɛ ne porɔ mu a.
*The silk-cotton (Bombax buonopozense) says that if he is of no use it is not so when he gets rotten.*
(Some people are of more use after death than when alive. Birds make their nests in holes in the rotten tree and insects thrive in it).

4848. [Onyina]/[ɔdupɔn] tutu a, bonkon na efiri ananmu.
*If the [silk-cotton (Bombax buonopozense)]/[great tree] is uprooted then the bonkon (fleurya aestuans) grows in its place.*
(Fleurya aestuans is a tall hairy herb. Hence: A lesser man takes over from a great one).

4849. Onyina-ase prammire na ɔmma ɔbɔfoɔ Yaw kum ɔnwam a, ɔdane gya kɔdi mmire nkwan.
*The cobra under the onyina tree prevents the hunter Yaw from killing the hornbill, so that he goes to eat mushroom soup.*
(If you are prevented from getting what you deserve, you have to make do with what you can get).

4850. Anyinaboaa, ogya bɛhi ato no.
*The wood beetle, once the wood is fired, will be consumed when the time comes.*
(Your time will come to face the fire).

**4851. "Onyini a ɔbɛgyae", na ɛmaa nkuraasefoɔ mma hyɛɛ wɔn ho bɔne**
*"When he grows up he will stop it", led the children of uncivilized people to become spoilt.*
("Nkuraasefoɔ" literally means country people or farmers, but it is also used disparagingly (rather like the English word "peasant") to mean an uncivilized person. Hence: If you are too lenient with people, they will grow up bad).

**4852. Worenyini a, na wonhunu, na woyɛ bɔne deɛ a wohunu.**
*When you are growing old, you don't notice it, but when you do bad things, you do notice it.*
(You cannot plead ignorance of intentional offense).

**4853. Worenyini no na wo mmusuo renyini.**
*As you are growing your bad luck is growing too.*
(As you get older your potentialities for good or bad develop too).

**4854. Yɛnnyinniiɛ a, yɛnsere akwatia.**
*If we are not full-grown, we don't laugh at a short man.*
(Don't ridicule someone you may yourself resemble).

**4855. Nyinsɛn nyɛ bayerɛ na abɔ akɔ fam.**
*Becoming pregnant is not a yam that can grow in the land.*
(There are some things that cannot be hidden).

**4856. Nyintoɔ yɛ ya.**
*Growing up is painful.*
(As children grow older, they compete with their parents and think they know better than them. This leads to strain in the family. It is this difficult relationship that the proverb illustrates).

- P -

**4857. Apa bɛkum aboa a, ɛfiri nyansa.**
*If a trap kills the animal, it is because of wisdom.*
(It needs planning to be successful).

**4858. Ɔpaani hwe ase a, okonkoni abɔ fam.**
*If a hired laborer falls down, then the rich man has fallen.*
(A man's prosperity depends on his workers).

**4859. Ɔpaani, yɛnsisi no sika-sese mu.**
*A hired laborer, we do not cheat him when changing his money.*
(A person who is always dealing in something cannot be cheated over it).

**4860. Mpaboa ansene wo a, ɛsene wo yɔnko.**
*If a sandal is not too big for you, it is too big for your companion.*
(One thing suits one person, another another).

**4861. Wopae dua na sɛ wontumi mpae a, wode nnaameɛ na ɛpaeɛ.**
*If you try and split wood and you can't, then you take a wedge to split it.*
(If you can't do a thing alone, get help).

**4862. Yɛpae afaseɛ a, Praa ada.**
*If we split up the water yam, then the Bosompra ntorɔ group doesn't worry (lit. has slept).*
(The water yam is taboo to this group. Hence: If something does not concern you, you don't worry about it).

**4863. Wopae nnuadowa mu di a, na womene memiremfi.**
*If you break into the garden egg to eat it then you chew the maggot.*
(Garden eggs are normally mashed up and used in that form; as a result, insects can be removed before it is eaten. Hence: If you go contrary to custom you experience what you are not expected to).

**4864. "Pae-mu-ka" yɛ ahomeka na fɛreɛ na ɛwɔ mu.**
*"Frankly speaking" is good but there is shame in it.*
(Speak the truth, even though it hurts).

**4865. "Pae-mu-se" yɛ fɛre, nso ɛyɛ ahodwoɔ.**
*We are ashamed to point out what we don't like, but it brings peace.*
(If you avoid telling people that you do not approve of what they are doing you can never improve the situation. It is better to tell them tactfully and so achieve peace).

**4866. Apafram nantwie se: "Mehwɛ Nyame".**
*The festival cow says: "I look up to God".*
(The cow is sacrificed. Hence: Only God can save the condemned).

**4867. Apagyapagya nti na owifoɔ ammɔ adere.**
*Collecting other peoples' things is why the thief did not forge a cutlass.*
(A lazy man depends on the work of others and does not bother to make his own way).

**4868. Apakyie akyire nkuronwi kwa; dodoɔ kyiri baako.**
*The back of the gourd has small hairs for nothing; many people hate one person.*

(In theory people like a stranger, but when an individual stranger appears, they mistrust him).

**4869. Apakyie akyi nkyerɛkyerɛwa se: "Dodoɔ kyiri baako".**
*The engravings on the back of the gourd say: "Many people hate one person".*
(An individual stranger is mistrusted by the crowd).

**4870. Apakyie mpaeɛ a, wompam.**
*If the gourd does not crack, you don't mend it.*
(A problem has to arise before you can look for a remedy).

**4871. Wopam aboa no na woannya no a, wose ne ho bɔn.**
*If you are unable to catch an animal in the chase, you say its body smells.*
(Sour grapes).

**4872. Apam foforɔ yɛpam firi dada ano.**
*The new clearing of wood, we begin from the end where we have collected before.*
("Apam afuo" is to complete the clearing of the ground, after the trees have been burned, by piling up the burned wood that remains. This is part of preparing land for farming in the forest. Hence: Work proceeds from where it has been left off).

**4873. Yɛpamo [kutukwaaku]/[pataku] ansa na yɛatu abirekyie fo.**
*We drive away the hyena before we give advice to the goats.*
(Get someone out of trouble before you try to give them advice).

**4874. Worepamo akokɔ (odwan) bɔne na akokɔ pa (odwan) di akyire.**
*If you drive away a bad fowl (sheep) the good follows after.*
(Be careful how you treat the bad member of a family or you may alienate the good).

**4875. Wopamo akyenkyena na woanto no a, na ɛfiri ne hɔ sereɛ.**
*If you chase the allied hornbill and you don't catch it, then it is because it is laughable.*
(It is difficult to punish an amusing person).

**4876. "Pamo no oo!" "Tware no oo!" ne nyinaa ne "Makye no!"**
*"Chase it!" (or) "Surround it" all amount to "I have caught it".*
(There many ways of achieving the same ends).

**4877. Ɔpampam nyɛ dua bi, nso yɛde no di asikadwini.**
*Albissia sassa is not much of a tree but we take it to do gold-smithing.*
(The wood is made into charcoal and used by goldsmiths in their work. Hence: Even a humble person can be very useful).

**4878. Ɔpampanya: wonyɛ ogya bi, na yɛde wo anane sika na yɛagyae de wo ayɛ biribiara.**
*Charcoal from the tree Albissia sassa: you are not such important fire wood that, although we take you to melt gold, we can use you for all other jobs.*
(Don't be above yourself. You may be good at one thing but not at everything).

4879. Apan mmɔ [Nyame]/[ɔsoro] soboɔ na ɔmmɔ Asaase nso soboɔ.
*The bat does not blame [God]/[the sky] and at the same time Mother Earth.*
(Don't offend all the gods at once!)

4880. Apan Kwaku, asɛm nyɛ wo ahomete, woda nkwan mu na woresere!
*Kwaku the bat, nothing worries you, while you lie in the soup, you still smile.*
(Said of someone who is foolishly cheerful).

4881. Apan sensɛne hɔ a ɔse: "Asaase frɛ me a, mɛte; na ɔsoro nso frɛ me a mɛte".
*The bat, hanging there, says: "If Earth calls me; I will hear; if the heavens call me I will also here".*
(Said of someone who follows two masters impartially).

4882. Pannɛɛ nim ntoma pam nso ne to tokuro.
*The needle knows how to sew a cloth but it can't sew its own hole.*
(Physician heal thyself).

4883. Pannɛɛ to ate nso ɔtɛ nkorɔfoɔ to.
*The needle's end has a hole in it, but it sews up other people's holes.*
(You may work for other people and still be unable to deal with your own problems).

4884. Ɔpanimmɔne na ɔhyɛ nsempowa-mmiɛnsa pieto.
*A bad elder wears cheap pants.*
(An unsuccessful person cannot afford the best).

4885. Ɔpanimmɔne na ɔtu fobɔne.
*A bad elder gives bad advice.*

4886. Mpanimfoɔ yɛ wo "dwane dwane" na wodwane a, akyire yi, wɔde sere wo.
*When the elders say to you "run off, run off" and you run off, afterwards they laugh at you.*
(You may do what you are told but be despised for it).

4887. Ɔpanin a, wammɔ ne bra yie na ɔbɔ borɔdedwo bosea.
*An elder who did not make a good living, borrows toasted plantain.*
(If you don't succeed in life you have to accept charity).

4888. Ɔpanin a wammɔ ne bra yie na ɔne nkɔdaa to nsa didie.
*If an elder did not acquire succed in life, then he eats from the same bowl as the children.*
(If you have achieved nothing, you are not respected).

4889. Ɔpanin a wanyini, ne dee wakɔ Serɛm aba, ne deɛ wakɔ Aburokyire aba, wɔn ne atorofoɔ a wɔwɔ ɔman mu.
*The elder who has grown old, he who has gone to the North and returned, and he who has gone overseas and returned, they are the liars in their own nation.*
(See Proverb 597. When there are no witnesses available, people are tempted to lie).

4890. Ɔpanin a watena fie ama nkɔdaa awe nanka no, sɛ yɛrekan a nanka anankawefoɔ ɔka ho bi.
*An elderly man who stays in the house and lets the children eat adders, if we are counting the adder-eaters, he must be counted also.*

(If an elder condones an act, he must be judged to be involved in it himself).

4891. Ɔpanin, yɛmmɔ no tonsuom.
*An elder, we don't create him in the blacksmith's shop.*
(Your acts determine your position in society and you do not suddenly become what you are).

4892. Ɔpanin ada no na ne nan gu adihɔ.
*When an elder sleeps, his legs are outside.*
(The head of the family is responsible for the actions of all its members.
If there is a troublesome member of the family then the whole family suffers from it. Hence: Being of good behavior yourself is not sufficient, you have to control those you are responsible for as well).

4893. Ɔpanin didi adidibɔne a, ɔyi n'ayowa hɔ.
*If an elderly man eats and eats greedily, he clears his own dish.*
(A warning against greed. It is customary for senior people to leave some pieces on the dish for the children of the house to share. If this is not done, then the children are reluctant to wash the dish).

4894. Ɔpanin didi nsɛm bebree akyi a, ɔman bɔ.
*If an elder involves himself in too many cases, the state is ruined.*
(Too much litigation spoils a community).

4895. Ɔpanin didi n'aso tokurom.
*An elder makes a living through the holes in his ears.*
(An elder profits from listening and giving advice).

4896. Ɔpanin-didifoɔ na ɔkuta ɛta.
*It is the greedy elder who handles the spoon.*
(If you ingratiate yourself too much it indicates self-interest).

4897. Ɔpanin due "Mante, mante".
*The elder wards of misfortune by saying: "I did not hear, I did not hear".*
(An elder considers what he knows or has heard directly, not mere gossip).

4898. Ɔpanin adwen na yɛde bu fie.
*An elder's thoughtfulness is used for running a home.*
(An elder brings stability).

4899. Ɔpanin fɛre ne ba na ɔnsuro no.
*An elder respects his child but does not fear him.*
(A senior man is not afraid to tell anyone junior to him the truth as he sees it).

4900. Ɔpanin fɛre ne mma a, na ne mma suro no.
*When an elder respects his children, then they fear him.*
(You respect those who treat you fairly).

4901. Ɔpanin gye abɔfra nsam akonnwa tena so, na nyɛ asaase a ɔte soɔ.
*Though an elder may take a stool a child is sitting on, he cannot take the ground it is sitting on.*
(You can take away a man's privilege but not his right to exist).

4902. Ɔpanin anhunu akonnwa so tena a, yɛtwe firi ne to.
*An elder who does not know how to sit on a stool has it taken from under him.*
(If you don't use authority properly, you lose it).

4903. Ɔpanin anhunu ta a, ɔwu.
*If an elder does not know how to fart, he dies.*
(Old people are full of wind and must get rid of it. You must sometimes do anti-social acts to survive. In Akan society it is very rude to fart in public).

4904. Ɔpanin hwere agyapadeɛ wɔ mansotwe mu.
*An elder squanders his heritage through litigation.*
(If you indulge in unprofitable activities you ruin your family).

4905. Ɔpanin ka na anyɛ yie a, yɛfrɛ no nkɔdaasɛm.
*If an elder says something and does not succeed, we say what he did was childish.*
(Failure is regarded as a lack of wisdom).

4906. Ɔpanin Kwame Nsia na ɔkaa n'asɛm sɛ: obi firi ahemfie bɛhem wɔ aboaboano a, na yɛmmɔɔ no sotorɔ a na wadi nkwandɛ.
*The elder Kwame Nsia said: if someone comes from the palace to blow his nose outside, if he has not been slapped, he has been eating good soup.*
(There are only two alternatives to explain a situation: either good or evil).

4907. Ɔpanin kye a, ɛdwo.
*When an elder fries something, it cools down.*
(A wise man knows how to settle disputes).

4908. Ɔpanin mee nsono.
*An elder can satisfy his hunger with his intestines.*
(An elder has his experience to live by and knows how to cope with difficult situations).

4909. Ɔpanin na obi nyɛɛ bi da a, na ɛnyɛ akɔdaa.
*Even if all people have not become elders, everyone has been a child.*
(There are some experiences that everyone shares).

4910. Ɔpanin ne mmɔfra hunu nante a, wɔsoa ne bɔtɔ.
*When the elder and the children know how to walk together, they carry his bag.*
(If an elderly person understands the young, then they will do anything to help him).

4911. Ɔpanin anim asɛm yɛ kana.
*It is not easy to speak face to face with an elder.*
(It is difficult to deceive someone with experience).

4912. Ɔpanin anim a atwetwe amantam no, ne nyinaa firi "Mereka akyerɛ wo, mereka akyerɛ wo".
*The fact that an old man's face is wrinkled is all because of: "I am going to tell you, I am going to tell you".*
(Constant listening to complaints ages a man).

4913. Ɔpanin nnim biribi a, ɔwɔ afotusɛm.
*If an elder has nothing else, he has admonition.*
(An elder is indispensable in society and if he can do nothing concrete he can at least warn people).

4914. Ɔpanin ano yɛ bosom.
*The mouth of the elder is the spirit of the shrine.*
(If you do not give heed to the elders, they can curse you or you will get into trouble with the spirits).

4915. Ɔpanin ano sene suman.
*The mouth of an elder is more potent than a charm.*
(Power and persuasion lie with the elders).

4916. Ɔpanin nyini, ɔdane ne mma.
*If an elder has grown old, he seeks the protection of his children.*
(Even a wise man must depend in his old age on younger people).

4917. Ɔpanin pa yɛ na.
*A good elder is rare.*

4918. Ɔpanin se na wanyɛ a, mmɔfra nsuro no.
*When an elder promises, but does not carry out his promise, the children do not respect him.*
(People respect consistency and the keeping of promises).

4919. Ɔpanin nsoma akɔdaa afidihwɛ mma anomaa nka no.
*An elder does not send a child to look at his trap and thus allow the bird to talk to him.*
(It used to be believed that animals could talk and such talk was taboo, as it meant bad luck. Sending a child into the bush to look at a trap would expose it to this risk. Hence: You don't entrust a task to someone and allow them to get into trouble).

4920. Ɔpanin su a, ɔsu ne tirim.
*If an elder cries, he cries in his head.*
(A senior man does not give way to grief in public).

4921. Ɔpanin ntena fie mma asefia mfɔ.
*The elder does not stay at home and allow the hearth to get wet.*
(A wise man foresees trouble and prevents it. An elder by his very nature acts responsibly).

4922. Ɔpanin tiri ho na yɛhɔn akuma.
*It is on the elder's head that we knock off the axe head.*
(It is the elders who are able to solve tricky problems).

4923. Ɔpanin to asa a, na ɛwɔ nkɔdaa deɛ mu.
*When an elder's bottom is flat, its fatness has gone to the children.*
(It is the older members of the community who care for the young. If they do not prosper later in life it is because of their children).

4924. Ɔpanin nto boɔ nhyɛ nto abɔfra nsam.
*An elder does not heat a stone and place it in the hand of a child.*
(A man in authority is not expected to harm those serving him).

4925. Ɔpanin ntie abansosɛm.
*An elder does not listen to gossip over the fence.*
(A senior man does not waste time on idle gossip).

4926. Ɔpanin nni biribi a, ɔwɔ abatwɔ.
*If an elder has nothing else, he has his elbow (to defend himself).*
(Everyone has some means of protecting themselves).

4927. Ɔpanin nni ntiamoa twɛdeɛ.
*An elder does not survive death's blow.*
(Death conquers all).

4928. Ɔpanin wu a, na ofie abɔ.
*If an elder dies, then his house is spoiled.*
(When the head of a household is not there, there is no one left to manage affairs).

4929. Ɔpanin yam adwansaeɛ aduasa. Asɛm a ɛyɛ ya to no a, ɔde bi hyira n'ano.
*An elder's stomach contains thirty sheep. When something that is painful meets him, he kills one to bless his mouth.*
(An old man has plenty of patience and when troubled by the family his experience keeps him calm).

4930. Ɔpantene nim dadeɛ bɔ a, anka ɔwɔ afuo.
*If the python knew how to forge iron, then he would have a farm.*
(If wishes were horses, beggars would ride).

4931. Apantweaa se ɔbɛsom afanu a, momma ɔnsom; na animguaseɛ ba a, na ɔbɛhunu.
*If the bat says it will serve two masters, let it do so; if disgrace comes, then it will know its position.*
(If someone thinks they can be on both sides in a quarrel, let them try and see the bad results).

4932. Papa akatua ne bɔne.
*The reward of goodness is evil.*
(In this life goodness does not always pay).

4933. Papa ne bɔne nyinaa mu wɔ adiadefoɔ.
*Both good and bad have heirs.*
(The good and evil that people do lives after them).

4934. Papa asusu de rekɔ no, na bɔne di akyire rekɔgye.
*While goodness is thinking where he will go, evil is following him to frustrate his efforts.*
(The bad man is always seeking to destroy the good man and his works).

4935. Ɔpapahwekwa tafere adeɛ bafua ho a, na wamee.
*If an unimportant (poor) man licks one thing, he becomes satisfied.*
(It doesn't take much to satisfy those who have little).

4936. Papayɛ dodoɔ yɛ mmusuo.
*Too much benevolence brings suffering (to the generous).*

4937. Papayɛ nkɔ akyiri.
*Well-doing does not spread.*
(Bad news spreads more widely than good news).

4938. Papayɛ ma onipa di aduane a wantɔ.
*Kindness allows a person to eat food he did not buy.*
(Virtue brings its rewards).

4939. Papayɛ wɔ akatua.
*Virtue brings its rewards.*

4940. Papayɛ nyɛ mfone.
*Virtue is not tedious.*

4941. Ɔpasopaso a ɔpa nwoma soɔ, ɛnyɛ no anumuɔdɛ, na ne yieyɛ na ɔpɛ.
*One who flays does not do it because of eating meat but because of doing it well.*
(You may work not because you want to profit from it but because the work needs doing).

4942. Wo mpasua si atɛkyɛ mu a, ɛhɔ ara na wofa.
*If your line of battle is stationed in a marsh, it is there that you pass.*
(You can't change things by wishful thinking).

4943. Wo pata bu a, agyinamoa dwane gya wo.
*If your roof breaks down, the cat runs off and leaves you.*
(If you are rich, people depend on you; if you become poor, they desert you for someone else).

4944. Wo pata adaban mmienu hyɛ gya mu a, baako hye.
*If you put two bars of iron in the fire, one gets burnt.*
(If you try to do two things at a time, one is never done well).

4945. Yɛmpata karawa mpata asibe, na ɔkwakuo nkɔtɔ egya mu.
*You don't please the mangabey and please the colobus, and show indifference when a monkey falls into the fire.*
(Karawa, asibi and kwakuo are kinds of monkey. Hence: Treat like people alike).

4946. Wopata nkokɔtɔkwa a, ohia mpa wo so da.
*If you stop a fight between chickens, you will never be free of poverty.*
(Don't involve yourself with quarrelsome people or you will never be free of trouble).

4947. Yɛmpata ntɔkwa abofuoso.
*We do not settle a quarrel by using bad temper.*

4948. Mpata kɔ a, ansa na abodwoɔ aba.
*If pacification leads, then tranquility follows.*
(Once a matter is settled there is peace and quiet).

4949. Apata-ase mpo wɔ ne hene.
*Even in the (produce storage) shed there is a chief.*
(There is a leader to every group).

4950. Patafoɔ di abaa.
*The peace-maker receives the stick.*
(If you want to be a peace-maker, you suffer).

4951. Ɔpatako nnye ɔko mmɔ ne bo.
*A mediator does not take the war to himself.*
(A mediator must not take sides).

4952. Pataku didi srɛso.
*The hyena feeds in the savannah.*
(Every man to his own place).

4953. Pataku ankɔbɔ nsaa mpo na ɔretu funu yi na ne sempoa bɛkɔ akɔdi mu yi!
*Even when the hyena did not pay a funeral contribution it was digging up the corpse, how much more when its threepence goes into the chest.*
(Could be said of someone who makes a nuisance of himself at a funeral. If he makes a donation, he may drink and cause even more trouble).

4954. Pataku ne n'akoa: ɔte ase a, ɔyɛ no akoa ɔwu a, ɔyɛ no nam.
*The hyena and its slave: when the latter lives it is [the hyena's] slave, when it dies it is [the hyena's] meat.*
(Said when something is always useful, whatever condition it is in).

4955. Mpatapaasɛm ne aturuturasɛm na ɛnam.
*Contrariness and quarrelsomeness move together.*
(Two vices are both evil).

**4956. Apaterɛ ahasa antere nkwan mu, na kusie basa na ɛbɛyɛ dɛn?**
*If three hundred apaterɛ fish do not make the soup sweet, how could the arm of a rat?*
(If the best won't do, why suggest something of poor value?)

**4957. "Ɔpatire" ne "atipa", ne nyinaa wɔ etiri hɔ.**
*"Something which causes baldness" and "Something which brings about baldness" are all on the head.*
(Whichever way you say a thing, the result is the same).

**4966. Apatrapa nse Apɔwotireho sɛ ne tiri ho akwanam.**
*A bald man should not tell a closely shaved man that his head is too bare.*
(The pot should not call the kettle black).

**4967. Wopatu kɔ kwan a, w'anim gu ase.**
*If you go on a journey without preparation, you are put to shame.*
(Prepare well before you face the outside world).

**4968. Wopatu yare a, wopatu wu.**
*If you are suddenly ill (i.e. you pretend to be ill), you die suddenly.*
(Don't tempt providence).

**4969. Ɔpatuo de n'ani hunahuna nkɔdaa nanso ɔnkye wɔn.**
*The owl uses its large eyes to frighten children but it does not catch them.*
(Some people's bark is worse than their bite).

**4970. Apatuprɛ ba nyɛ dana.**
*A bulbul's chick does not sleep with difficulty.*
(The nest is small and so it would fall out if it "tossed and turned." Hence: In straitened circumstances, one has to be careful of one's behavior).

**4971. Apatuprɛ gyansakyi, ɔdi mako na ɛhye no a, ɔdeyɛ ne to aduro.**
*The bulbul, if it eats pepper and feels its pungency, cures itself of disease on its bottom.*
(You have to suffer to be cured).

**4972. Apatuprɛ kɔsi mako nso na ɔtete bi di na wɔbisa no sɛ: "Adɛn nti na woreyɛ soeɛ–soeɛ?" Ose: "Efirisɛ merememene amu–amu ntira".**
*If the bulbul perches on the pepper plant and pecks some to eat and you ask it: "Why are you crying thus–soe–soe?" It replies: "Because I swallowed a pepper whole".*
(A stupid question requires a stupid answer).

**4973. Apatuprɛ se: "Ɔhɔhoɔ nim a, ɔmani nim."**
*The bulbul says: "If a stranger knows, a local man knows".*
(If someone outside a community knows what is going on, those inside should certainly do so).

**4974. Apatuprɛ se: ɔtete ntonkom a, ɔtete kɔ dua.**
*The bulbul says: if it plucks the big pepper, it plucks it to plant it.*
(What looks destructive to an observer, may in fact have a constructive motive).

**4975. Apatuprɛ se: "Ɔsɛɛ Mampɔn si ntoma a ɛfi, na enkyere tete".**
*The bullbul says: "Osei from Mampong washes his cloth whenever it's dirty, but it quickly becomes tattered".*
(Moderation in all things).

**4976. Mpatuprɛ na anya wɔn ayie na seekɔɔ deɛ wɔsi mu sɛn?**
*The bulbuls have their own funeral then how does it concern the small kingfisher?*
(Mind your own business!)

**4977. Mpatuwuo yɛ ya sene yarewuo.**
*Accidental death is more painful than death from illness.*
(If something could have been avoided you regret it, the unavoidable you accept).

**4978. Mpatuwuo yeaa nti na yɛkyere akokɔ a ɔsu.**
*Because of pain of sudden death the fowl cries when you catch it.*
(People often cry not because they are hurt but because of fear).

**4979. Yɛpɛ a yɛbɛhunu nti na yɛkyekyere boa.**
*It is in order to be able to find things that we tie them up together.*
(Said of a careful person who looks after their possessions).

**4980. Wopɛ a, ɛka wo.**
*If you want something too much, it bites you (i.e you suffer for it).*
(Desire brings suffering).

**4981. Worepɛ ɔbaatan biribi adi a, ne ba ka w'apampam twene.**
*If you wish to have intercourse with some motherly woman, her child will drum on your head.*
(If you really want somethin,g you have to put up with the associated inconveniences).

**4982. Worepɛ aberawa adi no a, na woma no egyansini.**
*If you wish to have intercourse with an old woman then you give her a piece of firewood.*
(If you want to get on with someone you give them what they need most).

**4983. Worepɛ obi aduane adi a, woyɛ w'ano feafea, na wonya bi a, wabae w'anom.**
*If you want to eat someone's food, you close your lips, and if you get some, you open your mouth.*
(i.e: you wait quietly for the food, and then give thanks when you get it. Hence: Good manners are rewarded).

**4984. Merepɛ obi akra no Saben na mehunu Agyaben a, ne nyinaa dane "ben."**
*I was looking for someone to take a message to Saben (the expert) but now I see Agyaben (the master mind), they are all the same kind.*
(Two things may be equally good, there are possible satisfactory alternatives).

**4985. Worepɛ obi tiri atwa a, ɔtwa wo deɛ.**
*If you want to cut off someone's head, he will cut off yours.*
(He who lives by the sword, shall die by the sword).

**4986.** Worepɛ obi two ahwɛ a, na wode n'adwaredeɛ kɔ toa no wɔ adwareɛ.
*If you want to see somebody's hydrocele, you take the things they use for bathing to them in the bathroom.*
(See Proverb 505. If you are sufficiently curious about something, you can find a way of getting to see it).

**4987.** Wopɛ asɛm a, na wonya asɛm.
*If you want trouble, you get trouble.*
(If you trouble trouble, trouble torubles you!)

**4988.** Worepɛ danka mu ahunu a, na wogorɔgorɔ no.
*If you want to see what is in the gourd, you shake it.*
(You have to stimulate someone to see how they react).

**4989.** Worepɛ adeɛ atɔ na wonya bi a, ɛte sɛ deɛ wɔde akyɛ woɔ.
*If you want to buy something and you get it, it is as if you have been given it free of charge.*
(If you really need something and you get it, you are delighted, whether you pay for it or not).

**4990.** Worepɛ w'aduane dɛ a, na wode nkyene to mu.
*If you like your food to be sweet, then you put salt into it.*
(If you want to prosper, you must put a lot into your work).

**4991.** Wopɛ habansɛm a, wotua ka-perennu.
*If you like an agreement decided on in the bush, you pay double price.*
(If you are not prepared to negotiate openly, then you have to risk being cheated).

**4992.** Wopɛ hɔhoɔ na woanhunu no a, na ɔkɔ ne kurom.
*If you need a stranger and you don't see him then he has gone to his own town.*
(A man can best be found in his own surroundings).

**4993.** Yɛrepɛ homa akyekyere adeɛ a, monutuo nka sɛ: "Mennya mo ase".
*If we need a rope to tie something up, the liana does not say: "Goodbye".*
(A servant should not seek to avoid his duties).

**4994.** Worebɛpɛ ahurihurie na woasuro anisobirie.
*You are going to enjoy being thrown into the air, but you already fear giddiness?*
(If you fear something you don't indulge in what brings it on. Said in a questioning tone).

**4995.** Wopɛ akasakasa a, na woware yerenom bebree.
*If you like frequent quarrels then you marry many wives.*
(If you ask for trouble, you get it).

**4996.** Worepɛ akɔdaa asoma no a, wokorɔkorɔ no.
*If you want to send a child on an errand, you pet it.*
(You flatter those whose help you need).

**4997.** Worepɛ kɔkɔɔ ayɛ a, na wode wo ho twere esie.
*If you want to become a red-skinned person, you rub yourself against an anthill.*
(If you want to succeed you keep company with people who are successful in what you want to do).

**4998.** Wopɛ nkɔmmɔ pii a, wodi nkɔmmɔ-mmim.
*If you like too much conversation, you monopolize the conversation.*
(Lack of moderation is always bad).

**4999.** Worepɛ ɔkra kurom akɔ a, na wofrɛ no Agya Kra.
*If you want to go to the cat's town, then you call him Father Cat.*
(You flatter those from whom you want favors).

**5000.** Worepɛ kuro bi mu atena a, wotutu mu nnunsini, na wonhyɛ mu mpam.
*If you want to live in a certain town, you pull up the stumps of trees there, you do not plant sharp things in the ground.*
(You don't shit on your own doorstep!)

**5001.** Wopɛ nkwannɛ a, wonsuro nantwie.
*If you like good soup, you don't fear the cow.*
(If you want something badly, you must be prepared to overcome any obstacles in your way).

**5002.** Wopɛ w'akyekyedeɛ mogya-dodoɔ a, na wode nsuo fra mu.
*If you want your tortoise's blood to increase, then you add water to it.*
(If you want to aggravate a situation, you add insult to injury).

**5003.** Wopɛ amaneɛ a, wonnya abadwadeɛ.
*If you like trouble you don't get arbitration fees.*
(A trouble-maker isn't asked to arbitrate).

**5004.** Worepɛ metini adi no nya a, wofrɛ no dorɔba.
*If you wish to use a driver's mate for something, you call him "Driver."*
(You flatter those you want to help you).

**5005.** Wopɛ ɛnim bebrebe a, wodi ntwo.
*If you like too much praise, you suffer defeat.*
(If you curry favour, people will not like you).

**5006.** Wopɛ nkwa bebrebe a, woka amamfoso.
*If you like a long life, you stay in a deserted town.*
(If you want more than your fair share, you suffer alone).

**5007.** Wopɛ nkwan a, ɛyɛ dɛ bebrebe a, ɛka mpa wo so.
*If you like too much good soup, you are always in debt.*
(If you overindulge you pay for it).

**5008.** Worepɛ w'ani so adeɛ ahunu a, womia w'ani kɔ Miawani.
*If you want to have experience in something, you try your best to go to the town of Try Your Best.*
(If at first you don't succeed, try, try, and try again).

**5009.** Worepɛ no yie a, wobrɛ.
*If you wish to do good, you suffer.*
(You have to suffer for what you believe in).

**5010.** Wopɛ papa abusua mu a, ɔberɛ mpa wo so.
*If you want a good reputation in your family, you get tired.*
(Family obligations are exhausting).

**5011. Worepɛ opepeni adi no nya a, wofrɛ no kramo.**
*If you wish to ask a man from the North to serve you, you call him a Moslem.*
(You flatter a person whose help you want).

**5012. Wopɛ pɛsewa atumpan a, yɛsene ma wo na yɛde bɔ wo abodin a, na wonteɛ.**
*If you want a very cheap drum you can get it, but when it is sounded for your appelations, you won't hear it.*
(Getting things on the cheap does not redound to your credit).

**5013. Worepɛ ɔpɛtɛ kosua a, woforo onyina.**
*If you want to have the vulture's egg, you have to climb the silk-cotton (Bombax buonopozense) tree for it.*
(You have to work hard to achieve a difficult project).

**5014. Worepɛ asa asa a, wosakra wo nanteɛ.**
*If you want to dance, you change your way of walking.*
(If you want to participate in an activity, you must conform to the rules governing it).

**5015. Wopɛ sɛ mmaa nto wo dwom da biara a, mmarima huro wo.**
*If you like women to mention you in their songs all the time, the men will scoff at you.*
(If you are too successful with one lot of people, the others dislike you).

**5016. Wopɛ sɛ wodaadaa obi kye no a, ɔdaadaa wo dwane.**
*If you want to cheat someone to catch him, he will cheat you to run away.*
(You get what you give).

**5017. Wopɛ sɛ dua mmu mmɔ kwakuo a, ɛnoa no si.**
*If you wish the tree to fall on the monkey, the tree will bend for it to escape.*
(If you ask someone's friend to harm him, he will help him instead).

**5018. Wopɛ sɛ yɛmfrɛ wo "Agyeman" a, ɛbɛwie aseɛ na yɛfrɛ wo "Ɔmammɔfoɔ".**
*If you want us to call you "Saviour," it may come to pass that we call you "One who brings mischief on the Nation".*
(If you are public-spirited, you may later be blamed for what you have tried to do).

**5019. Wopɛ sɛ ɛgu wo yɔnko so a, ɛgu wo so.**
*If you want something (dirty) poured on your acquaintance, it is poured over you.*
(If you wish evil on others, you get it yourself. Do as you would be done by).

**5020. Wopɛ sɛ wohunu dekodeɛ a ɛhyɛ dua bi ase a, wotu ne ntini ansa.**
*If you wish to see a particular thing, which is under the roots of a tree, you pull it out by its roots first.*
(You have to remove obstacles before you attain success).

**5021. Wopɛ sɛ wohunu nneɛma nyinaa a, w'ani fura.**
*If you want to see everything, you become blind.*
(Too much inquisitiveness is dangerous).

**5022. Wopɛ sɛ wonya biribi firi obi hɔ a, wode anyamesɛm na ɛdɛfɛdɛfɛ no.**
*If you want to get something out of someone, you use religious arguments to soften them up.*

**5023. Wopɛ sɛ wo sɛbeɛ yɛ tenten a, na woforo dua kɔne.**
*If you want your faeces to be long, you climb a tree to defecate.*
(If you want to court disgrace, then you make your faults obvious).

**5024. Wopɛ sɛ wote bese saka a, gye sɛ woforo dua no.**
*To pick a bunch of cola you must first climb the tree.*
(You must work to achieve success. First things first).

**5025. Wopɛ sɛ woyɛ ɔpanin pa a, wosisi w'aso, kata w'ani.**
*If you wish to be a real elder, you close your ears and cover your eyes.*
(An elder does not pay attention to idle gossip nor trivial events).

**5026. Worepɛ w'ase adi no atɛm a, na wone no di ɛtɔ.**
*If you want to insult your in-laws, then you and they eat mashed plantain.*
(When you make balls out of mashed plantain you stick out your thumb, which is an insult. Hence: If you want to insult someone with impunity, you can find the right occasion to do so).

**5027. Worepɛ w'ase paam ahwɛ a, na wo ne no to anɔpagya.**
*If you wish to see your mother-in-law's cleavage, you warm yourself with her at the early morning fire.*
(You must be intimate with a person to know all their secrets).

**5028. Worepɛ w'ase ntummɔnwi ahwɛ a, woma no bepɔ so afuyɔ.**
*If you want to see your father-in-law's hair on his buttocks, you give him a farm on a hillside.*
(If you want to do something questionable you achieve it in a roundabout way).

**5029. Worepɛ asɛm aka akyerɛ Nyame a, na woka kyerɛ mframa.**
*If you wish to tell anything to God, tell it to the wind.*
(If you want a man you fear to get to know something, you tell those who are intimate with him).

**5030. Worepɛ asɛm atie a, yɛka kyerɛ wo.**
*If you like to hear about matters, then we tell you.*
(If you are interested in information about something, then people will bother to tell you).

**5031. Wopɛ ɔsom bebrebe a, ɔsom ka wo kɔn mu.**
*If you like too much servitude, then servitude will hang round your neck.*
(If you have a slave mentality, you will be treated as a slave).

**5032. Wopɛ su a, na wodi funu akyire.**
*If you like to weep, then you follow the corpse.*
(If you like doing something, you go where you can do it).

**5033. Worepɛ "ta" a, ɛnte sɛ woanya "tatrata".**
*If you are after one thing, then what happens when you get more?*
(If a little satisfies you, a lot may overwhelm you).

**5034. Wopε taku na woanhunu no a, na wafra nsesa mu.**
*If you want a small coin and you don't find it, then it has hidden itself among the other small change.*
(If someone cannot be found, they have probably taken french leave).

**5035. Wopε ategɔ a wotɔ adwene.**
*If you like coco-yam fufu, you buy fish.*
(If you like something, you get what goes with it).

**5036. Wopε ntεm kɔ wo Nananom akurofoso kokae wo Nsamanfoɔ a, wɔkyekyere wo werε.**
*If you try and go quickly to you Ancestor's graveyard to remember your departed ones, they console you.*
(If you show pride in your ancestors, they will support you in life).

**5037. Wopε ntεm pii a, woka akyi.**
*If you like speed too much, you stay behind.*
(More haste, less speed).

**5038. Wopε "tie-ma-mense-wo a," na woware mmaa adodoɔ.**
*If you like "listen-and-let-me-tell you", you marry many women.*
(If you like trouble, become a polygamist!)

**5039. Yεrepε εtwε tuntum ade a aforo dua a, pobire mfa ne ho nsuma.**
*If we are after a black vagina to climb up a tree (to show the public), the black snail should not hide itself.*
(If you possess something admirable which is needed, you should not hide it).

**5040. Wopε atweε a, wonsuro nkekaboa.**
*If you like going on a hunting expedition, you do not fear the biting animals.*
(If you really want to do something, you take little notice of the dangers involved).

**5041. Wopε wo bosom na wonhunu no a, na wode w'ani toto wiem.**
*If you want your fetish and you don't find it, then you look in different directions in the sky.*
(Priests do this if possessed. Hence: When you can't get something at once, you try every means of getting it).

**5042. Wopε wo yere a, wodi ne mmara so.**
*If you love your wife, you obey her laws.*
(If you love someone, you behave as they would like you to).

**5043. Wopε wo yere bebrebe a, ɔma wo bɔ dam.**
*If you love your wife too much, she makes you go mad.*
(Too much of anything is dangerous).

**5044. Worepε wo yere aberewabɔ mu ahwε a, hwε w'ase.**
*If you want to know how your wife will look in old age, look at your wife's relations.*
(Like mother, like daughter).

**5045. Worepε wo yere agyae no a, na wose: "Meregye wo mpata piredwan".**
*If you want to get rid of your wife you say: "I am demanding a piredwan worth of pacification".*

(A piredwan is a large quanitity of gold-dust; a pacification fee is paid in recognition of wrong done. The idea is that a man may pretend to be seek reconciliation, but make the terms impossible for his wife to accept. Hence: If you want something to happen, you make the alternative unrealistic).

**5046. Wopε awoɔ a, wonsuro nkukutotɔ.**
*If you like giving birth, you don't fear buying of pots.*
(If you want a big family, you must be prepared to provide for it).

**5047. Worepε ayitoma akɔ ayie a, wonsiane εtwε ho, εfiri sε, εso nwi yε birisi, εtam ε εmo no nso yε kɔbene, εtwε no ara nso yε kɔbene.**
*If you want a funeral cloth to go to a funeral, you don't by-pass the vagina, because its hair is black cloth (birisi), the linen cloth on it is also orange (kɔbene), the vagina itself is also orange (kɔbene).*
(Birisi and kɔbene are funeral cloths. Hence: Don't go off looking for something, when what you need is right in front of you).

**5048. Worepε ayowa mu ahwε a, na wobɔ no.**
*If you are trying to look inside the pot, then you break it.*
(Too much curiosity leads to trouble).

**5049. Wompε ɔbaa bi a, na wobisa ne kunu.**
*If you do not love a certain woman, then you ask after her husband.*
(If you are not interested in someone, you make it quite clear).

**5050. Wompε asεm atie a, na wosisi w'aso.**
*If you don't like to listen to a question, you seal your ears.*
(It is up to your whether you pay attention or not).

**5051. Yεmpε sika nsi hɔ ansa na yεatwe manso.**
*We don't accumulate money before we indulge in litigation.*
(Whatever your position, if you are faced with a problem, you must solve it).

**5052. Pε-agorɔ na ɔsoa twene.**
*The music lover carries the drums.*
(If you are really interested in something, you are prepared to work for it).

**5053. Ɔpε, yεdi no ɔdɔ mu na yεnni no ahoɔfε.**
*Desire comes from love and not because of beauty.*
(It is affection that counts, not appearance).

**5054. Ɔpε kurom yε fε, na ɔkɔm na εwɔ hɔ.**
*The harmattan's town is beautiful but there is famine there.*
(The harmattan is the season of dry desert winds, starting at about Christmas time. There is a disadvantage to everything).

**5055. Ɔpε si a, na yεhunu akɔtɔbɔ mu mmarima ne mmaa.**
*When the harmattan comes, we know which of the crabs is male and which female.*
(In the dry season the ground is very hard and digging out crabs is a tough job; and when you bend over you may reveal your sex. Hence: In time of difficulty, a person's true character emerges).

5056. Ɔpɛ nsiiɛ no, na yɛhata adeɛ.
*Before the harmattan came, we spread things out to dry.*
(Things dry very quickly during the harmattan. Hence: Before the arrival of a benefactor, the poor man had his own way of living).

5057. Ɔpɛ bɛtoo ɔtwe na ne ho fitaa.
*The harmattan came to meet the duiker with its light skin.*
(During the harmattan people's skins get dry and often look white. Said of something which was in existence even before the circumstances which might have caused it).

5058. Pea hunu akyɛmpem a, ɛhɔn.
*If a spear sees an important man, it removes itself from the shaft.*
(If two powerful men meet, one must give way to the other).

5059. Apeaa nim su a, yɛmmoro no na wasu.
*If Apeaa knows how to cry, we don't have to beat her before she cries.*
(You don't expect someone to do something at the wrong time. "Crying" mourning songs is for funerals).

5060. Apeanimmaaa aburow-hono se: "Magye nim mama kankuwaa".
*The husk of maize in the Apeanimmaaa horn (used for drawing blood from a swelling) says: "I have won glory for the horn".*
(The husk is burnt to heat the horn before use. Hence: Used when someone who has contributed to the success of a project gets no credit for it).

5061. Apɛbi-anyabie nyinaa yɛ ɛka.
*To want something and get it all leads to debt.*
(What you get, you pay for).

5062. Apɛbiadifoɔ na ɔne ɔbɔfoɔ nanteɛ.
*Those who want a share in the food, walk with the hunter.*
(If you need something, you have to go to the source).

5063. Apeetɔɔ hyɛ Atwommaa bo, na wanyi a, ɔdidi a, na ɔrefe.
*If a woman is unable to express her disapproval, then if she eats, she vomits.*
(This way of expressing disapproval involves pushing the lips forward and making a small noise. Hence: You must have some way of letting off steam, or it bottles up inside you and makes you ill).

5064. Apem daadaa wo a, wodaadaa wo ho kɔ deɛ mpensa wɔ.
*If a thousand tricks you, you too find your way to where three thousand is.*
(If you are cheated of a lesser amount, you too have to cheat to get a larger one).

5065. Apem redaadaa wo akye wo a, wo nso wodaadaa no dwane.
*If a thousand is deceiving you in order to catch you, then you also deceive it to escape.*
(Avoid situations that will get you into trouble).

5066. Apem ase nhye da.
*The plantain's descendants are without end.*
(Said of a fruitful person or family).

5067. Mpempɛnsɔɔ yɛ wo dɛ a, w'asɛm ho nwini.
*If you like making hints, then your secrets are revealed.*
(If you can't keep quiet, you are bound to let out secrets).

5068. Apentemma, worekɔdi abenne a, nkra me.
*Apentemma, if you are going to engage in a serious fight, don't inform me.*
(Said to a trouble maker when you don't want to be involved).

5069. Pentene asaase da hɔ kwa a, yɛmfa no kwa.
*If the lands of Pentene village lie fallow, we don't seize them.*
(You don't take what does not belong to you, even if it is not used).

5070. Ɔpepɛɛni, yɛnsisi no animonoso.
*A miser, we don't cheat him in his presence.*
(It is difficult to cheat a mean man to his face).

5071. Mpepefoo de ahubaa gu bese so a, wonse sɛ: "Bese bɛtɔ."
*If Northerners are throwing sticks at the cola tree, you don't say: "There will be a good market for cola."*
(Many Northern Ghanaians buy cola nuts, which they chew as a stimulant, rather than collecting them for themselves. Hence: If people interfere with your expectations, you are not going to achieve success).

5072. Opepeni nya wo na ɔrenku wo a, hwɛ n'ani ase.
*If a Northerner gets you and he won't kill you, look at his cheek marks.*
(The people in Northern Ghana often incise marks on their faces, as a mark of their ethnic identity. If someone has suffered pain himself he is less likely to worry about giving you pain).

5073. Wopere adeɛ ho bebrebe a, ɛhwere wo.
*If you run about and make too much fuss, you miss it.*
(If you are over-anxious, you miss your chance).

5074. Wopere ɔkɔtɔ ho pii a, wote n'aperɛ.
*If you hurry too much too catch the crab, you break off its claws.*
(Too much haste defeats its own purposes).

5075. Wopere na woanya a, wosrɛ.
*If you struggle for something and you can't get it, you beg.*
(Some needs are so urgent that they have to be satisfied).

5076. Wopere wo man na woannya a, wopere wo kuro; wopere wo kuro na woannya a, wopere wo fie; wopere wo fie na woannya a, wopere wo nko ara wo ti.
*If you struggle for your state and you don't succeed, you struggle for your town; if you struggle for your town and you don't succeed, you struggle for your home; if you struggle for your home and you don't succeed, then you struggle for your own life.*
(If all opportunities fail, at least one's life must be preserved).

5077. Opereduasini na ɔyɛ nam.
*The one who has lost its tail is the ablest.*
(It is believed when an animal loses its tail or a dog is castrated, etc., it becomes stronger. Thus a person who has some physical disadvantage may have a strong character).

5078. Ɔperɛhwɛ yɛ ya sen ɛkam.
*Secret criticism hurts more than a wound.*
(To be hurt physically is less painful than being shamed).

5079. Apɛsɛ yɛ kɛse a, ɔyɛ ma dufɔkyeɛ.
*If the brush-tailed porcupine grows big, it does so on behalf of the rotten wood.*
(This porcupine eats grubs from rotten wood. The proverb expresses complete overlordship: a servant is not greater than the one who supports him).

5080. Pesewa nti na Dankyiraman bɔe.
*Because of a small amount the state of Dankyira fell.*
(Asante was a tributary state of Dankyira. The demand for tribute led to a war between Asante and Dankyira, which led to the reversal of the relationship. Hence: Because of a nail, the army was lost. Or: Carelessness in small things may bring about a great disaster).

5081. Pesewa nya amaneɛ a, piredwan ntumi ntua.
*If a small amount brings trouble, even a large sum cannot pay for it.*
(A small mistake may cause irreparable loss).

5082. Ɔpetɛ de ne ho hua bɔ ne ho ban.
*The vulture uses its scent to defend itself.*
(A thing which may be a disadvantage to one person, aids another).

5083. Ɔpetɛ ho ayɛ nkwasea ho deɛ, nanso ɔkyiri adwareɛ aniani.
*The vulture's body is ridiculous, but even he loathes incomplete bathing.*
(Because you are ugly, it does not mean you need to be dirty).

5084. Ɔpetɛ ne anene kra nsɛ.
*The vulture and the crow's souls are not alike.*
(You may do the same job as someone else but be unlike them in character).

5085. Ɔpetɛ takara twa ne wura nkontompo a, ɔtu twene.
*When a vulture's feather tells its owner a lie, he plucks it out and casts it away.*
(If your subordinate tries to trick you, you get rid of him. If your eye offends you, pluck it out).

5086. Ɔpetɛ nni biribi a, ɔwɔ dunsini a ɔsi anim.
*If the vulture has nothing else, it has the tree stump that it perches on.*
(Everyone has something they use and appreciate).

5087. Ɔpetɛ nni pirebuo nso ɔwɔ deɛ ɔda.
*The vulture has no nest but it has its sleeping place.*
(God provides for all).

5088. Apetebie didi soro na ɔsiane bɛdidi fam a, ɔtwe bɔ no soboɔ.
*If the striped squirrel which eats above climbs down to eat on the earth, then the duiker gives it a warning blow.*
(Each man to his own place. Don't encroach on another's territory).

5089. Apetebie rebɛkɔ wuo no ɔde ne ba ma aprɛnkensema sɛ ɔntete no, na wanka sɛ ɔmpoopoo n'ani nkyerɛ no.
*When the striped squirrel was on its deathbed it handed over its child to the bush baby to bring up, but it didn't say it should frighten it with its eyes.*
(The bush baby has very large eyes. If you inherit responsibility for someone's children, you should treat them as you would your own, and not abuse or exploit them).

5090. Apetebie na ɔkaa n'asɛm sɛ: akwankwaa nnante mma n'atifi nna hɔ kwa.
*It is the striped squirrel which said: a young gallant does not go around without covering over his head.*
(A young person dresses smartly when he goes out).

5091. Apetebie se: yɛfiri ahoma-ano na ɛsane.
*The striped squirrel says: we untie knots from the end.*
(We tackle a problem from its beginnings).

5092. Apetebie se: ɛsoro nni nkwanta a, anka ɔsi ahoma baako so a, anka ɔrensane mfa homa korɔ no so nsan mma.
*The striped squirrel says: if there were no cross-roads above, then if it took one liana strand, then it would not change and take another strand to come back.*
(The squirrels travel along the lianas in the forest; they are its "roads." Hence: If it is convenient, we continue to use the same old ways).

5093. Apetebie tɔ nsuo mu a, Onyame na ɔtware no asuo.
*If the striped squirrel falls into the stream, it is God who helps him out of the water.*
(God helps the helpless).

5094. Apetebie-kuru se: "Akɔnnɔ bɛkum hiani".
*The striped squirrel says: "The poor will die of longing".*
(The life of the poor is full of unfulfilled dreams and desires).

5095. Wopia wo dɔm a, na woko ma woɔ.
*If you spur on your battalion, then they fight for you.*
(People respond to encouragement).

5096. Pieto bɛtoo danta.
*Underpants came to meet the loincloth.*
(Every new thing replaces something older).

5097. Wopinkyɛ onyina a, na wohunu n'adukuro.
*If you approach the onyina tree, you see its buttress.*
(It is only when you get near someone that you learn their true nature).

5098. Wopinkyɛ pinkyɛ [obi]/[Ɔdasani] bebrebe a, ɔde woyɛ osuaa.
*If you attach yourself too closely to [someone]/[a human being] he treats you cheaply.*
(Osuaa is a small quanitity of gold dust. Hence: Familiarity breeds contempt).

5099. Piredwan a ɛda hɔ na menni bi, na deɛ ɛnenam hɔ deɛ, ebi wɔ hɔ.
*A piredwan which lies there (is saved) I don't have, but what walks about (spending money) I have.*
(Said when you are not rich enough to invest or save, but you do have enough to live on).

5100. Piredwan da man mu a, ɛwɔ amansan.
*If there is a piredwan in the state, it belongs to all its people.*

(Any wealth a citizen may have accrues to the general wealth of his state).

5101. Piredwan hwete abusua mu.
*A piredwan splits the family.*
(Money problems tear a family apart).

5102. Piredwan nya amaneɛ a, asuasa nna.
*If the piredwan brings trouble, asuasa does not rest.*
(Asuasa is a much smaller quantity of gold dust than a piredwan. Hence: If an important person is in trouble, a lesser person is in trouble too).

5103. Apiretwaa nni hɔ a, ɔbɔfoɔ nyɛ barima.
*If the hunter's bag is absent, the hunter is no man.*
(Even a strong man depends on his tools and servants).

5104. Apitie koko: "Huu-huu prɛm".
*The small tinker bird show its temper: "Agitation and then sudden calming down".*
(An extrovert calms down as quickly as he gets angry).

5105. Apitie se akwansosɛm dɛ nti na ɛboɔ bɔ no a, ɔnka ne ho, na ɛnyɛ gyimi na wagyimi.
*The tinker bird says because of a sweet tale from afar, when you throw a stone at it, it does not move about, it is not that it is foolish.*
(Some people have good motives for acting apparently unwisely).

5106. Mpitrapɔ wɔ Atwomaa bo a, abofono mpa.
*If resentment is in Atwomaa's heart, irritation is always there.*
(If you don't let your feelings out, they fester within).

5107. [Pitire]/[Ɔkaa] a n'ano yɛ hare na daawa bɔ no.
*A cat fish which is quick to snatch gets caught by the hook.*
(A warning against precipitate action and being too greedy).

5108. Pitire memene adeɛ a, ɔmemene ma ne wura.
*If the cat fish swallows anything, it swallows it for its master.*
(The cat fish's master is the crocodile, the most powerful creature in the water where they both live. Hence: The servant works for the benefit of the master; if he prospers, so does his master).

5109. Pitire memene nkawa a, ɔmene ma ne mma.
*When the cat fish swallows the young fish, it does so for its children.*
(A chief struggles for his subjects).

5110. Pitire nam yɛ dɛ, na ohia nti na yɛtɔn.
*The meat of the cat fish is sweet, but because of poverty we sell it.*
(We may like something very much but be forced to part with it in order to live).

5111. Pitire perepere a, ɔda kodoɔ mu.
*Even if the catfish flaps about, it still remains in the canoe.*
(There are some situations you cannot escape from even through struggling hard).

5112. Ɛpo so samini se: "Mehwɛ sakraka ne ne mma adowa a wɔregorɔ".

*The octopus in the sea says: "I am watching the big sea fish and its children as if they were playing adowa music".*
(A stranger stays outside the game and is only a watcher).

5113. Ɛpo anso adware a, Ɔfe renso.
*If the sea is not sufficient for bathing then the Offin river is not.*
(If the greatest is not enough, nor will the lesser be).

5114. Ɛpo ntwɛn asusuɔ ansa na ayiri.
*The sea does not wait for the rainy season before it overflows.*
(Some things do not depend on others, although it may seem likely).

5115. Ɛpɔ si wo mene ase a, wommɔ hwerɛma.
*If your throat has a goitre, you don't whistle.*
(If something is in your way, it is no good acting as if it were not there).

5116. Mpoano kɔtɔ dwane kɔ po mu na ɔnnwane nkɔ ɛserɛso.
*The crab on the sea shore scuttles to go into the sea, but it does not scuttle to go into the savannah.*
(If a man escapes, he escapes into his own element).

5117. Mpoatwa na ɛde ko ba.
*Defamation makes war come.*
(People fight in order to avoid losing face or being insulted).

5118. Mpoatwa na ɛma ɔsafohene di ako tɔ.
*Defamation makes the war leader fight to the death.*
(A man will do anything to protect his reputation).

5119. Mpobi di tɔ a, ne mene mu regono.
*If the fly eats mashed yam, its throat is loosened.*
(Don't bite off more than you can chew).

5120. Ɔpofoni se ɔbɛkɔ po a, yɛnnye no akyinnye.
*If the fisherman says he is going to sea, you don't contradict him.*
(You believe people when they tell you they are going to do what they normally do).

5121. Opoku mfa ne nku; medware a, me ho mpae.
*Let Opoku take his oil; if I bathe myself, let my skin be rough.*
(Used when you want to get rid of someone even if you apparently suffer by it).

5122. Opoku Frɛfrɛ na ɔse: "Biribi reba, biribi reba, ɛnyɛ ɔko a, ɛyɛ adeɛ".
*Opoku Frɛfrɛ says: "Something is going to come, something is going to come, if it is not war, then it is something good."*
(There are only two choices: good and bad).

5123. Pɔn tena kwan mu: yɛ kyiri!
*Remaining in the way after finishing a job: we abhor it!*
("Yɛ kyiri" means literally something like: we turn out backs on it. It is the verb used for things that are taboo. Hence: Used, for example, when someone has yielded control of a project, but is still interfering in it).

5124. Ɔpɔnkɔ abɔ dam a, ne wura deɛ ɔmmɔɔ dam.
*If a horse is mad, his master has not become mad.*
(Stupidity in a servant does not mean his master is witless too).

5125. Ɔpɔnkɔ de ne dua na ɛpra ne ho.
*The horse uses its tail to brush himself.*
(Everything has its special use).

5126. Ɔpɔnkɔ agyimi a, ɛnyɛ deɛ ɔte ne soɔ a.
*If the horse is stupid, it does not mean the rider is also so.*
(See Proverb 5124).

5127. Ɔpɔnkɔ agyimi a, nyɛ n'ammirika tuo ho a.
*If a horse is stupid, he is not stupid in running.*
(Everyone has some special quality).

5128. Ɔpɔnkɔ mmane kwa.
*A horse does not turn aside without cause.*
(A man must have a reason to deviate from his set course).

5129. Ɔpɔnkɔ ankɔ sa a, ne dua kɔ.
*If a horse does not go to war, its tail does.*
(Horse tails were used as part of a war leader's paraphernalia. Hence: Even if you are unable to attend a function personally, you can contribute to it).

5130. Ɔpɔnkɔ wɔ dua, ɛsono wɔ dua, nanso ɔpɔnkɔ deɛ kyɛn ɛsono deɛ kakra.
*The horse has a tail, the elephant has a tail, but the horse's tail is a little bigger than the elephant's.*
(Possession of talents does not depend on bulk).

5131. Aponkyerɛne se ɔbɔ soboɔ a, ɔbɔ ne to.
*The frog says if he wants to blame anything, he blames his buttocks.*
(Because of his flat bottom he could not get a wife like other animals. In time of disappointment you blame your own attributes).

5132. Aponkyerɛne se oni sɛ: "Hwɛ m'ani akeseɛ!" Na oni se: "Na me ɛ?"
*The frog says to its mother: "Look how big my eyes are!" Mother replies: "What about me?"*
(Said when someone boasts of something they have inherited through no merit of their own).

5133. Aponkyerɛne se: sɛ yereka ɛtoɔ ho asɛm a, ɔrenka bi.
*The frog says: if we are speaking of buttocks, he will not join us.*
(No one likes to discuss their own shortcomings).

5134. Aponkyerɛne se: "Mewo aduro a, anka manyɛ ananta?"
*The frog says: "If I had medicine, wouldn't I have taken it to enable me to walk".*
(Said by someone who is unable to do something and is criticized for it).

5135. Aponkyerɛne tɔ nsuohyeɛ mu a, na ɔhunu sɛ nsuo gu ahodoɔ.
*If the frog falls into hot water, he realizes that there are different kinds of water.*
(Experience teaches you to differentiate).

5136. Aponkyerɛne wɔ bafan aduro a, anka ne ba mmutu fam.
*If the frog had medicine to cure a cripple, then its child would not lie on its belly on the ground.*
(If you have the solution to a problem, you use it).

5137. Aponkyerɛne wu a, na yɛhunu ne tenten.
*If the frog dies, we see its length.*
(When things come to a head, we shall see how to act).

5138. Ɔpɔɔdɔ kakraka si hɔ a, obi nkɔ nsuo mfa ngu toa mu.
*If there is a big drinking water pot, a person doesn't go and fill the gourd.*
(Always use the best means available).

5139. Yɛpopa ntasuo na yɛnhanyan mu.
*We clean up the spittle but we don't spread it.*
(You settle a case and you don't allow its effects to spread).

5140. Apopobibire se ɔregye efie, na praeɛ nsoɛ?
*The black fungus says it is trying to capture the house, and what of the broom?*
(A black fungus grows where water is constantly poured and is hard to get rid of. It needs hard work to keep things in order. What are you doing about it?)

5141. Aporibaa da hɔ na ɔpanin anyi no hɔ a, yɛde hwe nkɔdaa ne mpanin.
*If a fighting stick is left somewhere and an elder does not pick it up, it is used to beat both children and elders.*
(Don't leave dangerous weapons around or they may be used against you).

5142. [Apɔsɔ]/[Nkutadene] se n'ahooden te nkutadene mu.
*The potto says its strength is in its ability to hold on.*
(Everyone has their own talent for self protection. Said of someone whose main ability is the holding onto what they are doing, whatever happens).

5143. "Apotɔ ama no afeɛ" nkyiri sɛ ɔde bɔ mu bie.
*"A masher who has prepared well" does not abhor taking part in eating it.*
(You are entitled to share what you have worked to achieve).

5144. "Potɔgumu" ne "hwiegumu" ne nyinaa ko kwansɛn korɔ mu.
*"Mash into it" and "pour into it" all go into one pot.*
(However you do it, the result is the same).

5145. Pɔweɛ bɔne dane kankane a, nkura we ne bɛhoma.
*If a bad tapper becomes a rich man, mice chew his climbing rope.*
(Objects not in use are often stored in the rafters, where the mice get at them. Hence: Don't despise the thing that helps you to succeed in life).

5146. Wopra pataso pra ɛfɔm a, na asɛm asa.
*If we sweep the rafters and then sweep the floor, the problem is solved.*
(Don't do a job first which may be spoilt by the second one. First things first).

5147. Praeɛ te anyanyaneɛ nso onnya ayɛ.
*The broom clears all stinking things away but it gets no praise.*

(Said of someone who does the dirty work but is not thanked for it).

**5148. Praeɛ teteaa ntumi nkum nwansena.**
*A single fibre of a broom cannot kill a fly.*
(Only cooperation brings success).

**5149. Praeɛ-tia wɔ hɔ yi wobu mu a, ɛmmu, nanso woyi no mmaako-mmaako a ɛbubu.**
*When single fibers of an old broom are put together, they don't break, but when you take them one by one they break in pieces.*
(United we stand, divided we fall).

**5150. Prako ba se: "Eno w'ano yi e!" Na ɔse: "Sɛ woreba".**
*The piglet says: "Mother what a big mouth you have." She replies: "You are also growing".*
(Be careful of blaming people for something which you too may indulge in when you reach their position).

**5151. Prako ne hwan a ɔne ɔsebo reko dompe ho?**
*Who is the pig to fight with a leopard over a bone?*
(How can a weak man challenge a very powerful one over something they both want?)

**5152. Prako nnom nsa mma abirekyie mmoro.**
*A pig does not drink for the goat to get intoxicated.*
(You don't do something for another to benefit ... or suffer).

**5153. Prako se: ɔfaa ne kwasea yi, ɛnyɛ n'atopa ho a.**
*The pig says: it is taken for a fool, but it does not mean it lacks skill in intercourse.*
(Stupid people can have certain talents).

**5154. Prako se: ɔnya danta a, anka ɔbɛbɔ, nanso ne dua nti?**
*The pig says: if it had a loin cloth, it would wear it, but what of its tail?*
(Man cannot hide his true nature).

**5155. Prako te ase dada a, ɔrepene, na ɔyare ne mu.**
*Even in normal times the pig groans, how much more when its chest is sick.*
(If a man always complains, he will do it even more when in real trouble).

**5156. Prako te ase dada a, ɔse ɔreburo dɔteɛ; na wɔabɛse no sɛ n'ase dan abuo.**
*If a pig normally stays in a place, it will churn the earth up; how much more so when it is told its in-law's building has collapsed.*
(If a person is troublesome, he will be even worse so in times of stress).

**5157. Ɔprammire a wasi kwan n'akyiri mmaa aduasa.**
*A black cobra blocking the path cannot avoid thirty strokes.*
(If a dangerous man exposes himself, he must take the consequences).

**5158. Ɔprammire firi bɔn mu firi a, na aboa biara nni mu bio.**
*If the black cobra comes out of its hole then no animal sleeps in it again.*
(People keep away from what they fear, even after the danger has gone).

**5159. Ɔprammire kyere mampam a, na ewiase reko awieɛ.**
*If the black cobra catches the monitor lizard, the world is coming to an end.*
(If the impossible happens, the end may be near).

**5160. Ɔprammire se: ɔkyiri ayuo, nanso abotokura di gu ne yam.**
*The black cobra says: it does not like guinea corn, but the striped mouse ate it to go into its stomach.*
(i.e. the mouse ate the corn and the snake ate the mouse. You may not sin directly yourself, but still profit from other people's sins).

**5161. Ɔprammire si kwan a, na ɔrekɔ ne baabi nso nnipa hu no a, na wɔredwane.**
*If a black cobra occupies the way when it is going on its own journey, then when people see it they flee.*
(A dangerous man is feared even when doing harmless things).

**5162. Ɔprammire si akwan, sɛ woanha no a, ɔnka wo.**
*If the black cobra blocks the path, if you do not disturb it, it won't bite you.*
(Let sleeping dogs lie).

**5163. Aprawa se: ɔnni ahoɔden nti na ɔde asrɛnnɛ abɔ ne ho ban.**
*The pangolin says: it is not strong and that is why it has fenced itself around with a raffia mat.*
(God provides for the weak).

**5164. Prebuo nyɛ nwonona a, anka apatuprɛ nna nnua mmienu so.**
*If it were not hard to build a nest, the bulbul would not have slept on two sticks.*
(You don't wittingly do without something which is easy to achieve).

**5165. Prɛkɛsɛ na ɛfiti kurotia a, na ne ho rebɔn afie mu.**
*Even if prɛkɛsɛ (Tetrapleura tetraptera) is on the outskirts of the town, its scent permeates the dwellings.*
(Prɛkɛsɛ has long brown four winged fruit which are used in soups and for cosmetics and have a pungent smell. Hence: A good reputation travels).

**5166. Prɛmo nhwere nnam.**
*A cannon does not miss game.*
(A powerful man gets what he wants).

**5167. Woprɛprɛ afiri-boa a, na worepɛ no asane no.**
*If you continue nudging a trapped animal, then you want to free it.*
(Said when someone who claims to have one goal is actully pursuing another).

**5168. Prokuo wo nta.**
*(Even) someone who has bad teeth gives birth to twins.*
(Your appearance does not indicate your ability).

**5169. [Prɔperaa]/[Kurukuroo] wɔ hɔ a, ɔbrane nne aku.**
*If he ought to run away, a man strong does not stay and fight.*
(Study the situation before you act).

**5170. Apuene ɔse: "Baabiara nyɛ".**
*Apuene says: "Nowhere is good".*
(Nothing is entirely good in life).

**5171. Opumpuni hwease a, ɔne ne kyɛ.**
*When a great man falls, he falls with his hat.*
(A head of Government falls with his advisors).

**5172. Apumpuo nkɔhyia nanka, nanka amma, apumpuo nso amma.**
*The centipede was to call the viper, the viper did not come, neither did the centipede.*
(A situation where neither of two things materializes).

**5173. Apumpuo anaa kɛtɛgo ɛmu biara nne animuonyam.**
*(Whether you use the name) apumpuo or kɛtɛgo (for the centipede), neither name is honorable.*
(You can't make a silk purse out of a sow's ear).

**5174. Apumpuo tɔprɛ-ampatu: "Mfumsɛm nti na meso me nneɛma.**
*The centipede: "Because of unforeseeable incidents I carry all my needs along".*
(It is good to be prepared for all eventualities).

**5175. Apupuo a ɔbɔɔ n'asuo da nsuakye.**
*The fresh water mussel that brought rain lies on the river bank.*
(This little creature brought rain by its prayers, but it was trampled underfoot in the mad rush of the animals for water. Hence: used to criticize ingratitude).

**5176. Opuro di ne berɛ papa so.**
*The squirrel reigns on the palm fronds.*
(A man is king of his own castle).

**5177. Opuro se: ɛkaa ɔno nko a, anka obiara kyiri nam.**
*The squirrel says: if it were left to it alone, all men should abhor meat.*
(We consider our own interests first).

**5178. Opuro se: ɔwɔ sekan a, anka nyɛ ɛne sɛ [domako]/[mmatatwene] akyere abɛ yi.**
*The squirrel says: if it had a knife then [the domako plant]/[the liana (Cercertis afzelii)] would not have strangled the palm-nut tree.*
(If you have no means of destroying an enemy you can only regret its actions).

**5179. Apurokuma regu nhyerɛne yi na ɛrekum akwaduo yi; na ɛbɛso abiribira.**
*Now that the apurokuma tree (Panda oleosa) is coming into flower, it is killing the yellow-backed duikers; how much more when it develops fruit.*
(If something apparently weak causes damage, how much more so when it is strong).

**5180. Apurukusu a waporɔ ateteɛ na ɔte sɛ oyoyo a n'ani da soɔ.**
*The electric fish that has rotted and torn is like the eel that is still living (lit. the eel that has hope).*
(i.e. they are both equally frightening. Said, for example, by a poor person when a rich person disparages him, meaning: I, with all my problems, am still as good as you).

**5181. Mapusu dɔte mansuro akrokra, na nyɛ mekɔpusu dunsini.**
*I have shaken the thicket and I did not fear the heavy dew, how much less hould Ifeat it, if I shake the tree stump?*
(If you don't mind heavy punishment, you don't fear lesser).

**5182. Wopusu dunsini a, wopusu wo ti.**
*If you shake the tree stump, you shake your own head.*
(If you try to do something useless, you yourself suffer).

**5183. Apusu-apusuo wie kokurobotie so.**
*Too much shaking causes hardship to the thumb.*
(It is the person most involved in something who suffers for it).

**5184. Putuo dadaa, yɛmfa nhyia ayeforoɔ.**
*An old hut, we don't take home a young bride to it.*
You make adequate provision before you embark on a new or long project. Don't put new wine into old skins).

## – S –

**5185. Wosa Krufie aduro a, na woawie asa.**
*If you use herbalist Krufie's medicine as an enema, then you have done with all other enemas.*
(If you have the best, you don't need anything else).

**5186. Wosa na wamfiri ntɛm a, yɛgu wo dwam.**
*If you dance and you don't cease in time, then we stop drumming abruptly (and put you to shame).*
(Overdoing anything is a disgrace. Don't overstay your welcome).

**5187. Woansa nsuo a, wonsa adwene.**
*If you don't scoop up the water, you don't scoop up the fish.*
(See Proverb 530. Hence: Unless you involve yourself in a project, you don't profit from it).

**5188. Ɔsa wɔkɔ no nkatae dodoɔ.**
*Many gun-lock covers go to war.*
(Success depends on adequate preparation and care of tools).

**5189. Ɔsa wɔkɔ no wɔn agya mma.**
*You go to war against your father's children.*
(You are more likely to quarrel with those you are close to. There is always a likelihood of the children of different mothers but the same father being hostile to each other as their mothers compete for the man's favors).

**5190. Ɔsa, yɛtwe no brɛbrɛ.**
*War, we pull it bit by bit.*
(You use wisdom and guile to achieve victory, it does not come all at once).

**5191. Asaase dɔre fi a, na wɔfrɛ no sie.**
*If the earth piles up dirt, we call it an anthill.*
(We judge by appearances).

**5192. Asaase nkosua, ebiara ne mankani.**
*One egg of the Earth is the cocoyam.*
(However insignificant you are, you are created by God)

**5193. Asaase kotokuo, obiara bɛkɔ mu.**
*Earth's bag, everyone must enter it.*
(We are all mortal).

**5194. Asaase nkyiri funu.**
*The earth does not abhor a corpse.*
(Death is natural and not to be feared).

**5195. Asaase so yɛ hye a, namɔn na ɛka.**
*If the earth is hot, the foot reveals it.*
(If you are in constant touch with a thing, you know its nature).

**5196. Asaase nyɛ bosom, nti na ɔnkyerɛ mmusuo.**
*The earth is not a god, it does not therefore tell fortunes.*
(If it is not your function to do something, you don't do it).

**5197. Asaase nyɛ kɛtɛ na yɛabobɔ.**
*The earth is not a mat that we can fold.*
(Some things cannot be moved).

**5198. Asaaseboa ɔdi asie nana ne me.**
*The earth creature that owns the world: its grandchild am I.*
(We all owe our existence to earth's bounty).

**5199. Asaaseboa ka wo na woante no anto gya mu a, woda a, w'ani nkum.**
*If the small ground insect bites you and you don't pick it off and throw it into the fire, if you sleep, you are wakeful.*
(Deal quickly with your enemies, or they will continue to trouble you).

**5200. Saben ba Yeboa se: "Wohunu kɛntɛn nwono a, mmaa bɔ wo se".**
*Saben's son Yeboa says: "If you know how to weave baskets well, women hail you".*
(According to oral tradition, Yeboa was the first person to weave baskets. Hence: If you make beautiful things, women appreciate you).

**5201. Ɔsabokwani yɛ sen ɔbɔdamfoɔ.**
*A drunkard is more than a madman.*

**5202. Asaboɔne nne nkwanta.**
*Bad dancing has no crossroads.*
(A bad dancer forges ahead regardless of the pattern of the dance. Hence: A warning against over-stepping the mark).

**5203. Nsaduaa num, ebi kyene bi.**
*Among five fingers, some are greater than others.*
(There is precedence in society).

**5204. Sadwa ase nsa, yɛbɔ ho puo da ase, na yɛmmɔ no puo mfa mmɔ aketekyiwa.**
*Palm wine at the tapper's shed, we leave the dregs and throw them to the ground and give thanks to the tapper, but we don't throw out the dregs and break the tapper's pot.*
(When you finish drinking palm wine, you tip out the dregs onto the earth. Hence: You don't harm a person who has helped you).

**5205. Sadweam kɔ Aburokyire a ɔremfa hwee mma.**
*If the drunkard goes overseas, he will never come back again.*
(See Proverb 597. A drunkard has lost all sense of belonging to a particular society and never has the means to return home).

**5206. Sadweam ne Taadweam kɔ Aburokyire, wɔamma.**
*The drunkard and the smoker go abroad, but they do not came back.*
(See Proverb 597. People who lead indulgent lives do not prosper).

**5207. Safo nsa ne ho.**
*The healer cannot heal himself.*
(A physician is unable to heal himself).

**5208. Safoa ne krado, panin wɔ mu.**
*Between the key and the lock one is senior.*
(There must be a leader even amongst equals).

5209. Ɔsafohene Kwame Brenya na ɔse: ɔrentwa asuo nko ahweɛ da, na sɛ pitire bɛtɔ n'aboboano deɛ a, ɔbɛfa.
*The Asafo Company leader Kwame Brenya says that he will never cross the river to fish, but if the cat–fish lands on his doorstep, he will take it.*
(This proverb is local to Assempanye-Assin. Said by someone who will never seek a quarrel, but who is prepared to fight if challenged).

5210. Ɔsafohene nsuae na wako.
*A war leader does not swear in before he fights.*
(If you are a leader you don't take instructions before you act).

5211. Ɔsafoɔ na sɛ yɛreka twene a, ne nammorɔ mu nnyae no hyehyeɛ da.
*It is the dancer who when you beat the drum, you see his legs are twitching.*
(Someone who really enjoys something shows signs of his desire to join in).

5212. Saka-saka nnam ɔha, nanso emu koro mpo bu a, na ɔrehuan apakye.
*The centipede has a hundred legs, but even if one amongst them breaks, he limps.*
(Even if you are well provided with something and you lose the smallest part of it, it may cripple you).

5213. Sakate mpobi, yɛreko won na wɔresɔ mmɛbɛ.
*We are fighting the soldier ant and he too is seizing the grasshopper.*
(A brave person does not give up easily).

5214. Asakyee na ɛma yɛhunu kraa ba.
*Skillful dancing makes us notice a slave's child.*
(Talent can be found even among the lowly).

5215. Asakyire-nan, obiara nnidi nnya bi.
*The four Asakyire groups, none eats without the other.*
(The four Asakyire groups make up the rear-guard of the Asante army. They are Akrokerri at the head, Bɔberase, Kusa and Odumase. They have a brass basin which is filled each year for all to drink from. The proverb is used when a group of people always share what they have).

5216. Asamando yɛ ɔman a, anka yɛnkɔ no animia.
*If the after-world were a state, then we would not go there reluctantly.*
(If you knew something was good, you would accept it willingly).

5217. Nsamampɔ mu adaka, wohwɛ ho a, fɛfɛɛfɛ, wobue so a, awerɛhoɔ nko ara.
*The box in the graveyard, if you see it there, it is beautiful, but when you open it you see only sadness.*
(Don't judge by outward appearances).

5218. Nsamampɔ mu Kwaku: wo nni ni a, wonwe nwa kobi.
*Kwaku whose parents lie in the cemetery (says): "If you have no mother, you don't eat the snail's liver".*
(This is the best part of the snail. Hence: If you are without parents, the rest of the family does not treat you well).

5219. Nsamampɔ mu soaduro: wo ni wu a, w'abusua asa.
*The act of carrying the corpse to the cemetery: if your mother dies, (it makes you realize) the family is finished.*
(It is at the actual moment of burial that you realize the extent of your loss).

5220. Nsamampom twene, yɛde nkontommire na ayere soɔ nanso yɛde dadeɛ nkonta na ɛbɔ.
*You make the cemetery drum with cocoyam leaves, but none the less you play it with iron sticks.*
(With intelligence we can do the seemingly impossible).

5221. Ɔsaman a ne nti yɛtoto apono mu no, ɔba fie a, ɛnyɛ hu bio.
*If the ghost because of whom we close doors, comes into the house, it is not frightening anymore.*
(If something is familiar you cease to fear it).

5222. Ɔsaman mfa nsa ho hwee.
*The ghost has nothing to do with drink.*
(Things may sound alike but be quite different).

5223. Ɔsaman ahoɔhwam ne nunum.
*The smell of ghosts is like the nunum plant.*
(Ocimum viride, the nunum plant, has a distinctive odor. Ghosts, too, are supposed to leave a smell behind. Hence: If you use something such as a scent which is peculiar to yourself, you indicate your presence).

5224. Ɔsaman kyɛ adeɛ na sɛ anyɛ yie a, ateasefoɔ sane kyɛ.
*If a departed spirit shares something and does not do it well, human beings share it again.*
(The living decide in this world not the dead).

5225. Ɔsaman pa di odwan.
*A good ghost eats mutton.*
(A well-respected person will be highly thought of even after he has died).

5226. Osaman pa hyira ne ba.
*A good departed spirit blesses its child.*
(If you have a journey to take or something dangerous to perform you may call on your ancestors to protect you. Your safety may depend on the support of these ancestors. Hence: Good relationships help one to get on in life).

5227. Ɔsaman pa na yɛsosɔ ne soɔ na nyɛ ɔsaman bɔne.
*A good ghost, we take trouble over but not over a bad one.*
(You show respect to those who have helped you, even after death. Those who have harmed you you forget quickly).

5228. Ɔsaman pa na yɛto no badin.
*It is a good departed spirit after whom we name a child.*
(If you are respected in life, you will be remembered in death. You only name children after those you wish them to emulate).

5229. Ɔsaman se: "Ɛnyɛ ɛnnɛ nko ara ne anadwo".
*The departed spirit says: "It is not today alone that night falls".*
(If you are able to outwit your enemy once, do not be too complacent, for he may find another way to defeat you).

**5230. Ɔsaman tene ne nsa kyea wo a, wopono wo deɛ mu.**
*When a ghostly spirit holds out its hand to greet you, you close your fist.*
(A warning against allowing yourself to be led into serious trouble).

**5231. Ɔsaman ntwɛn teasefoɔ ansa na wadidi.**
*The departed spirit does not wait for the living before it begins to eat.*
(People can care for themselves without waiting for charity).

**5232. Ɔsaman nni biribi a, ɔwɔ ahyehyɛwakyire.**
*If the spirit of the departed has nothing else, he has something to be inherited.*
(A person never dies without leaving something, good or bad).

**5233. Asamando yɛ ɔman a, anka obi mfiri hɔ mmɛbisa aduane ha.**
*If the after-world is a state, then no one comes from it to ask for food here.*
(It is difficult to prove what you have no physical evidence of).

**5234. Asamanfoɔ reyan wɔn twene a, wɔde dadeɛ nkonta, na ɛyan nanso ɔteasefoɔ de ne nsa bɔ mu a, ɛpae mmienu.**
*When the departed spirits are beating their drums, they use iron drumsticks, but if the living use their hands to beat them, the skin splits in two.*
(Every group of people has its own way of doing things without courting trouble. But if a non-initiate tries, it upsets everything).

**5235. Nsamanfoɔ mpo se wɔpɛ dodoɔ na ɛnte sɛ ateasefoɔ.**
*Even the ghostly spirits say they want a many people, how much more the living.*
(Human beings are gregarious. Also: In the old days, people desired their numbers to increase constantly).

**5236. Nsamanfoɔ twene ɛse: "Ɛwɔ do, ɛwɔ do, ɛbɛba".**
*The drum of the departed spirits says: "It is there, it is there, it will come back".*
(You cannot lose what you are destined to have).

**5237. Saman-kwan, ebi rekɔ na ebi reba.**
*The spirit road, someone is going on it but someone is also coming.*
(Spirits are sometimes believed to be reincarnated within the same family. Hence: Life is continuous, even if individuals come and go).

**5238. Samanta se: ɔnim pae a, ɛnte se atawa pa.**
*The oil bean of the spirits (Bussea occidentalis) says: if it knew how to explode, it could not do it like the real oil bean tree (Pentadethra macrophylla).*
(The bean-like pods of the Pentadethra macrophylla explode to throw out the seeds when ripe. Even if one was able to develop certain qualities, one would not be as good as the best).

**5239. Samina kukuo bɔ a, ɛmfa ɔkraman ho.**
*If the pot containing soap breaks, it does not concern the dog.*
(You are unlikely to spoil what has no interest for you).

**5240. Nsamu ma ɔdehyeɛ yɛ dɔm.**
*Lack of discrimination makes a royal revolt.*
(A man of standing insists on his rights).

**5241. Yɛsane kokurobotie mmɔ po.**
*We cannot tie a knot without the thumb.*
(Used, for example, to refer to people who are essential to a project).

**5242. Ɔsansa fa adeɛ na ayerɛmo te a, ɔdeto hɔ.**
*The hawk takes a bone, but if lightening strikes it, it drops it.*
(You cannot foresee how your actions may be frustrated).

**5243. Ɔsansa fa dompe a, ɛtua n'ano kwa, ɔkraman dea.**
*If the hawk takes a bone, it holds it in its beak in vain. It belongs to the dog.*
(What is useful to one person is useless to another).

**5244. Ɔsansa firi ahunum reba se: "Mekokyere nipa madi" na afei ɔkɔwia akokɔ.**
*The hawk swoops from the sky saying: "I am going to catch a man to eat", but in the end it steals a chicken.*
(Don't take any notice of the idle boasting of a bully. He will only attack those weaker than himself).

**5245. Ɔsansa kɔ abu a, ɔde n'akyi gya akorɔma.**
*When the kite goes to sit on its eggs, it leaves the hawk to keep watch.*
(When a paramount chief has to be away, there is always someone under him to take charge. Hence: Authority can be delegated when necessary).

**5246. Ɔsansa kurokotiako: ɔrebɛyɛ deɛn na ama woɔ a worebɔ no mmrane?**
*The kite: what is it coming to do for you that you sing its praise names?*
(Said of someone who praises a bad man in the hope that he may forward his cause).

**5247. Ɔsansa se: adeɛ a Onyame ayɛ nyinaa yɛ.**
*The kite says: everything God does is good.*

**5248. Ɔsansa se: akorɔnneɛ ɔnkyɛre wɔ nnipa nsam.**
*The kite says: a stolen thing does not stay long with a person.*
(Easy come, easy go).

**5249. Asansanfoɔ kuro nyɛɛ kɛse da.**
*The town of the ne'er-do-wells has never grown big.*
(Used as a warning to people who lead a bad life, that their community cannot prosper that way).

**5250. Ɔsansani due ne ho bo.**
*A good-for-nothing person is haughty.*
(A useless person shows off).

**5251. Ɔsansani nni animuonyam.**
*A good-for-nothing has no respect.*

**5252. Nsansono-dɔtɔ, yɛnto no pam.**
*The thicket of stinging plants, we do not give it a stake.*
(We do not encourage harmful things).

5253. Asantefoɔ ani bɛteɛ no, na Mosifoɔ awe ananka ama ananka asa.
*Before the people of Asante become aware, the Moshis have eaten all the puff adders (lit.: eaten the puff-adders and made the puff adders all get finished).*
(People often do not realise the value of their own things until they are all gone).

5254. Asantekwaa bɔtɔ, yɛnhwɛ mu kwa.
*The Asante citizen's sack, we don't look in it with impunity.*
(If you are the member of a strong family, people do not interfere with you).

5255. Wo santene yɛ tia a, wonnyae nkɔdi tentene mu.
*If your queue is short, you do not leave it to join a long one.*
(You don't desert a position of advantage to take up a worse one).

5256. Asanturofie abususɛm nti na yɛmfa no mma fie.
*Because of the nightjar's taboos, we don't bring it into the house.*
(You don't wittingly invite trouble into your home).

5257. Asanturofie anomaa, wofa no a, woafa mmusuo, wogyae no a, woagyae siadeɛ; na gyina hɔ merekɔ aba, nsoɛ?
*The nightjar, if you take it, you take trouble, if you free it, you lose good luck; what about (telling it) wait and I will come for you?*
(Used in reference to people who always bring trouble to their friends, but who are missed when they're not there).

5258. Sapɔ-funu yɛfa no hiada.
*The rotten sponge, we use it in times of need.*
(In time of need we use even those things which we normally discard).

5259. Nsapuo na ema yɛ hunu ɔnomfoɔ.
*How you pour out the dregs show us if you are a habitual drinker.*
(You can recognise a specialist by the way he acts).

5260. Sasabonsam a wabu akyakya na ɛte sɛ mmoatia ahasa.
*If the forest devil grows a hump, it is still like three of the little people (i.e. fairies).*
(See Proverb 461. Even in extremity, a great man excels his fellows).

5261. Sasabonsam ba wɔmfa no fo.
*No one takes the forest devil's child with ease.*
(If you want to wrest something from a powerful man, it is not easy).

5262. Sasabonsam ko ayie a, ɔsoɛ ɔbayifoɔ fie.
*If the Sasabonsam goes to a funeral, he stays in a witch's house.*
(Like seeks like).

5263. Sasabonsam te-ase dada a, ɔse ɔyɛ ɔbayifoɔ, na akɔwie sɛ ɔsi odum atifi na odum nso so mmoatia.
*In normal times they say that the forest devil is a witch, then how much more so when he is found sitting on an odum tree, that bears the fruit of dwarfs.*
(If you fear something in normal times, how much more so in times of trouble).

5264. "Sato, sato" na ɛmaa Akonnwa tɔn n'akoa.
*"Take and throw away, take and throw away" made the Stool sell its servant.*
(Too much giving away brings poverty).

5265. Ɔsatofoo nnim animka.
*The rogue does not understand criticism.*
(You cannot change the character of a bad man).

5266. Wo se akyi nyɛ wo dɛ a, ɛhɔ ara na wotaferɛ.
*The back of your teeth does not taste sweet, but you lick there just the same.*
(You have to accept circumstances as they are).

5267. Wose ɔbaa pɛ, na ɔsere bɔ ne nsam kyerɛ wo a, na wawie wo asɛm ka.
*If you say you love a woman, and she smiles and claps her hands at you, then she has already replied to you.*
(Actions speak louder than words).

5268. Yɛse biribi reba a, na ɛwɔ deɛ aba pɛn.
*If we say something is coming, it means what has happened before.*
(There is nothing new in the world, everything has happened before).

5269. Wose worenni akyire nso worenni anim, na sɛ ɛka wo nko a, wobɛyɛ dɛn?
*You say you won't keep to the back, neither will you lead, but if you are left alone, where will you be?*
(If you are too particular, you lose your friends).

5270. Yɛse: "Mahyɛ wo bosome" na yɛnka sɛ: "Mahyɛ wo nsoramma."
*We say: "I have given you the moon" but we do not say: "I have given you the stars".*
(I have given you a set time but not infinite license).

5271. Yɛse "ɛko" ansa na yɛase "ɛno".
*We say "one" before we say "two".*
(One thing at a time; first things first).

5272. Yɛse yɛnnkɔ ɔyarefoɔ ho a, na nyɛ deɛ ɔma no aduro.
*If we say we should not go near a sick person, it is not the person who gives the medicine.*
(There are exceptions to every rule).

5273. Yɛse yɛnkɔku wo a, ɛne wo mene mu, ɛntra nnuru wo moma so.
*If we say we are going to kill you, by cutting your throat, it won't reach your forehead.*
(You can only do your worst).

5274. Yɛse: "Akonta, gye", na yɛnka sɛ: "Akonta, bɔ mako mu".
*We say: "Brother-in-law take", but we don't say: "Brother-in-law use pepper to put in my eyes".*
(You give things to your brother-in-law but you also expect him to take your side in family matters).

5275. Yɛse: "Krɔkɔtoe" na yɛnse sɛ: "Krɔkɔseneɛe".
*We say: "Coming to meet you submissively" but we do not say: "Go and be arrogant over the person you have met".*
(If you go to share with someone's family, don't throw your weight about).

5276. Yɛse: "Ɔkwantenten akwaaba", na yɛnse: "Ɔkwantia akwaaba".

*We say: "Welcome from a long journey," but we do not say: "Welcome from a short journey".*
(If you achievement is great you are praised for it, but not for small successes).

**5277. Wose Akyea Mɛnsa nwuiɛ na ɔwɔ he?**
*You say that Akyea Mɛnsa has not died, but where is he?*
(Akyea Mensah was chief of Apadwa in Akim. In the early 1940's when the Ɔkyenhene died, he vanished and it was suspected he was beheaded to go with the Ɔkyenhene. A policeman by pretending to be a fetish priest uncovered all those guilty of his murder and they were prosecuted. Hence: If you swear something is true, you have to prove it).

**5278. Yɛse yɛrema adeɛ no abere na ayɛ dɛ, nanso sɛ ɛbere a, na ɛyɛ ya.**
*We say we are waiting for something to ripen before it becomes sweet, but when it ripens, it becomes bitter.*
(Things do not always live up to expectataions).

**5279. Yɛse yɛmma kramo yaakɔ nso yɛma daa.**
*We say we don't condole a Moslem, but we do it always.*
(No matter how strict a rule is, we are always breaking it).

**5280. Wose worepɛ mmirika atu, na wo nantwie te ahoma a, na wadom wo.**
*You say you want to run, so if your cow breaks her rope, she does you a favour.*
(An apparent misfortune sometimes works out for one's good).

**5281. Yɛse: "Yɛrepɛ twene-soafoɔ" a, ɔkyekye nso se: "Me na me tiri ho wɔ apɔ me na mɛsoa".**
*We say: "We are looking for someone to carry the drum", the broad-fronted crocodile says: "I've got bumps all over my head or otherwise I would have carried it".*
(Someone who wants to avoid work can always find an excuse for doing so).

**5282. Wose: "Pumpunu mpunu" a, na ɛpunu.**
*If you say "Let the storehouse swell up", it swells up.*
(It is easy to make a situation worse).

**5283. Wose wobɛsom Nyankopɔn a, som no prɛko, na mfrɛ biribi mmata ho.**
*If you say you are going to serve Almighty God, serve Him alone, but don't add anything to it.*
(You cannot serve God and also attend fetishes or other "gods". If you serve God you serve Him alone).

**5284. Wose ɔsrane anim nyɛ fɛ, na worekɔpopa anaasɛ worekosɛɛ no?**
*You say the face of the moon is not beautiful, but are you going to wipe it away or to destroy it?*
(Said when someone criticises to no purpose).

**5285. Yɛse yɛnsu a, na nyɛ okunafoɔ.**
*If we say we do not weep, this does not appply to widows.*
(There are exceptions to every rule).

**5286. Yɛse yɛnsu a, nteesoo deɛ, yɛteeso.**
*If we say we should not weep, still, as for sobs, we sob them.*
(If you can't do things one way, you do them another).

**5287. Yɛse wo bi a, tie, na kyenkyentakyi kuro yɛtu so a, yɛnwie yie.**
*If we advise you, listen, because if we vacate a town of litigation, we won't prosper.*
(Prolonged litigation, even if you are the winning party, leads to misfortune).

**5288. Yɛnse ɔsempɛfoɔ sɛ: "Bɛda na manna bi."**
*We don't say to an inquisitive person: "Come and sleep and let me sleep a bit".*
(You can't make a man act against his own nature).

**5289. Sɛ wo ba sane awoeɛ a, na wanha wo berɛ.**
*If your baby dies at birth, then it did not cause you trouble.*
(If something bad is destined to happen, it is better it happens quickly and you avoid extra suffering).

**5290. Sɛ ɔbaa se ɔhia awoɔ a, na ɔne kɔtedie.**
*If a woman says she needs a child then she is referring to sexual (lit.: penis) matters.*
(One thing leads to another. There are indirect ways of showing that you are ready to do something).

**5291. Se abɛ bere a, nnomaa nyinaa di bi.**
*When the palm nuts ripen, all the birds eat some.*
(When opportunity comes all people take advantage of it).

**5292. Sɛ wobɛn mmaa kwansɛn ase pii a, [wode ɛta bɔ wo]/[wɔ mma wonu nkwan mu.]**
*If you are always near the women's soup pot, [you are beaten with the ladle]/[you are asked to stir the soup.]*
(If a man hangs around women at work, he won't be treated with respect).

**5293. Sɛ aberewa wu na yɛde aberewa di n'adeɛ a, na owufoɔ no ayie na yɛatu ahyɛ da.**
*If an old lady dies and we take another old lady to inherit her, then it is the deceased's funeral that has been postponed.*
(It is better to replace something old with something new).

**5294. Sɛ obi ka sɛ "Saman kwan ware na wokɔ a, ma me nte wo ka" a, na ɔrempɛ wuo awie.**
*If someone says "The road to the spirit world si long, when you go there, send me a message", then that person does not want to die.*
(If someone asks for feed-back from where you are going, it means they are reluctant to go there themselves).

**5295. Sɛ obi kowu ɔbɔfoɔ nnanso a, ɛnyɛ ɔno na ɔkum no, nanso ɔno na ɔkyerɛ n'awusɛɛ.**
*If someone dies at a hunter's cottage, he did not kill him, but he has to explain the reason of the deceased's death.*
(If someone gets into trouble in your house, you cannot avoid becoming involved in his troubles).

**5296. Sɛ obi apa da wo nsa a, oni no na wodane no.**
*If someone's handcuff is round your wrists then you are at his mercy.*
(A person is in the power of the one who actually controls the situation).

5297. Sɛ obi repɛ fie bi mu akɔ ama woawo no, na wannya hɔ ankɔ a, na ɔkɔ hɔ awareɛ.
*If someone wishes to be born into a certain family and is unable to be so, then he will marry into the family.*
(The soul is supposed to have a choice as to where it is to be born. If it chooses a family and cannot be born into it, later on, when it is born elsewhere it will marry into that family. Through marriage you join your spouse's family. If you are determined to achieve something you will do so).

5298. Sɛ obi atofo kɛseɛ nti na wo kɔte asɔre a, ma no nna; na nyɛ ɛtwɛ nyininaa na odwamanfoɔ die.
*If it is someone's big behind that makes your penis rise, let it rest; because it is not all vaginas that a lecher can enjoy.*
(Don't get excited over something that has nothing to do with you).

5299. Sɛ aboa hahani se dompo ho bona, na ɔno nso, ɔdaa sɛn.
*If the stinking ant says the marsh mongoose smells bad, what about itself? (lit. but it too, how does it?)*
(The pot calling the kettle black).

5300. Sɛ aboa no tutu afuo ase na ɔtutu no yie a, ɔhunu nnipa a, ɔnnwane.
*If the animal uproots the farm and he does it well, when he sees a human being he does not run away.*
(If you work well, you are not afraid of criticism).

5301. Sɛ mmoa rekyerɛ ahoɔ fɛ a, wɔyi osebɔ.
*If the animals are holding a beauty contest, they take the leopard to be preeminent.*
(If you fear someone you praise them to their face).

5302. Sɛ mmoa nyinaa we borɔdeɛ a, wode hyɛ ɔdabɔ.
*If all animals chew plantain, you blame the bay duiker.*
(Why single out one person for blame when all do it?)

5303. Sɛ w'abɔgyeɛ rewae na yɛrekɔtwa ahoma abɛkyekyere ama wo a, wonse sɛ: "Moamma ntɛm a, meregyae mu!"
*If your jawbone is falling off and we are going to cut a string to tie it, you don't say: "If you don't come quickly, I am going to stop holding it!"*
(If someone helps you when you are in trouble, don't chivy them).

5304. Sɛ abosonnam yɛ ɔboafoɔ dɛ pii a, ne mfirikyiwa yera.
*If the priest's helpers like the fetish's meat too much, they lose their castanets.*
(Excess brings ill results).

5305. Sɛ wobu odwan mmɛn a, na woanya no.
*If you break the horns of the sheep, it is powerless.*
(If you remove a man's weapons, you can do as you like with him).

5306. Sɛ Oburoni annwansi wo yie a, obi nyɛ wo ayɛ yie.
*If the European does not sneeze in your interest, you cannot get a good omen for the day.*
(If a lucky person sneezes near you, you say, "I am watching your nose," meaning "I expect you to bring me luck". If the person you depend on does not show the necessary attention, you do not flourish).

5307. Sɛ ɔdabɔ di asɛm na ɔdi bem a, ɔde n'ani to ɔwansane hyire so.
*If the bay duiker has a case and is found not guilty, he relies on the white clay of the bush buck.*
(The white clay is needed to wear in the celebration of winning a case. Hence: When you need something you cultivate those who have it).

5308. Sɛ wode bɛgu aboa no kuro mu na ɔbɛtafere deɛ, fa gu ne tɛkrɛma so prɛko.
*If you intend to put something on an animal's sore, it will lick it off, so put it straight onto its tongue.*
(There is no point in helping a person who does not appreciate what you are doing. It is better to give him the means of helping himself).

5309. Sɛ yɛde ahoma hyɛ kontoa kon na sɛ ɛte a, yɛfrɛ no toateɛ.
*If we take a string and tie it round the neck of a gourd and if it breaks we call it "tied and broken".*
(If two people stay together and then separate their union is always remembered).

5310. Sɛ wode bɛka no bɔne na woasane aka no yie no, fa ka no yie prɛko.
*If you are going to say something bad and correct it, better to say the right thing at first.*
(Do what you do properly the first time and then you won't have to correct it).

5311. Sɛ yɛde akonnwa kɛseɛ na ɛdi ahene, a anka nkonnwasenfoɔ yɛ ahemfo.
*If we were to consider possession of a big stool as a qualification for being a chief, then stool-carvers would be chiefs.*
(Don't confuse the symbol with reality. The fact that you own something does not mean you have the right to use it).

5312. Sɛ yɛde "Mea, mea", na ɛdi hene a, anka obi nsiane akyenkyena ho nni akonnwa.
*If we consider "It is me, it is me", as a qualification to become chief, then no one can overtake the allied hornbill in gaining the stool.*
("Mea, mea", is the cry of this hornbill and also its nickname. Hence: Entitlement takes precedence over all else).

5313. Sɛ wode bɛyɛ onipa yie deɛ, fa yɛ aboa yie.
*Instead of being kind to a human being, be kind to an animal.*
(Human beings are ungrateful, it would be better to lavish your kindness on animals who appreciate it).

5314. Sɛ wo deɛ nyɛ no, saa ara na obi deɛ nyɛ.
*If your own thing is no good, in just the same way someone else's thing is of no use.*
(What is salt for the goose is salt for the gander).

5315. Sɛ wobɛdi adɔdɔdeɛ ahunu amane na woawu atɔfowuo deɛ, di abɛbrɛsɛ na wu w'akrawuo.
*If you are going to live a good life which leads you to commit suicide, then better suffer and die your natural death.*
(It is better to live simply and survive than have riches which lead to death).

5316. Sɛ wobɛdi afasɛɛ ama asɛm afa w'aseɛ deɛ, di nkamfoɔ ma yɛnkamfo wo.
*If you are eating water yam so that a case takes you by surprise, then it would be better to eat nkamfoɔ yam and let us congratulate you.*
(If you keep good company you prosper, whereas bad company brings trouble. A play on words. Afaseɛ is water yam; afa w'aseɛ means "take you by surprise". Nkamfoɔ means yam; yɛnkamfo means "let us congratulate you").

5317. Sɛ wodi akwakutire a, na ɛsoso wo daeɛ.
*If you eat a monkey's head, you will never stop having nightmares.*
(The meat on a monkey's head is considered bad. If you do bad things you will have trouble).

5318. Sɛ wodidi na woammee a, na ɛfiri wo sika.
*If you eat and you are not satisfied, it is because of your money.*
(What you pay for you get, no more, no less).

5319. Sɛ dɔm tu kɔ a, kagya na wɔde no gya amanfo so.
*When the army leaves, it is Griffonia simplicifolia that they leave at the deserted place.*
(An army may cut down the forest at its encampment, leaving only weeds, like Griffonia simplicafolia. Hence: Said of an apparently unimportant person, who is always hanging around somewhere).

5320. Sɛ odurugya hyɛn a, yɛnsɔ gya ano.
*When the flute is blown, we don't make fire.*
(On really serious occasions you don't bother about cooking and other niceties of life).

5321. Sɛ afafantɔ mpɛ nsa a, anka ɔnte sakwanso.
*If the butterfly does not like drink, then it does not remain on the road to the palm wine still.*
(Said of a man who protests he does not drink yet is always found around bars).

5322. Sɛ mframa fa adeɛ ma wo a, fa boɔ to so.
*If the wind brings you a present, put a stone on top of it.*
(Take care of what is given to you or it may go missing).

5323. Sɛ Egyaanam a ne se yɛ nam antumi ammɔ dompe mu a, nyɛ kakabo a kaka adidi ne sɛ ase na ɔbɛtumi.
*If Enduring-fire who has strong teeth has not been able to chew the bone, it is not a person with toothache whose teeth are broken who can do so.*
(If a strong person fails, a weak one cannot succeed).

5324. Sɛ wobɛgye odwan ama yɛadwan wo ho deɛ, firi fifire ma yɛmfa mfiri wo.
*If you are going to take a sheep so that we can make use of you later on, then better sweat so that we credit you.*
(It is better to work and earn, than to take something and be made to suffer for it).

5325. Sɛ ahennwa wo animuonyam a, na ɛnkyerɛ sɛ ɔhene a ɔte nso anim yɛ nam.
*Even if the stool is respected, it does not mean that the chief is worthy of respect.*
(A position can remain respected, even when its incumbent is unworthy).

5326. Sɛ ehia wo na deɛ ɔbɛhwɛ woɔ no nso, ehia no a, na adɛre wo.
*If you are in need and the person who is caring for you is also in need, you are in flames.*
(The needy cannot help the needy).

5327. Sɛ wo ho annwo wo a, na ɛfiri wo ara.
*If you are not content, it is because of your own self.*
(Content and peace of mind come as a result of your own actions, not those of others).

5328. Sɛ ahoma te na ɛtoa a, na ɛpɔ aba mu.
*If a long string breaks and you join it, a knot comes into it.*
(Relationships once broken can never be the same again).

5329. Sɛ wobɛhono abosom ama wo nkoa anom ama wɔasuro woɔ no, kum odwan ma wɔnni na wɔnnɔ wo.
*Instead of using herbal concoctions to give your servants to drink as a charm to make them fear you, kill a sheep and let them eat and they will love you.*
(It is better to make people act through love than fear).

5330. Sɛ wohunu sɛ obi te pɔnkɔdua so a, na ɛkyerɛ sɛ ɔrekɔpɛ biribi abɛdi.
*If you see that someone is on a log boat, it shows that he is looking for something to eat.*
(The pɔnkɔdua is a log used as a boat for fishing on Lake Bosomtwe. Hence: If you see a man with his working tools, you know he is trying to earn a living).

5331. Sɛ wohunu sɛ ɔnwamma-aba rehuru a, na brampoɔ ne no.
*If you see the ɔnwamma (Ricinodendron heullotii) fruit ferment, then it heralds the season of heavy rains.*
(Said when some sign shows that there will be trouble).

5332. Sɛ wohunu [awidie]/[ako] koro a, nto no boɔ, na ebia na ɔfiri dodoɔ mu.
*If you see a lone [grey parrot]/[parrot], don't throw a stone at it, for perhaps it is one of a flock.*
(No individual is without supporters, so be careful about attacking an apparently solitary man).

5333. Sɛ wobɛhuri asi w'anan mu deɛ a, fanyinam saa gyina hɔ ara.
*If you will jump and land on the same spot, then you had better stand there without jumping.*
(It is better to do nothing at all than to do something useless).

5334. Sɛ ahyehyewonsa nyɛ aserewa dɛ a, anka yɛmfa nsum no fidie.
*If the ahyehyewonsa fruit (Urera near mannii) was not sweet to the sunbird, then we would not take it to trap it.*
(If you want to attract someone, you have to offer them what they like).

5335. Sɛ yɛka adwene a, na koobi hyɛ dua ase.
*If we are talking of fish, there is koobi fish which is hiding among the tree roots (under water).*
(Adwene is a fish, but also means thought or idea. Hence: If we need wisdom, there is a source of it somewhere out of reach. So: You can't always get the help you need).

**5336. Sɛ woreka nokorɛ a, yɛnka sɛ wasem ware.**
*If you are speaking the truth, we don't say your speech is too long.*
(Truth is always satisfying).

**5337. Sɛ wobɛka atafere ama anya woɔ deɛ, di ma ɛnya wo.**
*If you are going to taste something so that you will get diarrhea, eat your fill so that you will get it.*
(In for a penny, in for a pound).

**5338. Sɛ ɔkafoɔ adeɛ kɔ amoamu a, ɔno ara na ɔtɔn.**
*If the debtor's property is going to be sold, he himself sells it.*
(It is you alone who control your own property and you should be responsible for your own actions).

**5339. Sɛ Ɔkanni rede ne nsa hwɛ soro na ɔka sɛ: "Nyame wɔ hɔ" a, ebia na ɔrekyerɛ ne gyedie, anaasɛ ɔde ne were na ɛrehyɛ Nyame mu ahwehwɛ mmoa afiri ne hɔ.**
*When an Akan person points to the sky and says: "God is there," maybe he is showing his faith, but maybe he is putting his trust in God to whisk animals off him.*
(Don't point to the skies and ask God to act for you, when you should be doing something yourself).

**5340. Sɛ koterɛ bɔ tɔfa ma wo a, nka sɛ ɛsua ɛfiri sɛ deɛ ne nsa tumi bɔ ara ne no.**
*If the lizard squeezes mashed yam to give you, don't say that there is not enough, because that is all its hand can press.*
(Be grateful when people do the best they can for you and don't expect more than they have to give).

**5341. Sɛ wokɔ baabi na koterɛ tare dan ho a, ɛnto boɔ mmɔ no ɛfiri sɛ ebia na ɛho dansifoɔ ne no.**
*If you go somewhere and find a lizard clinging to a house, don't throw a stone at it, for it may be the builder of the house.*
(Don't show disrespect to someone you don't know in a strange place).

**5342. Sɛ wobɛkɔ Kwaku Firi so, ama wɔagye wo adwan deɛ, fa tena Adudwan na di odwan.**
*If you are going to Kwaku Firi (a fetish) so that they collect a sheep from you, better to stay at Adudwan and eat mutton.*
(Make good use of what you own, rather than letting yourself be cheated out of it).

**5343. Sɛ yɛnko ayie-ase a, anikyerɛ deɛ yɛbu.**
*If we don't quarrel at a funeral, at least we can give insulting looks.*
(There is a way of getting around even things which are tabooed).

**5344. Sɛ ɛkɔm bɛkum wo biribi ama woasɛe sika ayɛ no ayie deɛ, ma no biribi nni na ɔnya akwa, na ɔnya akwa a, ɔte wo mpobiano.**
*If hunger is going to kill your relation to make you lose money on their funeral, give them something to eat so that they remain alive, because if they are alive they are there for your profit.*
(No living person is useless. It is better to keep people alive than to have to waste money on a funeral).

**5345. Sɛ akɔɔwere nyɛ ɔbaatan pa a, anka ɔbɛboro ne mma ama wɔawuwu.**
*If the Senegal kingfisher were not a really good mother, then it would beat its children to death.*
(This bird is always scolded by others. If someone were not patient, they would be unable to stand up to family troubles).

**5346. Sɛ kosua tɔ nkrane mu a, ma no nna mu, na wɔnam ho kwa.**
*If an egg falls amongst black ants, let it be, for they worry about it in vain.*
(If someone is well-protected, don't worry about them).

**5347. Sɛ nkosua mmienu bɔ mu a, Nyankopɔn nko ara na ɔte aseɛ.**
*When two eggs come together, they form what can only be understood by God.*
(God alone understands the mysteries of life).

**5348. Sɛ koteɛ ne ɛtwɛ di kokoam agorɔ a, ɔkra firi damparɛɛ bɛdi adanseɛ.**
*If the penis and vagina play about in secrecy, the soul (cat) from above will act as a witness.*
(The ɔkra or individual soul enters the body on conception. "Ɔkra" also means cat. Thus a person's destiny may depend on the casual actions of others. Hence: Any action, however frivolous may have serious results).

**5349. Sɛ wo koteɛ wu a, wontwa ntwene; wodwonsɔ mu.**
*If your penis dies, you don't cut it off; you use it to urinate.*
(Members of the family who are useless for one thing, may be useful for another. So, don't reject them).

**5350. Sɛ wokɔto aserewa sɛ ɔte ne fie a, nka sɛ ɔsua, ebia na ne panin mu ara ne no.**
*If you go and meet a sunbird in its house, don't tell it it is small, for it may be the elder there.*
(Every man is king of his own castle).

**5351. Sɛ kɔtɔkɔ wɔ hɔ a, apɛsɛ nkyerɛ mmusuo.**
*If the porcupine is present, the brush-tailed porcupine does not explain taboos.*
(Kɔtɔkɔ is the porcupine, symbol of the Asante nation. Apɛsɛ is a smaller animal. Hence: If the elder is present, you do not ask for the advice of an ordinary person).

**5352. Sɛ nkrane nni se a, anka wɔrenkeka nnipa.**
*If ants did not have teeth, they would not bite people.*
(We judge people by their actions).

**5353. Sɛ wo nkrantɛ hyɛ wo mmɔtoa mu na ɛfifiri tɔ a, wɔnto ntwene.**
*If your cutlass is under your arm and falls to the ground, you don't throw it away.*
(You look after your family whatever happens to them).

**5354. Sɛ wokum apɛsɛ na wode ne ti kyerɛkyerɛ kɔtɔkɔ a, na worebu no bɛ.**
*If you kill the brush-tailed porcupine and show its head to the crested porcupine, you will be speaking to it in proverbs.*
(Victory over a less important man will be taken as a warning by his superior).

5355. Sɛ wobɛkum toromo agye asasaduro deɛ, gyae no ma ɔnante ne hahan mu.
*If you are going to kill the bongo and you have to take a bath in protective medicine, then you had better leave it to wander in the bush.*
(The spirit of the bongo is very strong (sasa) and if you kill one you have to protect yourself by using medicines. Hence: Some things are best left alone, because of the trouble they entail).

5356. Sɛ kuntunkuni fata mmarima deɛ a, ɛnneɛ yaapeese nso bɛfata mmaa.
*If the brown (funeral) cloth suits men well, then the heavy black cloth (used for housework and farming) suits women.*
(If men claim that a cloth of ill-omen suits them, then women are suited by one that means hard work. If something inferior is admired, how much more something which is useful).

5357. Sɛ kurotwiamansa Kwadwo se wagyae ne nkwaseasɛm di a, na ɔnse sɛ Akua Abirekyie mmɛwo n'afikyire na ɔmfa ne ho mfa ne ba.
*If the leopard Kwadwo says he has stopped playing the fool, he does not say that Akua the goat should come and give birth in his back yard and go scot free with her child.*
(Don't tempt a reformed sinner!)

5358. Sɛ nkuruma sɛn ogya ani a, ɛsɛn hɔ ma ɔwansane.
*If the okro hangs over the fire, it hangs there for the bushbuck.*
(The seeds are dried and used the following season. When they are planted, animals raid them. Hence: Said when the person who benefits is not the intended one).

5359. Sɛ ɔkwasea bɛwu ama woayɛ no ayie deɛ, ɔyare a hwehwe no.
*If a fool is going to die so that you perform his funeral rites, rather look after him when he is ill.*
(Prevention is better than getting into debt).

5360. Sɛ yɛkyɛ animuonyam na woanya be a, animguaseɛ ba a, wonnya bi.
*If we share out honours and you don't get any, if ignominy comes you do not suffer from it.*
(If you don't have responsibility, you don't get blame).

5361. Sɛ woma ɔbaa kɔkɔɔ serem yɛ wo dɛ pii a, nkura de wo tirase yɛ twononoo.
*If you allow a fair-skinned woman's thighs to be too sweet to you, mice make a path over your head.*
(If you overindulge yourself, you lay yourself open to abuse).

5362. Sɛ woma wo bɔfo-twene yɛ wo dɛ bebrebe a, w'apretwa a te yera.
*If you allow your hunter's drum to be too sweet to you, your hunter's bag tears and goes astray.*
(If you overindulge in anything, you lose by it).

5363. Sɛ mogya wɔ abebeɛ mu a, anka nyɛ ɛne sɛ, wotu no a biribiara nni mu yi.
*If there were to be blood in the water snail, you would find it if you sucked it out (of its shell).*
(Said to a skeptic who doubts the truth of what you are saying).

5364. Sɛ mmusuo di w'akyi na ɛda onyina so a, wobɔ panhwam kɔfa.
*If you are followed by misfortune and it is in the branches of the silk-cotton (Bombax buonopozense) tree, you will by all means go there and take it.*
(If you are destined to suffer, you will suffer).

5365. Sɛ ɛna bɛwuo ama manya me ho deɛ, ɔntena hɔ na ɛnhia me.
*If mother is going to die for me to get my own things, it were better for her to remain there for me to be poor (lit. let her remain there and let me be poor).*
(Nothing replaces the value of a mother).

5366. Sɛ wonam asunam hwene so ku no a, ne dua deɛ ɛkɔ mfensa.
*If you aim at a fish's nose and kill it, its tail will go for ever.*
(If a man is destroyed, so are his followers).

5367. Sɛ yɛn ani bere a, na yɛfura kɔbene.
*If we are sad, we wear kɔbene.*
(Kɔbene is an orange funeral cloth. Hence: You dress according to how you feel; or according to the occasion).

5368. Sɛ wo ni ba ne [Akwasi Apɔɔfee]/[Abebeɛ] a, anka ɔba wo fie a, woremma no akonnwa sɛ ontena so?
*If your mother's child were [Kwasi Apɔɔfee]/[the Water snail] if he came to your house you would not offered him a seat to sit on.*
(The water snail does not have a flat bottom, so an offfer of a seat would be ridiculing it. Hence: Don't ridicule someone because of physical shortcomings).

5369. Sɛ wo nnɔbaeɛ anso wo ntoma tɔ mpo a, ɛso w'ano aduane.
*Even if your harvest is not enough to buy cloth, it is sufficient for you to eat it (lit: for your mouth's food).*
(Survival is more important than acquiring property).

5370. Sɛ anobrebrɛ nyinaa mu wɔ nokorɛdie a, anka obi nni asɛm nni fɔ.
*If all humility were to contain honesty, then no one would have litigation and be pronounced guilty.*
(Actions count more than words. You cannot judge a man by his words).

5371. Sɛ nokorɛ hyɛ wo ni twɛ mu a, fa wo kɔte kɔyi, na woyɛ saa a, na wonnii no.
*Even if truth is in your mother's vagina, use your penis to take it out, for when you do that you have not had sex with her.*
(It is best to tell the truth however difficult the circumstances are).

5372. Sɛ anomaa sua a, ɛnkyerɛ sɛ yɛwe ne ntakara.
*Even if a bird is small, that doesn't mean we should eat its feathers.*
(You need to pay attention to the proper solution of even small problems).

5373. Sɛ anomaa no retu afiri ne buo mu a, na ɔsɛe mu.
*If a bird is deserting its nest, then it fouls it.*
(If a man wants to leave his family he quarrels with them first).

5374. Sɛ anomaa-tawa se ɔbɛha nnomaa nyinaa a, ɛnyɛ ɔkɔrepɔn a.
*If the drongo says it will trouble all the birds, this does not include the eagle.*
(A man may cause trouble for many but avoids doing so to those who are more powerful than himself).

5375. Sɛ wo nua ne abobɔnnua a, ɔwu a, wobɛyɛ no ayie de a, tɔ akuma ma no ntɛm na mma no mmfa ne ti mmobɔ nnua mu nnwu.
*If your brother is a woodpecker and it dies, you perform its funeral rites; so but an axe for it immediately so that it may not die from knocking its head against a tree.*
(If you have a relation who is in trouble, help him at once. Hence: A stitch in time saves nine).

5376. Sɛ annuanom baanu nka mpo a, wɔda anadwo a wɔdi nkɔmmɔ.
*Even if two brothers are at loggerheads, when they go to bed they converse.*
(Family quarrels are settled with ease. Brothers often share bedrooms or even beds).

5377. Sɛ wonya adeɛ a, amankuo di bi, sɛ wonya eka deɛ a, na wadwane agya wo.
*If you have something the rhinoceros beetle eats a bit, but if you have a debt, it runs away and leaves you.*
(Said of people who are only fair–weather friends).

5378. Sɛ woannya wo wɔfa ba anaa wo se wɔfaase anware no a, wode no yɛ nua.
*If you are unable to marry your mother's brother's child nor your father's sister's child, you take them as sister or brother.*
(A thing remains within the family even if you do not yourself gain possession of it).

5379. Sɛ wɔpamo akyakyani na woanto no a, na ɛnyɛ ne mmirika-tuo ntira na mmom ne ho sereɛ ntira.
*If you chase a hunchback and you don't succeed, it is not because of his swiftness but because of his laughable figure.*
(Some apparent disadvantages bring advantages).

5380. Sɛ pampankwa da bamma ho, no wode huna ɔpanin na wannwane a, wode huna akɔdaa a, ɔnnwane.
*If the bush cutlass lies on the veranda and you threaten an elder with it and he does not flee, if you threaten a child with it, he also does not flee.*
(A child imitates the elders. If they do not fear, neither does he).

5381. Sɛ papa nyɛ hwee a, bɔne nso nyɛ hwee.
*If very good does not matter, then bad also does not matter.*
(If you don't care about good, you don't mind bad).

5382. Sɛ worepɛ akyekyedeɛ abɔ no atirimuɔden a, na wose no sɛ: "Hohoro wo nsa bra ma yɛnnidi".
*If you wish to be mean to the tortoise you say to it: "Wash your hands and come and dine with me".*
(You should not ask the impossible from someone. Don't taunt those who cannot help their shortcomings).

5383. Sɛ apoobɔ yɛ ahoɔden a, anka ɔkraman sene kurotwiamansa.
*If mere agressivenenss were to be valour, then the dog would be greater than the leopard.*
(Said of someone whose bark is worse than his bite).

5384. Sɛ [aponkyerɛne]/[atwerɛ] su sɛ: "Hwan na ɔbɛsee me? Hwan na ɔbɛsee me?" a, ɛdɔm tem dinn. Nanso sɛ ɔsu sɛ: "Hwan na ɔbedi m'adeɛ? Hwan na ɔbedi m'adeɛ?" a, ɔnya dɔm ma wɔgu no sɛ: "Mea, mea, mea".
*If the frog croaks: "Who will bury me? Who will bury me?," a crowd (lit. an army) is silent (lit. is silently silent). But if it croaks: "Who will inherit my estate? Who will inherit my estate?", then it gets a crowd that replies: "Me, me, me".*
(People want to share the good things not the bad).

5385. Sɛ ɔprammire firi ɛbɔn mu pue bese wo se: "Fa wo nsa hyɛ mu" a, nsuro, na wohunu sɛ biribiara nni mu bio.
*If the black cobra comes out of its hole to tell you: "Put your hand in it," don't be afraid, for you see that there is no longer anything left inside.*(Don't fear past dangers).

5386. Sɛ asamando wɔ amane a, anka ɔbaatan bi amane ne ba.
*If there was fortune in the spirit world then some good woman would remit to her child.*
(No mother will sit idle for her child to suffer if she has any means of helping).

5387. Sɛ [wo se]/[w'ase] funu amfɛre sɛ ɛsi wo a, wo nso womfɛre sɛ wosum no.
*If your [father's]/[in-law's] corpse does not respect you and hits you, you also do not respect it and push it away.*
(People believe than when a corpse is carried in the coffin through the village it will knock against the person responsible for its death. Hence: If someone who should respect you disgraces you, you retaliate).

5388. Sɛ wose wo kurom hene agyimi a, na wo ara na woagyimi.
*If you say that the chief of your town is stupid, then you yourself are stupid.*
(It is a fool who talks against the leaders of his community unless he is prepared to do something about it).

5389. Sɛ sebɛ bɛyɛ a, obiara bɛte ne nka.
*If a talisman is going to be good, everyone will hear about it.*
(A good thing makes itself known).

5390. Sɛ ɔsɛberɛbontu te Amporomfi anom asɛm a, ɔdi ahurisie.
*If the goat hears good news from the hyena, it jubilates.*
(Amporomfi is a byname for the hyena. Hence: If your enemy decides not to harm you, you rejoice).

5391. Sɛ woansene fie bi mu a, na ɛfiri wo suban.
*If you are not able to stay in the house, it is because of your character.*
(It is a man's character that directs his actions).

5392. Sɛ woansɔ w'afena mu anyɛ adwuma a, ɛkɔm ku wo.
*If you don't keep a firm hand on your sword to do work, hunger kills you.*
(There is dignity in labor. Or: We must work to live).

**5393. Sɛ asuo Bosomtwe ankame wo apaterɛ a, wo nso wonkame no kraman dompe.**
*If Lake Bosomtwe does not deny you apaterɛ fish, you do not deny it the bone of a dog.*
(One good deed deserves another. Dogs were sacrificed to Lake Bosomtwe).

**5394. Sɛ osuo muna na antɔ a, na ɛkyerɛ sɛ wakɔtɔ baabi.**
*If it clouds over and does not rain, then that means it has fallen somewhere else.*
(At least someone has benefitted).

**5395. Sɛ asuwa bɛfa woɔ deɛ, ma asukɛsee mfa wo.**
*If a streamlet is going to take you, rather let a great river take you.*
(In for a penny, in for a pound).

**5396. Sɛ yɛtete piredwan firi soro a, anka ahwenhema da aborɔsan so.**
*If we were to pluck a piredwan from above, then the white–nosed monkey would live in a story building.*
(A piredwan is a large amount of gold–dust. Hence: If it were easy to earn money, every Tom, Dick, and Harry would live well).

**5397. Sɛ wo tiri mu yɛ fufuo a, Ntuamoa nku wo.**
*If you have a clear conscience (lit.: if the inside of your head is white), the Ntuamoa fetish does not kill you.*
(A man of probity is not easily affected by evil).

**5398. Sɛ wobɛto ɔsebɔ tuo na wanwuo deɛ, fanyinam sɛ wobɛgyae no toɔ.**
*If you fire at a leopard and don't kill it, it would have been better not to have fired.*
(Don't arouse danger if you can't cope with it. Or: If you cannot do a job properly, don't do it at all).

**5399. Sɛ woto esum mu tuo a, wonsuro akyire.**
*If you fire a gun in the dark, you don't fear the consequences.*
(If you deliberately take risks, you should not be surprised at the results).

**5400. Sɛ woanto Ɔdomankoma Ɔbɔadeɛ na woto w'akora a, ne w'aberewa a, na woato no ara ne no.**
*If you don't meet the Creator but you see your father and mother, then you have indeed seen Him.*
(The security of the child is in his parents, for him they represent the Creator).

**5401. Sɛ wɔretɔn tumi a, tɔn w'aberewa kɔtɔ, na wo nsa ka no a, wode akɔgye no.**
*If they are selling power, sell your old mother to buy it, and when you get it, you can take her back.*
(If you get power, you can get everything else).

**5402. Sɛ tontronie anhunu dwa di a, ne dwetire deɛ ɛmmɔ no.**
*If an inexperienced trader does not make a profit, at least he does not lose his capital.*
(If you don't get a profit from an investment, at least you can withdraw your capital).

**5403. Sɛ tontroni kɔtɔn n'adwatonneɛ na ɛbɔ no, na dwerantwi nso tete tetare n'aduradeɛ mu a, na wanya mfasoɔ ara ne sa mprenu.**
*If a trader goes to sell wares and does not make any money, the burrs of the black jack planet (Bidens*

*pilosa) cling on to his clothing and then at last they have gained something.*
(Said, in consolation, when someone has not achieved what they were aiming for, pointing out that they nevertheless achieved something).

**5404. Sɛ "Tufoanteɛ" nyini bɛyɛ onipa pa a, na ɛfiri kasakyerɛ.**
*If a stubborn person grows into a good person, then it is because of admonitions.*
(Taking advice helps to keep you out of trouble).

**5405. Sɛ woretwa nkontompo a, ɛsɛ sɛ wode nkontompo to w'akyi na wo ho kyere wo a, wode atete wo ho.**
*If you tell lies, you must keep a lie (in reserve) behind you, so that when you are in difficulties, you can use it to get you out.*
(Once you are a liar you must be prepared to lie under all circumstances).

**5406. Sɛ etwe annyae dɛ yɛ a, kɔteɛ rennyae no die.**
*If the vagina does not stop being sweet, the penis will not stop enjoying it.*
(If a thing is attractive, people will not stop going after it).

**5407. Sɛ Tweneboa Kodua kɔwu gye Asanteman, mmaa mpene no a, ketrefeni a ɔkɔko dwane wɔ Banda na mmaa bɛpene no?**
*If when Tweneboa Kodua died for the Asante nation, women did not acclaim him, why should the women acclaim a weak person who went to fight and ran away at Banda?*
(If a courageous man gives his all for the nation and is not honored, how much less a coward).

**5408. Sɛ awareɛ yɛ dɛ o, sɛ ɛyɛ nwono o, deɛ wakɔ n'awareɛ na ɔnim.**
*If marriage is sweet or if it is bitter, it is the one who is married who can tell.*
(Experience is the best teacher).

**5409. Sɛ wobɛwe nankatia ayare tohwire no, fa we nankanini ma wo se ntutu prɛko.**
*If you are going to chew the short puff-adder to get ill with gaps in the teeth, much better to chew the great viper, so that your teeth will all come out at once.*
(In for a penny, in for a pound).

**5410. Sɛ wobɛwo mma tantan deɛ, fanyinam sɛ wokaa wo mmadwoa hyɛɛ wo yam.**
*If you give birth to nasty children, it would be better if you had kept to yourself.*
(A bad thing is worse than nothing).

**5411. Sɛ yɛwo wo to esie so a, wonkyɛrɛ tenten yɔ.**
*If you are born on an anthill, you don't take long to grow tall.*
(If you are born into a prominent family, you start with many advantages).

**5412. Sɛ woannwo awo pa a, wote twɛase ya.**
*If you don't give birth to a good child, you are constantly reminded of your labor pains.*
(If you produce something of bad quality, you are constantly reminded of its origins).

5413. Sɛ ɔwɔ kyere aponkyerɛne a, ɛnkyerɛ sɛ anomuodɛ na ɛyɛ no (na mmom ne borɔ ntira).
*If the snake catches the frog, it is not because of its sweet mouth (but for its poison).*
(The snake is supposed to get its poison from the frog. Hence: It is not always expectation of pleasure that leads people to take certain actions).

5414. Sɛ ɔwɔ wɔ ahoɔden a, anka ɔrennye aponkyerɛne borɔ mfa nni aninsɛm.
*If a snake were really strong, then it would not take poison from the frog in order to act in a manly way.*
(If you are really strong you do not depend on others to bolster you up).

5415. Sɛ yɛnni sika a, ɛnyɛ deɛ yɛde bɛto nkɔdaa kɔn mu a.
*If we have no money at all, it does not include that which we hang round children's necks.*
(Even if you are stone broke, you can find something for small courtesies).

5416. W'ase di wo atɛm a, di no bi, na ɔgye ne ba a, wobɛfa wo sika.
*If your in-law insults you, insult them a bit, but if they take their child, you will take your money.*
("Taking their child" is a reference to taking their daughter, your wife, back; i.e. to divorce. You are then entitled to redeem the money paid to the family at the time of your marriage. Hence: You may quarrel intermittently with someone, but if a contract is finally broken, you see you are paid in full).

5417. W'ase amfɛre sɛ ɔde bɔmmɔne bɛyɛ nkwan ama wo adi a, wo nso womfɛre sɛ wobɛse no sɛ "Ɛbɔn!"
*If your mother-in-law is not ashamed to use fermented fish to make soup to give you to eat, you also are not ashamed to tell her that: "It stinks!"*
(Tit for tat).

5418. W'ase repɛ ne ba agye no a, na ɔne wo de hye bɔna.
*If your in-law wishes to take his child from you, then he enters into litigation with you over a boundary.*
(Boundary disputes are common among the Akan and it is not always easy to define boundaries in the forest areas. Once more, "taking a child" refers to divorce. Hence: You find cause to quarrel with someone you are fed up with).

5419. W'ase repɛ wo atu wo a, na ɔse: "Yi wo kyɛmfrɛ awia mu".
*If your in-law wants to drive you away, she says: "Take away your broken pot from the sun".*
(People who dislike you, use every trivial excuse to discredit you).

5420. W'ase tane wo a, na ɔtane wo akyire yi.
*If your in-law hates you, they hate you from a later date.*
(People have to know you well before disliking you).

5421. Asɛɛ te sɛ bankye-fufuo, aba mpa mu da.
*A mother-in-law is like cassava fufuo, there is always lumps in it.*
(Men find it difficult to get on with their mothers-in-law, often finding something to quarrel over).

5422. Ɛse a ɛnhyia na yɛfrɛ no ɛgyerɛ.
*If all teeth do not come together, we call it a gap between the teeth.*

(In Asante, a sign of beauty is a gap between the two middle front top teeth. Thus what might appear to be a misfortune can be an advantage).

5423. Ɛse anna a, ɛyare kaka.
*If a tooth does not rest, it gets toothache.*
(Every man needs to rest to remain healthy).

5424. Ɛse hunu ne serefoɔ a, ɛsere.
*If a tooth sees someone it likes, it smiles.*
(You give recognition to those you like).

5425. Ɛse kɔ wuo a, ɔdi n'akyi gya abogyeɛ.
*If the tooth dies, it leaves the jaw to inherit.*
(The family is always there, even if individual members die).

5426. Ɛse antenten ne ɛse ntiantia didi prɛko.
*Long teeth and short teeth eat together.*
(It takes all kinds to make a world).

5427. Seantie dware Nkran.
*A stubborn child bathes in Accra.*
(Accra was some days journey from Asante in the old days and Accra would seem remote to an Asante. If you have a bad character, you tend to be driven from your home. Hence: A bad person lives far from home).

5428. Seantie funu, yɛnsie.
*A disobedient person's corpse, we don't bury.*
(A person who goes astray dies away from home).

5429. Seantie ne ɔnwam atikɔ pɔ.
*Stubbornness made the hornbill have a swollen head.*
(The tortoise was the wiseman and soothsayer of the forest. He was told to warn all creatures of danger. One day he found some young raffia palm trees by the river and he told the creatures to uproot them all but they laughed at him. The trees grew and grew and a hunter came along and took fibers from them to make rope for traps of various kinds - for fish, animals, and birds. The hornbill was caught and in struggling to escape hit its head so badly that it never recovered. Hence: If you are too stubborn and won't take advice, you suffer for it).

5430. Seantie nti na ɔdaammani tiri bɔ twene ho.
*Because of disobedience you find the youth's head hanging on the drum.*
(A young man who does not obey his elders risks serious trouble).

5431. Seantie nwo ɔba pa.
*Stubbornness does not give birth to a good child.*
(Like mother, like child).

5432. Oseberebontu abirekyie se: ɔrewo ne mma na ɔde wɔn ayɛ n'agodifoɔ.
*Oseberebontu the goat says: it is going to give birth to its young and use them as playmates.*
(Your children can be relied on more than outsiders).

5433. Ɔsebɔ ani anka fie no, na efiri Abirekyie.
*If the leopard was not happy at home, it was because of the goat.*
(The goat once found a wonderful patch of virgin forest and made a small clearing. The leopard saw the same patch of forest and built a house there. Both thought they were being helped by their ancestors: the goat thought his ancestors had built the house, the leopard

that his ancestors had made the clearing. When the house had two rooms, they moved in. Their children started playing together, but the leopard was unable to resist temptation and stalked one of the kids. The goat threatened the leopard, saying it had medicine in its rectum that killed on sight. The leopard and its family believed them and ran away, leaving everything to the goats. Hence: If you believe something, you act on it, even if it is untrue).

**5434. Ɔsebɔ repam yɛn, wobisa me sɛ: "Ɔyɛ onini anaa ɔbereɛ?"**
*The leopard is chasing us and you ask me: "Is it male or female?"*
(If you are in real trouble, make haste to get out of it; don't wait to analyze the situation).

**5435. Ɔsebɔ purokuo, wɔse no ɛfoɔ.**
*A leopard with rotten teeth can be revealed by the monkey.*
(The monkey is safe from the leopard, because it can't bite. Hence: Only a person who is both in the know and secure can reveal the weakness of a powerful man).

**5436. Ɔsebɔ se ohufoɔ na ɔyɛ barima.**
*The leopard says the fearful man is the courageous man.*
(Said of an astute man who retreats to fight again).

**5437. Ɔsebɔ se ɔnte asee sɛ wiram na ɔte a ɔmma efie, nanso onipa atoa no rebɛgye ne nsam aduane.**
*The leopard says he doesn't understand the fact that, though he lives in the forest and does not go to the house, people have followed him to take his food from his hands.*
(If you do not trouble a person, you do not expect them to harass you).

**5438. Asebu Amanfi na ɔwe aburopata.**
*It is Asebu Amanfi who can chew up a whole cornhouse.*
(A legendary Fante hero and strong man. The Asantes use this proverb to refer to someone who consumes too much or is a bully).

**5439. Aseda ne ayɛyɔ akatua.**
*Thanks are the reward for donations.*

**5440. Sɛdeɛ yɛdi nkɔntɔmfɛ, na saa ara na yɛnom ne nkorɔfɛ.**
*Just as we eat palm nuts so do we drink palm wine.*
(You cannot dislike someone and like their intimates).

**5441. Sɛdeɛ Kontromfi Gyasi-kumanini kɔkum kwagyansa a wamfa etuo no, saa ara na ne yere Amma Nhurudu-nhweaa kɔhuu kwagyansa a wamfa egya.**
*Just as the Baboon Gyasi-kumanini did not take a gun to go and kill the marsh mongoose, neither did his wife Amma, the tricky one, take wood to make a fire to singe the marsh mongoose.*
(If you don't complete the first part of a project, you can't go on to the next).

**5442. Sɛdeɛ memma me wɔfase mmo me ba no, saa ara na memma me ba nso mmo me wɔfase.**
*Just as I won't allow my nephew to beat my child, so I won't allow my child to beat my nephew.*
(Do as you would be done by. Because of the inheritance of nephews there is often jealously between children and their first-cousins which can lead to unpleasantness in family relations).

**5443. Sɛdeɛ nantwie dua anni gyina wɔ ne to no, saa ara na ɛnni gyina wɔ kɔmfoɔ nsam.**
*Just as the cow's tail does not stick to its bottom, so also it does not stay in the priest's hand.*
(A rolling stone gathers no moss).

**5444. Sɛdeɛ sekan teɛ no, saa ara na bɔha teɛ.**
*As the knife is, so also is the sheath.*
(You can tell a man by his friends).

**5445. Sɛdeɛ ɔtwekyɛ yera mpoano no, saa ara nso na ɔborɔkyɛ yeraa kwaeɛ mu.**
*Just as the antelope skin hat gets lost on the Coast, so the foreigner's hat got lost in the forest.*
(Man is master of his own territory).

**5446. Sɛdeɛ ɔwɔ nam no, saa ara na ɔda.**
*As a snake walks, so does it sleep.*
(Said when a man's character is unalterable and he should be content with it).

**5447. Asee na ɔni awuo, na seekɔɔ nso a wabɔ kɔbene mu yi ɛ?**
*The small woodpecker's mother died, but why does the bee-eater also put on funeral cloth?*
(Why does the stranger act like a member of the family?)

**5448. Asee ne hwan na ɔrekɔkom Kobi?**
*Who is the woodpecker that he would invoke the Kobi fetish?*
(This woodpecker is bald, and bald men were not allowed to invoke this fetish. Hence: Don't try to do what you are not entitled to).

**5449. Asee-patirapa: mpaningorɔ nti na ne tiri ho apa.**
*The bald-headed woodpecker: because of adult games its head became bald.*
(The woodpecker when young insisted on mixing with its elders and got its head knocked so often that it went bald. Hence: If you try to compete with your superiors, they gain advantage over you).

**5450. Asee apatirapa, ɔse: "Awu agya nti na me tiri ho apa".**
*The bald-headed woodpecker says: "Because of continual deaths I have become bald".*
(It is the custom to shave the head during funerals. Said by someone beset by troubles).

**5451. Nsee goro atipɛn-atipɛn.**
*Woodpeckers play according to their age groups.*
(People move with their own generation).

**5452. Nsee kɔ agyina a, wɔkɔ no deɛ borɔferɛ aberɛɛ.**
*If the woodpeckers sit in council, they look for a place where the pawpaw is ripe.*
(You seek to meet in congenial circumstances).

**5453. Ɛseɛ ne ka-gya nni aseda.**
*Promising without keeping the promise does not yield thanks.*
(Keep your promises. But: There is a piece of wordplay here, since kagya and ɛseɛ are the names of plants, so it could also mean: Between these two plants there is no giving of thanks. The proverb is most often used in circumstances where it is natural for one person to help another. In effect, it means: no need to thank me).

**5454. Ɛseɛ nyɛ akurofo na yɛatutu so.**
*A father is not like a deserted village that our belongings should be removed therefrom.*
(Whatever the circumstances you should always respect your father).

**5455. Ɔsɛɛ bɛku wo a, ɛnnim ntontotwe.**
*If Osei (the Asantehene) is going to kill you, you don't expect a lottery on your death.*
(Some fates are unalterable).

**5456. Ɔsɛɛ ne ne bua.**
*A statement has its reply.*
(There is an answer to everything).

**5457. Ɔsɛɛ ani ase kam, onipa na osaneɛ.**
*The cut below Osei's eye was done by a human-being.*
(Osei refers to the Asantehene. Even the most important people are vulnerable to some human-being).

**5458. Seekoɔ nyɛ anomaa bi, nso ɔboa ntwee-homaa ano.**
*The bee-eater is not any special bird, but at least it gathers small birds around it.*
(Said of someone who, though humble, attracts people).

**5459. Ɔsefoɔ anhunu se a, ɔtiefoɔ nhunu tie.**
*If the speaker does not know how to speak, the listener does not know how to listen.*
(A bad speaker makes a bad listener).

**5460. Asefunu nyɛ, akɔɔwɛre nyɛ, nso wowe kwaasansam.**
*You say the small kingfisher is not good, the bee-eater is not good, yet you eat the Senegal kingfisher.*
(Said when someone agrees to do one thing but refuses to take similar actions).

**5461. Asɛfunu se ɔmpɛ ne ho asɛm, nti na wabɔ funu.**
*The small kingfisher says it does not want trouble, so it looks defeated.*
(If you constantly run away from trouble, people disregard you).

**5462. Sɛkan a yɛde yii kokɔsakyi tiri ho a, amfu bio no, afe so na yɛrekeka a, na ntakaraboa redwane.**
*The knife which we used to shave the vulture and make it permanently bald, at the end of the year when we produce it, all the birds flee.*
(If something or someone has once been used with disastrous effect, all people avoid it or them).

**5463. Sekan a ɛnyɛ nam na ɛte sɛ papa.**
*A knife that is not sharp is like the stem of palm branch*
(A tool or person is not to be feared unless they are dangerous).

**5464. Sekan hyɛ bɔha mu a, na ɛho yɛ hu.**
*If the knife is in the sheath, it is feared.*
(You fear the outcome of an untried case).

**5465. Sekan ano nyɛ nam a, ɛnte sɛ akyire.**
*If the front of the knife blade is not sharp, it is better than the back.*
(The expert, even if disabled, is better than the ignorant).

**5466. Wo sekan bɛyɛ nam a, ɛnnim sɛ woatete ntasuo agu so.**
*If your knife is going to be sharp, it does not matter whether you spit on it.*
(A man who is determined to prosper will do so despite attempts to put him off).

**5467. Wo sekan nyɛ nam a, na wose hahan yɛ den.**
*If you cutlass is not sharp then you say the forest is hard.*
(A bad workman blames his tools).

**5468. Sɛkan nyɛ nam a, nyɛ sɛ yɛde retwa nku.**
*If a knife is blunt, it can still do to cut shea butter.*
(Everything or everybody has something he can achieve).

**5469. Sekan-Kuri Aboagye: "M'anim anyɛ nnam a, ɛte sɛ odwenini mmɛn".**
*Knife-without-handle: "If my blade is not sharp, it is like the horns of a ram".*
(Said of people who know how to fend for themselves, even if not by conventional means).

**5470. Wo sekantia bota wo a, wonto ntwene, wode hyɛ wo nkyɛn mu.**
*If your short knife cuts you, you don't throw it away, you keep it by your side.*
(You don't get rid of someone who normally helps, when they accidentally hurt you).

**5471. Sekantia gye ne ho abɔfra nsam.**
*A short knife frees itself from a child's hand.*
(Children learn by experience).

**5472. Sekantia Kofi, wobɛgye wo din a, gye no ntɛm. Ntena hɔ mma yɛnto wo ntwene ansa na woagye wo din sɛ wode sekan-kuri.**
*Kofi, the short knife, if you are going to make a name for yourself, do it early. Do not sit there for them to throw you away before you are labelled a rusty knife.*
(Good reputations are not made by hanging about but by working long and hard).

**5473. Osekufoɔ na odwan we ne borɔdeɛ.**
*An over curious person, the sheep chews his plantain.*
(Curiosity killed the cat).

**5474. Sɛkyerɛ akonkɔnini abankwa se: "Deɛ ɛbɛyɛ me ara na anya ayɛ me yi".**
*The Sekyere cock (which stretches its neck out) says: "The worst that can happen has already happened to me".*
(No worse can happen than that which has already occurred, so you have nothing further to fear. Sɛkyerɛ is a town near Dwaben; sekyere means to bend backwards and this proverb is given in connection with a goldweight of two cocks' heads twisted backwards on long necks).

**5475. Asekyerɛ ma onipa ani bere.**
*Tracing of origins makes a person angry.*
(People don't like revelations about ther ancestors unless they are to their credit).

**5476. Asɛm a ɛbi mma da na ɛnni mfatoho, na nyɛ asɛm a ɛbi aba pɛn.**
*A problem that has never come has no example, but this does not apply to a problem that has come before.*

(Could be used either when a problem is without precedent, or to indicate that a problem does have precedents).

**5477. Asɛm a ɛmfa wo ho no, na ɛfa obi ho.**
*If a matter does not concern you, it concerns someone else.*
(Everything concerns someone).

**5478. Asɛm a ɔhene bɛtie no, ɔkyeame te a, ɔsere.**
*News which the chief will hear, when the linguist hears it, he laughs.*
(A man profits from the affairs of his master).

**5479. Asɛm a, ɛhia Dankyira-Kyei na ɔde kɔ abɛɛ mu.**
*A matter which interests the minstrel Kyei from Dankyira, he includes in his chanting.*
(If you care very much about something, you make it known).

**5480. Asɛm a ehia Akanfoɔ no na Ntafoɔ de goro brɛkɛtɛ.**
*A matter which is serious to the Akan is a joke to the Northern people (lit. they take to play the brɛkɛtɛ drum).*
(Brɛkɛtɛ is one of the main Dagomba drums, which is danced to. Hence: What one lot of people regard as serious, another lot regard as a matter for entertainment).

**5481. Asɛm a ohiani bɛka ama yɛadwoo-dwoo no no, osikani ka ma yɛpene no.**
*An affair that a poor man talks of until we silence him, a rich man talks of to make us consent to him.*
(A rich man can get away with things a poor one can't).

**5482. Asɛm a ɔman bi ka su no, ɔman bi ka sere.**
*Something which makes one state somewhere weep, also makes another state laugh.*
(It takes all sorts to make a world).

**5483. Asɛm a Onyame adi abua no, ateasefoɔ ntumi nsesa no.**
*A case which God has tried and judged cannot be changed by living persons.*
God's judgement is unchangeable.

**5484. Asɛm a wobɛse na wobɛsan no, ma ɛnka wo tirim.**
*A statement which, when spoken you would wish to withdraw, should remain in your head.*
Think before you speak.

**5485. Asɛm a ɛsene ɔhene wɔ hɔ.**
*There is a problem which is beyond even the chief.*
(Some problems are impossible for human beings to solve).

**5486. Asɛm a wontumi nka wɔ abɔnten so no, wo ne wo yere te fie a, nka nkyerɛ no.**
*If there is anything which you cannot tell in public, when you and your wife are at home, don't tell it to her (there).*
(Something which is unrepeatable should not be repeated, even at home. Secrets revealed in the house have a way of getting out).

**5487. Asɛm a ɛwɔ anisoɔ na yɛde kɔ daeɛ mu.**
*A problem that is on the mind is what we dream of.*
(If we are anxious we have bad dreams. We worry about what concerns us most).

**5488. Asɛm a ɛyɛ dɛ bua ne wura bem wɔ fie, ansa na afiri adi.**
*A good case finds its master innocent at home before going outside.*
(If you are innocent from the onset, then you have confidence to carry the matter through).

**5489. Asɛm a ɛyɛ ahi nnim "Memfa ho".**
*A problem that is abhored does not know "I don't care".*
(Even if you are not personally concerned, you interfere when someone does what is universally disliked).

**5490. Asɛm a ɛbɛyɛ mmusuo na ɛsene abirikyie hwowa ho.**
*A problem which may become a disaster hangs on the testicles of a goat.*
(It is said that if you try and operate on a goat's testicles, it dies: so there can be no cure to diseases there. Hence: A warning against incurable diseases).

**5491. Asɛm a ɛyɛ pataku dɛ na ɔgye ho akyinnyeɛ.**
*A matter which concerns the hyena, he argues about.*
(If you are deeply concerned in something, you tend to question what people say about it).

**5492. Asɛm ba a, na abɛbuo aba.**
*When the occasion arises, a proverb comes to mind.*
(It is only at the right moment that we can remember the appropriate saying, quotation or proverb).

**5493. Asɛm ba a, na asisie aba.**
*If trouble comes, then cheating has come.*
(If you are in trouble, people take advantage of you).

**5494. Asɛm mmra na wɔnni wɔ hɔ yi, ɛnyɛ.**
*Let a case come and let's settle it, is not good.*
(Don't encourage trouble in the first place. Some people make a living from settling quarrels or cases in court but it is wrong to promote such quarrels deliberately to profit from them).

**5495. Asɛm baako mfa onipa nnante.**
*One purpose alone cannot make a person travel.*
(Problems never come singly).

**5496. Asɛm baako pɛ na ɛda ɔyarefoɔ so, wanwu a, ɔnya akwa.**
*There is only one problem for a sick person, if he does not die, he recovers.*
(There is only one alternative).

**5497. Asɛm bi safoa na ɛhini asɛm bi pono.**
*The key to one question acts as the key to another's door.*
(As in an interrogation; only when you have the answer to one question can you know the next to ask).

**5498. Asɛm bi nni adanseɛ a, yɛtwa ho bi yɛ danseɛ.**
*If an affair has no witness, we cut part of it as a witness.*
(Evidence comes out of the statement of a case).

**5499. Asɛm biara nhwere "twa"; yɛdekyɛ wo a, atwa; yɛgye wo sika a, atwa, yɛku wo a, atwa; na yɛde wo to afiase a atwa.**
*No case by-passes "settlement"; if we forgive you, it means it is settled; if we fine you, it is settled; if we kill you, it is settled; if you are imprisoned, it is settled.*
(Any solution is a solution).

**5500. Asɛm biara nni hɔ a ɛsene onipa tenten.**
*There is no case that is taller than a human being.*
(Nothing is beyond the power of man).

**5501. Asɛm biara yɛ den a, yɛmfa akuma na ɛtwa na yɛde ano na ɛka ma no twa.**
*However hard a case may be, we don't use an axe to cut it, but we settle it with our mouths.*
(Discussion, not force, solves problems).

**5502. Asɛm digya yɛ ya sene aduane digya.**
*A case tried in your absence is more painful than a meal having been eaten in your absence.*
(Justice is more important than food).

**5503. Asɛm ahi nti na dabodabo ne a, na wabɔ apee.**
*A vexatious case makes the duck make despising noises when it defecates.*
(No one acts without reason. Or: If you are angry, you show it).

**5504. Asɛm ho ba mfasoɔ a, na wo werɛ afi.**
*If a profit is made out of a matter, then you forget (your work).*
(Achievement makes you forget your toil).

**5505. Asɛm kɔ a, yɛnti no.**
*If a problem goes, we don't follow it.*
Let bygones be bygones

**5506. Asɛm nko, nyansa nko.**
*A problem is one thing, wisdom is another.*
(i.e the wisdom to solve it).

**5507. Asɛm kyɛre a, na yɛfrɛ no tetesɛm.**
*A past event, we call it from ancient times.*
(A current event soon becomes part of history).

**5508. Asɛm kyɛre a, na yɛhunu mu nokorɛ.**
*If a problem delays long, then we see truth in it.*
(If you think about some problem long enough, you can find its solution).

**5509. Asɛm ma wo akye a, na woma no due ne awɔ.**
*Only if a matter says good-morning to you, must you also condole it for passing through the cold.*
(If a problem comes to you, you meet it. An expression of sympathy for the cold is the standard response to an early morning greeting).

**5510. Asɛm na aba na kwaterekwa da agya na anka nyɛ n'apɛdeɛ ne no.**
*Because of unforseen circumstances a naked man is in the open, but that is not what he prayed for.*
(Circumstances sometimes reveal things which should remain hidden).

**5511. Asɛm na ɛde nnipa sɔreɛ.**
*It's a problem that makes people go out.*
(No one acts without a reason).

**5512. Asɛm na ɛde asɛm ba.**
*One problem brings on another.*

**5513. Asɛm nam anisoɔ na ɛkɔ asom.**
*A thing passes through the eye before it reaches the ear.*
(Seeing is believing).

**5514. Asɛm pa yɛ tia.**
*Truth is short.*
(If you have a good case, you don't need to spend too much time explaining it).

**5515. [Asɛm pa]/[Asentia] nyɛ kana.**
*A [good]/[short] case is not hard to state.*

**5516. Asɛm patafoɔ ne mpata.**
*The peacemaker in a case is atonement.*

**5517. Asɛm mpɛ onipa, onipa na ɔpɛ asɛm.**
*Trouble does not love a person, it is a person who loves trouble.*
Don't trouble trouble or trouble will trouble you.

**5518. Asɛm nsa da.**
*Problems never end.*

**5519. Asɛm nsansono hye wo a, wotiti.**
*If an irritating tale comes to you (lit: a problem or tale like a stinging nettle stings you), you scratch it (get involved).*
(Some things make you really annoyed and lose your control. Nsansono is a plant which makes you itch on contact).

**5520. Asɛm sɛ fitia mu a, yɛmfa nkɔ ahemfie.**
*If trouble should be settled in the private dwelling, you don't take it to the chief's palace.*
(Domestic problems should be settled at home).

**5521. Asɛm nsɛ asɛm a, yɛmfa nto ho nka.**
*One problem is not like another problem, you do not compare them.*
Problems differ.

**5522. Asɛm sɛe a, kwasea ka bi.**
*If a case is out of hand, a fool discusses it.*
(Everyone gossips about a public affair).

**5523. Asɛm sene wo panin na worebua ho bi a, wonhunu ne kasu.**
*If a problem is older than you (above your ability to solve) and you are saying something about it, you cannot do it properly.*
(Don't try and give advice which you are not capable of giving).

**5524. Asɛm ansene wo tirim a, ɛrensene wo yɔnko tirim.**
*If an affair does not remain secret in your mind, in just the same way it does not remain secret in your neighbour's mind.*
(If you cannot keep a secret, neither can others).

**5525. Asɛm suro Bɔdwesɛ (ɔbarima katakyie).**
*A case fears a Beard (brave man).*
(People tend to be afraid of others who are prepared to challenge them in a case).

5526. Asɛm te hɔ yi, yɛsina no sɛ ahweneɛ.
*Stating a case is like stringing beads.*
(A case must be put in logical order).

5527. Asɛm te sɛ anomaa, ɛnkyɛre na atu.
*News is like a bird, it travels swiftly.*
(News travels fast).

5528. Asɛm te sɛ nsafufuo, wofra mu pii a, ɛgyene.
*Telling a story is like fresh palm wine, if you add too much water it loses its taste (lit. it becomes clear).*
(If you talk too long, you spoil your story).

5529. Asɛm to wo a, ɔbakwasea na wo adwen.
*If you get into trouble, even a foolish person advises you.*
(People are free with advice, even when they don't really know the facts).

5530. Asɛm to wo a, na wohunu w'adɔfoɔ.
*If you get into trouble, then you see who your real friends are (lit. those who love you).*
(A friend in need is a friend indeed).

5531. Asɛm to wo mpofirim a, na fifi-bɔne firi woɔ.
*If you are unexpectedly drawn into a case, then you sweat heavily.*
(If you are not prepared to deal with a situation, it makes you afraid).

5532. Asɛm tɔɔ Takyiaforoboɔ fie a, wanhunu die nti na yɛfrɛɛ no Asantrofie (Asɛm-atɔ-wo-fie).
*When a case came to Takyi-climb-the-stone's house, he could not settle it and that is why we call him Asantrofie (A-case-has-remained-in-your-house).*
(There is a story of how the nightjar – Asantrofie – got its name. The proverb is used to say that if you don't settle a case quickly you get a bad name).

5533. Asɛm tɔ woso a, wo nyansa yera.
*If problems overwhelm you, you lose your wisdom.*
(Too much trouble defeats us).

5534. Asɛm antwa antwa a, ɛtwa.
*If a problem goes on being unsettled, in the end it is settled.*
(All's well that ends well).

5535. W'asem ware a, wonhwere nkommodifoɔ.
*If you are a good conversationalist, you never lose your listeners.*

5536. Asɛm nwira ba fie a, yɛde yɛn ano na ɛpra guo.
*If a dirty case comes to the house, we use our mouths to sweep it out.*
(You talk yourself out of trouble).

5537. W'asɛm yɛ dɛ a, ɛnnim sɛ woyɛ ɔbaakofoɔ.
*If your case is good, it does not matter if you are an unattached person.*
(Even if you have no family to back you, you can win a good case).

5538. Asɛm nyɛ dɛ a, yɛmmɔ so.
*If an affair is not interesting, we don't mention it.*
(If you are not interested in something, don't talk about it).

5539. W'asɛm nyɛ dɛ a, woma w'ano yɛ dɛ.
*If you are guilty, you use a soft tongue (lit: if your problem is not sweet, you let your mouth be sweet).*
(You should be humble, if guilty).

5540. W'asɛm nyɛ dɛ a, na wose: "Abadwafoɔ tan me".
*If your case is not a good one, you say: "The judges hate me".*
(You blame others for your own shortcomings).

5541. W'asɛm nyɛ dɛ na wode ahobrɛaseɛ ka a, yɛtie bi ma wo.
*If your case is not good, if you use humility to tell it, we listen.*
(Good manners lead to consideration).

5542. Asɛm nyɛ fɛ a, na nyɛ ne kakrawa.
*If an affair is not nice, at least there is something good in it.*
(You can find good in even the worst situation).

5543. Asɛm nyɛ kana, na deɛ ɔbɛtie bi ama woɔ?
*Affairs are not difficult to relate, but who will listen and bring them to you?*
(It isn't hard to state a case, but it is hard to find someone who will hear all the facts and tell them to you).

5544. Asɛm nyɛ kosua na yɛato amane.
*A problem is not an egg so that we can send it through someone.*
(You must solve your own problems).

5545. Asɛm nyɛ na, na asɛntiefoɔ ne asɛm.
*Cases are many, but listeners are rare.*
(A good listener is hard to find).

5546. Nsɛm nyinaa ne Nyame.
*Everything is God's.*

5547. Asɛmfrenkyem mu na yɛnam a, na yɛhunu dɔnkoni ase.
*Too much detailed investigation enables us to find out the origins of a slave.*
(If you talk too much about something, unpleasant facts may be revealed).

5548. Asɛmmɔne nka ɔkyeame fie.
*A bad case is not kept in the linguist's house.*
(If something is serious, it is dealt with by higher authority).

5549. Asɛmmɔne sɛ ohiani.
*Bad things are attributed to a poor man.*
(Poor-man-no-friend. A Ghanaian-English proverb).

5550. Asɛmmɔne nyɛ dina, na akyire asɛm.
*Wrong doing is easy, but it (has its) aftermath.*
(It's easy to do wrong, but hard to foresee the results).

5551. Nsɛmmɔne nti na yɛkyɛɛ din.
*Because of evil doing we shared names.*
(If you do wrong it is only you, yourself, who should suffer for it).

5552. Asɛmpa yɛ mmusuo.
*Comforting words are a calamity.*
(At times people suffer for their generosity).

5553. Asɛmpadie mu nni biribi a, ɛwɔ animuonyam.
*If there is nothing more to giving good advice, there is honour in it.*
(Monetary reward is not everything, an honourable position in society is even more important).

5554. Ɔsɛmpɛfoɔ kɔ bata a, ote ɔsɛmpɛfoɔ fie.
*If a garrulous person goes to trade, he stays in a garrulous person's house.*
(Like attracts like).

5555. Ɔsɛmpɛfoɔ na ɔnam a, ɔbɔ ntwoma.
*If a garrulous person walks around, he uses red clay (on his body).*
(If you want to talk too much, you do something to attract attention and make people ask questions).

5556. Asɛmpɔ hyɛ wo tirim a, wotowa kofie a, ɛnhyia.
*If your mind broods over something, when you raise a mound (for the yam) it is not completed.*
(If you worry too much, you can't concentrate on your work).

5557. Wobɛsɛn badwam a, wodi kan sɛn fie ma yɛhwɛ ansa.
*If you can hang in a public place, you first hang at home to let us see how you do it.*
(Before you do something ostentatious in public, be sure you are good at it).

5558. Ɛsɛn hwe ase a, n'afokyɛ ka fam.
*As soon as the herald falls, the monkey-skin hat touches the ground.*
(A man's dependents flourish or fall with him).

5559. Ɛsɛn keseɛ gye adedodoɔ noa, ɛnnye bi nni.
*The big pot takes a lot of food to cook, but it does not eat it.*
(A person may do a big job without profiting from it).

5560. Ɛsɛn se: "Mete Ɔhene akonnwa ho kwa, adeɛ na nkwamanfoɔ awie die yi!"
*The herald says: "I stay by the chief's stool in vain, the common people have finished everything off".*
(Said of someone who is always near the source of power but can never inherit it).

5561. Ɔsena firiiɛ ansa na nkrannyedua rebɛfiri.
*Dianium Guineense had grown before the physic nut started growing.*
(Dianium has a black fruit with a cover like velvet and a sweet yellow pulp which is edible and thirst quenching. The tall physic nut-Jatropha curcas-is used for many medicinal purposes and was originally brought in by the Portuguese and is not indigenous. Hence: Senority goes by age and origin, not size).

5562. Wosene obi asɛm a, ɔno nso sene wo nyansa.
*If you have more to say than someone, then he too has more wisdom than you.*
(We all have different gifts).

5563. Wosene me adidie a, mesene wo nna.
*You excel me in eating, but I excel you in sleeping.*
(We all have the things we are best at).

5564. "Mesene wo," yɛmfa mmu ɔman.
*"I am better than you," we do not use to run the state.*
(You don't build a good society by running other people down).

5565. Wosene wo se tenten a, nyɛ wo pɛn ne no.
*If you are taller than your father, he is not your coequal.*
(Seniority does not depend on physical attributes).

5566. Wosene wo yɔnko a, ɔtane wo.
*If you excel your companion, he hates you.*
(Jealousy causes hatred).

5567. Asɛnhia wɔ hɔ yi, yɛde dabɔne na ɛdie.
*If a case is serious we try it on a significant day.*
(We give something the respect it deserves. On dabɔne-lit. evil day-people do not go to their farms to work, for fear of meeting something terrible in the forest. They keep in the village and are therefore available for arbitrations).

5568. Nsɛnee mu wɔ biribi a, anka apan da apaken mu.
*If there were a reward for hanging, the bat would ride in a palanquin.*
(Said when someone excels at something which is not profitable).

5569. Ɔsenhyeɛ yɛ buana.
*A case which comes up suddenly is hard to solve.*
(You need time to deal with a new case properly).

5570. Ɔsenifoɔ na ɔdɔ afuo wɔ kwan kyɛn.
*It is a busy-body who makes his farm by the roadside.*
(An interfering person keeps his ear to the ground).

5571. Ɔsenifoɔ na ɛka sɛ no.
*A gossiper, a debt befits him.*
(A trouble-maker deserves trouble).

5572. Ɔsɛnkam yɛ ya sene kampa.
*A wounding word is more bitter than a physical wound.*
(Words hurt more than physical unkindness).

5573. Asɛnkeseɛ reba a, frankaa nsi so.
*When a serious event is about to take place, no flag is flown to announce it.*
(Used to warn people of simple events which may flare up and become serious).

5574. Asɛnkeseɛ kɔ da a, asɛnketewa na ɛnyane no.
*When a big affair is asleep, a little one awakens it.*
(Small troubles often lead to bigger ones).

5575. Asɛnkyerɛaseɛ bebrebe yɛ amammɔeɛ.
*Too much tale-bearing brings the destruction of the state.*
(Unsubstantiated gossip causes dissension).

5576. Ɔsɛnnahɔ wo mma.
*Apathy over a case gives birth to children.*
(Problems proliferate if they are not dealt with quickly).

5577. Asɛnnɛ nti na aberewa kotena dan-akyi.
*It is because of fresh news that the old lady goes to sit in front of her room.*
(If you want to hear something you must put yourself in a position to do so).

5578. Sensam na ɛfirii kane, na nkrannyedua abɛsene no tenten.

*Guinea grain grew from ancient times, but the physic nut is greater than it in height.*
(Amomum granum paradisi and Jatropha curcas - see Proverb 5561. The physic nut - Jatropha curcas - grows taller than the grain and is used medicinally. Seniority doesn't always correlate with size).

**5579. Sensam ne fie panin na nkrannyedua, brɛ wo ho ase.**
*Guinea grain is the elder of the house but the physic nut is submissive.*
(See Proverb 5578. Don't throw your weight about with your seniors, even if you believe yourself to be superior. )

**5580. Sensam ne sasabonsam din sɛ nanso wɔnsɛ honam.**
*Guinea grain and the forest devil have similar names but their appearance is not alike.*
(Names may resemble each other but characters differ).

**5581. Sensam sam bɛtene ase kwa, bɛtene yere ne aya.**
*Guinea grain gathers round the palm tree in vain, for the palm-tree's wife is the fern.*
(Guinea grain is a fern-like plant. The fern itself grows up the trunk of palm trees and between their branches. Hence: Said of someone who hangs around a married man trying to seduce him).

**5582. Asɛntoasoɔ bebrebe de onipa gyina dwa.**
*Too much repetition of a case causes a trial.*
(If you make too much fuss about something you get into serious trouble).

**5583. Ɛserɛ so dua kokrosabia se: ɛnyɛ ogya na ɛhye no afrinhyia biara a, anka ɔne odupon bi sɛ.**
*Cochlospermum Planchonii, bush of the savanna, says: if it were not for the fire that burns it every year, it would be the same size as the mahogany tree.*
(Because the grass is burnt annually, few trees survive to a great size in the savannah area. Hence: Circumstances are beyond human control or all people would flourish equally).

**5584. Wosere donko hwerɛma a, wonte ne dwom.**
*If you laugh at a slave's whistle you don't hear his song.*
(If you often interfere with someone who tries to please, when you do need him he won't cooperate).

**5585. Yɛsere wo nkonnwasoafoɔ a, na yɛasere wo.**
*If we laugh at your stool-bearers, then we have laughed at you.*
(If you ridicule someone serving some other person, you ridicule the person themselves).

**5586. Yɛnserɛɛ obi adeɛ a, yɛnka sɛ ne tirim yɛ den.**
*If we don't beg someone for something, we don't say they are hard-hearted.*
(Don't pass judgement unless you have ascertained the truth of what people say).

**5587. Ɛserem-seɛ resu a, kontromfi na ɔteatea no.**
*If the lion roars, it takes a creature like the baboon to shout at him.*
(Only someone out of reach of a powerful man can criticize him).

**5588. Ɔserefoɔ nnim n'awieɛ.**
*A mocker does not know how he will end.*
(If you laugh at other's suffering, your time may come to suffer too).

**5589. Aserɛnɛ a ɛsɛn dan ano, ɔse: "Madi wo hunkan."**
*The raffia mat which is hanging over the door says: "I have seen you first."*
(You cannot outwit a person who is always on the alert).

**5590. Ɔsereserefoɔ ho nyɛ ahi.**
*A cheerful person is not hateful.*
(A cheerful person does not arouse resentment).

**5591. Ɔsereserefoɔ se ayie a ɛmma.**
*If a joker announces a funeral, people don't come in numbers.*
(Wolf, wolf. If a person is known to be a joker, people don't take what he says seriously).

**5592. Aserewa a ɔbɛnyini koropɔn no, ɔsi hɔ a, na ne bo redwa.**
*If a sunbird is going to become an eagle, when it is perching on a tree, its chest shines.*
(Signs of coming greatness appear in youth).

**5593. Aserewa dɔdrohwedɔhwe ntu asuasu na ɔnnom adukurosuo.**
*The dainty sunbird does not make a well for it to drink from the buttress of a tree.*
(You don't labor in vain for others to benefit).

**5594. Aserewa bo tam kɛseɛ a, ɛtu no hwe.**
*If a sunbird puts on a big cloth, it will make it fall down.*
(Don't try and act beyond your capacity).

**5595. Aserewa se: w'ahunu bi pɛn, nti na ɔkɔgyegye ne ba a, ɔyi n'ani toto nkyɛn.**
*The sunbird says: it has experienced it before, that is why, when it is entertaining its child, it looks sideways.*
(Once bitten, twice shy).

**5596. Aserewa su agyenkuku su a, ne mene mu pae.**
*If the sunbird sings the song of the dove, its throat bursts.*
(If you try and imitate someone more talented than yourself or more important, you will only damage yourself).

**5597. Aserewa-Sikansuo se: "Ebi dɔ me, na ebi tan me".**
*The little sunbird says: "Some people love me and others hate me".*
(Not all people have similar likes and dislikes).

**5598. Nserewa aduasa buo baako, adeɛkye a, wɔkyinkyin kɔ ba nyinaa no, na ɔman siesie ntira.**
*Thirty sunbirds have one nest, when day breaks they move to and fro, all because of putting the state in order.*
(Communal labor helps the state).

**5599. Wosesa wo ho bebrebe a, wohwere daberɛ.**
*If you change your clothes constantly, you lose your sleeping place.*
(If you are too particular in life, people stop helping you).

**5600. Asesa rebɔ wo a, wose: "Mennim nante".**
*If laziness overcomes you, you say: "I don't know how to walk".*
(If you are too lazy, you can always find an excuse to do nothing).

**5601. Ɔsesea akurampɔn, ɔno na ɔdii afuo so kan, nso wannya adukuro.**
*Trema guineensis the small tree, which came first to the farm, also could not grow a buttress.*
(This small tree–Trema guineensis–has many medicinal uses. Used when the position which should be yours is usurped by a more recent–comer who is better qualified).

**5602. Ɔsesea si sie so, na woto boɔ sɛ wode rebɔ asee na ammɔ asee na ɛkɔbɔ sese a mu a, ne nyinaa dane "see".**
*Trema guineensis stands on the anthill and you throw a stone aiming at the woodpecker and it does not hit the woodpecker but hits the tree, they all make the same sound ("see").*
(Whomever you harm, the offense is the same. See Proverb 5601).

**5603. Ɔsese korɔ, ɔse: "Me nnaaseɛ ne ogya".**
*The lonely hut says: "My thanks is fire".*
(A solitary person lacks protection).

**5604. Asetena ya nyinaa ne ntɔdie.**
*Painful circumstances of life are all a question of expenses.*
(Money causes most of the difficulties in life).

**5605. Setie yɛ sene afɔrebɔ.**
*Obedience is better than harvest donations.*
(It's no good donating to religious causes, if you don't try and obey God's laws).

**5606. "Esi baabi a asi", yɛ amammɔeɛ.**
*"Come what may", is unpatriotic.*
(People should care about what happens in society).

**5607. Wosi atakwamedan mu na woankokwa ho a, nkura di mu ahurusie.**
*If you build a swish hut and you don't plaster it, the mice will rejoice inside.*
(If you don't finish a job properly, you will suffer for it).

**5608. Yɛbɛsi wo so a, anka yɛhyɛɛ wo ma.**
*If we intended to give you in full, we would have filled you up at first.*
(If you are only given a portion to start with, it means you are not intended to have more).

**5609. Wosi wo two so a, ɛhim wo.**
*If you keep hydrocele secret, it sways you about.*
(If you try to hide something which needs to be dealt with, it will be worse in the end).

**5610. Woansi wo dan no yie a, na wosunsum aseɛ.**
*If you do not build your house well, you have to prop it up.*
(If you don't do a job well, you have to keep going back to it).

**5611. Yɛnsi kontromfi nsɛma.**
*We don't set a trap for a baboon.*
(It is hard to trap a wise person).

**5612. Esia nko ara nyɛ kwaeɛ.**
*The stinkwood tree alone can't make a forest.*
(The stinkwood tree is Combretodendron macrocarpum. One tree does not make a forest).

**5613. Asiananta twene, wosa a, w'aberewa awu; woansa a, woyere awu.**
*Asiananta's drum, you dance, your old lady dies; but if you don't dance, your wife dies.*
(Hobson's choice).

**5614. Asiane nhyɛ da.**
*Misfortunes do not announce the day of their arrival.*

**5615. Asiane nsiane akoa nko.**
*Misfortunes do not only overcome slaves.*
(We are all subject to misfortunes).

**5616. Asiane nni nua ne wɔfaseɛ nti daa yɛbua no fɔ.**
*Because "Accident" has no brother nor nephew, that is why we always find him guilty.*
(A person without relatives is never respected).

**5617. Esiane sɛ ɛkɔm bɛba da bi, nti na nkurukutie kutiri koro ho sie.**
*Because famine will come one day, the woodpecker picks at the Albisia zygia tree to store.*
(Prepare for a rainy day).

**5618. Asibe se: kɔteɛ dɛ nti na ɔmmo tam.**
*The colobus monkey says: because of the sweetness of the penis it does not wear a loin cloth.*
(If you like something very much, you are always prepared for it).

**5619. Asibuo, yɛbu no ɔmanni.**
*Envious comparisons are only promulgated amongst fellow citizens.*
(It is easy to criticize those you know if they are better off than you).

**5620. Wosie obi asɛm a, ono nso sie wo nyansa.**
*If you hide a problem from someone, they too will conceal their good advice from you.*
(If you don't explain your problem, people can't help you).

**5621. Asie na ɔfa.**
*A keeper takes.*
(You know the whereabouts of something in your care better than anyone else, and so you can easily remove it).

**5622. Esie ho ba ɔkwan a, mmoadoma nyinaa kɔda mu.**
*If the anthill appears on the path, all animals go inside it to sleep.*
(If you make yourself available to people, they will take advantage of you).

**5623. Esie ho ba tokuro a, mmoa nyinaa wura mu bi.**
*If a hole comes in the anthill, all animals pass through it.*
(If you show up your weak point, people will take advantage of it).

**5624. Esie ho annwo no a, na ɛfiri okusie.**
*If the anthill has no peace it is because of the rat.*
(A troublesome person destroys peace in the house).

**5625. Esie ma ne ho kwan a, na mmoa di mu ahyɛnefiri.**
*If the anthill allows itself to be used as a path, then animals run in and out of it.*
(If you are too liberal, people take advantage of you).

**5626. Esie ne kagya nni aseda.**
*Between the anthill and Griffonia simplicafolia there is no need of thanks.*
(Griffonia simplicafolia often grows on anthills. Hence: people who are intimate do not need to thank each other. This is an expression of affection and acknowledgement of a warm relationship).

**5627. Esie animuonyam ne mmire.**
*The glory of the anthill is the mushrooms.*
(Mushrooms are often found on anthills. Hence: Said when someone is proud of their supporters or helpers).

**5628. Esie yera a, yɛbisa apakwaa (aduoku).**
*If the anthill gets lost we question the rat.*
(You question a person's intimates if you need information about them).

**5629. Asieɛ nyɛ kuro na yɛatu agya.**
*A cemetery is not a town to be deserted.*
(You cannot run away from final judgement).

**5630. Sika a yɛde tɔ donkɔ, ɛno ara na yɛde gye ɔdehyeɛ awowa.**
*Money which we take to buy a slave, is the money we take to release a royal person from being a pawn.*
(Money can do everything).

**5631. Sika bɛn wo a, ɛhoa.**
*When gold is near you, it pales.*
(Familiarity breed comtempt).

**5632. Sika da owuo afa.**
*Money sleeps with death.*
(If you are over greedy, you suffer for it).

**5633. Sika dabrɛ sua.**
*Where money sleeps is a small place.*
(Money comes and goes easily).

**5634. Sika dabrɛ nyɛ hunu nna, na mmɔdemmo na ɛhia.**
*It is not difficult to know the sleeping place of money, but you need to work hard.*
(Money is the reward for hard work).

**5635. Sika di ntomu, na ɛnni ntesoɔ.**
*Money needs adding to but not subtracting from.*
(You must learn to save, or you will lose everything).

**5636. Sika frɛ bogya.**
*Money calls blood relations.*
(If you are well-off, the family depends on you).

**5637. Sika nkɔdidi nsane mma kwa.**
*Money does not go out to eat and come back with nothing.*
(Money enables a man to achieve what he wants).

**5638. Sika [kutunsin]/[kukusin] nkɔ ahemfie.**
*A "headless" packet of gold dust does not go the the chief's palace.*

("Mataho" or "Kyekyerekon" were things tied onto or stuck into a larger packet of gold dust when it was used to pay fines. In the chief's palace, these went to the linguists. So a "headless" packet of gold dust - one without these additions - is not satisfactory for paying a fine. Hence: When you pay a debt there are usually small extras to be paid to witnesses or those who helped to collect it).

**5639. Sika Kwadwo a odi agorɔ mu, wonya bi a, amane, woanya bi a, amane.**
*Money Kwadwo which is part of the game (of life), if you get some, there is trouble, if you don't get some, there is trouble.*
(Money is the root of all evil).

**5640. Sika Kwadwo, woanhwɛ ne so yie a, ɛkɔ deɛ ɛfiri baeɛ.**
*Money Kwadwo, if you don't look after it well, it goes to where it came from.*
(You must look after money or you lose it).

**5641. Sika Kwadwo, na ɔma seporɔeɛ ka asomsɛm.**
*Money Kwadwo allows a man with rotten teeth speak into your ear.*
(Money leads you to accept what you would otherwise refuse).

**5642. Sika na ɛma ɔfɔdifoɔ di bem.**
*Money makes a guilty person become innocent.*
(Money can buy a person out of trouble).

**5643. Sika ne ɔhene.**
*Money is Chief.*
(Money rules all).

**5644. Sika nyini ne wura fotoɔ mu.**
*Gold increases in its owner's gold-weight bag.*
(You can take care of your own things and make profit from them).

**5645. Sika peredwan mu wɔ domponini.**
*In a peredwan's worth of gold there is also a small amount.*
(A piredwan is a large amount of gold-dust. Domponini is a very small amount of gold. Hence: If you have plenty of something, you can always spare a little).

**5646. Wo sika resa a, na w'ani teɛ.**
*If your money is coming to an end, you become prudent.*
(When you have only a little money, you are very careful how you use it).

**5647. Sika sene nkrantɛ nam yɛ.**
*Gold is sharper than the cutlass.*
(Money achieves more than the sword).

**5648. Wo sika sua a na w'asɛm nso sua.**
*If your money is small, your position is insignificant [lit. your affairs are also small].*
(A man's position in society depends on his wealth).

**5649. Sika te sɛ akoa, woanhunu ne so hwɛ a, ɔdwane.**
*Money is like a servant, if you don't look after it well, it runs away.*
(Money needs careful looking after).

**5650. Sika te sɛ hwenemunwi, wotu a, na woresu.**
*Money is like the hairs in the nose, if you pull them out, you cry.*
(It hurts some people to spend).

**5651. Sika te sɛ mpempena, ɔbaakofoɔ ntu.**
*Money is like the tiny mushroom, one person alone does not collect it.*
(When these small mushrooms grow everyone goes to pick them. Everyone is interested in money).

**5652. Sika nti na ɔkɔmfoɔ di nkontorɔ.**
*Because of money the fetish priest tells lies.*
(Men will do anything for money).

**5653. Sika ntini yɛde brɛbrɛ na ɛtwetwe.**
*The roots of money are usually pulled cautiously.*
(Money is acquired with care and caution).

**5654. Sika toto nnipa na nnipa ntam.**
*Money brings unfriendliness between men and men.*
(Money is the cause of much quarrelling).

**5655. Sika nni: "Ka wo nsa pɛ".**
*With money it is not just a case of: "Put out your hand and take".*
(You have to be careful how you deal with money; it is hard to come by and it should not just be handed out anyhow).

**5656. Sika nyansa nko, na asɛm nyansa nko.**
*Money wisdom is one thing and consultation wisdom is another.*
(What is profitable is not necessarily wise).

**5657. Sika nni adaagye a, yɛmfa mmɔ bosea.**
*If one has just sufficient money for one's own needs [lit. If (your) money has no rest], you do not loan out on interest.*
(You have to satisfy yourself before you satisfy others).

**5658. Sika yɛ fɛ, na ɔpagyafoɔ yɛ na.**
*Wealth is a good thing, but to find an heir is not easy.*
(Even if you are rich you cannot be sure that the person who will inherit you will be able to care for what you have toiled for).

**5659. Sika yɛ pɛna.**
*Money is difficult to find.*

**5660. Sika nyɛ owuo aduro.**
*Money is not an antidote to death.*

**5661. Sika dwuma, yɛyɔ no animia.**
*Working for money, we take it seriously.*
(Said when someone is prepared to face hardship to get money).

**5662. Sika dwuma nyɛ aniwu.**
*Working for money, is not shameful*

**5663. Osikani ba ne ohiani ba ɛnsɛ.**
*A rich man's child and a poor man's child are not alike.*
(Children from different environments differ).

**5664. Osikani deɛ, yɛnnwansi no bɔne da.**
*As for a rich man, we never sneeze badness at him.*
(See Proverb 5306. A man who is already lucky does not attract bad luck).

**5665. Osikani didi na ohiani nso didie.**
*A rich man eats and a poor man also eats.*
(Whatever one's status, one has to eat to live).

**5666. Osikani funu yɛ nyam a, sene ohiani teasefoɔ.**
*A rich man's corpse is more respected than a living poor man.*
(We pay less attention to the poor than the rich, alive or dead).

**5667. Osikani fura ntomago.**
*A wealthy man wears an old cloth.*
(A rich man can afford to behave as he likes).

**5668. Osikani na ɔdi akɔnnɔdeɛ.**
*A rich man eats sweet things.*
(Riches bring pleasure).

**5669. Osikani ne ohiani goro a, ɛnsɔ.**
*If a rich man befriends a poor man, it does not last.*
(Friendship between rich and poor seldom thrives).

**5670. Osikani ne panin.**
*The rich man is an elder.*
(Riches give you a good position in society).

**5671. Sikaniberɛɛ na ɛma kɔmfoɔ mene agyan.**
*It is the love of gold that makes the priest swallow an arrow.*
(People will do anything for money).

**5672. Sikaniberɛɛ nti na kɔmfoɔ de ne tiri hwe dan mu.**
*It is because of love of money that the fetish priest knocks his head against a wall.*
(Man will do anything for money however stupid).

**5673. Sikayie yɛ wo ya a, ɛkɔm ku wo.**
*If spending hurts you, hunger kills you.*
(A mean person does not thrive).

**5674. Simpa Panin hwɛ agyapadeɛ so nso ɔnni bi.**
*The elder from Winneba looks after valuables but has nothing.*
(A Winneba man who lived near the sea had his house used by all the fishermen to store their equipment. He did this for years but they never rewarded him. Hence: Said when people make use of someone without allowing them to profit).

**5675. Simpa prako na ɔde n'aso yɛ ne mmɛn.**
*The pig from Winneba uses its ears as its horns.*
(Winneba was well-known for its wild pigs which sometimes came into the market and acted aggressively, ignoring noisy attempts to scare them off. Hence: Used if someone refuses to listen to advice and becomes belligerent).

**5676. Sini awieeɛ na yɛhunu kyare.**
*The end of a cinema show enables us to see the hero.*
(We can only judge after anevent).

**5677. Yɛnsini boaboa afuo so kwa, mmaboa na ɛma egya dɛre.**
*Large pieces of firewood are clumped around the farm in vain, the little twigs make the fire flame up.*
(The most important are not always the most useful).

**5678. Wosiri ban yie a, wonya ahwedeɛ.**
*If you build a good dam you make a good catch (of fish).*

(See Proverb 530. Good preparations lead to a successful outcome).

**5679. Wosisi Ananse a, wosisi wo ho.**
*If you cheat the spider, you cheat yourself.*
(If you play a game by yourself you say: "Me ne Ananse tɔ..." or "I am playing with the spider". So, used to stop a child or other person cheating or playing truant. The only damage they do is to themselves).

**5680. Wosisi mu yɛ den a, na wosa akapimahwɛ.**
*If your waist is strong, then you bump bottoms when dancing.*
(If you are tough, you can do a tough job).

**5681. Wo sisi yɛ den a, na wodi abadwadeɛ.**
*If the lower part of your back is strong, you get your share of fees for attending an arbitration.*
(If you are prepared to sit it out and listen, you can help in arbitration work. If you are prepared to work, you can earn).

**5682. Asisie yɛ ya sene mako.**
*Cheating is more painful than pepper.*

**5683. Asisihamu mpo wɔ wura.**
*Even produce scattered in the bush has an owner.*
(Everything belongs to someone).

**5684. Asisirapɛ ne anomaa agorɔ nyɛ agopa.**
*The game between a winged white ant and a bird is not a good game.*
(When a man plays with his victim it is not good).

**5685. Sisire-kwabrafo se: ɔno deɛ, ɔmfa n'ahoɔden nsisi nnipa (na mmom ɔde wɛre ne ho).**
*The honey-badger says: as for him, he does not use his strength to cheat people (but he protects himself with his strength).*
(Some people may have the ability to harm others but rather use their talents for more positive purposes. Also, since asisie, meaning to cheat, sounds a little like sisire, the badger: Your name does not indicate your character).

**5686. Osisire ntutu nkɔtwere ɔnwamma.**
*The African tulip tree does not get uprooted to lean against the ricinodendron heullotii.*
(Ricinodendron heullotii is brittle and if the African tulip or flame tree – Spathodea campanulata – leans on it with force, the likelihood is that both will go down. Hence: One poor person should not depend upon another; both of them will soon be destitute).

**5687. Asisire dwaa pɛtɛ ani tua Oguaa, nso sommoro tua n'aniase a, ɔnhunu ntu.**
*The foolish vulture can see as far as Cape Coast, but it cannot see to remove the tick from under its eye.*
(Be concerned with your own shortcomings first).

**5688. Woso, woba so, anso wo di; na wokɔsrɛeɛ na ɛbɛso wo die?**
*You carry, your child carries, there is not enough to satisfy you; how much less when you go and beg will you be satisfied.*
(If hard work does not bring success, nor does begging).

**5689. Woso adaka a, na woso ne nemu adeɛ.**
*If you carry a box, you carry its contents.*

(If you wish to belong to a group, you must accept all its members and obligations).

**5690. Meso donno a, memmɔ mu.**
*If I carry the hour-glass drum, I do not beat it.*
(Acting on instructions is different from taking responsibility oneself).

**5691. Woso fruntum, so matatwene a, wonse sɛ: "Gye kwabɛtene kyekyere w'akyi".**
*If you carry the rubber tree, carry the liana (Cercertis afselii), then you don't say: "Take the tall palm tree to tie behind you".*
(If you have the means of doing a job, you don't go looking for something else to use).

**5692. Mebɛsoo gya na mammɛhwɛ nkwan mu.**
*I came to collect fire-wood but I did not come to look at the soup.*
(If you marry into a family, you should not interfere in its family affairs).

**5693. Woso, wonhunu mu, wobrɛ no ase a, wonhunu mu, na wohwie gu ɛ?**
*If you carry and can't see inside, you bring it lower, you still can't see inside; how about pouring it out?*
(If you want to solve a problem, you must really get to the bottom of it).

**5694. Woso kyɛnkyɛn si akɔnkɔn, ɛdɛ na woredie anaa woredi yea?**
*You are wearing bark cloth to sit on someone's shoulders, are you happy or are you suffering?*
(You are doing an uncomfortable and a pleasureable thing at the same time).

**5695. Meso me deɛ mentumi, wose: "Gye me".**
*I find it difficult to carry my own load, then you say: "Help me".*
(Said when someone already is in difficulties and is asked to give help to another).

**5696. Woso mpenu, woresu; na deɛ ɔso mpensa nyɛ dɛn?**
*You who carry two thousand are weeping; but how much more the one who carries three thousand.*
(If you suffer in doing a smaller job, how much more the person who does a larger one).

**5697. Woso nanka, wontumi a, womfa onini mmɔ kahyire.**
*If you carry the viper and you are unable to, you don't take the python to make a carrying pad.*
(See Proverb 550. Don't add insult to injury).

**5698. Yɛso asɛm pa a, yɛbɔ no kahyire.**
*If we bear good news, we make a carrying pad for it.*
(See Proverb 550. If you are a bearer of good news, you make sure everyone knows about it).

**5699. Yɛso atuduro a, yɛnom tawa.**
*Though we carry gunpowder, we smoke tobacco.*
(Even when in a dangerous situation a man has a right to the little luxuries of life).

**5700. Woso ɔtwe, me nso meso ɔtwe, wo se: "Ma menhwɛ wo twe to".**
*You are carrying a duiker, I also amd carrying a duiker, yet you say: "Let me see your duiker's bottom".*
(If you have something yourself, don't be envious of others).

5701. Woso awareɛ a, wotɔ wo prɛte.
*If you arrive at getting married, you buy your owm plate.*
(If you reach a certain status you must be able to look after yourself properly).

5702. Ɛso wo a na ɛyɛ akɔmmuo, wosoɛ a, na wo ho adwo wo.
*When you are carrying it your neck suffers, but when you put it down you become free.*
(No one suffers from a burden indefinitely).

5703. Woso, wo yere so, anyɛ yie, na wokɔfaa bi sɛn wo batri na ɛbɛyɛ dɛn?
*You carry, your wife carries, it is not a success, how much less the little that you have been able to hang from your shoulder.*
(If a major effort does not succeed, how can a small one).

5704. Wonsoo kokurodo tɔma mo a, wonsensan.
*If you have not reached the age of wearing big beads, you do not thread them.*
(If you can't use something you don't bother about it).

5705. Yɛsɔ afena tunu na ɛtwe afena.
*We grasp the hilt of the sword before drawing it.*
(First things first).

5706. "Sɔ me mu na menkum m'akoko a," wose: "Me yere ne me mma nkwaso".
*"Help me to kill my fowl," then you say: "Blessed be my wife and children."*
(Don't make use of other people to get what you want).

5707. Mesɔ wo mu abia nka me so.
*If I help you with something you don't leave it to me alone to do.*
(You don't desert your helper).

5708. Woansɔ bɔfuro ano na wotwa a, ɛgugu.
*If you don't close the mouth of the stomach sac well and you cut it, it pours out.*
(Carefulness avoids unpleasantness).

5709. Yɛnsɔ adwene dua mu, nse no sɛ: "Dware ma yɛnhwɛ".
*We don't hold a fish's tail and say: "Swim and let me see".*
(Don't ask someone to do something and then impede their doing it).

5710. Yɛnsɔ ogya foforɔ mfa nwa.
*You don't light a new fire and collect snails (at the same time).*
(It is a bad omen to pluck a snail on the first day of working on a new farm. Hence: Don't break taboos).

5711. Woanso [w'asɔtia]/[w'asɔ] mu anyɛ adwuma a, ɛkɔm de wo.
*If you don't stick to your short hoe and do some work you go hungry.*
(You must work to eat).

5712. Aso a akonnwa si mu na yɛka asɛm kyerɛ no.
*It is the ear that has a stool in it that we speak something through.*
(If someone is prepared to take advice and listen, we advise them).

5713. Aso da a, na afotosan reba.
*If the ears sleep, the moneybag will be loosened.*
(If you don't pay attention in court or in the business world, you may have to pay for it).

5714. Aso didi na ɛmmua nna.
*The ears eat and do not go fasting to bed.*
(You never stop hearing, whatever happens).

5715. Aso korɔ due.
*To a single ear: condolences*
(If you are the only elder in the family, you have no one to share your responsibilities in listening to and solving problems. You are therefore to be pitied).

5716. Aso ha ano.
*The ear troubles the mouth.*
(It is because of what one hears that one speaks. Or: Rude speech stimulates rude replies).

5717. W'aso ankɔ adidi a, wo tiri yera.
*If your ears don't go to eat (i.e. listen), your head gets lost.*
(If you are not attentive in life, you lose out).

5718. Aso mu nni nkwanta.
*There are no cross-roads in the ear.*
(One cannot accept truth and falsehood at the same time).

5719. Aso nyinaa mu wɔ kwan, nanso ɛnyɛ ne nyinaa na ɛte asɛm.
*There is a road to all ears but not all of them listen.*
(It is possible to speak with anyone, but not everyone will hear what you say and act on it).

5720. Aso pa nkyɛre asɛm te.
*A good ear does not delay in understanding things.*
(An intelligent person understands quickly).

5721. Aso si a, dua na yɛde yi mu, na ɛnyɛ fitiiɛ.
*If the ears are sealed, you use a stick to clear them and not a metal spike.*
(Don't be too drastic in your treatment of a problem).

5722. Aso sini so daeɛ na n'aso afefɛ.
*One whose ear is cut off dreamt that his ear had grown again.*
(We all hope for the best).

5723. Aso te sɛ nsania, woto mu, to mu a, ɛda.
*The ear is like a scale, if you go on dropping things into it, it gives way.*
(Persistent demands achieve their ends).

5724. Aso nte mma abogyeɛ nyera.
*The ear does not drop for the jaw to get lost.*
(You bear your own sufferings and not those of a stranger).

5725. Aso nni berɛ.
*The ears have no time (to spare).*
(Responsible people are seldom idle).

5726. Asɔ se: "Afe aso oo, na momma yɛnkɔ".
*The hoe says: "The year has come round, so lets get moving".*
(Said when it is time to start the farm work for the year).

5727. Ɔso nkra kon mmu.
*He who carries a message does not suffer from his neck.*
(i.e. he is not executed. Hence: The carrier of a message is not blamed for its contents).

5728. Woresoa obi adesoa a, wosoa no deɛ ɔbɛtumi.
*If you are helping someone to carry a load, you give him what he can carry.*
(Don't force someone beyond their capacity, it may be your turn next).

5729. Wobɛsoa odwan a, wosoa no ntɛm, na womma ɔnne mmɔ ne ho ansa.
*If you carry the sheep, carry it quickly, so that it does not have a chance to defecate on its body first.*
(Solve difficult problems urgently or they may get worse).

5730. Wosoa funu a, wosoa brɛ prenu.
*If you carry the corpse, you carry double tiredness.*
(A heavy load exhausts, but you may have to bear it).

5731. Wosoa pemee a, na wodi pemee.
*If you carry something heavy, then you eat something heavy.*
(Hard labor brings its rewards).

5732. Woansoa no tuntum so a, wosoa no fufuo so.
*If you don't carry it on black, you carry it on white.*
(Sooner or later, adversity comes to all).

5733. Nsoafoɔ yɛ sika a, anka nnipa nyinaaa anya bi pɛn.
*If youthful pride were to be money, then all men would have had some before now.*
(If wishes were horses, beggars would ride).

5734. Soakɔdi nyɛ ɔbrɛ.
*Carry-it-to-eat is not fatigue.*
(It is no hardship to work for your own benefit).

5735. Asɔbayerɛ nni hɔ a, na afaseɛ kɔ nkomena mu.
*If the good yam is not there, then the water yam is put into the pit.*
(Bayere is much preferred to afaseɛ. Hence: If you can't get the best, you make do with the second best).

5736. Asokuma nwoo ne ba Kwaku Ata na Dankyirahene wɔ ne nkonnwasoani.
*Asokuma had not given birth to her son Kwaku Ata when the Dankyirahene had his own stool-bearer.*
(You need not think you are the first person to be able to do a job).

5737. Asɔkwaa wɔ adeɛ a, akyenkyena di bi.
*If the white-crested hornbill has something, then the allied hornbill eats a little.*
(Members of the family share what it has).

5738. "Som wo ho" nyɛ akoa.
*"Serve yourself" does not mean slavery.*
(You enjoy the fruits of your own labors).

5739. Wosom akɛseɛ a, wokyima waa.
*If you (a woman) frequently have sex with a big penis (lit: if you serve a big one), your periods are prolonged.*
(If you do what is beyond your natural ability, you suffer the consequences).

5740. Wosom wo panini sompa a, ɔwu a, wonsuro ne mfofo mu.
*If you serve your elder well and he dies, you don't fear his cultivated farm.*
(i.e a place where you might meet his ghost. Hence: If you do your best, you don't fear judgement).

5741. Wosom Tanɔ, som Kobi a, obieku kye wo ku wo.
*If you serve Tano and Kobi at the same time, one of them catches and kills you.*
(Tano and Kobi are both important fetishes. Hence: You can't serve two masters at once).

5742. Wosom wo wura sompa a, ɔyi wo ayɛ.
*If you serve your master well, he rewards you.*
(A good servant makes a good master).

5743. "Mensom bi, mennan bi". Ɔse: "Asɛm bɛba da bi".
*"I won't serve someone, I won't go with someone". He says: "A problem will come someday".*
(If you refuse to help people, a day will come when you yourself will need help and will not get it).

5744. Wosoma obi akoa a, bɔ no mmrane, na ɔso nnoɔma a emu yɛ duru a, emu ayɛ ne hare.
*If you send someone's servant, give him appellations, so that if he is carrying a heavy load it becomes light for him.*
(You should make those who work for you happy so that they stay with you).

5745. Wosoma wo ba paadekyire na ɔkyɛre a, ɛnteetee; na ne ho we a, ɔno ara na ɔbɛba fie.
*If you send your child far away and he stays long, don't be worried; for when he is broke, he himself will come home.*
(When in need, you go to your family first for help).

5746. Yɛsoma banyansafoɔ na yɛnsoma nammɔntentene.
*We send a wise child but we don't send a long-shanks.*
(Wisdom is more valuable than speed in taking messages).

5747. Wosoma obi a, wo nan mu na ɛdwo woɔ, na wobo deɛ ɛnnwo wo.
*If you send someone, your legs are at peace, but you yourself are not at peace.*
(There is nothing like doing a job yourself).

5748. Wosoma ɔnammɔntenten a, wobɔ kaprenu.
*If you send someone who just takes long strides, you waste your money.*
(You need intelligence as well as speed to do a job properly).

5749. Yɛsoma wo dupɔn toɔ a, kɔto, na ebia na tokuro da mu.
*If you are sent to fell a big tree, go and fell it, it might be a hollow tree.*
(Don't shirk work because it looks hard. It may turn out to be easier than you think).

5750. Asomma nsene oni ta da.
*The young elephant does not ever excel its mother in farting.*
(An inexperienced person does not excel an experienced one).

**5751. Somankorɔ bini yɛ ketewa.**
*The one who is sent and does not go, produces small feces.*
(If you don't do what you are asked, you won't be fed).

**5752. Asommɛn firi sono yam.**
*The elephant's tusks come from its stomach.*
(Outward character flows from inner nature).

**5753. Asommɛn, yɛhyɛn no anoteɛ.**
*An elephant tusk horn, we play eloquently.*
(You need special talent to make the best out of your tools).

**5754. Asommɛn ma yɛhu ɔhene diberɛ.**
*The horns help us to know the rank of the chief.*
(The importance of a man can be judged by his followers, accoutrements and trophies).

**5755. Sommorɔ tua wo to. "Mente ma wo a". Wose: "Mɛta agu wo nsa ho".**
*A tick has attached itself to your buttocks. "Let me remove it". You say: "I will fart over your hand!"*
(If someone is trying to help you, you don't abuse him).

**5756. Asomorofi dwo a, na ɔkraman nya dabrɛ.**
*If the hearth becomes cold, the dog gets a sleeping place.*
(When the cause of a problem is dealt with, things can proceed normally).

**5757. Asɔmorɔdwe a ɔda nsa mu mmoroeɛ a, wo a wokɔɔ ho kwa mmoro nsa.**
*The palm beetle which lies in the drink is not drunk, then you who stand by should not be drunk.*
(If the one most involved is not affected, how can the observer be?)

**5758. Asɔmorɔdwe Akua Annɔ: "Wo bɔ annwo asɛm a, wo were mfiri".**
*The palm beetle Akua Anno: "If you don't cease to be angry over an event, you don't forget it".*
(You can't put an incident behind you, until you've put it out of your mind).

**5759. Asɔmorɔdwe Kwaa, ɔse: "Nnipa nni ayɛ".**
*The palm beetle Kwaa says: "Men have no gratitude".*

**5760. Asɔmorɔdwe se: ɔpɛ nsa nti na ɔda nsa mu.**
*The palm beetle says: it likes drink and that is why it lies in it.*
(Birds of a feather flock together).

**5761. Ɔsonam nna hɔ mma pataku nni namkɔm nkɔtwa nhwe fam nnwu.**
*The elephant's meat does not lie about to allow the hyaena to suffer from hunger and collapse and die.*
(If there is something available for you to benefit from, you don't suffer for lack of it).

**5762. Sɔneeɛ na ɛma obi di mmɛfe.**
*It is the sieve that leads one to eat the palm nut fibers.*
(Used when someone intimate to you lets you down).

**5763. [Ɔsonkurobia]/[Ananse adodewa] se ɔrekɔso bese, wannya anso, waso abemmen.**
*Cola caricifolia says that he goes to produce cola, he*

*does not produce it, but something similar.*
(Cola caricifolia, the monkey cola or fig-leaved cola is an edible nut not produced commercially. Said when someone has tried unsuccessfully to do one thing and has inadvertently succeeded in doing something close to his original aim).

**5764. Asono mmienu nya ntɔkwa wɔ kwaeɛ ase a, ɛhɔ nnua ne nhoma na ɛhunu amaneɛ.**
*If two elephants have a quarrel in the forest, the trees and leaves there are in trouble.*
(A fight between two important men, affects the lives of many).

**5765. Ɛsono a ɔbu akuma na fɛntemfrɛm amene no no.**
*The elephant that breaks the axe is swallowed up by the swamp.*
(However great you may be there is something which can destroy you).

**5766. Ɛsono a wayare afɔn no, ne twɛ a ɛbɔ ne toɔ sene ɔtwe.**
*An elephant which has become thin because of illness, its vagina behind its buttocks is greater than the duiker.*
(In all circumstances, the great are worth more than the small).

**5767. Ɛsono ba srɛ nkwa, na ɔnsrɛ kɛseɛ.**
*The elephant's child prays for a long life, but he doesn't pray for bulk.*
(If you have enough of something, you don't ask for more).

**5768. Ɛsono di adeɛ a, ɔgya [sibire]/[go].**
*If the elephant eats something, it leaves the plant Clinogyne leucantha.*
(Some things are left alone even by the powerful).

**5769. Ɛsono di adeɛ a, ɔde ne wedeɛ twa-adwa.**
*If the elephant is enstooled, it threatens with its skin.*
(i.e it bullies with its size. Hence: Someone who is too arrogant does not make a good leader).

**5770. Ɛsono di asawa.**
*The elephant eats asawa berries.*
(The asawe or sweet berry is much liked by elephants. Hence: Even little things are appreciated by the great).

**5771. [Ɛsono]/[Ɔtwe] dua yɛ tia, ɔde saa ara na ɛpra ne ho.**
*The elephant's (duiker's) tail is short, but it manages to whisk itself with it.*
(You have to make do with what you have been given in life).

**5772. Ɛsono afɔn a, yɛnnwa no ɛberɛ so.**
*If an elephant grows thin, we don't cut it up on a palm branch.*
(A great person, even when sick, remains great).

**5773. Ɛsono ho na yɛbɔ [apuruwa]/[namkum].**
*It is from the elephant that big lumps of meat are cut.*
(A powerful man means wealth).

**5774. Ɛsono nkɔ adidi nnya ne mma.**
*The elephant does not go to feed and leave its children behind.*
(A great man looks after his followers).

5775. Ɛsono kokurokoo, nanso adowa na [ɔman wɔ no]/[ne panin]/[ne hene].
*The elephant is enormous, but the royal antelope [owns the state]/[is senior]/[is chief].*
(The royal antelope is king of the beasts. Hence: Seniority does not depend on size).

5776. Ɛsono kokuroko hunu, adowa ne nkwan.
*The elephant is huge, but the royal antelope makes better soup.*
(Bulk does not ensure quality).

5777. Ɛsono kokuroko nso ɔnni se na ɔde aka.
*The elephant may be huge but it does not have teeth to bite.*
(Even the most powerful person has his weakness).

5778. Ɛsono akyiri nni aboa.
*After the elephant there is no other animal.*
(You can't compare the small with the great).

5779. Ɛsono akyiri aboa ne bɔfoɔ.
*After the elephant is the hunter.*
(Said of someone who takes over from a powerful man).

5780. Ɛsono nya wo a, adowa bɔ wo fɛ.
*When the elephant catches you, the royal antelope slaps you too.*
(Once you have been defeated by a big man, the small ones will turn on you too).

5781. Ɛsono nya wuo a, na efiri ɔkɔtɔ.
*If the elephant dies, it is because of the crab.*
(The crab is supposed to be able to kill an elephant by climbing inside its trunk. Hence: Even a small thing can cause the downfall of a great man).

5782. Ɛsono retea, ɔbɔfoɔ retea, hwan na ɔbɛkum baako akɔdie?
*The elephant trumpets, the hunter shouts, which of them will kill the other so that they may eat?*
(When two equal forces meet, the battle must end in the victory of one).

5783. Ɛsono tia fidie so a, [ɛnhwan]/[ɛbu].
*If the elephant treads on a trap [it does not spring]/[it breaks].*
(If the chief says something is not open for discussion any more, then the business is finished).

5784. Ɛsono tɔ fam a, aboa biara bɔ no bi.
*If the elephant falls, all the animals beat him.*
(When a great man becomes powerless, everyone abuses him).

5785. Ɛsono nni wiram a, anka ɛkoɔ ne ɔbɔpɔn.
*If the elephant is not in the forest, then the bush cow is the great animal.*
(When the great man is away someone else deputizes for him).

5786. Ɛsono bi nom adɔkonnie nko.
*Some people eat their kenkey differently from others.*
(Customs differ).

5787. Ɛsono dawuro, ɛsono dawuro, na ɛsono Akonna-kuma dawuro.
*There are many different gongongs but the Akonna-kuma has a special quality.*

(The construction "ɛsono A, ɛsono B" in this and the following proverbs means "A is one thing and B is another" or "A and B are different". Said of an exceptional person who cannot be compared to others).

5788. Ɛsono odum, na ɛsono ɔdan, na ɛsono kakapempen.
*Piptadenia africana is one thing, chlorophora excelsia is another and rauwolfia vomitoria is yet another.*
(These are three well-known forest trees. Hence: Everything has its own individuality and should be treated in its own way).

5789. Ɛsono fofoɔ mu dɔtɔ na ɛsono kwaeɛ-dɔtɔ.
*A thicket on a farm is one thing, a thicket in the forest is another.*
(Things may appear to be the same but have different functions).

5790. Ɛsono akoa na ɛsono akoa ba.
*A servant is one thing and a servant's child another.*
(People may resemble each other but be quite different in nature and position).

5791. Ɛsono sika na ɛsono ɔmmamma.
*Money is one thing and good citizenship is another.*
(Money alone does not make you a useful person).

5792. Ɛsono ntanka na esono agodie.
*It is one thing to take an oath, but another to play a game.*
(You can act either seriously or frivolously but not both at once).

5793. Ɛsono "Wo ho yɛ tan!" na ɛsono "Wo ho yɛ tan papa!"
*It is one thing (to say) "You are ugly", but it is another to say: "You are very very ugly".*
(A little criticism is not bad, but you don't need to be offensive).

5794. Nsono na ɔboa yafunu.
*The intestines help the stomach.*
(We are all interdependent within the family).

5795. Sonsono mpo wɔ ne pɛfoɔ.
*Even the worm has its fanciers.*
(Everyone is liked or admired by someone).

5796. Sonsono se ɔrenyini ansa na wafiri ani, ɛne no srataa.
*The worm says when it grows it will develop eyes, then it came to nothing.*
(Idle boasting will not achieve success).

5797. Asonsuasɔ ɔse: "Meresu me ho".
*The Senegal kingfisher says: "I am mourning for myself".*
(Said when someone sees nothing but bad in the future and is depressed).

5798. Nsoo nko nnɛre.
*Ash alone does not make a flame.*
(Some tasks cannot be done without help).

5799. Asoɔden nwo ba pa.
*Stubbornness does not give birth to a good baby.*
(A stubborn person does not make a success in life).

5800. Asoɔden yare ntisiaseɛ.
*Stubbornness suffers from refusal to listen.*
(An obstinate person does not take advice).

5801. Ɔsoodoni ka asomsɛm kyere ɔhene a, na nyɛ hwee sɛ aduane ho asɛm.
*If a chief's cook whispers to the chief, then it is not anything more than the talking of food.*
(Experts think more of their job than anything else).

5802. Ɔsoro adeɛ yɛ duro a, ɛnyɛ wɔnne atentrehuo.
*If things from above are heavy, leave out kapok.*
(There is an exception to every rule).

5803. Ɔsoro gye "tɛ!" a, asaase gye "tim!"
*If the heavens recieve "tɛ!" (i.e are shaken) then the earth receives "tim!"(i.e a blow).*
(If the person in authority is disgraced, then the people are doomed).

5804. Ɔsoro yi wo ma asaase yi wo a, wodi nnahia.
*If the heavens disown you and make the earth disown you, you don't have anywhere to rest (lit. you suffer from sleep-need).*
(If you are completely abandoned your life is not worth living).

5805. Wososɔ a, wode kɔma ne wura.
*If you repair, you return it to its owner.*
(What does not belong to you should be returned even if you have improved it).

5806. Sɔsɔ ammu, akuma ammu a, kwaeɛ si deɛ ɛsi.
*If the mattock does not clear and the axe does not clear, the forest stands where it is.*
(You can't get anywhere without work).

5807. Sɔsɔ ntu abɛ mma akuma mpene.
*The mattock does not uproot the palm tree for the axe to groan.*
(No one should suffer as a result of another's activity).

5808. Wososɔ ɛta so a, na ɛbɔn.
*If you are conscious of wind having been passed, then you smell it more.*
(Sometimes it's only when something is brought to your attention, that it worries you).

5809. Asosɔmu na ɛma okunafoɔ te ka ɔdeɛɛfoɔ soɔ.
*Constant help leads the widow to become attached to the helper.*
(If you constantly help people they become attached to you).

5810. Nsosɔsoɔ na ɛma kɔmfo-barima dwonsɔ-dwonsɔ ne ho badwam.
*It's flattery that makes the powerful fetish priest urinate on his body.*
(If you overdo things, you disgrace yourself).

5811. Ɔsotifoɔ nim ahwehwɛ mu hwɛ na ɔnte: "Fa ahwehwɛ ma me".
*A deaf person can look in a mirror but does not hear: "Bring me the mirror".*
(Seeing is one thing, hearing another).

5812. Asoto nti na yɛtu namɔn si awaresɛm soɔ.
*Because of false accusation, we put our foot on marriage squabbles.*
(Deal with family squabbles quickly so that they don't become real fights).

5813. Asoto yɛ ya sene ohia.
*False accusation is more bitter than poverty.*

5814. [Sotorɔ]/[Twedeɛ] bɛn wo a, wogye no ntɛm.
*If [a box]/[a blow]on the ear is coming to you, you take it at once.*
(If you know adversity is coming, go to meet it).

5815. Sotorɔ mmienu yɛ ani-hahane.
*Two slaps on the face give you a jolt.*
(Said when you find it difficult to face two difficult tasks at once).

5816. Asra kae ani awerɛhoɔ.
*Snuff reminds the eye of sadness.*
(Your eyes run when you take snuff. Some things are automatically evoked by certain actions).

5817. Ɔsrane mfiti prɛko ntwa ɔman mu.
*The moon does not on one occasion cross the state.*
(It takes time to achieve your purpose).

5818. Ɔsrane tan anadwo.
*The moon hates the night.*
(Said of something which enlightens).

5819. Ɔsrane bɛwu agya nsoromma.
*The moon will die and leave the stars.*
(Don't shun an old friend for a new, who may only last a short time).

5820. Asratoa Kofi adi asɛmpa nso yɛde ne tiri bɔ duam.
*Snuff-box Kofi has helped a great deal but we still knock his head against a tree.*
(Said of a useful person who is not appreciated but abused).

5821. Wosrɛ a, na wɔmfa mma woɔ, na wotɔ tua ka deɛ a, wo dea.
*If you beg for something and they don't give it to you and you buy and pay for something, it is yours.*
(What you pay for you own absolutely).

5822. Wosrɛ adeɛ na wobɛnya a, ɛnhia nkotodwe buo.
*If you beg for something and you are going to get it, you don't need to go down on your knees.*
(Don't be obsequious when it isn't necessary!)

5823. Wosrɛ kwasea adeɛ a, ɔmma wo mmrɛ.
*If you beg something from a fool, he does not make you regret.*
(It is easy to get things out of a stupid person).

5824. Wosrɛ na wobɛnya a, wontɔ.
*You beg and you are going to obtain (something) then you don't buy it.*
(If you can get something free, you don't pay money for it).

5825. Wosrɛ Nyame a, wose: obi nkɔka mmɛka wo.
*If you make a request to God, you say: let no one implicate you in a case.*
(We all pray to be free of trouble).

5826. Woasrɛ apesie, yɛrebu wo anikyie, wose: "Te abomuu to me so!"
*You beg for starch food, we look askance at you, you say: "Take some of the broth to add to it!"*
(If you can't get the main thing you want it is no good asking for what goes with it).

**5827. Srɛsrɛ-bidie nyɛ korɔnobɔ.**
*Constant begging for something to eat is not stealing.*
(It is not wrong to ask someone for something if you are in need).

**5828. Wosu gye a, yɛde ma wo; wosere gye nso a, yɛde ma wo; na akyire asɛm!**
*If you cry for it, we give it to you; if you laugh for it, we also give it to you; but the aftermath?*
(The future may depend on how you get your way, not on whether you get it).

**5829. Yɛresu anadwo su, wose "Ma menhwɛ w'ani ase nisuo".**
*We are weeping in the night, yet you say: "Let me see your tears".*
(Don't ask the impossible. Or: Don't make the situation worse).

**5830. Su nkwa, na nsu adeɛ.**
*Cry for life, but don't cry for riches.*
(As long as there is life there is hope).

**5831. Mesu wo brɛbrɛ na mense: "Sɛ wowu a, fa me kɔ".**
*I am weeping copiously for you, but I do not say: "If you die, take me along!"*
(Even if you like someone enough to warn them, it does not mean you are prepared to suffer with them).

**5832. Yɛnsu a, yetee so.**
*If we don't weep, at least we sob.*
(You can't control your emotions altogether).

**5833. Ɔresu su n'ani.**
*He who weeps, weeps from his own eyes.*
(Suffering is personal).

**5834. Esu a ɛyɛ dɛ na yɛfrɛ no awerɛhosu.**
*Weeping that is satisfying, we call it sad weeping.*
(The genuine thing is best).

**5835. Esu yɛdi no agyegye.**
*Weeping is contagious.*

**5836. Esu gu ahodoɔ: agorɔ su nko, ɛbora su nko, owuo su nko, na mpatu-su nko.**
*There are many kinds of weeping: weeping from a game is one thing, weeping from beating is another, weeping from death is yet another, and pretended weeping another.*
(There is a right time for every action).

**5837. Esu yɛ dɛ o, nyɛ dɛ o, ɛnnyane funu.**
*If weeping is pleasant, if it isn't pleasant, it does not wake up the corpse.*
(Sometimes mourners weep in a way that is satisfactory to those at the funeral, sometimes they don't. Either way, the deceased is still dead. Hence: said in circumstances where an act can be well or badly performed, but cannot change things fundamentally for the better).

**5838. Esu-frenkyemm ntua ka.**
*Weeping nicely does not pay debts.*
(See Proverb 5837).

**5839. Asua a annya ɔpatafoɔ na ɛtware kwan mu.**
*The stream which is not checked crosses the road.*
(If an angry man is not calmed down, he does damage).

**5840. Yɛsua ɔbra pa na yensua ɔbra bɔne.**
*We follow a good way of life but we do not follow a bad way of life.*
(You should aim for the best).

**5841. Wosua korɔno bɔ a, na woasua brɛbrɛ-womu-ase.**
*If you learn how to steal, then you have learned how to crouch and move slowly.*
(If you learn a profession, then you learn the skills that go with it).

**5842. Osua faa nnua nkɔnmu kɔyɛɛ afuo no, Kwaku Ananse de nyansa twaa kwan too ho de gyee ne nsa mu.**
*The white-nosed monkey from the top of the trees made a farm. Kwaku Ananse with cleverness cut a road to steal the produce.*
(A clever man may cheat you out of your just deserts).

**5843. [Osua]/[Ahwenhema] turu ne ba a, oturu no wɔ ne yafunu so.**
*If the white-nosed monkey carries its baby, it carries it on its stomach.*
(Akan people carry children on their backs. Hence: Customs differ).

**5844. Osua nwo ɛfoɔ.**
*The white-nosed monkey does not give birth to the colobus monkey.*
(Children resemble their parents, not strangers).

**5845. Nsuaeɛ nyɛ ɔko ampa.**
*Determination is not the same as actually going to war.*
(Making a decision is not the same as acting on it).

**5846. Yɛasuane pieto mu, na danta?**
*We have been able to tear the underpants, how much more the loin-cloth?*
(If you have destroyed a powerful person, you can easily deal with a lesser one).

**5847. Suban pa yɛ sene sika.**
*A good character is worth more than money.*

**5848. Osubɔdom nkɔbɔ nsɔwa ma yentwitwa akura aso.**
*The clawless otter does not go and take the catch from the fish trap so that we should cut off the mouse's ears.*
(A man should not be punished for another man's crime).

**5849. Asubɔtoɔ susu ne kɔte so na wabu ne pieto.**
*A person who measures the waist makes allowance for the penis before he makes the underpants.*
(Before embarking on a job, you have to consider all the elements involved).

**5850. Asudanna se: ɔte nsuo mu nti ɔda a, n'ani nkum.**
*The gaboon terrapin says: it lives in the water, so when it lies down, its does not sleep.*
(In some circumstances, you have to be constantly on the alert).

**5851. Osudwarefo na nsuo fa no.**
*The swimmer, the water takes him.*
(It is the person most intimately connected with something that is most likely to suffer through it).

5852. Sudwetire yɛ bɔna.
*Sobbing is hard to bear.*

5853. Sudwetire yɛ mmaa ahodeɛ.
*Sobbing is a woman's perquisite.*
(It is a woman's right to weep).

5854. Sudwetire nyɛ bɔna na osumafoɔ.
*Sobbing is not difficult, but whom to sob for?*
(It is not easy to find a worthy person to mourn).

5855. Nsufi tumi dum gya.
*Dirty water can put out fire.*
(Everyone can do something, however insignificant they are).

5856. Osufoɔ nyɛ na, na ɔkomafoɔ na ɔhia.
*A mourner is not rare, but those able to fight for you are most needed.*
(It is better to support someone when alive than to mourn for them when they are dead).

5857. Asugyadie yɛ animguasee.
*Bachelorship is a disgrace.*
(You need a wife to have a position in society).

5858. Osugyani didi aberaw-aberaw.
*An unmarried person eats scantily.*
(If you have no one to care for you, you look after yourself as best you can).

5859. Osugyani sɛ ne kɛtɛ ansa na waboro nsa.
*An unmarried person lays his own mat before he gets drunk.*
(If you have no one to care for you, you must plan ahead for yourself).

5860. Osugyani tirim wɔasɛm pa; nti na ɔne a, ɔpapa ne toɔ, na anka ɔne obi nni atunumuhwɛ.
*An unmarried person is sensible; that is why if he defecates, he cleans his behind, even though he and someone (else) do not look at each other's behinds.*
(i.e because he is not engaged with anyone in mutual inspection of behinds-as he might be if he were married. Hence: Some actions are taken for personal satisfaction and not to please others).

5861. Asuhina bɔ a, yɛmmisa koraa.
*If the water pot breaks, we don't ask for the calabash.*
(If the main source of supply is unable to provide, then the subsidiaries cannot).

5862. Asuhina ho hyehye no a, na nsuo na ɛwɔ mu.
*If the pot feels discomfort, it is because there is water in it.*
(A man's troubles emanate from the society in which he lives).

5863. Asuhina ntoto ne ho ase nkyɛre.
*The water pot does not run into danger for long.*
(If you know you are weak, keep out of trouble).

5864. Nsu-hunu yɛ ɔmee a, anka ɔkaa mfa daawa.
*If mere water were satisfying, then the fish would not take the hook.*
(Man is never satisfied but always seeking for something better).

5865. Suhyefa yɛmmua.
*Half a roof you cannot thatch.*
(Hear all sides of a case before giving judgment).

5866. Asuhyiayeɛ Tano se: "Deɛ ɛyɛ na ɛyɛ".
*Asuhyiayeɛ Tano says: "What is good, is good".*
(Asuhyiayeɛ Tano is one of the Tano fetishes. Hence: We should accept what is right).

5867. Asuhyiayeɛ Tano se: "Gye me dee na fa wo deɛ ma me, na wo deɛ no nyɛ".
*The Asuhyiaeɛ Tano says: "Take my thing and give me your thing, for your thing is worthless."*
(See Proverb 5866. You should be grateful if someone offers to exchange good for bad).

5868. Asuhyiayeɛ Tano se: "Wo ni te ase a, wose wo ne Mmɛm Boɔ pɛ".
*Asuhyiayeɛ Tano says: "If your mother is alive, you are as important as the Mmɛm Boɔ fetish".*
(Asuhyiayɛ Tano is one fetish and Mmɛm Boɔ is another. In a matrilineal society, the presence of the mother is of utmost importance).

5869. Asuhyiayeɛ Tano se: "Yɛwo tɔ yen ti".
*The Tano fetish says: "We give birth in order that if in difficulty it can be sacrificed".*
(See Proverb 5866. Used for instance if a baby dies in child-birth and the mother is saved. Hence: In time of need, we may have to sacrifice what is ours).

5870. Nsu-ketewa yɛ hye a, ɛso adware.
*If little water becomes hot, it becomes sufficient to bathe.*
(If something can be diluted, it goes a long way).

5871. Sukɔnkɔm ee! gyae dawuro bɔ na deɛ n'adeɛ yeraeɛ no, ɔpɛeɛ a, wahunu.
*Waterbird! stop beating your gongong, for even he whose property was lost, and who was searching, has found it.*
(Sukɔnkɔm is a heron. Used to restrain someone who makes too much fuss about something).

5872. Sukɔnkɔn se: se wanhyia asuo a, anka adidie abɔ no.
*The water bird says, if it were not for the help of the river, it would lose its eating-place.*
(See Proverb 5871. Some people exist on the charity of others).

5873. Asukɔnoma na ɔde sodeɛ ba.
*The baby at the breast brings about the first death of one's child.*
(One step can only follow another).

5874. Sukuu mfa adwareɛ ho hwee.
*School going is not connected with bathing.*
(Don't confuse separate functions).

5875. Osukwase anomaa nkɔdi Korɔbo ayuo na wɔnkyere Asanteni ntua ka.
*The Osukwase bird does not go to Kroboland to eat millet for an Asante to be taken as hostage.*
(You should not be make to suffer for what does not concern you).

**5876. Wosum borɔdeɛ a, sum kwadu, na wonnim dee ɔkɔm ba a ɛbɛgye wo.**
*If you plant plantain, plant some banana too, for you do not know when hunger will overcome you.*
(Don't put all your eggs in one basket).

**5877. Wosum aberewa a, wonhwɛ deɛ ɔbɛhweɛ.**
*If you push an old lady down, you don't bother where she has fallen.*
(If you deliberately commit an offense, you don't bother about the person you have offended).

**5878. Wosum nkontompo fidie a, woyi kasabrɛ.**
*If you set a lying trap, you catch nagging.*
(If you act badly, you attract constant blame).

**5879. Wosum aniha fidie a, woyi: "Agyawaadwo".**
*If you set a trap lazily, you catch: "Oh! dear".*
("Agyawaadwo" is an eclamation used when one is surprised. Hence: You suffer the consequences of your own bad work).

**5880. Suman kafirima nyɛ biribiara, na ɛyɛ amiadeɛ.**
*If the kafirima charm is good for nothing else, it has value as an ornament.*
(Even something which is apparently useless can serve a purpose).

**5881. Sumina de bɔkɔɔ na ɛhyeɛ.**
*The midden takes time to burn.*
(Slowly does it).

**5882. Sumina mu gya nhi da.**
*The fire on the rubbish heap never ceases.*
(Something which is adequately supplied lasts a long time).

**5883. Sumina na ɛkora nnebɔne.**
*It is the rubbish heap that keeps wickedness.*
(A despised person is given the worst tasks).

**5884. Suminaso dommo, ɔse: "Wobu me anikyeɛ a, merentɔ wo sɛn mu".**
*Mushroom in the midden says: "If you make rude gestures at me, I will never enter your cooking pot".*
(If you have no business with somebody, leave them alone).

**5885. Suminaso ntonkom se: sɛ apɔpe ammɔ no a, anka ɔne n'afɛfoɔ pɛ.**
*The big pepper on the midden says: if the splashing up of rain did not beat it, it would do as well as its counterpart on the farm.*
(We are slaves to our environments).

**5886. Suminaso ntonkom se: "Menyaa esie so siiɛ a, anka mɛso nnenkyeremma".**
*The pepper on the midden says: "If I could grow on an anthill then I would produce coral beads".*
(Given the best conditions you can produce wonders).

**5887. Suminaso anyɛ huam a, na ɛfiri fie.**
*If the rubbish heap stinks, it is from the house.*
(The origin of a person's shortcomings are from his family background).

**5888. Sunsum-Akwaboakwa-Trawa, wosɔre a, na wasɔre; wogyina a, na wagyina; nso wosoma no a, ɔnkɔ.**
*The flat shadow, if you get up, it gets up; if you stay still, it stays still; but if you send it, it does not go.*
(Some people are parasites: they depend on others but are not prepared to help them).

**5889. Sunsummɔne ba fie a, yɛde nkosua ɛne ɛtɔ na ɛpam no.**
*If a bad spirit comes to the house, we take eggs and mashed yam to drive it away.*
(We use tact to deal with a difficult person).

**5890. Yɛnsunti prɛko mmɔ ahina.**
*You don't stumble and break the pot simultaneously.*
(One things follows on another).

**5891. Asuo a ɔtae hɔ dinn na ɔfa nnipa.**
*It is the water which lies there calm that drowns men.*
(Still waters run deep).

**5892. Asuo a ɛte sɛ bosompo na nkyene akwam yi, na ɛwɔ aseɛ.**
*If a great body of water like the sea had too much salt, there must be a reason for it.*
(If even a great person is in trouble, how much more a humble one).

**5893. Asuo ba ne hweɛ a, na yɛhwɛ.**
*If a river is ready for fishing, we fish in it.*
(See Proverb 530. Hence: When our plans are ripe, we act).

**5894. Asuo bɔ biribi din na ɛwee.**
*Water utters the name of something and then dries up.*
(There is always a cause for someone's giving up the struggle).

**5895. Asuo bɔ asuo mu a, ɛdane asuwa.**
*If one stream runs into another, then it becomes a tributary.*
(If you serve a more important person, you come under his sovereignty).

**5896. Asuo refa ɔbakwasea a, ose: "Mereka sakere".**
*If the stream is taking a foolish person, he says: "I am riding a bicycle".*
(A foolish person does not recognize dangers).

**5897. Asuo fa wo a, na ɛho nnua nyinaa tane wo.**
*When a river is taking you, then all the trees (on the bank) hate you.*
(If you are in real trouble, people tend to desert you).

**5898. Asuo fa wo a, wonom bi.**
*When water is drowning you, you drink some.*
(You can't avoid being affected by a disaster, once you are implicated in it).

**5899. Asuo mfa masan.**
*The river does not drown a man who does not enter it.*
(If you are not involved with something, you don't suffer from it).

**5900. Asuo ho nni biribi a, ɛwɔ dware-ho-firi.**
*If a stream has nothing else, it has washing-from-itself.*
(If something can't be used for one thing, it can be used for another).

**5901. Asuo ho anwonoma ɔse: "Owia na meda no aseɛ".**
*Clinotyne filipas growing by the water says: "I give thanks to the sun."*
(The leaves of this plant are used in wrapping food at the market and are brought to town and sold in bundles for that purpose. You are grateful for what makes you thrive).

**5902. Asuo nam biribi so na ɛweɛ.**
*If the stream dries up it is for some reason.*
(Nothing happens without a reason).

**5903. Asuo ne asuo na ɛbɔ.**
*Two streams come together.*
(Two people with similar interests get on together).

**5904. Asuo ampinkyɛ wo a, wopinkyɛ no sa bi nom.**
*If a stream does not approach you, you approach it to drink something.*
(If the mountain does not come to Mohammed, Mohammed goes to the mountain).

**5905. Asuo ɔpo mpo a emu dɔ na nkyene atware mu yi, na deɛ ɛnni amena.**
*Even the ocean that is deep has an excess of salt, how much more the shallow ditch.*
(If a great man suffers, how much more the poor man).

**5906. Asuo bɛtoo abotan.**
*A river came to meet a stone.*
(Some people are senior to others).

**5907. Asuo tware kwan, ɔkwan tware asuo, ɔpanin ne hwan? Yɛbɔɔ kwan no kɔtoo asuo no, asuo no firi tete.**
*The stream crosses the path, the path crosses the stream, but which is the elder? We made the path to meet the river, the river is from creation.*
(Seniority takes precedence over power).

**5908. Asuo we a, ɛwɔ n'anwea mu.**
*If the water dries up, it is in its sand.*
(In times of difficulty, a powerful man still maintains his roots).

**5909. Asuo yiri a, na sukɔnkɔn kɔ atwee.**
*If the river overflows then the heron goes hunting.*
(Make the most of your opportunities).

**5910. Asuo yiri a, na nsunam yɛ ahantan.**
*If the river floods, the fish become proud.*
(In times of national wealth and success people tend to show off).

**5911. Asuo yiri a, ɛtwe.**
*If water overflows, then it subsides.*
(If something reaches its limits, then it loses force).

**5912. Nsuo a yɛde dum egya, yɛmpe no korɔgyee.**
*Water that we take to put out a fire, we don't expect to be clean.*
(What you need depends on what it is for).

**5913. Nsuo a yɛnni mu adee no yɛmfa mu nsoa.**
*The river from which we don't eat fish, we don't set traps in.*
(One should not expect to benefit from a project one does not support).

**5914. Nsuo a edɔ woɔ na ɛkɔ w'ahina mu.**
*It is the water that loves you which goes into your water pot.*
(If someone does not like you, he avoids you).

**5915. Nsuo a honam apoɔ nɔ, tɛkrɛma mfa nsie.**
*Water that has been rejected by the skin, the tongue should not keep.*
(A thing which is bad for one person is bad for others).

**5916. Nsuo a ɛnso adwareɛ no, eso nom.**
*Water which is not sufficient for bathing in is at least sufficient for drinking.*
(Be thankful for small mercies).

**5917. Nsuo a yɛnnwareɛ no, yɛnnom.**
*A river we would not bathe in, we do not drink from.*
(If you want to avoid something, avoid it altogether).

**5918. Nsuo a ɛwe ɔpeberɛ no, yɛfrɛ no "Dane–Nyame".**
*The river which dries up in the dry season we call: "At the mercy of God."*
(In times of trouble people wait for God to act).

**5919. Nsuo boro kramoni a, yɛmmisa ne batakari.**
*If rain beats a Moslem, we don't ask him about his batakari.*
(The batakiri is the smock worn in the North of Ghana, which will be soaked by the rain. Hence: If someone is in trouble, you don't rub it in).

**5920. Nsuo boro ɔpɛtɛ a, na ɔse: "Ɔkyena mesi me dan".**
*When rain beats the vulture it says: "Tomorrow I will build my house".*
(Said of people who constantly make promises they do not keep).

**5921. Nsuo dɔɔso nanso bosompo na ɔyɛ panin.**
*There are many waters but the sea is the elder.*
(People may appear similar but one is always the leader).

**5922. Nsuo hono ansa na agyene.**
*Water clouds before it becomes pure.*
(You must make a mistake before you can rectify it).

**5923. Nsuo hwe ɔsebɔ a, ne ho na efɔ; na ne nworanworan deɛ ɛmpopa.**
*When the rain beats the leopard, it wets it; but its spots it does not wash out.*
(Circumstances don't change a man's real nature).

**5924. Nsuo hwie gu a, na ahina mmɔeɛ.**
*The water can be poured out, but the pot does not break.*
(You can get rid of a temporary setback, but this does not mean that the main problem does not still exist).

**5925. Nsuo ka ano na nka nsa.**
*Water remains in the mouth but not in the hand.*
(Some people are able to retain and make use of wealth, others let it slip through their fingers).

**5926. Nsuo kyɛre ahina mu a, ɛbɔn.**
*If water stays long in the water pot, it stinks.*
(Familiarity breeds contempt).

5927. Nsuo mu panin ne kɔtɔ.
*In the river, the elder is the crab.*
(Said of a popular person).

5928. Nsuo pompono pompono a, ano twa.
*No matter how far the stream wanders, it must end somewhere.*
(Everything has its end).

5929. Nsuo pɔtɔpɔtɔ: tiatia mu na kɔsa nsu pa.
*Muddy water: pass through it and go and draw pure water.*
(Said of someone who has been of service but is being discarded for someone apparently better).

5930. Nsuo nsa anom nti ɔsansa fa adwene.
*Because there is always water in the mouth, the kite takes the fish.*
(Hunger compels a person to eat what they do not normally eat).

5931. Nsuo ansene ne egyina faako a, yɛfrɛ no tareɛ.
*If the stream does not flow but becomes stagnant, we call it a pond.*
(If someone does not fulfill expectations, we look down on them).

5932. Wo nsuo sua na wohunu adware a, ɛso wo.
*If you have little water and you are able to bathe, it is sufficient.*
(Enough is as good as a feast).

5933. Nsuo tae dɔtee so.
*The stream rests on the earth.*
(Everyone has his supporter).

5934. Nsuo atɔ atene susuan amfa mmusuo ankɔ, na ɔtareɛ na ɔbɛtumi ayɛ mmusuo dɛn?
*The falling rain that had drainage has not drained calamity away, how much less could a pool deal with calamity?*
(If an expert cannot deal with a problem, nor can the inexperienced).

5935. Nsuo tae aponkyerɛne a, ɔnna nyɛ wɔɔ.
*If the frog gets a surfeit of water, it does not lie there and croak.*
(Said for instance, when an offense is so overwhelming that the offended person is shocked into silence).

5936. Nsuo twe a, ɛda n'asumena mu.
*If the stream subsides, it rests on its own bed.*
(If you lose your position, you go back to where you came from).

5937. Nsuo nyiri mfa anomaa.
*The river does not flood out the bird.*
(Use appropriate measures).

5938. Osuo a ɛtɔ Korɔbo no, eno ara na ɛtɔ Siade.
*Of the rain which has fallen on the Krobo hills, some h as fallen on the Shai hills.*
(What is happening with me, is also happening with you).

5939. Osuo a ebetɔ nnim abosɛn.
*Rain that will fall does not care about juju.*
("Abosɛn" refers to stones hung up as a medicine to avert rain. Hence: Nature does not pay attention to such things).

5940. Osuo na boro boɔ a, ɛhohoro ho kwa.
*If water beats on a stone, it washes it in vain.*
(A strong man cannot be easily moved).

5941. Osuo aboro boɔ, ɛtim deɛ ɛtim.
*When rain beats a stone, it stands firm where it stands firm.*
(See Proverb 5940).

5942. Osuo aboro nkyene, nku resere no. Aboagyewaa nku, owia bɛbɔ na wodane sɛn?
*If water beats salt, shea butter teases it. Abogyewaa's shea butter, how will you be when the sun shines?*
(Don't laugh at another's troubles, your turn will come).

5943. Osuo boroo wo a, wose: "Ɔboroo me", na nka sɛ: "Ɔpampamoo me".
*If the rain beat you, you say: "It beat me", but not: "It drove me away".*
(Confess to the whole truth).

5944. Osuo na ɛma ntakraboa di tuo.
*The rain makes the birds receive the gun.*
(Misfortune makes you vulnerable).

5945. Osuo rebetɔ a, mframa di kan.
*If the rain is going to fall, the wind comes first.*
(There is always some warning before a major event).

5946. Osuo tɔ a, ɔtɔ gu po mu.
*If the rain falls, it falls to pour into the sea.*
(All waters feed the sea. The great benefit from the small).

5947. Osuo atɔ aboro asensɛ, ose: "Monnsere me, me ho bɛwo".
*The rain has fallen and beaten the hen with ruffled feathers: it says: "You need not laugh at me, I shall get dry".*
(Sometimes people try and make out that permanent ills are caused by something transitory which will clear up).

5948. Osuo tɔ gyae a, yensɔ nsuo.
*If the rain has fallen and stopped, we don't collect rain water.*
(You don't shut the stable door after the horse has bolted).

5949. Osuo tɔ hwe wo, na owia bɔ hye wo a, na wohunu abrabɔ yeaa.
*When the rain falls and beats you, and the sun comes out and burns you, then you see the troubles of life.*
(Experience is the great teacher).

5950. Osuo tɔ na ɔbɔfoɔ bekum aboa a, efiri ne katae.
*If it rains and the hunter kills an animal, then it is due to the gun cover.*(Used when an apparently unimportant person saves the day).

5951. Osuo tɔ na egu biribi so ansa na aka wo a, ɛnyɛ ya.
*If rain falls and drops on something else before reaching you, it is not painful.*
(If someone else takes the first blow in a disaster, you do not suffer too much).

**5952. Osuo retɔ na yɛnyiyi nneɛma a, ɛnyɛ yɛne boɔ.**
*If it is raining and we are told to collect things up, then it does not mean a stone.*
(Don't protect people who can protect themselves).

**5953. Osuo tɔɔ anadwo na woanhunu, na adeɛ kyee anɔpa nso ɛ?**
*The rain fell in the night and you did not notice it, but what about it at daybreak?*
(You don't make the same mistake twice).

**5954. Asuogya nko ne n'asaase.**
*The other side of the water is its own land.*
(What applies in one country does not apply in another. Customs differ).

**5955. Asuogya wɔ afanu.**
*The other side of the river has two sides.*
(You need a sense of balance in life).

**5956. Asuom wɔ "soa me!"**
*At the riverside there is "carry me".*
(Every place has its own idiom).

**5957. Nsuonwunu nyɛ: nsuohyeɛ nyɛ; gyimii nyɛ; nyansa nyɛ.**
*Cold water is no good; hot water is no good; foolishness is no good; wisdom is no good.*
(Nothing in the world is perfectly good).

**5958. Supurupu dom aberewa, na aberewa dom supurupu.**
*The turtle is useful to the old woman, and the old woman cares for the turtle.*
(Mutual help is good).

**5959. Suro deɛ ɔrepɛ wo hɔ biribi agyeɛ, na nsuro deɛ ɔbema wo biribi.**
*Fear him who wishes to take something from you, but do not fear him who wishes to give you something.*

**5960. Wosuro dibemma na asɛm to wo a, wonya kamafoɔ.**
*If you are afriad of apologies and something happens to you, you won't get a person to defend you.*
(Said in order to urge contrition).

**5961. Wonsuro dɔm anim a, wonsuro asɛm anim.**
*If you do not fear the battle front, you do not fear the front where words are weapons.*
(A courageous man does not fear criticism).

**5962. Wosuro dɔnkɔ bini ani a, wote no mprɛnsa.**
*If you fear a slave's feces, you sweep it up three times.*
(If you don't deal with something at once, the work accumulates).

**5963. Wosuro adwamsɛm a, w'abadwadeɛ yɛ ketewa.**
*If you fear to take part in public disputes, your share of fees (for attending) is small.*
(You can't expect to reap the benefit unless you take part in the action).

**5964. Wosuro ahennwareɛ a, wobɔ dɔfoa.**
*If you are afraid of marrying a chief, you attempt to hide yourself.*
(If you don't want to do something, you keep out of the way of those who may want you to).

**5965. Wosuro wo ho, na wonya amaneɛ a, wonya no ketewa.**
*If you are afraid of getting involved and you do get into trouble, you only get into a little (trouble).*
(If you are not a trouble-maker, you are judged leniently).

**5966. Wosuro "kai-kai" a, wonyɛn ayɛmmoa.**
*If you fear to shout "kai" in driving your animals, then you don't rear them.*
(If you are afraid of doing something, you don't succeed in it. "Kai" is used in shouting after a person or animal you are chasing).

**5967. Wosuro kwaeɛ bi mu a, wotwa mu ahoma a, wotwa no tenten.**
*If you are afraid of being in the forest, if you cut a rope, you cut a long one.*
(Ropes are made from forest creepers and so must be found in the forest. Hence: If you do something you fear, do it properly and you won't have to go back and do it again).

**5968. Wosuro akyekyere-sane a, wodi adwimpodie.**
*If you fear to tie and untie properly, you will bungle the job.*
(You need confidence in order to succeed).

**5969. Wosuro ananteanananteɛ a, wohwere adeɛ.**
*If you are afraid of going about you lose your fortune.*
(You must be active to succeed in life).

**5970. Wosuro nnatutuo a, wodi nnahia**
*If you fear changing your sleeping place, you experience the need of somewhere to sleep.*
(Sometimes its necessary to move on).

**5971. Wosuro nimo a, yɛde wo sekan dwa nanka.**
*If you fear adverse comment, your knife is used to cut up an adder.*
(In order to avoid publicity you may get into an unpleasant situation. Hence: Have the courage of your convictions).

**5972. Wosuro nnipa a, nnipa bɛsuro wo.**
*If you fear people, they too will fear you.*
(Fear begets fear).

**5973. Wosuro pepeni a, na wofrɛ no "Mallam".**
*If you fear a Northerner, then you call him a Moslem elder.*
(You flatter those you fear).

**5974. Wosuro w'ase a, wo yere nware wo.**
*If you fear your in-laws, your wife does not continue to marry you.*
(If you cannot stick up for yourself, you don't have the respect of a woman).

**5975. Wosuro asɛntenten a, wonte mpaninsɛm.**
*If you dislike a long story, you don't hear the talk of elders.*
(You need patience to hear wisdom).

**5976. Wosuro atɛkyɛ mpaboa a, wofira ne ntoma.**
*If you are scared of muddy sandals you wear a muddy cloth.*
(If you fear small things, worse will befall you).

**5977. Asusontire, yɛdi no apafɔ.**
*Playing in the rain leads to constant changing of clothes.*
(You have to be properly equipped to do certain things).

**5978. Yɛsusu aboa no kɔn na yɛabɔ ne homa.**
*You judge the size of an animal's neck before making a knot in the rope.*
(If you want to take action against someone, you first calculate what is necessary for you to do so).

**5979. Woresusu asuhina bɔdammɔ no, na nkantankantan kantan kwan mu. As you are collecting a pot full of water, a barrier is blocking your path. (However careful one is, the unexpected may interfere with one's plans).**

**5980. Yɛnsusu asɛm pa ho nkyerɛ asobrakyeɛ.**
*We don't suggest a good idea to a stubborn person.*
(You don't waste time over someone who does not want to take advice).

**5981. Nsusu bɔne ma onipa di hia.**
*Bad thoughts make a man poor.*
(If your attitude to life is negative, so will your results be).

**5982. Nsusuaa mpɛ sɛ obiara de n'ano ka no, nti na ɔyɛ nwono.**
*The little garden-egg does not want anyone to touch it with the mouth, that is why it is so bitter.*
(Said of a cantankerous person, who cannot get on with people).

**5983. Nsusuaa se: "M'ani mmere ntwuropo".**
*The little garden-egg says: "I don't envy the big garden-egg".*
(Used when an unimportant person has no desire to be in the position of an important one).

**5984. Susuan mforo bepɔ.**
*Water doesn't climb the hill.*
("Susuan" is the run-off after heavy rain. Hence: You can't go against nature).

**5985. Susuan de boɔ rekɔ, apakyie da wo ho so!**
*The running water is carrying away the stone, so gourd, be alert!.*
(See Proverb 5984. If someone more powerful than you is in trouble over something, be doubly careful yourself).

**5986. Susuan afa borɔdehono, ɛde no kɔ dee ɛmpɛ.**
*If the flood waters wash away the plantain skin, they take it where it does not want to go.*
(See Proverb 5984. Circumstances beyond your control may force you to do things you do not wish to do).

**5987. Susuan a ɛretene na ɛdi apaafoɔ.**
*The running water that overflows needs the service of laborers.*
(See Proverb 5984. A bad situation needs people to control it).

**5988. Susuan mu dɛnkyɛm ne aponkyerɛne.**
*In the flood waters, the frog is a crocodile.*
(See Proverb 5984. When helped along by stronger forces, a small man may act like a big one).

**5989. Susuan yɛ asubɔnten bi dehyeɛ.**
*The waters from the gutters are the royals of some rivers.*
(See Proverb 5984. Some people who are not well-regarded in one place are powerful in another).

**5990. Asusuɔ tue a, yɛnkyiri ɔwansane.**
*If the rainy season begins, we don't refuse to eat the bush buck.*
(It is believed that the bush buck leads to conflict. It is a "sasaboa," an animal with a bad spirit. Hence: In times of want, we may do what we would not risk in times of plenty).

**5991. Nsutafoɔ nya biribi di a, na Mampɔnfoɔ ho adwo wɔn.**
*If the Nsuta people have eaten their fill, then the Mampong people become peaceful.*
(The Nsuta royals belong to the royal Oyoko clan which is the Asantehene's clan. Therefore they were aggressive against their neighbor Mampɔn, who could not fight them because of the Asantehene. Hence: If a powerful man is well-fed, he is not likely to be so quarrelsome).

**5992. Nsuwa–nsuwa na ɛyiri asuo.**
*Small trickles of water make a flood.*
(Little drops of water make the mighty ocean).

**5993. [Osuwanku]/[dɔtɔ] dom osua na osua nso dom no.**
*The thicket helps the monkey and the monkey also helps it (i.e the thicket).*
(A monkey eats caterpillars and other insects and so helps protect the plants. Hence: You scratch my back, I'll scratch yours).

- T -

**5994. Ata ne Ata nka a, ɛnte sɛ Tawia ne Ata.**
*If Ata and Ata don't speak to each other, it is not like Tawia and Ata.*
(If twins don't speak to each other, it is not like one who is born after twins and a twin. "Ata" is the name given to male twins, "Tawia" to a boy born after twins. Even inside the family, some people are more intimate than others).

**5995. Ata ne Ata ntena hɔ mma Tawia nni adeɛ.**
*The twins do not stay there to allow the one born after them to inherit.*
(When the correct person is there, others do not usurp their position).

**5996. Ata-panin nni nkyene mma ɛntware Ata-kumaa anom.**
*The elder twin does not eat salt that it may trickle into the younger twin's mouth.*
(Even if very intimate, you do not do something for someone else to profit).

**5997. Nta ne Nta se wɔnnim wɔn ho, a ɛnte sɛ Ɔbampɔn ne Ntiamoa.**
*If two pairs of twins say they do not know each other, it is not as distant as Ɔbampɔn and Ntiamoa (Death and the Living).*
(Blood is thicker than water and twins are particularly close).

**5998. Ɛta fata kwansɛn.**
*The ladle suits the soup pot.*
(Some things go together).

**5999. Ɛta se ɔnim adeɛ pɔtɔ a, ɔmpɔtɔ dwoa, ma yɛnhwɛ, nyɛ nkontommire.**
*If the pestle spoon says it can grind, let it grind palm kernels and let us see and not the cocoyam leaf.*
(Said to someone who boasts, to make him justify his boasting. The pestle spoon would normally be used for grinding leaves but not nuts).

**6000. Ɛta to o, ano o, ne nyinaa ka nkwan.**
*Either the top or bottom end of the ladle can test the soup.*
(Said of someone who makes full use of themselves).

**6001. Ntaafoɔ mu kaakyire ne sedeɛ.**
*Amongst twins, the last born is the cowrie.*
(A twin has a shrine-abamo-which he keeps with him and which usually contains a cowrie. If you attach yourself too much to something it becomes personified).

**6002. Taapo nni aban mu (ahemfie mu).**
*There is not even half a string of cowries in the state (palace).*
(I'm stone broke).

**6003. Wotaataa ɛkoɔ a, ɔhem gu wo so.**
*If you trouble the bush cow, it snorts on you.*
(It is believed that froth from the bush cow's mouth will make you fall. Don't disturb a cantankerous man).

**6004. Wotaataa opuro bebrebe a, wowe aperenkensema.**
*If you chase the squirrel too much, you eat the bush-baby.*

(If you are over-keen on something, you make a mistake).

**6005. Wotaataa aboa no bebrebe a, ɔbɔ w'ahina.**
*If you chase an animal too much, it breaks your water pot.*
(If you make someone desperate, they will cause you harm).

**6006. Ɔtabiraa tare bɛtene ho a, ɔntare ho kwa.**
*If the black snail clings onto a tall palm tree, it does not do so without reason.*
(It would be out of reach of the picker. People act with reason).

**6007. Ɔtabiraa wɔ ne pɛfoɔ.**
*The black snail has its fanciers.*
(Even an unpopular person is liked by some).

**6008. Tabono se ɔnim nsuo ase a, ɔnte sɛ drawa.**
*If the paddle says it knows what is in the river, the fish hook knows more.*
(The real expert can be challenged only by someone even more expert).

**6009. Tadua kyɛnkyɛn gyae anomaa.**
*It is the bow of the trap which is too long that lets the bird escape.*
(Unless plans are made properly they will not be effective).

**6010. Atadwe ne ahwedeɛ yɛ mfremfremadeɛ, nanso ebi sene bi dɛ.**
*Tiger nuts and sugar cane are both sweet, but one is sweeter than the other.*
(Between two good things one is the best. Or: No two things are exactly alike).

**6011. Wotae aboa no, na woamma no dwanekɔbea a, ɔhuru fa wo kɔn ho.**
*If you chase an animal and you don't give it the chance to get away, it jumps over your shoulder.*
(If you repress people too much, they revolt).

**6012. Wotae akɔdaa na ɔdwane kɔ fasuo ase a, na ne kwan asi.**
*If you chase a child and if it runs into a well, that is the end of its journey.*
(It's a fair cop).

**6013. Wotafere afanu a, na womeeɛ.**
*If you lick on both sides, you become satisfied.*
(The harder you work, the better you do).

**6014. Tafo kukuo, abɔ na ɛsi hɔ.**
*The Tafo pot, it has fallen but it stands there.*
(Good quality things are not easily damaged. Tafo pottery was especially strong).

**6015. Ntaherafoɔ se: wokyekyere sie na woma so a tam.**
*The hornblowers say: if you prepare before action, you succeed.*
(If you plan before you act, you are more likely to succeed).

**6016. Ntakara na yede hunu anomaa.**
*It's the feathers by which we know a bird.*
(You judge a man by his appearance).

**6017. Ntakara pa na ɛma anomaa ho yɛ fɛ.**
*Fine feathers make a fine bird.*

**6018. Ntakuo mmiɛnsa nhwere okontomponi.**
*Three takuo are not out of reach of a liar.*
(Takuo is a small amount of gold dust. Hence: Even an unsuccessful liar makes something from his lies).

**6019. Takyi aforoben-anomaa werɛmfoɔ se: "Woamforo Tabi na woto akoraboɔ yiɛ?"**
*The mighty nightjar Takyi says: "If you did not climb over Tabi then why do you have a bullet in your bottom?"*
(Don't say that you have not done something when it is obvious that you have done so).

**6020. Takyi ankɔ, Takyi ansan a, Takyi ka nsensɛn-mu.**
*If Takyi did not go, and Takyi did not come back, then Takyi remains undecided in the middle.*
(This is a proverb from Lake Bosomtwe. Takyi is supposed to have disappeared in the whirlpool in the middle of the lake while crossing it. Hence: A man must be decisive or he will never get anywhere).

**6021. Takyimankuro bi de "Ɔba-Nsu-a-Yɛma-no-Num".**
*A town in the Takyiman area is known as: "If the baby does not cry we still give it the breast".*
(There really is a town of this name. Even though you don't ask for anything, it does not mean that you should not be given it if you need it).

**6022. Wo tam ano yɛ duru a, na woboa akobɔfoɔ ano.**
*If the corner of the loin cloth is heavy, you harbor vagabonds.*
(Money is sometimes tied into the corner of a cloth for safety. Hence: If you are wealthy, you attract hangers on).

**6023. Ntam mmoa nyɛ.**
*Encouraging someone to litigate is not good.*
("Ntam" is an oath sworn in order to bring a case to trial. Hence: Don't lead others into trouble).

**6024. Ntam nti na aberewa di nya.**
*Because of an oath the old woman possesses a slave.*
(If you lost a case in the past, you might have to give a relative as a "pawn," until you could recover them by paying the fine. This young relative might be made to serve an elder. Hence: People take advantages of others' misfortunes).

**6025. W'atamfo baasa kɔ agyina a, wɔbu wo fɔ.**
*When three people who hate you go to a council, they find you guilty.*
(Said when a decision is a foregone conclusion).

**6026. Wo tamfo wu anɔpa na wowu anwumerɛ a, ɛnyɛ hwee.**
*If your enemy dies in the morning and you die in the evening, it is no matter.*
(Even though we will all die, it is good to see your enemy die first).

**6027. Wo tamfo nya amaneɛ a, twitwa gye no, na ɔda wo ase a, na wonnye soɔ.**
*If your enemy is in trouble, help him, but if he thanks you, don't respond.*
(Don't trust your enemy, even if *you* are prepared to treat *him* reasonably).

**6028. Wo tamfo resua w'asa a, ɔkyea ne pa.**
*If someone dislikes you and copies your dancing, he bends his waist sideways.*
(A person who dislikes you, misinterprets you).

**6029. Wo tamfoɔ di w'asem ase kan a, woka nkyene a, ɛdane mako.**
*If those who hate you happens to know the inside of your case, if you talk salt, it turns to pepper.*
(A person who hates you will always do their best to misinterpret you).

**6030. Wo tamfoɔ repɛ wo atoto wo awe a, [wonhuri ntra ne gya]/[wankyini gya ho]. If those who hate you want to roast and eat you, [you don't jump over their fire]/[you don't come near the fire].**
(Keep out of the way of those who wish you ill).

**6031. Wotan kwakuo a, woyi n'akyea.**
*If you dislike the monkey, you exempt its gait.*
(You may dislike someone yet admire some quality they have).

**6032. Wotan onipa a, woma ɔyɛ nneɛma nyinaa.**
*If you dislike a man, you make him take the blame for all kinds of things.*

**6033. Wotan ɔpanin a, na wobisa n'akaseɛ.**
*If you hate an elder, you ask him the source of his debts.*
(If you wish to spoil a man's reputation, you make his secrets public).

**6034. Wotan sabokwani a, na wohyɛ no ahuhuro.**
*If you hate a drunkard, then you harass him.*
(It is only if you dislike someone very much that you bother to deal with them when they are drunk).

**6035. Wotan wo sapɔ a, w'anom bɔn.**
*If you dislike your chewing sponge, your mouth stinks.*
(If you dislike those who would help you, you lose by it).

**6036. Wotan sɔnsɔn a, woyi n'ammirika.**
*If you hate the Western Hartebeest, you leave out its ability to run.*
(Compare Proverb 6031. You can dislike a person yet admire certain of his qualities).

**6037. Wotan wo yɔnko a, wonnya wo ho animuonyam ara da.**
*If you hate your acquaintance you will not be trusted.*
(Hate is always unproductive).

**6038. Wotan wo yɔnko ba a, wo ba bu abugyen.**
*If you hate your companion's child, your child dies a sudden death.*
(When you think evil, you bring evil on yourself).

**6039. Yɛtan yɛn ho a, na yɛgye yen ho akyinnyeɛ.**
*If we hate each other then we dispute with each other.*
(Quarrelling is the result of dislike).

**6040. Ɔtan abotire bɔ wo tiri a, na ɛnkyerɛ sɛ obiara tane wo.**
*If a head gear of hatred is on your head, it does not mean that everyone hates you.*
(No one is hated by everyone).

6041. Ɔtan oduro ka ɛboɔ so.
*The enemy's medicine stays on the stone.*
(Medicine is ground on a stone. Hence: You don't help your enemies).

6042. Ɔtan firi nnompe mu.
*Hate is from the bones.*

6043. Ɔtan nnim akorɔ.
*Hatred does not recognize generosity.*
(Hatred does not acknowledge anything good in the hated).

6044. Ɔtan nni aduro.
*There is no medicine to cure hatred.*

6045. Ɔtan a ɔwoo ba na ɔnim n'adaeɛ.
*The parent who gave birth to a child knows where it sleeps.*
(The parents know best all about their children).

6046. Ɔtan ne ne ba mu mpae.
*A parent and their child are not separated.*
(Your family relationships are never broken).

6047. Ɔtan nni hɔ a, yenhyɛ ne ba dwee mu.
*If the parent is not there, we don't apply painful medicine to a child's yaws.*
(Be careful how you treat someone's children, even if your intentions are good).

6048. "Ɔtan bɛwu agya ne ba", yɛ dwom nso ɛyɛ su.
*"A parent will die and leave her child" is not only a song, but also a cry.*
(We may joke about a thing, but it is really serious).

6049. Ɔtan yam wɔ yea.
*A good parent is sympathetic.*

6050. Ɔtanhunu yɛ ya.
*Hatred without cause is bitter.*
(It is hard to be hated when you have given no cause for it).

6051. Ntamkɛseɛ te sɛ bayere amena, yento mu mfiri kwa.
*The Great Oath is like a yam hole, you don't fall into it and come out without injury (lit. just like that).*
(The Great Oath was the most serious oath in Asante, sworn in order to take a case before the Asantehene. If you swore it and were in the wrong, you could be executed. Hence: Court cases are costly, whether you are guilty or not).

6052. Ntan-kyinnykeɛ nti na ɔhene kum nnipa.
*Because of setting an oath at nought, the chief kills people.*
(If you are stubborn, you suffer the consequences).

6053. Ɔtannuro Abena: "M'afɛ kyiri me".The Trichilia Heudelothi tree says: "My contemporaries hate me".
(The plant's name-Ɔtannuro-means "the medicine that is hated." Hatred of someone is generated amongst his own age group).

6054. Ntansa annya din, na asuasa na ɛbeyɛ dɛn?
*If ntansa is not worthwhile, what can you use asuasa for?*
(Ntansa is a large weight, asuasa a small one. Hence: If a large sum is not sufficient for you, a smaller amount will be of little use).

6055. Tanseserewa nkyiri biribi a, ɛnyɛ ɛne taasɛn fi.
*If the processionary caterpillar does not taboo anything, we don't mean the old pipe.*
(The smoke of the pipe would make the caterpillar fall of the tree. Hence: Everybody has something he objects to strongly. Or: We differ in our taboos).

6056. Ntantai dodoɔ kum ɛdɔm.
*Many gun caps destroy the hostile army.*
(Many individuals, however humble, working together achieve success).

6057. Atantanneɛ nti na onipa tɔ dɔnkɔ.
*Because of filthy things a person buys a slave.*
(Because you are unwilling to debase yourself by doing certain work, you employ others to do it).

6058. Ɔtareɛ a ɔtae hɔ npo fa nnipa, na ɛnte sɛ asutene.
*If a pool of water that lies there calmly drowns people, but it isn't like (i.e. as dangerous as) a flowing stream.*
(If a weak person causes trouble, how much more a strong one).

6059. Wotase pii a, ɛfifiri gu.
*If you collect up a large amount, it pours out.*
(If you take too much of something, you lose some of it).

6060. Ntasuo mpa onipa anom.
*Saliva does not dry in a person's mouth.*
(Human beings are never without problems).

6061. Ntasu-kɔkɔɔ wɔ onipa anom, nso ɔgyae te fufuo.
*Red saliva is in a person's mouth, but it is white which is spat out.*
(If you act in anger you injure yourself; it is better to act humbly and avoid injury).

6062. Ntasuo nkɔ nnante.
*Saliva does not go walking.*
(Some things are never found away from their source).

6063. Tawa nteteho nsɛɛ tawa.
*Stripping the tobacco does not spoil it.*
(If you give what you can spare, it does not hurt you).

6064. Tawa wisie nni ahoɔden.
*Tobacco smoke has no strength.*
(The emanation from something does not have the force of the thing itself).

6065. Wote obi kodoɔ mu ma ɛrenwunu a, wonsesa mu nsuo?
*If you sit in someone's canoe and it leaks, don't you bail out the water?*
(You don't refuse to save someone else's property when its preservation is in your own interest).

6066. Worete aduane na ɛfiri wo nsa tɔ ayowa mu a, na ɛnkɔɔ baabi mmaeɛ.
*If when you are taking food it falls into the pot, it has not gone somewhere and not returned.*
(No harm done).

6067. Wote faako a, wote w'adeɛ so; nanso wonam nam a, wohyia.
*When you stay in one place, you sit on your wealth; but if you wander about, you are in need.*

(If you take care of things at home, you do better than if you are constantly away from home).

**6068. Yɛte ka so tua, na yɛnte so nto hɔ.**
*We ask for the reduction of a debt and pay, but we don't ask for a reduction and not pay.*
(If you can't pay, you don't argue over the price).

**6069. Wote akobɛn a, na asɛm aba.**
*If you hear the war horn, it means trouble has come.*
(You only give a serious warning when it is necessary).

**6070. Wote "konkon" a, asɛm a ɛyɛ dɛ no wopɛ te.**
*If you hear the sound of the gong-gong, it is a sweet thing that you hope to hear.*
(People are incurable optimists).

**6071. Wote Kumase na wɔbɛku wo a, woara na wonim.**
*If you live in Kumasi and they are going to kill you, it is you yourself that knows it.*
(If you decide to stay near danger, you have only yourself to blame for the consequences).

**6072. Wote me ho asɛm a, fa tam mu.**
*If you hear something about me, gird your loin cloth.*
(Prepare to act in support of a friend).

**6073. "Mate-ama," ne "mate-afa", nkwanta da mu.**
*"I have harvested for someone," and "I have harvested for myself"-there is a great difference.*
(The laborer is quite different from the self-employed man).

**6074. Wote puupuu a, wɔ bi di, na ebia na ɛyɛ amanetire.**
*When you hear the sound of pounding, you too may pound, because the kind of food may be the head of a heron.*
(Don't be afraid of participating in something as it may not be as hard as you think).

**6075. Wote sɛ obi awu a, bisa deɛ wawuo no din yie, na ebia na ɛnyɛ "Kwame Bi" a ɔte Bantama.**
*If you hear that someone has died, ask the name of the one who has died carefully, it may be that it is not "Kwame B". who lives at Bantama.*
("Kwame Bi" means literally "Some Kwame". Hence: Listen carefully before you act on information received).

**6076. "Mete sɛ, meteɛ ni?" yɛ asenka na nyɛ poatwa.**
*"Do I look as I used to?" is an expression but not a boast.*
(A simple question requires an answer, not a judgment).

**6077. Wote se wɔreto atuo a, mpɛ ntɛn nsere na ebia na wo se funu na ɛreba.**
*If you hear that guns are being fired, don't laugh too soon, for perhaps it is your father's corpse that is on its way.*
(Make sure what has happened before you celebrate it, for it may be unfortunate and not good).

**6078. Mete ase mannya adeɛ; na nyɛ mekɔwu a, na menya adeɛ.**
*I am alive and I have nothing; but it is not as if I am going to die and profit.*
(Things could always be worse).

**6079. Yɛte so a, yete gye amono.**
*If we reduce the price, it is because we want ready cash.*
(When people need money quickly, they have to sell cheaply).

**6080. Wote nsuo ho redware na ɔbɔdamfoɔ fa wo ntoma a, wohwewɛ bi ansa na woati no.**
*If a madman snatches your cloth while you are having a bath, put on some cloth before you pursue him.*
(If you are provoked, be careful not to act like those that provoke you, or you will be judged as they are).

**6081. Yɛnte deɛ yɛteɛ a, yɛnyɔ deɛ na yɛyɔ.**
*If we don't stay where we are, we don't do what we should do.*
(You cannot act if you are out of place).

**6082. Wontee afrɛse a, womfa abofu.**
*If you don't understand the reason for a call, you do not get angry.*
(Find out what something is about before you react to it).

**6083. "Ate a bisa", ne agorɔ.**
*"Hearing and asking" is a sign of good friendship.*
(If you are a good friend, you ask about what is reported before you accept it as true).

**6084. Atɛ korɔ nkɔ anwan.**
*One marble alone does not spin around.*
(One person alone cannot achieve anything in society).

**6085. Atɛ Akwasi se: yɛka sɛ ɔhene ata a, yɛnyi no adanseɛ ɛfiri sɛ ɔno na ɔte ne soɔ.**
*The leather stool Akwasi says: if we say the chief has farted, we should call him to bear witness, because it is on him that he sits.*
(It is your intimates who can vouch for you real character).

**6086. Ɔteasefoɔ na ɔma ɔsaman kɔn dɔ ɛtɔ.**
*It is the living who cause the departed spirit to long for mashed yam.*
(It is the one who gives the gift who creates the desire for it).

**6087. Ɛtɛ si w'ani a, na ɛnkyerɛ sɛ yɛmmɔ ɛtɛ din.**
*If you have a cataract on your eye, it does not mean that we should call out the name of the cataract.*
(Not everything that you notice should be mentioned).

**6088. Tɛfrɛ kuntu, ɔse: "Me ne akokɔ mpere hwee, na ɔtan na ɛnni aduro".**
*The cockroach says: "I have nothing with which to struggle with the chicken, for hatred has no medicine".*
(Said when someone constantly inconveniences another person who can do nothing about it).

**6089. Tɛfrɛ na ete dampareɛ kasa.**
*The cockroach understands the language of the rafters.*
(You understand the language of the people amongst whom you live).

6090. Tɛfrɛ se: ɛnyɛ deɛ yɛfa nyinaa na nkwagyeɛ wɔ; saa nti na wobɔ no to hɔ a, na woadane ne yam akyerɛ Onyame no.
*The cockroach says: it is not everywhere we go that is safe; that is why when you knock it down, it turns over on its back and shows its stomach to God.*
(A helpless person can only turn to God).

6091. Tɛfrɛ atɔ nkokɔ mu, ɔgyefoɔ ne hwan?
*When the cockroach falls among fowls, who is its savior?*
(You have no one to save you if you are in enemy hands).

6092. Tɛfrɛ atɔ nkokɔ mu, wodi no apretoɔ.
*When a cockroach falls among fowls, it is tossed here and there.*
(See Proverb 6091).

6093. Tɛfrɛ nni akokɔ anim bem da.
*The cockroach can never be innocent in the chicken's presence.*
(You enemy will always find you guilty).

6094. Nteho nti na yɛdi ahenkwaa.
*Because of obtaining a share of fines, people become stool servants.*(Everything is done for some profit).

6095. Tekakyerɛ bɔ kuro.
*Repeated gossip spoils the town.*

6096. Tɛkrɛma a yɛde tutu ka no, nyɛ ɛno na yɛde pɛ bosea.
*The tongue which we use to ask for time in paying debts is not that which we use for asking for a loan.*
(You change your tone according to the occasion).

6097. Tɛkrɛma bɛdeɛ fa adeɛ sene ɔhoɔdemfoɔ.
*A female tongue gets things more easily than a strong man.*
(A soft tongue works wonders).

6098. Tɛkrɛma mogya, woto bi gu na woamene bi.
*Blood on the tongue, you spit some out and swallow the rest.*
(Offenses may be criticized but should also be forgiven).

6099. Tɛkrɛma dane abogyeɛ.
*The tongue's strength depends on the jaw.*
(We are all interdependent).

6100. Tɛkrɛma reko a, ɔde ne werɛ twere abɔdwesɛ.
*If the tongue goes to war, it relies on the beard.*
(You need a strong backer before you become aggressive).

6101. Tɛkrɛma korɔ hia tɛkrɛma-pem a, ɛtɔ piti.
*If one tongue meets a thousand tongues, it faints.*
(One person cannot stand up to a crowd).

6102. Tɛkrɛma na ɛkum nnipa, gyae nnipa.
*It is the tongue that kills people but also releases people.*
(Talking can get you either in or out of trouble).

6103. Tɛkrɛma ne ɛse mpɔ wɔko.
*Even the tongue and the teeth fight.*
(Even intimate people fight, how much more enemies).

6104. Tɛkrɛma soa adeɛ a ɛyɛ hare na nyɛ dɛ ɛyɛ duru.
*The tongue carries what is light but not what is heavy.*
(You act according to your ability).

6105. Tɛkrɛma kwatri a, ɛsene nammɔn.
*A slip of the tongue is worse than a slip of the foot.*
(A bad remark does more harm than physical damage).

6106. Tɛkrɛma wɔ hɔ yi, yɛfrɛ no sakrama.
*The tongue as it is, we call it inconsistent.*
(People are good and bad at the same time).

6107. Ɔtɛkrɛmadɛfoɔ nyɛ yie da.
*A gourmand never achieves much.*
(If you are too greedy you do not succeed in life).

6108. Tɛkrɛma-ka yɛ ya sen kam-pa.
*The cut of the tongue is more hurtful than a real cut.*

6109. Tɛkrɛma-pa na yɛde wɛn tire.
*A good tongue we take to protect the head.*
(A discrete man keeps out of trouble).

6110. Temanmuhunu ho nhia ɔman.
*A good-for-nothing is not regarded in the state.*
(You have to earn your position in society by your actions).

6111. Tempɔn da hɔ a, akwamma da ho.
*If a highway is there, so is the by-way.*
(There is more than one way of approaching a matter).

6112. Tempɔn mu nni asomorofi.
*The highway has no hearths.*
(There's a difference between a public and a private one).

6113. Wotena dufɔkyee so di borɔfere a, woto fɔ, w'ano nso fɔ.
*If you sit on the rotten log to eat papaya, your bottom gets wet, and your mouth also gets wet.*
(If you are too greedy, you suffer for it).

6114. Wotena hɔ ma yɛde ɔkwasea bɛdi wo so hene a, wosom no.
*If you sit unconcerned for a foolish man to be enstooled, then you must serve him.*
(If you do not prevent something happening, you have to accept it when it comes).

6115. Tena hɔ na wobɛhunu, yɛ duabɔ.
*Stay here and you will see something, is a curse.*
(Take notice of warnings).

6116. Atena, wohunu a, ɛte sɛ ago, nso sɛ wɔyɛe no ara ne no.
*If you see a fishing net, it is like an old rag, but it is that which we use.*
(Put not faith in appearances).

6117. Wotena kuro bɔne mu a, woyi w'adadeɛ awigyina.
*If you stay in a bad town, you take your bag and baggage and flee in the afternoon.*
(Travelling in the afternoon is regarded as bad. Hence: In a bad situation we take extreme action).

6118. Yɛtena asɛm mu a, yɛhyɛ mu kena.
*If we sit on a case, we perform some action to witness to the fact (lit. we put a mark on it).*
(You need to keep some record of work you have done).

6119. Yɛtena tuo to na yɛntena tuo ano.
*We stay behind the gun and not in front of it.*
(You back a powerful man but you don't challenge him).

6120. Yɛntena ase mma yen apakan mmɔ yɛn.
*We don't sit idle to deprive ourselves of our carrying baskets.*
("Apakan" can mean a carrying basket or a palanquin. Hence: If you don't do a job properly, you will lose your chances).

6121. Tenabea nyinaa nsɛ.
*All dwelling-places are not alike.*
(Situations differ).

6122. Atena-nnufua rebɛtena akonnwa so, na yɛaye no dɛn?
*A person who sits on a log is now going to sit on a stool, what should we do to them?*
("Sitting on a stool" is a sign of status. Hence: Used when a formerly unimportant person takes over authority and you can do nothing about it).

6123. Wotene wo nsateaa hwɛ wo yɔnko so a, deɛ aka hwɛ wo so.
*If you point one finger at your companion, the rest will be pointing at yourself.*
(If you want to bring trouble on someone, you suffer more yourself).

6124. Ɛtene a awuo na n'ano yɛ nam.
*The dead sword-grass has a sharp edge.*
(Even a poor person has his legacy of influence).

6125. Atenfaako, yɛmmua.
*After listening to one side only, we don't give a verdict.*
(Wait until all the evidence is in).

6126. Atenkyema nya wuo a, nkura bo adwo.
*If the cat dies, the mice become satisfied.*
(When a persecutor dies the persecuted can be happy).

6127. Atɛnnie wɔ mframa mu.
*Abuse is in the wind.*
(Don't take any notice of spoken insults, since they are powerless and will soon be forgotten).

6128. Ɔtenten pono ne mu a, ɔne akwatia sɛ.
*If a tall man bends, he and a short person are alike.*
(It is only in reduced circumstances that a rich man resembles a poor one).

6129. Ɔtenten-teaa ne tiatia-pipiripie nyinaa nsɛ.
*A tall slender person and a short thick person are not alike.*
(It takes all sorts to make a world).

6130. Wotentene twa a, ɛgu w'ani so.
*If you cut above you, it falls into your eyes.*
(If you do something which is beyond you, you injure yourself).

6131. Atentirehuo nya baabi gyina a, ɔbisa mframa sɛ: "Worekɔ henefa?"
*If the silk-cotton seed has somewhere to rest, it asks the wind: "Where are you going to?"*
(If an insecure person becomes secure, he takes an interest in those less fortunate than himself).

6132. Atentirehuo atɔ nsuo mu, na ɛte sɛ ɔtamfoɔ ate wo ho asɛm.
*If the silk-cotton seed falls into the stream, it is like when an enemy has heard something about you.*
(i.e heard something bad. The silk-cotton seed is light, so it is carried swiftly. Hence: Bad news travels swiftly, particularly if carried by enemies).

6133. Atentirehuo tua wo to a, wonhuri ntra egya.
*If the silk-cotton seed is hanging from your buttocks, you do not jump over the fire.*
(The silk-cotton seed is highly flammable. Hence: If you know you are at a disadvantage, you should not take risks).

6134. Ɔte-pɔnkɔsoɔ nsunti.
*The horse-rider does not stumble.*
(If you are in a good position, you don't suffer, though perhaps your servant does).

6135. Wotare sie a, ɛnna nnwunu bio.
*If you have already mended it, then it does not leak any more.*
(Prevention is better than cure).

6136. Yɛretete abeteɛ no, na ne kye ara ne no.
*As we are taking abeteɛ (cassava dough) bit by bit, then we are sharing it in fact.*
(Take your share of something while it is available, or it may not be there in the future).

6137. Yɛtete ahahan tua ka na wɔrebɛgye a, wɔgye deɛ ɛso ano.
*If we gather leaves to pay a debt and they are going to take it, they take what is sufficient to pay the debt.*
(No one wants to lose over a transaction).

6138. Tete ara ne nnɛ.
*What was prevailing long ago, prevails today.*
(Conditions do not change fundamentally).

6139. Wobɛtete me kwan mu nnuadewa abɛtɔn ama me?
*Do you gather garden eggs from my farm and then sell them to me?*
(Said of someone who steal something and then tries to sell it to the owner).

6140. Tetehɔ no na kokromfi wura mmɔfra hwene mu na ɛnyɛ ɛnnɛ-mmerɛ yi a.
*It was in the old days that the praying mantis went into the nose of children and not at the present time.*
(Children used to be threatened that if they did not behave properly a praying mantis would get into their nose. The threat had a second part which said: "... it will only come out when your father has killed an elephant." Hence: men and times change).

6141. Atetekwaa we duaa a, ɔde wɔ ne se akyiri.
*If a stupid person chews a stick, he uses it to prick his upper gum.*
(A fool acts haphazardly).

6142. Tɛtia mfa abofuo mmoro nsa.
*The little black ant should not get angry and become drunk.*
(Insignificant people should be careful how they act, or they will get into trouble).

6143. Tɛtia, ɔkɔ obi bɔn mu, obi deɛ ɔntumi nkɔ ne bɔn mu.
*The small black ant goes into someone else's hole, but no one is able to go into its hole.*
(Some people benefit from you but you are unable to benefit from them).

6144. Tɛtia, ɔse: "Me kosɛ kosɛ wɔ me tirim."
*The little black ant says: "My thoughts are in my head."*
(Said by someone who does not want to say what they are doing or thinking).

6145. Ntɛtia bɔn: adeɛ tɔ mu a, wɔn ara na wɔyie.
*the little black ants' hole: if something falls into it, they themselves take it out.*
(You don't expect someone outside to settle your personal problems).

6146. Ntɛtia kɔkɔɔ nim akratɔ di, nso worekɔbubu mmabaa a, na wɔrekeka wo.
*The small red ants know how to eat mashed yam, but if you are going to collect firewood they bite you.*
(Akratɔ is the mashed yam used in the course of the ritual of "soul washing" and the ants will be able to eat it after the ceremony. But first you need firewood to cook it. Hence: Some people bite the hand that feeds them).

6147. Ntɛtia nsen, wowa nsen, na nsa no resa.
*The little ants pass by, the bees pass by, gradually you lose the palm wine.*
(If you are too benevolent, you lose your means of livelihood).

6148. Ti korɔ nkɔ agyina.
*One head does not make a council.*
(It takes more than one person to decide on community action).

6149. Wo ti anyini a, na wodi akoturowisie.
*If your head is matured, then you play at knocking heads.*
(This is a young person's game. Participants stand in a ring and one person bends his head down and others knock it in turn. You have to guess who it is and if you guess right, you change place with the knocker. Hence: You do not compete with someone who is not of the same standing as yourself).

6150. Wotia bamma so ansa na woakɔ dan mu.
*You tread on the threshold before going into the room.*
(One thing follows logically on another).

6151. Ntiamoa Sampanimako soa nimo kyɛ a, yɛkyi.
*If Ntiamoa Sampanimako carries the hat of constant accusation, it is very bad (lit. we taboo it).*
(You should not allow yourself to be constantly abused).

6152. Wotiatia obi deɛ so hwehwɛ wo deɛ a, wonhunu.
*If you trample on someone's property in looking for yours, you don't find it.*
(The selfish do not prosper).

6153. Tiatia na ɛbɔ ntowa.
*Small amounts make a big lump.*
(Little drops of water make the mighty ocean).

6154. Wo tiboaa bɔ wo kɔkɔ na woantie a, ɔbɔ wo fɛ.
*If your conscience warns you and you don't listen, it damages you.*
(If you don't pay attention to your conscience, you suffer for it).

6155. Ti-bɔne yɛfa no asaase so na yɛmfa no awoɔ mu.
*Bad luck is found on earth but it is not something one is born with.*
(Not all misfortunes are inherited).

6156. Ti-denso mmɔ adwabum.
*An easily-identified head should not join in a market riot.*
(If you are conspicuous, avoid getting into mischief or you will be caught

6157. Tidie abufufa ɔse: "Papiraa!" na wadwo.
*The tidie fish loses its temper, making an angry noise "papiraa", but it calms down quickly.*
(Quick tempered people also calm down quickly).

6158. Tie m'anom asɛm ansa na woase me kwasea.
*Listen to the words of my mouth, before you say I am a fool.*
(Wait until all the evidence is in).

6159. Wotie obi ano asɛm wie a, na wonya no kwaseaseberɛ.
*Only when you listen to what someone says to the end do you get the opportunity to abuse them.*
(You can only disagree with someone if you listen to their arguments).

6160. Yɛbɛtie ama wo a, ɛnim sɛ woatwa no tia.
*If we are going to listen to you, it does not matter if you cut it short.*
(A word to a helpful person is enough).

6161. Wotie nnipa ano dane aboa a, nnipa twa wɔn ho sere wo.
*If you follow people's criticism and become a fool, people in turn will mock you.*
(Don't take advice indiscriminately for you cannot please all the people all the time).

6162. Yɛbɛtie w'asɛm a, ɛnnim sɛ woaware w'asɛ.
*If we will listen to your affairs, it does not mean that you should draw them out.*
(You don't need to talk too much if your case is acceptable).

6163. Yɛtie asɛm pa de kɔ akuraa.
*We listen to good advice and take it to the village.*
(It is good things which should be spread).

6164. "Merentie, merentie", ne nnua ne "Ma yɛnkɔgya me dibemma".
*"I am not listening, I am not listening" brother is "Go and accompany me to render an apology."*
(A stubborn person ends up in trouble).

6165. "Mentie, mentie", so amaneɛ.
*"I won't listen, I won't listen" brings on a case.*
(If you are stubborn, you get into trouble).

6166. Atikɔ due "mante-mante".
*The back of the head is characterized by "I did not hear, I did not hear".*
(If you don't want to listen you turn your face away. You can talk to someone but you can't make them listen to you).

6167. Tikukuo nya ne twɛdeɛ a, ɛhɔ ara na yɛde bɔ.
*If the head deserves a blow, it is it that we hit.*
(You punish the person who has committed the crime, not another).

6168. Ntimmɔbɔ nti na yɛyi awirikwaa.
*Because of compassion we let the green parrot loose.*
(Used when out of kindness someone helps another with no ulterior motive).

6169. "Tin" ne "tan" yɛ bɔne korɔ.
*"Tin" and "Tan" are equally wrong.*
(Two similar sins are equally reprehensible).

6170. [Tipaeɛ]/[Tiyareɛ] ba kuro mu a, ɔkɔtɔ mfa ho.
*When there are headaches in town, the crab is not worried.*
(The crab does not have a head. Hence: You do not worry over troubles which cannot affect you).

6171. Atipaeɛ yɛ ani-adam.
*A headache is a red eye.*
(One thing leads to another).

6172. Etiri a adi kan ne panin.
*The head that tops the list is senior.*
(First come, first served).

6173. Etiri a ɛso daeɛ ne ɔdwendwenfoɔ.
*The head that dreams is wise.*
(A person of imagination and vision is likely to be the most successful).

6174. Etiri a ɛnyɛ, wo twa to nwunu mu a, ɛhuri kɔtɔ awia mu.
*If a head is bad, when you cut it off and put it in the shade, it jumps into the sunshine.*
(If someone is determined to misbehave they will do so at all times).

6175. Tiri bi resusuo na tiri bi rekeka.
*While some heads consult, others may be talking of it.*
(People may come to the same conclusions independently).

6176. Wo tiri kokuroko a, wonsan mmuna nka ho.
*If you are swollen-headed, you don't frown as well.*
(Don't add insult to injury).

6177. Wo tiri mu yɛ fufuo a, Ntuamoa nku wo.
*If your thoughts are pure (lit.: what is in your head is white) then Ntuamoa does not kill you.*
(The powerful fetish protects the virtuous).

6178. Etiri bi ne tiri bi nsɛ a, wɔnni akoturowisie.
*If two heads are not alike, they don't enter into a head-bumping game.*
(See Proverb 6149. You only compete against equals).

6179. Etiri nyinaa sɛ nanso emu nsɛm nyɛ pɛ.
*All heads look alike but what is in them is not the same.*
(You may resemble someone in looks but be quite different in character).

6180. Etiri yɛpere no mmaako-mmaako.
*Each of us protects his own head.*
(Each man cares for himself first).

6181. Etiri sɛe da koro.
*A head spoils in a day.*
(Even a man's character may change without warning).

6182. Wo tiri nsɛ Tete ayie a, wonse sɛ: "Yi me Tete ayie".
*If your head does not look like Tete's, you don't say "Give me Tete's hair style".*
(If you are not like someone, what suits them may not suit you).

6183. Wo tiri so a, enyɛ nneɛma nyinaa na wosoa.
*If your head is big, it is still not everything than you can carry.*
(There is a limit to everyone's capacity).

6184. Etiri te a, na asɛm asa.
*When a head is cut off, all troubles cease.*
(When a man has gone, his troubles and quarrels are no longer relevant).

6185. Etiri te sɛ adɔsoa, yɛnhwehwɛ mu adeɛ nhunu no da koro.
*A head is like bundle of things tied up for keeping, we don't take only a day to find what is inside it.*
(It is not possible to become familiar with a man's way of thinking all at once).

6186. Etiri nteeɛ a, yɛnnyae ekyɛ soa.
*If the head is not detached, we do not stop wearing a hat.*
(While you live you have to do what you ought to do).

6187. Etiri wɔ hɔ a, kotodwe nsoa kyɛ.
*If the head lives, the knee does not carry the hat.*
(Honor to whom honor is due).

6188. Etiri nni safoa na yɛahini ahwɛ.
*There is no key to a head so that we can unlock it and see inside.*
(A man's thoughts cannot be discovered from his face).

6189. Wo tiri yɛ a, na woto boɔ a, ɛkɔbɔ w'akontagye ba tirim.
*If you are fortunate and you throw a stone, it goes and hits your in-law's child's head.*
(If someone belongs to the same family as you and you harm him, he does not get you into trouble, but settles the matter in the home).

6190. Wo tiri yɛ a, na wo yam tu a, wo ne ɛhyɛn hyia.
*If you are lucky (lit. if your head is good), when you have a runny stomach, you meet the moonshine.*
(The latrines used to be at the edge of the village, so the moon would help you to see the way. Hence: If you are lucky you get a helper).

6191. Wo tiri nyɛ a, ebia na wo kraa yɛ.
*Even if you are unlucky perhaps your soul is lucky.*
(Physical and spiritual well-being differ).

6192. Wo tiri nyɛ a, woma Ɔnyame brɛ.
*If you are not lucky, you make God tired.*
(Said about someone who, despite hard work, does not prosper).

**6193. Etiri nyɛ borɔferɛ na yɛapae mu ahunu mu asɛm.**
*A head is not a papaya that we cut it open to see what is inside.*
(See Proverb 6188. You cannot see into the mind of man).

**6194. Tirim fɛreɛ sene fɛre-pa.**
*Shame in the head is worse than real shame.*
(Things felt inside you are worse than what happens outside).

**6195. Wo tirim yɛ den a, wonnya otubrafoɔ.**
*If you are hard-hearted you will not attract an expatriate.*
(It is the hospitable and warm-hearted people who attract visitors, not the hard ones).

**6196. Atirimusɛm-ka bebrebɛ ma ɔpanin adwene dane nkɔdaadwene.**
*Too much talking about everything that goes on in his head, makes an elder's thoughts become like a child's.*
(If an elder talks too much, he tends to become childish).

**6197. Otirimuɔdemfoɔ na ɔsom asra.**
*It is hard-hearted people who take snuff.*
(It is believed that snuff-takers are tough. Hence: You make assumptions about people on the basis of what you can see about them).

**6198. Atiti-atiti-ne-brafoɔti; obi mpɛ wo agoro a, tena w'ase. (Na ɔkɔtɔ bɔ pemme a, ɔsan n'akyi).**
*Atiti-atiti-ne-brafoɔti; someone does not want to play with you, keep to yourself. (For if the crab falls over, it returns to base).*
(It is not clear what "Atiti-atiti-ne-brafoɔti" means, though "brafoɔ" means executioner. But the proverb suggests: If you are not wanted, you had best return to where you came from).

**6199. Titiriku rekɔpe ɛtwɛ adi na wannya a, ne kɔte kuro mmere.**
*If the boar wishes to have sex and does not get it, the sore on its penis is not damaged.*
(If someone is entitled to something and does not get it, at least he has not suffered for it).

**6200. Wo to nyɛ a, ɛbare wo. Wontumi ntwa ntwene mma no nyɛ yie.**
*If there is something wrong with your buttocks, they still belong to you. You cannot cut them off and make them better.*
(What is an essential part of you, you have to make do with, for better or worse).

**6201. Yɛto mmɛta a, yempae mu.**
*If we fell twin palm trees, we don't separate them.*
(You cannot separate a family: if one suffers, all suffer).

**6202. "To wo bo ase, to wo bo ase" na ɛmaa ɔkɔterɛ bo yɛ traa.**
*"Be patient, be patient" made the lizard's chest flat.*
(If you are too patient, you suffer for it).

**6203. Woto wo bo ase a, woware ɔhene ayowa.**
*If you are patient, you marry the chief's young daughter.*
(Patience leads to success).

**6204. Woto wo bo ase, ma nsuo gyene, na wohwehwɛ ase adeɛ a, wohunu.**
*If you are patient and allow the water to become clear, if you look for something in it, you find it.*
(Patience brings rewards. Or: If you study a problem carefully, you will see your way out of it).

**6205. Woto aboa no na wansu a, sotia no so.**
*If you shoot an animal and it doesn't cry, you repeat the shot.*
(Try, try, try again).

**6206. Woto aboa tuo na ɔdwane ba fie a, wo kɔn mu na ɛdwo woɔ.**
*If you fire a gun at an animal and it runs to come to the house, your neck becomes free.*
(If something is done for you, it is no longer a burden).

**6207. Woto aboɔ mmienu kɔ soro a, ne sɔ yɛ sɔna.**
*If you throw two stones up high, it is difficult to catch them.*
(i.e catch them both. Hence: You cannot do two jobs at once).

**6208. Woto bopa twene w'akyi a, wohunu kɔfa.**
*If you throw a good stone behind you, you look and go find it.*
(You reap what you sow).

**6209. Woto adubɔne a, ebi ka w'ano.**
*If you administer poison, a little touches your mouth.*
(If you wish evil on others, it affects you too).

**6210. Woto ɔhene ntam mpɛn aduasa a, woyi no prɛko.**
*If you become a victim of a chief's oath thirty times, you pay for it only once.*
(If you pay the supreme penalty, you pay it only once. Hence: Said when someone is already in serious trouble. In for a penny, in for a pound).

**6211. Woto huu na obi annye wo so a, na woyera.**
*If you shout for help and no one responds, then you are lost.*
(If you don't get help, you suffer the consequences).

**6212. Woto mu nkyene bebrebe a, ɛtware mu.**
*If you put in too much salt, it is nasty.*
(You can have too much of a good thing).

**6213. Woto anadwo tuo a, wonsuro benabɔɔ.**
*If you fire off a gun in the night then you don't fear shouting.*
(You should be prepared for the natural consequences of your actions).

**6214. Woto anwea-ban a, wo nsa mpa ho da.**
*If you build a house of sand, your hand never rests.*
(Cheap work needs constant repair).

**6215. Woto pampim a, (na) woato kuro.**
*When you reach the barrier, (then) you have reached the village.*
(In the old days a barrier of logs was built across the path near the entrance to the village. A traveller would then know he was nearing habitation and would call out to announce his friendly approach. Hence: one thing leads to another).

**6216. Ɛto apenten a, na yɛfrɛ tibɔnkoso.**
*If trouble comes, we invite a foolish person.*
(Sometimes the foolish person is able to do what the wise cannot).

**6217. Ɛto apenten a, deɛ ɔwɔ ayera no ɔyera.**
*If trouble comes, anyone who has medicine for vanishing vanishes.*
(If you need to escape trouble, you use all your skill to do so).

**6218. Woto (sɛbe)/(tafrakyɛ) na woka asɛm bi a, yɛnkyiri.**
*If you excuse yourself before saying something, we don't taboo it.*
(Wise talking keeps you out of trouble. Sɛbe or sɛbe-o, is what you say before saying something which is unpleasant but not meant to be offensive, to let the person you are talking with know that no offense is intended).

**6219. Woto asɛm mu nkyene bebrebe a, yɛbua wo fɔ.**
*If you exaggerate a case too much, we find you guilty.*
(Exaggeration leads to disbelief).

**6220. Woto sonsono twene a, na ne dua di akyiri.**
*If you throw out a worm, its tail follows.*
(If you dispense with something, you dispense with everything about it).

**6221. Woto nsuo a, woso bi nom.**
*If you come to a stream, you collect some to drink.*
(You should make use of your opportunities when they come).

**6222. Woto ntasu-dan a, mframa na ebu no.**
*If you build a house with saliva, the wind will blow it down.*
(Do not build your house on sand).

**6223. Woto ɔtɔbrɔfoɔ adeɛ na woantua no ka a, nse sɛ woanya no fo na deɛ ɔnim wɔ ho.**
*If you buy something from a foolish man and you don't pay for it, don't think you have got it cheap, for there is someone who knows about it.*
(You cannot get away with dishonesty in the long run).

**6224. Yɛato tuo abɔ Baafi. Ammɔ no, amfom no, na akorabɔɔ ne wedeɛ mu a; na yɛreka no sɛn?**
*We have shot a gun at Baafi. It did not hit him but it did not miss either, but the bullets are still under his skin; then how shall we explain it?*
(Might be used in a situation where someone you do not like shouts a message at you, and you reply that you have heard it, even though you didn't really listen. He knows he has delivered the message but you don't even remember it).

**6225. Woto twene w'akyi a, ɛtɔ w'anim.**
*If you throw it away behind you it will be lying ahead of you.*
(Cast your bread upon the waters).

**6226. (Woto twene)/(Wowere firi) na wosan kɔfa a, yɛnkyiri.**
*If you (throw away/(forget) and you go back and take it, it is not taboo.*
(It is good to learn from or retrieve what you need from the past).

**6227. Ɛto wo a, ɛto wo ne wo ni.**
*If it happens to you, it happens to you and your mother.*
(Anything affecting the family affects the mother).

**6228. Woto wo dimmɔne a, ɛbra wo.**
*If you are given a bad name, it molds your character.*
(If you give a dog a bad name, it lives up to it. Be careful whom you name your children after or you may regret it).

**6229. Yɛto wo dua mu a, yɛsusu dammɔ ma wo.**
*If we chain you to a log, we suspect you of being a lunatic.*
(If you allow yourself to be molested, people suspect you).

**6230. Yɛto wo asesɛdwa na woantena so a, yɛde adammadwa ma wo tena so.**
*If we give you an important stool (made of the Ɔsesɛ tree) and you do not sit on it, then we will give you a cheap one to sit on.*
(If you do not take advantage of your opportunities or live up to expectations, you will not be treated with respect).

**6231. Yɛto wo so a, wonhono nsoo nnom.**
*If we accuse you, you don't dilute ash and drink.*
(The two things sound alike, but it does not mean they are related - this is entirely a play on words).

**6232. Wontoo ɔhene mmara a, asɛ ɔne wo ka.**
*If you have not become a victim of the chief's rules, you think he likes you.*
(If you have committed no offense, you feel free).

**6233. "Monto me ɔhene kwa", ma akɔdaa siane ɔpanin ho di adeɛ.**
*"You may just name me Chief" makes a child get round an elder to inherit the stool.*
(Determination and ambition get what they want in the long run).

**6234. Yɛnto ana na yɛmfa ɛsɛn foforɔ mmutu pataso.**
*We don't trace the history of our origins and then turn a new cooking pot upside down in the rafters.*
(If you were proud of your family, you would cook for them. Hence: You don't boast about your family and then not take care of them. Or, more generally: If your claims are sincere, your actions will confirm them).

**6235. Yɛnto ntasuo nto fam na yɛasan atafe.**
*We do not spit on the ground and go back and lick it up again.*
(If you discard something as useless, don't go back and collect it again).

**6236. Ɛntoo wo a, woda.**
*If it has not come to your turn, you sleep.*
(Don't worry about the future, though your turn may come).

**6237. Wobɛtɔ a, wonse adabraka.**
*If you are willing to buy, you do not ask for a reduction.*
(If you really want something, you are willing to pay the price for it).

**6238. Wotɔ ɔbaa abɔɔden a, ɛnnu wo ho, ɛfiri sɛ kuro mu da ne yam.**
*If you buy a woman dearly, don't regret it, for there is a town in her stomach.*
(A fruitful woman is worth a fortune).

**6239. "Ɛtɔ baabi a, ɛdum, ɛto baabi a ɛhye", nyɛ amammuo pa.**
*"If it (the fire) goes out in one place and burns in another" is not good government.*
(Partiality is not good in public life. Or: A good ruler should not be constantly changing his mind).

**6240. Ɛtɔ da bi a ohuruie tena badwam.**
*Sometimes the tsetse fly sits in state.*
(A treacherous man sometimes practices his treachery openly).

**6241. Ɛtɔ da bi a na ɔhene kɔn dɔ nhenkwaa aduane.**
*It sometimes happens that a chief feels like tasting the food of his court officials.*
(Sometimes a man in authority feels like behaving like an ordinary person).

**6242. Ɛtɔ da bi a na onipa-bɔnefoɔ ho yɛ nna.**
*It may happen one day that a bad man is rare.*
(Don't indulge in wishful thinking in the present even if you dream that things will be better in the future).

**6243. Ɛbɛtɔ da bi a na osikani renya ohiani ayɛ.**
*The day will come when the rich man envies the poor man.*
(Rich people have too many problems and envy the simplicity of the life of the poor).

**6244. Ɛbɛtɔ da bi na ewiem abae ama dufɔkyeɛ ayɛ agya.**
*The day will come when the clear sky will make the rotten log combustible.*
(Given the right circumstances, even a useless thing may become useful).

**6245. Ɛbɛtɔ da na akwagyinamoa tɔn adwene nanso ɔnnya bi nnwe.**
*There will come a day when the cat will sell fish but not have any to eat.*
(There will come a day when the seemingly impossible happens).

**6246. Wotɔ adeɛ de sika-mono tua ka a, ɛnnya wo dadwen.**
*If you buy something and use money to pay for it, you don't think about it anymore.*
(You should avoid worries by paying on the spot).

**6247. Wotɔ adeɛ na wotua ka a, yɛfrɛ wo okunini.**
*If you buy something and you pay, we call you distinguished.*
(Honesty breeds a good reputation).

**6248. "Matɔ!" ɛfiri opirafoɔ anum.**
*"I've bought it" comes from a wounded person's mouth.*
(Only a person who is affected by something really experiences the feeling of it).

**6249. Wotɔ ahwene mono na ɛkwan nnu mu a, wotene ho.**
*If you buy a new bead and there is not a big enough hole in it, you make it larger.*
(Where there is a will, there is a way).

**6250. Wotɔ kɛtɛ apem a, baako pɛ so na woda.**
*If you buy a thousand mats, it is on one only that you sleep.*
(You only really need what you can actually use).

**6251. Wotɔ okusie nam na wotua a, yɛde dabɔ nam firi wo.**
*If you buy rat's meat and pay for it, when you ask for antelope's meat on credit it is given to you.*
(Be honest in small things and you will be trusted in big).

**6252. Ɛtɔ akyire a, fa!**
*If it falls behind, take it!*
(Do not be afraid of drawing from the past).

**6253. Ɛbɛtɔ da na atɔwuo adane te-bese.**
*There will come a time when picking of cola nuts from the ground will be replaced by collecting from the trees.*
(In times of plenty everyone shares, but in times of shortage, ownership becomes important. We may be prosperous now but we should prepare for more difficult times).

**6254. Yɛtɔ ma wodi a, wose Kumase tena yɛdɛ.**
*When we buy for you to eat, you say, it is good to remain in Kumasi.*
(If people provide for you, then you enjoy life in the city).

**6255. Ɛtɔ mmerɛ bi a na gyimi mu wɔ nyansa.**
*A time comes when wisdom is found in foolishness.*
(There is method in some people's madness).

**6256. Yɛtɔ na yɛntua a, anka nkɔdaa bɔ akɔnhoma.**
*If we buy but we don't pay, then children are in a position to give a daily allowance.*
(Uneasy lies the head that wears a crown. Or: If you could live without accepting responsibility for what you do, life would be easy).

**6257. Yɛtɔ eni a, anka obiara bɛtɔ bi.**
*If we were to buy mothers, then everyone would buy one.*
(A mother is the most precious thing in life; if one could be replaced, then no one would do without).

**6258. Wotɔ nsuo mu a, yɛkan wo fra adwene.**
*If you fall into the water, we count you among the fish.*
(You are judged by the company you keep).

**6259. Wotɔ praeɛ a, woatɔ nanteɛ.**
*If you buy a broom, you buy walking.*
(Any tool brings labor).

**6260. Wotɔ aprawa a, na wonyaa nam bi ntɔeɛ.**
*If you buy a pangolin, then you have not got (good) meat to buy.*
(Said when someone takes on an unrewarding job).

**6261. "Ɛtɔɔ sɛsɛɛ" ba biara nyɛ ba pa.**
*The child "If-he-had-been-alive" is not a real child.*
(It is no good indulging in wishful thinking or vain regrets).

**6262. Ɛtɔ sikyi o, ɛtɔ mfuate o, yɛnya ɔkɔmfoɔ ku no.**
*Whether the die falls sikyi or whether it falls mfuate, we kill the fetish priest.*

(Sikya and mfuate are two different sides of a cube used in a game like dice. Hence: The decision has already been taken, so why debate over it)?

**6263. Wotɔ asuo mu a, woduru aseɛ prɛko.**
*If you fall into a river, you go under it at once.*
(i.e. Once you're in the river, why not go under and see what's there? Hence: Satisfy your curiosity when you can).

**6264. Wotɔ tam sie wo ni na woantua ka a, wonya w'aykie so aseda.**
*If you buy a loin cloth to bury your mother and you don't pay for it, you will get your thanks at the funeral!*
(If you don't carry out your obligations, you will suffer public disgrace).

**6265. "Mɛtɔ, mɛtɔ", nyɛ adetɔ; adetɔ ne sɛ woatua ka.**
*"I will buy it, I will buy it" is not buying it; buying something is when you have paid.*
(Don't count your chickens before they are hatched. Or: Don't make vain promises).

**6266. Yɛntɔ ahina mono ngu no hyɛ.**
*We don't buy a new drinking pot and then weld it.*
(When you acquire something, you make sure it is in good condition before you accept it).

**6267. Toa ho yɛ hye a, na nsuo wɔ mu.**
*Whenever the bottle gourd becomes bright, there is water inside it.*
(If you are fulfilling your proper function, you show it).

**6268. Toa mu wɔ adeɛ a, Amakye na ɔnim.**
*If there is anything profitable in a gourd, then Amakye knows about it.*
(Amakye is supposed to have been the first man to plant gourds, of which he sold very many. Hence: It is the creator who knows best the nature of his creation).

**6269. Toa fufuo abɔ, na gyanseɛ?**
*The vessel of white porcelain has broken, what about the glass?*
(If the most precious thing has gone, why worry about a lesser one?)

**6270. Ntoa te a, na danka abɔ.**
*If the belt breaks, the gunpowder flask is (also) broken.*
(The flask hangs on the belt; if the belt breaks, the flask falls and breaks also. Hence: One man's fate affects those dependent on him).

**6271. Wotoatoa kotepomponini ahaasa so na wɔne prammire tenten yɛ pɛ a, n'ano borɔ ntɔ prammire.**
*If you line up three hundred agama lizards to make them as long as a cobra, they cannot be as poisonous as a cobra.*
(You cannot make a person or thing what they are not, however you treat them).

**6272. Yɛtoatoa mu sɛ nkɔnsɔnkɔnsɔn, nkwa mu a yetoa mu, owuo mu a yɛtoa mu, abusua mu nte da.**
*If we are linked together like a chain, in life we are linked, in death we are linked, family links are never broken.*
(Family ties cannot be broken even by death).

**6273. Atofo keseɛ ntumi ɛta.**
*A large loin cloth bunched behind cannot stop farting.*
(If you make a law against nature, it will not be observed).

**6274. Ɔtɔfoɔ ba nnyini mmɔ akora.**
*A treacherous man's child does not grow into old age.*
(Like father, like son; the child is liable to suffer if the father does not).

**6275. Atɔfowufoɔ kyiri: "Na adɛn?"**
*A person who is going to commit suicide taboos: "Why?"*
(If you are going to break a taboo, you are not open to questioning).

**6276. Ntokɛsee na ɛnyane kɔtewuiɛ.**
*Big buttocks wake up an impotent penis.*
(It takes the right stimulus to get the right response).

**6277. Atokoo nte ntwire.**
*Sorghum does not hear criticism.*
(Its no good criticising someone who does not understand).

**6278. Tɔkwa denden afiti no, na mpata denden nam kwan so.**
*A bitter fight has begun, then forceful pacification is one its way.*
(Everything has its antidote).

**6279. Tɔkwa fono wo a, na wo werɛ afi akeka.**
*If a battle overcomes you, then you forget to bite.*
(Sometimes problems so overcome you, that you forget what the solution could be).

**6280. Wotɔɔkye, tɔɔkye a, obi nso tɔɔkye.**
*If you don't act forcefully, someone else will not act forcefully.*
(Weakness breeds weakness).

**6281. Ntoma na yɛpam no keseɛ, na ɛnyɛ ɛka.**
*It is a cloth that we sew large, but not a debt.*
(You don't work to your own disadvantage).

**6282. Ntoma pa ne nwera.**
*The best cloth is calico.*
(White calico is used all over Africa for celebrating victory and for rejoicing. Hence: Something which indicates happiness is always welcome).

**6283. Ntoma yɛ fɛ a, onipa na ɔfura.**
*If a cloth is beautiful, a human being wears it.*
(You cannot change human nature just by dressing it up).

**6284. Ntoma yɛ fi a, na enhyeeɛ.**
*If the cloth is dirty, it (still) is not burnt.*
(If someone is out of favor, it does not mean that they are good for nothing. Their reputations can always be cleansed).

**6285. Wo ntoma nyɛ a, wonkɔ adwabɔ ase.**
*If your cloth is bad, you don't attend a public function.*
(You try and keep up appearances in public).

**6286. Ɔtomasifoɔ nni biribi a, ne bɔwerɛ mu yɛ fitaa.**
*If washermen have nothing else, their nails are clean.*
(Everyone has something good to be said for them).

**6287. Ɔtomfoɔ bɔ mponterɛ a, ɔbɔ sɔsɔ nso.**
*When the smith makes hinges, he also makes the mattock.*
(You should have more than one iron in the fire).

**6288. Ɔtomfoɔ retono a, deɛ ɛhia no na ɔbɔ.**
*If the blacksmith is forging, wherever it is necessary, he hits.*
(If someone concentrates on something, it is because it is necessary to him and his work).

**6289. Tɔmma te a, yɛmmisa amoaseɛ.**
*If the bead girdle is broken, do not ask for the loin cloth.*
(The loin cloth is hung from a string of beads. Hence: One thing leads to another).

**6290. Tɔmma te a, na ɛtam afɛre.**
*If the bead girdle breaks, the loin cloth is shamed.*
(One person's downfall affects another near to him. See previous Proverb).

**6291. Wotɔn obi akoa di a, na wayɛ no bɔne; na sɛ wɔbɔ no safohene deɛ a, na wonyɛɛ no bɔne.**
*If you sell someone's servant, then you have committed an offense against them; but if you install them as commander in the army, then you have not offended them.*
(You are blamed if you harm someone, but not if you do them good).

**6292. Wotɔn adeɛ a ɛyɛ foɔ a, w'akyiri kwan nyera.**
*If you sell things cheaply, your whereabouts never gets lost.*
(If you are generous, people remember you).

**6293. Wotɔn adeɛ na yɛantɔ a, na ɛfiri wo ara.**
*If you sell something and we don't buy it, then it is your own fault.*
(If you don't make enough effort or don't plan well, you have yourself to blame if you do not succeed).

**6294. Yɛntɔn ɔdodoɔ na ɔnnibie atɔ bi.**
*We don't sell plenty so that one who has nothing can buy some.*
("Ɔdodoɔ" refers to a large family, "ɔnnibie" to someone who has no children. Hence: Families are not for sale or there would never be solitary people. Be content with your destiny in life).

**6295. Metɔn ne matɔ ahyia!**
*I am selling and I am buying have met!*
(An agreement has been reached).

**6296. Wotɔn wo fie ansa na wɔaku wo.**
*They sell you at home before they kill you.*
(Sudden death is the result of witchcraft in the family).

**6297. Wotɔn w'asɛm a, na wonya tɔfoɔ.**
*If you sell your case, you get a buyer.*
(When you explain your difficulties convincingly, you get help).

**6298. Wotɔn w'asɛm gye afotuo a, wommɔ akyire ka.**
*If you sell your problem (make it known) and get advice, you don't lose by it.*
(If you let people know what your problems are, they will help you to get out of them).

**6299. Wotɔn w'asɛm a, wonya ɔpatafoɔ gyina w'akyi.**
*If you sell your case, then you get a helper to stand behind you.*
(If you persuade someone to agree with you, they will help you solve your problem).

**6300. Wotɔn w'aso di asɛm a, wode w'animuonyam te dwaha.**
*If you sell your ear, you complete the agreement with your honor (i.e., you sell your honor too).*
("Te dwaha" refers to a traditional means of recording an agreement. On the making of an agreement, something was broken in half and the witnesses each took half so that at any time they could prove their participation. Hence: Used when an arbiter or judge is perverting justice).

**6301. Wɔretɔn wo a, wontɔ tuo.**
*If you are being sold, you don't buy a gun.*
(You don't ask for privileges if you are in the hands of the law).

**6302. Ntokom se: "Mesene abɛ kɔkɔɔ".**
*The long pepper says: "I surpass the palm nut in redness."*
(It is possible to make a soup or stew without palm nut but unthinkable without pepper! Hence: Said of someone who is conscious of his own indispensability).

**6303. Ntontom na ɔkɔɔ dwa na obi bisaa no sɛ: "Bayerɛ baɛ?" Ose: "Bayerɛ a ɛbaeɛ no, na ɛte sɛ me srɛ".**
*It is the mosquito who went to the market one day and on its return was asked: "Have the yams come?" It replied: "The yams that have come are as big as my thigh".*
(Don't pretend to be what you are not. Or: If you can't measure up to a situation do not try to do so).

**6304. Ntontom ne hwan, na ɔrekɔto onyina kɛsɛ.**
*Who is the mosquito, for it to trip up the great onyina tree?*
(Said of an insignificant person who takes on an important one).

**6305. Ntontom ne hwan a, na samee rekɔhono no?**
*Who is the mosquito for a boil in the groin to trouble it?*
(Big troubles should not affect small people).

**6306. Ntontom te hɔ dada a, ɔse ɔrepɛ n'ase fie akɔ na mframa akɔka no akyire.**
*The mosquito, as things are, proposes to go to his in-law's house and the wind carries and helps him on his way.*
(Used when you intend to do something at any rate and at the same time someone comes along and stimulates you to do it).

**6307. "Tɔn-Tɔnte, Tɔn-Tɔnte": yɛrenom nsa na yɛrefa adwen.**
*"The blind and the lame, the blind and the lame": as we are drinking we are planning ahead.*
(Reference to a tale in which a blind man carried a lame man to the palm wine tapper at his work and he gave them drink, telling them to wait for more. Realizing that more drink would prevent them from going home, they left while still sober. Hence: Even when enjoying yourself you should make sure of your future).

**6308. Atopa kɛseɛ gyina sisidenden so.**
*The shaking of the waist in intercourse depends on its strength.*
(You can only do what you are physically capable of).

**6309. Atopa kɛseɛ na ɛgye kɔteɛ agorɔ.**
*Much shaking makes the penis enjoy the game.*
(If you want something from someone, you do what pleases them).

**6310. Ɔtope se, akyekyedeɛ nka nkyerɛ anwonomo na anwonomo nso nka nkyerɛ mmatatwene, na mmatatwene nka nkyerɛ ɔman, ɛfiri sɛ yɛse, yɛse na ɛma asɛm trɛ.**
*The big snail tells the tortoise to tell the thatching reed, so that the thatching reed may tell the liana, for the liana to tell the state, because "we say, we say" makes news spread.*
(Because of constant gossip few things in society can be kept secret).

**6311. Tɔprɛ twene, yɛnka nni w'akyi a, wose ɛyɛ dɛ.**
*The tɔprɛ drum: if it is not played behind you, you say the music is sweet.*
(This drum was played behind people being led through the street and being tortured before execution. Hence: If you are not yourself involved you can enjoy a spectacle, even if someone else is suffering).

**6312. Tɔprɛ twene: yɛmpata no.**
*The tɔperɛ drum: we don't appease it.*
(See previous Proverb. Don't leave things until it is too late. Once past a certain point nothing can be done to better a situation).

**6313. Atɔprɛwuo nyɛ mpatuwuo.**
*Death by torture and execution is not unexpected.*
("Atɔprɛ" is the process of being tortured before execution. If you are being tortured it does not matter if you are strong or weak, death is the end. Hence: If you are guilty you should not be surprised by having to pay for it).

**6314. Ɔtɔprɛfoɔ na ɔyi ne ho agyamma mu.**
*A man who is being tortured before execution, disassociates himself from the children of his father.*
(See previous Proverb. If you are going to die a disgraceful death, you don't count yourself as one of your father's children. In extremity we are alone).

**6315. Ɛtorɔ baako seɛ nokorɛ apem.**
*One falsehood spoils a thousand truths.*
(By telling only one lie you can ruin your reputation for being truthful).

**6316. Ɛtorɔ yɛdi no ohia.**
*Telling lies is done out of need.*
(You lie to protect yourself or to obtain help when in real want).

**6317. Ɔtorofoɔ de mfeɛ apem tu kwan a, ɔnokwafoɔ de da koro ti no to no.**
*If a liar has a thousand years head-start on a journey, a truthful man can pursue and catch him in a single day.*
(Truth will always triumph over lies).

**6318. "Ɔtorofoɔ, gye adwa", ɔse: "Manya boɔ".**
*"Inveterate gossiper, take a seat"; he says: "I have got a stone."*

(A person being questioned by a fetish would be asked to sit on a stone which would make him speak the truth, thus if you let an inveterate tale bearer sit down, he will inevitably swear he is telling the truth. But this should not make you believe everything he says).

**6319. Ɔtorofoɔ mma ɔsensini.**
*A liar does not tell an uncompleted story.*
(A practiced liar is never without an excuse).

**6320. Ɔtorofoɔ na ɔse ɔkɔɔ Serɛm asusueberɛ na wɔde nku asi dan, nanso awia bɔeɛ na ɔwɔ Asanteman mu.**
*A liar says when he went North during the rainy season he saw that people used shea butter to build a house, but when the dry season came he was in Asante.*
(A liar finds a way of not having to prove a tall story).

**6321. Ɔtorofoɔ na ɔse: "Me dansefoɔ wɔ Aburokyire".**
*A liar says: "My witness is overseas".*
(See Proverb 597. If you wish to lie you say your witness is far away).

**6322. Ɔtorofoɔ nsɛm a ɛgu ahodoɔ nkyɛre gyina.**
*A liar's stories that are different do not exist for long.*
(Inconsistencies show up untruth).

**6323. Ɔtoromo mma sa a, ɔde ne mfɛfoɔ mma yɛ mma.**
*If the bongo's children are not there, he takes his friend's children as his.*
(A man may be feared and yet be kind and care for others).

**6324. Ɔtoromo pɛ ne ho kɔkɔɔ nti ma ɔ kɔ-tweree sie.**
*The bongo likes being red-colored, that is why it leaned against the ant hill.*
(If someone likes something, they try hard to get it).

**6325. Ntorowa se wamma dwam a, edwa ntumi nhuri.**
*If the rattle says he will not join the orchestra, the crowd does not become roused.*
(Said of something essential to the achievement of success).

**6326. Wototo akɔkono a, woyi no benebena.**
*If you roast the palm beetle grubs, you remove them stick by stick (from the fire).*
(They are cooked on sticks over a fire, like kebabs. Hence: Said of things that should be kept together).

**6327. Wototo akyenkyena a, na wohu wo hia da.**
*It is after you have roasted the allied hornbill that you realize that you are still poor.*
(All that glitters is not gold. The bird, because of its feathers, looks much bigger than it is).

**6328. Wototo we a, kyefrɛ afɛre.**
*If you roast and chew, the grill is put to shame.*
(If you circumvent someone by achieving your ends without them, you put them to shame).

**6329. Ɔtotɔ mfɔn.**
*The buyer does not starve.*
(The person who procures something satisfies himself first).

**6330. Totoanwoma retoto kɔrɔ no, na saneanwoma resane kɔ.**
*When a slanderer is going the rounds, then a defender is also going around.*
(Everything has its antidote. Or: Every negative has a positive).

**6331. "Etoto a, mɛsane" ne "Ɛba a, mɛsɔ ano": "Ɛba a, mɛsɔ ano" ne panin.**
*"When it gets entangled, I will straighten it out", and "When it comes, I will prevent it"; "If it comes, I will prevent it" is the elder.*
(Prevention is better than a cure. See Proverb 2).

**6332. Totobi kɔ ayie a, ɔda abɛnkwan afa.**
*If the rotted skin of an animal goes to a funeral, it sleeps in the same room as the palm-nut soup.*
(The skin is used to make soup. Hence: You keep company with those you get on with).

**6333. Totobi tere nkwan.**
*The rotted skin of an animal permeates the soup.*
(In the right place, an insignificant person is much appreciated).

**6334. Atotɔbɛ wɔwe no akɔnɔ.**
*A roasted palm-nut you eat it with good appetite.*
(A good thing deserves to be appreciated).

**6335. Tɔtɔborɔfoɔ! Ma w'ani nte na w'ani rete ayowam.**
*Idiot! Get wise to yourself, for you are concentrating too much on the pot.*
(Use your talents for more profitable things than self-indulgence).

**6336. Atotɔnsa nnom nsuo.**
*A person who buys strong drink does not drink water.*
(The owner shares what he has acquired. If you often entertain other people, they will entertain you in the same way).

**6337. Ɔtotopafoɔ hyia ne difoɔ.**
*A person desirous of having sex finally meets the person who will satisfy them.*
(If you try hard enough, you will succeed in getting what you want).

**6338. Wontraa deɛ ɛyɛ toro a, wonsere obi a wahwe ase torotorɔ mu.**
*If you have not left a slippery place, you don't laugh at someone who has slipped down there.*
(You wait until you know you are safe before you laugh at another's downfall).

**6339. Ntrama hia wo a, ɛsene apem.**
*If you are short of one string of cowries, it is worse than a thousand.*
(You mind much more missing something by a fraction than by a great deal).

**6340. Atrannɔ gyegyeegye samankrofi na ɔma ɔteasefoɔ nya odwantwerɛ.**
*The ghost who is always finding faults with people leads a living person into slaughtering sheep.*
(A troublesome member of the family, living or dead, leads you into unnecessary expense).

**6341. "Trara-trara" anyɛ mma, na "kokoko" ne ɛbɛyɛ deɛbɛn?**
*If heavy rain could not fill (the barrel) how much less will the drips be able to do so.*
("Trara-trara" and "kokoko" are onomatopoeic ways of referring to heavy and light rainfall, respectively. Hence: What the great cannot accomplish, the small cannot achieve either).

**6342. Yɛretu wo fo a, womposa wo hwoa.**
*If we are advising you, you don't scratch your testicles.*
(If you don't intend to take serious advice, don't make it obvious).

**6343. Yɛtu fo na yɛntu hyɛberɛ.**
*We give advice but we don't alter destiny.*
(You cannot interfere with fate).

**6344. Wotu mfofo mu agorɔ a, na watu kotokurodi suman.**
*If you are constantly playing among the aspilia latifolia, then you collect the wasp's fetish charm (i.e the wasp will sting you).*
(Aspilia latifolia is a plant with many medicinal uses. If you are on someone else's territory, you are subject to their whims).

**6345. Wotu agyan a, na wonkum ne borɔ.**
*You may remove the arrow but not the poison.*
(You can apologize for a bad word or deed but the effect remains).

**6346. Woretu ako ntakara a, womua n'ani.**
*If you are plucking out a parrot's feathers, you cover its eyes.*
(If you wish to break rules or do damage, do it circumspectly).

**6347. Woretu koneɛ-koneɛ no na obi nso retɛ kokoa-kokoa.**
*When you are creeping along, another person will be looking around.*
(Just as there are those anxious to commit a crime, so there are others anxious to prevent it).

**6348. Woretu korɔmfoɔ fo no na ɔte afikyire rebɔ ne bedɛ.**
*As you are advising a thief, then he sits behind the house and works at his woven basket (to steal with).*
(A bad man indicates he has no intention of taking advice).

**6349. Wotu kwan a, yɛ wo ho yie, na ehia na deɛ wobɛhyia no, woanhyia no bio.**
*If you are going on a journey, dress well, because the person you may meet on the way, you may not meet again.*
(Always make the best impression you can: you may not have a second chance).

**6350. Wotu amena ma wo yɔnko a, woto mu bi.**
*If you dig a trench to trap a companion, you too fall into it.*
(You get caught by your own trickery).

**6351. Wotu mmire a, wode kyerɛ esie.**
*If you uproot mushrooms, you show them to the anthill.*
(If someone is your benefactor, you keep him informed about your progress).

6352. **Wotu mmire na wo nko ara wodi a, yɛto wo so.**
*If you collect mushrooms and you eat them alone, we accuse you (of stealing).*
(Normally, you find mushrooms in the forest and you share them with the owner of the land. If you keep them to yourself people begin to suspect you of stealing from other farms. Hence: If you are mean you get accused of acts you have not performed).

6353. **Wotu mmirika na woanto wo bo ase a, wosunti.**
*If you run and you don't take care, you trip up.*
(If you are careless, you suffer for it).

6354. **"Montu-ntwene, montu-ntwene", (ka asomurofi)/(ɛka bokyia hunu).**
*"Throw away, throw away" results in an empty hearth.*
(If you are too critical, you are left with nothing to work with).

6355. **Yɛntu yɛn nan asuom nkɔtia atɛkyɛ mu.**
*We don't take our legs out of the water to step into the mud.*
(You don't exchange good for bad).

6356. **Wotua birekuo ntuahema a, ɔbɔ wa.**
*If you visit the clock-bird in early dawn, it coughs.*
(If you surprise someone suddenly, they react from shock).

6357. **Woretua ɛka a, na ɛyɛ ya; na nyɛ sɛ woreka asɛm.**
*If you are paying a debt, it is difficult; but when you are saying something it is not.*
(It is easy to talk but less easy to act).

6358. **Yɛtua owufoɔ ka wie ansa na yɛatua ɔteasefoɔ deɛ.**
*We finish paying a dead person's debt before we pay a live person's one.*
(You finish dealing with someone who you won't see again before dealing with those who are always with you. Also, the spirit of the dead may harm you. Hence, alternatively: You deal with the person you fear before you deal with others).

6359. **Atua nyɛ tuana, na ne nkatwom.**
*It is not difficult to insert medicine in your anus, but as for keeping it closed!*
(Peppers are sometimes inserted in the rectum as a treatment for constipation. Hence: Some things are easy to do, even if their results are hard to bear).

6360. **Etua wo yɔnko ho a, ɛtua dua mu.**
*Pain in your companion's body is like pain in a tree (to you).*
(You cannot experience the physical pain of another person, but that does not mean that you should not be sympathetic).

6361. **Otubrafoɔ nti na apopobire fam boɔ ho.**
*It is because of a settler that ground algae grows on the stone.*
(There needs to be a society before it attracts parasites).

6362. **Atuduro asa a ɛnyɛ Akwawua ntoa mu a.**
*If gunpowder was finished it was never so in Akwawua's belt.*
(Akwawua was a famous Bantamahene and general. Hence: A resourceful person never lacks means).

6363. **Atu-fanu hyia, asamankwan nna ntu.**
*If two opposing cannons meet, the road to the land of the dead is never deserted.*
(If war breaks out, death is inevitable).

6364. **Tufoanteɛ po afotuo, na ɔmpo ne funsie.**
*A person who does not listen to advice rejects advice, but he does not reject the burial of his corpse.*
(However stubborn you are, some things you cannot refuse. Or: If you don't heed advice, you pay the cost).

6365. **Otumfoɔ worɔ wo kawa a, ɔworɔ fa wo mmati.**
*If a very powerful man pulls off your ring, he pulls it over your shoulder.*
(There is no limit to the harm that power can do).

6366. **Tumi dodoɔ yɛ gyimi.**
*Too much power leads to stupidity.*
(If you are too powerful your head is turned).

6367. **Tumi nyinaa wɔ asaase so.**
*All power is from the land.*
(We are all utterly dependent on creation.

6368. **Tumi suman: yɛde gyimi na ɛsam soɔ.**
*The talisman of power: we use folly to cover it.*
(If you want power, you don't have to question your motives too much).

6369. **Mɛtumi aforo a, anka woammɛto me aseɛ.**
*If I were able to climb it, you would not have found me underneath.*
(If you can do something yourself, you don't wait for someone else to help you).

6370. **Wobɛtumi atɔ akoa, na worentumi ntɔ n'akoma (mu asɛm).**
*If you are able to buy a slave, you are unable to buy (what is in) their heart.*
(You can control people's bodies but not their feelings).

6371. **Wontumi biribi a, wommɔ kahyire nnye nsoa.**
*If you can't carry something, you do not prepare a pad to do so.*
(If you can't do a job, don't pretend you can).

6372. **Wontumi w'akɔmfo hyɛ a, wose: "Ɛnne yɛ dabɔne".**
*If you cannot kill yourself you say: "Today is a bad day".*
(If you have not the courage to do something, you make excuses for your inability to do so).

6373. **Wontumi akonnwasoa a, na wote wo wura so atua.**
*If you are unable to carry the stool, you revolt against your master.*
(Said when someone will not take on a job which he finds too much for him and therefore refuses to do it).

6374. **Wontumi wo ho a, na wose: "Abusuafoɔ anhwɛ me".**
*If you cannot manage your own affairs then you say: "My relatives did not look after me".*
(You tend to blame others for your own shortcomings).

6375. Wontumi nhua asera mma wo hwene ano nwo a, wode wo ntoma na ɛpepa.
*If you are unable to take snuff so that your nostril is cleared, you wipe it with your cloth.*
(Where there is a will there is a way).

6376. Wontumi akɔkono bɔ a, na wose: "Akɔ me tirim".
*If you cannot go to collect the palm beetle grub, you say: "I am tired of it".*
(Sour grapes).

6377. Wontumi kokuroko danta mo a, wonsane.
*If you are unable to wear an ostentatious loin-cloth (i.e., don't know how to put it on), you don't loosen it.*
(If you can't put something together, don't dismantle it).

6378. Wobɛtumi kokuroko tɔmma mo a, na wosensan.
*If you can wear the beads of a giant, then you thread them.*
(You only put work into what you have the power to use).

6379. Wontumi wo mmirikisie dɔ a, na wofrɛ no nsamampɔ.
*If you are unable to cultivate your heavy forest, then you call it a spirit grove.*
(If you cannot do something, you try and find a legitimate excuse not to do it).

6380. Wontumi mmorɔsonom a, wonom ahai.
*If you cannot drink foreign alcohol (i.e schnapps or rum), you drink corn beer.*
(If you cannot get the best from overseas, then you make do with home production).

6381. Wontumi wo nnoɔma a, na wose: "Me kahyire nyɛ".
*If you are unable to carry your things, you say: "My carrying pad is no good".*
(When you feel unequal to your duty, you blame someone else for it).

6382. Wontumi nsaa bɔ a, na wosa ayie ase asabrane.
*If you are unable to give a funeral donation, you dance funeral dances enthusiastically.*
(If you cannot do what is expected of you, you throw dust into the eyes of those involved).

6383. Wontumi nsi dan a, na wodane wo yɔnko.
*If you cannot build your own house, you depend on your companion.*
(What you can't do yourself, you must employ others to do).

6384. Wontumi awareɛ a, mfa nhye wo kora.
*If you can't make a (good) marriage, don't attribute it to your co-wife.*
(Don't blame others for your own shortcomings).

6385. Wontumi awareɛ a, na woware ababaawa.
*If you can't make a (good) marriage, then you marry a young wife.*
(You need patience and determination to make a marriage to an inexperienced girl successful. If you have no patience, do not embark on a course that needs it).

6386. Wontumi nyɛ somakorɔ a, na wokum wo ni ne wo se.
*If you are unable to obey orders to go here and there, you kill your mother and your father.*
(If what you are asked to do by your parents is too much for you, you still have to accept it).

6387. Wontumi ayikorɔ a, na wose: "Wɔammɛse me".
*If you are unable to go to a funeral, then you say: "They did not inform me".*
(You can always find an excuse not to do something you do not want to do).

6388. Otuntuma bu a, ɔdan fɛre.
*If the principal pole of the house breaks, the house becomes ashamed.*
(When the head of the house is no more, a family becomes weak).

6389. Etuo a, yɛde kɔ ɔko ka dɔm guo no, yɛmfa nni apiripiragorɔ.
*The gun that we go to war with and drive away the enemies, we don't use in child's play.*
(You take care of those who serve you well and treat them carefully).

6390. Etuo di mfoasoɔ.
*A gun earns a profit.*
(A good helper enables you to get on in life).

6391. Etuo di asia na woantɔ no asia a, woyɛ ho adeɛ ma no boro asia.
*If a gun is worth an asia and you don't give an asia for it, you will in the end pay more than an asia.*
(An asia is a weight of gold dust. Hence: You can't get good things cheap. If you do, it will cost you more in the end).

6392. Etuo kantamma nni baakofoɔ so.
*The cock of the gun is not meant for one man alone.*
(Life and death are for all).

6393. Etuo a ɛkum ɔbɔpɔn pane bankye-akorɛ.
*The gun which kills a great animal breaks the fork of the cassava plant.*
(The falling animal breaks the plant. Hence: You are responsible for the subsidiary results of your actions).

6394. Etuo mu ye sum.
*There is darkness in the gun.*
(It is difficult to know the mind of a treacherous person).

6395. Etuo nya okutafoɔ a, na ɛbɔ.
*If the gun gets a holder, it fires.*
(With encouragement you perform well).

6396. Etuo nya tiafoɔ a, na ɔdi mmarimasɛm.
*When a gun is adequately prepared, it performs warlike deeds.*
(When you have a good leader and prepare well, you perform well).

6397. Etuo (pae)/(ben) a, ɛsi ɔbarima bo.
*If a gun (bursts/(is shot), it is still on a man's chest.*
(A man is obliged to cope with the situation, however bad it is).

6398. Etuo pae ka ɔbɔfoɔ a, yɛmmisa deɛ ɔdii ɔbɔfoɔ nam.
*If the gun bursts and wounds the hunter, you don't ask him who has eaten the meat he has shot!*
(Don't add insult to injury).

6399. Etuo mpae wɔ Aburokyire mmɛka nnipa wɔ Abibirem.
*A gun does not burst in Europe to wound a man in Africa.*
(See Proverb 597. The cause of trouble can usually be found nearby).

6400. Etuo tim wo a, na wo nso wotim n'akantamma.
*If a gun conquers you, you too can conquer its hammer.*
(Everyone has something they can master).

6401. Etuo to a, na adeɛ abɔ.
*When a gun fires, trouble has come.*
(There is no smoke without a fire).

6402. Etuo bɛto a, ɛnnim sɛ yɛampopa mu.
*If a gun will fire, it does not matter if we clean it or not.*
(If something is destined to work, it will work).

6403. Etuo nto aboa bi nnyee nkɔhyehye aboa bi.
*A gun is not fired at one animal for another to receive the shot.*
(You don't attack one man for another to suffer).

6404. Etuo yɛnto no brɛɛ oo!
*You cannot shoot a gun without noise.*
(You cannot hide violence).

6405. Etuo yera nifa mu na ekɔfiri adɔnten mu a, na ɛnkɔɔ baabiara.
*When the gun is missing from the right flank of the battle and appears in the forefront, it did not go astray.*
(Providing a man is striving for the common good, he may do it in more ways and places than one).

6406. W'atuo sua a, na w'asɛm sua.
*If your guns are few, then your strength is small.*
(Unless you have the necessary resources you will not succeed).

6407. Etuo-tantia wotia a, ɛsi deɛ ɛsie.
*If you press the cap of a gun, it keeps its position.*
(A strong man holds his place).

6408. Aturuhweɛ mpaninsɛm nti na n'asefoɔ awu agya no amamfoso.
*Because of the mannikin's precocity, its relatives died and left it.*
(If you are too arrogant, you cause trouble for yourself and others).

6409. Aturuhweɛ su agyenkuku su a, ne to pae.
*If the mannikin sings the dove's song, his bottom bursts.*
(Don't try to do more than you are able to).

6410. Nturuhweɛ: "Yɛnim ko nso yɛsusua".
*The mannikins boast: "We know how to fight, but we are small".*
(Being small does not mean you lack courage).

6411. Aturukuku pɛ ɔbrɛ a, ɔbrɛ.
*If the turtle dove invites exhaustion, it gets tired.*
(This bird's monotonous call is supposed to sound like "better go home, better go home" ... "wobɛkɔ fie a, kɔ, kɔ." Hence: You get what you ask for).

6412. Woretutu, woredwiri a, wonse sɛ: "Gya me burodua ho."
*If you are removing the maize from the cob and you are scattering, you don't say: "Leave a little on the cob for me".*
(If you have everything, don't pretend to be in need).

6413. Woretutu, woredwiri; na deɛ ɛwɔ hene na ehia woɔ?
*You are removing the maize from the cob, you are scattering it; which of the two is the more important to you?*
(Set your priorities right before you act).

6414. Yɛntutu anomaa ho nkɔkyerɛ ɔpanin.
*We don't pluck a bird and show it to an elder (to identify).*
(You don't try and trick your seniors deliberately).

6415. Wotwa borɔdeɛ na ɛhwe fam birim a, wonse sɛ woabrim, wose: "Ewɔ aseɛ".
*If you cut plantain and it falls down hard, you don't say it has fallen down "bump," you say, "It is on the ground".*
(If you make a mistake, you don't speak the truth about it but try and make it sound less bad than it is).

6416. Wotwa borɔfere de yɛ atumpan a, ɛbɛyɛ yie na wode ma dammirifua a, na obi reteɛ.
*If you make a drum out of the pawpaw tree, it is possible, but when it is beaten to praise you, no one will hear it.*
(If you are lazy and use the easiest materials, it won't be to your credit. The pawpaw trunk is hollow and very soft).

6417. Wotwa ɔbrafoɔ tiri a, wɔsɔ na wɔmma ɛnto fam.
*If you cut the executioner's head off, he holds it, it does not fall to the ground.*
(Some people are so courageous that they stand up to any adversity).

6418. Wotwa wo nnunsini nyinaa gu a, wohwere wo soafoɔ.
*If you have chopped up all your tree stumps, you lose your helpers to carry.*
(When lifting a load, it is often put on a tree stump from which it is transferred to the head. Without the stump, lifting the heavy load is very hard. Hence: If you destroy your helpers, you have to do without help).

6419. Wotwa fufuo na ɛfiri tɔ ayowa mu a, na ɛnyeraeɛ.
*If you cut fufu and it falls into the soup pot, it is not lost.*
(You don't have to worry if something can be retrieved).

6420. Woatwa kɔntɔmoa kɛseɛ, yɛrebu wo anikyie; wosaa nkwan a, na woasa nnwanam.
*You cut off a big lump (of fufu), we have expressed disapproval; if you collect soup, you take twice your portion of tasty pieces of meat.*
(Don't add insult to injury).

6421. Wobɛtwa nkontompo ama yɛahuro woɔ deɛ, ka nokorɛ ma yɛmmpene wo.
*You are going to tell lies, so that we scold you, speak the truth and let us congratulate you.*
(It is better to earn praise than blame).

6422. Wotwa nkontompo a, na w'asɛm wareɛ.
*If you are dishonest, your problems are endless.*
(Dishonesty breeds chaos).

6423. Wotwa nkontompo a, na wosuro Kumase.
*When you tell a lie, you fear Kumase.*
(All serious crimes were tried at the Asantehene's court in Kumasi. Hence: A liar always fears being discovered and taken to justice).

6424. Wotwa nkontompo daa, na da-koro woka nokorɛ a, yɛnnye nni.
*If you indulge in falsehood all the time, and you speak the truth one day, we don't believe you.*
(A warning against perpetually telling lies. When the time of truth comes, no one will listen to you).

6425. Wotwa nkontompo ma wo safoa yera a, woda abɔnten.
*If through telling lies you lose your key, you sleep outside.*
(If you intentionally do wrong, you yourself suffer for it).

6426. Wotwa nkontompo nya wo ho afe a, ɛhia wo da koro pɛ.
*If you tell lies to become rich in a year, you become poor in a day.*
(Lies don't pay in the long run).

6427. Wotwa no tenten a, na wonya no fuaberɛ.
*If you cut it long, then you get somewhere to hold.*
(If you get plenty, you can make best use of what you get).

6428. Wotwa (ɔsahene)/(ɔdehyeɛ) ti kɔkyerɛ wo hene a, ɔma wo amo, nanso ɔtwa ne ho suro wo.
*If you behead the (enemy leader)/(royal) and go and show the head to your chief, he thanks you but he fears you in turn.*
(If a leader finds his follower is too powerful, he respects but fears him).

6429. Wotwa wo tɛkrema toto we a, na wonnyaa nam pa biara nweeɛ.
*If you cut your tongue and roast and eat it, you have not had any good meat to eat.*
(Don't do something stupid that brings little profit).

6430. Wotwa twemmɔne to asuoso a, ɛporie wo ara to asuo mu.
*If you build a bad bridge over a river, it rots and throws you yourself into the water.*
(If you do something bad, in the end it catches up with you).

6431. Wotwa ɔwɔ tiri a, deɛ aka yɛ homa.
*If you cut off a snake's head, the rest is rope.*
(If you deal with the leader of a group, it is easy to cope with his followers. Compare Proverb 1807).

6432. Atwa nso di a, yɛnhoro ngu.
*If there is not enough of wild yam for eating, you don't wash part away.*
(If there is not enough, you don't waste what there is).

6433. Atwamene suro ayeyada.
*A cut-throat is afraid to lie on his back.*
(A man fears what he inflicts on others).

6434. Wontwaree asuo nwieeɛ a, nka sɛ ɔdɛnkyɛm ano pɔ.
*If you have not finished crossing the stream, you don't say that the crocodile's mouth is deformed.*
(Get out of reach of a powerful person before you criticize them).

6435. Wotware Tanɔ a, na woaduru Bron.
*If you cross the Tano river you reach Brong.*
(The Tano river separates Asante from Brong. Hence: One thing follows logically on another).

6436. Atwarekwanawu amma akwannya anyɛ fo.
*The stinking shrew did not become satisfied with the roadside.*
(This animal is supposed to die if it crosses the road. Hence: If you are not content with what you have, you suffer for it).

6437. Wotwe biribi wɔ soro na ɛmma a, na biribi kuta mu.
*If you pull something from above and it does not come, then something is holding it.*
(If you don't get the expected results from an action, it means someone is interfering).

6438. Wotwe (afenatene)/(mpomponsuo) a, na woawie afenawe.
*If you pull (the long sword)/(the most important sword) out, you have finished the pulling of swords.*
(You have taken the final step in the matter. You can do nothing more drastic).

6439. Wotwe wiridi a, na werɛde taa toɔ.
*If you pull a string, it may have something on the end.*
(Warning that it is better not to interfere in another person's affairs, or you may not like what comes out of your interference. Note the assonance).

6440. Yɛretwe wo ase a, wonse sɛ: "M'akyiri kuro!"
*If we are dragging you along the ground, you don't say: "There is a sore on my back".*
(You don't complain of small things when you are in big trouble).

6441. Twe-ma-mentwe, na ɛma koraa bɔ.
*Pull and let me pull, breaks the calabash.*
(If there is a case between two people and they insist on dragging it on, the results may be even more serious).

6442. Ɛtwe bɔne, yɛdi no ɔhɔhoɔ.
*A bad vagina, we make use of it with a stranger.*
(Lack of knowledge may lead an innocent person to choose the wrong thing).

6443. Ɛtwɛ foforɔ nyane kɔtewuiɛ.
*A fresh vagina wakes up a weak penis.*
(Something new stimulates interest).

6444. Ɛtwɛ ho abrabɔ den na ɛyɛ nti na mmarima yɛ adwumaden.
*Because of difficulties in maintaining the vagina, that is why men do hard work.*
(Fulfillment is costly).

**6445. Ɛtwɛ hwe ase a, ne ba nte ntɔ.**
*If the vagina falls down, the clitoris does not fall apart.*
(When a great man falls, certain things always stay with him).

**6446. Ɛtwɛ anhyia ne ba a, anka ɛyare hwento.**
*If the vagina had not got a clitoris, then it would have suffered from a broken nose.*
(If you are not properly equipped, you are less attractive).

**6447. Ɛtwɛ nyini wie a, ensuro kɔtepɔn.**
*If a vagina is full grown, it is not afraid of a big penis.*
(If you can cope with a situation, you don't fear it).

**6448. Ɛtwɛ pɛ fɛyɔ nti na ɛfu nwi.**
*Because the vagina likes beauty, that is why it grows hair.*
(Because of your ambitions for the future, you take trouble).

**6449. Ɛtwɛ nni se, nanso ɔde brɛbrɛ we tam.**
*The vagina has no teeth, but it gradually chews up the loin cloth.*
(Slowly does it).

**6450. Ɛtwɛ yare a, kɔteɛ hyɛ akɔmfo.**
*If the vagina is sick, the penis hangs itself.*
(When someone vital to you can't help you, you become suicidal. Or: Without a woman's help, a man is nothing).

**6451. Ɛtwɛ yɛ eburo mpo a, ne ho te ma kɔteɛ.**
*If the vagina is thought dirty, it is neat to the penis.*
(Beauty is in the eye of the beholder).

**6452. Ɛtwɛ nyɛ dɛ a, ɛfekyere kɔtee.**
*If the vagina is not sweet, at least the foreskin contracts.*
(Things may not be perfect but at least they have some effect).

**6453. Ɔtwe bɛbrɛ, ɔbɔfoɔ nso bɛbrɛ,**
*The duiker will get tired, (but) the hunter will get tired as well.*
(If you trouble someone, you also are in trouble).

**6454. Ɔtwe redi nna atie wɔ ha mu na ɔrepɛ anatuo?**
*How big is the duiker staying in the forestfor it to be thinking of having fat calves on its legs.*
(If you know you are not staying long in a place, you don't bother to improve your situation).

**6455. Ɔtwe di twe, eyuo di ayuo.**
*The duiker eats beans, the black duiker eats guinea corn.*
(Tastes differ. A play on words).

**6456. Ɔtwe ankɔ dwa a, ne nwoma kɔ.**
*If the duiker does not go to the market, its skin does.*
(You can contribute to something without being there in person).

**6457. Ɔtwe Kwabena Agyanka a, ɔhyɛ mpaboakorɔ nanso ɔsi kɔn, na ɔkaa se: "Deɛ ɔbɛdi me nam na ɔsoa me bɛdɛ".**
*The duiker Kwabena Agyanka, which wears one sandal but limps, says: "The person who will eat my meat will have to carry my palm basket (with my carcass inside)".*

(If you really want something, then you have to do all the work which is necessary to obtain it).

**6458. Ɔtwe nhunu adukuru no, na ɔda.**
*Before the duiker found the buttress of the tree, it slept.*
(Man survived even without all modern conveniences).

**6459. Ɔtwe ne ɔtwe reko na wɔhunu gyahene a, wɔbɔ mu dwane.**
*If duiker fights duiker and they see a leopard, they join in flight.*
(Adversity brings even rivals together).

**6460. Ɔtwe ani anka, na ɛfiri ɔbɔfoɔ.**
*When the duiker is unhappy, it is because of the hunter.*
(Man suffers because he is persecuted).

**6461. Ɔtwe nya ahoɔden a, ɛfiri ɔbɔfoɔ.**
*If the duiker becomes strong, it is due to the hunter.*
(Adversity breeds strength).

**6462. Ɔtwe nya anantuo a, yekyiri.**
*If the calf of the duiker's leg is enlarged, we taboo it.*
(If something is deformed, we don't use it).

**6463. Atwe mmienu boro oyuo.**
*Two Maxwell's duikers defeat one black one.*
(Two weaker people can defeat a strong one. The advantage of joint action).

**6464. Ɔtwea nwo nto badwa mu.**
*A bitch does not give birth to its young in public.*
(If you respect yourself, you don't expose private affairs in public).

**6465. Tweapea afuo rehye a, Ɔburoni mfa ho.**
*If the chewing stick farm is burning, the European does not care.*
(If you don't use something, you don't mind losing it).

**6466. Tweefoɔ nu wɔn ho anwummerɛ.**
*Beaters repent in the evening.*
(Beaters are people who drive game towards huners. Hence: If you are unsuccessful, you regret the amount of work you have done).

**6467. Yɛtwɛn safoɔ ansa na yɛanom nsa.**
*We wait for the palm-wine seller before we drink.*
(Until something is produced, you can't consume it).

**6468. Atwene a ɛdwa na ɛtwetwe dɔm.**
*The drums that sound good invite the crowd.*
(A good thing attracts).

**6469. Atwene a ɛyɛ dɛ na ɔkɔmfoɔ gye ano nkɔmmoa.**
*If the drums are sweet, then the fetish priest collects fees.*
(Good publicity makes money).

**6470. Twene anim da hɔ a, yɛnyan nkyɛn.**
*If the drum has a head we don't beat its sides.*
(A bold man speaks out).

**6471. Twene nyɛ dɛ a, ɛnhwere pɔɔpɔɔ.**
*When the drum music is not good, at least it makes a sound.*
(Anything is better than refusing to speak).

6472. Twene nyɛ dɛ a, wosa ano saa ara.
*When the drum music is not good, you dance to it all the same.*
(You cannot always have the best. If you want to do something you do it even if conditions are not ideal).

6473. Ɛtwene da asuo so a, yɛnnyae nkɔfa nsuo mu.
*If there is a bridge over a river, we don't bypass it and go through the water.*
(If the way is easy, do not make it difficult).

6474. Tweneboa Kodua kɔwu gyee Asanteman no, mmaa ampene no, na ketrefeni kɔko dwane Bana a, na mmaa bɛpene no?
*Even when Tweneboa Kodua died for the Asante Nation, women did not congratulate him, how much less a weak person will plenty of sores who went to fight at Banda and ran away, will be congratulated by women?*
(If a courageous man who gives his all for the nation, does not get recognition, why should a coward and scoundrel?)

6475. Twenesoafoɔ nni adwamsɛm.
*The drum-carrier should not show off in a public place.*
(A servant does not show off in front of important people).

6476. Wotwere Oburoni a, wotwere borɔferɛ.
*If you lean against a European, you lean against a paw-paw tree.*
(Don't lean on a hollow reed).

6477. Twereboɔ na ɔma etuo di mmaninsɛm.
*Thanks to the flint the gun performs warlike deeds.*
(Even important people depend on humble ones to achieve success).

6478. Wotwetwe wo kunu kɔte a, ɛda wo to.
*If you continually pull your husband's penis, it lies on your buttocks (i.e vagina).*
(If you damage something you make use of, you yourself will suffer).

6479. "Atwetweakɔ-ne-atwetweba" nua ne "Biribi-abɛtɔ-mu".
*"You can't decide whether to go or come" has a brother "Something has cropped up".*
(Indecision leads to failure).

6480. Ɔtwɛntwɛnko a yɛretwɛn no ako mmadɛ a, yɛnko mma ɛnyɛ yie.
*If a person we are waiting to fight has not come, it is impossible for us to fight and do it well.*
(Some people are indispensible; you cannot act without them).

6481. Etwie ankum a, mɔnta nni.
*If the leopard does not kill, the bush-fly does not eat.*
(Said when someone depends on another's success for his maintainance).

6482. Etwie te ase a, damfo-adu nna kɔm.
*If the leopard is alive, the meat-fly does not go hungry.*
(Said when someone depends on another's success for his maintainance).

6483. Etwie nni hɔ a, yɛda ne nwoma so.
*If the leopard is absent (i.e. dead), we sleep on its skin.*
(If you no longer fear someone, you abuse them).

6484. Etwie nni twie.
*Leopard does not eat leopard.*
(Dog does not eat dog).

6485. Atwiretwi se: ɔnim nyansa nti na ɔda dua-tokuro mu.
*The doormouse says: it is wise, that is why it sleeps in a hole in a tree.*
(Wise people keeps themselves out of trouble).

6486. Twitɔn kakyerɛ ɔtokotaka sɛ ɔnnsa onyankyerɛne yareɛ nti na ɔno ara da awia mu.
*The bow-string hemp told the desmodium that it should not heal the sand-paper tree and therefore it, itself, now lies in the sun.*
(The Twitɔn-Sanevieria spp-is a stemless plant with long, dark green leaves mottled with white which occurs on gravelly soil. The leaves contain a fiber that is used as a thread and was formerly used for bowstrings; it was also used for making cloth in Asante and is medicinal. The Ɔtokotaka-Desmodium Lasiocarpum-is a shrub growing six to ten feet high and also grows in the more open forest and is medicinal. The Onyankyerɛn-Ficus Exasperata-is a tree of the secondary forest and is known as sand-paper tree as the leaves are used for polishing wood, etc. There is a story that its name was derived from the fact that it was the last tree in the forest to disclose its name so that it was thereafter called "onyankyerɛ" or "he has not explained". The sand-paper tree would provide shade for the others. Hence: If you advise someone not to help someone, you may yourself find that when you are in need you have no one to help you).

6487. Ɛtwo duru wo a, na wopɛ ne danta.
*If you get scrofula, then you find the loin cloth for it.*
(When the right time comes, you must find the means of doing something).

6488. Twɔtwɔ mu wɔ twɔ.
*Among blows there is the blow (that counts).*
(Even among intimate people some are more intimate than others).

6489. Twumasi ammɔ dam ante a, anka akɔm amma.
*If Twumasi had not become mad and been healed, then fetish possession would not have come.*
(Twumasi was reportedly the first person to be possessed and people thought him mad. When he recovered from possession he was able to perform wonders and people realized the value of possession. Hence: If someone becomes rich through help from another, then he should not refuse to give help in his turn).

- W -

**6490. Waduro se osuo tɔ a, apetampe, osuo antɔ a, apetampe.**
*The mortar says if it rains or not it is all the same to him.*
(Said of someone who could not care less; whatever happens he will not benefit from it).

**6491. Awaduro mmienu redi asie a, kosua se merakɔ pata?**
*If two mortars have a rough and tumble, does the egg say it is going to separate them?*
(If you are vulnerable, mind your own business and stay out of trouble).

**6492. Awaduwa kyinkyin-kyinkyin a, ɔnya abɛ wɔ.**
*If the small mortar wanders around too much, it gets (too many) palm nuts to grind.*
(Used as a warning to young girls who go around with men too much).

**6493. Awaha gyae ahim, awaha gyae ahim; asɛm a woahunu wiase no, ɛbɛfemfem wo.**
*Awaha (tall grass) stop trembling, awaha stop trembling. All the troubles you have seen in the world will give you much pain.*
(Said to someone who tries to carry everyone's troubles on his shoulders and finds it too much for him).

**6494. Nwamma-suo te a, na Ɔpɛ asi.**
*When the squall which brings down the ɔwamma (Vitex grandiflora) fruit ceases, the time for the Harmattan has come.*
(One thing presages another).

**6495. Ɔwansane Gyapomaa se: enyɛ ohia nti na ɔrefa egya mu akɔwuo.**
*The bush-buck Gyapomaa says: it is because of poverty that it will pass through the fire to die.*
(Even in times of dire need it is beter not to take unnecessary risk).

**6496. Ɔwansane Kwagyan, nsoroboa na anya ayie na wo deɛ woabɔ kuntunkuni mu yi. Wofa ho bɛn?**
*Meddlesome duiker, the tree animals have a funeral, but as for you, you've put on a funeral cloth. What business is it of yours?*
(Don't interfere in other people's business).

**6497. Ɔwansane mmɛn kuntann nanso ɛse ntua n'anom.**
*The horns of an antelope are widespread but it does not bite.*
(His bark is worse than his bite).

**6498. Ɔwansane se: osuo a abo no kwaeɛm nyɛ no ya sɛ emu akorokra na ɛku no.**
*The bush buck says: the rain that beat on it in the forest is not as painful as the drops from the trees that worry it.*
(The action of a person who joins in a quarrel or situation is more annoying than the original quarrel itself).

**6499. Ɔwansane antɔ nkuruma a, ɛwɔ ne tɔ da.**
*If the bush buck did not buy okro, there is its buying day (i.e. some day it will buy).*
(Someone day you may achieve success even if not now).

**6500. Ɔwansane nni afuo nso ɔwe nkuruma.**
*The bush buck has no farm yet it eats okro.*
(Some people always sponge on others).

**6501. Nwanwa dadu.**
*Wonders last only for a short time.*

**6502. Woware ɔbaa bɔne a, ɔdi w'ano kyeame.**
*If you marry a bad woman, she becomes your linguist.*
(If you are involved with a bad person, they will misrepresent you).

**6503. Woware ɔbaa tiatia a, wonnyae burogya tɔ da.**
*If you marry a short (little) woman, you never stop striking matches.*
(You cannot find her on the sleeping mat at night, so you have to strike a match to look for her! Small things may cause much trouble).

**6504. Awareɛ a tɔkwa wɔ mu na ɛsɔ.**
*A couple who quarrel intermittently make a successful marriage.*
(Love and hate are near together, a little quarrelling means you care).

**6505. Awareɛ a ɛnni kyigyinafoɔ na ɛguo.**
*If a marriage has no support it spoils.*

**6506. Awareɛ bɔ wo a, wonhwehwɛ mmaa mu yɛyerɛ.**
*If marriage eludes you, you don't look around amongst the women to find the best wife.*
(If you are not successful, you take what you can get).

**6507. Awareɛ bɔn a, yɛnna ho mma no nyɛ huam.**
*If a marriage stinks, we don't sleep with it so that the scent becomes good.*
(If a thing is bad, it is bad and you don't wait for it to become good).

**6508. Awareɛ yɛgyae no animia.**
*Marriage, we leave it reluctantly.*
(You have to think carefully before breaking up a profitable relationship).

**6509. Awareɛ ho mfasoɔ ne awoɔ.**
*The profit from marriage is birth.*

**6510. Awareɛ kwan ware.**
*The journey of marriage is a long one.*

**6511. Awareɛ rensɔ a, nyɛ ne foforɔ mu a.**
*If marriage is not going to prosper, it is not in its early stages.*
(It takes time to discover whether a relationship is going to last).

**6512. Awareɛ te sɛ nkateɛ, wopae mu a, na wohunu mu.**
*Marriage is like a ground nut, you must crack it to see what is inside.*
(You need to experience something before judging it).

**6513. Awareɛ yɛ, nanso adɔ ne adwuma.**
*Marriage is good, but to love is hard work.*

**6514. Awarebɔne deɛ, fanyinam sugya.**
*A bad marriage, bachelorhood is better.*

**6515. Awarebɔne sɛɛ ɔbaa pa.**
*A bad marriage spoils a good woman.*
(Women suffer most when a marriage breaks down).

**6516. Awarebɔne tete ntoma.**
*A bad marriage destroys the cloth.*

**6517. Awaredodoɔ yɛ ohia.**
*Polygamy (lit. too much marrying) is (nothing but) poverty.*

**6518. Awaredodoɔ ma ɔbarima tɛkrɛma bɔ nta.**
*Too many marriages make a man's tongue have twins.*
(If you owe allegiance to more than one person, it is impossible to please them all).

**6519. Awarefoforɔ na nkontagyeɛ di mu adɔdeɛ.**
*A new marriage, brother-in-law benefits from it.*
(Everything in the family brings benefit to someone. Because of the Akan family system, a woman's brothers will benefit indirectly from her marriage).

**6520. Awarefoforɔ te sɛ kookooahahan, ne foforɔ mu yɛ frɔmfrɔm, n'awieɛ yɛ dwann.**
*A new marriage is like cocoa leaves, its beginning is fine but it ends in disaster.*
(Things which begin well often end badly).

**6521. Awaregyaeɛ mmɔ kuro.**
*Divorce does not destroy the town.*
(Domestic matters are not of public importance).

**6522. Awaregyaeɛ ho akwan nyɛ na.**
*It is not difficult to get a divorce.*
(If you do not succeed the first time you can always start again. Divorce in Akan society is relatively easy, the children of the marriage belonging to the mother's family).

**6523. Awaresɛm, yɛdi no butaa-butaa.**
*Marriage arbitration, we settle it tactfully.*
(You deal carefully with a sensitive situation).

**6524. Ɔwaretoɔ na ɛmaa wɔkyeree Ntim Gyakari ne ne yere nnɔmum.**
*Playing of the game of ɔware led to the capture of Ntim Gyakari and his wife.*
(After the battle of Feyiase, the Dankyirahene Ntim Gyakari was reportedly captured while playing ɔware with his wife. Hence: You can never be careful. Or: Don't fool around when you should be on guard).

**6525. Awaretumi, wodi a, yɛtu so wo.**
*The power of marriage, if you exercise it, you are got rid of.*
(If you misuse power, you lose it).

**6526. Awaretumi nyɛ tumi pa.**
*The power of marriage is not real power.*
(Husband and wife have little real power over each other as marriage can be terminated easily and an Akan's allegience is first and foremost to his mother's family).

**6527. Watapuo–aba na ɛkyerɛ ɔtomfoɔ dadeɛ bɔ.**
*The fruit of cola gigantea teaches the blacksmith to forge.*
(The fruit is soft and pliable and can be molded to use for making shapes for casting. An adaptable person is useful).

**6528. Wowe dawuro a, n'abaa nyɛ wo wena.**
*If you eat the gong-gong, its stick is easy to consume.*

(If you do the most difficult thing, the rest comes easily).

**6529. Wowe dom fe a, na ɛkyerɛ sɛ bɔne nni wo tirimu.**
*If you vomit after taking dom, then it shows you have no evil in your head (a clear conscience).*
(There was a shrine at the Asantehene's palace before which women supposed to have committed adultery were taken. They were given a mixture known as dom to drink. If guilty they were supposed to swell up; if innocent they vomited up the mixture. Hence: a person with a clear conscience is not afraid of being investigated).

**6530. Worewe ɛfoɔ nsa a, hwɛ wo deɛ (nsa).**
*If you are eating a monkey's hand, look at your own.*
(If you speak ill of someone, or harm them, remember you too can become a victim).

**6531. Worewe wo ho ada a, wonsa mmaa mu.**
*If you are sleeping without a woman, you don't discriminate between women.*
(If you have nothing, you take what you can get).

**6532. Woawe kukusekunam, ayare agyemirekuto; yɛde akrampa nam retwam a, wose "Momma me sirɛko ntɔ!"**
*You have eaten the frog and suffered from mumps; when someone passes with vulture's meat, you still say: "Let me have a shilling's worth".*
(You have suffered from your own folly once, don't tempt providence again).

**6533. Wowe ɔkraman nan a, nanteɛ mpa wo so da.**
*If you chew the leg of a dog, you never stop roaming.*
(You take on the character of the company you keep).

**6534. Wowe Ananse a, wo din nna.**
*If you eat Ananse (the spider) your name is notorious.*
("To eat Ananse" is-idomatically-to do something to make yourself notorious. Said about someone whose actions cause gossip).

**6535. "Mawe anene, manwu". Yese: "Na wokasa sɛn?"**
*"I have eaten a crow and I have not died." We say: "What are you saying?"*
(You don't achieve anything by boasting of an unsavory action).

**6536. Wowe asɔmorɔdwe na sɛ sradeɛ nni mu a, fa w'ani to akɔkono anim.**
*If you eat the palm beetle and find no fat (juice) in it, consider the grub.*
(Both the palm beetle and the grub can be eaten. If one person does not satisfy you, remember they have a worthy relation who may do so).

**6537. Worenwe a, wonka.**
*If you won't eat, you don't bite.*
(Don't start something you don't intend to finish).

**6538. Wedeɛ reporɔ a, wommisa berɛboɔ.**
*If the skin is rotten, you don't ask for the liver.*
(If something durable is spoilt, you don't ask for something highly perishable attached to it).

**6539. Ɔwekɔ sene praeɛ animuonyam.**
*The old pot used for holding floor polish gets more respect than the broom.*

(Said of someone who does hard and dirty work but is not appreciated).

**6540. Awensaa se: "Deɛ ɔbɛdi me nam soa brɛfi".**
*The mouse says: "Whoever is going to eat my meat, carries the palm branches".*
(This kind of mouse lives in trees and is difficult to hunt, often having to be burnt out. Hence: If you follow a difficult person, you suffer. Or: If you take on a difficult case, you have to work hard at it).

**6541. Awereɛ na ɛkɔfaa ntoma pa baa fie.**
*The rough cloth went to bring the good cloth to the house.*
(By showing your poverty you get help).

**6542. Awerɛhoɔ kɔ agyina a, yafunu nkɔ bi.**
*If sadness goes to a meeting, the stomach does not accompany it.*
(Whatever your situation, you must eat).

**6543. Nwerɛnwerɛboa na ɔte anadwoboa kasa.**
*It is the cockroach that understands the gecko's language.*
(People who live in the same place understand each other).

**6544. Awesawesa sene sika ntansa.**
*To have enough to eat daily is better than to have much money.*
(Ntansa is three piredwan of gold dust, a very large sum. Hence: Regular good living is better than occasional riches).

**6545. Nwi nyɛ na a, anka akyekyedeɛ wɔ bi.**
*If hair were not hard to come by then the tortoise would have some.*
(Said when someone is in real trouble in obtaining what he wants).

**6546. Owia mu nni aduɔsan num.**
*The sun doesn't have seventy-five parts.*
(You cannot divide truth).

**6547. Owia wɔ sorosoro mpo na ɛhyehyeɛ yi na ɛbɛben fam?**
*The sun which is so far in the heavens, burns fiercely, how much more so were it to come close to the Earth.*
(If something can influence you from a distance, beware if you get too near to it).

**6548. Ewiaswe amaneɛ bebrebe nti na wowo akɔdaa a, ɔbɔ bena, efiri sɛ, ɔnnim abusua a, ɔreba mu, mu nsɛm.**
*Because of too many world problems, when you give birth to a baby, it wails, because it does not know the problems of the family it has entered.*
(Insecurity causes unhappiness).

**6549. Wiase, yɛtena no baanu baanu.**
*The world, we stay in it two by two.*
(Mankind is interdependent).

**6550. Awidie ano da nso.**
*The grey parrot, its beak is easy to identify.*
(Said of a well-known person).

**6551. Awidie se: ɛye no ya sɛ osuo rebɛtɔ ama adeɛ akye asa, na adekyeɛ mu asɛm na nnipa nim nanso adesae mu asɛm deɛ nnipa nnim.**
*The parrot says it pains it that it is going to rain, that day will break and night will fall, for man knows what day will bring and not that which comes in the night.*
(There is no logic in creation).

**6552. Ewiem nyɛ nsakrana.**
*It is not difficult for the weather to change.*
(Circumstances can alter at any time).

**6553. Awiemfoɔ pɛ ne sɛfoɔ na ɔne no agoro.**
*A self-respecting person finds someone like himself to play with.*
(Birds of a feather flock together).

**6554. Nwira a ɛte nsuo ani wɔ deɛ wɔn ntini wɔ.**
*Plants which grow on the water have their roots there.*
(You normally find people in their own environment).

**6555. Ɛwiram kenana yɛ mmoadoma fie.**
*Silent forest is the dwelling place of animals.*
(Everyone to their own place).

**6556. Ɛwiram mmoa nsaeɛ na ɔsebɔ akyere anomaa.**
*The forest animals are not finished for the leopard to catch a bird.*
(If the real thing is there, people are not satisfied with a substitute).

**6557. Awirefire na ɛmaa Ananse kaa sɛ ɔkyiri afaseɛ.**
*Forgetfulness made Ananse the spider say that he tabooed water yam.*
(When Ananse arrived late at his in-law's house, they gave him water yam to eat. He was so disappointed that he said that it was taboo to him. So they left him hungry. When he went to bath he kept his cloth on and they asked him why. He said that he was forgetful in the same way as he was when he said he could not eat the yam).

**6558. Awirikwa pagya ɔbrempɔn akonnwa a, ɔnim faako a ɔde sie.**
*If a stool servant lifts a chief's (his master's) stool, he knows where to place it.*
(A person working for you knows your needs).

**6559. Awirikwaa se adeɛ a ɛyɛ fɛ yɛ fɛ, nti na ɔde ne kɔkɔɔ abɔ ne moma so.**
*The green parrot says that something which is beautiful is beautiful, that is why it puts its red on its forehead.*
(Everyone uses beauty to adorn themselves if they can).

**6560. Awirikwaa se: sɛ wosom wo wura sompa a, ɔmfa n'agyapadeɛ nhunta wo.**
*The parrot says: if you serve your master well, he does not hide his family treasures from you.*
(Good service brings trust).

**6561. Awisiaa da ase anwummerɛ a, na adeɛ kye a, ɔnya foforɔ.**
*If an orphan gives thanks in the evening, when dawn breaks he receives more.*
(Gratitude, humbly expressed, brings its own reward).

**6562. Awisiaa deɛ ne kyɛmferɛ.**
*An orphan's possession is a broken pot*
(If you are without family your position is miserable).

6563. "Awisiaa woammee anaa?" Ɔse: "Womaa me sɛnea womaa wo ba a, anka memeeɛ".
*"Orphan, are you satisfied or not?" He says "If you gave me as much as you gave your own child, then I would have been satisfied".*
(It is only equality of treatment that satisfies).

6564. Awisiaa pere wedeɛ, na ɔmpere brɛboɔ.
*An orphan asks for the skin, but not the liver.*
(Compare Proverb 6538. An orphan seldom gets preferential treatment. Hence: If you are underprivileged you don't ask for the best).

6565. Awosiaa su a, ɔmmrɛ nisuo ho.
*When an orphan weeps, tears come easily.*
(An unfortunate person is easily upset).

6566. Wisie na ɛnim asaase mu kwan.
*Smoke knows the earthly roads.*
(Smoke can find its way through any crack. Hence: Some people always keep their ears to the ground and know what is going on).

6567. Wo na woma akyenkyena aduane die a, gyae no ma, na tannuro apae.
*If you are the one who feeds the allied hornbill, stop feeding it, for the seeds of the tannuro tree are ripe.*
(The bird is especially fond of this fruit. Hence: Don't continue to support someone who can support themselves).

6568. Wo na wose Apenten atuo apem, afei wose emu ahanum deɛ atwerehoɔ nni ano a, akyinnyeɛ nni mu.
*You who say that Apenten has a thousand guns, then you say five hundred of them are without flints, there is no point in arguing with you.*
(Apenten was a great warrior. Said when someone who has given you unreliable information in the past, then purports to be giving you the truth).

6569. Wo ne ɔbakwasea kɔ akusihu na wotu ne nsono ma no a, ɔde kɔkyerɛ ɔbanyansafoɔ.
*If you and a fool go to hunt rats and you give him the intestines, he takes them to show to a wise person.*
(Don't think you can cheat a fool and get away with it. His wise friends or members of his family will point out to him what you have done).

6570. Wo ne Ɔberɛmpɔn na ɛda a, anka wobɛte sɛ ɔsi apini anadwo.
*If you were to sleep with a paramount chief, you would hear that he sighs in the night.*
(Even the great have their troubles and anxieties).

6571. Wo ne obi di asɛm na ɔma wo dibem fie a, tie na ɛkɔ ahennim a, dibem korɔ no ara na wobɛnya.
*If you have an arbitration with someone and he apologizes at home, agree, because if you take it to the council of the chief, it is the same apology that you will receive.*
(It is better to settle out of court than to make a big and expensive case out of something).

6572. Wo ne obi kye adeɛ na ɔfa ɔhene a, na wasisi wo.
*If you and someone else divide something and he takes the chief, then he has cheated you.*
(If you have power behind you, you do not need anything else).

6573. Wo ne obi nni twaka a, ɔnkyerɛ wia nkyerɛ wo.
*If you are not intimate with someone, they can't say that they have committed adultery with you.*
(If you are too familiar with people you get accused of all sorts of things).

6574. Wo ne obi nsɛ a, wo ne no nni [asomsɛm]/[asrasom].
*If you and someone else are not alike, you and he do not [have close communion]/[take snuff] with each other.*
(Like cleaves to like).

6575. Wo ne aboa no goro a, na wohunu sɛ ne mmarane de "Krokotiaka".
*If you play with an animal you get to know that its appellation is "Betrayer".*
(Before you know someone well you do not know their real character and so should be careful how you trust them).

6576. Wo ne ɔdehyeɛ ba regoro a, na w'akoa bɔ wo tam ano.
*If you and the child of a royal are playing, then slavery is tied up in your cloth.*
(As your are enjoying temporary privileges, you must not go beyond certain bounds or you will suffer for it).

6577. Wo ne Ɔdomankoma-Wuo bu akonta a, wohwere w'ano.
*If you and Almighty-Death come to a reckoning, it is waste of time to talk.*
(You cannot argue with the inevitable).

6578. Wo ne hwan kɔka sɛ Zongohene ata, na woafa he akɔto bese?
*Who are you to say that the chief of the Zongo has farted, (for if you do so) where are you going to go to buy cola?*
(It is a taboo to fart in public. Cola is sold mainly by the Northerners whose chief is the chief of the Zongo area where many of the Moslems and Northerners live. Hence: If you insult a man, don't expect to get favors from him).

6579. Wo ne akɔdaa kɔ akɔtɔbɔ a, wodi kan bɔ bi hyɛ ne nsam.
*If you and a child go to hunt for crabs, you first catch one for him.*
(You should always help the weak before you help yourself).

6580. Wo ne kɔkɔte nam a, wommisa faako a awora da.
*If you travel with a red river hog, you don't ask where the swamp is.*
(This kind of pig lives in swampy ares. If you travel with someone who knows the way, you don't have to worry).

6581. Wo ne kontomponi nante a, ɔma wodi dansewia.
*If you and a liar walk together, he makes you perjure yourself.*
(Said to warn against associating with people of bad character).

6582. Wo ne korɔmfoɔ siane a, wobɔ korɔno.
*If you associate with a thief you steal.*

(Compare Proverb 6581: Said to warn against associating with people of bad character).

**6583. Wo ne ɔkraman bɔ abusua a, nisuo mpa w'ani ase.**
*If you have a dog as a member of the family, you are never without tears.*
(A troublesome relation causes endless worry).

**6584. Wo ne kwakuo yɛ aka a, wo borɔdeɛ na ɛnyini.**
*If you are "aka" with a monkey, your plantain is left to grow.*
(See Proverb 430. You don't lose from ceasing to be friends with a troublesome person).

**6585. Wo ne kwasea goro a, ne kwasea sane wo.**
*If you associate with a fool, you also become a fool.*
(Compare Proverb 6581: Said to warn against associating with people of bad character).

**6586. Wo ne kwasea gye akyinnyeɛ a, ɛka ne deɛ so.**
*If you and a fool have an argument, he succeeds.*
(A fool never changes his mind, so it is no use arguing with him).

**6587. Wo ne onifirani rekasa na sotorɔ anni kan a, ɔnhunu sɛ w'ani abere.**
*If you are talking with a blind person and you don't slap them, they do not realize how angry you are.*
(Said of someone who needs to be dealt with firmly).

**6588. Wo ne mpaninfoɔ hyia sadwaase, na wotɔ nsa ma wɔn a, na wo te adomankommasɛm.**
*If you meet the elders at the palmwine bar, and you buy a drink for them, then you hear words of wisdom.*
("Adomankommasɛm" means "the Creator's matters" and is used to refer to things that are only spoken of among elders. Consideration brings its rewards).

**6589. "Wo ne wo nua ntena", na ɛde abagyegyeɛ baeɛ.**
*"You and your brother should stay together", brought about child care.*
(It takes a whole family to raise the children).

**6590. Wo ne wo se akoa twa abɛ a, ɔfrɛ wo yɔnkoɔ.**
*If you and your father's slave tap the palm tree (together) he calls you companion.*
(If you share work with your subordinates, you are likely to lose their respect).

**6591. Wo ne asobrakyeɛ te a, w'asɛm ware.**
*If you stay with a stubborn person, you become talkative.*
(If someone refuses to take advice, you tend to go on talking and talking at them).

**6592. Wo ne asosiɛ te a, wonnya amane.**
*If you stay with a deaf person, you seldom quarrel.*
(We quarrel because we hear bad things. If you don't listen to bad gossip, you have nothing to quarrel about).

**6593. Wo ne wo wura nam, na ɔredi prako ano a, wura wiram bɔ bɛdɛ na wo ara na wobɛsoa.**
*If you are travelling with your master and he bargains over the price of a pig, go into the bush and make a basket for it, for it is for you to carry it.*
(Don't always wait to be told to do a job if you see it needs doing).

**6594. Wo ne wo yɔnko rebɛko a, wodi kan de wo twɛdeɛ toto ne deɛ ho ansa na woakyerɛ wo mmarinsɛm.**
*If you are going to fight your companion, you have to compare your fist with his before you show your manliness.*
(Weigh up a situation before you act).

**6595. Wo ne wo yɔnko te akonnwa korɔ so na woresɔre a, wobɔ no nkaeɛ.**
*If you and your companion are sitting on a stool, and you get up, warn him first.*
(If your actions are likely to endanger someone else, you should warn them before acting).

**6596. Wo nko wodidi a, wo nko wogoro.**
*If you eat alone, you play alone.*
(If you don't share, people won't want to associate with you).

**6597. Wo ara ankasa woyi wo tiri ho a, woyi wo ho ayibɔne.**
*If you cut your hair yourself, you will make a botched job of it.*
(You cannot do everything well on your own).

**6598. Wowo ɔbabɔne a, wofa kasabrɛ.**
*If you give birth to a bad child, you get tired of talking.*
(You have to admonish a bad child constantly. Hence: If you create a problem, you have to cope with it).

**6599. Wowo ba de no to "Bremawuo" a, ɔwu.**
*If you give birth to a child and call it "I am working for death," it dies.*
(If you anticipate danger or disaster, it comes).

**6600. "Mawo, mabrɛ", yɛkyiri.**
*"I have given birth, I have become tired", is a taboo.*
(Human life takes precedence over everything; you can never regret giving birth).

**6601. Wɔrewo ɔhene, na ɔpanin te ase.**
*When a chief was born an elder was already there.*
(Seniority is one thing, power another).

**6602. Yɛwo onipa a, na yɛwo ne tamfo.**
*If we give birth to a human being, we have given birth to his enemy.*
(Man is his own worst enemy).

**6603. Wɔwo "Merentie" anɔpa a, wɔwo "Gyae-ma-ɛnka" anwummerɛ.**
*If they give birth to "I won't listen" in the morning, then they give birth to "Give it up and let him speak" in the evening.*
(An obstinate person cools down in the end).

**6604. Wɔwo Tafoni ba no, na ɔnkutaa ta.**
*When a child was born in Tafo, he was not holding a spoon.*
(All talents are not inborn. Play on words).

**6605. Yɛwo wo di amim Kwasiada a, yɛwo wo yi adwo Adwoada.**
*If we give birth to you (in order that you should) cheat on Sunday, we give birth to you to kidnap and sell you on Monday.*
(If you order others to do wrong, the time will come when they will do the same to you).

**6606. Yɛwo wo na woannya din a, na wo ara na woampɛ.**
*If you are born and don't receive a name, it means you don't want it.*
(Only you yourself can build your own reputation).

**6607. Wowo awo bɔne a, wote wo twe nka.**
*If you give birth to a bad child, you hear of your vagina.*
(A bad child uses abuse and anyone retaliating may make rude remarks about its mother. A warning to control your children).

**6608. Wowo awopa a, wosa nkwan pa.**
*If you give birth to a good child, you eat good soup.*
(Children are an investment for the future).

**6609. Yɛnwo ba ne ɛse.**
*We don't give birth to a child with teeth.*
(Wisdom has to be learnt).

**6610. Yɛnwo nni.**
*We don't give birth to profit from it (lit. to eat).*
(Children don't exist for the benefit of their parents).

**6611. Awo bɔne na ɛma wɔkum asonetakom.**
*The birth of a bad child makes them kill the tumble-fly.*
(The tumble-fly is an insect that lays eggs which produce blood-sucking grubs that are harmful to people. Hence: A bad member of the family can destroy the reputation of the family and so must be dealt with).

**6612. Ɛwɔ obi a wohwɛ n'anim su a, nisuo ba.**
*Someone is there whom, when you look at them and cry, tears come.*
(There are some people you find really sympathetic and whose sufferings are as your own).

**6613. Wowɔ biribi a, na wodi ahantansɛm.**
*If you possess things, then you become arrogant.*
(Pride should not be dependent on possessions).

**6614. Wowɔ Boakye a, na wowɔ ayanneɛ.**
*If you have Boakye (an eminent goldsmith) under your control, you have a gold chain.*
(If you control the source of something good, it is always at your disposal).

**6615. Wowɔ aboterɛ a, wopɛ esum mu adeɛ a, wohunu.**
*If you have patience, if you search for something in the dark, you find it.*
(With patience, you can achieve many things).

**6616. Wowɔ aboterɛ a, na wowɔ nkwa.**
*If you have patience, then you have good health.*
(If you do not let life worry you too much, you don't get sick from worry).

**6617. Wo wɔ Aburowa, nkokɔyen wo nyɛ wona.**
*If you have corn, it is not hard to rear chickens.*
(If you are well-equipped, you can make a success of a job).

**6618. Ɛwɔ deɛ basini yɛ a ɔnu n'aso mu.**
*The one-armed man has a way to clear out his ear.*
(Even if you are at a disadvantage you can find a way to do something if you are determined to do so).

**6619. Ɛwɔ deɛ nantwinoma nya firi nantwie akyidie ho.**
*There is something the cattle egret gains from the cattle's rear.*
(The egret eats the insects that are found on or near cattle. Hence: You follow those whom you know can provide you with a living).

**6620. Wowɔ afuo a, na wowɔ nkwanseɛ.**
*If you have a farm then you have a boundary mark.*
(There is a definite limit to your possessions).

**6621. Wowɔ nkwa a, na wose: "Meredɔ adi".**
*If you are healthy, then you say: "I am cultivating to eat".*
(A healthy man is a hard-working one and an optimist).

**6622. Wowɔ nkwa a, na wowɔ adeɛ.**
*If you are robust, then you have good fortune.*
(Strength can leads to riches).

**6623. Wowɔ ahyehyɛdeɛ na wohyia ayeforɔ a, wommrɛ.**
*If you have storage vessels and you move to your husband's house, you don't worry.*
(If you plan well, you have no worries).

**6624. "Ɛwɔ me," ne "Ɛwɔ yɛn" nsɛ.**
*"It is mine" and "It is ours" are not the same thing.*
(Individual ownership is absolute, community ownership is not).

**6625. Ɛwɔ mu sɛ akokɔ ntakara na ɛma no yɛ kɛse deɛ, nanso ntakara bɔne deɛ, fanyinam kwaterekwa.**
*It is a fact that the feathers of a fowl make it big, but if the feather's are bad, it is better to go naked.*
(It is better to have nothing than something bad).

**6626. Wowɔ nneɛma mmienu a, na wode baako kyɛ.**
*If you have two things, then you can give one away.*
(Those who have, can afford to be generous).

**6627. Wowɔ mpenu, woresu na deɛ ɔnni bi nso nyɛ dɛn?**
*You who have two thousand are weeping, then he who has nothing, what will he do?*
(If the "haves" suffer, what about the "have-nots"?)

**6628. Wowɔ sika a, yɛfrɛ wo Nana.**
*If you have money, we call you "Nana" (Chief).*
(Money brings respect).

**6629. Wowɔ sika a, na wokae ɔsaman a wayɛ wo papa.**
*If you have money, you remember the departed who did you good.*
(A wealthy person should not forget those who helped him, because he has the means to be generous).

**6630. Wowɔ aso a, na woka asɛm kyerɛ onipa a, ɔteɛ.**
*If you have ears, when you tell someone something, they listen.*
(If you know how to take advice, people respect you when you give it).

**6631. Ɛnni baabiara a wotena we wisa pore gu suman so a, ɛnyɛ nnam.**
*There is no special place where one should sit and chew guinea pepper and blow it over one's charm to make it effective.*
(It is what you do that matters, not where you do it).

**6632. Ɛnni baabiara a wotena we atadwe a, ɛnyɛ dɛ.**
*There is not anywhere you can sit to chew tiger nuts for them not to be sweet.*
(If a thing is good, it is good wherever you are).

**6633. Wonni abayɛn sika a, wonware aberewa nana.**
*If you do not have money for a children's nurse, you do not marry an old lady's grand-daughter.*
(If you can't afford to look after your grandmother-in-law, don't marry her granddaughter).

**6634. Wonni obi tu wo fo, na wokɔto sɛ obi retu ne ba fo a, na wode ato wo kotokuo mu.**
*If you have no one to give you advice and you go to someone who is advising his child, then put it into your pocket.*
(Take advice where you can get it).

**6635. Ɛnni da biara a yemfrɛ no "ɛda-no".**
*There is no single day that we don't refer to as: "That day!"*
(Everything passes away).

**6636. Wonni biribi a, wonhoahoa wo ho.**
*If you have nothing, you don't flatter yourself.*
(A man is never proud without reason).

**6637. Wonni biribi de ma w'ase a, wɔmmɔ no korɔno.**
*If you don't have anything to give your in-laws, you don't steal from them.*
(Even if you have nothing to contribute to a situation, at least you don't make things worse).

**6638. Yɛnni biribi di a, yɛnnoa biribi.**
*If we have nothing to eat, we don't cook anything.*
(Said when you are lacking some essential tool for a task).

**6639. Wonni biribi hwɛ mu a, wohwɛ wo nsam.**
*if you have nothing to look into, you look into your hand.*
(An industrious person is never idle).

**6640. Yenni adaagye a, yɛngorɔ sanga.**
*If we have no time to spare, we don't play a sanga game.*
(Sanga is a beautiful dancing game that can go on for a long time. Hence: Said when obligations keep someone from a time-consuming but enjoyable activity).

**6641. Yɛnni adaagye a, yɛnkyere ɔdamfoɔ.**
*If we don't have leisure we don't catch a madman.*
(Some jobs take a great deal of time and care. Don't embark on them unless you have them).

**6642. Wonni adaagye a, wonturu ba yie.**
*If you don't have time, you don't fix the cloth that keeps the baby on your back properly.*
(You should take the time to do an important task. People have also misheard the proverb to say *Wonni adaagye a, wontu bayie*, which means "If you don't have time, you don't go in for witchcraft". This misheard proverb might be used to suggest that "idle hands do the devil's work").

**6643. Wonni adaagye a, wonnyegye asɛntoasoɔ so.**
*If you don't have leisure, you don't welcome constant telling of stories.*
(If you are busy you don't appreciate people constantly interrupting you with their problems).

**6644. Yɛnni adaagye a, yɛnto kwaduo tuo.**
*If we don't have time to spare, we don't shoot at the yellow-backed duiker.*
(The yellow-backed duiker is reputedly a chief and very difficult to kill. If you follow it, you may enter a strange twon and be arrested for homicide. Hence: You need time for a difficult task).

**6645. Yɛnni adwonkuo a, yɛnhuri asafo.**
*If we don't have a hip-bone we don't jump about to the asafo tunes.*
(You don't try to do what you are not equipped to do).

**6646. Wonni hɔ a, nka sɛ woɔ hɔ.**
*If you are not there, don't say you are there.*
(If you can't do something, don't say you can).

**6647. Yɛnni ani a, yɛnsina paneɛ.**
*If we don't have (good) eyes, we don't thread a needle.*
(If you are not qualified to do a job, you do not undertake it).

**6648. Wonni anɔpa-senaa a, wonnye abayɛn.**
*If you don't have a morning-cooking pot, you don't adopt a child.*
(If you have no means of caring for others, you don't attempt it).

**6649. Wonni panin a, due!**
*If you have no elder, condolences!*
(Elders are symbolic of wisdom and good advice. If you have no elder in the family, you have to advise yourself).

**6650. Wonni asia da hɔ a, wontene kankan tuo.**
*If you don't have any money (lit. if you don't have asia lying there), you don't aim a Dutch gun.*
(Asia is a small weight of gold-dust. The old name for Dutch Accra was Kankan and thus the Dutch were called Kankanfoɔ-Kankan-people or Kankan brɔfoɔ-Kankan-Europeans. European weapons were expensive commodities. Hence: You don't use something you cannot afford to purchase or maintain).

**6651. Wonni sika a, na ɛnkyere sɛ woagyimi.**
*If you have no money it does not show that you are a fool.*
(Money is one thing and wisdom or folly another).

**6652. Wonni sika a, na wose: "Ne boɔ yɛ den".**
*If you have no money then you say: "It is expensive".*
(If you can't afford something, then you complain of the cost).

**6653. Wonni sika a, na wo tiri te sɛ akokɔ ti.**
*If you have no money, then your head is like a chicken's head.*
(Chickens' heads are easily cut off! Hence: If you are poor, you are at everyone's mercy).

**6654. Wonni sika a, anka wofrɛ no anwea kwa.**
*If you have no gold dust, then you call it merely sand.*
(Sour grapes).

**6655. Yɛnni sika a, yɛnware ɔbaa.**
*If we don't have money we don't marry a woman.*
(You have to make adequate preparations before you embark on a difficult task).

6656. Yɛnni sisie a, yɛnkɔ asetena.
*If we have not a strong waist, then we do not attend a meeting.*
(Which entails much sitting around. Hence: If you do not have the means of doing something well, don't try to do it).

6657. Wonni [ntrama]/[sika] a, na wose nsa nyɛ dɛ.
*If you do not have [a string of cowries]/ [money], you say the drink is not sweet.*
(Sour grapes).

6658. Wonni ntumɔnwi a, wonnye ta agorɔ.
*If you have no hair around your anus, then you don't play at farting.*
(It is believed that if you have hair around your anus it helps you to fart without making a noise. Farting in public is a disgrace. Hence: If you have no protection, don't do what you should not).

6659. Wonni tuo a, wonsrɛ ntoa.
*If you do not have a gun, you don't beg for a gun belt.*
(First things first. If you don't have what is most necessary for action, you don't ask for subsidiary items).

6660. Yɛnni awaamu a, yenko abɔnten-tɔkwa.
*If we don't have a beautiful back, we don't fight in a public place.*
(You have to pull down your cloth to fight. Hence: If you know you can't make a good impression in public, keep out of the public eye).

6661. Ɛnni wo so a, wosuae.
*If it does not happen to you, you say you can solve it.*
(Easier said than done).

6662. Wonni wura a, aboa kye wo.
*If you have no master, a wild beast seizes you.*
(Everyone needs a strong protector).

6663. Wonni yaanom a, womfrɛ yaanom.
*If you have no comrade, do not call comrades.*
(If you have not friends to help you, don't look for them in time of need).

6664. Ɔnniwoɔ sɛ wo kɛtɛ fam.
*If someone does not know you well, he spreads your mat on the ground.*
(If you are not known, you are not respected).

6665. Ɔwɔ aduro yɛte no ahoɔhare.
*The herbs to apply to a snake bite we collect with speed.*
(Some actions are only effective if taken swiftly).

6666. Ɔwɔ foro adɔbɛ.
*The snake climbs the raffia palm tree.*
(A clever person can achieve the apparently impossible. The trunk of this tree is covered in spikes and sharp edges).

6667. Ɔwɔ ka aniberɛ.
*The snake bites in anger.*
(Let sleeping dogs lie).

6668. Ɔwɔ nka onipa kwa.
*A snake does not bite a person without cause.*
(There is no smoke without fire).

6669. Ɔwɔ nkosua nko ara na ɛbɛsuru wiram a, anka biribiara nsɛeɛ!
*If the snake's eggs alone go bad in the forest, then nothing is spoilt.*
(You can do without things which will cause future trouble).

6670. Ɔwɔ na obu bɛ se: "Ɔhiani nkyere hiani".
*The snake has a proverb which goes: "A poor man does not lay hold on (another) poor man".*
(Poor people stick together or dog does not bite dog).

6671. Ɔwɔ te sɛ ahoma nso yɛmfa nkyekyere gya.
*A snake is like a rope but it is not used for tying up fire wood.*
(Put not faith in appearances).

6672. Ɔwɔbie yɛ na.
*A rich person is rare.*
(No one will admit to being rich because of the obligations it brings).

6673. Ɔnnibie dane ɔwɔbie.
*He who has nothing seeks the protection of (lit. turns to) he who has something.*
(The poor seek the help of the rich).

6674. Ɔnnihɔ mfa asɛm ho hwee.
*Someone who was not there has nothing to do with a case.*
(If you are not a witness, you cannot give evidence).

6675. Ɔwoduo na ɔdi badu-dwan.
*A woman who can produce ten children eats the tenth child's sheep.*
(The sheep is a gift from people honor your fertility, perhaps as a sacrifice. Hence: If you do well, you are praised).

6676. Wɔfaaseɛ yɛ dɔm.
*Nephews are your enemies.*
(Those who are nearest to you can do you the most harm. Since a nephew inherits from his uncle, according to Akan custom, he may well wish him dead.

6677. Nwoma suane wɔ faako a ɛyɛ hare.
*Skin splits where it is thinnest.*
(A weak man is got at through his most vulnerable spot).

6678. "Awo-ni-oo," firi ɔkɔmfoɔ anom.
*"Pay attention!" is from the fetish priest's mouth.*
(Priests are sources of warnings from gods. Hence: Information direct from the source is best).

6679. Wɔn na ade pa ba a wokyɛ die no, ɛka ba a, wɔn ara na wɔkyɛ tua.
*Those who share good fortune, if debt comes, they also share the burden.*
(Share the good, you share the bad).

6680. Wɔn na wɔso kwadu bunu mpo, kwagyedu repamo wɔn: na ente sɛ wɔn na wɔso deɛ aberɛɛ.
*Even those who are carrying unripe bananas, the monkeys are making them fall: how much more those who carry ripe ones.*
(If even an unattractive thing attracts attention, how much more what is desirable).

6681. Ɔwonta nsuro kɔtepɔn.
*She who bears twins is not afraid of a big penis.*
(You do not fear what you have already experienced).

6682. Awoɔ yɛdi no nantinaka, na yɛnni no yɛn nua ba.
*Birth comes from one's own self (womb), but it does not come from a sister's child.*
(You own children are those nearest to you).

6683. Awoɔ ne wo yam.
*Birth comes from the womb.*
(Blood is thicker than water).

6684. Ɛwoɔ dɔre wo gyedua mu a, wode nyansa na ɛyie.
*If honey is maturing in your ficus Leprieuri tree, you use wisdom to get it out.*
(Ficus Leprieuri is a fig. You need wisdom to deal with a tricky situation).

6685. Ewoɔ sa ntafentafere.
*Honey gets finished with much licking.*
(Continuously using something exhausts it).

6686. Awoɔyɛ wɔ fie a, yɛmmisa deɛ ne ba ameeɛ.
*If a kindly woman is in the house, we don't ask whose child is satisfied.*
(Don't ask the obvious).

6687. Ɔworawora kɔtɔ se: "Me na menim sika dabere".
*The little crab says: "As for me, I know where gold is hidden".*
(Even humble people sometimes have valuable knowledge).

6688. Ɔwosoadɔtɔ nsuro akorokra.
*The one who shakes the thicket does not fear the drops of water.*
(A person who indulges in violent practices does not fear the results).

6689. [Wowa]/[Asɔmorɔdwe] kɔ asanom na sɛ wamma a, ɔnam dorobɛn mu.
*If a [bee]/[palm beetle] goes to drink and does not come back, it has gone through the tapping reed.*
(If you can't find a man, he is probably near the place he likes best).

6690. Wowa sa wo sa wo a, ɔbɔ wo.
*If the bee constantly chases you, it stings you.*
(If you allow someone to play about with you, they may get you into trouble).

6691. Wowa resen, nwansena resen, na sakoraa mu resa.
*The bee hangs about, the fly hangs about, the calabash of palm wine is finishing.*
(Followers-on leave when they have got all they can out of you).

6692. Wowɔwɔ a, ɛyɛ borɔdeɛ.
*However much you pound, it is still plantain.*
(Adversity does not change a person's nature).

6693. Wɔwu gya wo mpanin kasa a, wonnyae nkasa mmɔfra kasa.
*If you are left a legacy of the language of elders, you don't give it up to speak the language of children.*
(You don't change wisdom for ignorance).

6694. Wowu na w'ayie bɛba a, wohwɛ wo yareda hɔ mu.
*If you are going to die and your funeral will come (and be well attended), you foresee it from your sick bed.*
(If you are popular you can detect it when you are sick and in need of visitors. Hence: Times of trouble show who your real friends are).

6695. Yɛbɛwu nti yɛnna?
*We will die, but does that mean we should not sleep?*
(There's no point in worrying about the inevitable).

6696. Wowu atɔfowuo a, yɛsie wo atɔfosie.
*If you die an unnatural death, we bury you an unnatural burial.*
(People who die or are suppose to have died through witchcraft or who committed suicide are given a hurried burial. Hence: If you act abnormally, you are treated as a pariah).

6697. Owudifoɔ biara nni hɔ a wabɔ akwakora wɔ wiram. Ɛbere yera a, ɔbɛba fie abɛwuo.
*A fugitive from murder does not exist that hides himself for ever in the forest. If the time passes, he will come home to die.*
(There's no place like home. Or: Retribution will catch up with you in the end).

6698. Wonwuiɛ a, wonnim deɛ wobɛnya.
*If you do not die, you do not know what will happen to you.*
(While there is life there is hope).

6699. Woanwu adwa so a, yɛtu wo so.
*If you don't die on the stool, we remove you from it.*
(There is only one alternative).

6700. Owuo a ɛbaa wo fie nkɔeɛ a, wonsu sɛ: "Aka me nko".
*If Death has come to your house and has not gone, you don't complain that: "I alone remain".*
(Don't tempt providence).

6701. Owuo ba a, na yareɛ afɛre.
*If death comes, then sickness is shamed.*
(If the worst happens, lesser things are unimportant).

6702. Owuo biara dane owuo.
*Every kind of death is still death (lit. changes into death).*
(Used when you cannot bear your particular circumstances and are prepared to accept any risks to get away from them).

6703. Owuo brɛ onini ase.
*Death conquers the great man.*

6704. Owuo da amansan kɔn mu.
*Death hangs around the neck of all people.*

6705. Owuo de ne pasua fa fie mu a, ɔbosomfoɔ aduru dane nsuo.
*If Death encamps in the house, the priest's medicine becomes water.*
(If you are destined to die, nothing will save you).

6706. Owuo gyawurusie, obiara fura bi.
*Everyone has to put on Death's cloth.*
(No one can escape death).

**6707. Owuo ahenkwaa ne yarɛ.**
*Death's attendant is sickness.*
(Sickness prepares for death).

**6708. Owuo nhyɛ da.**
*Death does not give notice.*

**6709. Owuo bɛku wo na wofrɛ no "Agya" a, ɔbɛku wo; wofrɛ no "Ɛna" a, ɔbɛku wo.**
*If Death comes to kill you and you call him "Father", he will kill you; if you call him "Mother" he will kill you.*
(There is no escaping death).

**6710. Owuo nkum ɔyarefoɔ na mmom ɔkum nkrabea.**
*Death does not kill a sick man but he kills destiny.*
(If you are not destined to die at a certain time, illness won't kill you then).

**6711. Owuo kuta adeɛ mu a, nkwa ntumi nnye.**
*If Death is holding something, life cannot take it from him.*
(Death is omnipotent).

**6712. Owuo akyiri asɛm nti na onipa brɛ ne ho.**
*Because of what happens after death, people toil in life.*
(You work for your descendants).

**6713. Owuo ne nkwa mmɔ abusua.**
*Death and life do not form one family.*
(Good and bad do not agree).

**6714. Owuo ne w'ase hyɛ wo adwumayɛ a, owuo deɛ na wokɔ kane.**
*If both Death and your fathers-in-law appoint a day for you to do some work, it is Death's you go about first.*
(Death's call is immediate).

**6715. Owuo nim ne mma.**
*Death knows its children.*
(Death knows whom to take).

**6716. Owuo nnim adeɛ kyɛ.**
*Death does not know how to share things.*
(The estate is shared after a person's death. Hence: Said when there are difficulties in settling the division of property).

**6717. Owuo annya baabi ankɔ, nti na ɔkɔɔ asamando.**
*Death had no particular place to go, that is why he went to the Spirit world.*
(Said of someone who, because of bad activities, hides away somewhere from the community).

**6718. Owuo si aso.**
*Death seals the ears.*

**6719. Owuo to ababunu a, ɔnka sɛ "Aberewa ni na fa no kɔ".**
*If Death overtakes a young person, he does not say "Take away the old woman".*
(Death is no respecter of age).

**6720. Owuo atwedeɛ, ɔbaako mforo.**
*The ladder of death is not for one man alone to climb.*

**6721. Owuo wɔ ɔyamuɔnwonofoɔ adaka ano safoa.**
*Death has the key to open the miser's chest.*
(You can't take it with you).

**6722. Owuo yɛwu no da koro.**
*We die only on one day.*
(A brave man does not fear death).

**6723. Owuo nnye kɛtɛasehyɛdeɛ.**
*Death is not corrupt.*
(I.e. You can't bribe death).

**6724. Owuo nyɛ pie na yɛadi mu ahyɛnefire.**
*Death is not a sleeping-room that can be entered and come out of again.*
(Said when someone is doing something very risky and is warned it may leads to death).

**6725. Owuo nyɛ wuna, na deɛ yɛwu ma no na ɔyɛ na.**
*It is not difficult to die, but the one we die for is rare.*
(I.e. The one worth dying for. Hence: A good successor is rare).

**6726. Owuo nyɛ ya a, anka yɛde ahan dwane to gya ani a, ɛmpompono.**
*If death is not painful, when we hang a dry leaf above the fire, it would not fold up.*
(If experience is painful, it shows).

**6727. Wo wura bɔ wo boɔ a, na ɔnkum wo.**
*If your master hits you with a stone, he has not killed you.*
(The punishment of a superior officer is a correction, not an injury).

**6728. Wo wura dɔ wo a, na ɔma wo kye nkateɛ.**
*If your master likes you, he sets you to fry ground-nuts.*
(The person cooking nuts is bound to eat some too. Hence: If you are liked by someone they give you a job which enables you to share the proceeds).

**6729. Owura ne akoa ntam nni twe-ma-mentwe.**
*Between the master and slave there is no give and take. (Literally: the oath of master and slave is not pull-let-me-pull).*
(A slave's position is to do what he is told, not to argue about it).

**6730. Wo wura nya wo na ɔbeku wo a, ɔmmɔ wo boba.**
*If you master keeps you to be killed in the future, he does not hit you with a stone.*
(If someone wants to harm you they don't warn you first. In the old days, slaves were sacrificed on the death of an important man, to serve him in the next world).

**6731. Owura pa yɛ ahodeɛ.**
*Being a good master is an asset.*
(If you are a good master, you will easily get people to work for you).

**6732. Wo wura se koto ma ɔnni wo a, wonse sɛ: "Me sisi yɛ me ya".**
*If your master says you should bend down so that he can have sex with you, you don't say: "My waist hurts me".*
(A servant must in all circumstances do as he or she is told).

**6733. Wo wura tan wo a, na ɔfrɛ wo akoa dehyeɛ.**
*If your master hates you, then he calls you a slave aristocrat.*

(A master dislikes an arrogant servant and insults him).

**6734. Wo wura awu yɛanku wo ansie no, kɔ asatɔ a, wose: "Me mu yɛ me ya".**
*If your master has died and we have not killed you to bury (with) him, then we ask you to go and buy palm wine and you say: "I have chest trouble".*
(It is said to have been customary to kill slaves and bury them with a deceased master. Hence: If you are treated well, you should be obliging).

**6735. Wo wura awu, yɛanku wo ansie no. "Tua ayieasika" a, wose: "Menni bi". Yerekyɛ akunafoɔ a, wose: "Me deɛ ne kɔkɔɔ a ɔdi mu no".**
*Your master has died and we did not kill you to bury (with) him. If (we say) "Pay funeral dues," you say: "I have nothing". When we are sharing the widows you say: "Mine is the fair-colored one among them".*
(See Previous Proverb. Funeral dues are paid by all the family and friends of a dead person to pay for the cost of the funeral. Hence: Said when someone who has avoided their obligations, demands a benefit).

**6736. Wowura na sɛ wonsene a, wo ara na wosane.**
*If you enter and you cannot get through, then you are forced to return.*
(You either advance or retreat).

**6737. Awurawura bebrebe de animguaseɛ brɛ onipa.**
*Too much inquisitiveness brings about a person's disgrace.*
(Curiosity killed the cat).

**6738. Owurokosopinɔ se ɔrekɔpɛ mpete aduro, nanso mpete na ɛkum no.**
*The quack doctor says he is going to find a medicine for smallpox, but it is smallpox that kills him.*
(Said when someone boasts of a power, to challenge them to demonstrate it).

**6739. Awurukuo, gyae ahantan yɛ, ɛfirisɛ wo ho nni mfasoɔ wɔ badwam.**
*Red yam, stop being high and mighty, for you are good for nothing in a public place.*
(Said to rebuke or condemn showing-off).

- Y -

**6740. Ayaaka sɛɛ fie.**
*Refusal to communicate (making "aka") spoils the home.*
(See Proverb 430).

**6741. Yafummɔne nnim sɛ makɔsa.**
*A weak stomach does not respond to a suppository.*
(An incorrigible person cannot be cured by simple advice).

**6742. Ɔyafunu mu nni pumpuni.**
*There is no seniority in abdomens.*
(All men suffer alike).

**6743. Yafunu se: "Manya ntoma". Kotodwe se: "Ka me se (sɛ wanya ntoma)".**
*The belly says: "I have been given a cloth". The knee says: "Swear by my father (that you have got a cloth)".*
(Cloth was once very valuable and a treasure. The belly was boasting, but the knee knew if it were true, it too would be covered. When someone is boasting and you know it can't be true, you try to call his bluff).

**6744. Ɔyanfunu yɛ bɔtɔ, woanhunu no hyehyɛ a, ɛpae.**
*The stomach is a sack, if you don't look after its cleanliness, it bursts.*
(A warning against greed or indiscriminate eating).

**6745. Wo yam tim a, wokae nnuaba-nnuaba.**
*If you are constipated, you call to mind fruits (to purge you).*
(If you are ill, you remember previous cures).

**6746. Wo yam tu a, wokae deɛ wodiiɛ.**
*If you have diarrhea, you call to mind what you ate.*
(If you are in difficulty, you try and remember what you did to get into it).

**6747. Wo yam yɛ a, womfa wo yere nkyɛ.**
*If you are kind-hearted, you don't give your wife away as a gift.*
(There should be moderation, even in generosity).

**6748. Wo yam yɛ a, na ɔhooɔ bɛtena wo fie.**
*If you are good-hearted, then a stranger will stay in your house.*
(Good-heartedness attracts people to you).

**6749. Wo yam yɛ nwono a, na nyɛ deɛ ɔhua wɔ wo a.**
*Even if you are mean about food (lit. even if your stomach is bitter), this does not include the person who always eats in your house.*
(There are exceptions to every rule).

**6750. Ayamtubini, yɛmmɔ no boa.**
*We do not wrap up loose stools in a packet.*
(Some operations are too tricky to be performed).

**6751. Ɔyamuonwonofoɔ nkɔ ɔsa nni dɔm so.**
*When a miser goes to battle, he does not become victorious.*
(If you are not prepared to pay for them, you don't get good weapons. Said of someone who is not spending what is necessary to accomplish his goals).

**6752. Ɔyamuɔnwonofoɔ na ne fie gye apopobiririe.**
*A niggardly person's home attracts black algae.*

(A mean person gets no help in the house and it becomes dirty and unkept).

**6753. Ɔyamuonwonofoɔ na ɔtwɛn adekɛseɛ ansa na wayɛ ayɛ.**
*A stingy person waits for a big income before he donates.*
(A mean person only gives if he has a surplus from which to give).

**6754. Ɔyamuɔwonofoɔ wɔ ne yieyɔfoɔ.**
*A stingy person is someone's benefactor.*
(Even a mean person has his favorites).

**6755. Ɔyamuɔnwonofoɔ yɛyi no adwo.**
*A stingy person, we get rid of him.*
(A mean person is not fit to be in society).

**6756. Ayamyɛ yɛ sie, na yɛnyɛ nkyɛ.**
*Kindliness we do it to hoard, but we don't do it to give away.*
(If you help people, you hope for some return in the future).

**6757. Ɔyanfoɔ bi kuta nkonta nso ɔnyan.**
*The drummer holds the sticks but never beats a drum.*
(Used to describe a useless braggart).

**6758. Woyare anomuɔdɛ a, na woyare ntoto-ntoto.**
*If you are too greedy for meat, then you are always roasting.*
(If you have an excess of one thing, you have an excess of what goes with it).

**6759. Yareɛ a ɛkaa akokɔhwedeɛ maa ne nan ase worɔeɛ no, ɛno na ɛbɔɔ kɔkɔsakyi maa ne tiri ho paeɛ.**
*The disease that attacked the francolin and made its legs raw, it is the one that attacked the vulture and made his head bald.*
(Compare Proverb 1791. The legs of the francolin are red and look sore. Hence: Don't be in haste to criticize another. You too may be affected).

**6760. Yareɛ a ɛbɛku woɔ bɔ wo a, wonkae oduroyɔfoɔ.**
*If the illness which will kill you, attacks you, you do not remember the doctor.*
(If you are predestined to die, nothing can prevent it).

**6761. Yareɛ a ɛyeɛ kɔkɔsakyi a, amma ne tiri ho amfu no, sɛ bi yɛɛ [anene]/[asee] a, anka wuo na [ɔbɛwuo]/[ɔwuiɛ].**
*If the disease which affected the vulture, making it bald, had been caught by the [crow]/[woodpecker] then it would have died.*
(Don't laugh at other people's predicaments, you might have to face them yourself and suffer even worse).

**6762. Yareɛ reba a, ɛnam sibire ho, ɛrekɔ dee a, ɛnam babadua ho.**
*When sickness is coming, it takes its way through the reeds, when it is going, it takes its way through the babadua (Thalia near geniculata) (thicket).*
(Compare Proverbs 171-173. A thicket of babadua is almost impenetrable. Hence: Evil is quick to come and slow to go).

**6763. Yareɛ biara nyɛ yarewa.**
*No illness is a small illness.*
(All illness causes some suffering).

**6764. Yareε mmɔɔ wo a, wose wo ho yε den.**
*If you have not been ill before, you say you are tough.*
(Lack of experience leads to boasting).

**6765. Yareε yεnko no ahantan so.**
*Illness is not cured by being arrogant.*
(If someone is trying to cure you, you should accept his treatment in humility).

**6766. Yareε nkɔreeε a, yεnnye aboadeε.**
*If illness is not healed, we don't ask for a financial reward.*
(A doctor must be worthy of his fee before he is paid).

**6767. Yareε anku wo a, n'aduro nyε na.**
*If a sickness does not kill you, it is easy to get medicine for it.*
(A situation which is temporary should not be taken too seriously).

**6768. Yareε nim ba na εnnim kɔ.**
*Illness knows "come" but it does not know "go".*
(Evil is quick to come and slow to go).

**6769. Yareε sεe akyamfoɔ.**
*Sickness destroys (even) the most worthy.*
(If you are really sick, you lose your position in society).

**6770. Yareε wɔ wo so a, εyε anyamesεm, na εnyε w'abusuafoɔ na wɔreyε woɔ.**
*If you are ill, it is the way of providence, and it is not your relatives that is killing you.*
(Many illnesses are put down to witchcraft, whereas they are really infections that should be treated with medicine. Hence: Do not blame your relations if you get ill, but go to the doctor).

**6771. Yareε rebεyε kɔkɔte a, na n'ani yε no hyene.**
*If the bush pig is going to be ill, it begins to suffer from the eyes.*
(Symptoms are evidence of troubles to come).

**6772. Yaredahɔ na εma yεhunu Ɔdomankomawuo nkaebɔ.**
*A serious illness makes us know the warning of Almighty Death.*
(A warning makes you aware of your real position).

**6773. Ɔyarefoɔ a ɔnni obiara na ɔnante kɔpε aduane bεdie.**
*It is a sick person that has no one who walks to fetch his own food to eat.*
(If you have no friends, you are forced to look after yourself).

**6774. Ɔyarefoɔ toto ne kuro a, ɔtoto no mmantwea.**
*If a sick person dresses his sore, he does so in a hidden corner.*
(If you are in an unpleasant situation, you try to hide it).

**6775. Yare-kεseε nko na kεse pa nko.**
*Fatness as a result of illness is one thing and healthy fatness is another.*
(Things are not always as good as they appear to be. Don't judge by appearances).

**6776. Yareε kεseε ase na yεsa nyarewa-nyarewa.**
*By curing a serious disease we get rid of the less serious ones.*

(If you cure the root cause of a trouble, all the minor discomforts go with it).

**6777. Yarewuo na εyε ya na nyε didiwuo.**
*Death from sickness is worse than death from overeating.*
(You are prepared to suffer for something you have caused yourself but not if you are innocent).

**6778. Woyε obi deε yie a, na wo deε yε yie.**
*If you look after someone's things well, your property will prosper.*
(Virtue brings its rewards).

**6779. Woyε obi adeε yie a, εka wo so.**
*If you maintain someone's thing well, it becomes yours.*
(If you look after someone well, they become attached to you).

**6780. Woyε ɔbarima bebrebe a, yεko gya wo.**
*If you are a real man, we fight and leave you.*
(If you are too brave, you get killed).

**6781. Woreyε biribi a, wohwε wo mmati ansa.**
*If you are doing something, you look over your shoulder first.*
(Forewarned is forearmed).

**6782. Woyε biribi na anyε yiye a, womfa nka asεm.**
*If you do something and it does not turn out well, you don't take it to make a case about.*
(You don't publicize a failure).

**6783. Yεayε abiribiriwa, obiara so ne kyε.**
*We have become (like) the fruit of Lannea acida, everyone wears his own hat.*
(The fruit of this tree has the appearance of a head wearing a hat. Hence: Said when people are acting independently or taking care of themselves).

**6784. Woyε aboro a, aboro bo wo.**
*If you are envious, envy will beat you.*
(In the long run, you suffer from your own shortcomings).

**6785. Woyε adeε na woyε no yie a, yεnka w'akyi asεm.**
*If you perform a task and do it well, we do not talk against you.*
(Virtue is rewarded not blamed).

**6786. Mayε odemmerefua, me ho ayε hwam.**
*I have become like a marsh mongoose, I smell nicely!*
(Said when someone has to take part in an unsavory affair and feels contaminated by it).

**6787. Woyε den bebrebe a, wohwere tɔkwakofoɔ.**
*If you are too tough, you are denied a competitor.*
(Someone who is aggressive will lack companions).

**6788. Woyε dɔm aborɔ a, εkɔm ku wo.**
*If you refuse to do anything for the benefit of others, you will die of hunger.*
(A mean man suffers from his own meanness).

**6789. Woyε adɔyε bebrebe a, yεde w'anim yi kwan.**
*If you are too benevolent, we use your face as a path way (worry you).*

**6790. Mayɛ adukurosuo, nnomaa nyinaa boro me.**
*I am like water collected in the stump of a tree, all birds beat me.*
(The birds beat the water with their wings while bathing. Hence: Said by someone everybody makes use of, but who gets no thanks for it).

**6791. Woyɛ adwenhare a, yɛbɔ w'ano abira.**
*If you talk frivolously, we misinterpret you.*
(Always be careful what you say, or people will get you wrong).

**6792. Woyɛ adwuma na woannya mu sɛnkyerɛneɛ a, yɛkyiri.**
*If you have worked and you don't get anything to show for it, we taboo it.*
(No one should be expected to work for nothing).

**6793. Woyɛ fikorɔ mu kuna mprɛnsa a, yɛfrɛ wo busufoɔ.**
*If you celebrate widow's rites three times in the same family, people will call you a devil.*
(If bad things happen too often in a family, people will blame you for witchcraft. If you have too much bad luck, people will blame it on you).

**6794. Woyɛ [hmm hmm]/[anofɔforɔtɔ] a, yɛde wo sekan dwa nanka.**
*If you are inarticulate, we use your knife to skin the adder.*
(If you are too weak, you will be abused).

**6795. Woyɛ wo ho bɛsensono a, obi mmɔ wo kyɛm so.**
*If you behave like a wild boar [which thinks it is greater than the elephant], everyone disregards you.*
("Bɛsensono" is a name of the wild boar and contains the words "sene" (better) and "ɛsono" (elephant). Hence: If you throw your weight around too much, people keep away from you).

**6796. Woyɛ wo ho bɔbɔmfradaa a, yɛse wo fa baabi twi ɛtɔ mu, sane de wo yɛ amamneɛ a ɛkeka ho.**
*You have made yourself look like the krobonko fruit, we take part of you to mix in mashed yams, and then use you again to make a story to tell.*
(The krobonko is an edible gourd. Its seeds are used to make soups. Hence: Used to compliment a useful or popular person whose name is destined to live after them).

**6797. Woyɛ wo ho dufɔkyeɛ a ɛda kwan mu a, obiara tena wo so.**
*If you behave like a rotten log across the path, everyone sits on you.*
(If you leave yourself open to abuse, people abuse you).

**6798. Woyɛ wo ho akokɔ, na wodidi de w'ano twitwiri fam.**
*If you behave like a chicken, if you eat, you rub your beak on the ground.*
(If you lower yourself too much, you behave in a vulgar way and are regarded as inferior).

**6799. Woyɛ nkɔmmɔmum a, wohwere sɛmɔdɛbɔfoɔ.**
*If you are too silent, you lose the friendship of a good talker.*
(If you don't cooperate, you lose by it).

**6800. Woyɛ akwadworɔ a, na w'adwumadeɛ yɛ akwadworɔ.**
*If you are lazy, then your implements are also lazy.*
(Like master, like man).

**6801. "Mereyɛɛ ama wɔasere", na ɛde nkwaseasem baeɛ.**
*"I am acting for you to laugh", brings foolishness.*
(Playing the clown may bring laughter but people cease to repect you).

**6802. Woyɛ "me-nko-medi" a, wonya asaman-nhunuiɛ.**
*If you are an "eat by myself" kind of person, you will often see a spirit.*
(It is customary to cook food and put it in the room where the family stools are stored for the ancestors to enjoy. If you don't do this and you eat your food alone, you may be visited by the ancestors' spirits, and then you may die. Hence: selfishness leads to disaster).

**6803. Woyɛ nnam bebrebe a, yɛtwa wo tiri so dwira.**
*If you are too well-informed, we celebrate the Odwira festival on your head.*
(In the past, you might be sacrificed at the Odwira festival, if you challenged those in power. Hence: Used to warn someone whose success threatens those in power).

**6804. Woyɛ mpepafemee a, wota burodua ho.**
*If you are too assiduous you fart on the corn-husk.*
(Overdoing something brings trouble. The corn-husk is used as toilet paper in the villages).

**6805. "Mereyɛ na mayɛ" nua ne "Akahɔ".**
*"I-will-do-it-later's" brother is "Not done".*
(Procrastination ends in inaction).

**6806. ["Mereye na maye"]/[Mmɔtohɔ] nti na sonsono annya ani.**
*["I will do it later"]/[Procrastination], that is why the worm did not get eyes.*
(According to a folk tradition, the worm when young kept on saying that it would grow eyes but it never did. Hence: Procrastination leads to failure).

**6807. Woyɛ na ɛyɛ yie a, na yɛbɔ wo din.**
*If you do something and you do it well, your name is talked about.*
(Good work earns a good reputation).

**6808. Woyɛ na anyɛ yie a, yɛfrɛ wo ayɛbiaguo.**
*If you do things and they don't go well, we call you a good-for-nothing.*
(You are judged by the results of your actions and not by your motives and efforts).

**6809. Woyɛ nkɔnkɔnsa ma yɛkum ɔkra a, nkura we wo nam.**
*If by treachery you kill the cat, the mice chew your meat.*
(Be careful how you treat those who can help you or you will suffer).

**6810. Mayɛ konturo, me na medi ani kan.**
*I am like the konturo fish, I am always the first to be caught.*
(Used of someone who does not know how to cheat and if he does is always caught. This fish has the reputation of being easily caught).

6811. Woyɛ anantenanteɛ a, wodi w'akyiwadeɛ.
*If you are a gadabout you eat what you taboo.*
(If you wander around too much, you get into trouble).

6812. Mayɛ anene kwaakwaa, ɛnyɛ sɛ me su kwa, asɛm yea na mede "yɛ saa".
*I am like a crow, I don't cry for nothing, but because of bitterness I cry: "Has it come to this!"*
(The crow lost his position as God's messenger and chief priest because he was tempted by groundnuts to delay delivering a message. Hence: This is said by someone in despair who is forced to voice out his complaint).

6813. Woyɛ "Menim ka, mɛka" a, yɛfrɛ wo ɔsɛntentenfoɔ; wotwa no tiawa nso a, yɛbua wo fɔ.
*If you act "I know how to speak, I will speak," we call you long-winded, but if you cut it short, we count you guilty.*
(Whatever you do, someone will criticize you).

6814. Woyɛ w'anim asika-si-kyie a, yɛbisa wo bosea.
*If you act like a rich man, we ask you for a loan.*
(If you pretend to be rich, people will try and get money out of you. Hence: We act on the basis of appearances).

6815. Woyɛ papa a, woyɛ to w'akyi.
*If you do good, you do it behind you.*
(Your reputation lives after you).

6816. Woyɛ papa na obi anhunu bi a, na woayɛ agu.
*If you do good and no one witnesses it, then you have toiled for nothing.*
(We do good to make a name for ourselves).

6817. Woyɛɛ papa mpo na ɛkɔsii sɛn na woreyɛ bɔne.
*Even when you did good it did not bring good results, how much less if you do something bad.*
(If virtue does not succeed how much less vice).

6818. Woyɛ Simpa Panin a, na yɛde asɛm yi wo akwa.
*When you behave like an elder of Simpa, then we bypass you with an incident.*
(A chief of Simpa-Winneba-in the old days was not respected by his subjects. They did not want to destool him, but told him nothing of what was going on. Hence: If you are not respected, people won't come to you with their problems).

6819. Woyɛ ɔtan ba dɛn ara a, ɔbɛko oni hɔ.
*Whatever you do for somebody's child, they will return to their mother.*
(Blood is thicker than water).

6820. Woyɛ tenantuo wɔ obi kuro so a, ɔbu wo kɔsankɔbi.
*If you stay too long in someone's town, he regards you as a good for nothing.*
(Familiarity breeds contempt).

6821. Woyɛ wo to aborɔ a, wota wo yam.
*If you are unkind to your anus, you let air into your stomach.*
(If you refuse to share something with the right person, it may go sour on you).

6822. Woyɛ yie a, wode gya wo mma; wo sɛɛ bɔne nso a, wode gya wo mma.
*If you do good, it lives in your descendants; if you do bad, it also lives in them.*
(The good and evil that men do lives after them).

6823. Nyɛ mmaa a wɔn ho yɛ fɛ nyinaa na wɔnim adeyɔ.
*Not all women who are beautiful are good at house work.*
(Don't judge by looks alone).

6824. Nyɛ ɔbaakofoɔ nko ara na ne nana ne aberewa.
*It is not one person alone whose grandmother is an old woman.*
(We share many problems in common with other people).

6825. Nyɛ ɔbaakofoɔ na ɔnim adeɛ a, ɛyɛ dɛ.
*It is not just one person who knows something is sweet.*
(We all seek after what is pleasurable).

6826. Nyɛ barima ne barima, barima ne deɛ ɔkɔtie bɛseɛ.
*An (ordinary) man is not a (real) man, a (real) man is he who goes to listen and then report.*
(If you face up to a situation, then you have real courage).

6827. Nyɛ bayerɛ a ɛhwere pam ne nkamfoɔ.
*It is not the nkamfo yam which finds it difficult to get a stick (to climb).*
(Someone useful can always get help).

6828. Nyɛ obi biribi ne obi, obi biribi ne deɛ wayɛ no yie.
*Just anyone is not another person's relative, one's relative is the one that has done good to one.*
(Affection grows out of good deeds and intimacy).

6829. Nyɛ obi aburowpata nti na kɔtɔkɔ fifiri se.
*It is not for someone else's corn granary that the porcupine grows teeth.*
(Man is intended to look after himself but not to use his talents dishonestly).

6830. Nyɛ obi na ɔkum Antwi, Boasiako no ara na ɔde ne tiri gyee akyerɛma.
*It was no one who killed Antwi, it was Boasiako (Antwi) who offered his head for execution.*
(During one of the Asante wars a royal returned and found his wife pregnant. He questioned her but she refused to say who was the guilty man. The lady was questioned by the counsellors in the presence of the Asantehene. One Duodu Antwi (Boasiako) knew that the Asantehene was the culprit. He whispered to him that he would take responsibility and claimed publicly that he was the guilty man. Even his unknown loyalty to the Asantehene could not save him from execution. However, a short horn was made in his honor which has, ever since, indirectly praised him for his self-sacrifice. Hence: Used when someone needlessly takes punishment due to another).

6831. Nyɛ obi na ɔmaa odwan twɛ kɔbɔɔ ne to.
*It was not anyone who caused the sheep's vagina to be at the back (exposed).*
(Things are as God made them).

**6832. Nyɛ obi na ɔma nkanka nsuo ma ɔde si aborɔsan.**
*Nobody gives the white ant water to build its storey-building.*
(Used to show you are independent and do not depend on anyone to succeed).

**6833. Nyɛ obi na ɔbɛnya ɛsono tunumu akakaduro.**
*No one can get enough ginger to put up an elephant's anus.*
(Ginger root is used as a suppository. Hence: If you ask for too much, people will not be able to help you).

**6834. Nyɛ obi na ɔse obi sɛ: "Tɔ nkyene di na w'anom akum".**
*No one tells someone else: "Buy salt and eat because you have lost appetite".*
(You don't advise people to do the obvious).

**6835. Nyɛ obi na ɔse ɔkwasea sɛ: "Tɔ gya a efua wo twene na ɛbɛhyɛ wo".**
*No one advises a fool: "Throw away the fire you are holding or it will burn you".*
(No matter how foolish a person is, he will do some things automatically).

**6836. Nyɛ obi na ɔyɛ bafan adeɛ ma no.**
*Nobody does a cripple's everyday business for him.*
(Every person has to live their own life).

**6837. Nyɛ obi na ɔyɛɛ akokɔ mmusuo maa dwonsɔ bɔɔ no.**
*It is no one who has bewitched the fowl so that it cannot urinate.*
(Some disadvantages are God-given).

**6838. Nyɛ obi ne bɔfoɔ na ɛkɔɔ wiram.**
*No one went to the bush with the hunter.*
(Said when there are no witnesses to an event).

**6839. Nyɛ wo biribi ne bɔdamfoɔ na ɔreharam a, wose: "Ɔnɔkwa ne no, ɔde reba!"**
*If a mad person is not your relative, when he yawns you say: "He is well-known, he is doing it again".*
(You misunderstand those outside your family and are prepared to cause trouble for them).

**6840. "Nyɛ biribi", yɛnse no abodwo.**
*"It's all right", we don't say it wholeheartedly.*
(Saying we don't mind something does not mean we don't feel it).

**6841. Nyɛ mmoa nyinaa na wɔwɔ teberɛ.**
*Not all animals have a good dwelling-place.*
(Not all people are equally lucky).

**6842. Nyɛ borɔdeɛ bɛtem na ɛbɛso kuro-mu die.**
*It is not one finger of plantain that can satisfy the whole town's population.*
(Used when what is produced is not sufficient for the occasion).

**6843. Nyɛ Aburownko na dɔkono nko.**
*Corn and kenkey do not differ.*
(Kenkey is made from ground corn. Hence: Members of a family share the same interest).

**6844. Nyɛ wo busuani ne akyakyani a, wonhunu sɛdeɛ ɔsi da.**
*If a hunchback is not your relative, you don't know how he lies down to sleep.*
(You only know intimate things about those close to you).

**6845. Nyɛ da a yɛfua bayerɛ no ara na yɛsi no pam.**
*It is not the same day that yam is planted that we give it a stake.*
(Plans take time to mature).

**6846. Nyɛ da a woato boɔ atware Firaw na mpafe si woɔ.**
*It is not the day that you have successfully thrown a stone across the Volta river, that you suffer from your shoulder.*
(If you commit an offense and are not caught at once, it does not mean you will not be caught later).

**6847. Nyɛ da biara na ɔbɔfoɔ mma twa wɔn anom.**
*It is not everyday that the hunter's children eat well.*
(Life has its ups and downs).

**6848. Nyɛ da biara na yɛdɔ onipa.**
*It is not everyday that we like someone.*
(Don't overtax friendship. People sometimes need to be alone).

**6849. Nyɛ da biara na ɔkwasea dwane a ɔpa ne ntoma guo.**
*It is not everyday that a fool runs away and discards his cloth.*
(You don't expect even a fool to be caught twice at the same thing).

**6850. Nyɛ daa na aponkyerɛne huri a, ɔgye ta.**
*It is not always that the frog will hop and land.*
(You cannot always be successful in life).

**6851. Nyɛ daa na ɔtwe bɛwo a bedeɛ.**
*It is not always that the duiker gives birth to a female fawn.*
(You cannot always repeat your successes).

**6852. Nyɛ nna nyinaa na ɛyɛ nna pa.**
*It is not all days which are good days.*
(We all have our ups and downs in life).

**6853. Nyɛ dam nyinaa na ɛyɛ dam pa, ɛbi yɛ "bɔdamaniateɛ".**
*It is not all madness that is real madness, some of it is "pretending to be mad when you are not".*
(Sometimes people pretend to be mad to protect themselves from responsibilities or the consequences of their own actions).

**6854. Nyɛ danta ne danta, danta ne deɛ sika bɔ ano.**
*It is not the loincloth that is the (real) loincloth, but the loincloth is the one with money tied into its end.*
(Compare Proverb 6826. People store money tied in a corner of a cloth. But not all cloths have money tied in them. Hence: It is not appearance but achievment that matters).

**6855. Nyɛ deɛ mmoa adi kɔ na ɛhia, na deɛ aka na yɛbɔ ho ba.**
*It is not what the animals have eaten and gone which is important, but that which remains we must take good care of.*
(It is no good regretting the past, you must plan for the future).

6856. Nyɛ deɛ yɛbu no sɛ ɔyɛ kwasea biara na wagyimi.
*It is not every person whom we suspect of being a fool, who is (in fact) dimwitted.*
(We should not be too sure of our first judgment of a person).

6857. Nye deɛ adeɛ atɔ n'ani no ara na ɔyie.
*It is not the person who has something in their eye who can take it out.*
(A physician cannot always heal himself, he may need someone to help him).

6858. Nyɛ deɛ odwan ntee bi da ne "Monkye no nku no".
*The thing which the sheep has never heard is not: "Let us catch it and kill it".*
(Some people are never free of disasters).

6859. Nyɛ deɛ adwene pɛ ne sɛ ɔho gya so.
*It is not the wish of the fish that it should be found smoking over the fire.*
(No one willingly seeks their own downfall).

6860. Nyɛ deɛ ɛdwono wɔ ne tirim nkoara na adwen wɔ ne tiri mu.
*It is not only the person who has grey hair on his head who has wisdom.*
(Age is not the same as wisdom).

6861. Nyɛ deɛ akokɔbaatan nhunu bi da ne ne awommawuo.
*What the hen has never before seen is not the death of her children.*
(Compare Proverb 6858. Said to urge someone to accept that they must cope with a recurrent misfortune).

6862. Nyɛ deɛ kokobuo siɛ na ɔbata bɔ mprɛ.
*It is not around the hen coop that the wild cat plays his drum.*
(You do not advertise your presence in the enemy camp.

6863. Nyɛ deɛ yɛkum odwan die na yɛgu hɔ nwira.
*It is not where we kill the sheep to eat that we put our rubbish.*
(You do not spoil the place where you enjoy yourself).

6864. Nyɛ deɛ kusie nhunu bi da ne: "Monnɔ ntrɛ mu".
*What the rat has never experienced is not: "Clear the area wider".*
(Some people are used to persecution).

6865. Nyɛ deɛ n'ani ayɛ kɔkɔɔ nko na n'ani aberɛ.
*It is not only the person who has red eyes who becomes angry.*
(You don't only judge a person's state of mind by his appearance).

6866. Nyɛ deɛ onipa anhunu nyinaa na ɔka.
*It is not everything a man has seen that he speaks of.*
(Some things are better kept private).

6867. Nyɛ deɛ Saforotwe akoa nhunuu bi da ne manniamfrɛ ɔha.
*What chief Saforotwe's servant has never seen is not gagging a hundred times.*
(You are not surprised at what you are familiar with. Chief Saforotwe would close his servant's mouths so that they could not reveal his secrets).

6868. Nyɛ deɛ n'atadeɛ yɛ hyɛnhyɛn nko ara na ɔyɛ osikani.
*It is not only someone who has beautiful clothing who is rich.*
(Appearances can be deceptive).

6869. Nyɛ deɛ ɔtan abotire bɔ ne ti nko ara na ɛdɔm tan no.
*It is not the one that inspires hatred (lit. that hatred falls on his head) alone that everyone (lit. the army) (should) hate.*
(Do not judge by appearances).

6870. Nyɛ deɛ ɔtwe nhunuu bi da ne "Montware no".
*It is not what the duiker has never heard: "Let us intercept him".*
(Compare Proverb 6858. You are not surprised at experiencing what you are used to).

6871. Nyɛ adeɛ a kuruwaa ntee bi da ne "Tuii!"
*It is not a thing which the chamber pot has never heard: a fart.*
(Compare Proverb 6858. If you are familiar with something, you are not shocked by it).

6872. Nyɛ adeɛ a nammɔn ntuu bi da ne kunkumabɔɔ.
*It is not the soil which has become hardened that has never been kicked by the foot.*
(Someone who has been through a difficult experience is toughened by it).

6873. Nyɛ dua a esi ne ho soɔ ne odum.
*The tree which hides itself is not the odum tree.*
(You can't hide a conspicuous person).

6874. Nyɛ nnua nyinaa na ɔbɔfoɔ te.
*It is not all trees that the hunter hides behind.*
(You discriminate even between like people and things).

6875. Nyɛ [duaba]/[aburow] a atɔ aseɛ nyinaa na ɛfifiri.
*It is not all [fruit]/[corn] that has fallen under the [tree]/[plant] that germinates.*
(Not all projects are successful).

6876. Nyɛ aduane a ɛyɛ dɛ nyinaa na onipa die.
*It is not every sweet food that a man eats.*
(Because a thing is good, it is not automatically used by everyone).

6877. Nyɛ aduane na ɛsono nya di kyɛn adowa nti na ɔyɛɛ kɛse kyɛn no.
*It is not because the elephant has more to eat than the antelope that it became bigger than the antelope.*
(It is heredity that controls man's stature, not food).

6878. Nyɛ dwa nyinaa na yɛtɔn aseɛ nnoɔma.
*It is not in every market that we sell things.*
(Not every place is suitable for the same activity).

6879. Nyɛ edwa pa bi ne mpɛsewa-dwa.
*Good business is not a matter of a small amount (pennies).*
(You must deal with large quantities if you are to succeed in a big way).

6880. Nyɛ adwene daberɛ ne bokyea so.
*The hearth is not the sleeping-place of the fish.*
(Each man to his own place. If a man is in the wrong place, it is not for his own benefit).

**6881. Nyε faako a obi da na yεpε daberε.**
*It is not in the same place that someone sleeps that we look for a resting place.*
(We don't cause trouble by demanding from people what is theirs).

**6882. Nyε agorɔ nyinaa na yεko asee.**
*It is not every kind of game that we squabble over.*
(Some things we need to take seriously and not fight over).

**6883. Nyε ɔhene nko na ɔdi asekantwa.**
*It is not only a chief who cuts with a knife.*
(It is not only those at the top who can punish).

**6884. Woanyε ɔhene bɔne a, ɔnku wo.**
*If you do not offend the chief, he does not kill you.*
(If you do not antagonize, you will not be harmed).

**6885. Nyε ohia nko ne ka.**
*It is not only the poor who are indebted.*
(Rich people also get into debt. It is not because you have nothing that you borrow. It may be that what you want money cannot buy).

**6886. Woanyε "hunu" a, wonyε "nnam".**
*If you don't become a good-for-nothing first, you don't become a better person later.*
(You cannot be truly good unless you have a knowledge of bad).

**6887. "Nyε hwee" na ɔbarima gyina deε ɔmpε.**
*"It does not matter" leads a man to stand where he does not want to be.*
(Things often matter more than we are willing to admit. You should take help if you are offered it and not be too proud to accept it).

**6888. "Nyε hwee, nyε hwee", na abusuafoɔ resa.**
*"It does not matter, it does not matter", makes members of a family go short.*
(Lack of care leads to want).

**6889. Nyε ɔkafoni yɔnko ne ɔdefoɔ.**
*The debtor should not make the rich man his friend.*
(You make friends with your equals not with those above you).

**6890. Nyε tεkrεma na εbɔɔ nantwie a amma wanhunu kasa.**
*It is not because it was denied a tongue that the cow cannot speak.*
(People always have a reason for not doing something, but you have do find the right one).

**6891. Nyε ɔko nyinaa na yεfa mu sadeε.**
*It is not all wars that we take plunder from.*
(You cannot be successful all the time).

**6892. Nyε ɔkɔmfoɔ biribi ne Dɔmena a, anka ɔrento dwom mfrε no.**
*If Domena had no relationship to the priest, he would not have included his name in the song.*
(You do not mention a person's name without reason, or if you have no knowledge of them).

**6893. Nyε konkontibaa nti na yεhwe asuo.**
*It is not because of the tadpole that we sieve the water.*

(We don't take trouble to obtain something which is useless to us).

**6894. Nyε akonnwa pa bi, na mpεsεwa–dwa.**
*It is not a stool to be reckoned with, the stool worth a few pence.*
(You don't respect a worthless man).

**6895. Nyε εkoɔ piesie ne Dankyira.**
*Dankyira is not the eldest son of the Ɛkuona clan.*
(Everyone has their rightful place in society and no one should try and usurp another's).

**6896. Nyε kunadan mu na yεfa kunafoɔ.**
*It is not inside the house of mourning that we take the widow.*
(You should only act on the appropriate occasions. Or: Don't act too soon).

**6897. Nyε akunafoɔ nyinaa na yεgye wɔn na nyε akunafoɔ nyinaa na yεware wɔn.**
*It is not all widows that we let go and it is not all widows that we marry.*
(There is no general rule about how we should act).

**6898. Nyε [kusie]/[ɔtwe] nko ne ne bεdε mu.**
*It is not the [rat]/[duiker] alone that the basket is for.*
(Don't think you are the only one to suffer).

**6899. Nyε okusie yɔnko ne dadefidie.**
*A rat is not a companion to the iron trap.*
(Used of traditional enemies).

**6900. Nye kwaeε koro na yεkɔ mu adommiretwa.**
*It is not in one forest alone that we go to collect cane (for basket making).*
(You are not restricted to one place for your means of livelihood).

**6901. Nyε kwan nyinaa na onipa kɔ bie.**
*It is not every journey that a man should go along on.*
(You should pick and choose what you do).

**6902. Nyε akyeame mma nyinaa na wɔnim kasa.**
*It is not all linguists' children who know how to talk.*
(Not all a man's children inherit the same talents).

**6903. Nyε "Mame kakra menni" na yεde dɔ Asiampɔn kwaeε.**
*It is not "Give me a little to eat" that we use to weed the Asiampɔn forest.*
(This forest is very thick and needs hard work to clear. Hence: A hard job needs a good reward).

**6904. Nyε Memeneda nko ara na yεmene adeε.**
*It is not on Saturdays alone that we swallow things.*
(Play on words. You can try your luck any day)

**6905. Nyε mmorɔsa dε nti na yεtɔ.**
*It is not only because foreign drink is sweet that we buy it.*
(Veneration and respect lead us to take certain actions and not always our personal taste. Imported drinks are regarded as being in some way special and are preferred for prestige reasons).

**6906. Nyε amumuyɔ a akwantimfi dunsini nyεε bi da ne sε ɔrema ne ho kwan ama nammɔn apori no.**

*It is not unusual that the stump of a tree in a pathway becomes an obstacle for people to stub their toes against.*
(Some people's propensities for trouble are well known).

**6907. Nyɛ muna nko ara na ɛyɛ abofuo ho nsɛnkyerɛnneɛ.**
*It is not grimacing alone that gives warning of someone's anger.*
(It is not from the face alone that we judge a person's state of mind).

**6908. Ɛnyɛ na wɔnkɔto ntwene a, wɔmfa nto fie.**
*If something is bad and should be thrown away, you don't bring it into the house.*
(What is not good enough to keep should be got rid of).

**6909. Ɛnyɛ nam dodoɔ na ɛma nkwan yɛ dɛ.**
*It is not a great quantity of meat that makes the soup good.*
(It is quality, not quantity, that counts).

**6910. Ɛnyɛ ɛnam dodoɔ na ɛma ani bere amoakua.**
*It is not the quantity of its meat that makes the ground squirrel much sought after.*
(But because of its tail. It is not only bulk that counts).

**6911. Nyɛ nantwie nko na ɔfiri Sraha baeɛ.**
*It is not only cattle that come from Salaga.*
(Salaga was once the center of the slave trade with the North and the Asantes used this proverb to stress their overlordship).

**6912. Nyɛ animuonyam ne sɛ ɔkɔmfo barima fua bodua di funu anim.**
*It is not dignified that a fetish priest (male) should hold a cow's tail and lead (the procession) in front of the corpse.*
(You do not break your own taboos and retain respect).

**6913. Nyɛ nnipa nyinaa na yɛde asaeɛ hyɛ wɔn nsam a, wɔtumi de bɔ dadeɛ soɔ.**
*It is not all people when you give them the hammer, they can strike iron.*
(Not everyone can do a skilled job).

**6914. Nyɛ nnipa nyinaa na yɛne wɔn di atirimsɛm.**
*It is not everyone with whom one can share secrets.*
(Be careful who you share secrets with as many people are not reliable).

**6915. Nyɛ nnipa nyinaa na wɔnim sɛ osuo retɔ a, wɔsɔre kɔ dan mu.**
*It is not everyone who knows that it is raining and gets up to go under a shelter.*
(Some people do not know that a solution can be found to their troubles).

**6916. Nyɛ nnipa nyinaa na wɔbɛnya Frempɔn-mmanson adakabere asie wɔn sienom.**
*It is not everyone who can afford the kind of golden coffin bought by Frempong's seven sons to use for burials.*
(See Proverb 503. There's a difference between the achievements of the rich and the poor).

**6917. Menyɛ anomaa a me pirebuo si m'akyi.**
*I am not a bird to carry my nest on my back.*
(If someone owes you money and you meet him in public and demand payment, he might say this).

**6918. Nyɛ nisuo nyinaa na ɛkyerɛ awerɛhoɔ.**
*It is not all tears that show sadness.*
(The are real tears, crocodile tears and tears of joy. Hence: Don't judge by appearances).

**6919. Nyɛ nwanwa sɛ onifrani bɛtɔ ahwehwɛ.**
*It is not surprising for a blind man to buy a mirror.*
(You must know the reason for something before you find it odd).

**6920. Nyɛ nwanwa sɛ nnoma nyinaa di koropatuo mpammorɔ.**
*It is not surprising that all birds come together to harrass the eagle owl.*
(People band together against the oppressor).

**6921. Nyɛ nwanwa sɛ ɔbofoɔ bɛkum sono ne wawe abotokura.**
*It is not surprising that the hunter who will kill an elephant has eaten a striped mouse.*
(Some rich people enjoy simple pleasures. Or: Many people, even among the affluent, have once known want).

**6922. Nyɛ ɔpanin ne panin.**
*Not every elder is a real elder.*
(All that glitters is not gold).

**6923. Nyɛ apɛsɛwedeɛ kakra a mɛwe nti na merebɛfrɛ kuntunu sɛ "Wɔfa".**
*It is not the small quantity of brush-tailed porcupine's skin that I will chew that will make me call the long stick in the trap "Uncle!"*
(Some people object to using flattery to get things, even if it is to their advantage to do so).

**6924. Nyɛ apotoyowa mu na yɛtu domo.**
*We do not find mushrooms in the clay mashing bowl.*
(Look for things in the appropriate place).

**6925. Wonyɛ prako na woawo ba adi.**
*You are not a pig to give birth to a child and eat it.*
(A man should treat his children with respect and not exploit them).

**6926. Nyɛ sadwaase na yɛbɔ abusua.**
*It is not at drinking bars that we create a family group.*
(Cadgers do not make good friends).

**6927. Nyɛ sɛ deɛ ɔbarima si di ne yere na ɔdi ne mpena.**
*It is not the same way that a man has intercourse with his wife as he has it with his concubine.*
(You treat something temporary less carefully than something which is permanent).

**6928. Nyɛ sɛ ɔkraman pɛ dompe kyɛne nam pa, na deɛ ɛso ne so ara ne no.**
*It is not that the dog prefers bones to meat, but only because that is all that is left for it.*
(Beggars cannot be choosers).

**6929. Nyɛ sɛ wotwe dompɔ ase a, ɔdɔre, nti na wonnyae no asetwe.**
*It is not because if you drag the marsh mongoose, it will become fat, that you don't stop dragging it.*
(The Akans believe that if you kill the marsh mongoose in the forest and you wish it to become fat, you have to drag the carcass home. Hence: You must not be too greedy in your demands on a benefactor).

**6930. Nyɛ nsɛm nyinaa na yɛde to badwam.**
*It is not every subject that we use to make songs about.*
(Some matters are not suitable for public discussion and should be kept private).

**6931. Nyɛ sika bi akoa ne sika bi.**
*One man's money is not the slave of another man's money.*
(Money brings independence).

**6932. Nyɛ sika nyinaa na yɛdie.**
*It is not all money that we use.*
(Be careful from whom you take money or you may get into trouble).

**6933. Nyɛ osikani nko ara na nyansa wɔ ne tirim.**
*It is not only a rich man who has wisdom in his head.*
(Money and wisdom do not necessarily equate).

**6934. Nyɛ osisire na ɛbɛtumi akisikuro.**
*It is not "false tears" that can cure an old sore.*
(The bark of the tree Spathodia Campanulata is highly medicinal. A small sum given to a debtor will not get you out of trouble).

**6935. Nyɛ nsuo a yɛsa nyinaa na ɛkɔ ahina mu.**
*It is not all the water we scoop up that goes into the pot.*
(Not all life's work is successful).

**6936. Nyɛ nsua nyinaa na yɛdwareɛ mu.**
*It is not all rivers that we bathe in.*
(Sometimes an apparently appropriate action is actually inappropriate).

**6937. Nyɛ Ata nko na ɔtɔn atadwe.**
*It is not only the twin who sells tiger nuts.*
(Play on words: Ata (twin) and ata–dwe (tiger-nut). Hence: Used when something is done by an unexpected person).

**6938. Nyɛ Ata anim na yɛtare adeɛ.**
*It is not in front of Ata that we seal something.*
(See previous Proverb. Play on words: Ata (twin), tare (to seal)).

**6939. Nyɛ ntam nteho na ɛma aberewatia nsa kɔ n'ano.**
*It is not fees paid for oath-swearing that makes the old lady's hand go to her mouth (earn her living).*
(You may benefit from something without it being your only source of support).

**6940. Nyɛ Tanɔ mma nyina na wɔkɔm.**
*It is not all Tano's children who know how to be possessed.*
(Not all a person's children follow in their footsteps. The Tanɔ fetish is one of the most important in Ashanti).

**6941. Nyɛ ntɛtia yɔnko ne nkrane.**
*The black ant is not an equal (lit.: a companion) of the small ant.*
(There are classes in every society).

**6942. Nyɛ ɛtɛ a ɛsi onipa ani so na yɛhwɛ de hunu ne yɔsuo.**
*It is not the cataract that covers a person's eyes that we consider in judging a person.*
(Judge by action, not appearance).

**6943. Nyɛ ntɛtoɔ ase na yɛbɔ abusua.**
*It is not where we play marbles that we have our family.*
(Where there is strong competition there can be no intimacy).

**6944. Nyɛ ɔtofoɔ nko na ɔkum aboa.**
*It is not the shooter alone who kills an animal.*
(There are many ways of doing something).

**6945. Nyɛ ɔtomfoɔ nko ne adabraka.**
*It is not only the blacksmith who demands a higher price.*
(Most people charge as much as they can for services or goods).

**6946. Nyɛ ɔtwe a ɔbɛhwere dowa ne Boasare.**
*Boasare is not the kind of duiker to be denied a rope.*
(If you are of exceptional quality, you will be picked out).

**6947. Nyɛ ɔtwe tiri ho na yɛyi nwanam.**
*You do not look for small pieces of meat from a duiker's head.*
(You cannot get help from a needy man. Nnwanam are the less valued but tasty pieces of meat given to the person flaying an animal as a reward for his work).

**6948. Nyɛ ɔtwea yɔnko ne prako.**
*The bitch is not a companion of the pig.*
(Pigs may try to eat the young of other animals. Hence: People who have little in common are not likely to make friends).

**6949. Nyɛ "Maware, maware", na yɛde ware ɔbaa.**
*It is not "I have married, I have married" that we use to marry a woman.*
(It's actions, not words, that count).

**6950. Nyɛ "Merewu nnɛ, merewu ɔkyena", na yɛde yɛ ayie.**
*We don't use "I am dying today, I am dying tomorrow" in performing funeral rites.*
(You don't announce an event until it finally happens).

**6951. Nyɛ wora korɔ mu na yɛyi daha.**
*It is not from one part of the bush alone that we take the adɔbɛ palm leaves.*
(Used to point out that there is an alternative source of something).

**6952. Nyɛ owuo baako a mɛwuo nti na mede me nsa mmienu rekɔdwa kɔmfoɔ.**
*It is not because of one death that I am going to die that I am going to use my two hands to greet the fetish priest.*
(One does not demean oneself beyond a certain point whatever happens).

6953. Yɛnyɛ yareɛ sɛ ɔhene a ɔda abeɛ mu.
*We don't nurture sickness like a chief who is hearing his appellations.*
(We do not encourage a bad thing by praising it).

6954. Nyɛ wo yɔnko ne deɛ aseɛ kye a, ɔtumi bɔ w'ano akɔnhoma.
*Your companion is not the person who can provide you with a daily allowance.*
(If you depend on people you tend to feel inferior to them).

6955. Ayeferɛ sika, yɛmfa nkɔ aban mu.
*We do not use the money taken as compensation for adultery to pay into the State coffers.*
(Some things are dealt with traditionally, others by modern state procedures. Render unto Caesar the things which are Caesar's).

6956. Ayeferɛ sika ntumi ntua mpoaka.
*The money taken as compensation for adultery cannot pay many debts.*
(Compensation for adultery has always been a small amount. You do not depend on casual emoluments to defray your general expenses).

6957. Ayeferɛ sika ntwa poa.
*Adultery fees cannot be used for boasting.*
(If you have obtained your position shamefully, you cannot boast about it in public).

6958. Ayɛmeda ba, yɛyɛ no, na Ahwɛmeda ba yɛahwɛ no.
*The child of someone who has once abused us, we abuse, but the child of one who has helped us, we care for.*
(Do as you would be done by. As others treat you, you treat their relations).

6959. [Yendihene]/[Yaanehene] se ɔbɛkɔ Sraha a, ɔne ne pɔnkɔ nansini.
*If the Yendi chief says he will go North (lit. to Salaga) he does so with his three-legged horse.*
(See Proverb 2485).

6960. Yɛne akokɔ da a, yɛmpɛ no dabrɛ.
*If we sleep in the same place as the chicken, we don't have to search for its sleeping-place.*
(You don't have difficulty in finding those you live with).

6961. Yɛne ɔkorɔmfoɔ te a, yɛmpae adeɛ.
*If we stay with a thief, we don't shout for our things.*
(If you know someone is unreliable, you treat him as such).

6962. Woyera kwaeɛ mu a, susu ma no nyɛ wo ya na, ne nyinaa yɛ wira mu hwehwɛ.
*When you lose your way in the forest, try not to worry too much for it is a good way to get to know the forest.*
(Every cloud has a silver lining. Or: Look on the bright side).

6963. Wo yere a ɔnyɛ no, na ɛte sɛ obi adwaman.
*If your wife is not good, she might as well be someone else's harlot.*
(If something is not serviceable, it does not matter if other people play about with it).

6964. Wo yere gyee wo "Yaa-dwo" na ɛyɛɛ dɛn, na waka sɛ: "Ka na mɛte!"
*Even when your wife gave you the response "Things are normal" it meant nothing. How much less when she says: "You'd better tell me".*
(If you get nothing out of good behavior, you expect nothing from bad).

6965. Wo yere kɔ asuo ba na ɔse "Soɛ no" a, soɛ no, nasɛ da bi wobɛkɔ bi anom a, wonnim.
*If your wife goes for water and returns and asks you to help her unload, help her to unload, for you do not know when you may have to go to the water to drink yourself.*
(Do as you would be done by).

6966. Wo yere noa aduane na ɛnyɛ dɛ a, ka kyerɛ no na deɛ wobɛdi da biara ne no.
*If your wife cooks you food and it is not good, tell her so, for this is the very food you will eat all your life.*
(Don't be afraid of telling the truth or you will suffer for it).

6967. Wo yere nyiniɛ a, wontutu mmirika nkɔhyia no.
*Before your wife has reached puberty you don't run to meet her.*
(Natural growth takes its time, so you must be patient).

6968. Wo yere apem a, w'asɛm apem.
*If you have a thousand wives, you have a thousand troubles.*
(Don't multiply your troubles unnecessarily).

6969. Wo yere awu a, ka sɛ: "Me yere awu", nka sɛ: "Yɛn yere awu".
*If your wife dies, say: "My wife has died", don't say: "Our wife has died".*
(Experience is personal, don't presume to share it around).

6970. Wo yere nyɛ a, ɛnte sɛ wo nko ara woda.
*If your wife is no good it does not mean that you sleep alone.*
(Any wife is better than none!)

6971. Ɔyere bɔne te sɛ ntoma a ayɛ fi, wodi nam a, wo ho nte.
*A bad wife is like a dirty cloth, if you wear it and walk outside, you are not admired.*
(A bad wife gets you a bad reputation).

6972. Ɔyere dada na ɔnim ne kunu yam kɔm.
*An old wife knows what her husband likes best (lit.: his stomach's hunger).*
(Long familiarity with someone leads you to know them better than anyone else).

6973. Ɔyere kɔ a, ɔba ba.
*If a wife goes away, a child stays.*
(You may lose your original investment and still get to keep the proceeds).

6974. Ɔyere pa yɛ ahodeɛ.
*A good wife is wealth.*

6975. Ɔyere pa sene sika.
*A good wife is more precious than gold.*

6976. Ɔyere te sɛ kuntu; wode kata wo ho a, wo ho keka wo, woyi gu hɔ nso a, awɔ de wo.
*A wife is like a woollen blanket; if you cover yourself with it, it irritates you, and if you take it away, you feel cold.*
(Every relationship has its ups and downs).

6977. Wo yerenom yɛ edu a, wo tɛkrɛma yɛ edu.
*If you have ten wives, you have ten tongues.*
(Divided loyalties lead to lies).

6978. Ɔyɛyerɛ biara ho nyɛɛ fɛ da.
*No first wife is ever beautiful.*
(Men find their first wives less glamorous than later rivals. Hence: The other man's grass is always greener).

6979. Ayeyesɛm akoa ne adɔnnyɔ.
*The slave of contrariness is rebellion.*
(If the master acts in one way, the servant imitates him).

6980. Woyi obi ayibɔne a wo din nna.
*If you cut someone's hair in a bad shape your name will be constantly mentioned.*
(If you do bad to someone you get a bad reputation).

6981. Woyi dadu wɔ borɔdeɛ a, ɛnnane bayerɛ da.
*If you take ten days to pound plantain, it will never change into yam.*
(You can't change a person's nature however hard you try).

6982. Woyi w'ahina ayɛ pii a, ɛbɔ.
*If you praise your water pot too much, it breaks.*
(Too much flattery spoils a servant).

6983. Yɛayi wo agorɔ mu a, wonnyina kurotia mpusu w'awan.
*If you have been dismissed from the dance you don't go and stand at the outskirts of the town to shake your shoulder.*
(If you are told you are not wanted, don't try and force yourself to continue).

6984. "Mɛyi mono" na ɛde nkurobɔ ba.
*"I will select the new" brings litigation.*
(If you are not entitled to something and try to take it, there will be trouble).

6985. Woyi sika na ɛyɛ wo ya a, ɛkɔm de wo.
*If you dislike taking out your money, you become hungry.*
(A miser punishes himself).

6986. Yɛyi wo baabi a, kɔ baabi.
*If you are dismissed from somewhere, go somewhere else.*
(There is always an alternative).

6987. Yɛreyi wo agorɔ mu a, wonse sɛ: "Makae dwom".
*If you are being dismissed from a group of players (dancers) you don't say: "I have remembered a song".*
(If you are dismissed, however good your advice, it will not be taken).

6988. Yɛnyi aboa yan mprɛnu.
*We don't take the breast of an animal twice.*
(The breast meat is the tastiest. Hence: Some priveleges can only be enjoyed once).

6989. Worenyi me ayɛ a, nsɛɛ me din.
*If you won't show me gratitude at least do not spoil my good name.*
(Used when someone is slandering a benefactor).

6990. Yɛnyi atɛn a, yɛnto ntam.
*If a charge is not brought against us, we do not have to answer to the oath.*
(If you are not charged, you do not have to put up a defense).

6991. Oyi rekeka na oyi rekeka, na wɔn nyinaa ka bom a, ɛgye fɔmm.
*This one announces and that one announces and all come together in peace.*
(Life is like an orchestra, you should play in tune).

6992. Ayiase ntɔkwa, ne nyinaa firi ɛkɔm.
*If there is much fighting at the funeral, then it is all because of hunger.*
(People are not supposed to eat during a funeral, but they can drink and this leads to quarrels. Family matters are settled and inheritors are chosen after funerals and the poorer members of the family have to fight to get something. Everything has root cause).

6993. Ayie ba a, na yɛfrɛ ɔbɛtwani sɛ: "Nana".
*If a funeral comes we call the palm wine tapper: "Chief".*
(An insignificant man has his day).

6994. Ayie fɛ ne ka.
*A beautiful funeral is a debt.*
(Something ostentatious is expensive).

6995. Ayie ne n'ani krakra na ɛma mfomsoɔ ba.
*Funeral celebration accompanied by a lack of concentration brings mistakes.*
(We can all make mistakes when under stress).

6996. Ayie, yɛsɔ no aba–aba.
*Everyone helps to carry the burdens of a funeral.*
(We should all help each other in times of need).

6997. "Yieyɛ" yɛ aseda, na "bɔneyɛ" yɛ aseda.
*Kindliness has its reward and unkindliness also has its reward.*
(We get what we give in life).

6998. Ayi-fɛɛfɛ nnyane funu, nanso ɛyɛ asɛnka.
*Grand funeral celebrations do not awake the corpse but it becomes memorable.*
(Some things are not done for profit but for honor).

6999. Woyiyi wo se ase di a, na wonnyaa nam pa biara nniɛ.
*If you lick around your teeth and eat what you get, then you have not got any good food to eat.*
(If you try to exploit your relatives, you don't gain anything).

7000. Oyoko ne Dakɔ nnipa dapaafoɔ, kwabusafoɔ bosua na yɛdi awareɛ.
*People of the Oyoko and Dako clans are depraved for they marry one another.*
(These two clans are related and marriage inside related clans is not normally permitted. However, this case is an exception. Hence: If you commit taboos people do not respect you, even if according to your own rules it is all right).

7001. Ɔyokoman bɛkɔ sumina soɔ no, na ɛnam nyansa mu.
*If the Ɔyokoman woven kente cloth is going to the rubbish heap, it does it through wisdom.*
(Wise people know how to get around awkward situations without giving offense. In the old days when an important person died they would be dressed up in a kente cloth. On the way to the grave-yard this would be left on the rubbish heap to be collected on the return journey by the mourners. However it was realized that this made the cloth dirty and they are very difficult to clean, so the habit was adopted of covering the coffin with the cloth and passing the cloth over the rubbish heap on the way to the graveyard and on the way back, so people could say it had been on the rubbish heap, but it did not get spoiled).

7002. "Yɔ-ma-menhwɛ!" yɛ yɔna.
*"Make it and let me see" is difficult.*
(It is difficult to make a success of a job if someone is watching).

7003. Wo yɔnko da ne wo da.
*Your companion's day (of death) is your day (of death).*
(Show sympathy to your neighbor, it may be your turn next).

7004. Wo yɔnko di wo amim na woanni no bi a, ɛyɛ a na ɔsusu sɛ wosuro no.
*When your companion helps himself to the larger share when sharing something with you and you (when sharing something with him) do not do the same, he thinks you fear him.*
(Don't let people get away with cheating or they will not respect you).

7005. Yɔnkoɔ mu wɔ yɔnkoɔ.
*Among companions some are (better) companions (than others).*

7006. Yɔnkoɔ wu a, yɔnkoɔ nkɔ ayie.
*If a companion dies, a companion does not go to the funeral.*
(If you don't know someone's family, you don't know whom to condole).

7007. "Yɔnko, yɔnko" na ɛma asɛm trɛ.
*"Friend, friend" makes news spread.*
(Friends don't keep secrets from each other and so even private information tends to become public. Hence: Used to warn people not to speak to someone they think they can rely on).

7008. Ayɔnkofoɔ baanu goro ɔbaa koro ho a, ntoto ba.
*If two friends play with one woman, it leads to misunderstanding.*
(Two men cannot share one woman).

7009. Ayɔnkogorɔ te sɛ mpaboa, sɛ wohyɛ na ankɔ wo a, woworɔ gu hɔ.
*Playing with friends is like sandals, if you put them on and they do not suit you, you cast them away.*
(Ayɔnkogorɔ literally means having a good time with friends. If you cease to get on with your friends, you part with them. You stop doing what is unprofitable to you).

7010. Ayɔnkogorɔ nti na ɔkɔtɔ annya tire.
*Because of friendship, the crab lost its head.*
(If you waste too much time with your friends you suffer for it. When the crab went to get its head from God, it delayed while looking for friends to go with and when it reached God, there were no heads left).

7011. Ayɔnkogorɔ nti na nsiammoa kaa nam mu.
*Because of friendship the larvae remains in the flesh.*
(Friendship holds you in one place).

7012. Ayɔnkogorɔ yɛ fɛ sene ɛna-mma.
*Friendship is more beautiful than a mother's child.*
(Friendship is better than blood relationships).

7013. Eyuo nkɔ, na apupuo nka.
*The black duiker does not depart and leave its rustling noise behind.*
(If traces are cut, they should be cut completely).

7014. Eyuo ne wansane gyina hɔ a, na yɛhunu deɛ ɔwee aberewa nkuruma.
*It is only when we get the black duiker and the bush buck together that we can tell which one ate the old lady's okro.*
(You must hear both sides of a case before giving judgment).

7015. Eyuo Kwasi se ɔnim sɛ wansane bedane kɔmfoɔ a, anka wansɛe ne hyire.
*The black duiker Kwasi says if it could have forseen that one day the bush buck would be a fetish priest, it would not have wasted its white clay.*
(The black duiker is supposed to have given the bush buck its white stripes. Hence: If you had known in advance that someone would become a nuisance then you would not have wasted time in helping them).

# Bibliography

Akrofi, C.A. *Twi Mmɛbusɛm.* London: Macmillan, 1958.

Antuban, K. *Ghana's Heritage of Culture.* Leipzig: Koehler and Amilag, 1963.

Cansdale, G.S. *Animals of West Africa.* London: Longmans, 1960.

Christaller, J.G. *Dictionary of the Asante and Fante Language.*
         Second Edition. Basel: Basel Evangelical Missionary Society,1933.

----. *Three Thousand Six Hundred Ghanaian Proverbs: From the
Asante and Fante Languages.*, Basel: Basel Evangelical Missionary Society, 1879.

Daaku, K.Y. *Oral Traditions of Adanse, Assin-Twifo, Dankyira,
Sefwi, Ahwiaso and Bekwai.* Legon: Institute of African Studies, University of Ghana, 1974.

Danquah, J.B. *The Akan Doctrine of God.* Second Edition. London: Frank Cass & Co., 1968.

Garrard, T.F. *Akan Weights and the Gold Trade.* London: Longmans, 1980.

Kyerematen, A.A. Y. *Kingship and Ceremony in Ashanti. Dedicated to the Memory of
Otumfour Sir Osei Agyeman Prempeh II, Asantehene.* Kumasi: UST Press, nd (c), 1970.

----. *Panoply of Ghana.* London: Longmans, 1964.

Mensah, J.S. *Asantesɛm ne Mmɛbusɛm Bi.* Kumasi, Private Printing, 1966.

Nketia, J.H. *Funeral Dirges of the Akan People.* Achimota: James Townsend and Sons, 1955.

Rattray, R.S. A*kan-Ashanti Folk-Tales.* Oxford: Clarendon Press, 1930.

----. *Ashanti.* Oxford: Clarendon Press, 1923.

----. *Ashanti Law and Constitution*: London: Oxford
         University Press, 1929.

----. *Ashanti Proverbs.* Oxford: Clarendon Press, 1916.

----. *Religion and Art in Ashanti.* Oxford: Clarendon Press, 1927.

Reindorf, C.C. *The History of the Gold Coast and Asante.* Second Edition. Basel: Basel
Evangelical Missionary Society, 1895.